Visual Basic® .NET
XML Web Services
Developer's Guide

About the Author

Roger Jennings is a principal of OakLeaf Systems (http://www.oakleaf.ws), a northern California consulting firm. His primary consulting activities are designing and programming Visual Basic .NET client/server and XML/XSLT database applications, and data-intensive XML Web services. Roger's books on Windows database, operating system, and multimedia topics have more than 1.25 million English copies in print and have been translated into some twenty languages. His latest books include *Admin911: Windows 2000 Group Policy* (McGraw-Hill/Osborne), *Special Edition Using Access 2002* (Que), *Special Edition Using Windows 2000 Server* (Que), and *Database Developer's Guide with Visual Basic 6.0* (Sams).

Roger is a columnist for Fawcette Technical Publications's family of Web sites, including the .NET*Insight* and XML & Web Services *Insight* newsletters, and a contributing editor for *Visual Studio Magazine* (http://www.fawcette.com/vsm/). He's also contributed content to the Microsoft Developer Network (MSDN), *Microsoft Developer News*, Tech*Ed, and TechNet. Contact Roger at Roger_Jennings@compuserve.com.

About the Reviewer

Darshan Singh holds a Master's Degree in Computer Science (MCS) from India's Pune University. He started his programming career at Spectrum Business Support Ltd. (http://www.sbsworld.com) where he built software for a full text search engine written in C and Visual C++/MFC. He then joined Persistent Systems Private Limited (http://www.pspl.co.in), where he worked on projects such as COM-based integration of Microsoft Outlook third-party software. Darshan came to the United States in 1999 to work with Microsoft's SQL Server Technical Support Group. In 2000, he joined InstallShield (http://www.installshield.com) as Senior Developer in the research and development division.

Darshan contributed a white paper about Microsoft SQLXML 3.0 and its .NET and XML integration features to the SQL Server 2000 Web Services Toolkit. Microsoft distributed the Toolkit CD-ROM, which included Darshan's sample Projects/Tasks Tracking System XML Web service and client, at Visual Studio .NET release events in March 2002.

Darshan is a founder of PerfectXML.com, a community Web site dedicated to XML topics. He has coauthored several books on MSXML, .NET XML, and SQLXML topics, and acted as technical editor for many more computer-related books. Darshan specializes in .NET XML and database design and development. Along with the rest of the PerfectXML team, Darshan is currently pursuing several .NET consulting projects. You can reach him at darshan@PerfectXML.com.

Visual Basic® .NET XML Web Services Developer's Guide

Roger Jennings

McGraw-Hill/Osborne

New York   Chicago   San Francisco
Lisbon   London   Madrid   Mexico City   Milan
New Delhi   San Juan   Seoul   Singapore   Sydney   Toronto

McGraw-Hill/Osborne
2600 Tenth Street
Berkeley, California 94710
U.S.A.

To arrange bulk purchase discounts for sales promotions, premiums, or fund-raisers, please contact **McGraw-Hill**/Osborne at the above address. For information on translations or book distributors outside the U.S.A., please see the International Contact Information page immediately following the index of this book.

Visual Basic® .NET XML Web Services Developer's Guide

1234567890 FGR FGR 0198765432

ISBN 0-07-222369-3

Publisher	Brandon A. Nordin
Vice President & Associate Publisher	Scott Rogers
Acquisitions Editor	Ann Sellers
Project Editor	Lisa Wolters-Broder
Acquisitions Coordinator	Timothy Madrid
Technical Editor	Darshan Singh
Copy Editor	Chrisa Hotchkiss
Proofreader	Susan Carlson Greene
Indexer	Claire Splan
Computer Designers	Carie Abrew, Kelly Stanton-Scott
Illustrators	Michael Mueller, Lyssa Wald
Series Design	Roberta Steele
Cover Series Design	Greg Scott
Cover Illustration	Eliot Bergman

This book was composed with Corel VENTURA™ Publisher.

This book is dedicated to my wife, Alexandra.

Contents at a Glance

Contents

Acknowledgments

Thanks to Microsoft Corporation for *finally* releasing the .NET Framework and Visual Studio .NET. Experienced Visual Basic developers might find the initial transition from Visual Basic 6.0 to .NET to be daunting. But—as this book demonstrates—adopting a fully object-oriented version of this venerable programming language isn't as challenging as one would expect. Visual Studio .NET's developers worked long and hard to make the transition as painless as possible. Their efforts are much appreciated.

Technical editor Darshan Singh caught my technical gaffes and made valuable suggestions for improving the book's coverage of XML Web services. Any errors or omissions you encounter, however, fall directly on my shoulders.

Thanks to McGraw-Hill/Osborne's Wendy Rinaldi, editorial director, and Ann Sellers, acquisitions editor, for having the foresight to publish this book. Tim Madrid, acquisitions coordinator, shepherded the manuscript through the labyrinthine editing and publishing process. Chrisa Hotchkiss, copy editor, corrected my grammar and capitalization lapses. Lisa Wolters-Broder, project editor, transformed the manuscript into the book you're holding now. The very professional Osborne publishing team made writing this book an unusually enjoyable experience.

Introduction

This book is devoted entirely to designing and coding XML Web services and consuming applications with Visual Basic .NET, plus a bit of Visual Basic 6.0 code in the early chapters. You won't find a single line of C# in its 500-plus pages. Nor will you encounter primer chapters devoted to XML basics, writing XSL transforms, or designing XSD schemas from scratch. Adequately covering these topics requires entire works of at least this book's length. Instead, *Visual Basic .NET XML Web Services Developer's Guide* concentrates on teaching you how to create, test, and deploy real-world, production-quality, data-intensive XML Web services. The only trivial example you'll find in this book is ASP.NET's default "Hello World" service at the end of Chapter 1.

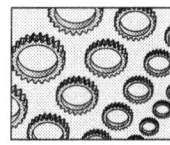

NOTE

This book uses the term consumer *or* consuming application *or* project *in preference to* client *to avoid inference that XML Web services adhere to the client/server model. Although most of this book's example services communicate with Windows or Web form clients, the majority of production XML Web services will probably communicate server-to-server, and many will invoke complementary Web services.*

Exclusive use of Visual Basic code isn't intended to reignite programming language wars or to denigrate C# in any way. C# is a new language that's intended to lure C++ and Java programmers to Visual Studio .NET's managed code and the Common Language Runtime (CLR). Visual Basic is a mature language; millions of programmers around the globe use Visual Basic 6.0, VBScript, and VBA to create enterprise-grade applications and components. C# offers the ability to add XML-style comments and write unsafe code, which Visual Basic .NET doesn't support. Otherwise, there's little or nothing that you can do with C# that you can't handle with Visual Basic .NET. Omitting C# examples permits this book to cover a much wider range of XML Web service topics.

It's a safe bet that at least 95 percent of all production XML Web services will connect to one or more relational databases. Trivial services that emulate four-function calculators, convert units of measure, or return the quote-of-the-day don't represent commercial products.

Neither are services that, given an ISBN, scrape other sites' screens to return book prices. The early adopters of XML Web services will be organizations that are attempting to reduce the cost and extend the life cycle of enterprise application integration (EIA) projects. EIA middleware is *not* simple.

Adoption of W3C-standard XML, XSD, and XSL/T, and industry-standard SOAP 1.1+ and WSDL 1.1+ promises to topple today's Tower of Interop Babel, minimize EIA consultant fees, and extend the life of EAI middleware beyond the next revision of the software that the project connects. B2B and, to a lesser extent, B2C supply-chain applications, will lead the second stage of XML Web service migration. Almost all EAI, B2B, and B2C middleware has a database at one or both ends.

All but one example XML Web service in this book connects to one or more SQL Server or MSDE 2000 databases having base tables that range in size from about 35,000 to 200,000 rows and contain real or simulated real-world data. Sample applications let you increase the size of some databases to the limit of available disk space. Use of moderate to large databases lets you compare the performance of XML Web services with varying programming approaches, such as substituting ADO.NET for MDAC 2.7 COM components. Chapters 2 through 10 of this book emphasize performance tests with both local and remote XML Web services.

The sample XML Web services you create on your test computer have production counterparts running on the OakLeaf Systems XML Web service demonstration site at http://www.oakleaf.ws. The OakLeaf site currently has a 1538/727-kbps ADSL connection to the Internet, which has sufficient bandwidth to emulate sites connected by T-1 lines having moderate traffic loads. Availability of remote XML Web services lets you demonstrate and compare your SOAP consumer applications' performance with Internet- and intranet-based services. All sample ASP.NET consuming applications include detailed tracing pages for precise determination of remote and local XML Web service method execution times.

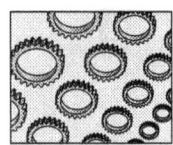

NOTE

Western Samoa, now just Samoa, owns the .ws TLD, but it's likely that many commercial XML Web service providers will adopt .ws in lieu of .com.

Who Should Read This Book

This book is intended for seasoned Visual Basic 6.0 developers, but not Visual Basic .NET experts. Experience writing and deploying Visual Basic ActiveX components is helpful but not essential. The book assumes no familiarity with VBScript, ECMAScript, or ASP programming. Chapter 6 shows you how to migrate conventional Windows form XML Web service consumer code to ASP.NET Web Forms. If you haven't worked with ASP.NET, you'll be surprised how easy Visual Studio .NET makes emulating conventional Windows forms with ASP.NET Web Forms.

Chapters 3, 4, and 5 show you how to use the Microsoft SOAP Toolkit 2.0+ with Visual Basic 6.0 components, and then migrate the component to Visual Basic .NET and ASP.NET Web Service projects. Visual Studio .NET's Visual Basic .NET Upgrade Wizard does a remarkably good job of migrating well-written Visual Basic 6.0 code to Visual Basic .NET. Many Visual Basic experts, such as Desaware's Dan Appleman, contend that there's little or no economic justification for upgrading production Visual Basic 6.0 applications and components to Visual Basic .NET. Chapter 4 demonstrates a considerable performance gain when you convert XML Web services from ActiveX components with a SOAP wrapper to ASP.NET. Chapter 5 illustrates a more modest improvement by substituting ADO.NET for COM-based ADODB objects.

TIP

For Dan's viewpoint on porting Visual Basic 6.0 code to Visual Basic .NET, see his "Stop! Don't Port That Code" editorial in the March 2002 issue of .NET Magazine (http://www.fawcette.com/dotnetmag/2002_03/magazine/departments/guestop/).

What's in the Book

This book is divided into twelve chapters and two appendixes. The chapters follow the sequential process that a typical Visual Basic 6.0 developer might follow when adopting Visual Studio .NET for the express purpose of learning to write and deploy production-quality XML Web services.

▶ Chapter 1, "Introducing XML Web Services and the .NET Framework," provides an overview of the roles of and markets for XML Web services in EIA, B2B, and B2C applications, gives you a preview of the book's sample services and consumers, and describes important future trends in extensions to XML Web services.

▶ Chapter 2, "Getting a Grip on SOAP and WSDL," explains the basics you need to know about the current SOAP 1.1 and WSDL 1.1 de facto industry standards that form the foundation of XML Web services. The chapter concludes with a simple XML Web service example based on an upgraded Visual Basic 6.0 ActiveX component and the Northwind SQL Server 2000 sample database.

▶ Chapter 3, "Working with the Microsoft Soap Toolkit 2.0," shows you how to apply a SOAP wrapper to—and generate WSDL files for—ActiveX components that serve as XML Web services and still retain their COM/DCOM middle-tier capabilities. You also learn to use the Toolkit's Trace Utility to inspect SOAP request and response messages that use the rpc/encoded format. The techniques you learn in this chapter also apply to version 3.0 of the Toolkit.

▶ Chapter 4, "Upgrading to ASP.NET Web Services," illustrates the upgrade, copy, and paste technique for migrating from Visual Basic 6.0 components to ASP.NET document/literal XML Web services. You also learn how to add Web References to Windows form clients, and debug XML Web services and their consumers.

▶ Chapter 5, "Moving from ADO 2.5+ to ADO.NET," describes the differences between ADO.NET and its `ADODB` predecessor, and shows you how to use `SqlClient` objects to gain a significant performance boost. The chapter also introduces you to ADO.NET's `DataSet` and `DataTable` objects and illustrates the Visual Basic.NET code required to create and consume them.

▶ Chapter 6, "Converting XML Web Service Test Clients to ASP.NET," explains the copy-and-paste migration process from Windows forms to Web Forms with moderately complex Visual Basic .NET code behind the form. You add ASP.NET `DataGrid` server controls to the form and analyze their effect on consumer performance.

▶ Chapter 7, "Navigating System.Web.Services and System.Xml," is a guided tour of the primary .NET Framework namespaces that support ASP.NET XML Web services. The chapter also covers working with SOAP headers and using the `XmlTextReader` class in conjunction with the attribute-centric XML documents returned by XML Web services you create with Microsoft's SQLXML 3.0 add-in.

▶ Chapter 8, "Delivering Reports with XML Web Services," moves to XML Web services that employ element-centric XML documents as SOAP request and response messages. You learn how to create XML Web services that generate XML crosstab report documents from conventional Transact-SQL aggregate queries.

▶ Chapter 9, "Designing the Presentation Layer with ASP.NET," proposes a four-phase process for designing Web pages that rival those of graphic arts professionals. The chapter's example shows you how to design an ASP.NET consumer application that displays a crosstab document's values in a fully formatted table. The chapter also describes how to create Crystal Reports XML Web services to display crosstab values as tables and graphs in an ASP.NET consumer, and use of the Office XP Web Services Toolkit to generate formatted Excel 2002 worksheets from XML Web services that return summary values.

▶ Chapter 10, "Applying Advanced XML Web Service Techniques," introduces you to generating and applying XSD schemas to validate XML request and response documents and their element datatypes with the `XmlValidatingReader` class. You also learn how to change ASP.NET's document/literal SOAP format to rpc/encoded, serialize complex datatypes as element-centric XML documents, consume asynchronous XML Web services, and work with SOAP extensions.

▶ Chapter 11, "Advertising Public Web Services with UDDI," tours the Microsoft public UDDI 1.0 registry and shows you how to register your XML Web services so that Visual Studio .NET's Add Web References dialog will find them. The chapter includes a Visual Basic .NET port of a Microsoft C# sample application for searching UDDI 1.0 registries programmatically.

▶ Chapter 12, "Interoperating with Third-Party Web Services," explains the role of the fledgling Web Services Interoperability (WS-I) organization in promoting XML Web service interoperability based on profiles of standards compliance. The chapter also discusses interoperability issues with services created by SOAP toolkits other than Microsoft's.

▶ Appendix A, "Installing the Sample Databases," contains detailed instructions for downloading, attaching, and configuring the six SQL Server/MSDE 2000 sample databases that support most of the XML Web services you create and modify as you proceed through this book. The appendix also describes how to install and configure the optional CFRSQL database to support a local version of the OakLeaf Code of Federal Regulations XML Web services and consuming pages.

▶ Appendix B, "Expanding the CFRSQL Database with the CFRClient Program," explains how to use the Visual Basic 6.0 and .NET versions of an application that lets you populate a local copy of the CFRSQL database. If you don't download Appendix A's CFRSQL sample database, don't bother reading this appendix.

Typographical Conventions

This book uses the following conventions in body text and Visual Basic code examples:

▶ Replaceable elements in text, such as filenames, are italicized, as in *ServiceName*.asmx.

▶ Ellipsis precede filenames when the path to the file has been specified previously, as in ...\Reports.asmx, in place of D:\VBWS08\ReportsWS\Reports.asmx.

▶ A pipe symbol separates menu choices, such as Add | Add Existing Item.

▶ Text you type in text boxes and at the command line is set in **boldface**.

▶ Namespaces, including URIs and some URNs, class names, method/property names and values, and Visual Basic .NET code is set in a `monospace` font.

▶ Square brackets surround optional argument and other values in text and generic code examples, such as `ObjectName.MethodName(strArg1[, intArg2[, blnArg3]])`.

▶ French braces surround and pipe symbols separate alternate values of required arguments (usually of overloaded functions), as in *ObjectName.MethodName({strArg1|intArg1|blnArg1})*.

▶ Visual Basic datatype abbreviations, such as `str` or `int`, follow conventional Visual Basic 6.0 Hungarian notation standards; a `typ` prefix indicates that the datatype isn't specified in the context. Prefixes that represent .NET Framework class members, such as `xtr` for `XmlTextReader`, are arbitrary. The `obj` prefix is used only to identify instances of the generic Visual Basic or .NET `Object` datatype or when assigning different object types to the same identifier.

Sample Code Downloads

The sample code for this book is available from the McGraw-Hill/Osborne download page at http://www.osborne.com/downloads/downloads.shtml. Scroll the page to the Source Code entry for this book, which has the following links in the second level of the bulleted list:

▶ **VBWSReqd.zip**   Contains all required sample code files for this book in a single archive. VBWSReqd.zip creates a set of VBWS## and VBWS_OCE folders in the drive's root directory. (## is the two-digit chapter number). The size of the file is about 18MB, which expands to about 70MB when you unzip it.

 **TIP**

Many Visual Basic .NET samples are hard-coded to the D:\ drive, so unzipping this or the individual chapter sample files to a D:\ logical drive will make your life much easier.

▶ **VBWS##.zip**   Contains individual archives of the sample code for a single chapter. You must create the individual \VBWS## folder into which to expand the files. Entries in the download list display the .zip and expanded file sizes. Expanded sample code files range from 8 to 11,671kB.

▶ **VBWS_OCE.zip**   Contains the six databases to support the OakLeaf Consumer Electronics (OCE) sample XML Web services and consumers. You must download this 10.8MB .zip file, which expands to 42.3MB, to gain any significant hands-on coding benefit from this book. You attach the databases to SQL Server or MSDE 2000, so the directory in which you expand the .mdf and .ldf files isn't important. Appendix A has the SQL Server/MSDE 2000 installation instructions.

► **VBWS_CFR.zip**   Provides a "starter" version of the OakLeaf Code of Federal Regulations database. If you download and install this database, be sure to download VBWSAB.zip to populate the database from the U.S. Government Printing Office's Electronic CFR (e-CFR) beta site. The .zip file is 8.5MB, which expands to 51MB. Appendix A includes installation instructions.

► **VBWSAB.zip**   Contains Visual Basic 6.0 and .NET versions of the CFRClient Windows form application for populating the CFRSQL database. The name and location of the subfolder into which you unzip the files isn't important. The .zip file is 850kB, which expands to 3.2MB. The CFRClient project required a *lot* of Visual Basic code and required about two months to write and test. Downloading and transforming all sections of the U.S. Code of Federal Regulations requires about ten days with a high-speed (T-1 or equivalent) Internet connection.

Introducing XML Web Services and the .NET Framework

IN THIS CHAPTER:

Beyond the Web Services Hype

Web Services Architectures

Core XML Web Service "Standards"

XML Web Services Support in .NET

A week seldom goes by without a deluge of press releases, online and print articles, and white papers covering the "Web services revolution." Information technology pundits and computer journalists breathlessly proclaim Web services to be the "next big thing" in computing technology. For example, Gartner Group, a leading technology analysis and advisory firm, rates Web services as one of "... four key emerging technology trends for the next decade." Following is an excerpt from Gartner's October, 2001, press release:

> By packaging business processes as software components, Web services will drive much of the still-to-be-developed e-business landscape. Web services will facilitate much faster software development and integration. They will also enable businesses to become more agile, and help them focus on their core competencies while outsourcing other functions. Web services are likely the hottest trend of 2001 and 2002, and are probably still an underestimated technology.

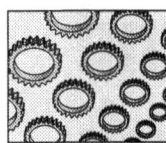

NOTE

For a comprehensive list of Gartner's Web service reports and news articles, go to http://www3.gartner.com/ and search for "Web Services."

"[P]ackaging business processes as software components" is old hat. Visual Basic developers have been packaging business processes as business logic components since 1995, when Microsoft added the ability to create COM DLLs to Visual Basic 4.0. Microsoft Transaction Server enabled multiple COM components to enlist in distributed database transactions, which made three-tier application architecture a reality and enabled Visual Basic developers to write enterprise-class applications. Active Server Pages and server-side VBScript or ECMAScript deliver the presentation layer to browser-based, "thin" clients that connect to middle-tier business-process components. Any Internet-based application that takes advantage of object-oriented architecture and uses HTTP or other standard Internet protocols to communicate with other servers or deliver the presentation layer to clients qualifies as a generic Web service. Web-based collaboration schemes and peer-to-peer sharing of idle computer resources can also qualify as Web-based services. Thus, generic Web services aren't a new technology.

A critical prefix is missing from most of today's Web services prose. The technology that writers and analysts are gushing over is *XML* Web services. Industry-standard Extensible Markup Language (XML) documents, the Simple Object Access Protocol (SOAP), and Web Services Description Language (WSDL) files distinguish XML Web services from their operating system–specific, protocol-constrained, and language-dependent predecessors. This book is about *XML* Web services running under Windows 2000+ and is intended for Visual Basic 6.0 and current or prospective Visual Basic .NET and ASP.NET developers. The XML Web services you create and test as you progress through this book are accessible to any client or server that can communicate via HTTP, HTTPS, or SMTP and process the XML content of a WSDL file.

Beyond the Web Services Hype

Most press and analyst reports, including .NET propaganda from Microsoft, have focused on electronic commerce (e-commerce) as the driving force behind the development of [XML] Web services. It's impossible to accurately determine how many billions of dollars now-bankrupt dot-coms have thrown into business-to-consumer (B2C) e-commerce's bottomless money pit. To date, business-to-business (B2B) e-commerce participants, such as commodity- and industry-specific exchanges (and their software suppliers) haven't fared much better than their B2C predecessors. Today's most serious impediment to adoption of XML Web services technology by IT management is the early e-commerce stigma.

Enterprise (application) integration is the key to initial deployment of XML Web services. Enterprise integration currently has much broader scope than e-commerce applications. The goal of enterprise integration is interoperability of distributed computing systems of all types and sizes, not just B2C or B2B projects. The overwhelming majority of distributed systems involve interaction between databases that reside on mainframes, UNIX boxes, and Windows NT/2000 servers. XML Web services map the route to the Holy Grail of Database Interoperability and Software Reusability, and promise a substantial increase in the return on investment (ROI) of software development projects.

ARC Advisory Services, a strategic planning and technology assessment firm, pegs the 2006 enterprise integration software and services market at $3.9 billion in 2000, $4.8 billion in 2001, and over $11 billion by 2006. The increase in the enterprise integration market stands in sharp contrast to the cutbacks in overall information technology spending in late 2001 and early 2002. ARC's October, 2001, press release states:

> Web [s]ervices are on the horizon with strong support from the J2EE-based suppliers as well as Microsoft with its .NET platform. Web services will provide a standard communications interface between heterogeneous platforms, and is well suited for Internet-based applications and [e]nterprise [i]ntegration.

In March 2002, Gartner Group projected that the overall market for Web services will reach $28 billion by 2006. If both the ARC and Gartner estimates are correct, B2B and B2C Web services will garner more than $17 billion in 2006. Market size predictions for new technologies are notoriously inaccurate, but B2C and, to a lesser extent, B2C services will probably gain the largest share of IT spending for Web services by 2004.

TIP

If you (or, more importantly, your bosses) believe an article printed in the Harvard Business Review *is to business management as a paper published in the* New England Journal of Medicine *is to health care, spend $6.00 to download the PDF version of the October 2001 "Your Next IT Strategy" article by John Hagel III and John Seeley Brown from http://www.hbsp.harvard.edu/hbsp/prod_detail.asp?R0109G. The article, which is directed at corporate and IT management, not developers, describes an analogy between "service grids" of XML Web services and electrical power distribution grids. Put all members of your organization's upper management on the distribution list for this article.*

Web Services Architectures

Web services permit programming objects to communicate across a public network (the Internet) where the endpoints (hosts) are located behind firewalls. Virtually all firewalls permit HTTP request-response response operations by clients on TCP port 80, and many support encrypted communication by the Secure Sockets Layer (SSL) API and secure HTTP (HTTPS) protocol on port 443. HTTP is a stateless (also called connectionless) protocol, which contributes to the scalability of Web-based applications; thus, all Web services are said to be "loosely coupled." In this respect, Web services are related to messaging services, but not to message queuing or store-and-forward applications. If your Web-based applications require maintaining session-level or application-level state, the Web server, not the Web service, stores state information for the client.

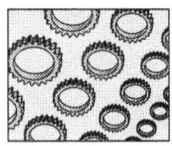

NOTE

The term "Web service" implies the "World Wide" prefix and conformance with applicable World Wide Web Consortium (W3C) recommendations, such as those for HTML and XHTML. Services using Internet transport protocols other than HTTP, TCP, and UDP or remote procedure call (RPC) methods are beyond the scope of Web services. Specifically, FTP and SMTP transports aren't covered in this book.

Another characteristic of all Web services is that, unlike most ActiveX controls and Java applets, Web services don't interact directly with the user interface, and many Web services are intended only for server-to-server communication. Thin (browser-based) and thick (Windows application–based) clients provide the UI. You compile Visual Basic 6.0 ActiveX DLLs that participate in Web services with the Unattended Execution and Retained in Memory options. The Unattended Execution option prohibits inclusion of forms in your DLL, and use of message and input boxes in your code. Similar restrictions apply to XML Web services you create with ASP.NET and Visual Basic .NET.

The following sections describe by example the differences between generic and XML Web services.

Generic Web Services

Internet Information Server's SQLXML 3.0 add-on provides the capability to create data-related generic Web services. A COM or .NET DLL can use connectionless HTTP or HTTPS wire protocols to POST the text of a conventional SQL query with a FOR XML AUTO modifier appended. The FOR XML AUTO modifier returns the query result set as an XML document. Template queries enhance the data-retrieval process by defining a Transact-SQL query that accepts WHERE clause constraints expressed as arguments of HTTP requests. SQL Server 2000 XML updategrams handle connectionless updates to remote databases and support transactions.

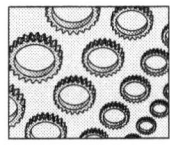

NOTE

Formatting a query result set or updategram as an XML document doesn't qualify either of the two processes as an XML Web service, as defined in the following section. Microsoft could have chosen any standard text format, such as comma-separated values (CSV) or Rich Text Format (RTF) files, to enable data transport via HTTP. Remote Data Services (RDS), which Microsoft now terms a "deprecated" (read "no longer supported") technology, uses MIME encoding to pass lightweight `ADOR.Recordset` *objects through firewalls.*

Figure 1-1 illustrates three approaches to retrieving data from and updating remote SQL Server databases protected by firewalls:

▶ A client's browser issues a `GET` or `POST` request to an .asp or .aspx (ASP.NET) page over an intranet. The page's VBScript or Visual Basic .NET code sends an HTTP `GET` request to the virtual directory to specify the SQL Server template and the parameter value(s). SQL Server returns the query result set as attribute-centric XML, which the component transforms to an HTML or, preferably, XHTML table. A `Response.Write str[X]HTML` instruction sends the table to the client's browser.

▶ A client's browser opens an HTML page that uses dynamic HTML to generate a template query based on user input. The browser sends the HTTP request directly to a different template, which specifies an XSL file to transform the XML to an HTML table on the remote server. The server responds to the client directly.

▶ A Visual Basic application running on a Windows client connects to a remote ActiveX DLL via DCOM. The component translates client requests for data into template queries and updates into updategrams. Template queries return XML data to the component for translation into a format that's compatible with the client application. For example, the component can append the XML query result set to a set of custom header and schema elements and deliver a persistable XML `ADODB.Recordset` object to the client.

TIP

For more details on SQLXML template queries and transforms, go to http://www.oakleaf.ws/articles and click the Enterprise 2001 link.

The first two of the preceding data access scenarios are operating system–independent. For example, an Opera browser running under Linux or Internet Explorer (IE) on a Macintosh delivers the same result as IE on Windows desktops. The second data access method doesn't depend on ASP or ASP.NET, so this approach is totally operating system–agnostic. The last example is Windows-centric and the most difficult to deploy. Configuring DCOM proxies on thousands of Windows 95, 98, Me, NT, and 2000 clients is a *very* difficult and costly project. Dispensing with DCOM is one of the primary incentives for adopting XML Web services as your standard component access technology.

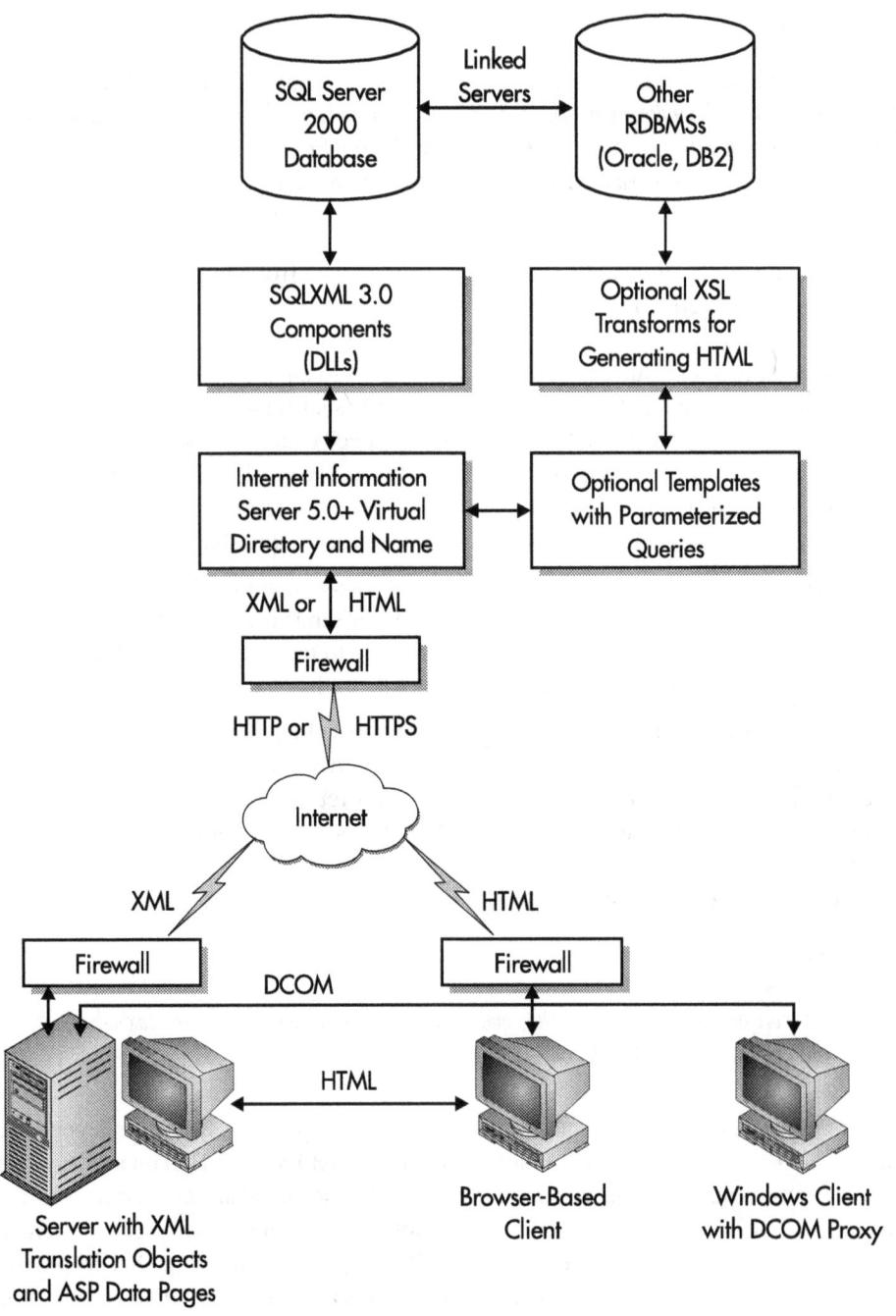

Figure 1-1   IIS' XML for SQL Server add-on enables Web servers and browser-based or Windows clients to access remote, firewall-protected SQL Server databases by HTTP GET and POST operations.

XML Web Services

"XML Web services" is Microsoft's official term for the subject of this book, although you're likely to see "Web services," ".NET Web services," and "ASP.NET Web Services" in early Microsoft .NET Framework documentation and developer presentations. XML Web services require use of SOAP for communication, WSDL files for definition of functionality, XML for content (called *payload*), and XML Schema Definition (XSD) language for datatype definitions. ASP.NET Web Service projects, which generate instances of `System.Web.Services` objects, conform to these requirements, so you can consider .NET and ASP.NET a synonym for XML in this context. Plain "Web services" appears mostly in early Microsoft publications that haven't been reedited to conform to today's terminology.

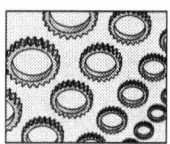

NOTE

When you create a new ASP.NET Web Service project, Visual Studio .NET generates its WSDL file automatically. Early beta versions of Visual Studio .NET employed Microsoft's proprietary Service Description Language (SDL). Use of the term "ASP.NET Web Service" in this book refers only to ASP.NET projects for creating XML Web services that use SOAP messaging, with a few explicit exceptions. The "System.Web.Services Namespaces" and "ASP.NET Web Service Projects" sections near the end of this chapter offer more detailed coverage of this issue.

Figure 1-2 illustrates the following data-related XML Web service scenarios that correspond approximately to those shown in Figure 1-1:

▶ A browser-based client issues an HTTP `GET` request for a page from a Windows Web server with the .NET Framework installed. The ASP.NET page has a SOAP client proxy—called a *Web Reference*—that stores a locally cached copy of a WSDL document on a remote server. The page calls a function (`WebMethod`) defined by the cached WSDL file. For this example, executing the `WebMethod` sends a SOAP request message to an ASP.NET XML Web service, which returns an XML-encoded SOAP response message to the ASP.NET server. Visual Basic .NET code behind the ASP.NET page transforms the XML content to an XHTML table and sends the XHTML document to the browser.

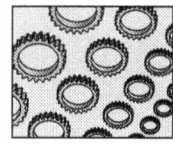

NOTE

For an example of the preceding type of XML Web service, go to http://www.oakleaf.ws/cfr/. Clicking the Contents link returns an XHTML document that represents the top-level table of contents of the U.S. Code of Federal Regulations.

▶ Alternatively, the ASP.NET page executes a Transact-SQL (T-SQL) stored procedure that has a similar WSDL file and SOAP wrapper. SQLXML 3.0, which Microsoft also calls SQL Server 2000 Web Services Toolkit for Microsoft .NET, includes a feature that automatically creates WSDL files and SOAP wrappers for SQL Server or MSDE 2000 `SELECT` stored procedures. Chapter 7's "Creating XML Web services with Microsoft SQLXML 3.0" section shows you how to use this new feature.

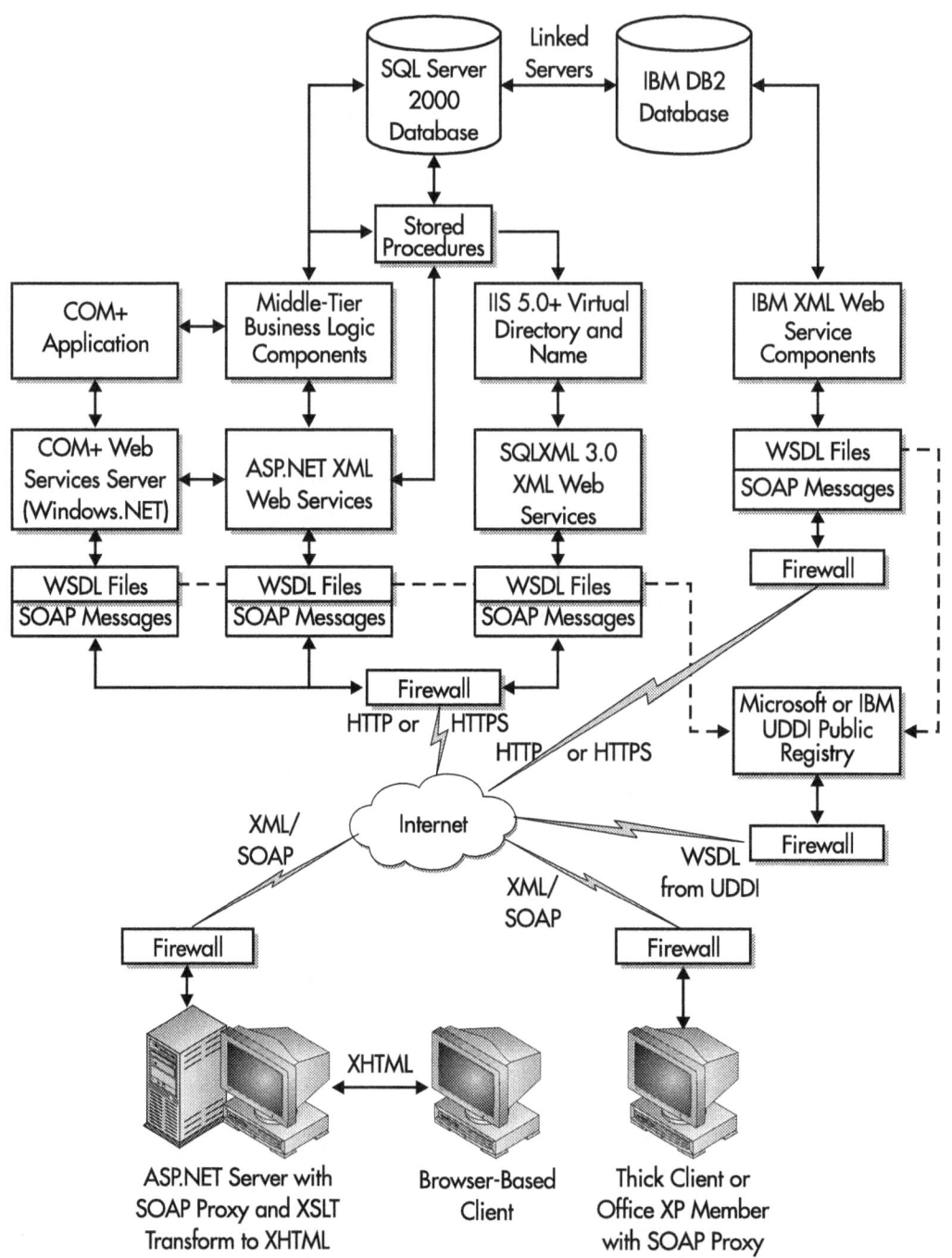

Figure 1-2 *ASP.NET and new SOAP-based toolkits for Microsoft SQL Server 2000 and Office XP enable Web servers and Windows applications to consume XML Web services.*

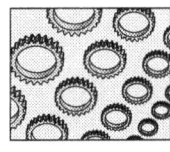

NOTE

Go to http://www.oakleaf.ws/SQLXML3/ for a demonstration of an SQLXML 3.0 XML Web service. Select the Top 100 option, mark the Amplifiers, DVD Players, and Receivers (Home) check boxes, and click the Retrieve Data button to execute the GetTop100 stored procedure.

▶ A client running a Windows forms application refers to a cached WSDL file and sends a secure HTTPS POST request to the entry function of a COM+ business-process application running under Windows .NET Server's COM+ Web Services Server. Windows .NET Server lets you SOAP-enable a COM+ component by marking a configuration check box.

▶ An Excel 2002 application that's been SOAP-enabled by the Office XP Web Services Toolkit searches a public Universal Description, Discovery, and Integration (UDDI) 1.0 registry for an XML Web service that connects to a remote IBM DB2 database of demographic information. After locating the service by a keyword or business name search, the Excel application connects to the WSDL file and executes the specified Enterprise JavaBean function to retrieve SOAP-encoded data for a particular Metropolitan Statistical Area (MSA). Excel VBA code transforms the XML payload of the SOAP message to a named range.

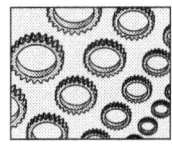

NOTE

Chapter 9's "Using the Office XP Web Services Toolkit with Excel 2002" section shows you how to use the Toolkit to display formatted financial reports generated by an ASP.NET XML Web service.

With the exception of the Office XP example, all the preceding processes are operating system–agnostic on the client side. The browser and thick client can run on any version of Linux, UNIX, or the MacOS that supports SOAP 1.1 client proxies.

The primary technical and economic benefits of XML Web services derive from mandatory adherence to a set of industry standards. Adopting operating system–and programming language–agnostic W3C specifications lets developers create object packages that are accessible to anyone, anywhere, who needs and is willing to pay for the services they provide. Thus, the potential market for commercial XML Web services is much larger than that for components based on proprietary technologies, such as ActiveX controls, but the business models differ greatly. You purchase a one-time, design-mode license, which includes unlimited run-time distribution, for most commercial ActiveX controls. Providers of XML Web services are more likely to charge a pay-per-use or subscription fee, often with a one-time setup charge.

Standards-based object invocation methods are also important to corporate IT management, because the investment in developing XML Web services survives organizationwide or departmental platform changes and development tool transitions. Depending on internal accounting policies, departments using corporate XML Web services might be assessed setup, usage, or both types of fees.

XML Web Service Examples

Many developers write example XML Web services and make them accessible from SOAP-enabled clients by registration in one of the two public UDDI 1.0 registries run by Microsoft and IBM. Public UDDI registries replicate their data each day, so you need to register your services on only one site. Several sites act as informal registries that provide lists of links to HTML pages that describe the service and provide a link to the developer's WSDL file. The XMethods site (http://www.xmethods.net/), for example, offers a comprehensive list of sample XML Web services, most of which execute trivial functions, such as area code lookup or units conversion.

The following sections describe Microsoft's first commercial XML Web services and the nontrivial Visual Basic sample services and SOAP-enabled clients you create as you proceed through the chapters of this book.

.NET Passport

The most controversial member of Microsoft's commercial XML Web services is .NET Passport for user authentication. (Microsoft added the .NET prefix to the Passport service in late 2001.) .NET Passport provides single-sign-on services for Microsoft's HotMail, public UDDI registry, and other Web sites that subscribe to the Passport service. Microsoft claimed in late 2001 to have more than 200 million identities stored in their "Passport Vault" and 10,000 servers to process up to 1.5 billion authentications per day.

The next version of Passport .NET, scheduled for implementation sometime in 2002, adds Kerberos v5 authentication to the original cookie-based system and enables organizations to establish their own .NET Passport servers. If your organization meets Microsoft's security standards and pays a substantial yearly fee, you can "federate" your .NET Passport servers via a cross-domain trust with the Microsoft service. Get further information on .NET Passport and download version 2.0+ of the .NET Passport SDK for Windows 2000/XP/.NET at http://www.microsoft.com/myservices/.

Web privacy organizations and, of course, Microsoft's competitors question whether Microsoft can be trusted to preserve the sanctity of Passport user-supplied information, such as credit card and demographic data, as well as prevent safecrackers from gaining access to the vault. Sun Microsystems, IBM Corporation, and other major players in the hardware and software business obviously covet Microsoft's high-profile status in the Web identity market. Sun and 30-some other organizations have formed the Liberty Alliance project to create an "open, federated identity solution," which translates to "alternative to Passport." (Go to http://www.projectliberty.org/ for details.) When this book was written, the Liberty Alliance was in the formative stage and collecting membership fees to "... architect, develop, market, and adopt a new, open solution for federated network identity." Most industry observers doubt that "identity by committee" will overcome the "identity by Microsoft" momentum.

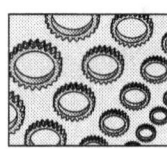

NOTE

Go to http://techupdate.zdnet.com/techupdate/stories/main/0,14179,2830300,00.html for a March 2002 compendium of ZDNet articles on the Passport versus Liberty Alliance battle.

.NET My Services

.NET My Services (formerly codenamed HailStorm) is a suite of Microsoft-hosted XML Web services, most of which are scheduled for commercial deployment in 2002. Version 1.0 of .NET My Services encompasses 15 personal data services for consumers and corporate users, all of which will use .NET Passport's Kerberos authentication mechanism in the release version. Many of the services duplicate features of Microsoft Exchange, Outlook, and Outlook Express. Following are brief descriptions of the most useful V.1 services:

- ▶ **.NET Notification** is the first of the new .NET My Services to go online at eBAY, MSN, and a few other third parties. The .NET Notification service uses the Windows or MSN Messenger service to deliver simple notifications to PCs and mobile devices.

- ▶ **.NET Calendar** handles time and task management and lets you share your free/busy schedule with others.

- ▶ **.NET Contacts** is a server-based address book that's adaptable to a wide range of devices, such as Pocket and Tablet PCs, Palm-style organizers, and cell phones.

- ▶ **.NET Inbox** stores e-mail and voice mail messages on Microsoft's server instead of your organization's Exchange server. Some industry analysts equate .NET My Services with Exchange 2000 Server outsourced to Microsoft as the application service provider (ASP).

- ▶ **.NET Wallet** is the successor to the Microsoft Wallet (integrated with Passport) and stores credit card information to support the Passport Express Purchase service. Microsoft will probably add some type of micropayment system to .NET Wallet to eliminate credit card transaction fees imposed on pay-per-use Web services.

- ▶ **.NET Profile** is a service migrated from the original Passport Profile component, which stores user demographic data, such as names, addresses, telephone numbers, public e-mail addresses, birthday and anniversary dates, and even photographs.

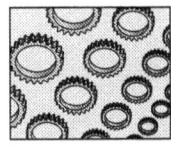

NOTE

For a complete list of the version 1.0 services, go to http://www.microsoft.com/myservices/ services/faq.asp. You can download the .NET Passport SDK v2.1 from MSDN Downloads; search for "Passport."

Subsequent to release of a beta version of the .NET My Services SDK and specification at Microsoft's October 2001 Professional Developer's Conference, company officials appear to be reconsidering the business model for the product. A February 2002 *CINET News* article quotes Microsoft vice president Jim Allchin's description of the original My Services plan as "not thought out" and the result of unclear thinking. Read the entire "Is Microsoft Getting Ahead of Itself?" article at http://news.com.com/2100-1001-839853.html.

OakLeaf Systems' Online Code of Federal Regulations

The OakLeaf Online Code of Federal Regulations (CFR) ASP.NET sample project is an example of a large-scale content syndication service supported by six Visual Basic .NET

XML Web services. The Federal government describes the U.S. Code of Federal Regulations as "a codification of the general and permanent rules published in the Federal Register by the Executive departments and agencies of the Federal Government." The print version consists of 204 volumes and costs $1094 for a one-year subscription.

The U.S. Government Printing Office (GPO) and the National Archives and Records Administration (NARA) publish the Electronic CFR (e-CFR), an online version of the CFR, which is updated daily. The e-CFR Web site (http://www.access.gpo.gov/ecfr/) lets you browse the CFR's 50 titles, 28 subtitles, 375 chapters, 799 subchapters, 7920 parts, and 172,800 sections and appendixes. Sections contain the CFR's text, which is available in HTML and Standard Generalized Markup Language (SGML) formats. The GPO site also offers full-text search of the sections.

The data source for the CFR site is a 1GB SQL Server 2000 database, which contains a table for each element of the CFR hierarchy. The Titles, Subtitles, Chapters, Subchapters, and Parts tables store tables of contents (TOCs) as well-formed XML documents. TOCs provide the foundation for navigating the CFR hierarchy. The Sections table contains a structured XML document with a header, body, and, when applicable, additional elements for each CFR section. Sections and appendixes range in size from a single short paragraph to very complex, 1+ MB documents. SQL Server 2000's full-text search service emulates a Web-based search for individual words and complete phrases. The full-text index files for TOCs and section text consume about 150MB of disk space.

TIP

The Home and About pages of the CFR site at http://www.oakleaf.ws/cfr/ offer detailed explanation of the structure of the U.S. CFR, samples of generated XML and XHTML documents, and example WSDL files. The Help page explains the navigation process and has links to CFR sections of general interest.

ASP.NET and the XML Web services transform the XML documents to XHTML for the browser presentation layer. (*XHTML* is HTML composed as a well-formed XML document so as to be valid for an XML Web service payload.) Alternatively, the XML Web services supply XML documents that subscribers to the syndicated content can transform to HTML, Compact HTML (cHTML), and Wireless Markup Language (WML) to accommodate multiple devices.

Figure 1-3 is a diagram of data flow through the CFR project; the XML Web service components are shaded.

Following are brief descriptions of the major components of the CFR project:

▶ A Visual Basic .NET administrative client application downloads the SGML text of CFR sections and transforms the flat SGML typesetting format to XML documents, which are stored in the CFRSQL database's Sections table. The transformation components translate SGML named character references, such as `&thnsp;`, to their ISO 8879 numeric entity equivalents (` `). Section body text is transformed to a hierarchy of paragraphs in unconventional outline format: (a), (1), (i), (A).

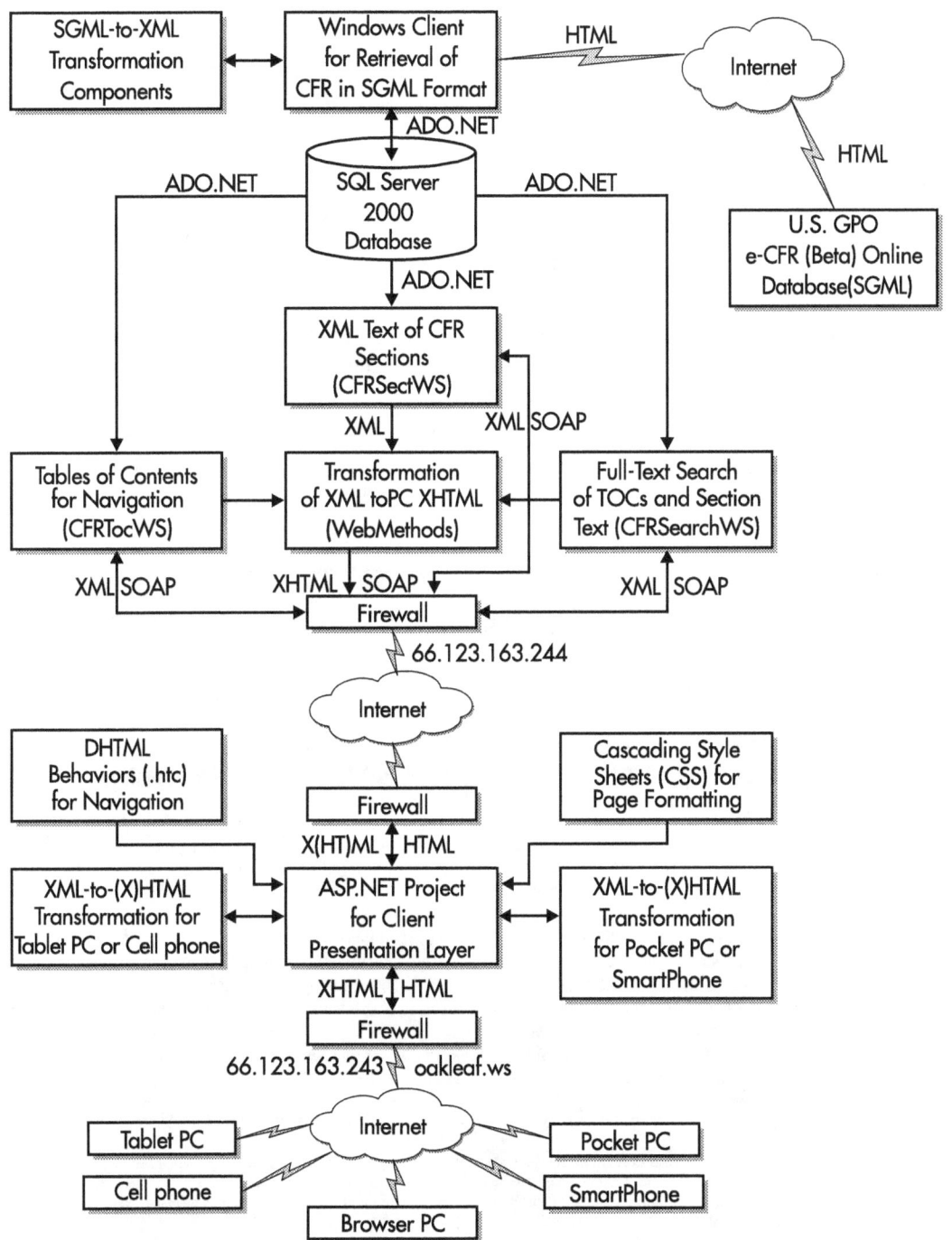

Figure 1-3   *This diagram of the OakLeaf Code of Federal Regulations (CFR) project describes the data flow between its components. XML Web services are shaded.*

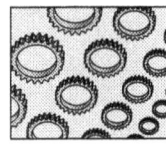

NOTE

Appendix A provides instructions for downloading and attaching the sample CFRSQL database to your local instance of SQL Server or MSDE 2000. Appendix B describes how to use the CFRClient.exe application to populate the CFRSQL database on your development machine.

▶ Clients connect to the home page of the CFR Web site, which offers TOC-based navigation, full-text search, and links to Help and About pages. (See Figure 1-4.)

▶ Clicking the Home page's CONTENTS link to the default title/subtitle TOC or a TOC element at a lower level begins a typical XML Web service request-response operation.

▶ The CFRTocWS service's `TransformXMLToc` method generates the well-formed (but not validated) XHTML code to display the requested TOC table. (See Figure 1-5.) Alternatively, the ASP.NET page can request the source XML document and locally invoke the `XfrmXMLToc` method for PC devices.

▶ The OpenToc.aspx page routes requests for section text to the CFRSectWS service, which obtains the requested XML document from the Sections table and passes it to

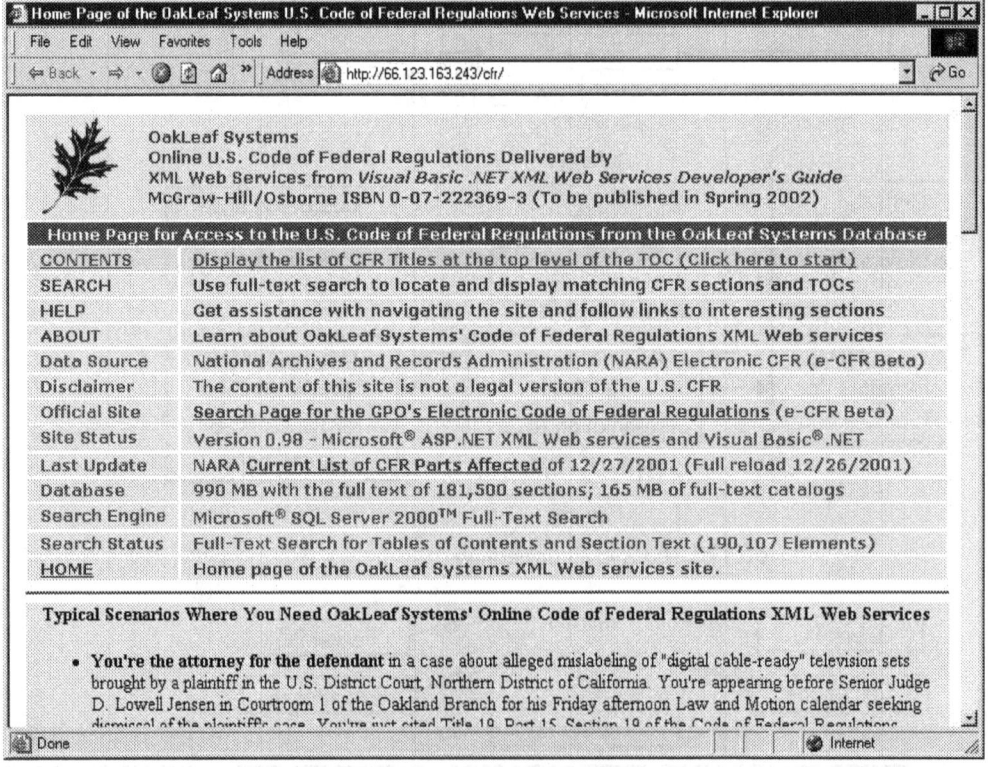

Figure 1-4 *The Home page of the OakLeaf Online CFR site uses a combination of DHTML table rows, CSS, and JavaScripted DHTML behaviors for navigation.*

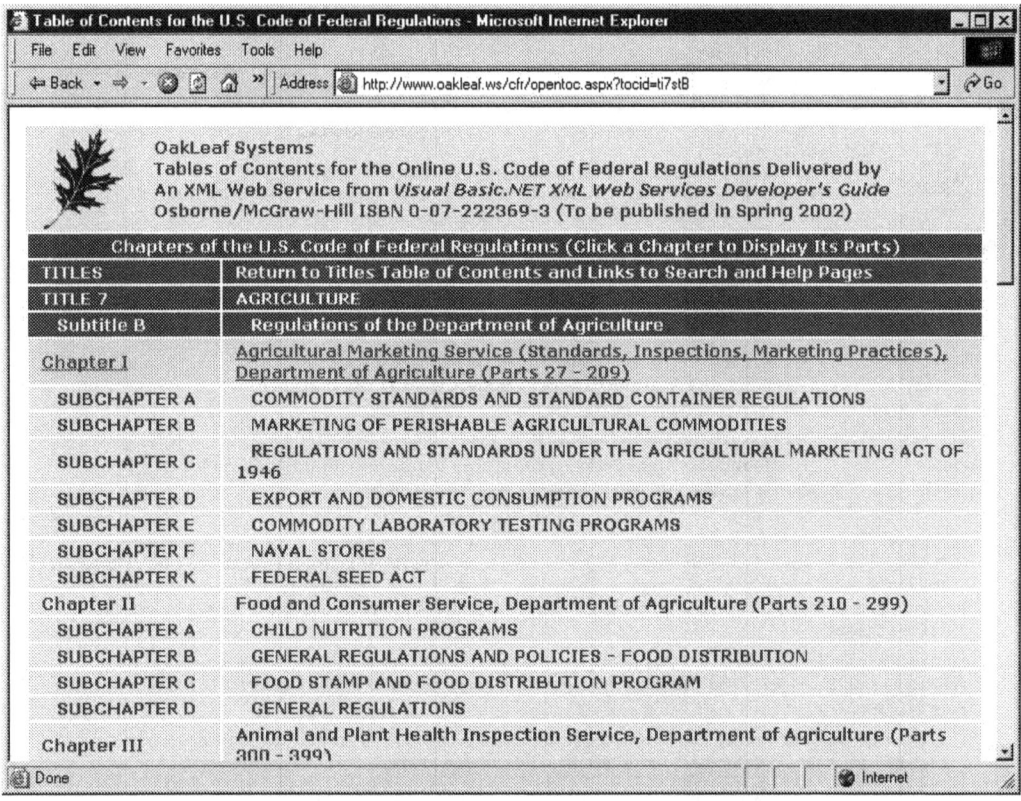

Figure 1-5   *Navigation by TOC passes the TocId attribute value (in this case, ti7stB for title 7, subtitle B) to the CFRTocWS service's GetTocById function.*

the XfrmSectWS service to format the header and text as XHTML. (See Figure 1-6.) XML paragraph subelements determine indentation of nested paragraphs.

▶ The Search.aspx page (see Figure 1-7) contains a table-based form that lets you enter a search expression, restrict the search to TOCs or section text, specify all CFR titles or a single title, determine the depth of TOC searches, and limit the number of hits returned. Figure 1-8 shows part of the results returned by a search with the default "satellite NEAR broadcast" search term.

NOTE

*Microsoft and IBM UDDI 1.0 registries contain fully documented entries for the three XML Web services that support the OakLeaf CFR application. Go to http://uddi.microsoft.com/ and type **oakleaf** in the Search text box. Click the OakLeaf Systems link to open the Business Details page, which has links to the individual services.*

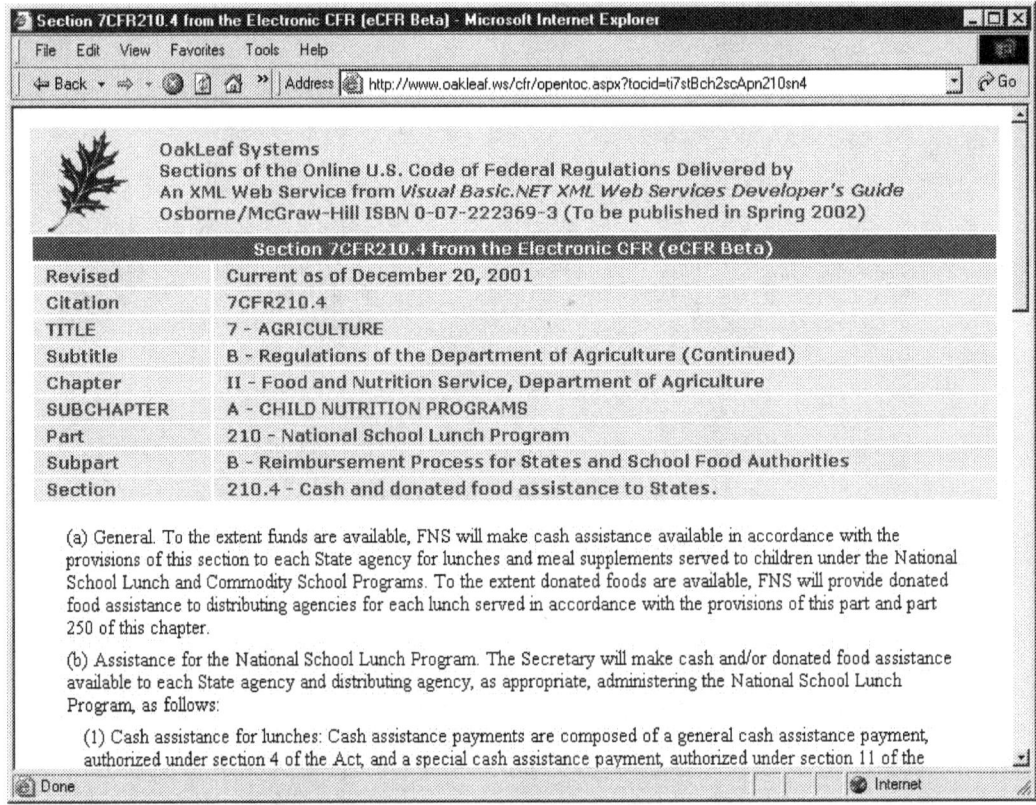

Figure 1-6   *When you click a TOC element at the lowest (section) level of the hierarchy, the JavaScript behavior code passes the SectID attribute value to the CFRSectWS services' GetSectById function.*

The ASP.NET version of the CFR project is the result of a three-stage upgrade from the original Visual Basic 6.0 components and conventional ASP technology. The CFR-COM version uses ActiveX DLLs. COM components of the CFR-SOAP version are upgraded to XML Web services with the SOAP Toolkit 2.0. The next step was CFR-ASPX, which uses ASP.NET in ASP compatibility mode to consume the COM-based XML Web services. You can access the original and the three upgrade versions of the project from the default page at http://www.oakleaf.ws. There is little difference in the appearance or performance of the four versions.

Chapter 9's "Drilling Down with DHTML Navigation" section explains how the CFR client application works. The chapter's downloadable sample code includes the complete ASP.NET code and other files for the client side. You can install the client on your test machine and consume OakLeaf's remote CFRTocWS, CFRSectWS, and CFRSearchWS XML Web services.

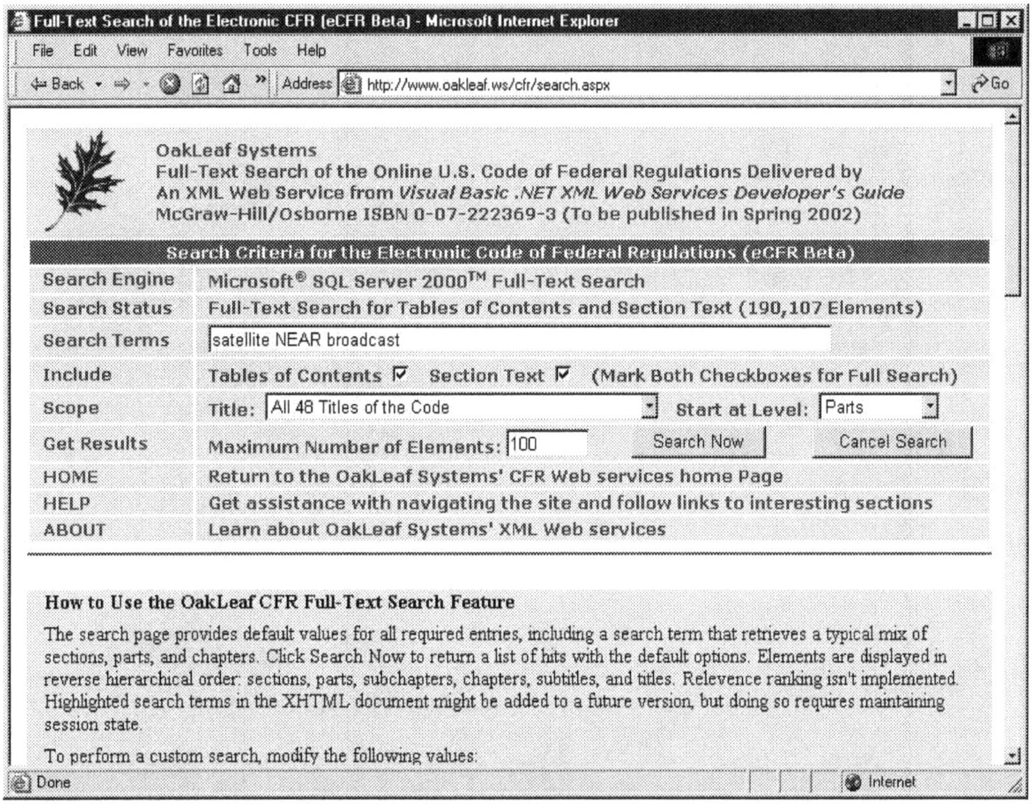

![Full-Text Search of the Electronic CFR (eCFR Beta) - Microsoft Internet Explorer browser window showing the Search.aspx page. Address: http://www.oakleaf.ws/cfr/search.aspx]

OakLeaf Systems
Full-Text Search of the Online U.S. Code of Federal Regulations Delivered by
An XML Web Service from *Visual Basic .NET XML Web Services Developer's Guide*
McGraw-Hill/Osborne ISBN 0-07-222369-3 (To be published in Spring 2002)

Search Criteria for the Electronic Code of Federal Regulations (eCFR Beta)

Search Engine	Microsoft® SQL Server 2000™ Full-Text Search
Search Status	Full-Text Search for Tables of Contents and Section Text (190,107 Elements)
Search Terms	satellite NEAR broadcast
Include	Tables of Contents ☑ Section Text ☑ (Mark Both Checkboxes for Full Search)
Scope	Title: All 48 Titles of the Code Start at Level: Parts
Get Results	Maximum Number of Elements: 100 Search Now Cancel Search
HOME	Return to the OakLeaf Systems' CFR Web services home Page
HELP	Get assistance with navigating the site and follow links to interesting sections
ABOUT	Learn about OakLeaf Systems' XML Web services

How to Use the OakLeaf CFR Full-Text Search Feature

The search page provides default values for all required entries, including a search term that retrieves a typical mix of sections, parts, and chapters. Click Search Now to return a list of hits with the default options. Elements are displayed in reverse hierarchical order: sections, parts, subchapters, chapters, subtitles, and titles. Relevence ranking isn't implemented. Highlighted search terms in the XHTML document might be added to a future version, but doing so requires maintaining session state.

To perform a custom search, modify the following values:

Figure 1-7   *The Search.aspx page generates a full-text search on TOCs, section text, or both.*

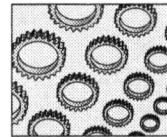

NOTE

Writing the Visual Basic data delivery components, designing the .asp pages, and upgrading the project to XML Web services and, eventually, to ASP.NET and ADO.NET was a piece of cake compared to the effort involved in writing the code to translate the GPO's SGML into well-formed XML for populating the database. SGML is intended primarily for typesetting and doesn't adhere to XML's strict requirements for well formedness, such as matching opening and closing element tags. The GPO has established a very detailed Document Type Definition (CFRDOC.DTD) for a future XML version of the CFR, which you can review at http://www.access.gpo.gov/ecfr/cfrxmldtd.txt.

OakLeaf Consumer Electronics' B2C and B2B Project

The OakLeaf Consumer Electronics (OCE) project is an example of a Visual Basic .NET/ASP.NET B2C retail application that incorporates a B2B supply-chain system. The OCE sample project is typical of distributed applications that use vendors' XML

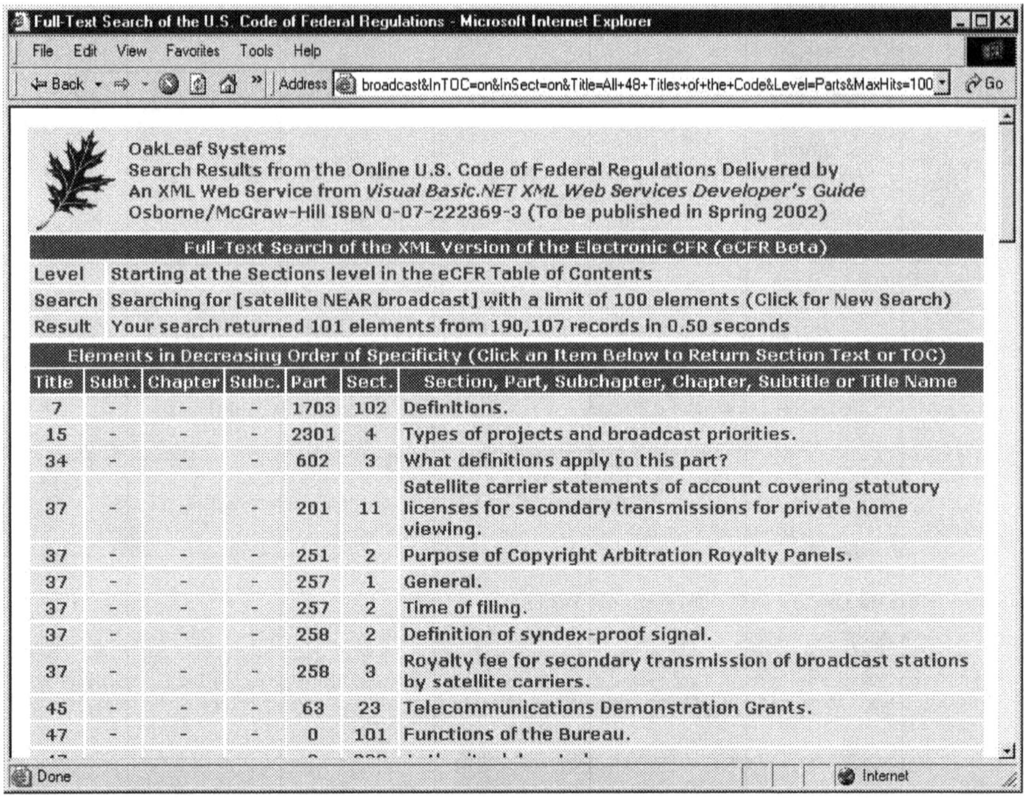

Figure 1-8   The Results.aspx displays the first few sections of the 101 hits returned by the default search specification shown in Figure 1-7.

Web services to perform credit card transactions, manage shipping operations, replenish inventory, and fulfill nonstock or special orders directly from vendors' inventory. Figure 1-9 illustrates the interconnections between OCE customers, service providers, and suppliers. In B2B-speak, these organizations are called "business partners." Partnership infers joint and several liability of partners, so "vendors" or "suppliers" and "service providers" are more accurate terms for third-party participants in sales transactions.

You build the Visual Basic .NET XML Web services and consuming client applications for the OCE project in Chapters 2 through 10 of this book. The databases have a sufficient number of records to determine relative performance of different data access methodologies. Following are brief descriptions of the databases and processes involved in the OCE project:

▶   The Customers/Orders database contains a Customers table with 25,344 customer names, postal addresses, phone numbers, e-mail addresses, and account passwords.

▶   The Products/Inventory database contains a Products table listing 695 consumer electronics products from 26 manufacturers. The products are purchased from three local distributors (Alpha Electronics, Beta Electronics, and Gamma Electronics), each of which offers automated order processing implemented as XML Web services.

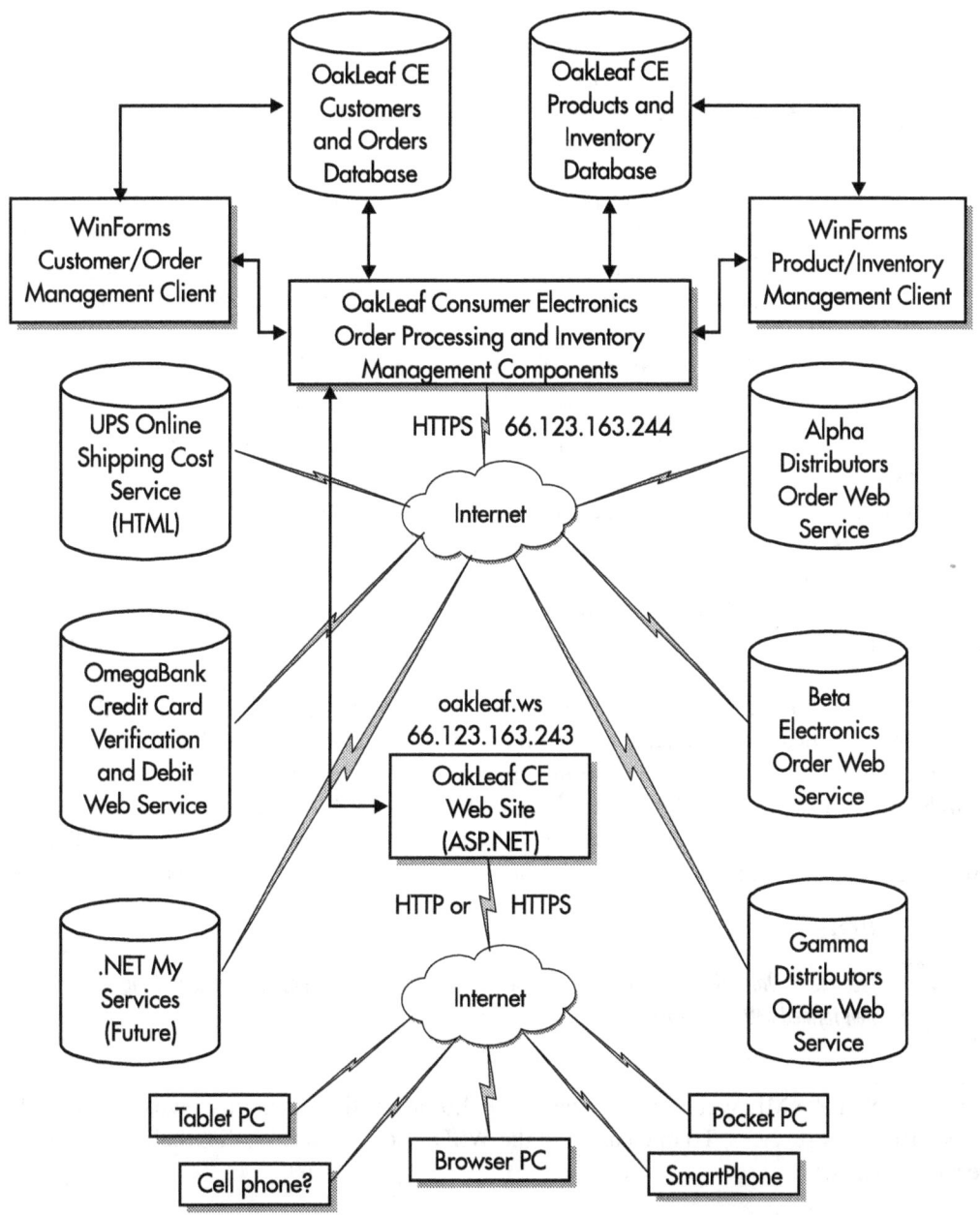

Figure 1-9   *The OakLeaf Consumer Electronics project emulates a large-scale distributed supply-chain application that uses third-party XML Web services for transactions with suppliers and service providers.*

▶ OmegaBank's Authorization database contains 38,188 fictitious American Express, Discover, MasterCharge, and Visa credit cards for OakLeaf's 25,344 customers. The record for each card includes ChargeLimit, Charges, Holds, and Available (credit) fields.

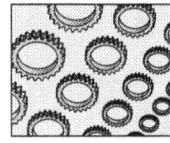

NOTE

All customer and credit card information in the databases is fictitious. The products offered represent actual consumer electronic devices from the manufacturers specified in the database, but price and cost data don't represent actual retail and distributor prices.

▶ When a customer places an order, the ASP.NET project verifies the customer's credit card and available credit, checks product inventory (locally or at the distributor), and computes and adds the shipping charge and sales tax, where applicable. If the products are in inventory, the initial transaction places a hold for the total amount of the order against the credit card, classifies the products ordered as committed inventory, issues a ship order to the warehouse or distributor, and sends an acknowledgment of the order to the customer as an e-mail message or .NET Notification.

▶ Upon shipment of the goods, the final transaction removes the hold, debits the customer's credit card, decrements the products' inventory level, and sends another message or .NET Notification to customers with shipment and tracking information.

Each step in the initial and final transactions is subject to business rules implemented by Visual Basic .NET Windows form and Web Form clients. For example, the initial transaction aborts if the customer's credit card number is invalid, expired, or canceled, or the customer has insufficient credit availability for the purchase.

Figure 1-10 shows the ASP.NET Web Form version of the client consumer for the OmegaBank, AlphaDist, BetaDist, and GammaDist XML Web services. The ALPH entry in the Dist column for the first of the two line items in the figure indicates that shipment of the item has been outsourced to Alpha Distributors, Inc. To test drive the Web Form version of the OCE_Client application, go to http://www.oakleaf.ws/oce/ and click the ASP.NET page's Add One Order button repeatedly to add orders to the remote OCE and distributor databases.

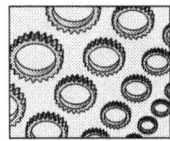

NOTE

Technically, OmegaBank isn't an XML Web service because it returns a cookie-like text string, not a well-formed XML response document.

Like the CFR XML Web services, the UDDI 1.0 production registries have entries for the three distributor services. To open and test the WSDL document for a distributor XML Web service, do this:

1. Go to http://uddi.microsoft.com and search for **Alpha Dist**. Alternatively, click the Advanced Search link, type **oakleaf** in the Search For text box, and choose Business Identifier from the list to display a page that has links to all four services registered by OakLeaf Systems.

2. Click the link to the Business Identifier page, and then click a Name link in the Services list to open the Service Details page.

3. Click the Access Point link to open the service's WSDL page, AlphaDist for this example, which has HTML-formatted service documentation. (See Figure 1-11.)

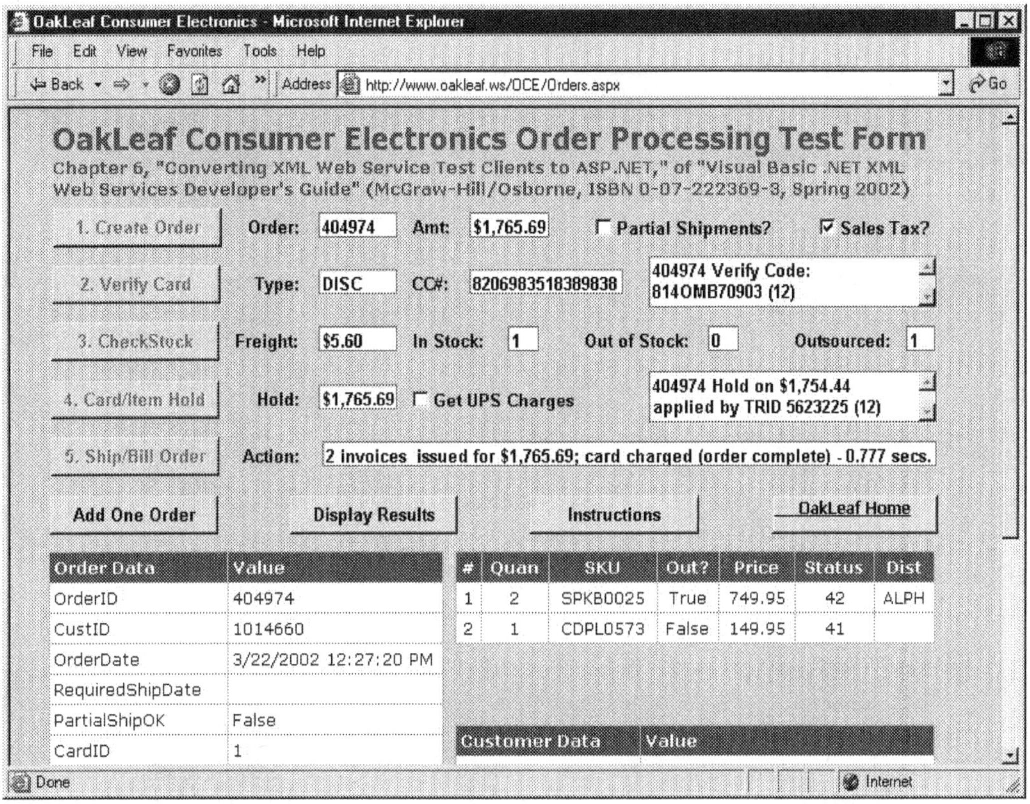

Figure 1-10   *The ASP.NET version of the OCE_Client application consumes ASP.NET XML Web services for credit card and outsourced order processing.*

4. Click the Service Description link to display the WSDL document.

5. Return to the WSDL page and click the Check Stock link to open a test form that uses the HTTP GET protocol to return an XML response document generated by the CheckStock method.

6. Type the five values shown in boldface into the test form's corresponding text boxes.

7. Click Invoke to display the XML response document. (See Figure 1-12.)

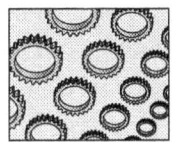

NOTE

Chapter 11 shows you how to navigate the UDDI 1.0 public registries and register your XML Web services.

The Role of XML Web Service Providers

Remote hosting of high-volume public Web sites by major Internet service providers, such as IBM, AT&T, and Exodus, has been common since the late 1990s. The usual approach to remote hosting has been co-location, where the Web site owner rents space (a cage) and

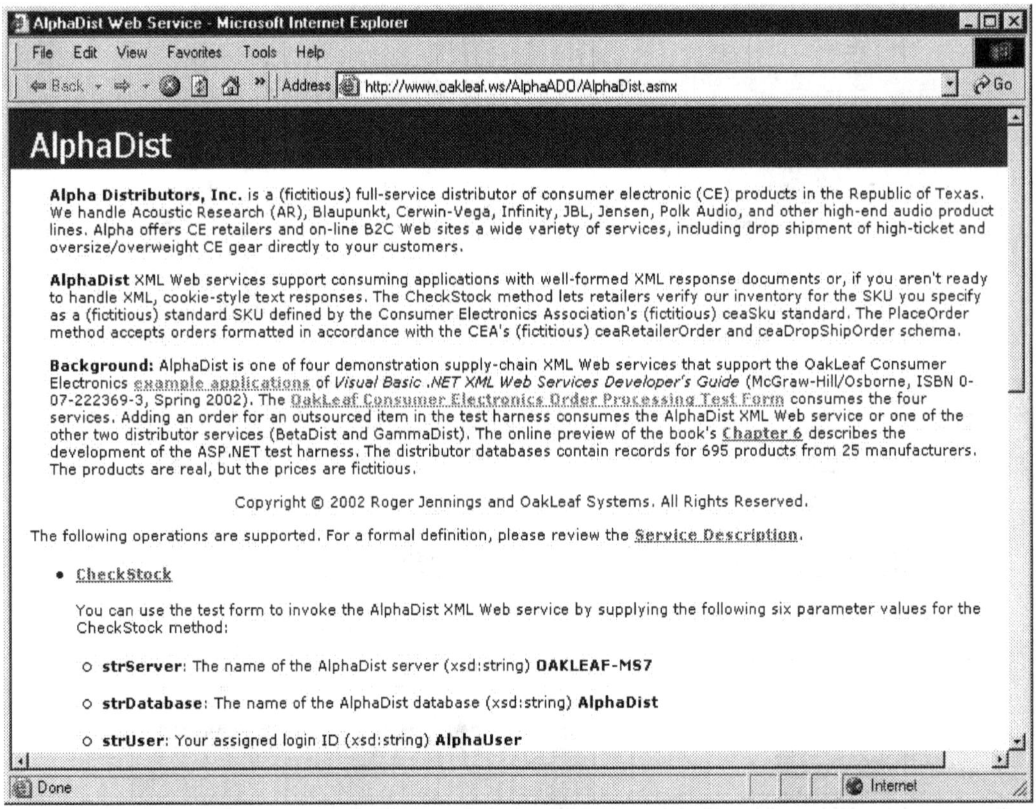

![AlphaDist Web Service - Microsoft Internet Explorer browser window showing the AlphaDist Web Service page]

AlphaDist Web Service - Microsoft Internet Explorer

File Edit View Favorites Tools Help

Back ▾ ⇒ ▾ ⊗ ⊗ ⌂ » Address http://www.oakleaf.ws/AlphaADO/AlphaDist.asmx ▾ ∂Go

AlphaDist

Alpha Distributors, Inc. is a (fictitious) full-service distributor of consumer electronic (CE) products in the Republic of Texas. We handle Acoustic Research (AR), Blaupunkt, Cerwin-Vega, Infinity, JBL, Jensen, Polk Audio, and other high-end audio product lines. Alpha offers CE retailers and on-line B2C Web sites a wide variety of services, including drop shipment of high-ticket and oversize/overweight CE gear directly to your customers.

AlphaDist XML Web services support consuming applications with well-formed XML response documents or, if you aren't ready to handle XML, cookie-style text responses. The CheckStock method lets retailers verify our inventory for the SKU you specify as a (fictitious) standard SKU defined by the Consumer Electronics Association's (fictitious) ceaSku standard. The PlaceOrder method accepts orders formatted in accordance with the CEA's (fictitious) ceaRetailerOrder and ceaDropShipOrder schema.

Background: AlphaDist is one of four demonstration supply-chain XML Web services that support the OakLeaf Consumer Electronics <u>example applications</u> of *Visual Basic .NET XML Web Services Developer's Guide* (McGraw-Hill/Osborne, ISBN 0-07-222369-3, Spring 2002). The <u>OakLeaf Consumer Electronics Order Processing Test Form</u> consumes the four services. Adding an order for an outsourced item in the test harness consumes the AlphaDist XML Web service or one of the other two distributor services (BetaDist and GammaDist). The online preview of the book's <u>Chapter 6</u> describes the development of the ASP.NET test harness. The distributor databases contain records for 695 products from 25 manufacturers. The products are real, but the prices are fictitious.

Copyright © 2002 Roger Jennings and OakLeaf Systems. All Rights Reserved.

The following operations are supported. For a formal definition, please review the <u>Service Description</u>.

- <u>CheckStock</u>

  You can use the test form to invoke the AlphaDist XML Web service by supplying the following six parameter values for the CheckStock method:

  ○ **strServer**: The name of the AlphaDist server (xsd:string) **OAKLEAF-MS7**

  ○ **strDatabase**: The name of the AlphaDist database (xsd:string) **AlphaDist**

  ○ **strUser**: Your assigned login ID (xsd:string) **AlphaUser**

Done   Internet

Figure 1-11   *ASP.NET Web service projects generate ServiceName.asmx files, which have links to the WSDL document and test forms to test the service.*

Internet bandwidth from the provider. Security issues and the cost of Web server management have created a market for complete Internet (and often intranet) infrastructure management by independent firms called application service providers (ASPs).

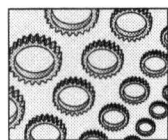

NOTE

The term ASP originally applied to organizations that outsourced server-based applications, such as Microsoft Exchange, customer relationship management programs, e-mail systems, and the like, on the ASP's hardware. Outsourcing a Web server farm, regardless of who owns the equipment, is similar to outsourcing any other application, so ASP has grown to encompass services that manage customers' Internet, intranet, or both operations.

Third-party XML Web service providers are ASPs that specialize in hosting XML Web services and, in many cases, their underlying databases. Some WSPs offer support for multiple platforms, such as Linux, Windows, and various UNIX flavors, and rent space on Oracle, IBM, Sybase, and other database servers. Others specialize in a single technology, such as Microsoft's .NET Framework and SQL Server 2000. The advantages of outsourcing

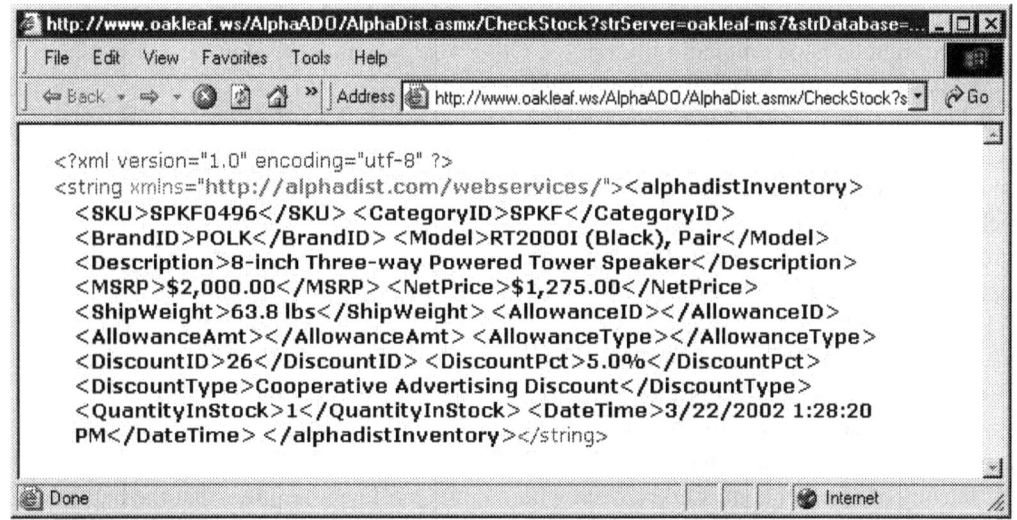

```
<?xml version="1.0" encoding="utf-8" ?>
<string xmins="http://alphadist.com/webservices/"><alphadistInventory>
  <SKU>SPKF0496</SKU> <CategoryID>SPKF</CategoryID>
  <BrandID>POLK</BrandID> <Model>RT2000I (Black), Pair</Model>
  <Description>8-inch Three-way Powered Tower Speaker</Description>
  <MSRP>$2,000.00</MSRP> <NetPrice>$1,275.00</NetPrice>
  <ShipWeight>63.8 lbs</ShipWeight> <AllowanceID></AllowanceID>
  <AllowanceAmt></AllowanceAmt> <AllowanceType></AllowanceType>
  <DiscountID>26</DiscountID> <DiscountPct>5.0%</DiscountPct>
  <DiscountType>Cooperative Advertising Discount</DiscountType>
  <QuantityInStock>1</QuantityInStock> <DateTime>3/22/2002 1:28:20
  PM</DateTime> </alphadistInventory></string>
```

Figure 1-12   *The WSDL page's test form returns the response document of XML Web services that support HTTP GET requests.*

XML Web services, and to a lesser extent, data storage, are similar to those for outsourcing Web farms—availability, reliability, scalability, and, most importantly, security.

Mike Amundsen's Eraserver.net (http://www.eraserver.net) is one of the first WSPs to specialize in hosting .NET XML Web services. Hosting XML Web services on Eraserver.net starts at $9.95 per month; add $10.00 for 10MB of SQL Server database space and another $10.00 for domain hosting. For a list of hosting services that support the .NET Framework and ASP.NET XML Web services, go to http://www.gotdotnet.com/resourcecenter/resource_center.aspx, and select Web Hosting from the Type list. Few, if any, of these hosting firms, however, provide availability and performance guarantees.

Enterprise-level hosting services that offer availability and performance guarantees do so through service-level agreements (SLAs). An SLA specifies guaranteed availability, usually expressed as an uptime percentage—typically 99.9 percent ("three nines"), 99.99 percent ("four nines") or 99.999 percent ("five nines"). Four- or five-nine availability usually requires server clusters and multiple Web server front ends. Hardware-based firewalls provide security against intrusion and site hacking. If the service fails to meet the guaranteed availability level, the customer receives a partial or complete refund for a specified period of time. Charges for enterprise-level hosting services with stringent SLAs start at $10,000 per month or more. Initial hardware and setup charges, which are becoming more common as enterprise-level ASPs burn through their original venture capital, often exceed $100,000.

XML Web Service Pitfalls

One potential drawback of XML Web services is versioning problems. A primary tenet of COM component design is that interfaces are immutable. That is, after you've created a production object, never alter the name or arguments of its public methods. Fixing internal bugs and recompiling a Visual Basic component, however, is allowable if you compile with the appropriate version compatibility option. Otherwise, you must recompile and redeploy every client app to accommodate the updated version.

When your application integration projects involve external XML Web services, which are under the control of another organization and its developers, you can't count on the outside developers to adhere to the immutable component interface rule. Beware of XML Web services that carry "subject to change without notice" in their licensing or subscription agreements. A minor change to a single XML Web service can bring your entire enterprise application integration system to an abrupt halt.

Internet latency and reliability issues are another major concern when your distributed system relies on external XML Web services. Even if the provider of the XML Web service offers a four-nines SLA, the uptime applies only to the remote site, not your ability to connect to it from your server. Quality of Service (QoS) contracts for both endpoints (servers, in this case) can minimize latency over a fixed route, but provisioning QoS is costly to implement. The latency of Internet connections, even with a high QoS level, requires that the database supporting the XML Web service be either local to the site or connected by a dedicated, high-speed (T-3 or better) connection.

Stringent security and snappy performance are mutually exclusive objectives. Until the W3C establishes final security standards for SOAP messages, SSL versions 2.0 and 3.0—which implement the Public Key Infrastructure (PKI), and HTTPS as the transport protocol—are the best (and often the only) choice to maintain security with an Internet connection. Endpoint authentication and message encryption add a substantial amount of overhead to XML Web service connections. Tests with typical request-response operations against moderate-sized databases indicate that HTTPS transmission time increases by about 50 percent of the HTTP round-trip time. There's no guarantee that proposed IBM/Microsoft/VeviSign WS-Security SOAP extension or the W3C's XML Signature and XML Encryption standards will be significantly faster or more secure than traditional SSL and HTTPS.

Another issue developers often raise when discussing the merits of XML and its dialects is the wire overhead added by XML's requirement for human-readable text, long-winded Uniform Resource Identifiers (URIs) for namespace declarations, and other baggage carried by XML-derived languages. Fortunately, HTTP 1.1 text-compression algorithms for readable text and, especially, repetitive tag names and attribute values are very efficient. Performance penalties when substituting XML Web services for DCOM components, for example, are insignificant in most cases. Increases in LAN and WAN performance during XML Web services' commercial gestation period will more than overcome the wire overhead imposed by WSDL/SOAP encoding.

Core XML Web Service "Standards"

XML Web services rely on the W3C specifications (couched as "recommendations") for XML and XSD, but SOAP currently has the status of a W3C note. WSDL, which isn't mentioned in the SOAP note, is a W3C note that's derived from an amalgam of IBM's Network Accessible Services Specification Language (NASSL), DevelopMentor's Component Description Language (CDL), and Microsoft's Service Description Language (SDL) and Service Contract

Language (SCL). UDDI is an invention of the "committed industry leaders" who founded UDDI.org, and doesn't have even W3C note status. The amount of press coverage devoted to a new and largely unproven technology based on pseudostandards is surprising, to say the least. Publicity alone has made SOAP a de facto industry standard.

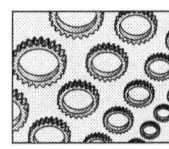

NOTE

Version 1.1 of SOAP and WSDL were current when this book was written. W3C's Web Services Activity, which incorporated the XML Protocol Activity in January 2002, is responsible for establishing a SOAP 1.2 recommendation. You can read the current working draft of the two-part SOAP 1.2 specification at http://www.w3.org/TR/soap12-part1/ and http://www.w3.org/TR/soap12-part2/.

This book doesn't waste pages with an "XML primer" or other introductory XML content. It's assumed that you're at least familiar with XML fundamentals or are willing to gain your XML vocabulary by immersion as you progress through this book. XSD coverage is limited to those elements applicable to WSDL and SOAP request/response documents. The following sections provide an introduction to the XML-based pseudostandards, which Microsoft calls "baseline XML Web service standards," and the W3C recommendations that support or complement XML Web services.

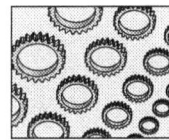

NOTE

Chapter 2 covers the SOAP and WSDL 1.1 specifications in detail. Chapter 10's "Validating XML Request and Response Messages with XSD Schemas" and "Applying Element Datatype Checking to XML Web Services" sections describe how to validate SOAP request and response documents.

Simple Object Access Protocol (SOAP)

SOAP is a specification for a wire protocol designed primarily for invoking methods of objects with a combination of XML and HTTP as the invocation mechanism. The SOAP specification describes an XML vocabulary for representing methods, parameters, return values, and errors (exceptions). SOAP is a standards-based substitute for proprietary RPC protocols, such as DCOM and Internet-InterORB Protocol (IIOP), which aren't well suited to transmission via the public Internet. One of the primary benefits of SOAP is use of HTTP 1.0+ as its transport; all firewalls allow HTTP connections on TCP port 80. Although SOAP supports other transports, use of HTTP is the "Open Sesame" that let the XML Web services genie out of the bottle.

The origins of SOAP extend back to early 1998, when Dave Winer of Userland Software (http://www.userland.com/), Don Box, and members of Microsoft's COM+ (then COM/MTS) group drafted an early version of the current specification. According to Don Box (see http://www.xml.com/pub/a/2001/04/04/soap.html), who's now an architect in the Microsoft .NET Developer and Platform Evangelism group, disagreements between Microsoft's XML and COM+ groups caused a hiatus in the specification development process. To fill the gap, Dave Winer published in April 1998 an XML-RPC specification (http://www.xmlrpc.com/) from a subset of the original SOAP proposal. XML-RPC quickly gained implementations in all major Web-based programming languages and platforms.

Microsoft's subsequent decision to "embrace and extend" XML, which is similar in scope to the firm's December 1995 "embrace and extend" manifesto for Internet-enabling Windows, sped up the authoring process, and the SOAP version 1.0 specification shipped in late 1999. Version 1.1, which gained contributors from IBM and its Lotus subsidiary, was published as a W3C note dated May 8, 2000 (http://www.w3.org/TR/SOAP/). Version 1.1 incorporated some minor technical clarifications and changes; the only new feature added in SOAP 1.1 was the optional `actor` attribute.

A SOAP message is a one-way transmission between endpoints, called *sender* and *receiver*. A SOAP request message usually results in a SOAP response message delivered as an HTTP response to the sender on the request connection. SOAP messages consist of the following three basic elements:

▶   `<SOAP-ENV:Envelope>` is the top element of all SOAP messages and is mandatory.

▶   `<SOAP-ENV:Header>` is an optional element. If present, this element must be the first child element of `<SOAP-ENV:Envelope>`. Header elements enable SOAP messaging to handle extensions, such as WS-Security or WS-Routing, which are described in the later " Microsoft Global XML Web Service Architecture Extensions" section.

▶   `<SOAP-ENV:Body>` is a mandatory element that contains the payload, which must be a well-formed XML document, and an optional single instance of a `<SOAP-ENV:Fault>` element for handling exceptions. Today, the most common payload for a request message is an object method call; the response message's payload is the result of the method's execution, such as a simple string or numeric value. As XML Web services mature, use of XML documents for request and response messages will become more common.

The following two sections illustrate a real-life (nontrivial) pair of SOAP request and response messages. The samples are for a Visual Basic 6.0 ActiveX DLL with a SOAP wrapper applied by the Microsoft SOAP Toolkit 2.0. The Toolkit's Trace Utility (MsSoapT.exe) captured the two messages that result from clicking the Search Now button of the CFR project's .Search.aspx page.

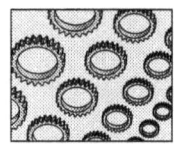

NOTE

You might question why the examples of this chapter use Visual Basic 6.0 components instead of ASP.NET Web Service projects. The answer is that most Visual Basic developers will cut their XML Web services eyeteeth with existing ActiveX DLLs and the SOAP Toolkit. Even if your DLL doesn't emit well-formed XML, it's reasonably easy to modify the DLL code to send the result as unparsed `CDATA` or base64-encoded characters.

SOAP Request Message Example

The following document is a sample SOAP message that requests the XML source document for the default full-text search against the CFRSQL database shown in Figure 1-7, except for a 10-hit (rather than 100-hit) limit. The `GetSearchResults` method of the `CFRSearch` object has nine arguments: `strConnect`, `strSearch`, `intMaxHits`, `intMinLevel`, `intMaxLevel`, `strTitleID`, `lngTOCItems`, `lngSectItems`, and `strSearchType`.

For this example, the value of `strSearchType` is XML; substituting XHTML returns the corresponding XHTML document for browser presentation.

```
<?xml version="1.0" encoding="UTF-8" standalone="no" ?>
  <SOAP-ENV:Envelope SOAP-ENV:encodingStyle=
        "http://schemas.xmlsoap.org/soap/encoding/"
        xmlns:SOAP-ENV="http://schemas.xmlsoap.org/soap/envelope/">
    <SOAP-ENV:Body>
      <SOAPSDK1:GetSearchResults
            xmlns:SOAPSDK1="http://oakleaf.ws/message/">
        <strConnect>
          Provider=SQLOLEDB;Data Source=OAKLEAF-MS9;
          Initial Catalog=CFRSQL;UID=CFRUser;PWD=charon?123
        </strConnect>
        <strSearch>
          satellite NEAR broadcast
        </strSearch>
        <intMaxHits>
          10
        </intMaxHits>
        <intMinLevel>
          0
        </intMinLevel>
        <intMaxLevel>
          7
        </intMaxLevel>
        <strTitleID />
        <lngTOCItems>
          9179
        </lngTOCItems>
        <lngSectItems>
          172801
        </lngSectItems>
        <strSearchType>
          XML
        </strSearchType>
      </SOAPSDK1:GetSearchResults>
    </SOAP-ENV:Body>
  </SOAP-ENV:Envelope>
```

The assignment of the method name and its argument values to XML elements is straightforward and easy for any Visual Basic developer to interpret. In this example, the argument values are simple strings and numeric types, which don't require datatype definitions in the message. Chapters 2 and 10 deal with these and more complex datatypes, such as structures and arrays. Chapter 3 shows you how to use the Microsoft SOAP Toolkit 2.0.

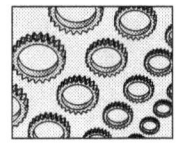

NOTE

When this book was written, the SOAP Toolkit 3.0 was in the prebeta stage. Version 3.0 of the Toolkit should be available as a beta or release version in mid-2002.

SOAP Response Message Example

Sending the preceding request message results in the following SOAP response message, which contains a well-formed XML document as its `<SOAP-ENV:Body>` payload. The SOAP wrapper appends `Response` to the name of the method and delivers the document within the `<Result>` subelement. The `<Header>` subelements generate the first four rows of the table shown in Figure 1-8; the `<ColHeads>` subelement specifies the number of columns and column names for the search hits. Result elements at the `<Sections>` level include `id` attribute values for navigation and populating the ten result rows.

```
<?xml version="1.0" encoding="UTF-8" standalone="no" ?>
<SOAP-ENV:Envelope SOAP-ENV:encodingStyle=
      "http://schemas.xmlsoap.org/soap/encoding/"
      xmlns:SOAP-ENV="http://schemas.xmlsoap.org/soap/envelope/">
   <SOAP-ENV:Body>
      <SOAPSDK1:GetSearchResultsResponse
            xmlns:SOAPSDK1="http://oakleaf.ws/message/">
         <Result>
            <?xml version="1.0" encoding = "UTF-8" ?>
            <CFRSearch xmlns:CFRSections=
                  "http://www.oakmont.org/CFR/Search" >
               <Header>
                  <Head>
                     Full-Text Search of the XML Version of the
                     Electronic CFR (eCFR Beta)
                  </Head>
                  <Level>
                     Starting at the Sections level in the eCFR
                     Table of Contents
                  </Level>
                  <Search>
                     Searching for [satellite NEAR broadcast] with
                     a limit of 10 elements
                  </Search>
                  <Result>
                     Your search returned 10 elements from 181,980
                     records in 0.12 seconds
                  </Result>
                  <ColHeads>
                     4:Title:Part:Section:Section Name
                  </ColHeads>
```

```
      </Header>
      <Body>
         <Sections>
            <Section id='ti7pn1703sn102'>
               102 - Definitions.
            </Section>
            <Section id='ti15pn2301sn2'>
                2 - Definitions.
            </Section>
            <Section id='ti15pn2301sn4'>
                4 - Types of projects and broadcast priorities.
            </Section>
            <Section id='ti34pn602sn3'>
               3 - What definitions apply to this part?
            </Section>
            <Section id='ti37pn201sn11'>
                11 - Satellite carrier statements of account
                covering statutory licenses for secondary
                transmissions for private home viewing.
            </Section>
            <Section id='ti37pn251sn2'>
                2 - Purpose of Copyright Arbitration
                Royalty Panels.
            </Section>
            <Section id='ti47pn0sn283'>
               283 - Authority delegated.
            </Section>
            <Section id='ti47pn0sn51'>
               51 - Functions of the Bureau.
            </Section>
            <Section id='ti47pn1sn4000'>
               4000 - Restrictions impairing reception of
               television broadcast signals, direct broadcast
               satellite services, or multichannel multipoint
               distribution services and restrictions impairing
               reception or transmission of fixed wireless
               communications signals.

            </Section>
            <Section id='ti47pn11sn33'>
                33 - EAS Decoder.
            </Section>
         </Sections>
      </Body>
   </CFRSearch>
```

```
        </Result>
      </SOAPSDK1:GetSearchResultsResponse>
    </SOAP-ENV:Body>
  </SOAP-ENV:Envelope>
```

Compare the text of the preceding source XML document with the tabular results shown in Figure 1-8. Most <Result> subelements correspond to those of Figure 1-8; differences are the result of specifying 10 instead of 100 as the maximum number of hits.

SOAP Message Attachments

Conventional SOAP messages consist of a well-formed XML document; if the message isn't well formed, XML parsers reject the entire envelope. In many cases, it's desirable to include nontext attachments, such as fax and bitmap images, with the SOAP payload. Microsoft's SOAP Messages with Attachments specification defines "SOAP message packages" that contain a primary (XML) document and attachments of the MIME Multipart/Related media type (IETF RFC 2557, http://www.ietf.org/rfc/rfc2557.txt). You can read Microsoft's W3C note at http://www.w3.org/TR/SOAP-attachments.

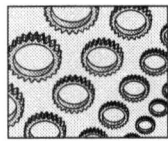

NOTE

SOAP Messages with Attachments isn't a "core" XML Web services protocol, but it shares W3C note status with SOAP and WSDL. An alternative to base64 encoding non-XML content or incorporating a MIME attachment is to provide a URL for the attachment and rely on the consuming application to retrieve the binary data.

In May 2001, Microsoft published a specification for Direct Internet Message Encapsulation (DIME), which you can read at http://www.gotdotnet.com/team/xml_wsspecs/dime/dime.htm. The specification's authors describe DIME as a "lightweight, binary encapsulation format that can be used to encapsulate multiple application-defined entities or payloads of arbitrary type and size into a single message construct." The DIME specification is intended to improve the performance of SOAP messages with attachments by eliminating the need to parse an entire MIME enclosure to determine if and how the enclosure applies to the message. Microsoft submitted DIME and Encapsulating SOAP in DIME as Internet drafts to the IETF on February 1, 2002. You can read both drafts at http://gotdotnet.com/team/xml_wsspecs/dime/default.aspx.

Web Services Description Language (WSDL)

WSDL (commonly pronounced "whizdle") is a standardized metadata language—developed jointly by Microsoft and IBM—for defining XML Web services in terms of service endpoints (ports) to which clients connect with a specified protocol (binding), object invocation (operation), and message format (SOAP). You can read the WSDL version 1.1 specification, which was current when this book was written, at http://www.w3.org/TR/wsdl.

The WSDL 1.1 specification provides examples only for SOAP 1.1, HTTP GET/POST, and MIME. Given a sufficiently detailed WSDL file, an application can automatically generate a SOAP client proxy from the WSDL document. The SOAP Tookit's WSDL Generator utility (Wsdlgen.exe) generates WSDL 1.1 files named *WebServiceName*.wsdl.

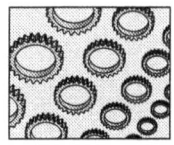

NOTE

When you create an ASP.NET Web Service project with the `<WebService>` class attribute, ASP.NET creates a WebServiceName.asmx page that contains a WSDL document, not a freestanding .wsdl file.

As you can see from the following Toolkit-generated CFRSearchWS.wsdl file for the CFR project's full-text search page, writing a custom WSDL file in Notepad isn't a trivial task:

```
<?xml version='1.0' encoding='UTF-8' ?>
<!-- Generated 10/08/01 by Microsoft SOAP Toolkit WSDL File Generator,
     Version 1.02.813.0 -->
<definitions name='CFRSearchWS' targetNamespace='http://oakleaf.ws/wsdl/'
             xmlns:wsdlns='http://oakleaf.ws/wsdl/'
             xmlns:typens='http://oakleaf.ws/type'
             xmlns:soap='http://schemas.xmlsoap.org/wsdl/soap/'
             xmlns:xsd='http://www.w3.org/2001/XMLSchema'
             xmlns:stk='http://schemas.microsoft.com/soap-toolkit/
                   wsdl-extension'
             xmlns='http://schemas.xmlsoap.org/wsdl/'>
  <types>
    <schema targetNamespace='http://oakleaf.ws/type'
            xmlns='http://www.w3.org/2001/XMLSchema'
            xmlns:SOAP-ENC='http://schemas.xmlsoap.org/soap/encoding/'
            xmlns:wsdl='http://schemas.xmlsoap.org/wsdl/'
                   elementFormDefault='qualified'>
    </schema>
  </types>
  <message name='CFRSearch.GetSearchResults'>
    <part name='strConnect' type='xsd:string'/>
    <part name='strSearch' type='xsd:string'/>
    <part name='intMaxHits' type='xsd:short'/>
    <part name='intMinLevel' type='xsd:short'/>
    <part name='intMaxLevel' type='xsd:short'/>
    <part name='strTitleID' type='xsd:string'/>
    <part name='lngTOCItems' type='xsd:int'/>
    <part name='lngSectItems' type='xsd:int'/>
    <part name='strSearchType' type='xsd:string'/>
  </message>
  <message name='CFRSearch.GetSearchResultsResponse'>
    <part name='Result' type='xsd:string'/>
  </message>
  <portType name='CFRSearchSoapPort'>
    <operation name='GetSearchResults'
                   parameterOrder='strConnect strSearch intMaxHits
                   intMinLevel intMaxLevel strTitleID lngTOCItems
                   lngSectItems strSearchType'>
```

```
      <input message='wsdlns:CFRSearch.GetSearchResults' />
      <output message='wsdlns:CFRSearch.GetSearchResultsResponse' />
    </operation>
  </portType>
  <binding name='CFRSearchSoapBinding' type='wsdlns:CFRSearchSoapPort' >
    <stk:binding preferredEncoding='UTF-8'/>
    <soap:binding style='rpc'
                  transport='http://schemas.xmlsoap.org/soap/http' />
    <operation name='GetSearchResults' >
      <soap:operation soapAction='http://oakleaf.ws/action/
                      CFRSearch.GetSearchResults' />
      <input>
        <soap:body use='encoded' namespace='http://oakleaf.ws/message/'
            encodingStyle='http://schemas.xmlsoap.org/soap/encoding/' />
      </input>
      <output>
        <soap:body use='encoded' namespace='http://oakleaf.ws/message/'
            encodingStyle='http://schemas.xmlsoap.org/soap/encoding/' />
      </output>
    </operation>
  </binding>
  <service name='CFRSearchWS' >
    <port name='CFRSearchSoapPort' binding='wsdlns:CFRSearchSoapBinding' >
      <soap:address location='http://66.123.163.243/cfr/CFRSearchWS.WSDL' />
    </port>
  </service>
</definitions>
```

NOTE

This book often uses IP addresses instead of domain names to invoke XML Web services. The use of hard-coded IP addresses improves service performance by eliminating DNS lookup operations. The oakleaf.ws domain provides a unique URI for the `targetNamespace` *attribute of the top* `<definitions>` *element. The .ws (Western Samoa) top-level domain will undoubtedly become popular for sites offering commercial Web services.*

If you skip the laundry list of namespace declaration attributes at the beginning of the sample WSDL document, it's easy to associate WSDL elements with the two SOAP messages of the two preceding sections. The `<portType>` section's `<input>` element includes the programmatic ID (`ProgID`) registered for the ActiveX DLL. (A registered copy of the DLL or, less commonly, a DCOM proxy, must exist on the machine that hosts the WSDL file.) A `<part>` element specifies each parameter's name and datatype; parameters require XSD datatype identifiers, many of which correspond to Visual Basic .NET's elementary datatypes. The later "XML Schema Definition (XSD) Language" section has more information on XSD datatypes. The `<portType>` element's `<operation>` section defines `<input>` (request)

and <output> (response) message names. The <binding> element specifies the wire
protocol (HTTP), and <service> adds the URL to which clients connect to read the
WSDL file and execute the method.

Web Services Meta Language (WSML) defines a Microsoft proprietary XML syntax
required for SOAP-enabled COM components. When you create a WSDL file, Wsdlgen.exe
writes the corresponding WSML file and uses the information it contains to generate the final
WSDL file. ASP.NET Web Service projects don't need a WSML file.

```xml
<?xml version='1.0' encoding='UTF-8' ?>
  <!-- Generated 10/08/01 by Microsoft SOAP Toolkit WSDL File Generator,
       Version 1.02.813.0 -->
<servicemapping name='CFRSearchWS'>
  <service name='CFRSearchWS'>
    <using PROGID='CCFRSearch.CFRSearch' cachable='0'
           ID='CFRSearchObject' />
    <port name='CFRSearchSoapPort'>
      <operation name='GetSearchResults'>
        <execute uses='CFRSearchObject' method='GetSearchResults'
                 dispID='1610809344'>
          <parameter callIndex='1' name='strConnect'
                     elementName='strConnect' />
          <parameter callIndex='2' name='strSearch'
                     elementName='strSearch' />
          <parameter callIndex='3' name='intMaxHits'
                     elementName='intMaxHits' />
          <parameter callIndex='4' name='intMinLevel'
                     elementName='intMinLevel' />
          <parameter callIndex='5' name='intMaxLevel'
                     elementName='intMaxLevel' />
          <parameter callIndex='6' name='strTitleID'
                     elementName='strTitleID' />
          <parameter callIndex='7' name='lngTOCItems'
                     elementName='lngTOCItems' />
          <parameter callIndex='8' name='lngSectItems'
                     elementName='lngSectItems' />
          <parameter callIndex='9' name='strSearchType'
                     elementName='strSearchType' />
          <parameter callIndex='-1' name='retval'
                     elementName='Result' />
        </execute>
      </operation>
    </port>
  </service>
</servicemapping>
```

TIP

Connect to http://66.123.163.243/cfr/cfrsearchws.wsdl to open the Toolkit's version of the WSDL file in IE 5.0+. The other WSDL files for the CFR project at this URL are CFRTocWS.wsdl (to return TOCs) and CFRSectWS.wsdl (to return section text). To open the ASP.NET version, use http://66.123.163.243/cfrtocws/cfrtocws.asmx?wsdl as the address. The Toolkit creates rpc/encoded .wsdl files; ASP.NET uses document/literal format. Chapter 2's "Exchanging SOAP Messages" section describes the differences between rpc/encoded and document/literal formats.

XML Schema Definition (XSD) Language

All XML documents that participate in XML Web services must be well formed. Being *well formed* means that the document complies with the grammar and syntax rules of the W3C XML 1.0 specification. XML parsers, such as MSXML v3+, report errors when opening a malformed XML document. MSXML v3+ has a `parseError` object that you can interrogate to determine whether an error has occurred, and, if so, what caused the error. Being well formed, however, doesn't mean the XML document is valid for its intended purpose. *Validation* is the process of assuring that the document's contents conform to a particular structure and a specific set of rules for the document's class.

XML is a derivative of the SGML document formatting language, which uses Data Type Definition (DTD) documents for validation. Thus, it's not surprising that the first validation method for XML documents also used DTDs. DTDs are intended primarily for describing text-based documents, are very complex, and are exceedingly difficult to write correctly. As developers adopted XML for exchanging data between database servers and applications, it became clear that DTDs weren't suited to validating documents that contained datatypes other than text strings. Another disadvantage of DTDs is that they aren't written in XML, so they're difficult to read and parse.

XML-Data was the first attempt to replace DTDs with schemas for defining and documenting object classes within XML documents. Microsoft was the primary sponsor of the XML-Data specification, which was published as a W3C note in 1998 (http://www.w3.org/TR/1998/NOTE-XML-data/). XML-Data provided XML `<elementType>` declarations having an optional `<description>` element for documentation, and `<key>` elements to support one-to-many relationships. XML-Data also defined datatype attributes, such as `dt:dt="int"` and `dt:dt="string"`. Microsoft adopted a subset of XML-Data—named XML-Data Reduced (XDR)—as the standard schema definition language for SQL Server 2000's XML features, BizTalk server, and other XML-based programs. The MSXML parser released with IE 5.0 handles document validation by XDR schemas.

After a long gestation period in the XML Schema Working Group, W3C published the final recommendations for XML Schema in May 2001. The specification consists of three documents: XML Schema Part 0: Primer (http://www.w3.org/TR/xmlschema-0/), XML Schema Part 1: Structures (http://www.w3.org/TR/xmlschema-1/), and XML Schema Part 2: Datatypes (http://www.w3.org/TR/xmlschema-2/). Microsoft has adopted XSD in all newly released products; XDR is supported by the .NET Framework but is relegated to "legacy" status. MSXML 4.0 Core Services, released in September 2001, validates documents with XSD or XDR. SQLXML 2.0+ supports both XSD and XDR schemas for XPath queries, and you can use the `XMLSchemaCollection` member of the .NET Framework's `System.Xml.Schema` namespace to validate XML documents against XSD or XDR schemas.

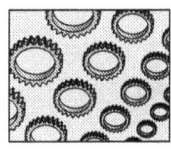

NOTE

Chapter 10's "Validating XML Request and Response Messages with XSD Schemas" section has examples of XSD schemas and shows you how to validate XML request and response messages with the .NET Framework's `XmlValidatingReader` *class.*

The Datatypes section of the XML Schema specification is of most interest to XML Web service developers, because it defines the simple datatypes you can assign to method arguments and elements of SOAP response documents. Following are the three primary classes of XML Schema datatypes:

▶ **Built-in primitive datatypes** include `string`, `decimal`, `float`, `double`, `boolean`, `base64Binary`, and `hexBinary`, many datatypes for date, time, and duration, and miscellaneous types, such as `anyURI`, `QName`, and `NOTATION`.

▶ **Built-in derived datatypes** represent subclasses of primitive datatypes defined by values of *constraining facets* that restrict a datatype's value. For example, `integer` is derived from `decimal` with the `fractionDigits` facet value set to 0. Each primitive datatype has a collection of valid constraining facets. Subclasses of `integer` include `long`, `int`, `short`, `byte`, `negativeInteger`, `nonPositiveInteger`, `positiveInteger`, `nonNegativeInteger`, `unsignedLong`, `unsignedInt`, `unsignedShort`, and `unsignedByte`. Both types of built-in datatypes are called *atomic*.

▶ **User-derived datatypes** are made up of atomic datatypes and include list and union datatypes. The most common application for simple user-derived datatypes is data validation by `<pattern>` elements that use regular expressions to define valid data. Individual list values are separated by whitespace, so list elements can't contain spaces or newline characters.

The preceding three categories of simple datatypes are capable of handling most method arguments and values returned from relational databases. Complex type definitions, which Part 1: Structures describes, support objects representing business documents, such as purchase orders, or rows of relational data.

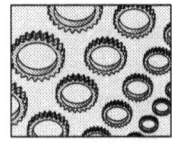

NOTE

Chapter 10's "Specifying XSD Datatypes in XML Request Documents" and "Applying Element Datatype Checking to XML Web Services" sections show you how to create strongly typed documents and validate their elements' datatypes.

Section 5.2 of the SOAP 1.1 specification adopts all built-in datatypes of XSD, plus XSD enumerations. The SOAP specification additionally defines two compound datatypes: `Struct`, which is similar to an XSD complex type, and `Array`. The `Array` datatype supports multidimensional and sparse arrays, which are useful for adding or updating records of tables having one-to-many relationships. Don Box observes that the SOAP 1.0 specification would have been only three or four pages long if the XSD specification had been completed prior to finalizing the SOAP W3C note.

Universal Description, Discovery, and Integration (UDDI)

UDDI is the result of a joint effort by Microsoft, IBM, and others to provide a means for potential users to locate XML Web services that perform a particular function. UDDI consists of specifications for data structures, a programmer's API, and replication, together with XSD schemas for each type of document. You can download version 2.0 of the complete set of UDDI specifications from http://www.uddi.org/specification.html. The UDDI.org site also offers white papers and technical/executive backgrounders.

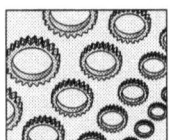

NOTE

Unlike WSDL, there's no generally accepted pronunciation for UDDI. Some developers say "ooh-dee" and others stick with more formal "u-d-d-i."

Microsoft and IBM operate public UDDI version 1.0 registries, which use replication to keep the individual sites in sync. UDDI registrars assist users with registering their services in one of the public registries and searching for third-party services. (The Microsoft registry requires .NET Passport authentication). Chapter 11 shows you how to register and search for services from your browser or by using the Microsoft UDDI Toolkit, which you can download from http://www.microsoft.com/downloads/release.asp?ReleaseID=35982.

As mentioned in the earlier "XML Web Service Examples" section, you can search Microsoft's UDDI 1.0 registry for a specific company name or by several different industry classification schemes (http://uddi.microsoft.com/search.aspx). Most UDDI registrations are blatant advertisements and have no XML Web service registrations. Controlling spam in the registries presents a major problem for UDDI operators. One possibility is to drop registrations that don't point to a valid WSDL file within 30 days of adding the company information.

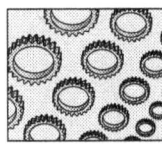

NOTE

UDDI 2.0 was in the beta testing stage when this book was written, and several additional organizations run public UDDI 2.0 nodes. Chapter 12 discusses the pros and cons of moving to a beta version of UDDI 2.0. Windows .NET Server Beta 3 and later supports private UDDI 2.0 directories; Microsoft no longer offers a private UDDI 1.0 implementation.

UDDI public registration of XML Web services is optional and, depending on the nature of the services you offer, might not be advisable. For example, if your XML Web services provide access to your organization's inventory data and enable automated order entry, your marketing department undoubtedly knows the potential consumers of the services. Advertising the service in a public UDDI registry is likely to invite more hackers and competitors than prospective customers to take advantage of your commercial XML Web services. On the other hand, if you offer a general-purpose XML Web service, such as a sales tax rate lookup application, you might benefit by adding an entry for the service in a public UDDI registry.

W3C Security Standards: XML-Signature, XML Encryption, and XML Key Management Specification (XKMS)

HTTPS is currently the only universal (and thus currently practical) method for XML Web service consumer authentication and securing the communication channel for XML Web services that deliver confidential information. For an overview of XML Web service authentication and authorization issues in the Visual Basic 6.0 environment, read the "Building Secure Web Services with Microsoft SOAP Toolkit 2.0" paper at http://msdn.microsoft.com/library/en-us/dnsoap/html/soapsecurity.asp. Most of the recommendations in this paper also apply to ASP.NET Web Service projects.

One of the primary concerns of potential publishers of XML Web services is assuring the security of the services and their underlying data sources. Thus, W3C working groups and member organizations are busy preparing recommendations and position papers on XML-related security technology. Following are two specifications and one proposal for enhancing the security of XML Web services beyond what is offered by HTTPS:

▶ **XML-Signature Syntax and Processing** is a W3C recommendation, which was adopted on February 12, 2002. XML-Signature describes methods for attaching digital signatures to individual elements of an XML document or the entire document. PKI-based digital signatures are intended to verify the identity of the source of the data, such as a person authorizing a debit to a checking account. In this case, signing the SOAP request message and verifying the signature of the bank in the response message provides two-way verification.

▶ **XML Encryption Syntax and Processing**, as of March 4, 2002, is a W3C candidate recommendation for, according to the abstract, "a process for encrypting data and representing the result in XML. The data may be arbitrary data (including an XML document), an XML element, or XML element content. The result of encrypting data is an XML Encryption element which contains or references the cipher data." The candidate recommendation is at http://www.w3.org/TR/xmlenc-core/.

▶ **XML Key Management Specification** (XKMS) is W3C note-authored by VeriSign and others for use of XML-Signature to identify cryptographic keys and authenticate request and response messages, and for use of XML Encryption to protect the confidentiality of message payload. XKMS is specifically intended to be "layered over SOAP and WSDL." You can read the note at http://www.w3.org/TR/xkms/ and search the http://www.verisign.com with **xkms** to find links to Verisign's marketing propaganda for XKMS.

Microsoft Global XML Web Service Architecture Extensions

Microsoft announced in October 2001 a set of four proposed extensions to SOAP, which have come to be known as "SOAP bubbles." These extensions add support for SOAP-based security and message routing. Microsoft and IBM released an additional XML Web Service extension, WS-Inspection, on November 2, 2001. The five extensions were the first members of what Microsoft calls Global XML Web Services Architecture (GXA). For a long-winded description of the objectives of GXA, go to http://gotdotnet.com/team/xmlwebservices/gxa_overview.aspx.

Microsoft GXA Extensions

Following are brief descriptions of the purposes of the four original Microsoft GXA extension proposals:

▶   **WS-Security** Defines headers that convey the identity of XML Web service consumers and specify the methods that are used to assure confidentiality and integrity for SOAP messages.

▶   **WS-License** Defines headers that identify the consumer's credentials (licenses) to use an XML Web service. WS-License is incorporated in the new WS-Security specification described in the next section.

▶   **WS-Routing** Defines headers for indicating the path by which SOAP messages are to be routed from one SOAP node to another.

▶   **WS-Referral** Defines headers that allow an individual SOAP node to specify the route to the next node, rather than including the routing information in the SOAP message header data.

At http://www.gotdotnet.com/team/XMLwebservices/gxa_overview.aspx, you can read an October 2001 white paper that describes the preceding four GXA members. The page at http://msdn.microsoft.com/library/default.asp?url=/library/en-us/dnsoapspec/html/wsspecsover.asp has links to the four preceding specifications and their schema.

The IBM/Microsoft/VeriSign WS-Security Specification

IBM, Microsoft, and VeriSign announced on April 11, 2002, a new version of the WS-Security specification that combine basic elements of the original WS-Security and WS-Licensing specs. The objective of WS-Security is to provide end-to-end message integrity, confidentiality, and non-repudiation. (HTTPS provides point-to-point security but doesn't provide non-repudiation, which requires a digital signature for the SOAP message payload.) WS-Security specifies a set of custom SOAP headers to implement the W3C XML Encryption recommendation and XML Signature proposed recommendation. The XML Key Management Specification (XKMS) 2.0—a working draft when this book was written—will play an important role in implementing WS-Security.

IBM and Microsoft also announced a "Web services security roadmap" that includes the following six future specifications:

▶   **WS-Policy** for defining constraints applied by Web service security policies

▶ **WS-Trust** for establishing direct and brokered trust relationships

▶ **WS-Privacy** for stating and implementing Web service privacy practices

▶ **WS-Secure Conversation** for managing security context and deriving session keys

▶ **WS-Federation** for brokering trust relationships in heterogeneous service environments

▶ **WS-Authorization** for defining and management of authorization data and policies

Microsoft and IBM have published at http://msdn.microsoft.com/ws-security/ a "Security in a Web Services World: A Proposed Architecture and Roadmap" white paper which describes and has links to the new WS-Security specification. Microsoft announced at Tech*Ed 2002 that sample .NET implementations of WS-Security *might* be available by late 2002.

WS-Inspection

The WS-Inspection specification is the result of a joint effort between Microsoft and IBM to develop a Web Service Inspection Language (WSIL). The objective of WSIL, according to the authors, is to "facilitate the aggregation of references to different types of service description documents, and then provides a well-defined pattern of usage for instances of this grammar." Unlike the GXA members of the preceding sections, WS-Inspection doesn't involve headers.

WSIL is the replacement for Microsoft's proprietary disco(very) service, which was the standard inspection method for .NET XML Web services prior to the Visual Studio .NET release version. You can read the full text of the proposed WS-Inspection specification at http://msdn.microsoft.com/library/en-us/dnsrvspec/html/ws-inspection.asp.

Other Proposed XML Web Service Languages

Web services tool vendors appear to be intent on erecting a modern-day Tower of WS-Babel. Proposals for new XML grammars to support real or imagined needs of XML Web services developers surface every week or two. Microsoft and IBM cooperate on many XML fronts, but the interests of IBM and its other partners often diverge from Microsoft's. Following are three IBM-sponsored proposals that might gain widespread support:

▶ **Web Services Flow Language** (WSFL) is an XML grammar for orchestrating interaction between multiple XML Web services. WSFL defines a service flow model by layering WSFL over WSDL. WSFL appears to compete with Microsoft BizTalk Server's XLANG for defining document workflow. The proposed WSFL specification is at http://www-4.ibm.com/software/solutions/webservices/pdf/WSFL.pdf. A series of IBM white papers about WSFL start at http://www-106.ibm.com/developerworks/webservices/library/ws-ref5/.

▶ **Web Services Endpoint Language** (WSEL) defines properties of endpoints, such as QoS, execution time limits, and escalation methods in the event of endpoint failure. The WSFL specification alludes to, but doesn't define, a future WSEL implementation. WS-Endpoint might be a candidate for a future GXA extension.

▶ **Web Services Component Model** (WSCM) is a project intended to standardize the browser interface for XML Web services that are directed to end users rather than servers. WSCM is based in part on Epicentric's Web Service User Interface (WSUI) for corporate portals (http://www.epicentric.com). IBM will contribute its Web Service Experience Language (WSXL) to the project (http://www-106.ibm.com/developerworks/library/ws-wsxl/index.html). The Organization for the Advancement of Structured Information Standards (OASIS) will handle the standardization process (http://www.oasis-open.org/news/oasis_news_10_22_01.shtml).

OASIS' primary claim to XML fame is sponsorship—in conjunction with the United Nations Centre for Trade Facilitation and Electronic Business (UN/CEFACT)—of the electronic business XML (ebXML) standards. ebXML is a very complex messaging standard that's built on top of SOAP. Microsoft arch-enemy Sun Microsystems is one of the outspoken proponents of ebXML, and the majority of ebXML implementations are Java-based.

Sun joined the general-purpose XML Web services bandwagon well after Microsoft and, when this book was written, was playing catch-up in the SOAP public relations space. Sun vice-president Rich Green said in late October 2001, "As standards are defined for the next generation of networked services—what we call *services on demand*—Sun ONE will have a comprehensive set of industry standards–based capabilities to offer" (emphasis added; http://www.sun.com/smi/Press/sunflash/2001-10/sunflash.20011023.5.html). When this book was written, Sun didn't appear to be convinced that SOAP 1.1 and WSDL 1.1 were de facto industry standards because of their Microsoft/IBM heritage. Perhaps Sun plans to wait for the W3C XML Protocol Working Group to issue a formal recommendation for SOAP 1.2 before offering their "services on demand."

XML Web Services Support in .NET

Microsoft's .NET Framework and Visual Studio .NET represent a major departure from the company's traditional dependence on proprietary technologies, such as COM and ActiveX, for interobject communication in the Windows environment. Standards-based XML is the *lingua franca* of .NET, and XML Web services are destined to be the plumbing for loosely coupled distributed applications that communicate with HTTP. .NET Remoting is the DCOM replacement for tightly coupled componentized applications. The .NET Framework, ASP.NET, and Visual Basic .NET combine to ease the transition from "legacy" COM-based components to XML Web services written in managed Visual Basic code and deployed by simple XCOPY methods.

System.Web.Services Namespaces

The .NET Framework Class Library treats *everything* as an object type. Even elementary datatypes are structures defined within the `System` object namespace. For example, the `System.Int16` structure represents Visual Basic 6.0's `Integer` datatype, which corresponds to `Short` in Visual Basic .NET.

TIP

To explore the namespaces applicable to XML Web services, in Visual Studio. NET, choose Help | Contents, and expand the Visual Studio .NET, .NET Framework, Reference, Class Library, and System.Web.Services nodes.

The .NET Framework implements XML Web service elements, specifically SOAP messages and WSDL files, as classes. Transforming a class instance to its corresponding XML document or stream is called *XML serialization*; the reverse process is called *XML deserialization*. Following are brief descriptions of the primary namespaces you use when creating XML Web services and their clients:

▶ `System.Web.Services` contains the classes for objects that participate in the creation and consumption of XML Web services. The `System.Web.Services.WebMethodAttribute` class added to a `Public` method enables the method to be called by remote clients. The `System.Web.Services.WebService` class provides access to the ASP.NET `Application` object and `HttpSessionState` instance of the `Session` object.

▶ `System.Web.Services.Description` is the object representation of the WSDL file for a service. This class has 65 subclasses, which correspond to elements and attributes of WSDL documents. The `System.Web.Services.Description.Mime...` classes implement the SOAP Messages with Attachment specification.

▶ `System.Web.Services.Discovery` contains subclasses for implementing Microsoft's DISCO machine-level service discovery mechanism, not UDDI or WS-Inspection. This class became obsolete with the release of Visual Studio .NET.

▶ `System.Web.Services.Protocols` provides the object representation of SOAP messages as `System.Web.Services.Protocols.Soap...` subclasses. `System.Web.Services.Protocols.HTTP...` subclasses support the simple HTTP `GET` and `POST` operations for generic Web services.

▶ `System.Xml.Serialization.XmlSerializer` controls serialization and deserialization of XML documents and streams. `System.Xml.Serialization.Soap...` classes let you customize serialization of SOAP element attributes.

Chapter 7 provides a detailed view of the `System.Web.Services` and `System.Xml` classes applicable to XML Web services.

ASP.NET Web Service Projects

Conventional XML Web services rely on HTTP as their transport, so the services you create with .NET run from IIS 5.0+ virtual directories. ASP.NET is Visual Studio .NET's framework for writing Web-based applications with managed code. ASP.NET automates the basic steps required to create XML Web services that are deployed as an assembly of *WebServiceName*.asmx and supporting files.

TIP

Make sure the IP address of your local Default Web Site is set to (All Unassigned), not a fixed IP address, and IIS 5.0+ is running before you attempt to create your first ASP.NET Web service. The sample Web service uses localhost as the server name; if the site is bound to a fixed IP address, you receive "not found" errors when you attempt to create or run the Web service.

When you open a new ASP.NET Web Service project using Visual Basic .NET, a *WebServiceName*.asmx.vb file contains the code behind the .asmx file. Figure 1-13 shows the default `Public Class Service1` with the `<WebService()>` attribute applied to define the project as a Web service, but not an XML Web service that meets this book's definition. The `http://oakleaf.ws/testws/` namespace URI replaces the default `http://tempuri.org/` URI. The `<WebMethod()>` prefix to the `Public Function HelloWorld()` declaration makes the method visible to the WSDL document.

TIP

"tempuri" isn't the plural form of "tempura." It's an abbreviation for "temporary Universal Resource Identifier" (URI). Replace tempuri.org with your domain name and, optionally, a virtual directory name to assure that your XML Web services have their own globally unique namespace. The URI you choose need not be accessible from the Internet; you can also use Uniform Resource Names (URNs) such as [urn:]oakleaf-ws:testws. If you compile and run the project with tempuri.org as the URI, you receive a message that suggests changing the name.

The *WebServiceName*.asmx file contains only the following single line of compiler directives:

```
<%@ WebService Language="vb" Codebehind="Service1.asmx.vb" _
Class="WebService1.Service1" %>
```

The `@ WebService` directive tags the file as supplying a Web service; `Language="vb"` specifies Visual Basic .NET as the language for the service; `Codebehind` designates the file containing the Visual Basic code, and the `Class` entry provides the equivalent of a COM object's ProgID.

ASP.NET also adds a standard set of .NET Framework references to the project and generates a host of other supporting files in the folder linked to the IIS virtual directory, most of which appear as nodes in the Solution Explorer window. C:\DefaultSite\WebService1 is the default folder for the assembly. Double-clicking a file node displays the contents of the file in a help page of the main tabbed window.

When you uncomment the function code block and press F5 to compile and run the Web service, a test page opens in IE 5.0+ with a Service Description link to the autogenerated WSDL file. (Scan the WSDL file for the `<portType>`, `<binding>`, and `<service>` elements for the three invocation methods.) The HelloWorld link opens a page that lets you test the generic HTTP `GET` version of the service. (See Figure 1-14.) Clicking the Invoke button displays "Hello World" on an IE page. The test page also includes XML and HTML code examples for SOAP, HTTP `GET`, and HTTP `POST` request/response operations.

This brief introduction to ASP.NET's implementation of Web services in general and XML Web services in particular offers only a very limited preview of ASP.NET's

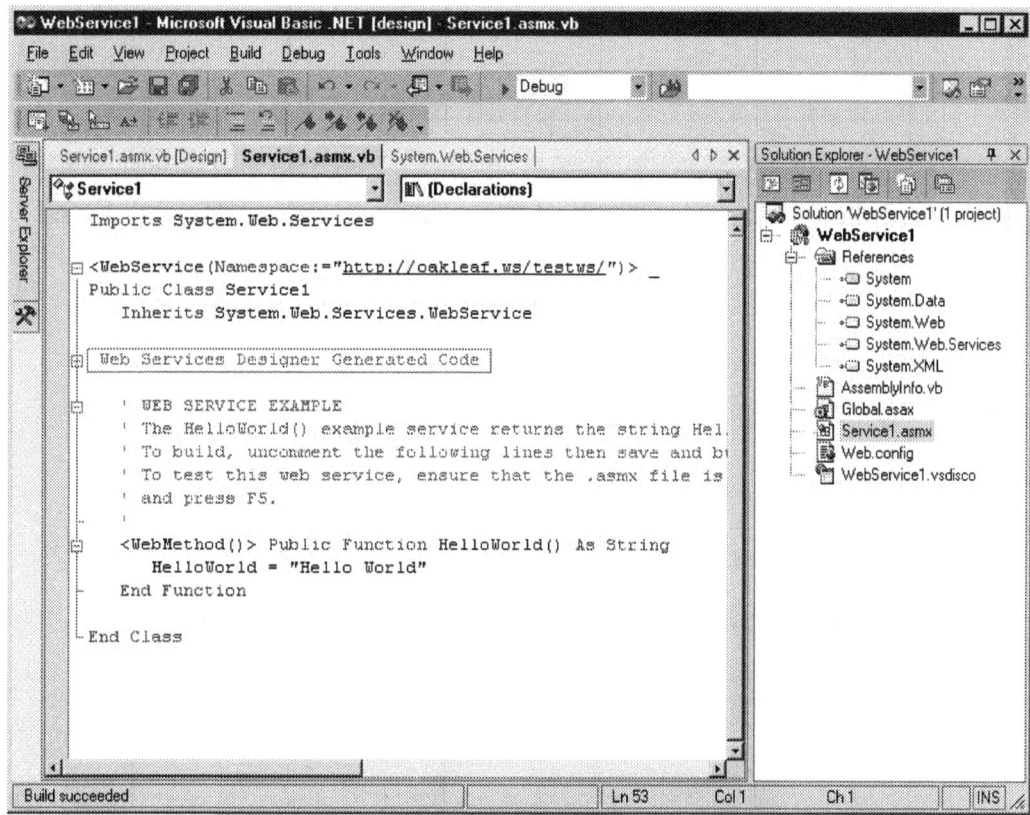

Figure 1-13 *Opening a new ASP.NET Web Service project with Visual Basic .NET as the selected language displays the Visual Basic code for a sample HelloWorld WebMethod.*

capabilities, and is typical of trivial sample Web services that litter UDDI and private Web service registries. This book concentrates on creating and testing production-class XML Web services that deliver meaningful information and perform useful operations on SQL Server database back ends. Chapter 8, for example, shows you how to write production-grade, data-intensive B2B and B2C XML Web services with Visual Basic .NET methods and ADO.NET.

ASP.NET Pages and COM-Based XML Web Services

It's often not worth the time and effort to upgrade production Visual Basic 6.0 SOAP-enabled COM components to Visual Basic .NET. The CFR-ASPX version of the CFR application demonstrates that you can use ASP.NET pages with managed Visual Basic .NET code behind them as clients for SOAP-enabled Visual Basic 6.0 COM components. You can use the conventional ASP-style, late-bound `CreateObject("MSSOAP.SoapClient")` code shown in Figure 1-15 and take advantage of the .NET Framework's COM Interop feature to return an XHTML page of full-text search hits from the CFRSearchWS service.

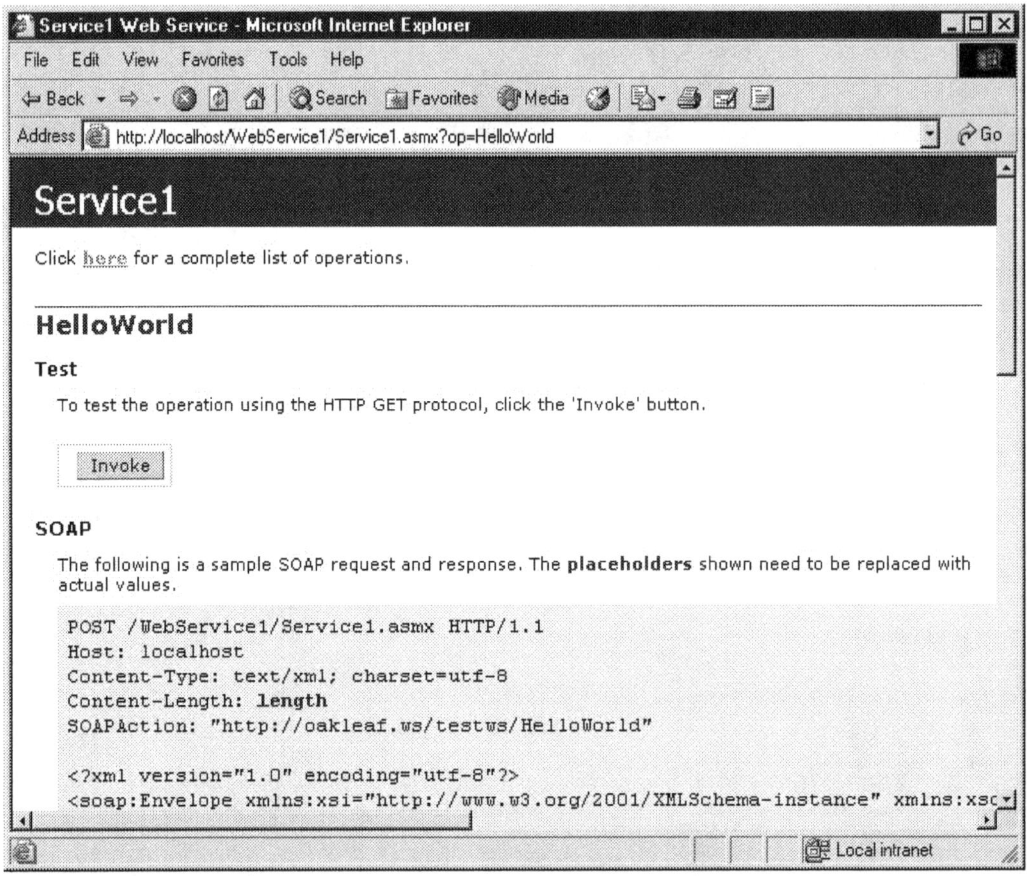

```
Service1 Web Service - Microsoft Internet Explorer                      _ □ ×

File   Edit   View   Favorites   Tools   Help

← Back  ▾  ⇒  ▾  ⊗  🗋  🏠  | 🔍 Search  📷 Favorites  🎬 Media  🎶 | 🔖▾ 🎛 🖼 📄

Address  🗋 http://localhost/WebService1/Service1.asmx?op=HelloWorld        ▾   🔗 Go
```

Service1

Click here for a complete list of operations.

HelloWorld

Test

To test the operation using the HTTP GET protocol, click the 'Invoke' button.

    [Invoke]

SOAP

The following is a sample SOAP request and response. The **placeholders** shown need to be replaced with actual values.

```
POST /WebService1/Service1.asmx HTTP/1.1
Host: localhost
Content-Type: text/xml; charset=utf-8
Content-Length: length
SOAPAction: "http://oakleaf.ws/testws/HelloWorld"

<?xml version="1.0" encoding="utf-8"?>
<soap:Envelope xmlns:xsi="http://www.w3.org/2001/XMLSchema-instance" xmlns:xsc▾
```

```
🜨                                                      🖳 Local intranet
```

Figure 1-14   *This IE 6.0 test page for the HTTP GET service implementation includes samples of SOAP, HTTP GET, and HTTP POST operations.*

One of Visual Studio .NET's most useful features is the capability to early-bind XML Web services, regardless of their location, the tool used to create them, or the operating system that hosts them. Choosing Project | Add Web Reference opens a dialog of the same name with links to the Microsoft production and test UDDI registries. Typing the IP address of a .wsdl, .asmx, .disco, or .vsdisco file in the Address text box lists the available service(s) as View Contract links in the right pane and displays the contents of the WSDL file you select in the left pane. (See Figure 1-16.) Clicking the Add Reference button adds a Web References node to the Solution Explorer list. The default name of the reference you add is WebReference1; you can rename the reference to something more descriptive.

TIP

You can add a remote Web Reference to a sample project by typing http://www.oakleaf.ws/cfr/ CFRSearchWS.wsdl or http://66.123.163.243/cfr/CFRSearchWS.wsdl in the Add Web Reference's Address text box.

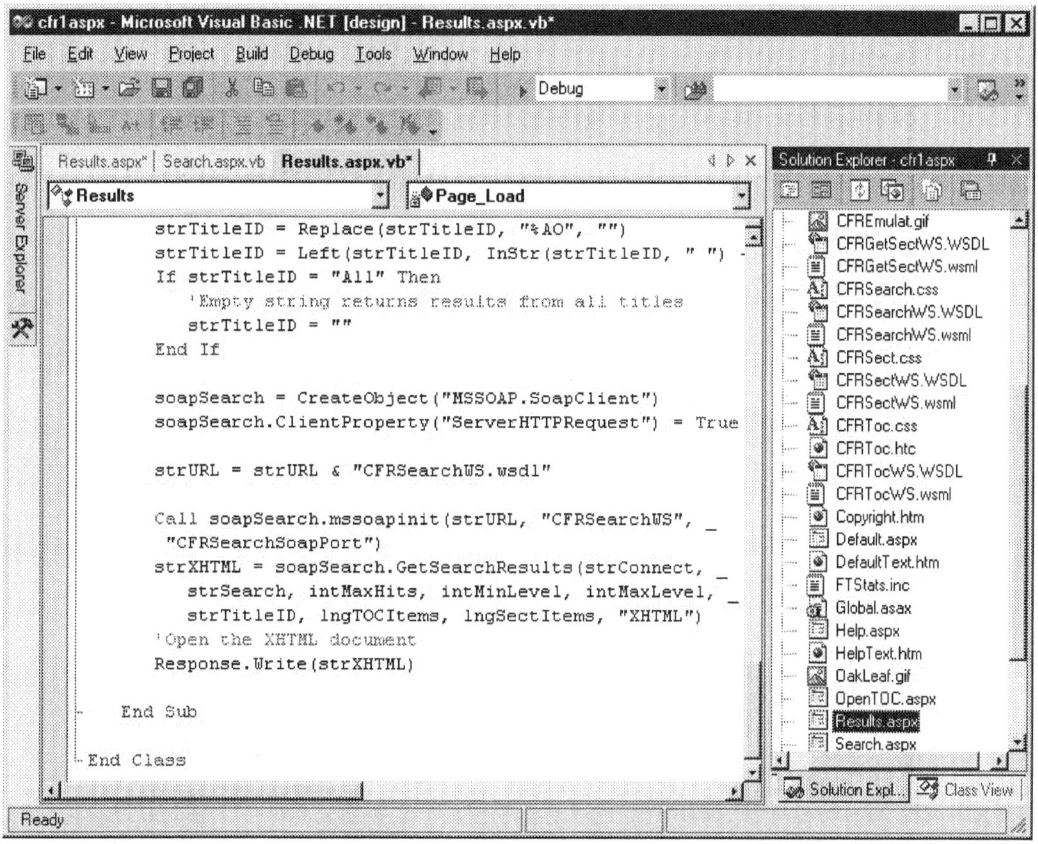

```
cfr1aspx - Microsoft Visual Basic .NET [design] - Results.aspx.vb*
File   Edit   View   Project   Build   Debug   Tools   Window   Help

Results.aspx* | Search.aspx.vb | Results.aspx.vb* |

Results                                 Page_Load

        strTitleID = Replace(strTitleID, "%AO", "")
        strTitleID = Left(strTitleID, InStr(strTitleID, " "))
        If strTitleID = "All" Then
            'Empty string returns results from all titles
            strTitleID = ""
        End If

        soapSearch = CreateObject("MSSOAP.SoapClient")
        soapSearch.ClientProperty("ServerHTTPRequest") = True

        strURL = strURL & "CFRSearchWS.wsdl"

        Call soapSearch.mssoapinit(strURL, "CFRSearchWS", _
          "CFRSearchSoapPort")
        strXHTML = soapSearch.GetSearchResults(strConnect, _
            strSearch, intMaxHits, intMinLevel, intMaxLevel, _
            strTitleID, lngTOCItems, lngSectItems, "XHTML")
        'Open the XHTML document
        Response.Write(strXHTML)

    End Sub

End Class
```

Solution Explorer - cfr1aspx

- CFREmulat.gif
- CFRGetSectWS.WSDL
- CFRGetSectWS.wsml
- CFRSearch.css
- CFRSearchWS.WSDL
- CFRSearchWS.wsml
- CFRSect.css
- CFRSectWS.WSDL
- CFRSectWS.wsml
- CFRToc.css
- CFRToc.htc
- CFRTocWS.WSDL
- CFRTocWS.wsml
- Copyright.htm
- Default.aspx
- DefaultText.htm
- FTStats.inc
- Global.asax
- Help.aspx
- HelpText.htm
- OakLeaf.gif
- OpenTOC.aspx
- Results.aspx
- Search.aspx

Solution Expl... | Class View

Ready

Figure 1-15   *This Visual Basic .NET code behind the Search.aspx ASP.NET page late-binds the CFRSearchWS XML Web service with a COM-based MSSOAP.SoapClient proxy.*

Adding the Web Reference to your Web or Windows form project adds a Web References folder to the assembly with a subfolder for each reference. The subfolder contains a local copy of the service's WSDL file, a Reference.map file for the service location, and a Reference.vb file, which contains the code for synchronous and asynchronous SOAP client proxies. The local copy of the WSDL file eliminates a round trip to retrieve its contents from the source site. Early-binding the Web Reference reduces the number of lines of code to retrieve the SOAP message payload from six to two. (See Figure 1-17.) A simple function call passes the required arguments to the SOAP request message and delivers the response message payload to an ASP.NET Web page. You also gain the benefits of statement completion with autolist members and parameter data.

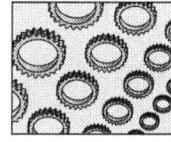

NOTE

An interesting feature of ActiveX DLLs with SOAP wrappers applied by the SOAP Toolkit 2.0 is that the underlying object isn't affected. You can invoke the object by a conventional method call or a SOAP client proxy. The CFR project's CFR-COM, CFR-SOAP, and CFR-ASPX implementations share a single set of Visual Basic 6.0 ActiveX DLLs.

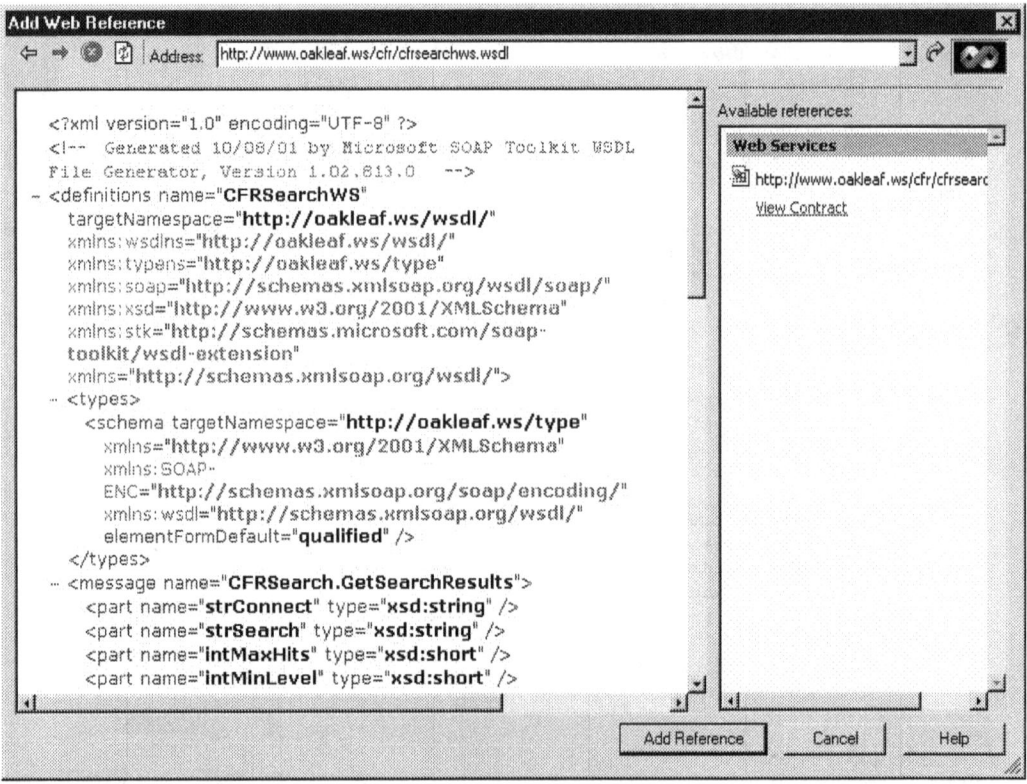

Figure 1-16 *The Add Web Reference dialog lets you take advantage of early-binding by automatically generating a SOAP client proxy from the WSDL file you select.*

Your "take-away" from these few brief sections that describe .NET support for XML Web services, as well as much of the chapter's earlier content, should be this:

> Visual Studio .NET's developers have made use of XML Web services transparent to Visual Basic developers. Invoking an XML Web service written in Java, COBOL, C++, C#, or Visual Basic that's accessible from any Web server anywhere on the Internet is as easy as instantiating a local COM or Visual Basic .NET component.

Following are the obligatory action steps:

▶ Consider SOAP-enabling all your existing ActiveX DLLs that deliver data as XML documents.

▶ Write all new Visual Basic .NET components as ASP.NET [XML] Web Services, unless you have a good reason to do otherwise.

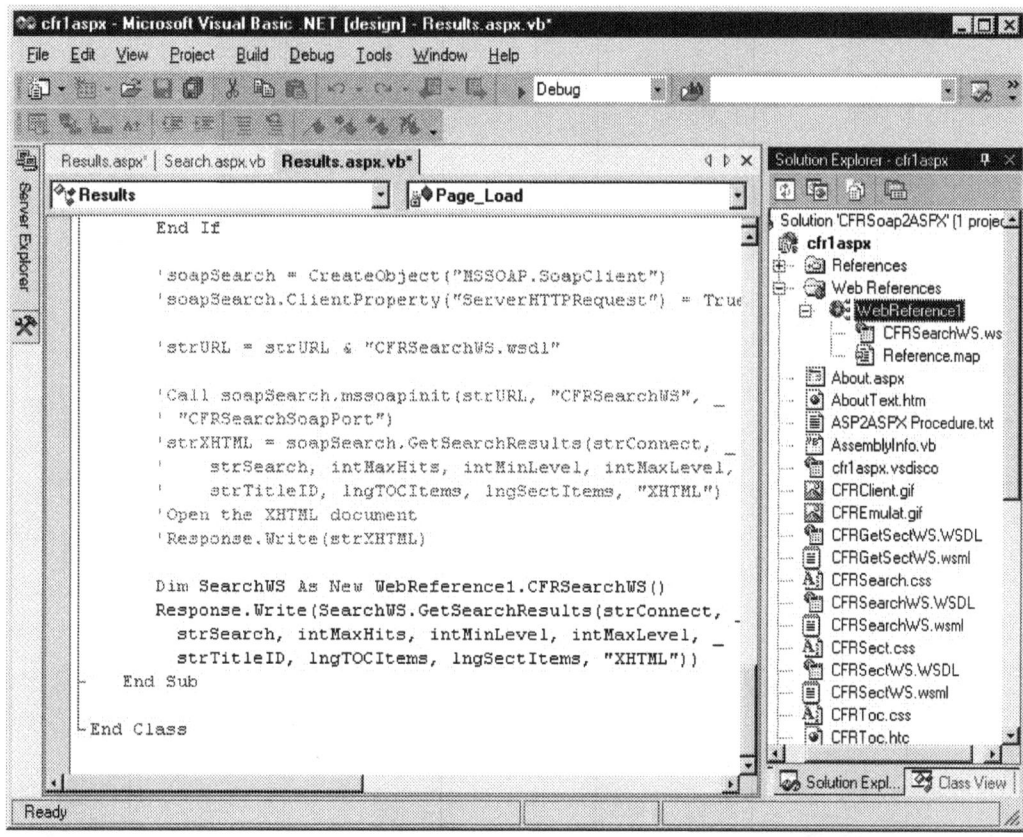

Figure 1-17   *Early-binding XML Web services makes their invocation as simple as that for traditional early-bound COM objects.*

▶ Decide which SQL Server stored procedures to enable for direct XML Web service access.

▶ Take advantage of early-bound XML Web services in all new .NET Web and Windows form clients.

▶ Read the rest of this book and try the example code to prepare for the "next big thing" in distributed computing.

Getting a Grip on SOAP and WSDL

IN THIS CHAPTER:

Comparing SOAP/WSDL and DCOM Implementations

Exchanging SOAP Messages

Invoking Methods with RPC-Style Messages

Handling SOAP Faults

Dissecting WSDL Files

Extending SOAP Messages with Header Elements

Previewing the GetNwindOrder ASP.NET Web Service

I t's conceivable that you could create production-quality XML Web services without understanding—or even reading—the current SOAP and WSDL specifications. ASP.NET's built-in support for creating new XML Web services handles all SOAP-related coding chores for you. The SOAP Toolkit 2.0 does the same for your existing ActiveX DLLs. Plowing through the 33 printed pages of turgid prose of the SOAP 1.1 spec is an exercise that borders on masochism. The WSDL 1.1 specification weighs in at 48 pages and is an even tougher read for most folks than the SOAP note. Like the W3C's XML 1.0 specification, the SOAP and WSDL documents are intended primarily to guide implementers, not developers. XML parsers must conform to the grammar of XML 1.0; similarly, XML Web service implementations, such as those provided by the .NET Framework and the SOAP Toolkit 2.0, must satisfy the requirements of the SOAP specification and the WSDL schema.

The goals of this chapter are to present the salient features of the SOAP 1.1 and WSDL 1.1 specifications from the Visual Basic developer's viewpoint. Significant changes to SOAP 1.1 anticipated in version 1.2 of the specification appear as notes. Chapter 1 observed that almost all XML Web services connect—either directly or indirectly—to relational databases. Thus, the XML Web service examples in this chapter involve message content persisted in database tables, rather than as XML documents stored as .xml files.

Comparing SOAP/WSDL and DCOM Implementations

Visual Basic 6.0 component developers tend to share a myopic view of distributed computing architecture: if your preferred (or only) component development tool has been Visual Basic 6.0 and earlier, everything looks like an ActiveX DLL. Java 2 Enterprise Edition (J2EE), Enterprise JavaBeans (EJB), and Common Object Request Broker Architecture (CORBA) don't generate blips on *your* radar screen. XML Web services extend your object horizon to alternative object architectures and operating systems. The SOAP and WSDL standards open your Visual Basic client and middle-tier applications, and VBScripted Web pages to interaction with SOAP-enabled clients that are written in any language and located anywhere on the Internet.

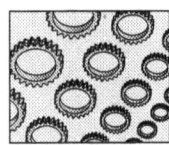

NOTE

The ability to process SOAP messages supplied by external (third-party) sources depends on the SOAP implementation. If an external XML Web service uses SOAP extensions that your SOAP client implementation doesn't support, you receive a SOAP `Fault` message, and communication terminates. Proprietary SOAP extensions, such as Microsoft's WS-Inspection, WS-Security, and WS-Routing, require implementation for the server and the client sides.

In the SOAP context, the term client (also called the consumer) refers to the process that initiates a SOAP request; the server (also called the listener) hosts the XML Web service and responds to the request. Clients can be conventional Windows applications, ASP or ASP.NET pages, components, or other XML Web services.

The SOAP 1.1 specification describes two operating methods: an inherently one-way messaging system that transports XML documents over HTTP, and a two-way RPC approach. The RPC method uses the HTTP request-response mechanism in most cases but isn't limited to HTTP as the transport. Sections 6 and 7 of the SOAP specification describe how to use SOAP with HTTP messaging and RPC method calls, respectively. Microsoft's implementations of the SOAP RPC mechanism resemble DCOM's RPC implementation but avoid the deployment problems and platform-dependence imposed by the Windows Registry.

Visual Basic programmers are a pragmatic lot; most focus on a new component design methodology's implementation before attacking its theory and specifications. Thus, implementation examples precede an analysis of the SOAP and WSDL specifications in this chapter. Figure 2-1 compares Microsoft's DCOM implementation for ActiveX DLLs with Visual Basic 6.0 and ASP.NET SOAP 1.1 RPC implementations. The following

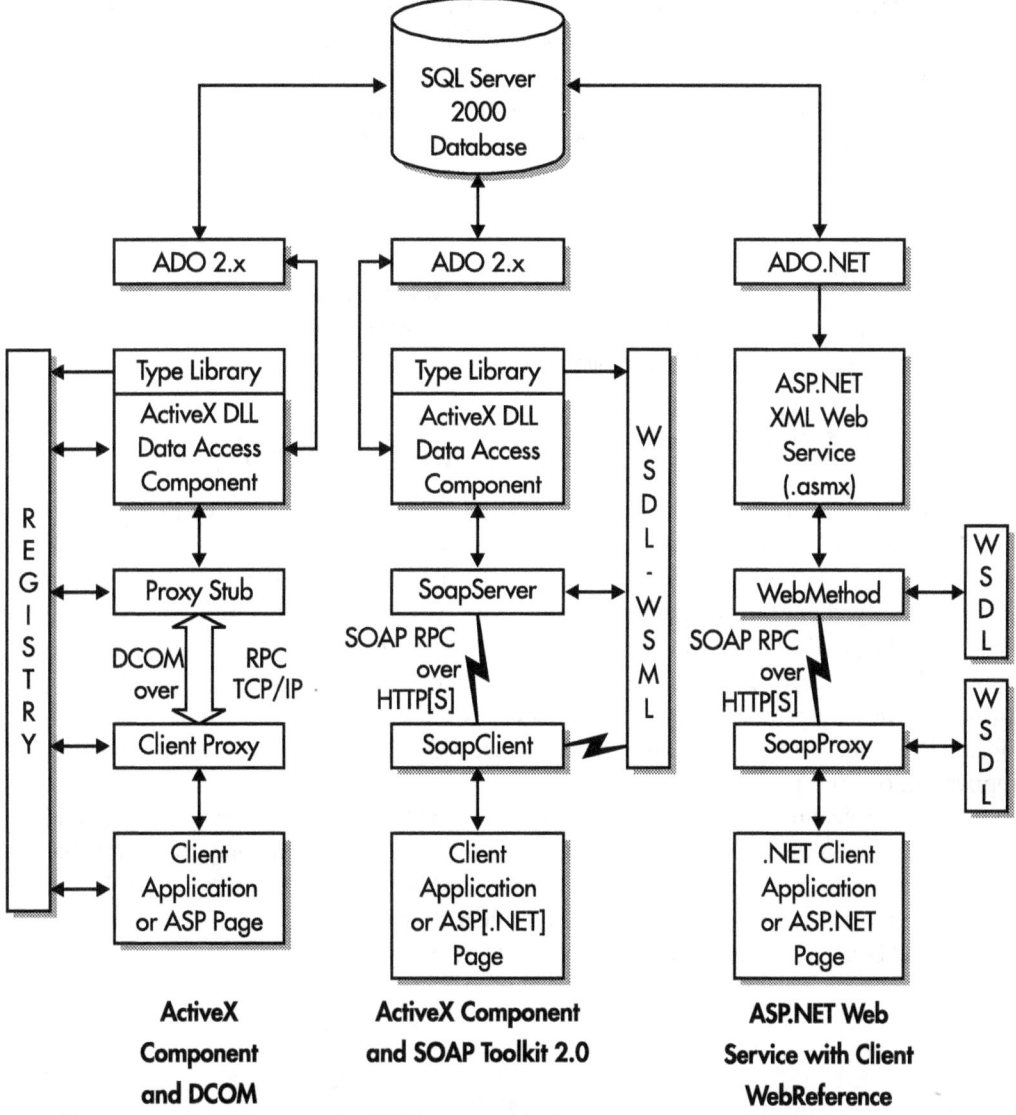

Figure 2-1   *This diagram compares traditional DCOM implementation with Visual Basic 6.0 and ASP.NET XML Web service counterparts.*

three sections explain the similarities and differences between the DCOM and SOAP implementations.

Visual Basic 6.0 ActiveX DLL with DCOM

DCOM RPC employs a proxy stub on the component server and a client proxy on each client machine, both of which have a local instance of the Service Control Manager (SCM). The client proxy includes the name of the remote server and the GUID of the proxy stub, which points to the remote object's DLL. The requesting client marshals method parameter values with the Object RPC (ORPC) wire protocol, and the server unmarshals the values for use by the component. The server responds by marshaling the result of object execution on the wire, and the client unmarshals the return value for use by the client application or Web page. Microsoft's optimization of the ORPC protocol is responsible for the generally excellent performance of DCOM when method parameters are marshaled by value.

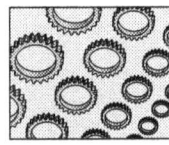

NOTE

.NET Remoting replaces DCOM for new middle-tier components. .NET Remoting provides a much wider range of transport and marshaling options than DCOM. COM and DCOM, like the Jet database engine, are relegated to legacy status with the arrival of .NET.

Visual Basic 6.0 ActiveX DLL with the SOAP Toolkit 2.0

This configuration substitutes a server-side WSDL file for the Registry entries added by compiling the DLL; the WSDL file also provides the equivalent of a type library for the SOAP messages it defines. You create the WSDL file by running the SOAP Toolkit 2.0 Wizard (Wsdlgen.exe). `SoapServer` and `SoapClient` objects, which are supplied by the Toolkit's MSSOAP1.dll, correspond to DCOM's proxy stubs and client proxies, respectively. The `SoapSerializer` object handles request marshaling (serializing) for the SOAP wire protocol (HTTP, in most cases), and `SoapReader` unmarshals (deserializes) the response message to deliver the SOAP message (payload) to the client application or Web page.

Adding a project reference to the MSSOAPLib type library (\Program Files\Common Files\ MSSoap\Binaries\MSSOAP1.dll) lets you use Object Browser to display the library's objects, properties, methods, and enumerations, as shown here. Most MSSOAPLib objects are represented by XML Document Object Model (DOM) objects, such as `IXMLDOMElement`, `IXMLDOMNode`, or `IXMLDOMNodeList`.

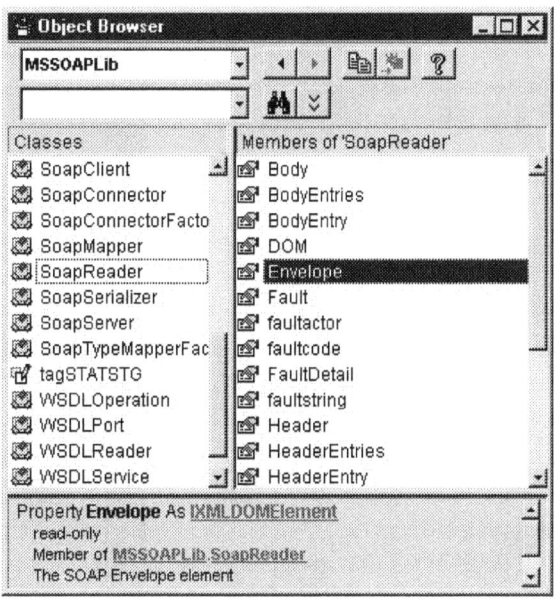

You must install and register MSSOAP1.dll's type library on every machine that supplies or consumes XML Web services that you SOAP-enable with the SOAP Toolkit 2.0 Wizard. (Installing the Toolkit automatically registers the type library). All clients must connect to and deserialize the remote WSDL file with the `WSDLReader` object so they can serialize the method call and its parameters correctly in the request, and deserialize the response message's payload to a return value. Obtaining a client-side instance of the WSDL file requires an extra round trip to the server. Fortunately, the UTF-8-encoded WSDL files created for COM objects are quite small—usually less than 5KB for an object with one or two methods.

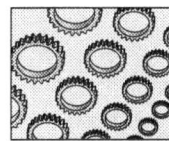

NOTE

Chapter 3 provides a much more detailed explanation of interactions between the objects defined by the MSSOAP1.dll type library.

ASP.NET Web Service with a .NET Client Web Reference

The "ASP.NET Web Services" section in Chapter 1 describes how the XML Web services you create as ASP.NET Web Services expose public functions as `WebMethods`. ASP.NET automatically generates a local WSDL definition document for the service and updates the document with `WebMethod` changes each time you build your Visual Basic .NET project code.

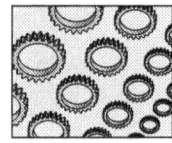

NOTE

You can SOAP-enable components you design with .NET Remoting by specifying HTTP as the transport, which sets SOAP as the default serializer.

All .NET clients connect to XML Web services by a proxy class that serves the same purpose as the client proxy provided by the SOAP Toolkit's MSSOAP1.dll and its MSSOAPLib type library. The primary benefit of the `WebReference` proxy is the local copy of the WSDL file for the service, which lets you early-bind the XML Web service object. The local WSDL file copy eliminates a round trip to the server, but the client copy must be updated manually for each change to the remote WSDL file. Adopt the golden rule of COM interfaces: never alter the `WebMethods` of a production XML Web service.

TIP

You can early-bind SOAP-enabled Visual Basic 6.0 components with Microsoft's Web Services Proxy Wizard (http://msdn.microsoft.com/library/en-us/dnvs600/html/webservproxwiz.asp). The Proxy Wizard is a Visual C++ 6.0 ATL Object Wizard, which generates a proxy class from the component's WSDL file. You add a reference to the proxy to your Visual Basic 6.0 client application.

Exchanging SOAP Messages

Section 2 of the SOAP 1.1 specification defines a *message path* between the sender and receiver of the message, which can include intermediate nodes. Unlike version 1.0, the SOAP 1.1 specification doesn't mandate a transport protocol. HTTP is currently the most common transport; HTTP and HTTP-M, which implements the HTTP Extension Framework, are the only transports the specification addresses (in section 6).

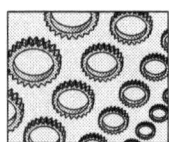

NOTE

The SOAP 1.0 specification provides for HTTP M-POST transport, if the receiver rejects a conventional HTTP POST operation with a 501 Not Implemented or 510 Not Extended error message. The HTTP Extension Framework is an experimental IETF RFC intended to define the identity of a recipient and how the recipient should handle custom extensions. Section 6.3 of the SOAP 1.1 specification names the extension identifier for SOAP (http://schemas.xmlsoap.org/soap/envelope/). You can read RFC2774 for the Framework at http://www.ietf.org/rfc/rfc2774.txt.

SOAP message processing falls into two fundamental styles: exchanging XML documents and RPC method invocation. The bulk of the SOAP 1.1 specification deals with documents; section 7 defines how SOAP-RPC encapsulates remote procedure calls within SOAP documents. This book and the WSDL specification use the term *document style* when referring to the SOAP specification's default method for exchanging business documents within the `Body` element of the SOAP envelope, and *rpc style* when referring to remote method invocation.

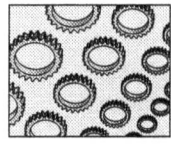

NOTE

The name Simple Object Access Protocol implies that SOAP is intended primarily to invoke remote objects. Version 1.2 of the SOAP specification removes the earlier versions' apparent bias toward RPC by replacing all references to the full protocol name with SOAP. When version 1.2 gains full recommendation status, SOAP won't be an acronym.

Another characteristic of SOAP messages is their encoding method, which this book and the WSDL specification define as *literal* and *encoded*. Section 5 of the specification permits specifying value data types by an associated XSD or other schema, an `xsi:type` attribute, or a SOAP-encoded `arrayType` attribute. Literal encoding requires the receiver to interpret data types from their accessor tag names by reference to a schema, which is designated by an attribute value in URI format, or by interpretation by code in the receiving application.

Document-style messages most commonly use literal encoding, and RPC exchanges are either literal or encoded. If a SOAP-RPC message uses literal encoding, it must have an embedded or associated XSD schema to specify the data types of the method's parameters and return value.

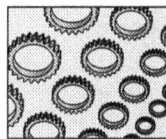

NOTE

The WSDL 1.1 specification defines `style` *and* `use` *attributes in* `document/literal`, `document/encoded`, `rpc/literal`, *and* `rpc/encoded` *combinations. The most common message formats are* `document/literal` *and* `rpc/encoded`.

Sending a Literal SOAP Document

Typically, the sender issues an HTTP `POST` request to transmit the message to the receiver. The receiver extracts the SOAP `Body` element, parses the payload, and, optionally, returns a SOAP message to the sender.

If the receiver can't process the incoming SOAP envelope, the receiver returns a SOAP `Fault` element as the message body. The "Handling SOAP Faults" section later in this chapter describes the structure of `Fault` messages. If an error occurs when processing the payload, the receiver can respond with a custom SOAP `Fault` element or return an error message in the SOAP `Body`. Document-style messaging is unidirectional; the response message, if sent, is independent of the request message. For example, a message that requests an update to a database need not send a response message confirming the update. It's more common, however, to acknowledge all incoming messages with a response message.

Serializing Data Structures

The first step in generating a SOAP message is defining the structure of the XML payload document. Section 5 of the SOAP specification defines a set of rules for serialization of SOAP elements. The basic rule is this: All values are represented as element content. The effect of this rule is that SOAP messages are element-centric, rather than attribute-centric, so each value must be enclosed within a tag pair, which the specification calls an *accessor*.

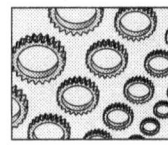

NOTE

Saving *ADODB.Recordset* objects with the `adPersistXML` option creates attribute-centric XML representations of result sets. SQL Server 2000's T-SQL `FOR XML AUTO` clause delivers attribute-centric documents unless you add the `ELEMENTS` modifier. If you want to pass attribute-centric XML in a SOAP `Body`, enclose the document in a `<!CDATA[ ... ]]>` element so the receiver doesn't attempt to parse the content.

A typical business-document exchange scenario is generating invoices from sales orders when the order ships. Many Web-based marketing sites employ third-parties to fulfill their orders. The Web site sends a copy of the customer's order as a SOAP message to the fulfillment house, which ships all or part of the order directly to the customer and sends a SOAP message to the Web site when the order ships. The Web site then prepares an invoice and debits the customer's credit card; in most cases, the invoice is for internal accounting purposes.

Most current COM or DCOM middle-tier objects for processing orders return `Recordset` objects, arrays, or other data structures, not XML documents. Returning the XML representation of an order requires adding new serialization methods to the existing objects. Modifying orders or generating invoices requires adding deserializing methods. The following document represents a Northwind Traders order serialized from records in the SQL Server 2000 Northwind sample database. In this case, the `xmlns` namespace attribute of the `Order` accessor specifies the location of and XSD schema for an `Order` document. Even without a schema, data types of the values can be inferred from their accessor names or obtained from the **Type** property of each **Field** object.

```
<Order xmlns='http://schemas.oakleaf.ws/order/'>
   <OrderID>10251</OrderID>
   <OrderDate>7/8/1996</OrderDate>
   <ShippedDate>7/15/1996</ShippedDate>
   <Freight>41.34</Freight>
   <CustomerID>VICTE</CustomerID>
   <ShipName>Victuailles en stock</ShipName>
   <ShipAddress>2, rue du Commerce</ShipAddress>
   <ShipCity>Lyon</ShipCity>
   <ShipRegion></ShipRegion>
   <ShipPostalCode>69004</ShipPostalCode>
   <ShipCountry>France</ShipCountry>
   <LineItems>
      <Item>
         <ProductID>22</ProductID>
         <Quantity>6</Quantity>
         <UnitPrice>16.8</UnitPrice>
         <Discount>0.05</Discount>
      </Item>
      <Item>
         <ProductID>57</ProductID>
         <Quantity>15</Quantity>
```

```
            <UnitPrice>15.6</UnitPrice>
            <Discount>0.05</Discount>
        </Item>
        <Item>
            <ProductID>65</ProductID>
            <Quantity>20</Quantity>
            <UnitPrice>16.8</UnitPrice>
            <Discount>0</Discount>
        </Item>
    </LineItems>
</Order>
```

The preceding `Order` document represents the message sent from the fulfillment house on shipment; customer information (other than the `CustomerID` value and shipping address) isn't included. In the case of a partial shipment, missing items have a 0 `<Quantity>` value. Documents for backorder shipments include only the `<LineItems>` subelement(s) in each subsequent shipment.

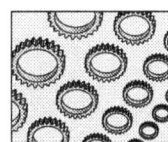

NOTE

The code required to serialize query result sets to element-centric XML documents isn't complex, especially if you retain the table's field names as accessor names. Deserializing XML documents to alter table values, however, is a more involved process. The "Previewing the GetNwindOrder ASP.NET Web Service" section, near the end of this chapter, lists the VB.NET code that serializes the preceding XML document. Chapter 3 provides examples of Visual Basic 6.0 code for serializing more complex `ADODB.Recordset` objects and deserializing XML documents to perform `UPDATE` and `INSERT` operations with T-SQL statements.

Adding a Simple SOAP Envelope

The simplest SOAP message you can send to a SOAP receiver adds a top-level `soapEnv:Envelope` element that defines the SOAP `Envelope` namespace, and a second-level `soapEnv:Body` element that contains the message elements, which the SOAP specification calls *parts*. The specification uses `SOAP-ENV` as the namespace prefix of the top-level accessor name, but you can substitute any name you want; it's `Envelope` that's important.

Following is the serialized `Order` document with the top message part named `ShipNotice` instead of `Order`. In this case, the receiver interprets the message, which adheres to the same schema as the preceding example, as notification of shipment. Alternatively, a top-level `Order` document can use `http://schemas.oakleaf.ws/shipnotice/` or the like to indicate how to interpret and process the message. In this case, the receiver uses the document to prepare the invoice and add the freight charge to the customer's credit-card debit.

```
<soapEnv:Envelope
      xmlns:soapEnv='http://schemas.xmlsoap.org/soap/envelope/'>
    <soapEnv:Body>
        <ShipNotice xmlns='http://schemas.oakleaf.ws/order/'>
```

```
        <OrderID>10251</OrderID>
        <OrderDate>7/8/1996</OrderDate>
        <ShippedDate>7/15/1996</ShippedDate>
        <Freight>41.34</Freight>
        <CustomerID>VICTE</CustomerID>
        <ShipName>Victuailles en stock</ShipName>
        <ShipAddress>2, rue du Commerce</ShipAddress>
        <ShipCity>Lyon</ShipCity>
        <ShipRegion></ShipRegion>
        <ShipPostalCode>69004</ShipPostalCode>
        <ShipCountry>France</ShipCountry>
        <LineItems>
            <Item>
                <ProductID>22</ProductID>
                <Quantity>6</Quantity>
                <UnitPrice>16.8</UnitPrice>
                <Discount>0.05</Discount>
            </Item>
            <!-- Other two <Item> subelements here -->
        </LineItems>
    </ShipNotice>
  </soapEnv:Body>
</soapEnv:Envelope>
```

Sending a Response Message

It's not obligatory to send a response to incoming document-style messages, but it's a generally accepted practice to do so. For the preceding example, the response message might consist of a subset of the originating message that uniquely identifies that message. In this case, the `OrderID` and `ShippedDate` values serve to identify the transaction. The receiver of this message updates the database with the date and time of the acknowledgment obtained from the system clock or the message's HTTP header. Asynchronously processing pairs of one-way messages, which emulate the DCOM event-based callback mechanism, requires that the two message endpoints act as SOAP message listeners, which requires a Web server on both ends.

Following is a simple response message, which acknowledges the `ShipNoticeAck` message:

```
<soapEnv:Envelope
     xmlns:soapEnv='http://schemas.xmlsoap.org/soap/envelope/'>
  <soapEnv:Body>
    <ShipNoticeAck xmlns='http://schemas.oakleaf.ws/order/'>
        <OrderID>10251</OrderID>
        <ShippedDate>7/15/1996</ShippedDate>
    </ShipNoticeAck>
  </soapEnv:Body>
</soapEnv:Envelope>
```

The preceding SOAP message examples barely qualify as a real-world exchange. Actual messages undoubtedly would contain custom `Header` element(s) preceding the `Body` element. Header elements might contain the number of retries, a transaction ID value, or other information specific to the types of messages exchanged. Header elements are the subject of the "Extending SOAP Messages with Header Elements" section later in the chapter.

NOTE

WSDL files aren't required for document-style messaging between two well-known endpoints. There's no reference to WSDL in the SOAP 1.1 or 1.2 specifications. A well-known recipient's message processor is expected to understand the `Body` document schema and use the schema to interpret accessor names and namespaces. The WSDL specification encompasses document-style SOAP messages, but it hasn't been a common practice to provide WSDL files for them. WSDL files enable automatic proxy generation and, for ASP.NET XML Web services, early binding by Web References. As document-style SOAP messaging gains momentum, WSDL files will become a universal standard.

Invoking Methods with RPC-Style Messages

Section 7 of the SOAP 1.1 specification sets out the rules for exchanging bidirectional RPC messages, which form the foundation of most of today's XML Web services. If the method you invoke by a SOAP request message has parameters of simple XSD-defined data types, such as `xsd:string`, `xsd:int`, `xsd:short`, and the like, it isn't necessary to encode the request document with data type information. In most cases, the method's return value is a `String` variable of XML text, but it's also possible to return values having other data types recognized by the SOAP specification. Many demonstration XML Web services return only an integer, such as the sum or product of two integers you supply. In this case, the value is the single SOAP `Body` element. The WSDL file for the RPC message pair specifies the parameter and return value data types, so you don't need to add the `xsd:datatype` attributes to the request message.

The following RPC message examples use element names and namespaces defined by the Toolkit code. The Toolkit's Trace Utility (MSSoapT.exe) captured the HTTP `POST` header and SOAP `Envelope` contents. SOAP-RPC message exchange isn't limited to the HTTP, HTTPS, or HTTP-M protocols, but HTTP and HTTPS are the only protocols commonly used today for XML Web services. In all cases, `oakleaf.ws` replaces the default `tempuri.org` component of namespace URIs.

POSTing the RPC Request

Following is the HTTP `POST` header for a typical RPC request for XML-encoded data shown in the earlier "Serializing Data Structures" section. The header contains the relative path to the WSDL file for the service and a `SOAPAction` header that firewalls and applications can inspect to decide whether to pass and process the message.

```
POST /ch02/GetOrder.WSDL HTTP/1.1
Content-Type: text/xml; charset="UTF-8"
```

```
Host: localhost
SOAPAction: http://oakleaf.ws/action/GetOrder.GetXMLOrder
Content-Length: 480
```

The SOAP request `Envelope` encapsulates the argument names and values for the
`GetOrder.GetXMLOrder` method within the `<SOAPSDK1:GetXMLOrder>` accessor.
The first three parameters' data type is `xsd:string`; the fourth parameter is `xsd:short`,
which corresponds to Visual Basic 6.0's `Integer` data type. None of the examples of the
SOAP 1.1 specification include the standard `<?xml version="1.0" ... ?>` document
declaration, but the Toolkit's `SoapClient` object adds it for you. The `standalone="no"`
document declaration indicates the presence of external markup declarations.

```
<?xml version="1.0" encoding="UTF-8" standalone="no" ?>
<SOAP-ENV:Envelope

SOAP-ENV:encodingStyle="http://schemas.xmlsoap.org/soap/encoding/"
     xmlns:SOAP-ENV="http://schemas.xmlsoap.org/soap/envelope/">
  <SOAP-ENV:Body>
    <SOAPSDK1:GetXMLOrder
         xmlns:SOAPSDK1="http://oakleaf.ws/message/">
      <strServerName>OAKLEAF-MS7</strServerName>
      <strUserName>NwindUser</strUserName>
      <strPassword>Nwind$123</strPassword>
      <lngOrder>10251</lngOrder>
    </SOAPSDK1:GetXMLOrder>
  </SOAP-ENV:Body>
</SOAP-ENV:Envelope>
```

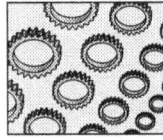

NOTE

*Sending database login names and passwords as clear text in a SOAP request message invites security
breaches. The server name and other connection string values are included in the message because you
need to change the argument values supplied by the client application to suit your particular SQL Server
configuration.*

Processing the RPC Response Message

When the receiver's Web server detects an HTTP `POST` header containing a `SOAPAction`
header component, the server instantiates a SOAP handler object to process the message.
The SOAP Toolkit provides a choice between a default Internet Server API (ISAPI) listener
for direct request message processing and an ASP listener for invoking an ASP script to
preprocess the request message. Figure 2-2 illustrates the steps required to process request
messages to a COM object that's been SOAP-enabled by the SOAP Toolkit 2.0. ASP.NET
Web Services follow a similar pattern but don't use a WSML file.

Methods of MSSOAPLib's `SoapServer` object deserialize the incoming message into
an XML DOM structure and load the WSDL into another DOM structure. Another method

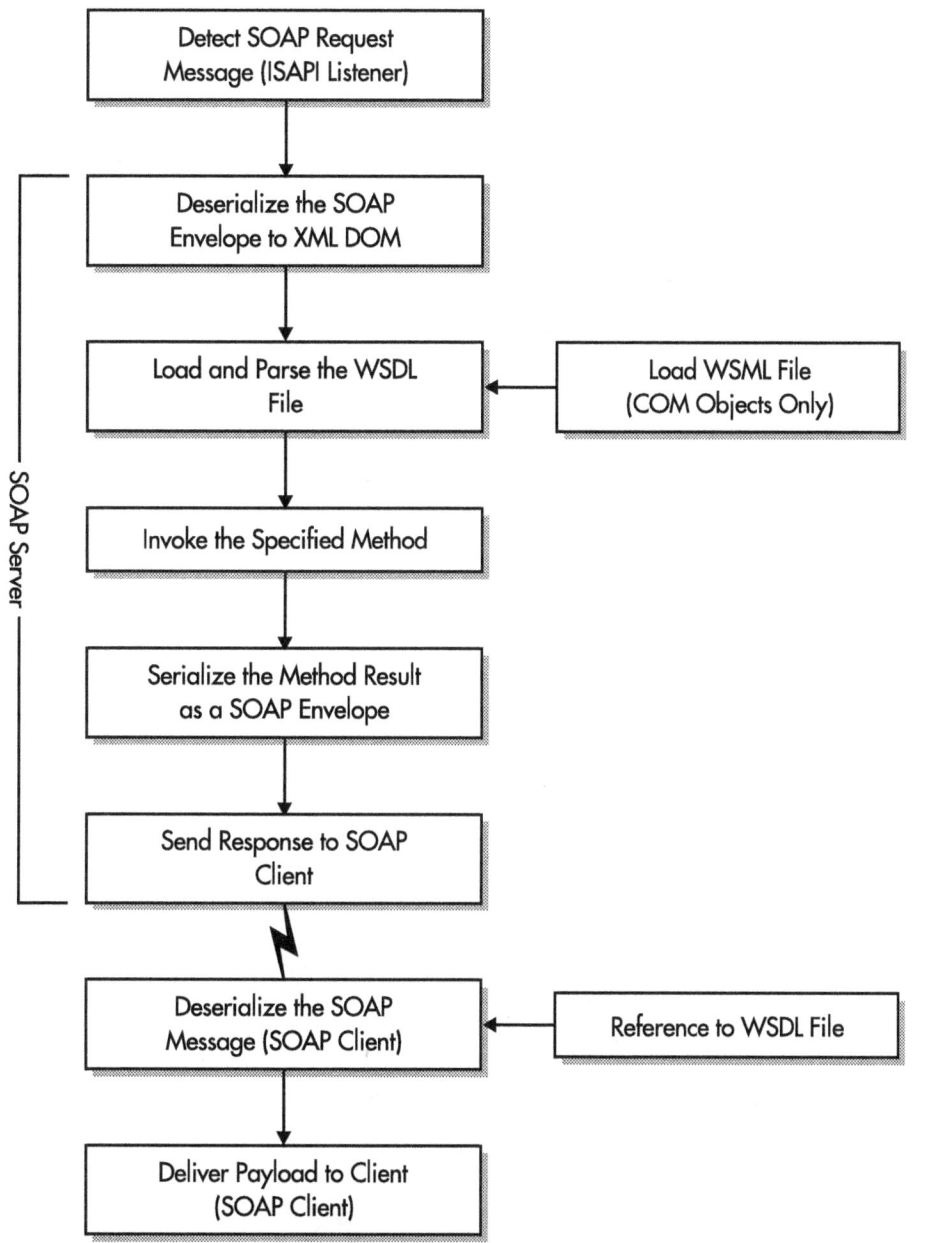

Figure 2-2   *Processing an incoming SOAP request message and returning a SOAP response message involves the basic steps shown here.*

extracts the COM method's name and argument values and invokes the method to obtain the return value. The final `SoapServer` method serializes the return value within the body of a SOAP response message and sends the response to the requesting client. Microsoft calls the `SoapServer` object a high-level API for processing SOAP requests.

Following is the HTTP header and SOAP `Envelope` response generated by the request message in the preceding section:

```
HTTP/1.1 100 Continue
Server: Microsoft-IIS/5.0
Date: Mon, 12 Nov 2001 20:30:37 GMT

HTTP/1.1 200 OK
Server: Microsoft-IIS/5.0
Date: Mon, 12 Nov 2001 20:30:37 GMT
Content-Type: text/xml; charset="UTF-8"
Content-Length: 1691
Expires: -1;

<?xml version="1.0" encoding="UTF-8" standalone="no" ?>
<SOAP-ENV:Envelope

SOAP-ENV:encodingStyle="http://schemas.xmlsoap.org/soap/encoding/"
      xmlns:SOAP-ENV="http://schemas.xmlsoap.org/soap/envelope/">
   <SOAP-ENV:Body>
      <SOAPSDK1:GetXMLOrderResponse
            xmlns:SOAPSDK1="http://oakleaf.ws/message/">
         <Result>
            <Order xmlns='http://schemas.oakleaf.ws/order/'>
               <OrderID>10251</OrderID>
               <OrderDate>7/8/1996</OrderDate>
               <ShippedDate>7/15/1996</ShippedDate>
               <CustomerID>VICTE</CustomerID>
               <ShipName>Victuailles en stock</ShipName>
               <ShipAddress>2, rue du Commerce</ShipAddress>
               <ShipCity>Lyon</ShipCity>
               <ShipRegion></ShipRegion>
               <ShipPostalCode>69004</ShipPostalCode>
               <ShipCountry>France</ShipCountry>
               <LineItems>
                  <Item>
                     <ProductID>22</ProductID>
                     <Quantity>6</Quantity>
                     <UnitPrice>16.8</UnitPrice>
                     <Discount>0.05</Discount>
                  </Item>
                  <!-- Other two <Item> subelements here -->
               </LineItems>
            </Order>
         </Result>
```

```
        </SOAPSDK1:GetXMLOrderResponse>
      </SOAP-ENV:Body>
</SOAP-ENV:Envelope>
```

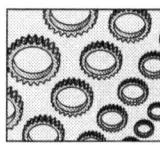

NOTE

The SOAP 1.2 working draft of October 2001 replaces references to `schemas.xmlsoap.org/soap/` *in URIs for the SOAP namespace prefixes with* `www.w3.org/2001/09/soap`*-namespace, where* `namespace` *is replaced by* `envelope`*,* `encoding`*,* `faults`*, and* `upgrade`*, without the trailing virgule (*`/`*). The final URIs will probably drop the month identifier (*`/09`*) and change the year element to reflect the final recommendation date. URIs with the* `www.w3.org` *prefix unambiguously indicate version 1.2 (or later). Version 1.2 also allows application of the* `encodingStyle` *attribute to individual sections of the SOAP message, not just the* `Envelope`*.*

The receiver verifies that the response message is in SOAP format, refers to the instance of the WSDL file employed by the request operation, and deserializes the SOAP message to deliver the Body payload to the client. Additional code in the client deserializes the Body document to an XML DOM structure from which it extracts the element values to members of a structure, array, or set of individual variables. Alternatively, you can use XSLT to transform the XML document into [X]HTML or more easily readable text.

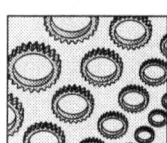

NOTE

Chapter 7 describes how to replace `SoapServer` *and* `SoapClient` *objects with the .NET Framework's* `System.Web.Services` *classes and serialize and deserialize payload documents with the* `System.XML` *classes.*

Handling SOAP Faults

If the receiver can't process the SOAP message for any reason, a method of the `SoapServer` object returns a single `Fault` message contained in the SOAP `Body` element. Section 4.4 of the SOAP 1.1 specification defines the structure and content of the `Fault` message, which has the following basic structure:

```
<SOAP-ENV:Fault>
   <faultcode>
      <!-- Section 4.4.1 requires one of the following values:
           Client, Server, MustUnderstand, and Version -->
   </faultcode>
   <faultstring>
      <!-- Required by section 4.4 to provide a human-readable
           explanation of the fault. -->
   </faultstring>
   <detail>
```

```
    <!-- Required for errors occurring during processing of
           the Body element, not Header elements. -->
  </detail>
</SOAP-ENV:Fault>
```

Implementations can extend any of the required `faultcode` values to return more explicit information on the type of error. For example, you might use `Client.Authentication` to indicate that the client's credentials don't permit sending SOAP requests. Similarly, `Server.Authentication` might indicate failure of a user name or password submitted to the database server that supplies the result set for the method's return value.

Following is an example of an error message generated by a defective GetOrder.wsml file:

```
<?xml version="1.0" encoding="UTF-8" standalone="no" ?>
<SOAP-ENV:Envelope

SOAP-ENV:encodingStyle="http://schemas.xmlsoap.org/soap/encoding/"
   xmlns:SOAP-ENV="http://schemas.xmlsoap.org/soap/envelope/">
  <SOAP-ENV:Body>
    <SOAP-ENV:Fault>
      <faultcode>SOAP-ENV:Server</faultcode>
      <faultstring>WSDLOperation: Instantiating the dispatch object
                 for method GetXMLOrder failed</faultstring>
      <faultactor>http://localhost/ch02/GetOrder.WSDL</faultactor>
      <detail>
        <mserror:errorInfo
           xmlns:mserror="http://schemas.microsoft.com/soap-
           toolkit/faultdetail/error/">
          <mserror:returnCode>-2147221164</mserror:returnCode>
          <mserror:callStack>
            <mserror:callElement>
              <mserror:component>WSDLOperation</mserror:component>
              <mserror:description>Instantiating the dispatch object
                for method GetXMLOrder failed</mserror:description>
              <mserror:returnCode>-2147221164</mserror:returnCode>
            </mserror:callElement>
          </mserror:callStack>
        </mserror:errorInfo>
      </detail>
    </SOAP-ENV:Fault>
  </SOAP-ENV:Body>
</SOAP-ENV:Envelope>
```

In this instance, the content of the `<detail>` element regurgitates the `<faultstring>` value and includes two entries for the `<mserror:returnCode>` value. The `<faultactor>` element points to the WSDL file despite the fact that the WSML file was the culprit.

If you specify an incorrect IP address or the recipient machine is out of service, you receive the following `<faultstring>`:

```
WSDLReader:Loading of the WSDL file failed HRESULT=0x80070057 -
WSDLReader:XML Parser failed at linenumber 0, lineposition 0,
reason is: System error: -2147012867. HRESULT=0x1
```

Like many other Microsoft error messages, the `<Fault>` message responses provide no indication of which actions you might take to fix the error. In most cases, you must add code to the receiving application to detect the fault during the deserializing process and, if possible, take appropriate action to resolve faults. The pragmatic approach to writing error handlers for SOAP `Faults` is to simulate errors with defective messages and WSDL and WSML files. It's up to you to translate the resulting `<Fault>` messages to readable error messages for clients with UIs or add appropriate error handlers to middle-tier components. Visual Basic .NET's structured exception handling finally brings order to the chaos of `On Error GoTo` spaghetti code.

Dissecting WSDL Files

WSDL defines the syntax of an XML document for specifying the XML Web services offered by a Web server at a specified URL. A WSDL document, which you persist as a *ServiceName*.wsdl file, serves as a contract between clients and the server. The Web Services Definition Language 1.1 specification permits a single WSDL file to contain definitions of services provided by multiple objects contained in a single DLL. The contract specifies that the server will deliver a SOAP response message to a SOAP request message that's constructed in accordance with the contract's terms and conditions.

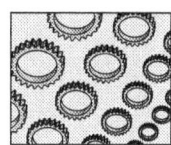

NOTE

The server breaches the contract if it's out of commission due to power or hardware failures, blue screens of death, viruses, or denial-of-service attacks. What's missing from the WSDL contract are the usual "weasel" clauses that publishers commonly incorporate into software licenses. Future versions of the WSDL specification might include the equivalent of a `<weasel>` element having a several-page `<eula>` child element. In today's litigious society, boilerplate in WSDL contracts is inevitable; the WSDL 1.1 specification provides for a `<wsdl:document>` element in which you can store your terms and conditions today. Chapter 4 shows you how to add HTML-formatted information to the `<wsdl:document>` element.

A WSDL file consists of five sections divided into hierarchies of abstract definitions and concrete descriptions, which must be present in a specified order. Definitions relate to a set of SOAP messages without reference to the site that processes them. Descriptions contain site-specific information, such as the transport, encoding method, and URL of the WSDL file.

Abstract Definitions Sections

The following three sections briefly describe the abstract definitions sections, including WSDL document fragment examples from a sample WSDL file.

The Types Section   The `<types>` section has a `<schema>` element whose attributes specify type definition namespace shortcuts to URIs for namespaces used elsewhere in the document. The `<schema>` element also contains XSD schema for document/literal messages and rpc/encoded messages that have complex data types, such as arrays or structures (structs, user-defined functions). The root `<definitions ...>` element and the `<types>` section are usually the same for all WSDL documents created by a particular authoring tool. The only section whose name is the same as the element is `<types>`.

```
<types>
  <schema targetNamespace='http://oakleaf.ws/type'
    xmlns='http://www.w3.org/2001/XMLSchema'
    xmlns:SOAP-ENC='http://schemas.xmlsoap.org/soap/encoding/'
    xmlns:wsdl='http://schemas.xmlsoap.org/wsdl/'
    elementFormDefault='qualified'>
  </schema>
</types>
```

The Messages Section   The Messages section contains one `<message name='objectName.methodName'>` element for each request and response message, with `<part name='argumentName' type='xsd:dataType'>` child elements for arguments and return values; `objectNameResponse` identifies the return value message. Following is an example for a method having four parameters:

```
<message name='GetOrder.GetXMLOrder'>
  <part name='strServerName' type='xsd:string'/>
  <part name='strUserName' type='xsd:string'/>
  <part name='strPassword' type='xsd:string'/>
  <part name='lngOrder' type='xsd:int'/>
</message>
<message name='GetOrder.GetXMLOrderResponse'>
  <part name='Result' type='xsd:string'/>
</message>
```

The PortTypes Section   The PortTypes section contains one `<portType name='objectNameSoapPort'>` element having one `<operation name='methodName'`

parameterOrder='*partName1, partName2, ...*'> child element for each method, plus <input message='wsdlns:*messageName*'> and <output message='wsdlns:*messageName*Response'> elements.

Here's an example <portType> section:

```
<portType name='GetOrderSoapPort'>
  <operation name='GetXMLOrder' parameterOrder='strServerName
      strUserName strPassword lngOrder'>
    <input message='wsdlns:GetOrder.GetXMLOrder' />
    <output message='wsdlns:GetOrder.GetXMLOrderResponse' />
  </operation>
</portType>
```

The structure of the abstract definitions sections is hierarchical, because <messages> obtains the *dataType* reference from <schema>; <portType> obtains the *objectName* and *methodName* from <message> attributes and each parameterOrder *partName#* from a corresponding <part> element.

Concrete Description Sections

Concrete descriptions are divided into the following two sections, which depend on <portType> elements.

The Bindings Section   The Bindings section has a <binding name='objectNameSoapBinding' type='wsdlns:*objectName*.SoapPort'> element for each object. The first two child elements, <stk:binding...> and <soap:binding...>, specify the encoding for the message (UTF-8), style (RPC), and transport (HTTP). One <operation name='methodName'> element exists for each method with <soap:operation...>, <input>, and <output> child elements. The <soap:operation...> element provides the soapAction HTTP header, and <input> and <output> define the encoding style of the SOAP Body element.

Following is an example of binding the GetOrder object to the HTTP transport and specifying RPC/encoding style:

```
<binding name='GetOrderSoapBinding' type='wsdlns:GetOrderSoapPort' >
  <stk:binding preferredEncoding='UTF-8'/>
  <soap:binding style='rpc'
      transport='http://schemas.xmlsoap.org/soap/http' />
  <operation name='GetXMLOrder' >
    <soap:operation
        soapAction='http://oakleaf.ws/action/GetOrder.GetXMLOrder' />
    <input>
      <soap:body use='encoded' namespace='http://oakleaf.ws/message/'
          encodingStyle='http://schemas.xmlsoap.org/soap/encoding/' />
    </input>
    <output>
```

```
      <soap:body use='encoded' namespace='http://oakleaf.ws/message/'
        encodingStyle='http://schemas.xmlsoap.org/soap/encoding/' />
    </output>
  </operation>
</binding>
```

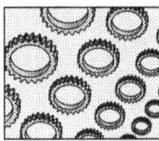

NOTE

The WSDL specification defines bindings for HTTP GET *and* POST*, and MIME, in addition to SOAP. HTTP and MIME bindings haven't gained widespread acceptance and don't qualify as XML Web services protocols, which, by definition, use SOAP binding. As mentioned in Chapter 1's "ASP.NET Web Services" section, ASP.NET automatically adds HTTP* GET *and* POST *bindings to the WSDL document for ASP.NET Web services.*

The Services Section   The final Services section has a `<service name='`*objectName*`'>` element for each object with a `<port name='objectNameSoapPort' binding= 'objectNameSoapBinding'>` child element, which in turn has a `<soap:address location='http://`*url*`/`*fileName*`.wsdl'>` child element that specifies an endpoint. In this case, the endpoint is the site-specific location of the WSDL file.

This example specifies the endpoint for requests to instantiate the `GetOrder` object:

```
<service name='GetOrder' >
  <port name='GetOrderSoapPort'
binding='wsdlns:GetOrderSoapBinding' >
    <soap:address location='http://localhost/ch02/GetOrder.WSDL' />
  </port>
</service>
```

Analyzing the GetOrder.wsdl File

It's clear from the preceding WSDL section descriptions that rolling your own WSDL files isn't a walk in the park, especially if you must support several objects having multiple methods in a single file. The probability of making one or more fatal typographical errors when typing a WSDL file in Notepad is close to 100 percent. Ambiguous SOAP `Fault` messages complicate debugging errors in hand-hewn WSDL files. Fortunately, the SOAP Toolkit 2.0 and Visual Studio .NET include tools for automatically generating WSDL files and documents based on the type library for the DLL that implements them.

The complete GetOrder.wsdl file for the simple `GetOrder` COM object and its `GetXMLOrder` method offers further evidence that writing a WSDL file in a text editor is, at best, a chancy process. Following is the WSDL document that the Soap Toolkit 2.0 creates from the ActiveX DLL (axGetOrder.dll) for the `GetOrder` object:

```
<?xml version='1.0' encoding='UTF-8' ?>
<definitions name='GetOrder' targetNamespace='http://oakleaf.ws/wsdl/'
  xmlns:wsdlns='http://oakleaf.ws/wsdl/'
```

```
xmlns:typens='http://oakleaf.ws/type'
xmlns:soap='http://schemas.xmlsoap.org/wsdl/soap/'
xmlns:xsd='http://www.w3.org/2001/XMLSchema'
xmlns:stk='http://schemas.microsoft.com/soap-toolkit/wsdl-extension'
xmlns='http://schemas.xmlsoap.org/wsdl/'>
<types>
  <schema targetNamespace='http://oakleaf.ws/type'
    xmlns='http://www.w3.org/2001/XMLSchema'
    xmlns:SOAP-ENC='http://schemas.xmlsoap.org/soap/encoding/'
    xmlns:wsdl='http://schemas.xmlsoap.org/wsdl/'
    elementFormDefault='qualified'>
  </schema>
</types>
<message name='GetOrder.GetXMLOrder'>
  <part name='strServerName' type='xsd:string'/>
  <part name='strUserName' type='xsd:string'/>
  <part name='strPassword' type='xsd:string'/>
  <part name='lngOrder' type='xsd:int'/>
</message>
<message name='GetOrder.GetXMLOrderResponse'>
  <part name='Result' type='xsd:string'/>
</message>
<portType name='GetOrderSoapPort'>
  <operation name='GetXMLOrder' parameterOrder='strServerName
      strUserName strPassword lngOrder'>
    <input message='wsdlns:GetOrder.GetXMLOrder' />
    <output message='wsdlns:GetOrder.GetXMLOrderResponse' />
  </operation>
</portType>
<binding name='GetOrderSoapBinding'
    type='wsdlns:GetOrderSoapPort' >
  <stk:binding preferredEncoding='UTF-8'/>
  <soap:binding style='rpc'
      transport='http://schemas.xmlsoap.org/soap/http' />
  <operation name='GetXMLOrder' >
    <soap:operation
      soapAction='http://oakleaf.ws/action/GetOrder.GetXMLOrder' />
    <input>
      <soap:body use='encoded'
        namespace='http://oakleaf.ws/message/'
        encodingStyle='http://schemas.xmlsoap.org/soap/encoding/' />
    </input>
    <output>
```

```
        <soap:body use='encoded'
          namespace='http://oakleaf.ws/message/'
          encodingStyle='http://schemas.xmlsoap.org/soap/encoding/' />
      </output>
    </operation>
  </binding>
  <service name='GetOrder' >
    <port name='GetOrderSoapPort'
      binding='wsdlns:GetOrderSoapBinding' >
      <soap:address location='http://localhost/ch02/GetOrder.WSDL' />
    </port>
  </service>
</definitions>
```

XML Web service clients view the WSDL file from the bottom up, starting at the Services section, which defines the ports available to access the service. For example, the `location` attribute's URL might differ from the URL at which you open the WSDL file for inspection. If the service has multiple bindings, for example, the client inspects each binding name to find a preferred protocol. Finally, the client iterates the `<message>` elements to obtain a list of parameter names and data types for use in the request message.

Visual Studio .NET's client proxy handles the WSDL inspection process for you and provides early binding to a local file copy of the .asmx file's WSDL document. Late binding to the WSDL file is the general rule for ASP and Visual Basic 6.0 clients. An exception is a WSDL proxy for Visual Basic 6.0 client that you can create with the Web Service Proxy Wizard, which the earlier "ASP.NET Web Service with a .NET Client WebReference" section mentions and Chapter 3 describes in greater detail.

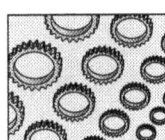

NOTE

WSDL files for SOAP RPC messaging aren't mandatory. You can write custom ASP or ASP.NET SOAP servers and clients, as well as Visual Basic 6.0 or Visual Basic .NET clients, to perform the serialization and deserialization operations without reference to a WSDL file. WSDL files or documents are required for all XML Web service discovery processes, however, including UDDI. Thus, a WSDL file or document is necessary to qualify a SOAP-based RPC-style (or document-style) messaging application as an XML Web service.

Reviewing the SOAP Toolkit's Autogenerated WSML File

The SOAP Toolkit 2.0 Wizard generates a Web Services Meta Language (WSML) file with the same filename and a .wsml extension for each WSDL file. WSML files are specific to XML Web services based on COM objects; there's no specification, W3C note, or formal grammar documentation for WSML files. The purpose of the WSML file is to specify the programmatic ID (ProgID) of the COM object to load for the service. The WSML file is the only platform-dependent component of an XML Web service. XML Web services that you create with ASP.NET or .NET Remoting don't require WSML files.

The WSML file maps the objects, methods, and parameters defined by the ActiveX DLL's type library to the WSDL file's `<portType><operation>` element. Following is the Wizard-generated WSML file for axGetOrder.dll:

```xml
<?xml version='1.0' encoding='UTF-8' ?>
<servicemapping name='GetOrder'>
  <service name='GetOrder'>
    <using PROGID='axGetOrder.GetOrder' cachable='0'
        ID='GetOrderObject' />
    <port name='GetOrderSoapPort'>
      <operation name='GetXMLOrder'>
        <execute uses='GetOrderObject' method='GetXMLOrder'
                 dispID='1610809344'>
          <parameter callIndex='1' name='strServerName'
                     elementName='strServerName' />
          <parameter callIndex='2' name='strUserName'
                     elementName='strUserName' />
          <parameter callIndex='3' name='strPassword'
                     elementName='strPassword' />
          <parameter callIndex='4' name='intOrder'
                     elementName='intOrder' />
          <parameter callIndex='-1' name='retval'
                     elementName='Result' />
        </execute>
      </operation>
    </port>
  </service>
</servicemapping>
```

The `dispID` attribute value of the `<execute>` element is an optional shortcut to the COM dispatch ID for the method. Providing the `dispID` value eliminates a cross-process call to `GetIDsOfNames` to obtain the dispatch ID for binding the method. The only parameter that has a `<message><part>` name that differs from the `<parameter name>` attribute value is the method's return value (`retVal`), which maps to `Result`.

TIP

If you receive an instantiation error message, one of the first of the service components to check is the WSML file. If the WSML file is corrupted or out of sync with the object or WSDL file, your COM-based XML Web service breaches its contract with the client. Recreating the WSDL/WSML combination with the SOAP Toolkit 2.0 Wizard usually solves the problem.

Extending SOAP Messages with Header Elements

This chapter's SOAP and WSDL examples represent a basic XML Web service that's understandable by simple SOAP 1.1–compliant clients that support WSDL 1.1, is written in any programming language, and is run under any operating system. The GetOrder.wsdl file includes all the information required by a Java programmer, for example, to write a SOAP client that runs under UNIX or Linux. Executing the GetXMLOrder method requires that the programmer know the server name, user name, and password for the database, as well as the range of current intOrderID values.

The first step in making your XML Web service inaccessible to potential casual users (and hackers) is to take advantage of SOAP's optional extensibility features, which are implemented in the <SOAP-ENV:Header> element. For example, you can add an authentication header for submitting a password or other credential in the request message. In this case, you might use the strUserName and strPassword argument values to authenticate the client prior to executing a database query. An even more secure approach is to require a different user name and password or a client certificate. If you decide to implement SOAP headers, the <SOAP-ENV:Header> element must appear immediately after the root <SOAP-ENV: Envelope ...> tag.

Following is a SOAP request message to invoke the GetXMLOrder method only for valid user name/password combinations, which the message header supplies as values of the <Auth:UserID...> and <Auth:Password...> elements:

```
<?xml version="1.0" encoding="UTF-8" standalone="no" ?>
<SOAP-ENV:Envelope
      SOAP-ENV:encodingStyle="http://schemas.xmlsoap.org/soap/encoding/"
      xmlns:SOAP-ENV="http://schemas.xmlsoap.org/soap/envelope/">
  <SOAP-ENV:Header>
      <Auth:UserID xmlns:Auth="http://oakleaf.ws/auth/"
                  SOAP-ENV:mustUnderstand="1">
        NwindUser
      </Auth:UserID>
      <Auth:Password xmlmns:Auth="http://oakleaf.ws/auth/"
        SOAP-ENV:mustUnderstand="1">Nwind$123
      </Auth:Password>
  </SOAP-ENV:Header>
  <SOAP-ENV:Body>
      <SOAPSDK1:GetXMLOrder
            xmlns:SOAPSDK1="http://oakleaf.ws/message/">
        <strServerName>OAKLEAF-MS7</strServerName>
        <strUserName>NwindUser</strUserName>
        <strPassword>Nwind$123</strPassword>
        <lngOrder>10251</lngOrder>
```

```
      </SOAPSDK1:GetXMLOrder>
    </SOAP-ENV:Body>
</SOAP-ENV:Envelope>
```

In the preceding example, the value of the `SOAP-ENV:mustUnderstand` attribute is 1, which requires the receiver to process the `Header` element. If the receiving application doesn't recognize or can't process a `Header` element, it must return a `SOAP-ENV:Fault` message with `MustUnderstand` as the value of the `<faultcode>` element.

The SOAP Toolkit's high-level API doesn't support headers, and the SOAP Toolkit 2.0 Wizard doesn't create the WSDL entries required to define header operations. The .NET Framework's `System.Web.Services.Protocols.SoapHeader` class provides the infrastructure for adding header processing to XML Web services and supplying header values to SOAP request messages. When you add headers to an ASP.NET Web Service, Visual Studio .NET automatically generates the required WSDL elements. Chapters 7 and 8 show you how to add header processing to XML Web services that you create with ASP.NET and Visual Basic .NET.

Previewing the GetNwindOrder ASP.NET Web Service

Up until now, this chapter's examples have been based on a Visual Basic 6.0 COM component. The Visual Studio .NET Upgrade Wizard makes converting simple COM components to ASP.NET Web methods a snap. Here's the drill:

1. Open the Visual Basic 6.0 project—axGetOrder.vbp for this example—in Visual Studio .NET to start the Upgrade Wizard. Click Next three times (accepting the defaults), click Yes when asked if you want to create a folder for the upgraded project, and click Next again to start the upgrade engine.

 **TIP**

Download Vbws02.zip from this book's entry at http://www.osborne.com/downloads/downloads.shtml if you want to create the sample GetNwindOrder solution. Vbws02.zip contains the axGetOrder.vbp project files; verify the reference to the Microsoft ActiveX Data Object 2.7 Library, and compile the project after extracting the files. You must be able to connect to an SQL Server 7.0 or 2000 instance with the Northwind sample database to run the resulting Web service. The Microsoft Desktop Engine (MSDE) instance installed by Visual Studio doesn't include the Northwind database. If you use an MSDE instance installed by Access 2000 or 2002, change the `InitialCatalog` value of `strConnect` to `NorthwindCS`.

2. When the Wizard completes the upgrade, fix any errors and investigate warnings reported in the ToDo window, choose Build | Build Solution to confirm your changes, and save the solution.

3. Open a new instance of Visual Studio .NET, and choose File | New | Project to open the New Project dialog. Select Visual Basic Projects in the Project Types list, and select the ASP.NET Web Service icon in the Templates list. In the Location text box, replace WebService1 with the name of the new IIS virtual directory to host the service—GetNwindOrder for this example, as shown here. Click OK to close the dialog and open the new solution and project.

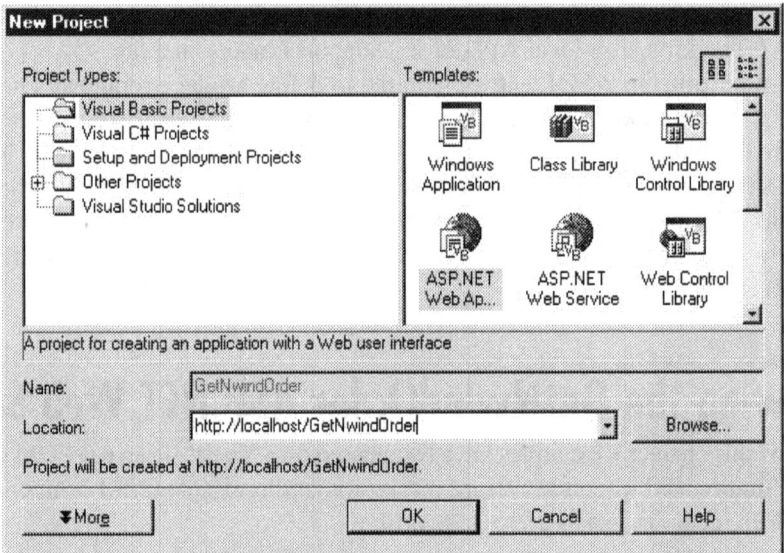

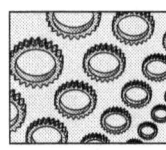

NOTE

When you click OK, ASP.NET automatically creates Inetpub\wwwroot\serviceName and Inetput\wwwroot\serviceName/bin folders, and a serviceName virtual directory of the machine Default Web Site. The default solution file is \Documents and Settings\UserName\My Documents\Visual Studio Projects\serviceName\serviceName.sln.

4. Click the code view link to open the Service1.asmx.vb code-behind page. Replace `tempuri.org` with your preferred namespace URI prefix, **oakleaf.ws/order** for this example. Change the class name from `Service1` to **objectName (GetOrder)**, which changes the service name to GetOrder.asmx.

5. Select all the commented `WEB SERVICE EXAMPLE` code, switch to the other instance of Visual Studio .NET, copy the `Public Function` code to the clipboard, return to the ASP.NET instance, and replace the commented code with the function code. Add **`<WebMethod()>`** as a prefix to the `Public Function` line. Here's Visual Studio .NET's window at this point in the process.

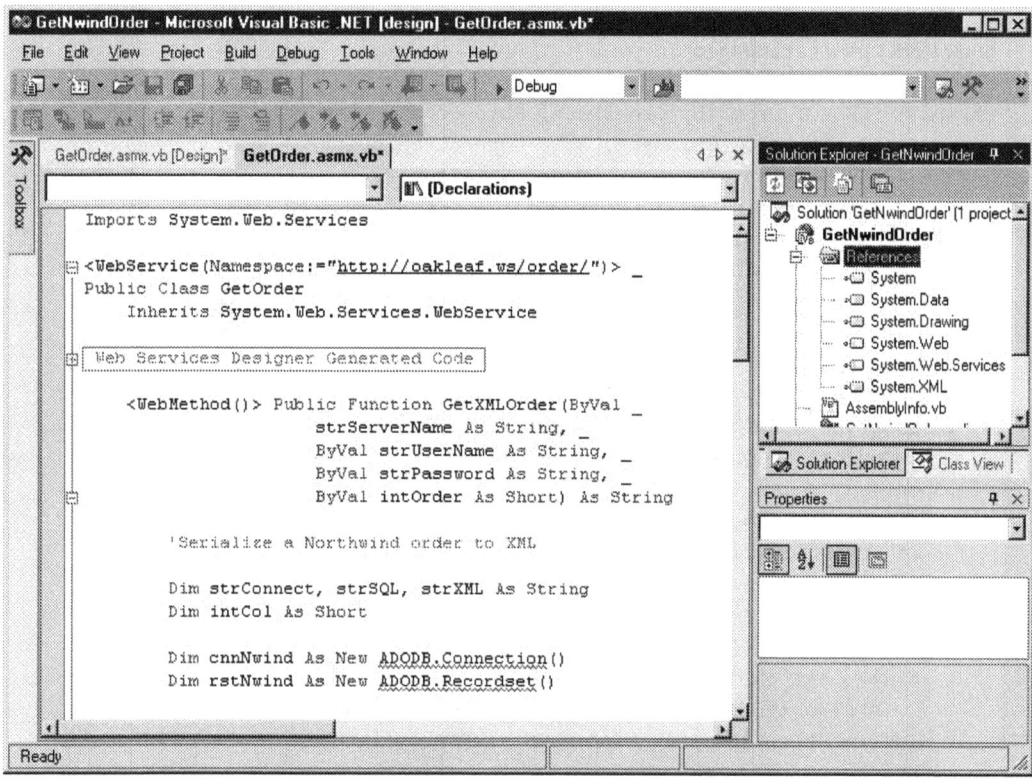

Following is the Visual Basic .NET code for the `GetOrder` class of the GetNwindOrder Web service. Minor changes to the code reflect new Visual Basic .NET features, such as streamlined multiple declarations of variables of a single data type and the new C-style += operator for string concatenation.

```
Imports System.Web.Services
<WebService(Namespace:="http://oakleaf.ws/order/")> _
Public Class GetOrder
    Inherits System.Web.Services.WebService
#Region " Web Services Designer Generated Code "
#End Region
<WebMethod()> Public Function GetXMLOrder(ByVal _
    strServerName As String, ByVal strUserName As String, _
    ByVal strPassword As String, ByVal intOrder As Short) As String
    'Serialize a Northwind order to XML
    Dim strConnect, strSQL, strXML As String
    Dim intCol As Short
    Dim cnnNwind As New ADODB.Connection()
    Dim rstNwind As New ADODB.Recordset()
    On Error GoTo ErrGetXML

    strConnect = "Provider=SQLOLEDB;Data Source=" & strServerName & _
        ";Initial Catalog=Northwind;UID=" & strUserName & _
```

```
                          ";PWD=" & strPassword
        cnnNwind.Open((strConnect))

        strSQL = "SELECT OrderID, OrderDate, ShippedDate, Freight, " & _
                 "CustomerID, ShipName, ShipAddress, ShipCity, " & _
                 "ShipRegion, ShipPostalCode, ShipCountry " & _
                 "FROM Orders WHERE OrderID = " & CStr(intOrder)
        'First line of serialized Order data
        strXML = "<Order xmlns='http://schemas.oakleaf.ws/order/'>" & vbCrLf

        With rstNwind
            .ActiveConnection = cnnNwind
            .CursorLocation = ADODB.CursorLocationEnum.adUseClient
            .CursorType = ADODB.CursorTypeEnum.adOpenStatic
            .let_Source(strSQL)
            .Open()
            For intCol = 0 To .Fields.Count - 1
                If IsDBNull(.Fields(intCol).Value) Then
                    'Empty Region or PostalCode value
                    strXML += " & CStr(.Fields(intCol).Name) & _
                        ">" & "</" & CStr(.Fields(intCol).Name) & ">" & vbCrLf
                Else
                    strXML += "   <" & CStr(.Fields(intCol).Name) & ">" & _
        CStr(.Fields(intCol).Value) & _"</" & CStr(.Fields(intCol).Name) & ">" & vbCrLf
                End If
            Next intCol
            .Close()
        End With

        'Add the line items as nested elements
        strSQL = "SELECT ProductID, Quantity, UnitPrice, Discount " & _
                 "FROM [Order Details] " & "Where OrderID = " & CStr(Order)
        strXML += "   <LineItems>" & vbCrLf
        With rstNwind
            .ActiveConnection = cnnNwind
            .CursorLocation = ADODB.CursorLocationEnum.adUseClient
            .CursorType = ADODB.CursorTypeEnum.adOpenStatic
            .let_Source(strSQL)
            .Open()
            Do Until .EOF
                strXML = strXML & Space(6) & "<Item>" & vbCrLf
                For intCol = 0 To .Fields.Count - 1
                    strXML += Space(9) & "<" & CStr(.Fields(intCol).Name) & ">" & _
                            CStr(.Fields(intCol).Value) & "</" & _
                            CStr(.Fields(intCol).Name) & ">" & vbCrLf
                Next intCol
                strXML += Space(6) & "</Item>" & vbCrLf
                .MoveNext()
            Loop
```

```
      .Close()
   End With
   cnnNwind.Close()

   strXML += "   </LineItems>" & vbCrLf & "</Order>"
   GetXMLOrder = strXML
   Exit Function

ErrGetXML:
   GetXMLOrder = "Error: " & Err.Description
   Exit Function
End Function
End Class
```

Completing and Testing the Web Service

Do the following to run a preliminary test of a copied function that contains ADODB object
variables:

1. Choose Project | Add Reference to open the Add Reference dialog box, click the
    COM tab, and double-click Microsoft ActiveX Data Object 2.7 Library. Expand
    the Component Name column to make sure you select the correct library,
    as shown here.

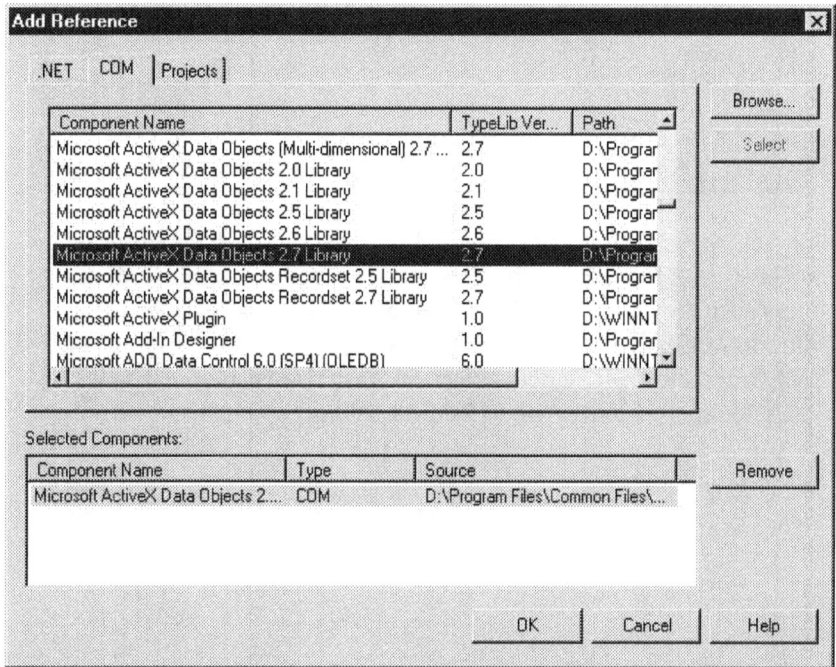

2. Click OK to add the reference and close the dialog, and then press F5 to build and
    run the Web service. After a second or two, if your code is clean, IE 6.0 opens

the ASP.NET Web Service page (GetOrder.asmx). If not, fix the problem(s) and press F5 again.

3. Click the link to the function name (GetXMLOrder) to open the GetOrder form, which has four text boxes to enter the parameter values. Type the server instance name, login ID, password, and order number (10250 or greater), as shown here.

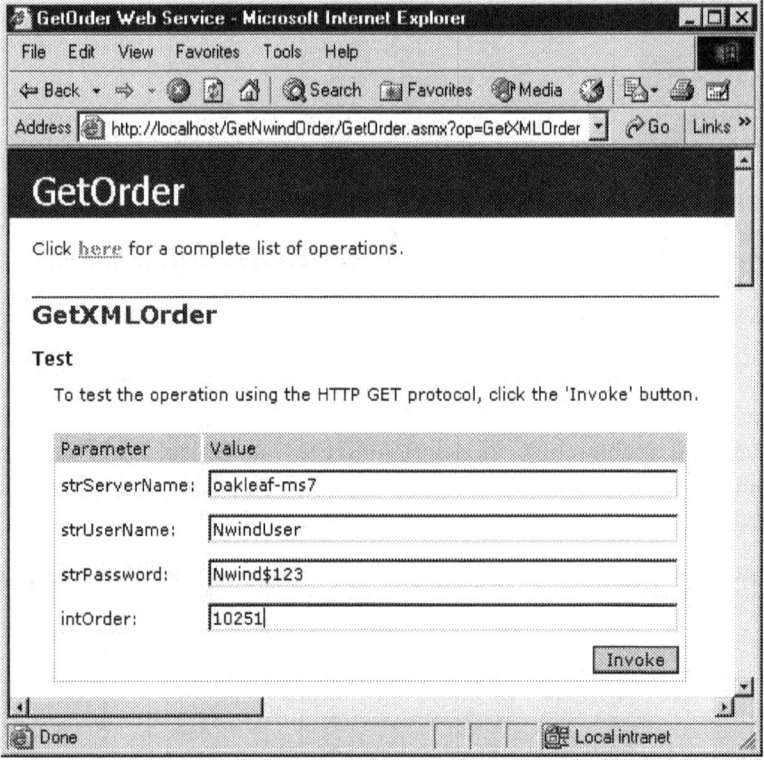

4. Click Invoke to use HTTP **GET** protocol binding to display an unformatted version of the XML document in IE 6.0, shown in the next illustration. A typical URL for the **GET** operation on the GetNwindOrder service is http://localhost/GetNwindOrder/GetOrder.asmx/ GetXMLOrder?strServerName=oakleaf-ms7&strUserName= NwindUser&strPassword=Nwind%24123&intOrder=10251.

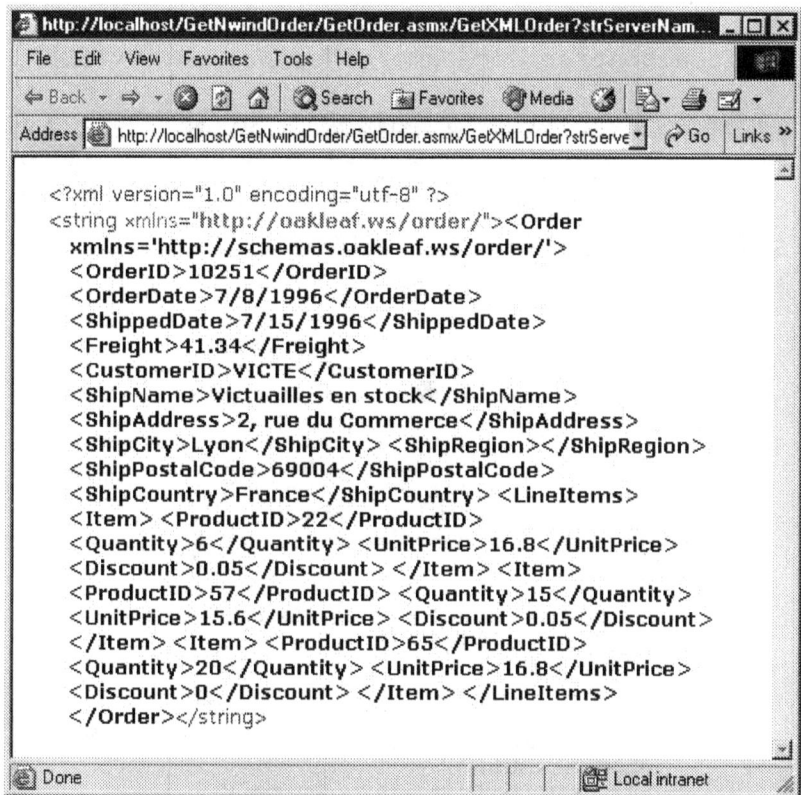

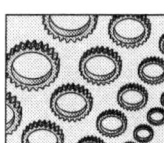

NOTE

Enclosing the payload document with `<string>...</string>` tags causes IE's XML stylesheet to ignore document whitespace, which includes spaces and newline characters external to the document elements. The resulting document is just a sequence of payload element tags and their values.

5. Close the document window, click Back, and click the Service Description link to display the contents of the service's WSDL document, shown in the next

illustration. The default URL to display the ASP.NET WSDL document is
`http://localhost/`*serviceName*`/`*objectName*`.asmx?WSDL`.

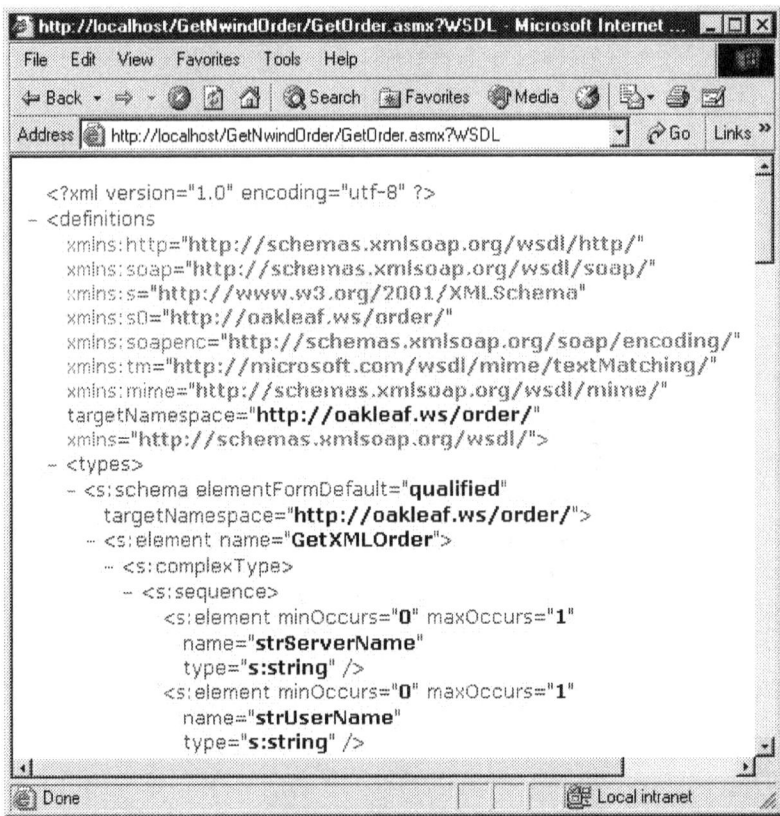

Scrolling the WSDL text demonstrates that the autogenerated WSDL document for an
ASP.NET Web Service differs substantially from the SOAP Toolkit's WSDL file for the
COM version of the `GetOrder` components.

Analyzing ASP.NET's WSDL Document

ASP.NET doesn't persist the WSDL document for the GetNwindOrder service as a
GetNwindOrder.wsdl file. Instead, the service generates the WSDL dynamically when you
specify `WSDL` as the argument of a `GET` operation on the .asmx file. Dynamic generation
permits immediate changes to the WSDL document when you alter your Visual Basic .NET
code behind the ASP.NET page.

TIP

*You can persist the .asmx page's WSDL document as a WSDL file by creating a client application and adding
a Web Reference to the .asmx page.*

Following are additional differences between ASP.NET Web Services and XML Web services based on COM objects:

▶ The web service is delivered by an ASP.NET page, which corresponds to the ASP page required when you specify the ASP listener instead of the ISAPI listener with the SOAP Toolkit 2.0 Wizard.

▶ The ASP.NET page for the GetNwindOrder service (GetOrder.asmx) contains a single directive to identify the language, code file, and service class. The directive for the sample service is `<%@ WebService Language="vb" Codebehind= "GetOrder.asmx.vb" Class="GetNwindOrder.GetOrder" %>`. This directive takes the place of the Toolkit-generated WSML file.

▶ The default style of ASP.NET Web Services is document/literal; the SOAP Tookit's high-level API supports only rpc/encoded style. HTTP `GET` operations require document/literal messaging. Chapter 10 describes how to use .NET Remoting with the HTTP channel type and SOAP formatter to create rpc/encoded-style XML Web services.

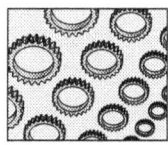 **NOTE**

Most current third-party Web services use rpc/encoded style. Making document/literal ASP.NET's default SOAP messaging style will accelerate the transition from rpc/encoded to document/literal style for production XML Web services.

▶ Document/literal style requires an embedded XSD schema for the document. Thus, the `<types>` section of the WSDL document includes an `<s:schema>` subsection to define the sequence and data types of the `GetXMLOrder` method's arguments.

▶ ASP.NET adds `<message>`, `<portType>`, `<binding>`, and `<port>` elements for HTTP `GET` and HTTP `POST` operations, which the WSDL 1.1 specification describes in section 4. These operations MIME-encode the result string in accordance with section 5 of the specification. Neither of these operations qualify as XML Web services, which require SOAP as the messaging protocol.

Following is the complete WSDL document for the GetNwindOrder service. Compare the contents of this document with the relatively simple WSDL file for rpc/encoded messaging in the earlier "Dissecting WSDL Files" section.

```
<?xml version="1.0" encoding="utf-8" ?>
<definitions xmlns:http="http://schemas.xmlsoap.org/wsdl/http/"
    xmlns:soap="http://schemas.xmlsoap.org/wsdl/soap/"
    xmlns:s="http://www.w3.org/2001/XMLSchema"
    xmlns:s0="http://oakleaf.ws/order/"
    xmlns:soapenc="http://schemas.xmlsoap.org/soap/encoding/"
    xmlns:tm="http://microsoft.com/wsdl/mime/textMatching/"
    xmlns:mime="http://schemas.xmlsoap.org/wsdl/mime/"
    targetNamespace="http://oakleaf.ws/order/"
    xmlns="http://schemas.xmlsoap.org/wsdl/">
```

```xml
<types>
  <s:schema elementFormDefault="qualified"
      targetNamespace="http://oakleaf.ws/order/">
    <s:element name="GetXMLOrder">
      <s:complexType>
        <s:sequence>
          <s:element minOccurs="0" maxOccurs="1"
              name="strServerName" type="s:string" />
          <s:element minOccurs="0" maxOccurs="1"
              name="strUserName" type="s:string" />
          <s:element minOccurs="0" maxOccurs="1"
              name="strPassword" type="s:string" />
          <s:element minOccurs="1" maxOccurs="1"
              name="intOrder" type="s:short" />
        </s:sequence>
      </s:complexType>
    </s:element>
    <s:element name="GetXMLOrderResponse">
      <s:complexType>
        <s:sequence>
          <s:element minOccurs="0" maxOccurs="1"
              name="GetXMLOrderResult" type="s:string" />
        </s:sequence>
      </s:complexType>
    </s:element>
    <s:element name="string" nillable="true" type="s:string" />
  </s:schema>
</types>
<message name="GetXMLOrderSoapIn">
  <part name="parameters" element="s0:GetXMLOrder" />
</message>
<message name="GetXMLOrderSoapOut">
  <part name="parameters" element="s0:GetXMLOrderResponse" />
</message>
<message name="GetXMLOrderHttpGetIn">
  <part name="strServerName" type="s:string" />
  <part name="strUserName" type="s:string" />
  <part name="strPassword" type="s:string" />
  <part name="intOrder" type="s:string" />
</message>
<message name="GetXMLOrderHttpGetOut">
  <part name="Body" element="s0:string" />
</message>
<message name="GetXMLOrderHttpPostIn">
  <part name="strServerName" type="s:string" />
```

```xml
      <part name="strUserName" type="s:string" />
      <part name="strPassword" type="s:string" />
      <part name="intOrder" type="s:string" />
</message>
<message name="GetXMLOrderHttpPostOut">
    <part name="Body" element="s0:string" />
</message>
<portType name="GetOrderSoap">
    <operation name="GetXMLOrder">
      <input message="s0:GetXMLOrderSoapIn" />
      <output message="s0:GetXMLOrderSoapOut" />
    </operation>
</portType>
<portType name="GetOrderHttpGet">
    <operation name="GetXMLOrder">
      <input message="s0:GetXMLOrderHttpGetIn" />
      <output message="s0:GetXMLOrderHttpGetOut" />
    </operation>
</portType>
<portType name="GetOrderHttpPost">
    <operation name="GetXMLOrder">
      <input message="s0:GetXMLOrderHttpPostIn" />
      <output message="s0:GetXMLOrderHttpPostOut" />
    </operation>
</portType>
<binding name="GetOrderSoap" type="s0:GetOrderSoap">
    <soap:binding transport="http://schemas.xmlsoap.org/soap/http"
        style="document" />
    <operation name="GetXMLOrder">
      <soap:operation soapAction="http://oakleaf.ws/order/GetXMLOrder"
          style="document" />
      <input>
        <soap:body use="literal" />
      </input>
      <output>
        <soap:body use="literal" />
      </output>
    </operation>
</binding>
<binding name="GetOrderHttpGet" type="s0:GetOrderHttpGet">
    <http:binding verb="GET" />
    <operation name="GetXMLOrder">
      <http:operation location="/GetXMLOrder" />
      <input>
        <http:urlEncoded />
```

```
      </input>
      <output>
        <mime:mimeXml part="Body" />
      </output>
    </operation>
  </binding>
  <binding name="GetOrderHttpPost" type="s0:GetOrderHttpPost">
    <http:binding verb="POST" />
    <operation name="GetXMLOrder">
      <http:operation location="/GetXMLOrder" />
      <input>
        <mime:content type="application/x-www-form-urlencoded" />
      </input>
      <output>
        <mime:mimeXml part="Body" />
      </output>
    </operation>
  </binding>
  <service name="GetOrder">
    <port name="GetOrderSoap" binding="s0:GetOrderSoap">
      <soap:address location=
          "http://localhost/GetNwindOrder/GetOrder.asmx" />
    </port>
    <port name="GetOrderHttpGet" binding="s0:GetOrderHttpGet">
      <http:address location=
          "http://localhost/GetNwindOrder/GetOrder.asmx" />
    </port>
    <port name="GetOrderHttpPost" binding="s0:GetOrderHttpPost">
      <http:address location=
          "http://localhost/GetNwindOrder/GetOrder.asmx" />
    </port>
  </service>
</definitions>
```

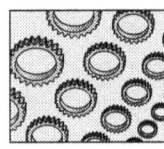

NOTE

The `nillable="true"` *attribute of the* `string` *element near the beginning of the document isn't a misspelling of nullable. If* `nillable="true"`, *the element may contain no value. The XML Schema Part 1: Structures (http://www.w3.org/TR/xmlschema-1/) provides a somewhat abstruse description for the use of* `nillable`.

Despite the size and complexity of the WSDL document for ASP.NET Web Services, ASP.NET is the easiest and fastest method for creating and deploying conventional Visual Basic .NET XML Web services. The alternative, .NET Remoting with HTTP as the transport, adds design flexibility to XML Web services at the cost of writing a substantial amount of Visual Basic .NET support code.

Working with the Microsoft SOAP Toolkit 2.0

IN THIS CHAPTER:

Analyzing Workflow of a Typical B2C/B2B Project

Using the OCE_Orders Project's Test Client

Installing the Microsoft SOAP Toolkit 2.0 and Running the Sample Code

Creating ActiveX DLLs for Web Services

SOAP-Enabling ActiveX Components with the SOAP Toolkit 2.0 Wizard

Invoking XML Web Services with the SoapClient Object

Using the Trace Utility for Debugging Messages

Deploying XML Web Services to a Production Server

The SOAP message and WSDL examples in Chapters 1 and 2 gave you a preview of the capabilities of the Microsoft SOAP Toolkit 2.0 and its Trace Utility. This chapter's primary objective is to show you how to use the Toolkit's high-level APIs to SOAP-enable moderately complex ActiveX middle-tier components that manage data persisted in multiple databases. Components that emulate real-world transactions are much more meaningful to experienced Visual Basic developers than "Hello World" or "Add Two Numbers" examples. Sample Web services that read from and update multiple databases let you compare the performance of conventional and SOAP-enabled ActiveX components in a simulated production environment. Later chapters compare performance of Web services based on ActiveX components, native ASP.NET implementations, and ADO versus ADO.NET data access.

The "OakLeaf Consumer Electronics' B2C and B2B Project" section in Chapter 1 briefly describes the databases that support this chapter's examples. This chapter's sample code includes a Visual Basic 6.0 test client for creating and updating B2C orders and invoices, verifying and charging credit cards, and conducting B2B transactions with consumer electronics distributors. The Web services you create in this chapter with the SOAP Toolkit 2.0 will handle credit-card and B2B transactions with simulated business partners and a fictional credit-card processing network.

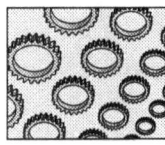

NOTE

Download the SQL Server 2000 databases for this chapter as VBWS_OCE.zip (10MB) from http://www.osborne.com/downloads/downloads.shtml. The six databases consume about 50MB of disk space. Appendix A describes how to attach the databases to an instance of SQL Server or MSDE 2000 and set up server logins and user permissions. VBWS03.zip contains this chapter's Visual Basic 6.0 and .NET sample code.

TIP

If you want to dive directly into working with the SOAP Toolkit 2.0 and its sample service and client, skip to the "Installing the Microsoft SOAP Toolkit 2.0 and Running the Sample Code" section.

Analyzing Workflow of a Typical B2C/B2B Project

The OakLeaf Consumer Electronics (OCE) sample project emulates a Web-based storefront. The OCE organization is split into two divisions: Customer Service and Order Fulfillment. The Customer Service division, which is located in Dallas' Oak Cliff neighborhood, runs the Web site and owns the OCE_Cust customer relationships management (CRM) database. The Order Fulfillment division owns the OCE_Prod products and inventory database and manages the Garland warehouse. A leased T-1 line connects the office and warehouse LANs.

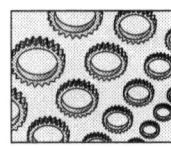

NOTE

Most of this chapter's sample code runs from a Visual Basic 6.0 client project, OCE_Orders.vbp, which is archived in VBWS03.zip. The sample code uses dynamically generated SQL statements for all queries and updates. Production applications ordinarily employ stored procedures for these tasks. Dynamic SQL code makes the operational code examples more evident and lets you change data-related functions without rewriting stored procedures.

Order Processing

The OCE Web site requires customers to register before placing an order; registration requires a valid e-mail ID and a customer-specified password. Placing an order requires the customer to provide a valid American Express, Discover, MasterCharge, or VISA credit-card number, cardholder name and address, and expiration date. Chapter 9 shows you how to use ASP.NET Web forms for registration and entry of customer information.

TIP

Even if you don't download VBWS_OCE.zip and attach the databases, this section and the sections that follow will make much more sense if you download and extract the sample code for review in Visual Basic 6.0. For consistency with code for later chapters, create a \VBWS02 folder to hold the contents of VBWS02.zip. Several OCE_Orders classes have references to Microsoft XML 4.0 for parsing XML documents. If you don't have this version installed, search for and download Microsoft XML Core Services 4.0 from the MSDN web site.

Figure 3-1 illustrates the order-processing workflow for a typical order received from the OakLeaf Web site and entered in the OCE_Cust database. The OCE_Cust database's Customers table has records for 25,344 current customers, which have records for 31,188 fictitious credit cards in the CustCards table and a single physical shipping address in the ShipAddresses table.

Figure 3-2 is the SQL Server 2000 database diagram for the OCE_Cust database. The OrdersInvoices relation table is required because drop shipments from distributors and partial shipments generate multiple invoices for a single order.

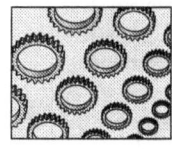

NOTE

Production-grade B2C applications usually store credit-card data in a separate, very secure server. Combining the credit card with customer data lets you use a single server and OCE_Cust database. The credit-card numbers are fictitious.

The following four sections describe the business rules that apply to orders for which all line items are in OCE warehouse inventory.

Create New Order

Customers specify products by stock-keeping unit (SKU) and quantity, which translate to order line items. The test client form's Create Order button (`frmOrders.cmdNewOrder_Click`) generates an order for a random customer; each order has one to four line items selected at random from the 695 products in the Products table of the OCE_Prod database. A local transaction assures that the order record added by the `clsAddOrder.AddOrderConn` method has the correct number of line items added by the `clsAddOrder` `.AddLineItemConn` method. If not, the transaction rolls back. The "Using the OCE_Orders Project's Test Client" section describes the objectives of the test form and how to use it.

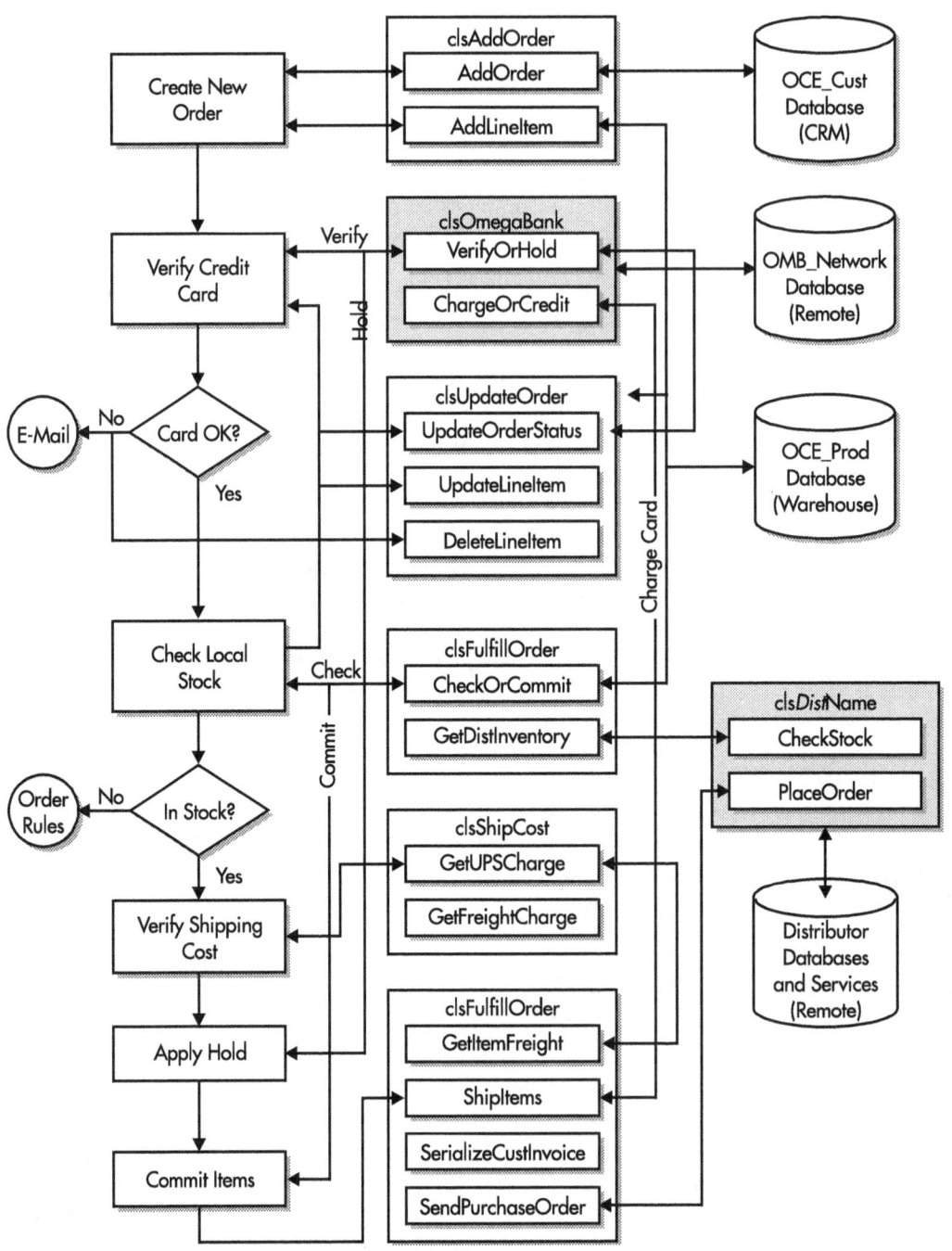

Figure 3-1 Processing orders follows the path shown in this flow diagram, which doesn't include backorder handling. Classes for B2B transactions implemented as Web services are shaded.

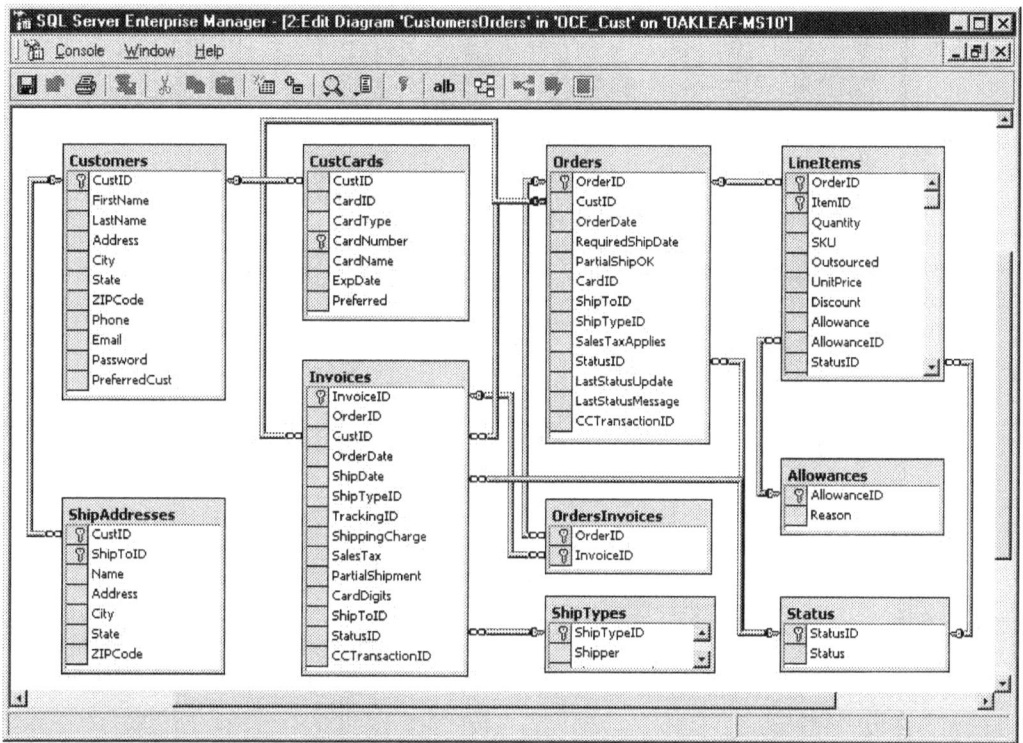

Figure 3-2   *The OCE_Cust database contains all customer, order, and invoice data for this book's B2C sample code.*

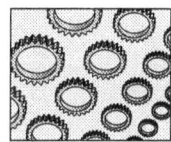

NOTE

The two preceding methods share a common `ADODB.Connection` *object passed by reference to enable transactions. The* `clsAddOrder.AddOrder` *and* `clsAddOrder.AddLineItem` *methods open a new connection for each invocation, which is consistent with the methods of the other classes. The latter two methods require a COM+ application to manage a distributed transaction.*

The client computes the total amount of the order from return values of the `clsAddOrder.AddLineItemConn` method and adds sales tax if the customer resides in Texas. The total order amount includes a preliminary estimate of 5 percent of the order amount for freight.

Verify Credit Card and Credit Availability

OCE has a merchant account with the fictitious OmegaBank credit-card network. Figure 3-3 is the diagram for the OMB_Network database. The Authorize table contains one record for each customer credit card. Operations, such as placing holds for pending transactions and applying charges, add a record to the Transactions table. Invoking the `clsOmegaBank.VerifyOrHold` method with the `blnHold` parameter set to `True` compares the issuer and card number, cardholder name, ZIP code, and expiration date with data in the OCE_Cust database's CustCards table.

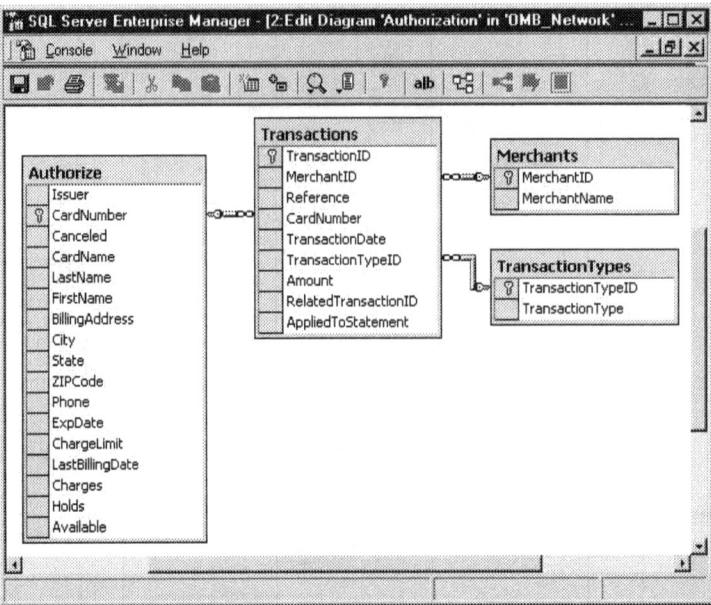

Figure 3-3 The OmegaBank OMB_Network database holds credit-card data for verification and dynamically adjusts credit availability as cardholders make purchases and payments on accounts.

If the preceding values match, the method checks the expiration date and determines whether credit availability is at least equal to the estimated transaction amount, which includes sales tax for shipments to Texas destinations and a freight allowance of 5 percent of the total amount of the order. If a mismatch occurs, the method returns a string like this:

```
50345 Declined: Expiration date mismatch (15)
```

If the card passes muster, the method returns a string similar to this:

```
50346 Verified: $454.36 419OMB24347 (12)
```

If the cardholder attempts to overspend the credit line, the method returns the following:

```
50351 Declined: Insufficient credit availability (14)
```

The verification string consists of a reference number (OrderID), pending transaction amount, randomly generated verification code, and a parenthetical status code. OmegaBank assumes its customers aren't prepared to parse XML documents at this point, so the option to return an XML document isn't implemented until you reach Chapter 7.

Order Status Update

If the credit card bounces, the `clsUpdateOrder.UpdateOrderStatus` method marks the line items as deleted and updates the order's StatusID, LastStatusUpdate, and LastStatusMessage fields. Another method, which isn't implemented at this point, sends a "We're sorry to inform you …" e-mail message to the customer. OrderID is an `int` `identity` column, so every order receives a unique OrderID. CRM rules and auditors require rejected order records to be retained. Other operations update the status fields; a StatusID value of 99 indicates a software-generated error. The Status table stores a list of StatusIDs and their meaning.

Check Local and Distributor Stock

If the credit card passes the initial test, the client invokes the `clsFulfillOrder.CheckOrCommit` method and queries the OCE_Prod database's Products table to determine if the items are in stock in the warehouse or from a distributor's stock. Figure 3-4 is the database diagram for the OCE_Prod database. If the `blnCommit` parameter is `False`, the method returns the total weight of the order. If `True`, the function adds the LineItem Quantity value to the Committed field.

OCE and its distributors ship each item in the manufacturer's packaging. For items weighing 50 pounds or less, invoking the `clsShipCost.GetUPSCharge` method uses the `ServerXMLHTTP` method to execute an HTTP `GET` request to the UPS Web site, which returns each item's shipping charge (shown in bold) within a string similar to this:

`UPSOnLine3%GNDRES%75041%US%50316%US%005%25%10.05%0.00%`**`10.05`**`%-1%`

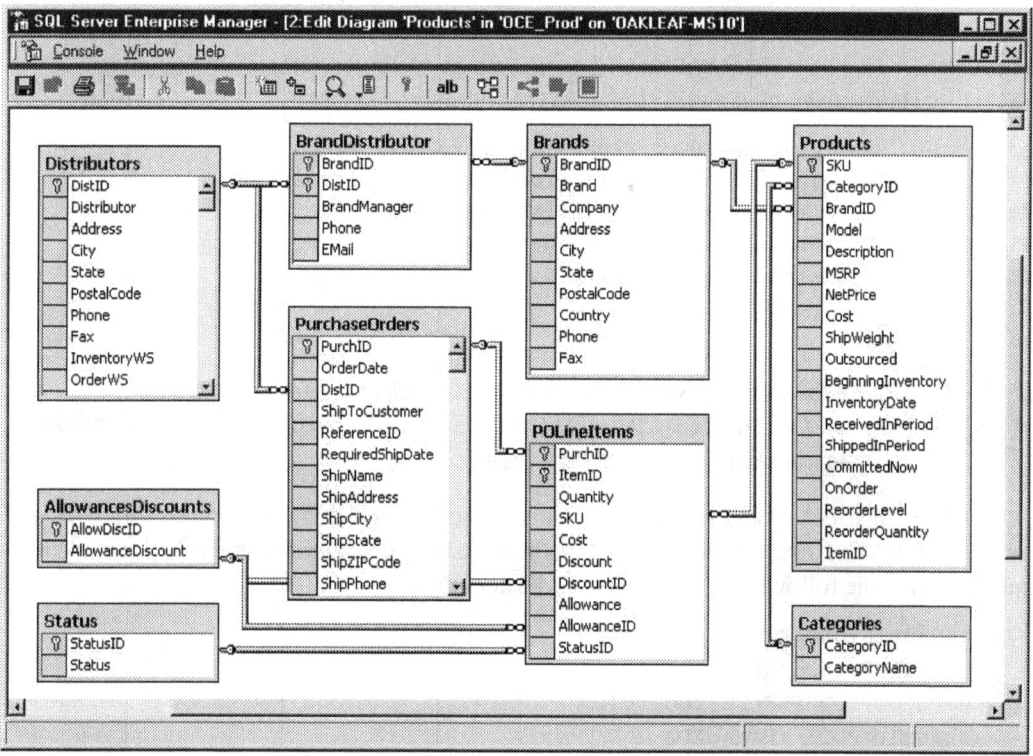

Figure 3-4 *The OCE_Prod database contains tables for managing and replenishing product inventory and issuing purchase orders to distributors for direct shipments.*

The numeric suffix 3 indicates a valid request; GNDRES is UPS Ground, residential service; US indicates a U.S. location; 75041 is the ZIP code of the Garland warehouse; 50316 is the destination ZIP code; 25 is the weight in pounds; the first 10.05 is the standard charge; 0.00 represents surcharges, such as insurance; and −1 is a second status code.

Items weighing more than 50 pounds are shipped by less-than-truckload (LTL) freight companies, such as Con-Way. The examples of this chapter use $0.50 per pound as the typical LTL shipping charge.

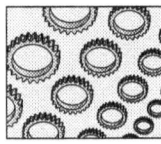

NOTE

Shipping cost and delivery time calculations are logical candidates for implementation as XML Web services. When this book was written, no package delivery or truck transportation firms had UDDI-registered XML Web services. UPS offers XML-based "OnLine Tools" (http://www.ec.ups.com), but not SOAP-based XML Web services. UPS prohibits publication of sample code to use their "Tools" because, in the words of a UPS attorney, "[S]uch publication could also constitute an infringement of UPS' copyrights and other proprietary and intellectual property rights." Fortunately, Microsoft doesn't prohibit publication of sample code for its "intellectual property."

The clsFulfillOrder.GetDistInventory method checks distributor stock of outsourced items by sending the item's SKU to distributors from which OCE purchases products. Records in the BrandDistributors table determine which distributor(s) to query for a particular SKU. The clsNameDist.CheckStock method returns a cookie-style inventory status string by default, similar to the following example:

```
AlphaDist inventory for SKU=SPKF0489;Category=SPKF;Brand=POLK; _
Model=RT1000I (Black), Pair;Description=6-1/2-inch Three-way _
Powered Tower Speaker;MSRP=$1,200.00;NetPrice=$750.00; _
ShipWeight=37.5 lbs;AllowanceFor=Cooperative Advertising;Amount=$15.00; _
DiscountFor=Cooperative Advertising Discount;Percent=15.0%;InStock=100
```

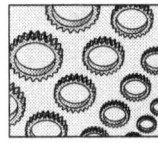

NOTE

The three distributors and their class and filenames are AlphaDist (clsAlphaDist, AlphaDist.cls), BetaDist (clsBetaDist, BetaDist.cls) and GammaDist (clsGammaDist, GammDist.cls).

All three distributors are well ahead of OmegaBank on the XML technology curve. If you set the clsNameDist.CheckStock method's blnXML argument to True, an inventory query returns the following well-formed XML document:

```
<AlphaDistInventory>
   <SKU>SPKF0489</SKU>
   <CategoryID>SPKF</CategoryID>
   <BrandID>POLK</BrandID>
   <Model>RT1000I (Black), Pair</Model>
   <Description>6-1/2-inch Three-way Powered Tower Speaker</Description>
```

```
    <MSRP>$1,200.00</MSRP>
    <NetPrice>$750.00</NetPrice>
    <ShipWeight>37.5 lbs</ShipWeight>
    <AllowanceID>13</AllowanceID>
    <AllowanceAmt>$15.00</AllowanceAmt>
    <AllowanceType>Cooperative Advertising</AllowanceType>
    <DiscountID>26</DiscountID>
    <DiscountPct>5.0%</DiscountPct>
    <DiscountType>Cooperative Advertising Discount</DiscountType>
    <QuantityInStock>100</QuantityInStock>
    <DateTime>11/27/2001 12:55:36 PM</DateTime>
</AlphaDistInventory>
```

If more than one distributor stocks the outsourced item, it's easy to select the distributor with the lowest net cost, including discounts and allowances. The `clsNameDist.CheckStock` method adds the winner's DistID code (ALPH, BETA, or GAMM) to the LineItem record's OrderFrom field. Records of the distributors table store the server name, database name, user name, and password, which distributors require to connect to their XML Web service. The records also store the URL for the two services.

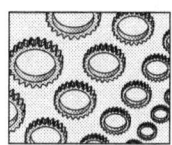

NOTE

Production B2B XML Web services require only a user name and password for authentication. Adding server and database names accommodates installation of the sample distributor databases on your server with database names you choose. The version of the distributor Web services running on the OakLeaf site disregard server and database names.

If all items are in warehouse or distributor stock, or the customer permits partial shipments and at least one item is in stock, the `clsFulfillOrder.CheckOrCommit` method commits warehouse inventory and the `clsOmegaBank.VerifyOrHold` procedure places a hold for the total amount of the order, with the actual freight cost, on the customer's credit card. Up to this point, the test client application maintains state for the transaction.

Shipping and Invoicing

The `clsFulfillOrder.ShipItems` method has more than 600 lines of code to perform the following sequential operations:

1. Update the LineItems records for warehouse items to StatusID 41 (Item Shipped from Warehouse).

2. Add the line item Quantity value to the ShippedInPeriod field of the Products record and subtract the value from the CommittedNow field.

3. If the item is outsourced, generate an XML purchase order document for the item, and change LineItems StatusID to 42 (Item Shipped from Distributor).

4. Recalculate the total amount of the order, and invoke the `clsOmegaBank` `.ChargeOrCredit` method with the `blnCredit` parameter set to `False` to reduce the hold amount and charge the customer's credit card. If the order is complete, setting the `blnReleaseHold` parameter to `True` reverses the original hold amount.

5. Generate an invoice for the customer, which serves as the packing list for shipment from the warehouse, plus one invoice for items shipped by each distributor. An order with all items in stock in the warehouse or at distributors can generate one to four invoices.

6. Generate an XML representation of the invoice for outsourced item(s) to the purchase order with the `clsFulfillOrder.SerializeCustInvoice` method. Sample code for this method follows. The distributor prints the invoice and includes it with the drop shipment as a packing list. A few orders require fulfillment by two or three distributors.

7. Invoke the `clsFulfillOrder.SendPurchaseOrder` method to serialize the purchase order(s), including the customer invoice, as a well-formed XML document.

8. Return a distributor invoice or out-of-stock report from the distributor(s) by invoking the `clsNameDist.PlaceOrder` method.

Following is an example of typical serialization code for records from tables with a one-to-many relationship, such as Invoices and LineItems. The code finds the invoice, generates invoice header elements, iterates the line items to find one or more items that are drop shipped by the distributor, and adds an `<Item>` element for each line item. Database field names provide the nested element tag names. The code adds indentation for readability; production applications seldom add the whitespace overhead incurred by indenting child elements.

```
Private Function SerializeCustInvoice(ByVal lngInvoiceID As Long, _
                               ByVal lngOrderID As Long, _
                               ByRef cnnCust As ADODB.Connection, _
                               ByRef cnnProd As ADODB.Connection, _
                               ByRef rstInvoice As ADODB.Recordset, _
                               ByRef rstCust As ADODB.Recordset, _
                               ByRef rstShipTo As ADODB.Recordset _
                               ByRef strDistID As String) As String
    'Distributors require customer invoices (packing lists) in a
    'standardized XML format for printing and enclosure in shipment
    'Implemented as Private Function to reduce length of ShipItems function
    Dim rstItems As New ADODB.Recordset
    Dim rstProd As New ADODB.Recordset
    Dim strXML As String
    Dim intCol As Integer
    Dim strSQL As String
```

```
With rstInvoice
   If .EOF Then
      strXML = "Error: Can't find invoice " & lngInvoiceID
   Else
      'Serialize the invoice, starting with invoice header
      strXML = "   <CustomerInvoice>" & vbCrLf & Space$(6) & _
               "<Header>" & vbCrLf
      For intCol = 0 To CInt(.Fields.Count) - 2
         strXML = strXML & Space$(9) & "<" & _
                  CStr(.Fields(intCol).Name) & _
                  ">" & CStr(.Fields(intCol).Value) & _
                  "</" & CStr(.Fields(intCol).Name) & ">" & vbCrLf
      Next intCol
      strXML = strXML & Space(6) & "</Header>" & vbCrLf & _
               Space(6) & "<BillingAddr>" & vbCrLf

      'Add billing address
      With rstCust
         'Combine first and last name
         strXML = strXML & Space$(9) & "<Name>" & _
                  CStr(.Fields(1).Value) & _
                  " " & CStr(.Fields(2).Value) & "</Name>" & vbCrLf
         For intCol = 3 To 6
         strXML = strXML & Space$(9) & "<" & _
                  CStr(.Fields(intCol).Name) & _
                  ">" & CStr(.Fields(intCol).Value) & _
                  "</" & CStr(.Fields(intCol).Name) & _
                  ">" & vbCrLf
         Next intCol
      End With
      strXML = strXML & Space(6) & "</BillingAddr>" & vbCrLf & _
               Space(6) & "<ShippingAddr>" & vbCrLf

      'Add shipping address
      With rstShipTo
         For intCol = 2 To CInt(.Fields.Count) - 1
         strXML = strXML & Space$(9) & "<Ship" & _
                  CStr(.Fields(intCol).Name) & _
                  ">" & CStr(.Fields(intCol).Value) & _
                  "</Ship" & CStr(.Fields(intCol).Name) & ">" & vbCrLf
         Next intCol
      End With
      strXML = strXML & Space(6) & "</ShippingAddr>" & _
               vbCrLf & Space(6) & "<LineItems>" & vbCrLf
```

```
'Add outsourced line items
strSQL = "SELECT * FROM LineItems WHERE OrderID = " & lngOrderID
Set rstItems = cnnCust.Execute(strSQL, , adCmdText)
With rstItems
    Do Until .EOF
        If CBool(.Fields("Outsourced").Value) Then
            If CStr(.Fields("OrderFrom").Value) = strDist Then
                'Item is outsourced, get product info
                strSQL = "SELECT BrandID, Model, Description " & _
                        "FROM Products " & _
                        "WHERE SKU = '" & CStr(.Fields(3).Value) & "'"
            Set rstProd = cnnProd.Execute(strSQL, , adCmdText)
            If rstProd.EOF Then
                strXML = "Error: Can't find product record"
            Else
                strXML = strXML & Space$(9) & "<Item>" & vbCrLf
                'Add ItemID, Quantity, SKU
                For intCol = 1 To 3
                    strXML = strXML & Space$(12) & "<" & _
                            CStr(.Fields(intCol).Name) & _
                            ">" & CStr(.Fields(intCol).Value) & _
                            "</" & CStr(.Fields(intCol).Name) & _
                            ">" & vbCrLf
                Next intCol

                'Add BrandID, Model, Description
                For intCol = 0 To 2
                    strXML = strXML & Space$(12) & "<" & _
                    CStr(rstProd.Fields(intCol).Name) & _
                        ">" & CStr(rstProd.Fields(intCol).Value) & _
                        "</" & CStr(rstProd.Fields(intCol).Name) & _
                        ">" & vbCrLf
                Next intCol

                'Add UnitPrice, Discount, etc.
                For intCol = 5 To CInt(.Fields.Count) - 4
                    strXML = strXML & Space$(12) & "<" & _
                    CStr(.Fields(intCol).Name) & _
                        ">" & CStr(.Fields(intCol).Value) & _
                        "</" & CStr(.Fields(intCol).Name) & _

                        ">" & vbC CrLf
                Next intCol
                strXML = strXML & Space$(9) & "</Item>" & vbCrLf
            End If
```

```
                    End If
                End If
                .MoveNext
            Loop
        End With
        If InStr(strXML, "Error:") = 0 Then
            '& appears occasionally in addresses
            strXML = Replace$(strXML, "&", "and")
            strXML = strXML & Space(6) & "</LineItems> " & _
                vbCrLf & "   </CustomerInvoice>"
        End If
    End If
  End With
  SerializeCustInvoice = strXML
End Function
```

The next section's XML document includes an example of the document generated by the preceding code.

XML Purchase Order Documents

Distributors require an electronic purchase order to be submitted in accordance with a standard schema for the consumer electronics industry. The `clsFulfillOrder` `.SendPurchaseOrder` method handles this chore. Following is an example of a drop-shipment purchase order formatted to the fictional schema:

```
<PurchaseOrder>
  <Header>
     <PurchID>28306</PurchID>
     <OrderDate>11/27/2001 5:18:52 PM</OrderDate>
     <ShipToCustomer>True</ShipToCustomer>
     <RequiredShipDate>11/27/2001</RequiredShipDate>
     <ShipPhone>503-642-9605</ShipPhone>
     <ShipByID>11</ShipByID>
     <PartialShipOK>False</PartialShipOK>
  </Header>
  <BillingAddr>
     <CompanyName>OakLeaf Consumer Electronics</CompanyName>
     <Attention>Accounts Payable</Attention>
     <Address>415 W. Jefferson</Address>
     <City>Dallas</City>
     <State>TX</State>
     <ZIPCode>75208</ZIPCode>
     <Phone>214-555-2345</Phone>
  </BillingAddr>
  <ShippingAddr>
```

```
        <ShipName>Walt Woodcock</ShipName>
        <ShipAttn></ShipAttn>
        <ShipAddress>453 Pepper Rd</ShipAddress>
        <ShipCity>Berthoud</ShipCity>
        <ShipState>CO</ShipState>
        <ShipZIPCode>80513-1342</ShipZIPCode>
    </ShippingAddr>
    <LineItems>
        <Item>
            <ItemID>1</ItemID>
            <Quantity>1</Quantity>
            <SKU>TVRC0366</SKU>
            <Cost>825</Cost>
            <Discount>0</Discount>
            <DiscountID>0</DiscountID>
            <Allowance>0</Allowance>
            <AllowanceID>0</AllowanceID>
            <StatusID>32</StatusID>
        </Item>
    </LineItems>
    <CustomerInvoice>
        <Header>
            <InvoiceID>140287</InvoiceID>
            <OrderID>305807</OrderID>
            <CustID>1024484</CustID>
            <OrderDate>11/27/2001 5:18:51 PM</OrderDate>
            <ShipDate></ShipDate>
            <ShipTypeID>11</ShipTypeID>
            <TrackingID></TrackingID>
            <ShippingCharge>$16.50</ShippingCharge>
            <SalesTax>0</SalesTax>
            <PartialShipment>False</PartialShipment>
            <CardDigits>5642</CardDigits>
        </Header>
        <BillingAddr>
            <Name>Walt Woodcock</Name>
            <Address>453 Pepper Rd</Address>
            <City>Berthoud</City>
            <State>CO</State>
            <ZIPCode>80513-1342</ZIPCode>
        </BillingAddr>
        <ShippingAddr>
            <ShipName>Walt Woodcock</ShipName>
            <ShipAddress>453 Pepper Rd</ShipAddress>
            <ShipCity>Berthoud</ShipCity>
```

```
                <ShipState>CO</ShipState>
                <ShipZIPCode>80513-1342</ShipZIPCode>
            </ShippingAddr>
            <LineItems>
                <Item>
                    <ItemID>1</ItemID>
                    <Quantity>1</Quantity>
                    <SKU>TVRC0366</SKU>
                    <BrandID>PANA</BrandID>
                    <Model>CT-32SX31</Model>
                    <Description>Dual Tuner PIP 32-inch Television</Description>
<UnitPrice>1099.95</UnitPrice>
                    <Discount>0</Discount>
                    <Allowance>0</Allowance>
                    <AllowanceID>0</AllowanceID>
                </Item>
            </LineItems>
        </CustomerInvoice>
</PurchaseOrder>
```

TIP

Assign table field names that correspond to XML element names to minimize serialization code, whether you use the technique described in the preceding section or the XML Document Object Model (DOM). The `clsFulfillOrder` *class'* `SerializeCustInvoice` *and* `SendPurchaseOrder` *methods demonstrate the simplicity of serializing the preceding document. All the document's element names are the original or slightly modified field names.*

Verifying Serialized XML Documents

It's good programming practice to verify that the XML document payload of all messages are well formed. Otherwise, you receive an error message instead of the response document you expect from the XML Web service. Checking the payload document with the MSXML parser takes only a few lines of code. Here's an example extracted from the SendPurchaseOrder method:

```
Dim docOrder As New MSXML2.DOMDocument40
With docOrder
    strServiceURL = "http://localhost/"
    .loadXML strXML
    If .parseError.errorCode = 0 Then
        'Send the purchase order document
    Else
        SendPurchaseOrder = "Error: Parse error '" & _
            .parseError.reason & "' in order document."
    End If
End With
```

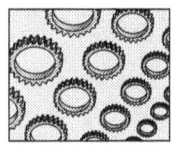

NOTE

The preceding approach only verifies the document as well-formed, not that its structure is what your client code expects. To validate the document's structure and contents, you must provide an XSD schema and specify the SchemaName.xsd file to be used.

Sending an XML document to the distributor offers you the choice of implementing an rpc/encoded or document/literal XML Web service. The SOAP Toolkit 2.0 Wizard supports only RPC-style messaging, so this chapter uses rpc/encoded style messaging.

Distributor Order Processing

At this point in the development of the order processing system, it's assumed that distributors make shipments of in-stock products immediately upon receipt of an order. Examples in later chapters introduce a delay between receipt of an order and its shipment.

The `clsDistOrder.PlaceOrder` method with the `blnXML` parameter set to `False` returns a string similar to the following:

```
OrderID=32004;Date=11/30/2001;Item=1;SKU=SPKF0022;Shipped=2;Status=Complete
```

With `blnXML` set to `True` and all items in stock or partial shipments allowed, the method generates an invoice from the order document and returns the following XML document:

```
<Invoice>
   <Header>
      <InvoiceID>54858</InvoiceID>
      <InvoiceDate>11/30/2001</InvoiceDate>
      <PurchID>32025</PurchID>
      <OrderDate>11/30/2001 2:38:06 PM</OrderDate>
      <ShipToCustomer>True</ShipToCustomer>
      <RequiredShipDate>11/30/2001</RequiredShipDate>
      <ShipPhone>520-290-8203</ShipPhone>
      <ShipByID>11</ShipByID>
      <PartialShipOK>False</PartialShipOK>
      <OrderStatus>Shipment Complete</OrderStatus>
   </Header>
   <BillingAddr>
      <CompanyName>OakLeaf Consumer Electronics</CompanyName>
      <Attention>Accounts Payable</Attention>
      <Address>415 W. Jefferson</Address>
      <City>Dallas</City>
      <State>TX</State>
      <ZIPCode>75208</ZIPCode>
      <Phone>214-555-2345</Phone>
   </BillingAddr>
   <ShippingAddr>
      <ShipName>Tony Lewis</ShipName>
      <ShipAttn></ShipAttn>
```

```
            <ShipAddress>Masonic Bl</ShipAddress>
            <ShipCity>Estancia</ShipCity>
            <ShipState>NM</ShipState>
            <ShipZIPCode>87016</ShipZIPCode>
        </ShippingAddr>
        <LineItems>
            <Item>
                <ItemID>1</ItemID>
                <Quantity>1</Quantity>
                <SKU>RCVA0380</SKU>
                <Cost>900</Cost>
                <Discount>0</Discount>
                <DiscountID>0</DiscountID>
                <Allowance>0</Allowance>
                <AllowanceID>0</AllowanceID>
                <StatusID>42</StatusID>
                <Backordered>0</Backordered>
            </Item>
        </LineItems>
</Invoice>
```

Otherwise, the method returns a slightly modified version of the original purchase order with an `<OrderStatus>Canceled</OrderStatus>` element. In all cases, the method updates all `<StatusID>` element values to reflect the status of the order and its line items.

Following is the code for the `clsAlphaDist.PlaceOrder` method that generates the preceding XML document. The method employs the `appendChild` and `insertBefore` methods of the `MSXML2.IXMLDOMNode` class to add the required nodes at their proper location in the document.

```
Public Function PlaceOrder(ByVal strServer As String, _
                           ByVal strDatabase As String, _
                           ByVal strUser As String, _
                           ByVal strPassword As String, _
                           ByVal strXML As String, _
                           ByVal blnXML As Boolean) As String


    'Send purchase order to distributor as XML document
    'Return invoice if order processed, updated order if not
    '(This procedure is identical for each distributor)

    Dim cnnOrder As New ADODB.Connection
    Dim rstOrder As New ADODB.Recordset
    Dim docOrder As New MSXML2.DOMDocument40
    Dim lstNodes As MSXML2.IXMLDOMNodeList
    Dim nodParent As MSXML2.IXMLDOMNode
```

```vb
    Dim nodChild As MSXML2.IXMLDOMNode
    Dim nodBackOrd As MSXML2.IXMLDOMNode
    Dim nodInvoice As MSXML2.IXMLDOMNode

    Dim strOrderConn As String
    Dim strCustInvoice As String
    Dim strOrderID As String
    Dim strOrderDate As String
    Dim strPartShip As String
    Dim strQuan As String
    Dim astrItems(10, 2) As String
    Dim intItems As Integer
    Dim intCtr As Integer
    Dim strSQL As String
    Dim lngReccnt As Long
    Dim strRetMsg As String
    Dim blnAllInStock As Boolean

On Error Resume Next
With docOrder
    .loadXML strXML
    If .parseError.errorCode <> 0 Then
        PlaceOrder = "Error: Parse error '" & .parseError.reason & _
                    "' in order document"
        GoTo ExitPlaceOrder
    End If
End With

'Connect to the distributor database
strOrderConn = "Provider=SQLOLEDB;Data Source=" & strServer & _
    ";Initial Catalog=" & strDatabase & ";UID=" & strUser & ";PWD=" & _
    strPassword
cnnOrder.Open strOrderConn
If Err.Number <> 0 Then
    'Can't connect
    PlaceOrder = "Error: Can't connect to " & strServer & " database."
    GoTo ExitPlaceOrder
End If

'Remove and save the customer invoice for printing (only removed here)
If InStr(strXML, "<CustomerInvoice>") > 0 Then
    strCustInvoice = "    " & Mid$(strXML, _
                    InStr(strXML, "<CustomerInvoice>"))
    strCustInvoice = Left$(strXML, InStr(strXML, "</CustomerInvoice>") _
        + 17)
```

```
        strXML = Trim$(Left$(strXML, InStr(strXML, "<CustomerInvoice>") - 1))
        strXML = strXML & "</PurchaseOrder>"
    End If
    With docOrder
        If Len(strCustInvoice) > 0 Then
            'Reload the document without the customer invoice
            .loadXML strXML
            If .parseError.errorCode <> 0 Then
                PlaceOrder = "Error: Parse error '" & .parseError.reason & _
                             "' in order document"
                GoTo ExitPlaceOrder
            End If
        End If


        'Return string headers
        Set lstNodes = .getElementsByTagName("PurchID")
        Set nodParent = lstNodes.Item(0)
        strOrderID = nodParent.Text
        Set lstNodes = .getElementsByTagName("OrderDate")
        Set nodParent = lstNodes.Item(0)
        strOrderDate = nodParent.Text
        If InStr(strOrderDate, " ") Then
            'Trim the time
            strOrderDate = Left$(strOrderDate, InStr(strOrderDate, " ") - 1)
        End If
        Set lstNodes = .getElementsByTagName("PartialShipOK")
        Set nodParent = lstNodes.Item(0)
        strPartShip = nodParent.Text

        Set lstNodes = .getElementsByTagName("SKU")
        'Create an array of SKUs and quantities for inventory test
        intItems = lstNodes.length - 1
        For intCtr = 0 To intItems
            Set nodParent = lstNodes.Item(intCtr)
            astrItems(intCtr, 0) = nodParent.Text
        Next intCtr
        Set lstNodes = .getElementsByTagName("Quantity")
        For intCtr = 0 To intItems
            Set nodParent = lstNodes.Item(intCtr)
            astrItems(intCtr, 1) = nodParent.Text
        Next intCtr
    End With

    blnAllInStock = True
    For intCtr = 0 To intItems
```

```vb
        'Check SKU current inventory
        strSQL = "SELECT Quantity FROM Products WHERE SKU='" & _
                astrItems(intCtr, 0) & "'"
        Set rstOrder = cnnOrder.Execute(strSQL, , adCmdText)
        With rstOrder
            If .EOF Then
                PlaceOrder = "Error: " & strServer & _
                            " has no record of SKU '" & _
                            astrItems(intCtr, 0) & "'"
                GoTo ExitPlaceOrder
            Else
                strRetMsg = strRetMsg & "SKU=" & astrItems(intCtr, 0) & ";"
                If CInt(.Fields(0).Value) >= CInt(astrItems(intCtr, 1)) Then
                    'Decrement the inventory quantity for the product
                    strSQL = "UPDATE Products SET Quantity = Quantity - 1 " & _
                            "WHERE SKU='" & astrItems(intCtr, 0) & "'"
                    'DistUser is allowed to update the distributor database
                    cnnOrder.Execute strSQL, lngReccnt, adCmdText
                    If CLng(lngReccnt) = 0 Then
                        'Internal distributor error (not handled here)
                    End If
                Else
                    'Out of stock
                    astrItems(intCtr, 1) = "0"
                    blnAllInStock = False
                End If
            End If
            .Close
        End With
    Next intCtr

    If blnXML Then
        Set lstNodes = docOrder.getElementsByTagName("Item")
        For intCtr = 0 To lstNodes.length - 1
            Set nodParent = lstNodes.Item(intCtr)
            'Quantity child node
            Set nodChild = nodParent.childNodes(1)
            strQuan = nodChild.Text
            nodChild.Text = astrItems(intCtr, 1)

            'Status child node
            Set nodChild = nodParent.childNodes(8)
            If blnAllInStock Then
                nodChild.Text = "59" 'Order Complete
            Else
```

```vb
      If astrItems(intCtr, 1) = "0" And strPartShip = "True" Then
         nodChild.Text = "51" 'Partial Shipment 1
      Else
         nodChild.Text = "88"
      End If
   End If


   'Add the Backordered node to each line item
   Set nodBackOrd = docOrder.createElement("Backordered")
   If blnAllInStock Then
      nodBackOrd.Text = "0"
   ElseIf strPartShip = "True" And astrItems(intCtr, 1) = "0" Then
      nodBackOrd.Text = strQuan
   Else
      nodBackOrd.Text = "0"
   End If
   nodParent.appendChild nodBackOrd
Next intCtr


'Add the OrderStatus element and value
Set nodChild = docOrder.createElement("OrderStatus")
If blnAllInStock Then
   nodChild.Text = "Shipment Complete (59)"
ElseIf strPartShip = "True" And astrItems(intCtr, 1) = "0" Then
   nodChild.Text = "Partial Shipment 1 (51)"
Else
   nodChild.Text = "Canceled (88)"
End If
Set lstNodes = docOrder.getElementsByTagName("Header")
Set nodParent = lstNodes.Item(0)
nodParent.appendChild nodChild


If blnAllInStock Or strPartShip = "True" Then
   'Add the invoice date first to simplify adding the invoice number
   Set nodChild = docOrder.createElement("InvoiceDate")
   nodChild.Text = CStr(Date)
   Set lstNodes = docOrder.getElementsByTagName("Header")
   Set nodParent = lstNodes.Item(0)
   Set nodInvoice = lstNodes.Item(0).firstChild
   nodParent.insertBefore nodChild, nodInvoice

   'Add the distributor invoice number
   Set nodChild = docOrder.createElement("InvoiceID")
   'Use random distributor invoice numbers for simplicity
   nodChild.Text = CStr(1000000 + Int(100000 * Rnd))
```

```vb
         Set lstNodes = docOrder.getElementsByTagName("Header")
         Set nodParent = lstNodes.Item(0)
         Set nodInvoice = lstNodes.Item(0).firstChild
         nodParent.insertBefore nodChild, nodInvoice
      End If
      'Return the document as a string
      strXML = docOrder.xml
      'Fix up the formatting of the added elements
      strXML = Replace$(strXML, "</InvoiceID>", "</InvoiceID>" & _
         vbCrLf & Space$(6))
      strXML = Replace$(strXML, "</InvoiceDate>", "</InvoiceDate>" & _
         vbCrLf & Space$(6))
      strXML = Replace$(strXML, "</Backordered>", "</Backordered>" & _
         vbCrLf & Space$(6))
      strXML = Replace$(strXML, "</OrderStatus>", "</OrderStatus>" & _
         vbCrLf & Space$(3))
      If blnAllInStock Or strPartShip = "True" Then
         'Generate an invoice
         strXML = Replace$(strXML, "PurchaseOrder>", "Invoice>")
      End If
      If Err.Number = 0 Then
         PlaceOrder = strXML
      Else
         strXML = "Error: Internal invoice document generation error.
      End If
   Else
      strRetMsg = "OrderID=" & strOrderID & ";Date=" & strOrderDate & ";"
      For intCtr = 0 To intItems
         strRetMsg = strRetMsg & "Item=" & CStr(intCtr + 1) & _
                     ";SKU=" & astrItems(intCtr, 0)
         If blnAllInStock Then
            strRetMsg = strRetMsg & ";Shipped=" & astrItems(intCtr, 1)
         ElseIf strPartShip = "True" And astrItems(intCtr, 1) = "0" Then
            strRetMsg = strRetMsg & ";Backordered=" & astrItems(intCtr, 1)
         Else
            strRetMsg = strRetMsg & ";Shipped=0"
         End If
      Next intCtr
      If blnAllInStock Then
         strRetMsg = strRetMsg & ";Status=Complete"
      ElseIf strPartShip = "True" And astrItems(intCtr, 1) = "0" Then
         strRetMsg = strRetMsg & ";Status=PartialShipment"
      Else
         strRetMsg = strRetMsg & ";Status=Canceled"
      End If
```

```
            PlaceOrder = strRetMsg
        End If


ExitPlaceOrder:
    'Cleanup
    Set docOrder = Nothing
    Set lstNodes = Nothing
    Set nodParent = Nothing
    Set nodChild = Nothing
    Set nodBackOrd = Nothing
    Set nodInvoice = Nothing

    With rstOrder
        If .State = adStateOpen Then
            .Close
        End If
    End With
    Set rstOrder = Nothing
    With cnnOrder
        If .State = adStateOpen Then
            .Close
        End If
    End With
    Set cnnOrder = Nothing
End Function
```

The preceding code is typical of B2B XML Web services that are designed for order processing and shipment confirmation.

Using the OCE_Orders Project's Test Client

For Web-based projects with many components, it's often more effective to write a Windows test client than to design an ASP or ASP.NET site to emulate the workflow. A properly designed Windows test client (also called a *test harness*) form lets you run multiple instances of the components to test scalability and simplifies component debugging by keeping IIS 5+ out of the testing loop. You can reuse some Visual Basic 6.0 and almost all Visual Basic .NET client code in your Web pages, as demonstrated by the Chapter 6 ASP.NET example.

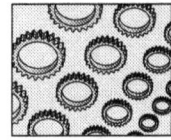

NOTE

As mentioned earlier, you must download and install the sample databases to run the test client. Search for (local) *in the form code, change the string values to your server name, and compile the project. If you select the Check UPS Charge check box, you must have an Internet connection to obtain the UPS freight charges. Otherwise, the code calculates UPS charges at $0.25 per pound.*

The OakLeaf Consumer Electronics Order Test Harness

The OCE_Orders project's single `frmOrders` form, shown in Figure 3-5, has the following five command buttons to enable stepwise execution of the order-processing workflow:

▶ **1. Create Order**   Generates a random order with one to four line items, as described in the "Create New Order" section earlier. This button is enabled throughout the workflow process to allow generating uncompleted orders.

▶ **2. Verify Card**   Tests credit-card validity and credit availability. If the card passes muster, the two DataGrid controls display values of the Orders and LineItems records for the order, and the Check Stock button is enabled.

▶ **3. Check Stock**   Tests warehouse and distributor inventory. If all items are in stock (or any item is in stock and the customer allows partial shipments), the code updates order and line-item StatusID values, and enables the Card/Item Hold button. Otherwise, order processing terminates with an e-mail message to the customer.

▶ **4. Card/Item Hold**   Commits the warehouse inventory, places a hold on the customer's credit card for the total amount of the order, and enables the Ship/Bill Order button. If the credit-card hold fails, the order terminates with an e-mail message to the customer.

▶ **5. Ship/Bill Order**   Executes the `clsFulfillOrder.ShipItems` method, completes the order process, and sets the order status to Shipment Complete or Partial Shipment 1 and the line-item status to Shipped From Warehouse, Shipped From Distributor, or Item Backordered.

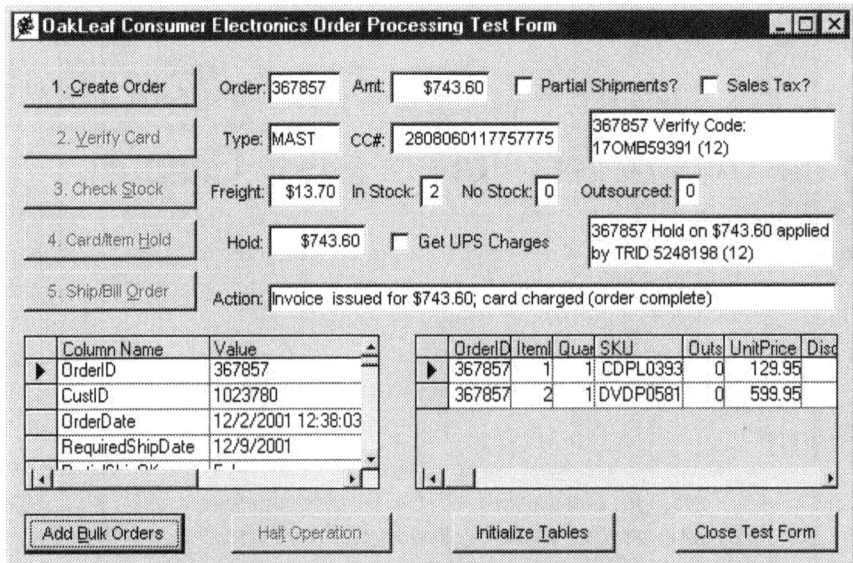

Figure 3-5   *The client test form displays the typical data shown here after clicking the Ship/Bill Order command button.*

The test form and its classes execute about 4,500 lines of Visual Basic 6.0 code for a completed order. You might consider the OCE_Orders project to be excessively complex for your initial foray into XML Web services. Most real-world B2C and B2B applications, however, are *much* more complex than the OCD_Orders project at this stage in its development. As mentioned at the beginning of the chapter, creating typical "Hello World" or "Add Two Numbers" Web services isn't representative of the services you require for a production project. To qualify as an XML Web service, the service must return a well-formed XML document as its payload, not a simple string. Lengthy projects also demonstrate issues that arise when upgrading Visual Basic 6.0 projects to Visual Basic .NET, as Chapter 4 demonstrates, and lengthy projects make performance comparisons of original and upgraded projects realistic.

Continuous Order Processing

Clicking Add Bulk Orders executes the preceding steps at a rate of one order per second, if you have a fast server and don't enable UPS freight-charge lookup. With a high-speed Internet connection, and the Get UPS Charges check box marked, order addition takes 2 or 3 seconds. Clicking Halt Operation stops order addition and displays the average execution time for completed orders.

You can run multiple copies of the client on the server and workstations to verify scalability of the components. Adding a large number of orders results in an increasing number of credit-card rejections and out-of-stock items. Clicking Initialize Tables returns all the databases to their original state.

TIP

Use Enterprise Manager to shrink the OCE_Cust, OCE_Prod, and OMB_Network databases after adding more than 10,000 records and clicking Initialize Tables. Click the Shrink Database - DatabaseName dialog's Files button to open the Shrink File - DatabaseFile dialog, and click OK to free all unused space in the database file. Repeat the process for the databases' log file to regain the maximum amount of free space.

Installing the Microsoft SOAP Toolkit 2.0 and Running the Sample Code

If you don't have the final (June 2001) version of the SOAP Toolkit 2.0 installed, download the required files from http://msdn.microsoft.com. You must download the sample code separately.

TIP

Microsoft has a tendency to reorganize the MSDN site periodically, so do an exact-phrase search for "SOAP Toolkit 2.0 SP2" as of 6/21/2001, which was current when this book was written. Uninstall any previous version of the SOAP Toolkit before installing version 2.0 SP2, which Microsoft also calls gold code. Download the samples and, if you need to support SOAP client applications, download the redistributable files. The Toolkit download includes the documentation.

Running soaptookit20.exe adds a Microsoft SOAP Toolkit choice to your Programs menu with Readme, Samples, Trace Utility, User Guide, and WSDL Generator submenus. The readme file and online help contain more than you're likely to want to know about the Toolkit at this point. Bypass the SOAP Sample Applications in the online help file, which use scripts instead of Visual Basic clients to execute a trivial high-level and low-level service. These two samples require copying and pasting a substantial amount of code. You install the Visual Basic 6.0 and Visual C++ examples by running soaptoolkit20samples.exe.

Installing the Toolkit with soaptoolkit20.exe is a snap compared to installing, registering, and running the Visual Basic 6.0 samples included in soaptoolkit20samples.exe. Installing the sample files creates a jungle of subfolders under the \Program Files\MSSOAP\ folder for multiple versions of both client and server projects. The samples demonstrate RPC- and document-style SOAP messaging using ISAPI and ASP servers, and verify that the `SoapClient` and `SoapServer` objects are operable. Choose Programs | Microsoft SOAP Toolkit | Samples to open a page with the list of sample SOAP clients and servers.

Assigning a IIS Virtual Directory and Server Name

Testing the sample services requires a specified pair of IIS virtual directory and server names: MSSoapSamples and MSSoapSampleServer. After running the sample setup application, do the following to enable the sample Web services:

1. Launch Internet Services Manager, right-click Default Web Site, and choose New | Virtual Directory to start the Virtual Directory Wizard. Click Next.

2. Type **MSSoapSamples** in the Alias text box, and click Next.

3. Click Browse, navigate to your \Program Files\MSSOAP\Samples folder, click OK, and click Next.

4. Click Next to accept the default virtual directory access permissions, and click Finish to dismiss the Wizard.

5. Open the MSSoapSamples Properties dialog, click the Configuration button on the Virtual Directory page to open the Application Configuration dialog, and click the App Options tab.

6. Clear the Enable Session State check box to improve Web service performance, and verify that the Enable Buffering check box is marked. Application buffering is required for SOAP-enabled COM components. Click OK twice to close the dialogs, and then close Internet Services Manager.

7. Launch Explorer, navigate to \WINNT\system32\drivers\etc, and open the hosts file in Notepad. Below the `127.0.0.1      localhost` line, type **127.0.0.1**, press TAB, and type **MSSoapSampleServer**, as shown here. Close Notepad and save your changes. All Toolkit samples use http://MSSoapSampleServer/MSSoapSamples/ *SampleName*/Service/*Type*/…Vb as the location for the *SampleName*.wsdl file.

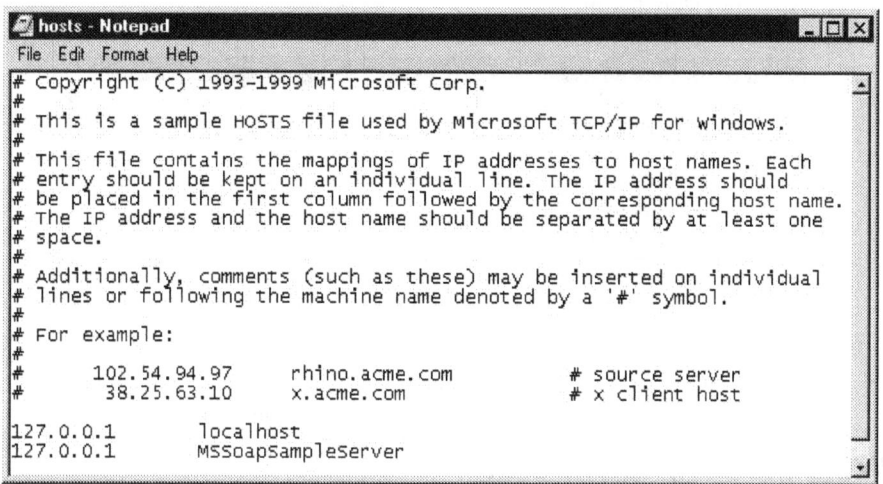

Running the Visual Basic Calc RPC Application

The Visual Basic sample applications consist of a pair of client and server projects in separate subfolders. The simplest sample is Echo, which sends and returns a string. The slightly less trivial Calc sample emulates an ancient four-function calculator. To verify that your virtual directory and hosts file additions work properly, run the Calc sample by following these steps:

▶ In Explorer, navigate to \Program Files\MSSOAP\Samples\Calc\Service\Rpc\VbSrv and double-click CalcSvcRpcVb.vbp to open the project. The `Calc` class has four mathematical functions.

▶ Choose File | Make CalcSvcRpcVb.dll to recompile and register the DLL. Close the project.

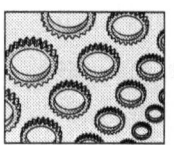

NOTE

Although the SOAP Toolkit's help file states that you must compile ActiveX DLLs with the Unattended Execution and Retained In Memory options, none of the Visual Basic samples abide by this rule.

▶ Navigate to \Program Files\MSSOAP\Samples\DataType\Client\Rpc\Vb and double-click CalcCliRpcVb.vbp to open the client project.

▶ Run the client and verify that the WSDL combo box contains the default http://MSSoapSampleServer/MSSoapSamples/Calc/Service/Rpc/IsapiVb/ _ Calc.wsdl item, as shown here. This URL points to the only WSDL file for the DLL you registered in step 2.

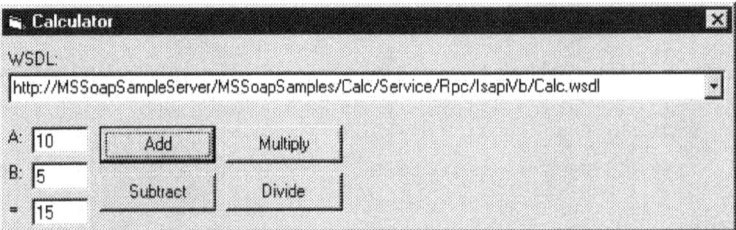

▶ Click each button to verify that the client can connect to the WSDL file and execute the function.

Analyzing the SOAP Client Code

Most of the samples have high-level and low-level SOAP API versions. The high-level API requires you to create an instance of the **SoapClient** object and pass the URL for the Web service's WSDL file as the argument value of the **SoapClient.mssoapinit** method.

TIP

Open the d:\Program Files\MSSOAP\Samples\Calc\Service\Rpc\IsapiVb\Default.htm page and double-click the Service Document Description link to display Calc.wsdl inIE.

After you connect to the service, you execute a service's method, as follows:

```
typReturnMessage = objSoapClient.MethodName(typArg1[,typArg2[, …]])
```

For example, clicking the + button of the Calc sample form executes the following code:

```
Private Sub cmdAdd_Click()
   On Error GoTo ErrorHandler
   Me.MousePointer = vbHourglass
   Connect
   txtEquals.Text = CStr(Client.Add(CDbl(txtA.Text), CDbl(txtB.Text)))
   Me.MousePointer = vbDefault
   Exit Sub
ErrorHandler:
```

```
    Me.MousePointer = vbDefault
    MsgBox Client.faultstring, vbExclamation
End Sub
Private Sub Connect()
    If sConnectedWSDL <> cbWSDL.Text Then
        Set Client = New SoapClient
        Client.mssoapinit cbWSDL.Text
        sConnectedWSDL = cbWSDL.Text
    End If
End Sub
```

If the service specified by the WSDL file encounters a problem with the client request, `SoapClient` throws a runtime error and identifies the source of the problem by `faultcode` and `faultstring` values, and in some cases, a `faultactor` value. For example, if you temporarily remove the `CDbl(txtB.Text)` argument, the Calc client returns a "Client: Incorrect number of parameters supplied for SOAP request" `faultstring` message. The value of the SOAP-specified `faultcode` is `Client`, which isn't very informative.

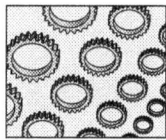

NOTE

Document-style messaging and use of the SOAP Toolkit's low-level SOAP API with Visual Basic 6.0 code is beyond the scope of this book. Chapters 8 and later in the book demonstrate document-style messaging and working with SOAP headers using Visual Basic .NET and ASP.NET.

Creating ActiveX DLLs for Web Services

The SOAP Toolkit 2.0 requires that ActiveX DLLs meet the following requirements:

▶ Visual Basic 6.0 classes must be compiled with the Unattended Execution option. The Toolkit's online help file states that the Retained In Memory option is required, but none of the Visual Basic server samples have the Retained In Memory check box marked.

▶ The DLL must be registered and contain a type library.

▶ All function parameters must be passed by value. The Visual Basic 6.0 default is `ByRef`, so all function parameter declarations must include a `ByVal` prefix.

▶ Function parameters and return values can't be user-defined data types (struct[ure]s).

▶ The class must be stateless and not rely on COM+ or MTS to preserve state between invocations.

Most production-grade ActiveX DLLs conform to the preceding requirements; however, the inability to pass parameters by value and handle structures means that XML Web services can't replace all DCOM implementations.

Compiling the B2B Classes as ActiveX DLLs

All OCE_Orders classes and functions except `clsFulfillOrders.CheckOrCommit` meet the preceding requirements. If you don't implement functions that require values passed by reference, which also include `clsAddOrder.AddNewOrderConn` and `clsAddOrder.AddLineItemConn`, you can use the Toolkit to wrap DLLs created from every class. At this point, you need to create ActiveX DLLs only for the B2B classes: `clsOmegaBank`, `clsAlphaDist`, `clsBetaDist`, and `clsGammaDist`. Optionally, you can compile the remaining classes as ActiveX DLLs to emulate middle-tier database components.

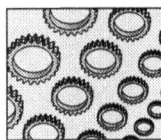

NOTE

Creating the Visual Basic 6.0 version of the XML Web services for the OakLeaf CFR Web site, described briefly in the "OakLeaf Systems' Online Code of Federal Regulations" section in Chapter 1, followed the process described here. The initial code consisted of a single Visual Basic 6.0 application with many private classes. Development of the site began with ASP pages calling Visual Basic 6.0 ActiveX components derived from the classes. The second step moved from traditional ASP to ASP.NET pages and SOAP-enabled components. The final version uses Visual Basic.NET components and ASP.NET for the XML Web services. You can run each of the four CFR versions at the OakLeaf Systems Web site: http://www.oakleaf.ws/.

To create a set of new Visual Basic 6.0 executable and ActiveX DLL projects and compile the sample OmegaBank and distributor classes, perform these steps:

1. Save OCE_Orders.vbp with a new name, OCE_OrdersAX.vbp, in the same folder as OCE_Orders.vbp.

2. Remove `clsOmegaBank`, `clsAlphaDist`, `clsBetaDist`, and `clsGammaDist` from the new project.

3. Open the Project Properties dialog, change the Project Name value to OCE_OrdersAX, verify that the folder is correct, and save the project.

4. Choose File | New Project, and double-click ActiveX DLL Create A New Project1.

5. Open the Project1 - Project Properties dialog and change the Project Name value to AlphaDist. Add an optional Project Description value if you want.

TIP

Make multiple references easier to find by adding a common prefix, such as OCE in this case, to each Project Description value. Doing so places references to all the DLLs in one location in the References dialog.

6. Mark the Unattended Execution check box, and clear the Upgrade ActiveX Controls check box, as shown here. At this point, the remaining default options are satisfactory, so click OK.

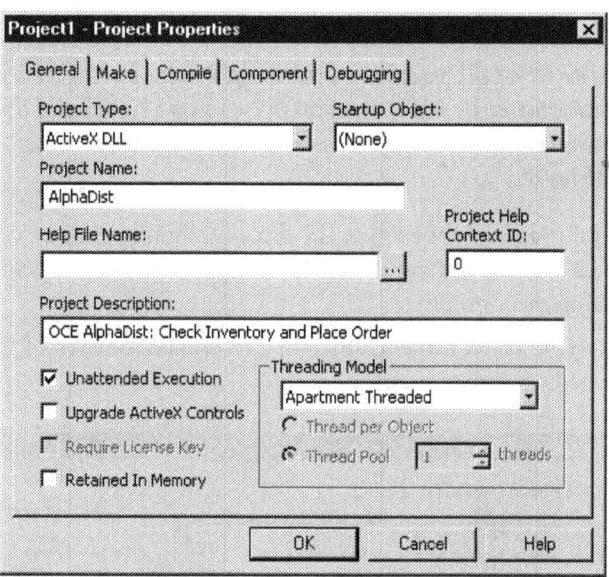

7. Right-click Class 1, and choose Remove to delete the empty class from the project without saving it.

8. Right-click the AlphaDist project, and choose Add | Class Module to open the Add Class Module dialog.

9. Click the Existing tab, and double-click AlphaDist to add the class to the project.

10. Open the Properties dialog for `clsAlphaDist`, and set the `Instancing` property value to 5 - MultiUse.

11. Choose Project | References, and add a reference to Microsoft ActiveX Data Objects 2.7 Library and Microsoft XML v. 4.0.

12. Choose File | Save AlphaDist.cls As, verify that the folder is correct, and change the filename from AlphaDist.cls to AlphaDistAX.cls.

CAUTION

If you overwrite AlphaDist.cls with the altered class compilation properties, OCE_Orders.vbp throws a "ClassName can't be public..." message and changes the `Instancing` property of the class to 1 - Private.

13. Choose File | Make AlphaDist.dll, accept the default DLL filename, verify that the folder is correct, click OK to compile and register the DLL, and close the project, saving your changes.

CAUTION

*Do **NOT** add the ActiveX DLL projects to a project group. Doing so prevents the WSDL files you create from instantiating the objects. Adding an ActiveX DLL project to a Visual Basic 6.0 project group is one of the most common problems developers encounter when migrating applications to XML Web services with the SOAP Toolkit.*

14. Repeat steps 4 through 13 for each of the three remaining classes, `clsBetaDist`, `clsGammaDist`, and `clsOmegaBank`, changing the Project Name and Project Description values accordingly.

15. Open the OCE_OrdersAX project, and add a reference for each of the four ActiveX DLLs you created, as shown here.

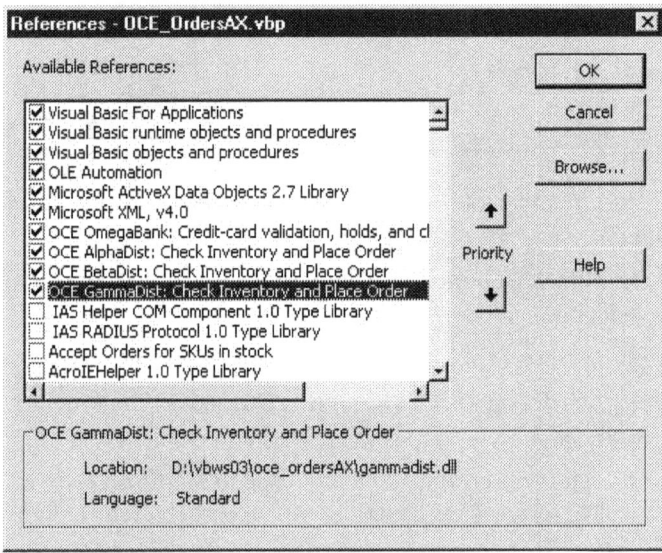

16. Choose Run | Start With Full Compile to verify that you completed the preceding steps correctly. Fix the compilation errors, which usually result from a missing reference, rerun the project, and click Add Bulk Orders to test your work so far.

17. Click Make OCE_OrdersAX.exe, accept the default options, verify that the folder is correct, and click OK to compile the project.

A production project might use separate DLLs for the `CheckInventory` and `PlaceOrder` methods, because instantiating two smaller objects conserves memory and improves the project's scalability.

TIP

You can save the few minutes required to create OCE_OrdersAX.vbg yourself by opening OCE_OrdersAX.vbp in the [\VBWS03]\OCE_OrdersAX subfolder. OCE_Orders_AX.vbp relies on its parent folder for the test client objects. Recompile each of the seven ActiveX DLL projects and reestablish the OCE_OrdersAX.vbp references to their libraries. If your subfolder path doesn't match that for the sample files, specify the path to each DLL for Project Compatibility on the Component page of the ProjectName Properties dialog. Finally, compile and run the project group.

SOAP-Enabling ActiveX Components with the SOAP Toolkit 2.0 Wizard

The procedures for adding virtual directories and generating WSDL files that are described in the following three sections apply to any COM object that meets the Toolkit's requirements. In this case, you use the DLLs you created for the OCE_OrdersAX project.

Adding Virtual Directories for the OCE_OrdersAX Services

COM-based and ASP.NET XML Web services require IIS virtual directories that point to the folder that contains the service. Individual directories emulate on a single machine each OCE B2B service. To add the four virtual directories for the remote XML Web services, do this:

1. Launch Internet Services Manager and expand the Default Web Site node.
2. Right-click the Default Web Site node, and choose New | Virtual Directory to start the wizard. Click Next.
3. Type **Omega** as the name of the virtual directory, and click Next.
4. Browse to the directory that contains the OCE_OrdersAX DLLs, \VBWS03\OCE_OrderAX for this example, and click Next and Finish.
5. Repeat steps 2 through 4 three times, replacing Omega with Alpha, Beta, and Gamma, respectively.

When you complete the preceding exercise, Internet Services Manager appears more or less as shown here. Only the Omega, Alpha, Beta, and Gamma virtual directory items are significant.

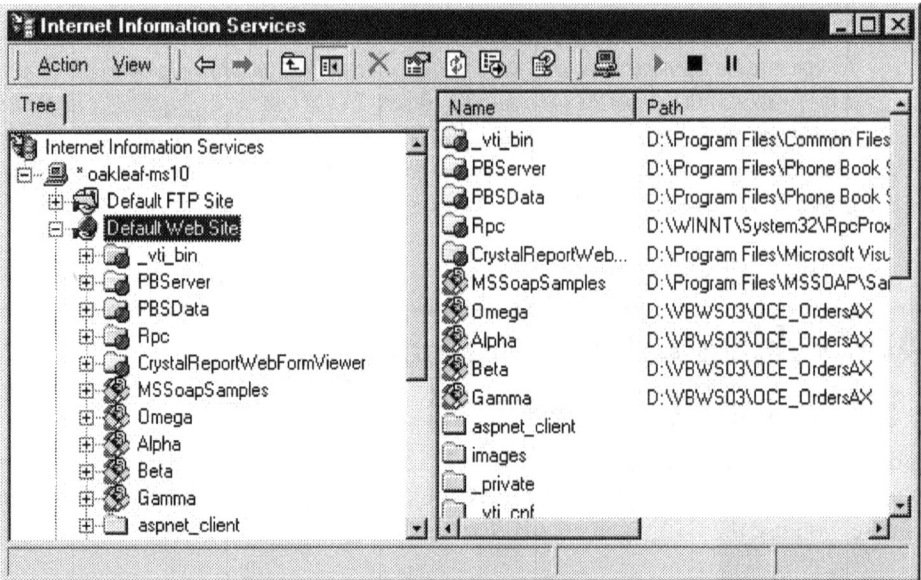

Using the Wizard to Create the WSDL Files

The SOAP Toolkit 2.0 Wizard makes creating the WSDL files for the DLLs a cinch. Here's the drill:

1. Choose Programs | Microsoft Soap Toolkit | WSDL Generator to start the Wizard, and click Next.

2. Type the name of the DLL as the name of the XML Web service, **OmegaBank** for the first file.

3. Click Select COM Object, navigate to the folder that contains the DLL to wrap, \VBWS03\OCE_OrdersAX for this example, and double-click the corresponding DLL. (See the Select The COM .dll File To Analyse page.) Click Next.

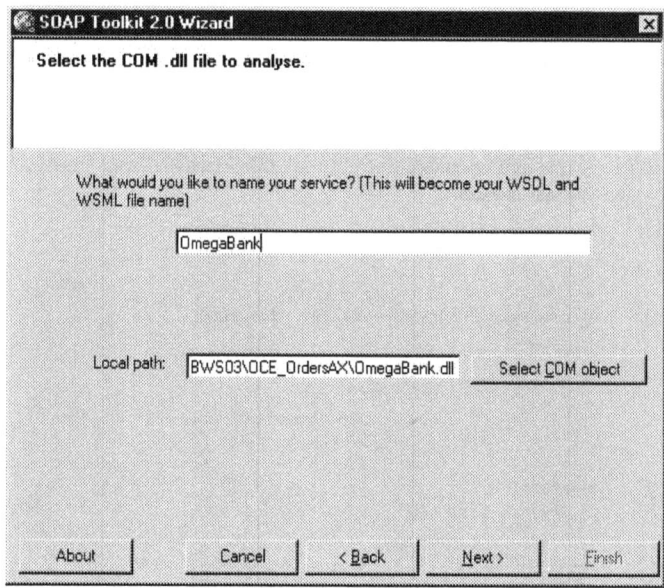

4. Mark the check boxes corresponding to the DLL's name and its class, which marks the class' method(s), as shown in the Select The Services You Would Like To Expose page. If you don't want to expose a public method as a service, clear its check box. Click Next.

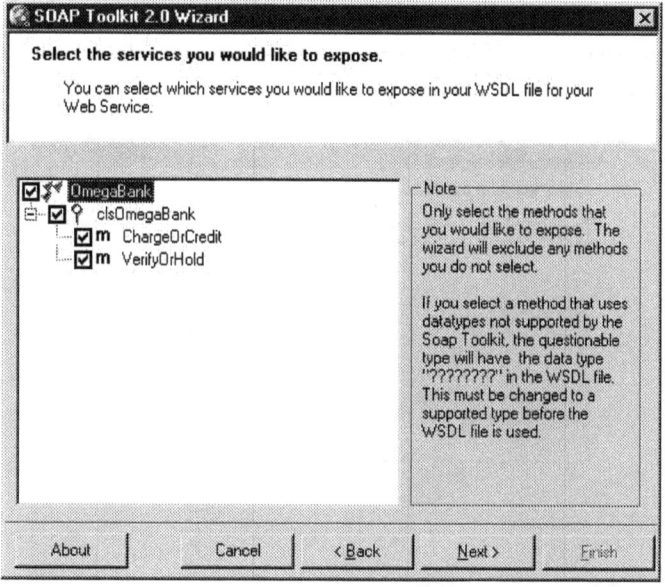

5. Type the URI to the appropriate virtual folder you added in the preceding section, including the final virgule, and accept the default ISAPI Listener option and the 2001 XSD Schema Namespace option. (See the SOAP Listener Information page.)

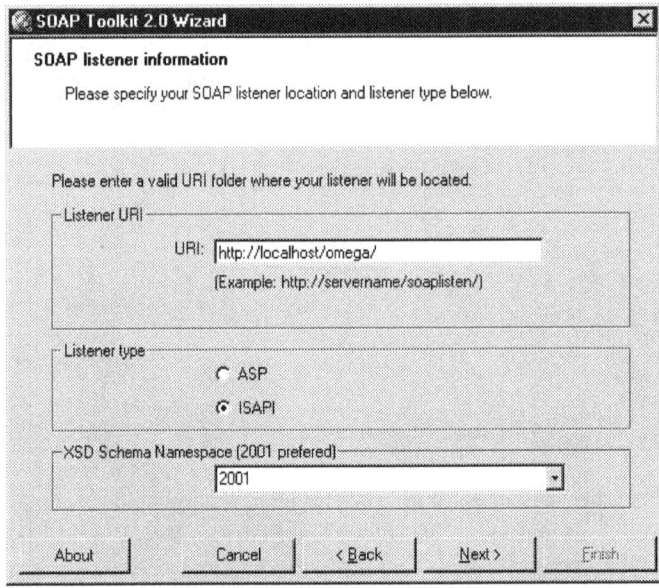

6. Accept the default UTF-8 Character Set option, click Select, and navigate to the folder that contains the source DLL. (See the Specify The Location For The New WSDL And WSML Files page.) Click Next and Finish to generate the *DLLName*.wsdl and *DLLName*.wsml files, and dismiss the Wizard.

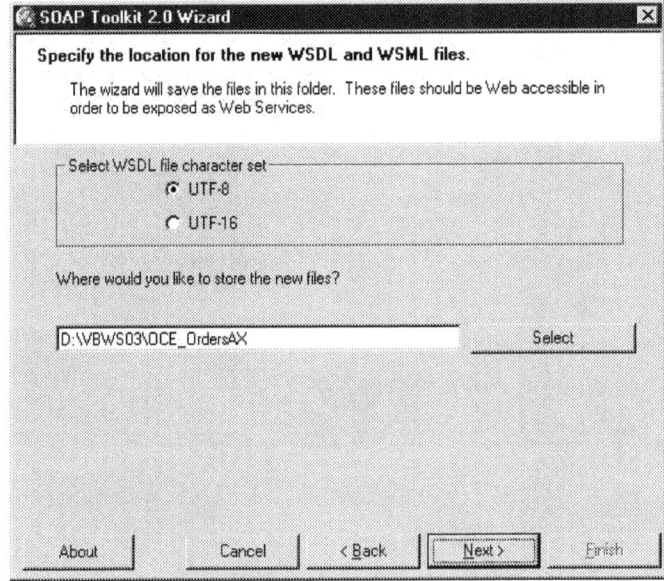

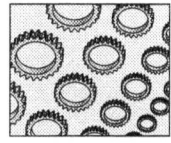

NOTE

When you click Next during creation of the OmegaBank.wsdl file, you receive an error message regarding data types. Click OK; the next section discusses fixing unsupported data type problems.

7. Repeat steps 1 through 6 for the AlphaDist, BetaDist, and GammaDis DLLs to assign a pair inventory and order services to the Alpha, Beta, and Gamma virtual directories.

The naming conventions for this example are arbitrary, but assigning the name of the component as the XML Web service name is the simplest approach.

TIP

All the preceding WSDL files are included in the \VBWS03\OCE_OrdersAX\ subfolder, but it's a good idea to overwrite at least the OmegaBank.wsdl and .wsml files so you can make the corrections described in the following section.

Fixing Wizard-Created WSDL Files

The Wizard doesn't offer a text box for replacing the default `tempuri.org` namespace URI. Thus, you should open each WSDL file and assign the appropriate URI, such as `omegabank.com` or `alphadist.com`. If you've installed Visual Studio .NET, double-clicking a WSDL file opens it in the Visual Studio IDE. Visual Studio wants to save a solution along with the modified WSDL file, so open the file in Notepad. Replace `tempuri.org` with the URI of your choice, and save the changes.

If you specify an argument or return value data type that the XSD Schema specification doesn't support, you see the following error message, which advises that the unsupported data type values will be replaced with question marks in the WSDL file. The XML Schema specification doesn't support the `Currency` data type, so you receive this message when generating the OmegaBank.wsdl file.

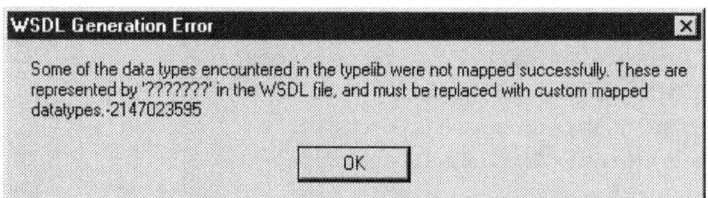

The logical replacement for the `Currency` data type is `xsd:decimal`, which is the data type Visual Basic .NET substitutes for `Currency` when upgrading Visual Basic 6.0 projects. The canonical representation of the `xsd:decimal` data type requires a decimal point and at least one digit before and after the decimal point. Additional leading and trailing zeroes and the plus sign are prohibited. You're likely to encounter currency values with trailing .0 or .00 values, so the safe approach is to replace the two instances of `???????` with `float` (the equivalent of Visual Basic's `Single` data type), as shown here.

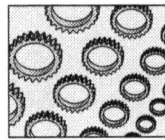

NOTE

Sections 3.2.3 and 3.2.4 of the XML Schema: Part 2 Datatypes specification describe the `xsd:decimal` *and* `xsd:float` *primitive data types. The canonical restrictions on* `xsd:decimal`'s *leading and trailing zeroes is in section 3.2.3.2. Testing indicates that* `xsd:decimal` *and* `xsd:float` *behave identically. The Microsoft implementation of both data types introduces occasional rounding errors in the Amount field (*`money` *data type) values of the OMB_Network database's Transactions table.*

```
OmegaBank.WSDL - Notepad                                    _ □ X
File  Edit  Format  Help
  </types>
  <message name='clsOmegaBank.VerifyOrHold'>
    <part name='strServer' type='xsd:string'/>
    <part name='strUser' type='xsd:string'/>
    <part name='strPwd' type='xsd:string'/>
    <part name='lngMerchantID' type='xsd:int'/>
    <part name='lngRefNum' type='xsd:int'/>
    <part name='strIssuer' type='xsd:string'/>
    <part name='strCardNumber' type='xsd:string'/>
    <part name='strCardName' type='xsd:string'/>
    <part name='strZipCode' type='xsd:string'/>
    <part name='strExpDate' type='xsd:string'/>
    <part name='curTransactAmt' type='xsd:float'/>
    <part name='blnApplyHold' type='xsd:boolean'/>
    <part name='blnUseWS' type='xsd:boolean'/>
  </message>
  <message name='clsOmegaBank.VerifyOrHoldResponse'>
    <part name='Result' type='xsd:string'/>
  </message>
  <message name='clsOmegaBank.ChargeOrCredit'>
    <part name='strServer' type='xsd:string'/>
    <part name='strUser' type='xsd:string'/>
    <part name='strPwd' type='xsd:string'/>
    <part name='lngMerchantID' type='xsd:int'/>
    <part name='lngRefNum' type='xsd:int'/>
    <part name='strCardNumber' type='xsd:string'/>
    <part name='lngRelTransactID' type='xsd:int'/>
    <part name='curTransactAmt' type='███████'/>
```

Here's the final version of the modified OmegaBank.wsdl file:

```xml
<?xml version='1.0' encoding='UTF-8' ?>
<!-- Generated 12/03/01 by Microsoft SOAP Toolkit WSDL File Generator,
  Version 1.02.813.0 -->
<definitions  name ='OmegaBank'   targetNamespace =
      'http://omegabank.com/wsdl/'
  xmlns:wsdlns='http://omegabank.com/wsdl/'
  xmlns:typens='http://omegabank.com/type'
  xmlns:soap='http://schemas.xmlsoap.org/wsdl/soap/'
  xmlns:xsd='http://www.w3.org/2001/XMLSchema'
  xmlns:stk='http://schemas.microsoft.com/soap-toolkit/wsdl-extension'
  xmlns='http://schemas.xmlsoap.org/wsdl/'>
  <types>
    <schema targetNamespace='http://omegabank.com/type'
      xmlns='http://www.w3.org/2001/XMLSchema'
      xmlns:SOAP-ENC='http://schemas.xmlsoap.org/soap/encoding/'
      xmlns:wsdl='http://schemas.xmlsoap.org/wsdl/'
```

```
    elementFormDefault='qualified'>
  </schema>
</types>
<message name='clsOmegaBank.VerifyOrHold'>
  <part name='strServer' type='xsd:string'/>
  <part name='strUser' type='xsd:string'/>
  <part name='strPwd' type='xsd:string'/>
  <part name='lngMerchantID' type='xsd:int'/>
  <part name='lngRefNum' type='xsd:int'/>
  <part name='strIssuer' type='xsd:string'/>
  <part name='strCardNumber' type='xsd:string'/>
  <part name='strCardName' type='xsd:string'/>
  <part name='strZipCode' type='xsd:string'/>
  <part name='strExpDate' type='xsd:string'/>
  <part name='curTransactAmt' type='xsd:float'/>
  <part name='blnApplyHold' type='xsd:boolean'/>
  <part name='blnUseWS' type='xsd:boolean'/>
</message>
<message name='clsOmegaBank.VerifyOrHoldResponse'>
  <part name='Result' type='xsd:string'/>
</message>
<message name='clsOmegaBank.ChargeOrCredit'>
  <part name='strServer' type='xsd:string'/>
  <part name='strUser' type='xsd:string'/>
  <part name='strPwd' type='xsd:string'/>
  <part name='lngMerchantID' type='xsd:int'/>
  <part name='lngRefNum' type='xsd:int'/>
  <part name='strCardNumber' type='xsd:string'/>
  <part name='lngRelTransactID' type='xsd:int'/>
  <part name='curTransactAmt' type='xsd:float'/>
  <part name='blnReleaseHold' type='xsd:boolean'/>
  <part name='blnCredit' type='xsd:boolean'/>
  <part name='blnUseWS' type='xsd:boolean'/>
</message>
<message name='clsOmegaBank.ChargeOrCreditResponse'>
  <part name='Result' type='xsd:string'/>
</message>
<portType name='clsOmegaBankSoapPort'>
  <operation name='VerifyOrHold' parameterOrder='strServer
      strUser strPwd lngMerchantID lngRefNum strIssuer
      strCardNumber strCardName strZipCode strExpDate
      curTransactAmt blnApplyHold blnUseWS'>
    <input message='wsdlns:clsOmegaBank.VerifyOrHold' />
    <output message='wsdlns:clsOmegaBank.VerifyOrHoldResponse' />
  </operation>
```

```
      <operation name='ChargeOrCredit' parameterOrder='strServer
          strUser strPwd lngMerchantID lngRefNum strCardNumber
          lngRelTransactID curTransactAmt blnReleaseHold blnCredit blnUseWS'>
          <input message='wsdlns:clsOmegaBank.ChargeOrCredit' />
  <output message='wsdlns:clsOmegaBank.ChargeOrCreditResponse' />
      </operation>
    </portType>
    <binding name='clsOmegaBankSoapBinding'
        type='wsdlns:clsOmegaBankSoapPort' >
      <stk:binding preferredEncoding='UTF-8'/>
      <soap:binding style='rpc'
          transport='http://schemas.xmlsoap.org/soap/http' />
      <operation name='VerifyOrHold' >
        <soap:operation soapAction=
            'http://omegabank.com/action/clsOmegaBank.VerifyOrHold' />
        <input>
          <soap:body use='encoded' namespace='http://omegabank.com/message/'
              encodingStyle='http://schemas.xmlsoap.org/soap/encoding/' />
        </input>
        <output>
          <soap:body use='encoded' namespace='http://omegabank.com/message/'
              encodingStyle='http://schemas.xmlsoap.org/soap/encoding/' />
        </output>
      </operation>
      <operation name='ChargeOrCredit' >
        <soap:operation soapAction=
            'http://omegabank.com/action/clsOmegaBank.ChargeOrCredit' />
        <input>
          <soap:body use='encoded' namespace='http://omegabank.com/message/'
            encodingStyle='http://schemas.xmlsoap.org/soap/encoding/' />
        </input>
        <output>
          <soap:body use='encoded' namespace='http://omegabank.com/message/'
            encodingStyle='http://schemas.xmlsoap.org/soap/encoding/' />
        </output>
      </operation>
    </binding>
    <service name='OmegaBank' >
      <port name='clsOmegaBankSoapPort'
          binding='wsdlns:clsOmegaBankSoapBinding' >
        <soap:address location='http://localhost/omega/OmegaBank.WSDL' />
      </port>
    </service>
  </definitions>
```

Invoking XML Web Services with the SoapClient Object

The preceding "Analyzing the SOAP Client Code" section briefly describes the Visual Basic 6.0 code for instantiating an early-bound COM object with the `SoapClient` object. Visual Basic's Auto Quick Info and Auto List Members features enabled by early binding operate on the `SoapClient` object, not the COM object. You can use early- or late-binding of `SoapClient` objects; in either case, the COM object is late-bound.

Late-Binding the SoapClient Object

Scripted Web pages and ASP require late-bound invocation of XML Web services. Following is a generic example of a late-bound method call:

```
Dim objSoapClient As Object
Set objSoapClient = CreateObject("MSSOAP.SoapClient")
[objSoapClient.ClientProperty("ServerHTTPRequest") = True]
Call_
objSoapClient.mssoapinit("http://URL/VirtualDirName/ServiceName.wsdl")
If Err.Number = 0 Then
    typReturnValue = objSoapClient.MethodName(typArg1[,typArg2[, …]])
Else
    'Unable to connect to WSDL file
End If
```

If you remove the `As Object` type identifier, the preceding code fragment is valid for VBScript. The `ClientProperty` line is required for ASP clients and optional for Visual Basic 6.0 clients. Setting `ServerHTTPRequest = True` specifies use of "server-safe" MSXML components to open the WSDL and WSML files.

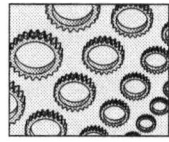

NOTE

There is only a slight performance penalty for late-binding the `SoapClient` object. The ASP version of the OakLeaf CFR project at http://www.oakleaf.ws/cfr-soap/ uses VBScript similar to the preceding example to invoke the project's XML Web services.

Handling Runtime Errors

Dealing with runtime errors thrown when invoking XML Web services is a bit more complex than conventional COM objects. You might encounter any or all of the following errors when executing early- or late-bound calls to a service:

▶ Runtime errors initiating the `SoapClient` object with the `mssoapinit` method. These errors occur if the server-side MSXML components can't open the WSDL or WSML file, or either file isn't a well-formed XML document.

▶ Runtime errors executing the method of the underlying COM object. These errors occur if the number of arguments passed to the method isn't correct, the COM object throws an unhandled exception, or, in some cases, if the data type of an argument is wrong.

▶ Client or server errors reported by the `SoapClient.faultstring` property value. Whether a runtime error occurs depends on the type of error.

For runtime errors, the `SoapClient.faultstring` property value is a variation on the `Err.Description` theme. For example, when the `mssoapinit` method can't open the requested WSDL file, `Err.Description` returns the following string:

```
WSDLReader:Loading of the WSDL file failed HRESULT=0x80070057 -
WSDLReader:XML Parser failed at linenumber 0, lineposition 0,
reason is: System error: -2147012889.
```

and the value of the `SoapClient.faultstring` property is:

```
WSDLReader: XML Parser failed at linenumber 0, lineposition 0,
reason is: System error: -2147012889.
```

In many cases, `faultstring` is more informative than `Err.Description`. Following are the `Description` and `faultstring` values for a call with an incorrect number of arguments:

```
Invalid procedure call or argument
Client: Incorrect number of parameters supplied for SOAP request
```

and here are the values for an incorrect data type:

```
Type mismatch
Client: Type conversion failure for element curTransactAmt
```

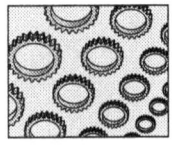

NOTE

You receive a type mismatch or type conversion error if you substitute a string value for a numeric value, but not the reverse. You can pass a value of any Visual Basic data type (except objects) to a parameter having the `xsd:string` data type.

Some server-side errors don't generate a runtime error in the client. For example, the COM object might return the `Err.Description` value in the event of an internal error. The OCE_OrdersAX project's DLLs use this approach for inline exception handling and reporting other types of internal problems. The error strings have an uppercase `ERROR:` prefix for exceptions and `Error:` for problems.

To assure that your client-side error-handling process traps any error generated by the `SoapServer` or a COM object that returns a `String` value, use a statement such as the following:

```
If Len(objSoapClient.faultstring) > 0 Then
    'Handle SOAP client or server-side errors
    'Handle runtime errors with the faultstring value
ElseIf InStr(UCase$(strResult), "ERROR") Then
    'Handle internal COM object problems
ElseIf Err.Number <> 0 Then
    'Handle runtime errors
End If
```

Verifying the Services with the OCE Test Client

The OCE test harness offers sample code for invoking local and remote XML Web services. Running OCE_OrdersAX.vbp with the OmegaBank.dll and OmegaBank.wsdl files in the application folder enables the following three check boxes:

▶   **Use XML Web Services**   Marking this check box sets the `blnUseWS` flag to `True`, uses the `SoapClient` object and the WSDL files to instantiate the ActiveX DLLs, and makes the following check box visible. This feature lets you compare conventional COM object and XML Web service execution times.

▶   **Use Remote oakleaf.ws Services**   Marking this check box sets the `blnUseOakLeaf` flag to `True`, changes the URLs and the WSDL files to virtual directories on the OakLeaf Web site, such as http://www.oakleaf.ws/omega/omegabank.wsdl, and exposes the following check box. This feature lets you compare local and remote XML Web service execution times.

▶   **Use IP 68.123.163.243 (Not DNS)**   Marking this check box sets the `blnUseIP` flag to `True`, which lets you determine the performance penalty for DNS lookup. There's no significant penalty if your operating system caches DNS lookups.

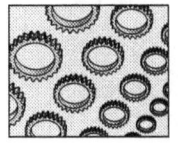

NOTE

The OakLeaf SQL Server uses the default login IDs (NetUser, AlphaUser, Beta User, and GammaUser) and passwords (Net#123, Alpha#123, Beta#123, and Gamma#123) for the local databases. These users have very restricted SELECT, UPDATE, and INSERT access to the three databases. The sample databases reinitialize daily at midnight.

OCE_OrdersAX.vbp's `frmOrders` form and classes use late-binding to invoke the `SoapClient` method to avoid dependence on a reference to the `MSSOAPLib` library. Following is an example of the code from `frmOrder`'s `cmdVerifyCard` subprocedure to invoke the OmegaBank `VerifyOrHold` method, which demonstrates use of the three check-box options:

```
Dim objOmegaBank As Object
…
If blnUseOakLeaf Then
   'Use OakLeaf's remote Web service
   If blnUseIP Then
      'Test time difference with DNS lookup
      strURL = "http://" & strNetIP & "/omega/OmegaBank.wsdl"
   Else
      strURL = "http://www.oakleaf.ws/omega/OmegaBank.wsdl"
   End If
   'oakleaf.ws SQL Server name (usual login IDs and passwords)
   strServer = "OAKLEAF-MS7"
Else
   strURL = "http://localhost/Omega/OmegaBank.wsdl"
   strServer = strNetServer
End If
Set objOmegaBank = CreateObject("MSSOAP.SoapClient")
objOmegaBank.ClientProperty("ServerHTTPRequest") = True
Call objOmegaBank.mssoapinit(strURL)
strVerify = objOmegaBank.VerifyOrHold(strServer, strNetUser, _
            strNetPwd, 151203, lngOrderID, strCardType, _
            strCardNumber, strCardName, strZipCode, _
            strExpDate, curOrderTotal, False, blnUseWS)
If Len(objOmegaBank.faultstring) > 0 Then
   strVerify = "ERROR: " & objOmegaBank.faultstring
End If
Set objOmegaBank = Nothing
```

To implement early-binding, add a reference to the Microsoft Soap [sic] Type Library, change the `Dim` statement to `Dim objOmegaBank As New SoapClient`, and delete or comment out the `Set` statement.

Using the Trace Utility for Debugging Messages

Chapters 1 and 2 mentioned the SOAP Toolkit's Trace Utility for capturing messages on the SOAP server. The Trace Utility intercepts messages sent to or from a nonstandard HTTP TCP port (usually port 8080), displays formatted or unformatted messages in two windows, and redirects the messages to port 80. You temporarily add the port designator to the `<soap:address location=http://… />` element's URL attribute value. The primary purpose of the unformatted (binary) mode is to display HTTP headers. Formatted messages are the better choice for most debugging operations.

Now that you have some interesting messages to view, give the Trace Utility a test drive by following these steps:

1. Open the WSDL file for the XML Web service in Notepad. Navigate to the end of the file and add `:8080` to the server name element of the `<soap:address location=http://… />` element URL. For this example, which uses the AlphaDist service, the change appears as shown here:

```
<soap:address
location='http://localhost:8080/alpha/AlphaDist.WSDL' />
```

2. Save the WSDL file and choose Programs | Microsoft SOAP Toolkit | Trace Utility. Choose File | New | Formatted Trace or press CTRL-F to open the Trace Setup dialog.

3. Accept the default Listen and Forward To values and click OK to open an MDI child window to display the messages.

4. Invoke an XML Web service to send and receive messages. For this example, mark the OCE_OrdersAX's Use XML Web Services check box, and click Add Bulk Orders. When the program encounters an outsourced line item, message nodes appear in the left pane. Specifying `localhost` as the server name identifies the nodes with the IP loopback address (127.0.0.1).

5. After you've intercepted a few messages, stop the application, expand one of the message nodes, and double-click the Message #1 item to display the messages sent and received in the two right panes.

6. When you complete the tests, remove the `:8080` port designation from the WSDL file and close the Trace Utility.

OCE_OrdersAX sends an initial and preorder `CheckInventory` message, followed by a `PlaceOrder` message, if the outsourced item is in distributor stock. Figure 3-6 shows the messages sent to and received from the `AlphaDist.PlaceOrder` method. The XML purchase order document is in the top pane and the resulting invoice is in the lower pane.

Deploying XML Web Services to a Production Server

After you've debugged your XML Web services with a client test harness, here's the drill for deploying the ActiveX DLLs to a production server and enabling the services:

1. Install the SOAP Toolkit 2.0 on the production server, if it's not already installed.

2. Add a new folder for the DLL, WSDL, and WSML files on the server. Grant the anonymous Internet users, IUSR_*SERVERNAME* and IWAM_*SERVERNAME*, Read and Execute, List Folder Contents, and Read permissions.

3. Add one or more new virtual directories for the services.

4. Copy the Web Service DLLs, WSDL, and WSML files to the new production server folder.

5. Register each DLL by running **Regsvr32** "*Foldername/Dllname*.**dll**".

6. If your WSDL file doesn't have `localhost` in the `<soap:address location='http://localhost/...` /> line, Launch the Toolkit's WSDL generator and create new WSDL and WSML files for each DLL.

7. Correct any unsupported data type issues, and replace `tempuri.org` with the appropriate namespace.

8. Verify proper operation of the production services with your test harness.

The preceding process set up the DLL, WSDL, and WSML files on the oakleaf.ws Web site. The SQL Server Enterprise Manager Copy Database Wizard generated the production copies of the four databases on the OAKLEAF-MS7 server.

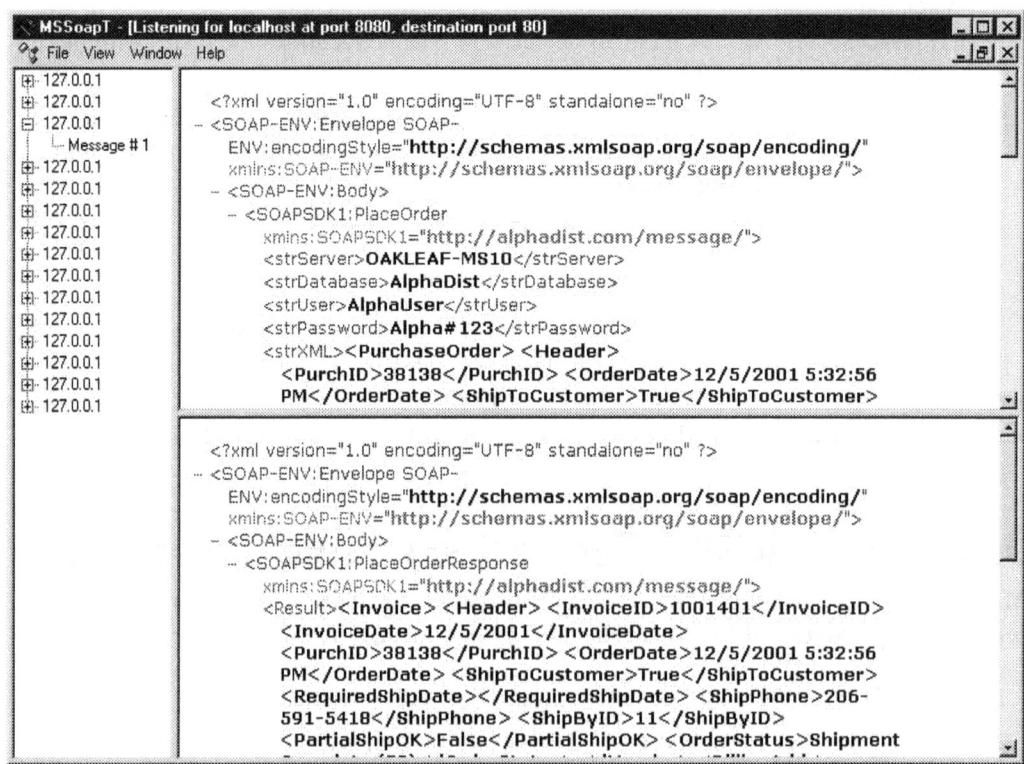

Figure 3-6 *The Trace Utility displays the request message in the top pane and the response message in the lower pane.*

Upgrading to ASP.NET XML Web Services

IN THIS CHAPTER:

It's probably safe to say that most Visual Basic 6.0 developers give Visual Studio .NET its first full test drive by upgrading existing projects to Visual Basic .NET. This is especially true for database front-end and middle-tier component developers who need to make preliminary performance and scalability comparisons of the two platforms. While upgrading to Visual Basic .NET doesn't generate optimized code that takes total advantage of the full gamut of .NET Framework features, migrating existing code gives developers a chance to uncover undocumented "gotchas" and potential workarounds. The results of initial test upgrades often become the basis for establishing IT department budgets—or lack thereof—to support future .NET training and project expenditures.

Moving from conventional COM components to XML Web services is another incentive for migrating client and middle-tier applications to .NET. Wrapping COM components with the SOAP Toolkit 2.0 adds the overhead of instantiating a `SoapClient` object, which, in turn, instantiates the remote component. Chapter 3 demonstrates that it's easy to create simple RPC-style XML Web services with the Toolkit, but handling complex argument data types or document-style messaging requires a substantial investment in writing Visual Basic 6.0 code for type mappers, the low-level SOAP API, or the SOAP Messaging Object (SMO).

Visual Studio .NET and the .NET Framework's `System.Web.Services` and `System.Xml` namespaces deliver a much more straightforward approach to coding complex XML Web services. Moving to ASP.NET services generates a .disco file for finding XML Web services installed on individual servers and adds `GET`, `POST`, and `MIME` transport options.

Another benefit of moving clients and XML Web services to Visual Studio .NET is integrated debugging for .NET services. The Visual Studio .NET debugging process is similar to that provided for COM objects that you include in Visual Basic 6.0 project groups. Integrated debugging isn't available for COM-based services that you create with the SOAP Toolkit, so heavy-duty XML Web services with a lot of complex code are also good candidates for upgrading to .NET-based services.

If your production XML Web services require a lot of code, the upgrade "clincher" is substantially improved performance compared with SOAP-enabled COM components. The "Evaluating Performance of Upgraded .NET Clients and XML Web Services" section, at the end of this chapter, compares the performance of COM and ASP.NET components and XML Web services. You can gain further performance improvement by following the Chapter 5 recommendations to upgrade ADO/OLE DB-based SQL Server access to ADO.NET's `SqlClient` objects.

Taking a High-Level View of the Upgrade Process

The primary objective of this chapter is to demonstrate the simplest process for upgrading Windows client applications, COM-based middle-tier components, and XML Web services from Visual Basic 6.0 to Visual Basic .NET. A secondary objective is to compare the performance of COM-based and ASP.NET XML Web services of moderate complexity.

TIP

Upgrade Visual Basic 5.0 and earlier projects to version 6.0 before you use the Visual Basic .NET Upgrade Wizard. (The Upgrade Wizard isn't included in the Visual Studio .NET Standard Edition.)

Following are the basic steps in the upgrade process:

1. Process the client application or test harness with the Upgrade Wizard to create the Visual Basic .NET version.

2. Upgrade the projects that create the COM DLLs for the XML Web services. Upgrading the projects for other DLLs is optional but highly recommended.

3. Test the upgraded client with the upgraded Visual Basic .NET DLLs.

4. Use the ASP.NET Web Services template to generate a virtual directory and an empty .asmx file for each XML Web service.

5. Copy and paste the DLLs' Visual Basic .NET code to the .asmx.vb files and add a `<WebMethod()>` attribute (also called a *processing directive*) to each `Public Function` you want to expose as an XML Web service method.

6. Add the references required to build the .asmx code and create the ASP.NET DLL for each service, which replaces the SOAP Toolkit 2.0 version.

7. Optionally, move the folders containing the upgraded ASP.NET services from subfolders of \Inetput\wwwroot to your project's subfolders.

8. Add a Web Reference to the client project for each local service. If the client relies on remote XML Web services, add their Web References.

9. Change the client code to instantiate the XML Web services instead of the original COM objects, or, in the case of COM-based services, `SoapClient` objects.

10. Run the client to test your changes and verify that the new and remote XML Web services execute as expected.

11. Develop and execute a test regimen to compare the performance and scalability of the two implementations under simulated database and Web server loads.

This chapter uses the OCE_OrdersAX.vbp project for its examples. This project is sufficiently complex to emulate upgrading a production-grade three-tier application to Visual Basic .NET and ASP.NET XML Web services. Another benefit of using moderately complex data-driven components for the examples is the ability to compare performance and potential scalability of the COM and .NET versions in a simulated production environment.

Upgrading XML Web Service Clients to Visual Basic .NET

Testing ActiveX DLLs upgraded from Visual Basic 6.0 to Visual Basic .NET requires a test harness to verify that your upgraded DLLs work correctly before you use the code to create

XML Web services. Upgrading 3,100 lines of moderately complex Visual Basic 6.0 code also illustrates some of the obscure problems you're likely to encounter when moving your Visual Basic 6.0 projects to Visual Basic .NET and Windows forms. You need the Visual Basic .NET version of the client project to substitute Web References for the ASP.NET version of the XML Web services. Another advantage of upgrading client applications is the ease with which you can debug components, local ASP.NET XML Web services, and, if you have proper credentials, remote ASP.NET XML Web services.

Downloading This Chapter's Sample Files

The VBWS04.zip file, which you can download from the book's entry at http://www.osborne.com/downloads/downloads.shtml, contains a modified (self-contained) copy of the Chapter 3 OCE_OrdersAX.vbp project in the \OCE_OrdersAX folder. Create a new VBWS04 folder and expand the archive's contents into the folder. The four ActiveX DLL projects, which are required to support local XML Web services, are included. If you didn't compile the four DLLs as you progressed through the Chapter 3 examples, you must do so now.

 **CAUTION**

Don't compile VBWS04.zip's versions of AlphaDist.vbp, BetaDist.vbp, GammaDist.vbp and OmegaBank.vbp if you previously compiled the versions from the Chapter 3 VBWS03.zip file. Compiling two sets of DLLs having the same class names and descriptions clobbers the original Registry entries and creates a nasty example of DLL hell.

This chapter's version of OCE_OrdersAX.vbp replaces the Use IP 66.123.163.243 (Not DNS) check box with a Use Remote ASP.NET Services check box. Marking this check box routes XML Web service requests to ASP.NET WSDL files on the OakLeaf server at http://www.oakleaf.ws/oce/. The "Consuming ASP.NET XML Web Services with SoapClient Objects" section, near the end of this chapter, describes the changes to the OCE_OrdersAX.vbp code required to consume ASP.NET XML Web services.

The VBWS04.zip archive also contains the fully upgraded version of OCE_OrdersAX in the OCE_OrdersNET folder. It's strongly recommended, however, that you perform the upgrade exercises in the following few sections if you haven't upgraded several complex Visual Basic 6.0 database front-end and middle-tier components successfully.

Moving from Late to Early Binding

One of the objectives of .NET in general and of ASP.NET in particular is to eliminate all late-binding. The OCE_OrdersAX.vbp project uses late-binding of the `SoapClient` object, which lets the program run without installing the SOAP Toolkit 2.0. Visual Studio .NET supports late-binding in upgraded Visual Basic 6.0 and ASP code, but the equivalent of COM-style early-binding is the rule for all Visual Studio .NET projects. If you don't change to early-binding, you receive many warnings that the Upgrade Wizard can't determine the default property of late-bound objects.

TIP

Making the change to early-binding in your Visual Basic 6.0 code is much easier than changing the Wizard-generated Visual Basic .NET code.

Making the change to early-binding is optional, but it takes only about 5 minutes. Most of the following process for VBWS04.zip's OCE_OrdersAX.vbp project applies to all Visual Basic 6.0 clients that implement late-binding of any COM object type:

1. Add a reference to the Microsoft Soap [sic] Type Library.

2. Replace all occurrences of `As Object` in the project with `As New ObjectName`, `SoapClient` for this example. Searching for "early-binding" in the current project finds these lines.

3. Delete all `Set objName = CreateObject("ProgID")` lines, and save your project changes. For this example, `ProgID` is `MSSOAP.SoapClient`. These lines also have "early-binding" comments.

4. Compile and run the project to verify the changes.

TIP

Run OCE_OrdersAX.vbp in each of its three configurations — COM, and local and remote XML Web services — with bulk order addition. Add at least 50 new orders to make sure that all three distributor DLLs execute at least once.

Using the Upgrade Wizard to Create the OCE_TestClient

The Visual Basic .NET Upgrade Wizard does a remarkably good job of upgrading production-quality Visual Basic 6.0 code to Visual Basic .NET. The OCE_Orders example in this section typifies upgrading a simple three-tier database front end.

TIP

Review the "Preparing a Visual Basic 6.0 Application for Upgrading" online help topic and its subtopics if you haven't upgraded a moderately complex project.

To upgrade the OCE_OrdersAX test client project to Visual Basic .NET, do this:

1. Compile and run OCE_OrdersAX.vbp if you haven't done so previously. You're not likely to be able to upgrade a Visual Basic 6.0 project that won't compile due to missing references or other faults.

2. Launch Visual Studio .NET and close the last project or solution, if present.

3. Choose File | Open | Project, and navigate in the Open Project dialog box to the subfolder where OCE_OrdersAX.vbp is located. Double-click the OCE_OrdersAX.vbp file to start the Upgrade Wizard. Click Next twice.

4. Edit the default D:\VBWS03\OCE_OrdersAX\OCE_OrdersAX.NET folder location in the text box to **D:\VBWS04\OCE_OrdersNET\TestClient**.

5. Click OK to create the new folder, and then click Next to start the upgrade, which takes about 5 minutes on an 866-MHz PIII box.

6. In Solution Explorer, change the name of the solution and project to **OCE_TestClient**, and press CTRL-SHIFT-S to save all the project files with default names.

7. Open the _UpgradeReport.htm page and verify that 0 errors occurred. (See Figure 4-1.) You can disregard the 20 or so warnings, which relate primarily to default properties of XML Web service methods invoked by the `SoapClient` object and changes to Visual Basic 6.0 events and methods in Visual Basic .NET. Close the Upgrade Report page.

8. If the Task List isn't visible, choose View | Show Tasks | All to display about 30 items, 20 of which are warnings related to an array passed by reference to the `FulfillOrders` class and the size of the array. Comments prefixed with "ToDo" also appear in the list.

9. Press F5 to build and attempt to run the project. Click No when asked if you want to continue despite the build errors.

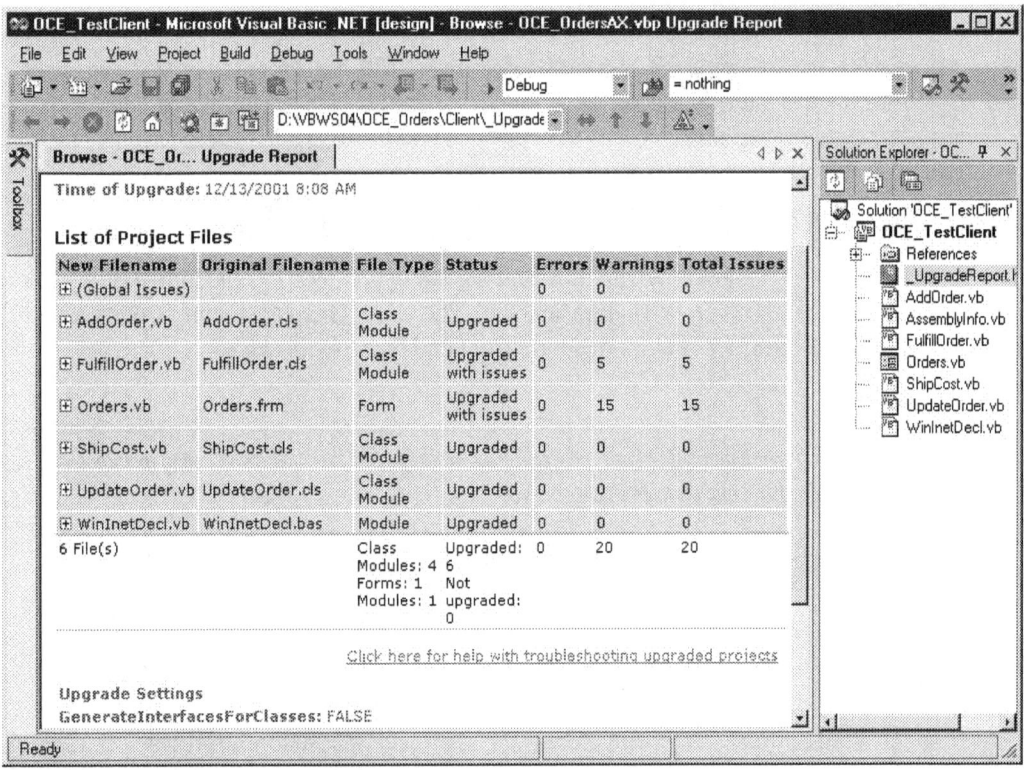

Figure 4-1 *The Upgrade Report page lists errors and warnings resulting from the upgrading process. You disregard warnings initially, but errors prevent building the project.*

Correcting Build and Runtime Errors

If your source code doesn't contain arrays passed as argument values, you're likely to encounter only a few fatal errors that prevent you from building the upgraded project. It's usually easy to correct these flaws based on the Task List's Description items. Correcting runtime errors that throw exceptions is also straightforward in most cases, despite the obscurity of many error messages. It's considerably more difficult to correct runtime errors that *don't* throw exceptions and instead return unexpected values.

The show-stopper that prevents building the executable file for Orders.vb is the `astrLineItems` array passed by reference from `frmOrders.CheckOrHoldStock` to `FulfillOrders.CheckOrCommit`. Issues with object destruction and `ADODB.Connection` objects passed by reference cause runtime exceptions.

To make the Visual Basic.NET version of the client operational, do this:

1. Open Orders.vb, navigate to the `CheckOrHoldStock` subprocedure, and change `Dim astrLineItems() As String` to **`Dim astrLineItems(5, 3) As String`**. You must specify the number of dimensions when declaring a .NET array, but you aren't required to set the number of elements in the declaration. Thus, `Dim astrLineItems(, ) As String` is also acceptable.

2. Open FulfillOrder.vb, navigate to the `Public Function CheckOrCommit` line, and change `ByRef astrLineItems() As String` to **`ByRef astrLineItems(, )`** to designate a two-dimensional array. This and the preceding step remove the build errors.

3. In Orders.vb, comment out or delete the `cnnCard.Close()` statement at the end of the `cmdVerifyCard_Click` event handler. Under Visual Basic .NET, executing this line closes the connection for `rstItems Recordset`, which throws a runtime error in the `cmdIssueHolds_Click` event handler.

4. With all the .vb files open, search for and remove all instances of *objName* = `Nothing` in each class, including Orders.vb. The CLR garbage collector automatically handles object destruction.

5. Remove the `If Len(Dir(VB6.GetPath & "\OmegaBank.dll"))`... and `End If` lines from the `frmOrders_Load` and `cmdInitialize_Click` event handlers, if present, to make the XML Web Services check boxes visible: these lines aren't present if you upgrade from the version of OCE_OrdersAX.vbp from the VBWS04.zip archive.

6. In the Orders.vb file, change `" (ActiveX Web Services)"` to `" (.NET XML Web Services)"` and save all files.

7. Press F5 to build and run the project in debug mode.

8. Run the client in the COM and local and remote XML Web service modes to test interoperability with the existing DLLs and WSDL files you created in Chapter 3 and the COM-based XML Web services from the OakLeaf Web site. Make sure that "Invoice issued..." messages and occasional "2 invoices issued..." messages appear in the Action text box. If not, you probably skipped step 3.

TIP

If you encounter runtime errors, temporarily comment all On Error Resume Next instructions to break on the line that causes the error.

Conforming Assembly Names and Namespaces

Changing the solution and project names from OCE_OrdersAX to OCE_Client doesn't change the project's namespace or the name of the executable file. Upgraded projects retain the original values. It's good design practice to use the same name for all elements of the project and, especially, the executable file.

To synchronize the project assembly and executable names with the new project name, right-click the project and choose Properties to open the OCE_TestClient Property Pages dialog. On the Common Properties, General page, change OCE_OrdersAX to **OCE_TestClient** in the Assembly Name and Root Namespace text boxes, as shown here, and click OK.

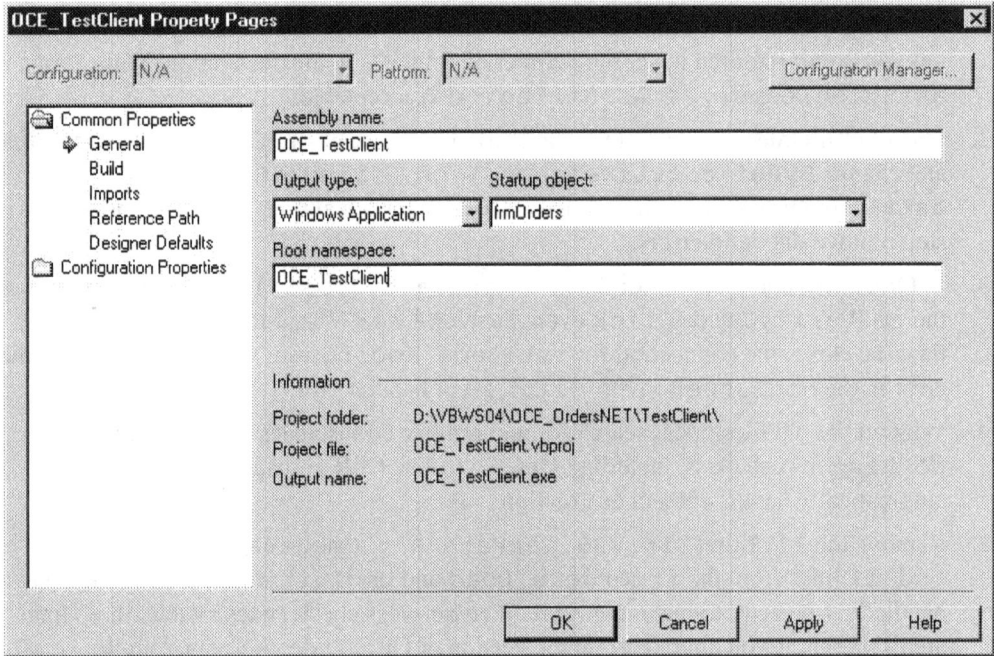

TIP

The Configuration Properties, Optimizations page has an Enable Optimizations check box. Marking this check box causes the compiler to reduce the size of the output file and improves execution speed. The downside is that enabling compiler optimization rearranges your code, which interferes with debugging operations. Mark this check box only after you've completed testing the project.

Upgrading ActiveX DLLs to Visual Basic .NET Components

Migrating ActiveX components to Visual Basic .NET follows the same course as upgrading the client. The number of upgrade warnings and errors depends on the quality of the code and complexity of the component, but you usually receive fewer items in the component's Task List. The following sections describe how to upgrade and test COM components using the four COM DLLs of the OCE_OrderAX.vbp project as examples.

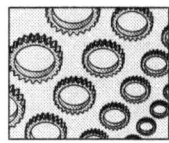

NOTE

Unlike Visual Basic 6.0, you can include XML Web service component projects in the client solution. Visual Studio .NET doesn't cause the XML Web service instantiation problems that occur from including ActiveX DLL projects in a Visual Basic 6.0 project group that contains the client project. It's good design practice, however, to create a separate solution that contains the projects for all upgraded components.

Creating a Solution Containing the Upgraded ActiveX DLLs

Visual Studio .NET solutions, like Visual Basic 6.0 project groups, contain multiple related projects. The advantages of grouping projects in a solution are easy access to individual components of member projects and the capability to rebuild all member projects with a single F5 keystroke. This example's Services.sln solution contains all upgraded Visual Basic .NET components and, ultimately, ASP.NET projects for XML Web services.

Here's the drill for upgrading the four Visual Basic 6.0 components to Visual Basic .NET:

1. Close the client solution, choose File | Open | Project, and double-click OmegaBank.vbp to start the Upgrade Wizard. Click Next.

2. The Wizard proposes to create a DLL and offers the option to generate default interfaces for all public classes. Select the check box, and click Next.

3. Specify a location parallel to the client project for the component, **D:\VBWS04\OCE_OrdersNET\TestServices\OmegaBank** for this example, click OK to confirm the new folder, and click Next to complete the upgrade.

4. Check the _UpgradeReport page for errors and warnings. Upgrading the OmegaBank project generates a single warning about use of `IsNull()`, which you can disregard. The Task List shows only a single ToDo element.

5. Change the name of the solution to **TestServices**, and press CTRL-SHIFT-B to build the solution and save the solution file as **TestServices.sln** in the \VBWS04\OCE_OrdersNET\ TestServices folder. You use this folder because the solution will contain all upgraded component projects.

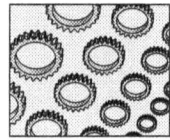

NOTE

If you press F5 to run the project, you receive a "nocando" message. Runtime tests require a test client to instantiate the object and invoke its methods.

6. Choose File | Add Project | Add Existing Project to open the Add Existing Project dialog, double-click AlphaDist.vbp, click Next, and repeat steps 2 through 4, but change OmegaBank to **AlphaDist** in step 3.

7. Repeat steps 2 through 4 and Step 6 for BetaDist and GammaDist, if you have the patience.

TIP

You can continue to use the COM versions of BetaDist and GammaDist, if you want to save some time. If you don't upgrade these two components, don't change the references to them in the later "Changing Client References to Upgraded Components" section.

8. Press CTRL-SHIFT-B to build and save the entire solution.

Building the four components creates a DLL file in the …\bin folder of each assembly. Unlike Visual Basic 6.0, building COM-compatible .NET components doesn't register the type libraries of the DLLs. One of the primary advantages of the .NET Framework is the elimination of DLL hell by eliminating reliance on the Windows Registry.

Defeating Evil Type Coercion in Your Components

Setting `Option Strict On` is the first step in preparing your upgraded component code to meet full .NET standards. The plethora of errors that occur when you first build an upgraded component are most commonly caused by Visual Basic's Evil Type Coercion (ETC) "feature." The Visual Basic 6.0 source code for the four components minimizes type-coercion errors by applying `CType` functions to conform `Recordset` property values of the `Variant` type to the appropriate Visual Basic 6.0 data types in preparation for upgrading.

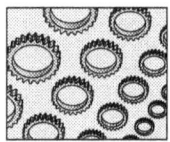

NOTE

Type-coercion errors in the four components of the Services solution in the \OCE_OrdersNET folder have been corrected and `Option Strict` is set to `On`.

To track down and fix type-coercion errors in your components, change `Option Strict Off` to `Option Strict On` in the .vb file of each component and then build the component. The Task List reports the errors and provides the line number of the statement in which each error occurs. Task List items disappear as you correct the errors. If you have more than one component in a solution, start with the first project and continue with the others; don't turn strict type checking on for all components at once.

Changing to `Option Strict On` can cause side effects, which result in runtime errors that don't throw exceptions. An example is the use of the `RecordCount` argument when executing SQL statements with `ADODB.Connection` and `ADODB.Command` objects. For example, the `OmegaBank.VerifyOrHold` method contains the following code to add a credit-card hold record to the Transactions table:

```
strSQL = "INSERT Transactions(MerchantID, Reference, CardNumber, " & _
    "TransactionDate, TransactionTypeID, Amount) " & "VALUES(" & _
    CStr(lngMerchantID) & ", " & CStr(lngRefNum) & ", '" & _
    strCardNumber & "', '" & strDateTime & "', 31, " & _
    CStr(curTransactAmt) & ")"
cnnVerify.Execute(strSQL, lngReccnt, ADODB.CommandTypeEnum.adCmdText)
If lngReccnt = 1 Then
    strSQL = "SELECT TransactionID FROM Transactions " & _
        "WHERE Reference = " & CStr(lngRefNum) & _
        " AND TransactionDate = '" & strDateTime & "'"
    rstVerify = cnnVerify.Execute(strSQL, , ADODB.CommandTypeEnum.adCmdText)
    With rstVerify
      If .EOF Then
        VerifyOrHold = CStr(lngRefNum) & _
            " Error: Unable to apply hold (99)"
      Else
        lngTransactID = CInt(.Fields(0).Value)
        VerifyOrHold = CStr(lngRefNum) & " Hold on " & _
        Format(-curTransactAmt, "$#,##0.00") & _
            " applied by TRID " & CStr(lngTransactID) & " (12)"
      End If
      .Close()
    End With
Else
    VerifyOrHold = CStr(lngRefNum) & " Error: Unable to apply hold (99)"
End If
```

The Task List reports "Option Strict On disallows implicit conversions from 'System.Object' to 'Integer'." The most obvious correction is to change `lngReccnt` to `CInt(lngReccnt)` in the `cnnVerify.Execute…` line of the preceding snippet, and remove the `CInt` data type conversion function from the succeeding line. Coercing the data type to `Integer` solves the build error. The `Execute` method, however, returns 0 regardless of whether the insert succeeds, and the function always returns an error message.

The solution to this sneaky problem, which you're likely to encounter in any code that uses the `RecordCount` argument, is to change `Dim lngReccnt As Integer` in the Declarations section to **`Dim lngReccnt As Object`** and `If lngReccnt = 1` back to **`If CInt(lngReccnt) = 1`**.

Changing Client References to Upgraded Components

Testing upgraded components requires replacing the reference to the COM DLL with a reference to the component's assembly. The .NET Framework lets you add references in .NET applications to .NET components without interacting with the Registry. You add a reference to the component project's DLL on the Projects page tab of the client application's Add References dialog.

Following is the procedure for adding project references to a client application, in this case, the OCE_OrdersAX test client you upgraded in the earlier sections:

1. Expand the References node of the client project, and delete the reference(s) to the original ActiveX component(s): AlphaDist, BetaDist, GammaDist, and OmegaBank, for this example.

TIP

Don't delete the BetaDist or GammaDist references if you didn't upgrade the components.

2. Choose Tools | Add Reference to open the Add Reference dialog.

3. Click the Browse button to open the Select Component dialog, which accepts .dll, .tlb, .olb, .ocx, and .exe files in the …\bin folder of existing projects.

4. Navigate to the …\bin folder of the component you want to reference and double-click the .dll file, AlphaDist.dll, in the \VBWS04\OCE_OrdersNET\TestServices\AlphaDist\bin folder for this example, to add the file to the Selected Components list.

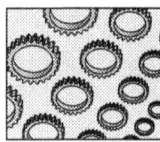

NOTE

Be sure to select the components you upgraded in the …\TestServices folder.

5. Repeat step 4 for each additional component to add: BetaDist, GammaDist, and OmegaBank, for this example. (See Figure 4-2.)

6. Click OK to add the reference(s) to the client project.

7. In Solution Explorer, right-click the item for the new reference, choose Properties to open its Properties window if necessary, and verify that the Path value points to the path of the added reference, as shown here. After checking all the replaced references, close the Properties window.

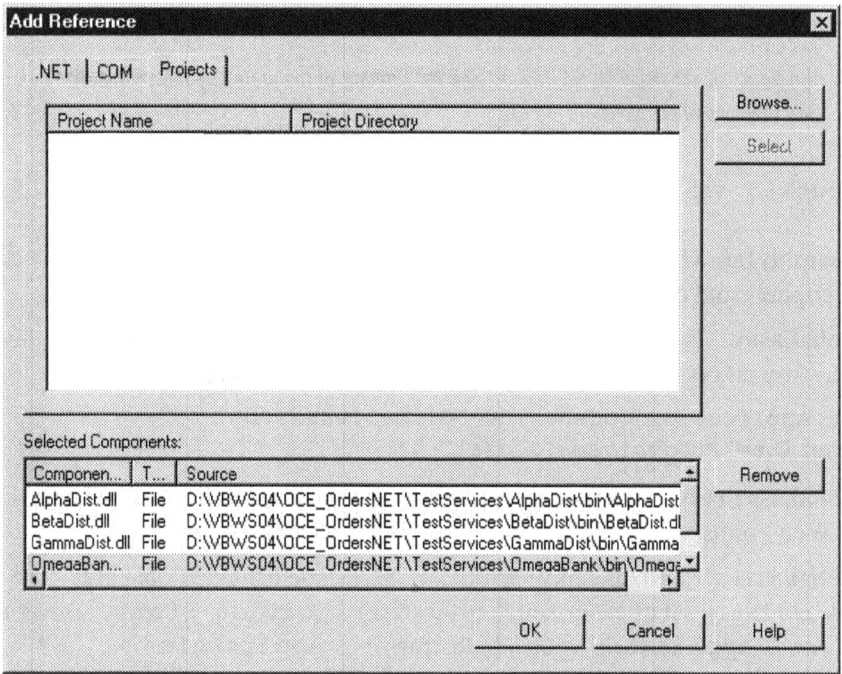

Figure 4-2   *Add references to the components' DLL files on the Projects page of the Add Reference dialog.*

8.   Build and run the project to test the new references.

The upgraded OCE_Orders client uses the new references if you don't select the Use XML Web Services check box. Services remain COM-based until you complete the next five sections, which describe how to create, test, and relocate ASP.NET XML Web services from upgraded COM components.

Creating ASP.NET Web Services from Imported Component Code

The "ASP.NET Pages and COM-Based XML Web Services" section in Chapter 1 briefly introduced you to generating XML Web services with the ASP.NET Web Services project template. The template automatically creates the files required to support a new XML Web service. All you need to do is add the Visual Basic .NET code to provide the services methods and build the project. Upgraded Visual Basic 6.0 code that runs properly in a component class is almost certain to produce a functioning ASP.NET service.

TIP

Use Notepad, not Visual Studio .NET, to view the contents of the preceding files. Some file types generate new solutions when opened in the IDE.

The ASP.NET Web Services template generates the following files:

▶ **AssemblyInfo.vb**   Holds optional information about the assembly, such as its title, description, and copyright information.

▶ **Global.asax**   Is the counterpart of ASP's Global.asp file. It contains only the following processing directive that points to the Global.asax.vb file:

```
<%@ Application Codebehind="Global.asax.vb" _
Inherits="ProjectName.Global" %>
```

▶ **Global.asax.resx**   Is a template resource file that contains an XSD schema document for Web Forms.

▶ **Global.asax.vb**   Holds the Visual Basic .NET code behind Global.asax. The template code contains a set of event-handler stubs: `Application_Start`, `Session_Start`, `Application_BeginRequest`, `Application_AuthenticateRequest`, `Application_Error`, `Session_End`, and `Application_End`. You declare application-level (global) variables in this file.

▶ *ProjectName*.**vbproj**   Is the standard project file for all Visual Basic .NET projects.

▶ *ProjectName*.**vbproj.webinfo**   Stores the URL for *ProjectName*.vbproj in the following format:

```
<Web URLPath = "http://localhost/ProjectName/ProjectName.vbproj" />
```

▶ *ProjectName*.**vsdisco**   Is the Disco[very] file for the project. In the Add Web Reference dialog box, you search for these files to create a list of local .asmx files. The Disco file is identical for all ASP.NET Web services.

▶ **Service1.asmx**   Is the default name for the ASP.NET Web page and its embedded WSDL file. This file contains the `WebService processing directive`:

```
<%@ WebService Language="vb" Codebehind="Service1.asmx.vb" _
Class="ProjectName.Service1" %>
```

▶ **Service1.asmx.resx**   Is a resource schema that's identical to Global.asax.resx.

▶ **Service1.asmx.vb**   Holds the Visual Basic .NET code behind Service1.asmx.

▶ **Web.config**   Is an XML configuration document, which stores processing directives for debugging, custom error messages, authentication, authorization, trace logging, session state, and globalization.

Only the AssemblyInfo.vb, *ServiceName*.asmx, *ServiceName*.vsdisco, Global.asax, and Web.config files appear in Solution Explorer. Choosing Project | Show All Files doesn't add items for resource files or the Service1.asmx.vb file to Solution Explorer. Renaming the project or .asmx file in Solution Explorer or the class name in *ServiceName*.asmx.vb automatically updates the corresponding files.

Adding ASP.NET XML Web Services and Copying Method Code

Creating ASP.NET XML Web services from Visual Basic .NET code is a simple point-and-click, copy-and-paste exercise. The entire process takes fewer than five minutes for a service, regardless of the number of methods the service supports or the complexity of the code that implements the methods.

In this example, you copy and paste the Visual Basic .NET component code you upgraded earlier in the chapter to new Visual Basic .NET projects in the TestServices solution. Follow this procedure to add the ASP.NET XML Web services to the TestServices solution:

1. With the TestServices.sln solution open, choose File | Add Project | New Project to open the Add Project dialog.

2. Select the ASP.NET Web Service icon, and, for this example, replace WebService1 in the Location text box with **OmegaWS**. As you change the text, the entry in the disabled Name text box changes to match your service location.

3. Click OK to create a new IIS virtual directory named OmegaWS. By default, the template saves the files it generates in the \Inetpub\wwwroot\OmegaWS folder.

4. Change the Services1.asmx filename to a more descriptive name. In this case, use the same name as the WSDL file you generated with the SOAP Toolkit in Chapter 3: **OmegaBank.asmx**.

5. Right-click the OmegaBank.asmx item, choose View Code to open OmegaBank.asmx.vb, and change the namespace in the `<WebService(Namespace:= "http://tempuri.org/")>` line to a unique URI, **http://omegabank. com/ webservices/**, for this example.

6. Change the name of the class from `Service1` to **OmegaBank**.

7. Delete the commented code that creates a "Hello World" service. (See Figure 4-3.)

8. Replace the deleted code with Visual Basic .NET code that implements the services methods. For this example, copy the code for the `OmegaBank.VerifyOrHold` and `OmegaBank.ChargeOrCredit` functions in OmegaBank.vb and paste it below the `Web Services Designer Generated Code` line.

9. Prefix with `<WebMethod()>` each `Public Function` statement for the methods you want to expose to the XML Web service.

10. If function declarations include a trailing `Implements` statement, delete them. The two functions of OmegaBank.vb have `Implements` statements.

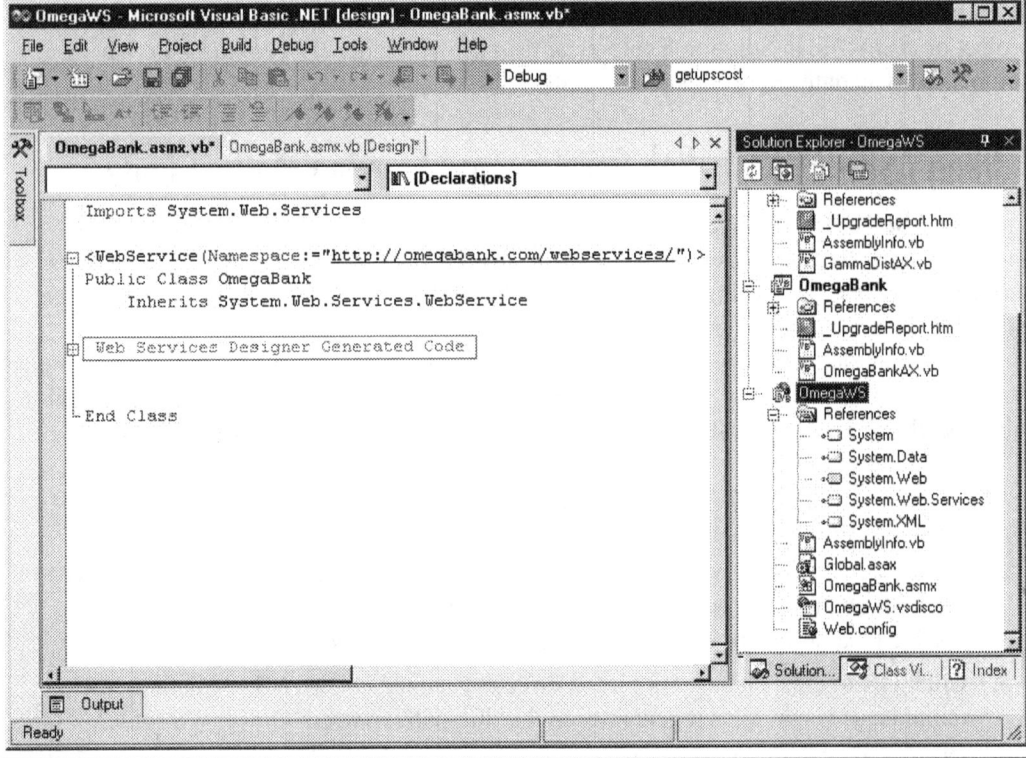

Figure 4-3   Modify the ASP.NET Web Services template code as shown here to prepare for importing the Visual Basic .NET code to implement the methods.

TIP

The ASP.NET Web Services template doesn't add `Option Explicit` and `Option Strict` directives as the first two lines of the ServiceName.asmx.vb file. The reason for this omission is probably to minimize the number of errors you incur when importing VBScript from ASP files. It's good programming practice to add these two lines to the top of each .asmx.vb file, even if you set `Option Strict` to `Off`.

11. If your component accesses databases with ADODB objects, choose Project | Add Reference, click the COM tab of the Add References dialog, and double-click Microsoft ActiveX Data Objects 2.7 Library. Click OK to add the reference.

TIP

Be sure to add the Microsoft ActiveX Data Objects 2.7 Library, not the Microsoft ActiveX Data Objects Recordset 2.7 Library or Microsoft ActiveX Data Objects (Multidimensional) 2.7 Library. Expand the Component Name column to display the entire reference name.

12. Press CTRL-SHIFT-B to build the solution.

13. Repeat steps 1 through 12 to add the AlphaWS, BetaWS, and GammaWS projects, replacing OmegaBank with **AlphaDist**, **BetaDist**, and **GammaDist**, respectively. See step 6 as an example.

TIP

After you modify and build the AlphaDist.asmx.vb code, copy that code to the clipboard and paste it to BetaDist.asmx.vb and GammaDist.asmx.vb. If you upgraded only AlphaWS, don't create BetaWS and GammaWS.

14. In addition to the ADODB reference you add in step 11, add a reference to Microsoft XML 4.0 for each distributor service.

15. Remove all instances of the VB6. prefix of Format functions.

16. Press CTRL-SHIFT-B to build the solution.

17. Finally, press CTRL-SHIFT-S to make sure you save all the new files.

Solution Explorer contains eight projects after you upgrade all components and create their ASP.NET counterparts.

NOTE

At this point, OmegaBank is technically a Web service, not an XML Web service, because neither of its methods return an XML document. The distributor services return XML documents if the blnXML parameter value is set to True.

Checking the .asmx File's WSDL Document

It's a good quality-control practice to verify that the WSDL document generated by the new *ServiceName*.asmx files expose the functions you designate as WebMethods. For example, if you forget to add the <WebMethod()> prefix to the Public Function line, the WSDL document contains only a few lines and is obviously defective.

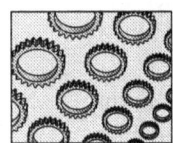

NOTE

If you opted to use the prefabricated Services.sln solution in the \OCE_OrdersNEW folder instead of following the instructions in the preceding sections to create the TestServices solution, you must create virtual directories for the four XML Web services in the ...OCE_OrdersNET\Services folder at this point. Use Internet Services Manager to create IIS virtual directories named OmegaWS, AlphaWS, BetaWS, and GammaWS. Specify the corresponding subfolders of ...OCE_OrdersNET\Services\ as the location of the files.

Adding a ?WSDL element to the URL for the *ServiceName*.asmx page displays its WSDL document. For example, typing **http://localhost/omegaws/omegabank.asmx?wsdl** as the address displays the WSDL document shown in Figure 4-4.

WSDL documents generated by .asmx files include everything *and* the kitchen sink. ASP.NET WSDL documents support MIME, HTTP GET, and HTTP POST protocols, in addition to conventional SOAP. A complete listing of the WSDL document for

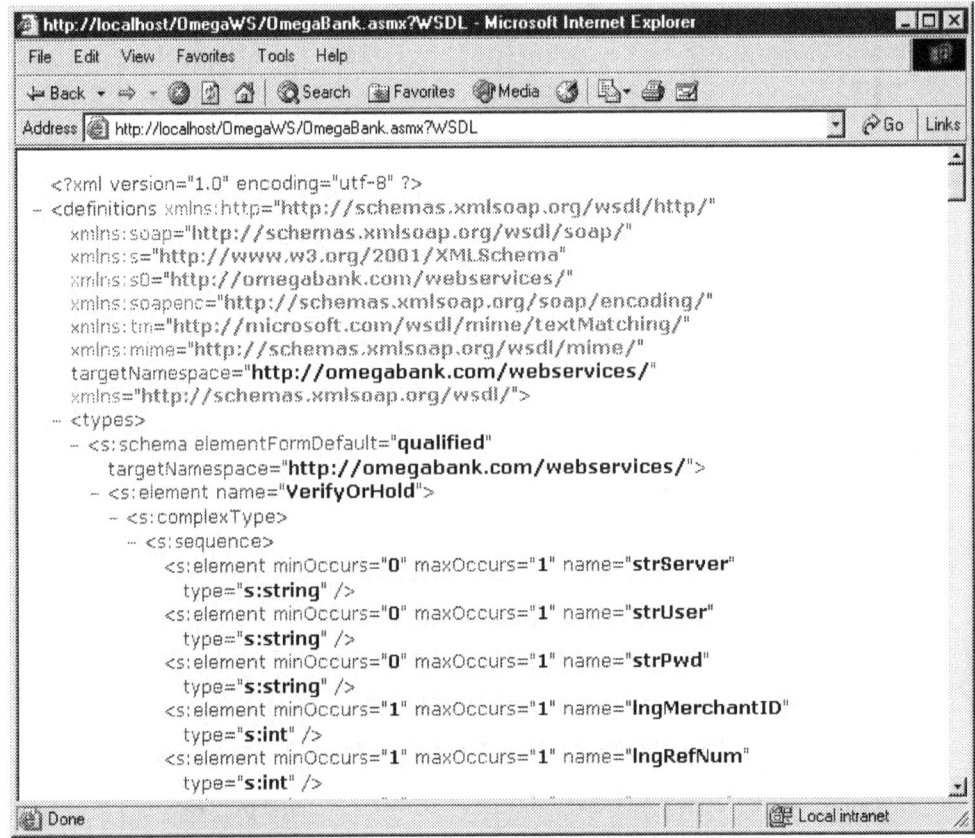

Figure 4-4   *The WSDL document generated by the OmegaBank.asmx file differs considerably from that generated by the SOAP Toolkit 2.0 Wizard.*

OmegaBank.asmx would consume nine pages. Therefore, only the most important SOAP-related differences between WSDL files created by the SOAP Toolkit 2.0 Wizard and the ASP.NET Web Methods template appear in the following listings. The comparison includes elements only for SOAP transport. As mentioned in Chapter 1, alternate transports don't qualify as XML Web services by this book's definition.

If you compare the contents of the two-page OmegaBank.WSDL file, listed in the "Fixing Wizard-Created WSDL Files" section in Chapter 3, with the WSDL document generated by OmegaBank.asmx, the most evident changes occur in the namespace declaration attributes of the `<definitions>` and `<schema>` elements. Most of the namespace declarations differ, and the `<s:schema>` element includes a full XSD schema for two OmegaBank methods. Here's the beginning of the WSDL document with the namespace and schema definitions:

```
<?xml version="1.0" encoding="utf-8" ?>
<definitions xmlns:http="http://schemas.xmlsoap.org/wsdl/http/"
    xmlns:soap="http://schemas.xmlsoap.org/wsdl/soap/"
    xmlns:s="http://www.w3.org/2001/XMLSchema"
    xmlns:s0="http://omegabank.com/webservices/"
```

```
      xmlns:soapenc="http://schemas.xmlsoap.org/soap/encoding/"
      xmlns:tm="http://microsoft.com/wsdl/mime/textMatching/"
      xmlns:mime="http://schemas.xmlsoap.org/wsdl/mime/"
      targetNamespace="http://omegabank.com/webservices/"
      xmlns="http://schemas.xmlsoap.org/wsdl/">
<types>
  <s:schema elementFormDefault="qualified"
    targetNamespace="http://omegabank.com/webservices/">
    <s:element name="VerifyOrHold">
      <s:complexType>
        <s:sequence>
          <s:element minOccurs="0" maxOccurs="1" name="strServer"
            type="s:string" />
          <s:element minOccurs="0" maxOccurs="1" name="strUser"
            type="s:string" />
          <s:element minOccurs="0" maxOccurs="1" name="strPwd"
            type="s:string" />
          <s:element minOccurs="1" maxOccurs="1" name="lngMerchantID"
            type="s:int" />
          <s:element minOccurs="1" maxOccurs="1" name="lngRefNum"
            type="s:int" />
          <s:element minOccurs="0" maxOccurs="1" name="strIssuer"
            type="s:string" />
          <s:element minOccurs="0" maxOccurs="1" name="strCardNumber"
            type="s:string" />
          <s:element minOccurs="0" maxOccurs="1" name="strCardName"
            type="s:string" />
          <s:element minOccurs="0" maxOccurs="1" name="strZipCode"
            type="s:string" />
          <s:element minOccurs="0" maxOccurs="1" name="strExpDate"
            type="s:string" />
          <s:element minOccurs="1" maxOccurs="1" name="curTransactAmt"
            type="s:decimal" />
          <s:element minOccurs="1" maxOccurs="1" name="blnApplyHold"
            type="s:boolean" />
          <s:element minOccurs="1" maxOccurs="1" name="blnUseWS"
            type="s:boolean" />
        </s:sequence>
      </s:complexType>
    </s:element>
```

```xml
          <s:element name="VerifyOrHoldResponse">
            <s:complexType>
              <s:sequence>
                <s:element minOccurs="0" maxOccurs="1" name="VerifyOrHoldResult"
type="s:string" />
              </s:sequence>
            </s:complexType>
          </s:element>
          <s:element name="ChargeOrCredit">
            <s:complexType>
              <s:sequence>
                <s:element minOccurs="0" maxOccurs="1" name="strServer"
                  type="s:string" />
                <s:element minOccurs="0" maxOccurs="1" name="strUser"
                  type="s:string" />
                <s:element minOccurs="0" maxOccurs="1" name="strPwd"
                  type="s:string" />
                <s:element minOccurs="1" maxOccurs="1" name="lngMerchantID"
                  type="s:int" />
                <s:element minOccurs="1" maxOccurs="1" name="lngRefNum"
                  type="s:int" />
                <s:element minOccurs="0" maxOccurs="1" name="strCardNumber"
                  type="s:string" />
                <s:element minOccurs="1" maxOccurs="1" name="lngRelTransactID"
type="s:int" />
                <s:element minOccurs="1" maxOccurs="1" name="curTransactAmt"
                  type="s:decimal" />
                <s:element minOccurs="1" maxOccurs="1" name="blnReleaseHold"
                  type="s:boolean" />
                <s:element minOccurs="1" maxOccurs="1" name="blnCredit"
                  type="s:boolean" />
                <s:element minOccurs="1" maxOccurs="1" name="blnUseWS"
                  type="s:boolean" />
              </s:sequence>
            </s:complexType>
          </s:element>
          <s:element name="ChargeOrCreditResponse">
            <s:complexType>
              <s:sequence>
```

```
        <s:element minOccurs="0" maxOccurs="1"
          name ="ChargeOrCreditResult" type="s:string" />
      </s:sequence>
    </s:complexType>
  </s:element>
  <s:element name="string" nillable="true" type="s:string" />
</s:schema>
</types>
<!-- Many more pages -->
</definitions>
```

The ASP.NET template adds `<s:complexType>` subelements to `<MethodNameResponse>` elements despite the fact that the response message is an XSD `simpleType`.

Adding schemas for the methods simplifies SOAP `<message>` elements by substituting a reference to the schema element for the individual `<part name='paramName' type ='xsd:dataType' />` of the Toolkit's WSDL file., as illustrated by the following fragment:

```
<message name="VerifyOrHoldSoapIn">
  <part name="parameters" element="s0:VerifyOrHold" />
</message>
<message name="VerifyOrHoldSoapOut">
  <part name="parameters" element="s0:VerifyOrHoldResponse" />
</message>
<message name="ChargeOrCreditSoapIn">
  <part name="parameters" element="s0:ChargeOrCredit" />
</message>
<message name="ChargeOrCreditSoapOut">
  <part name="parameters" element="s0:ChargeOrCreditResponse" />
</message>
```

HTTP `GET` and `POST` transports don't benefit from the preceding simplification. These transports require a `<part>` element for each argument.

`<PortName>` elements no longer require the `parameterOrder` attribute values, because the `<s:sequence>` subelements of the schema define the parameter sequence, as illustrated by this fragment:

```
<portType name="OmegaBankSoap">
  <operation name="VerifyOrHold">
    <input message="s0:VerifyOrHoldSoapIn" />
    <output message="s0:VerifyOrHoldSoapOut" />
  </operation>
  <operation name="ChargeOrCredit">
    <input message="s0:ChargeOrCreditSoapIn" />
    <output message="s0:ChargeOrCreditSoapOut" />
```

```
    </operation>
</portType>
```

Another major difference from the Toolkit's WSDL file is substitution of document/literal style for RPC/encoded style messaging in the `<binding>` elements, as this snippet illustrates:

```
<binding name="OmegaBankSoap" type="s0:OmegaBankSoap">
  <soap:binding transport="http://schemas.xmlsoap.org/soap/http"
      style="document" />
    <operation name="VerifyOrHold">
      <soap:operation soapAction="http://omegabank.com/_
          webservices/VerifyOrHold" style="document" />
      <input>
        <soap:body use="literal" />
      </input>
      <output>
        <soap:body use="literal" />
      </output>
    </operation>
    <operation name="ChargeOrCredit">
      <soap:operation soapAction="http://omegabank.com/_
          webservices/ChargeOrCredit" style="document" />
      <input>
        <soap:body use="literal" />
      </input>
    <output>
      <soap:body use="literal" />
    </output>
  </operation>
</binding>
```

Instead of pointing to a WSDL file, the `<soap:address>` element's `location` attribute specifies the *ServiceName*.asmx file, as shown in the following fragment at the end of the WSDL document:

```
<service name="OmegaBank">
  <port name="OmegaBankSoap" binding="s0:OmegaBankSoap">
    <soap:address location="http://localhost/OmegaWS/OmegaBank.asmx" />
  </port>
  <!-- Elements for HTTP ports removed -->
</service>
```

The `System.Web.Services.Protocols` namespace provides access to objects for all supported transports. One of the namespace's more useful objects is `SOAPException`, which provides customized error handling for client applications. Chapter 7 shows you how to take advantage of `System.Web.Services` objects to customize your XML Web services.

Adding XML Web Service Descriptions

Other developers who use your XML Web services need documentation to describe the purpose of the service and its methods, method parameters, and return document format or schema. If you decide to advertise your XML Web services in the public UDDI registries, a complete and accurate description of each service is essential.

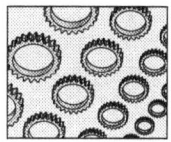

NOTE

There's no rule against adding marketing material to the description, but excessive hype is likely to turn off prospective users and, especially, developers.

You add descriptive text for your service as the value of the `Description` property of the `<WebService()>` and `<WebMethod()>` attributes. Unfortunately, you can't declare `String` variables, assign their values, and specify the name of the variable as the value of the `Description` property. The property requires what Microsoft calls a "constant expression" but most developers call a literal value. As you've undoubtedly discovered, the CLR doesn't support named constants. Thus, you must type the literal value of the description text within the `<WebServices()>` or `<WebMethod()>` attribute, which is not fun.

TIP

Use XHTML tags to format descriptive text for readability. Keep your formatting simple because unclosed tags or other XHTML transgressions bomb your WSDL document.

Rebuild the solution after adding each `Description` text block. If your text entry isn't perfect, you receive a barrage of build errors in the Task List. Figure 4-5 shows the start of the code in the OmegaBank.asmx.vb file from the ...\Services\OmegaWS folder, which has verbose descriptions for the `<WebServices()>` and `<WebMethod()>` attributes of all four services.

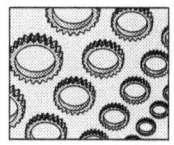

NOTE

You advertise the final version of these XML Web services in the Microsoft UDDI Registry when you complete the procedures described in Chapter 11. The descriptions of the prefabricated XML Web services and their methods contain more text than you're probably willing to type at this point.

The `Description` property values you type become the values of `<Documentation>` subelements of the `<service>` and `<portType>` elements of the WSDL document.

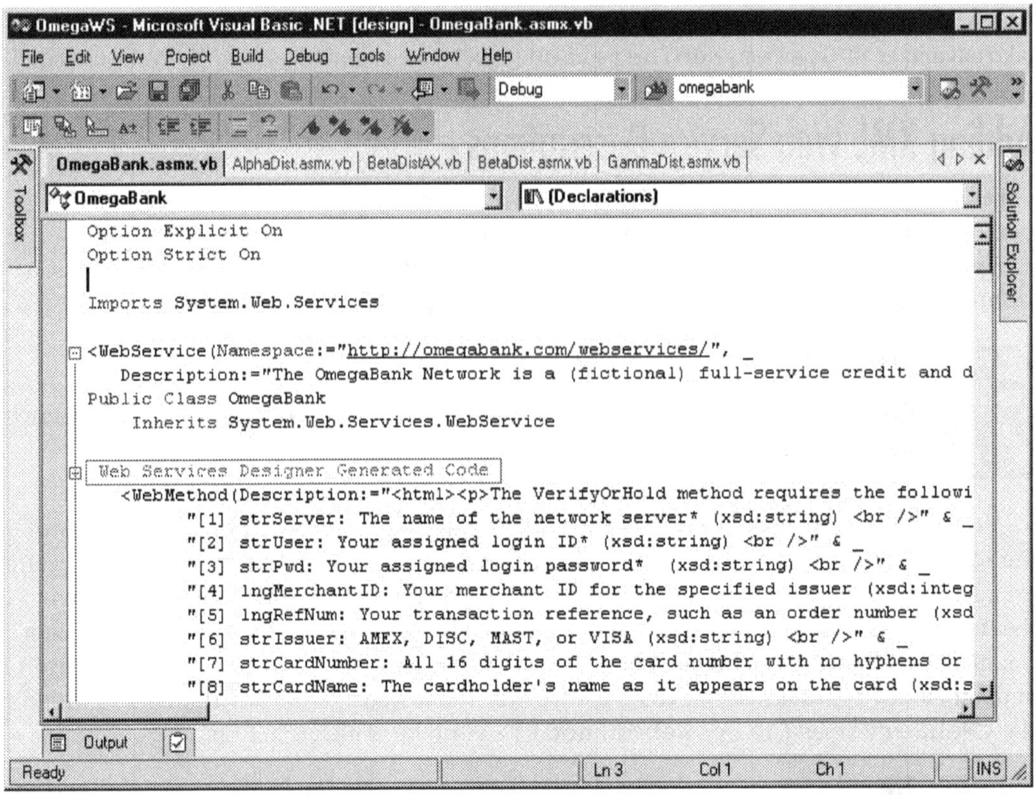

![Visual Basic .NET IDE showing OmegaBank.asmx.vb source code]

```
OmegaWS - Microsoft Visual Basic .NET [design] - OmegaBank.asmx.vb

File   Edit   View   Project   Build   Debug   Tools   Window   Help

                                              Debug          omegabank

OmegaBank.asmx.vb | AlphaDist.asmx.vb | BetaDistAX.vb | BetaDist.asmx.vb | GammaDist.asmx.vb

OmegaBank                                      (Declarations)

    Option Explicit On
    Option Strict On


    Imports System.Web.Services


  <WebService(Namespace:="http://omegabank.com/webservices/", _
      Description:="The OmegaBank Network is a (fictional) full-service credit and d
  Public Class OmegaBank
      Inherits System.Web.Services.WebService


    Web Services Designer Generated Code
      <WebMethod(Description:="<html><p>The VerifyOrHold method requires the followi
          "[1] strServer: The name of the network server* (xsd:string) <br />" & _
          "[2] strUser: Your assigned login ID* (xsd:string) <br />" & _
          "[3] strPwd: Your assigned login password*  (xsd:string) <br />" & _
          "[4] lngMerchantID: Your merchant ID for the specified issuer (xsd:integ
          "[5] lngRefNum: Your transaction reference, such as an order number (xsd
          "[6] strIssuer: AMEX, DISC, MAST, or VISA (xsd:string) <br />" & _
          "[7] strCardNumber: All 16 digits of the card number with no hyphens or
          "[8] strCardName: The cardholder's name as it appears on the card (xsd:s

Output

Ready                                         Ln 3        Col 1        Ch 1        INS
```

Figure 4-5   *Adding descriptions for your XML Web services and their methods requires typing the text within the **Description** property value.*

(See Figure 4-6.) Each <portType> element has its own copy of the WebMethod's Description text; long descriptions greatly increase the size of the WSDL document.

TIP

Take advantage of Microsoft Word's spelling checker when you write WebService and WebMethod descriptions for use by others, especially if you plan to advertise your Web services in a UDDI registry. Paste the text between the quotes of the Description:= ""property assignment statement, removing line feeds, if present.

The <WebService()> attribute has only a required Namespace property and an optional Description property. The <WebMethod()> attribute has several optional properties in addition to Description, such as EnableSession and TransactionOption. With the cursor within the <WebMethod()> declaration, press CTRL-F1 to open the "Using the Web Method Attribute" help page for a list of the attribute properties. For now, the default property values are adequate.

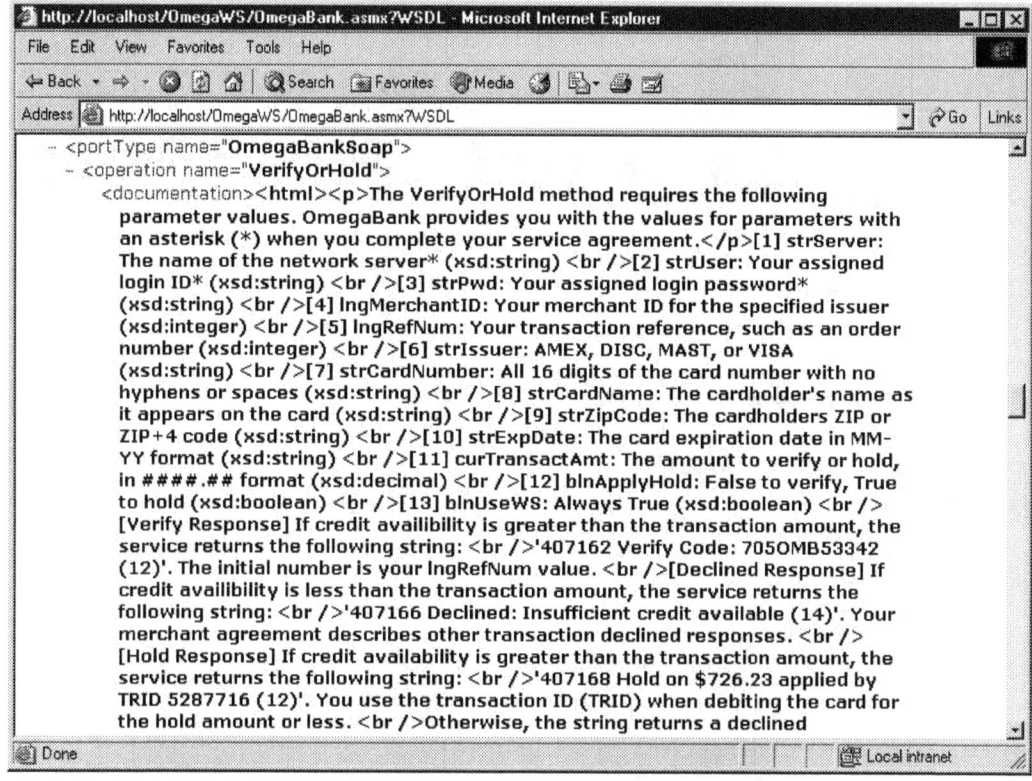

Figure 4-6   *The descriptions you add to the service and its methods generate*
<Documentation> subelements in the WSDL document.

Testing XML Web Services with Help Pages

Opening an .asmx page in Internet Explorer without adding the ?WSDL parameter displays
a help page, which has a Service Description link to the WSDL document. Each method
has a link to a form in which you enter parameter values to return a result string or XML
document. Figure 4-7 shows the help page for the OmegaDist XML Web service, which
has XHTML formatting applied. The link to the `ChargeOrCredit` method is below the
bottom of the window.

The AlphaDist XML Web service's `CheckStock` method is easier to test, because it has
fewer parameters than either of the two OmegaBank methods. Type **http://localhost/alphaws/
alphadist.asmx** as the address, and click the CheckStock link to open the CheckStock page,
which has a test form below the description. Type the values shown in Figure 4-8 in the
form, but substitute **(LOCAL)** (with parentheses) or your SQL Server instance name for
`OAKLEAF-MS10`. You can't use the default [LOCAL] (with brackets) server name with the
HTTP `POST` protocol; you receive an error message from the service if you try. Change the
`blnXML` value to `True`, and click Invoke to open a new page with an XML document as
the result string.

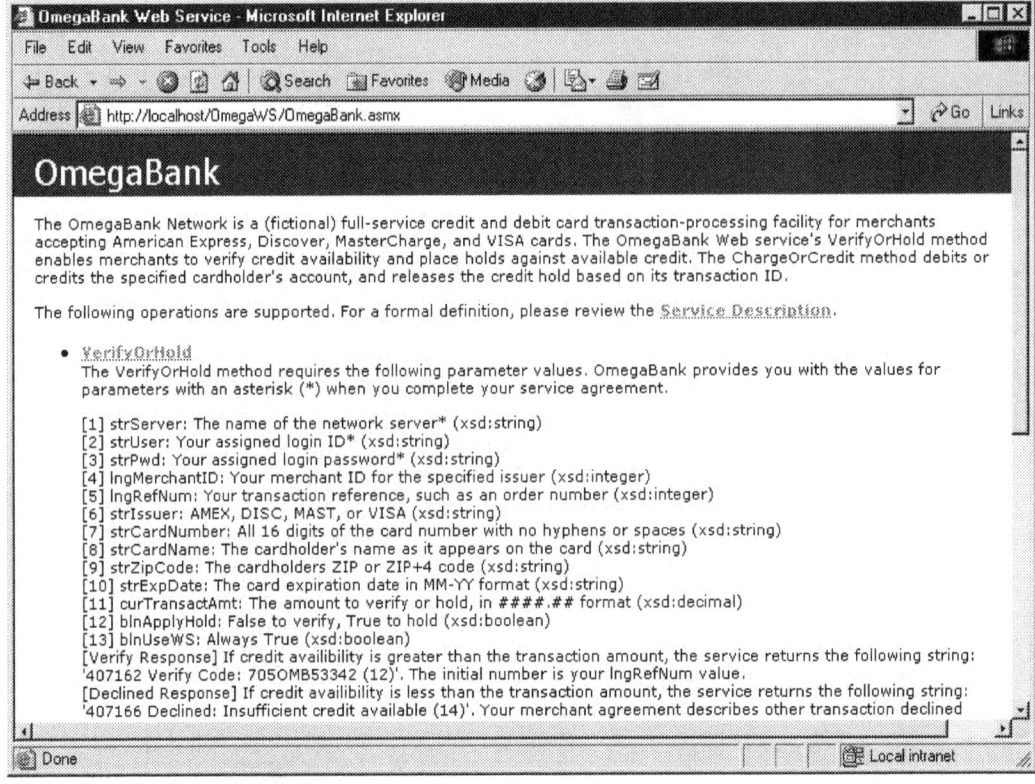

Figure 4-7 *XHTML formatting tags make complex .asmx help pages more readable.*

The ability of prospective users to give your .ASP.NET XML Web services a test drive is another benefit from migrating COM-based services to .NET. The test page also explains why Microsoft provides the HTTP GET protocol in the WSDL document. It's possible to type an XML document as a parameter value, but doing so is likely to be a frustrating and unrewarding exercise.

Moving or Copying ASP.NET Project Files to a New Location

The ability to move or deploy projects by the "XCOPY" method is another highly touted feature of Visual Studio .NET. The ASP.NET Web Services template generates project code in the \Inetpub\wwwroot*ProjectName* folder. For security reasons, most Web site administrators don't store code or any other production files in \Inetpub\wwwroot subfolders.

An example of redeploying project files is moving the TestServices solution's …WS projects to \VBWS04\OCE_OrdersNET\TestServices subfolders. Here's the process:

1. Close Visual Studio .NET.

2. Copy \Inetpub\wwwroot\OmegaWS and the three other …DistWS folders to the clipboard.

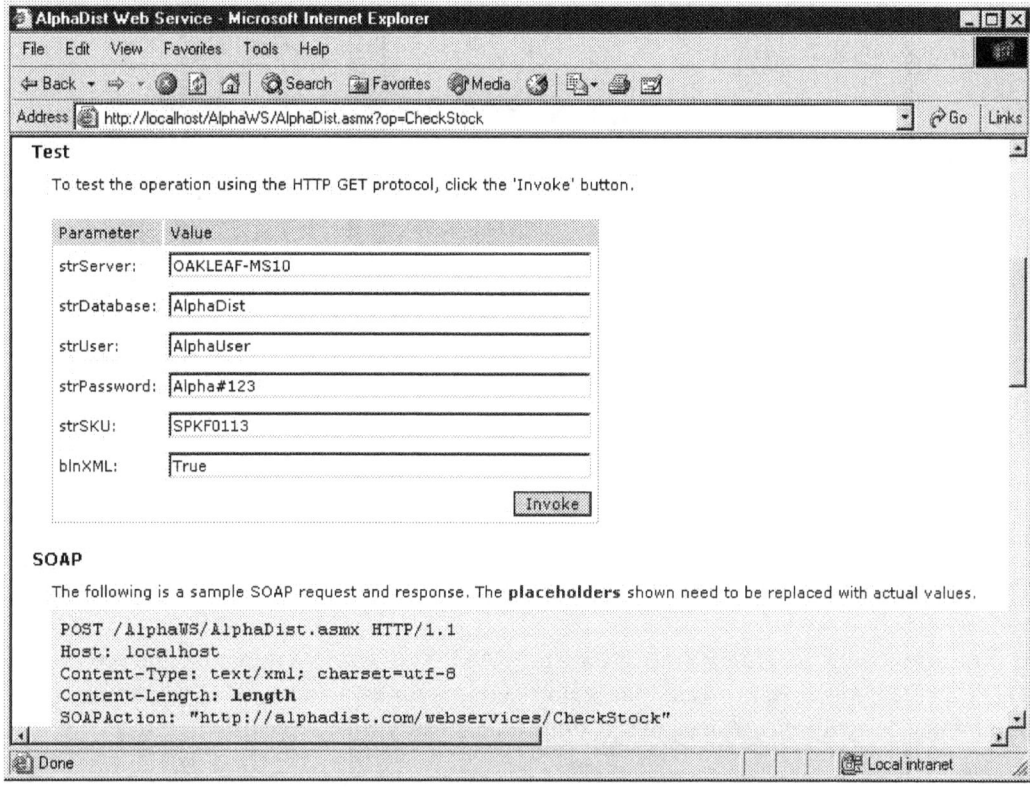

Figure 4-8   *Type parameter values for the method and click Invoke to test the XML Web service with the HTTP **POST** protocol.*

3. Paste the folders to \VBWS04\OCE_OrdersNET\TestServices.

4. Launch the Internet Services Manager, and delete the AlphaWS, BetaWS, GammaWS, and OmegaWS virtual directories that the template generated. Deleting the virtual directories moves the corresponding directories to the Recycle Bin.

TIP

If you receive an "access denied" message when attempting to delete the virtual directories, you probably need to reboot your server to remove locks on the DLL files. Stopping IIS doesn't release the locks, but running `iisreset` *at the command prompt usually works.*

5. Recreate the four virtual directories, specify the new \…WS subfolders as the location of the files, and accept the Wizard's default permissions.

6. When you relaunch Visual Studio .NET and open TestServices.sln, you receive a Web Access Failed dialog box.

7. Mark the Retry Using A Different Share Path option, as shown here, click the browse button, and type the path to the appropriate folder in the text box.

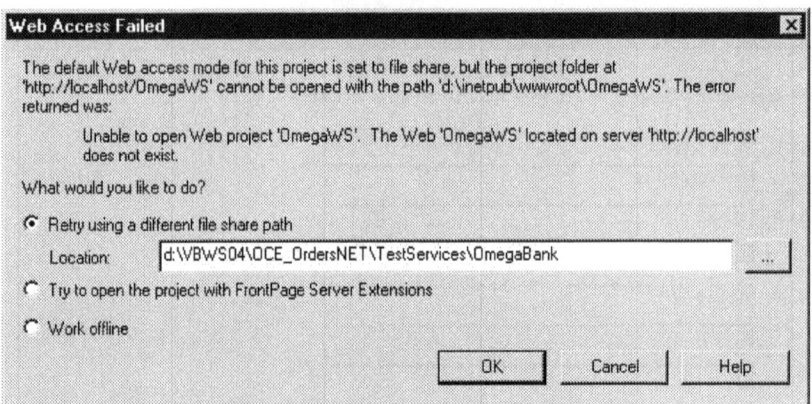

8. Repeat step 7 for each of the remaining three virtual directories.
9. Build and test the relocated XML Web services with their help pages.

You also use the preceding process to deploy ASP.NET services to production servers. This technique was used to create four remote services for the Orders_OCE project at http://www.oakleaf.ws/oce/omegaws/ and the three other virtual directories.

TIP

If your production server assigns fixed IP addresses to sites (most do) or the virtual directory hierarchy on your production server isn't the same as that of the development server, open the ProjectName.vbproj.webinfo file in Notepad. Alter the URL to correspond to your production virtual directory structure. Substitute the production server's IP address for `localhost`. Otherwise, you can't open the .asmx file to generate the WSDL document, nor can you open the ASP.NET project or add the project to a new solution you create on the server.

Migrating Visual Basic .NET Client Applications to Web References

A *Web Reference* is a proxy class that Visual Studio .NET generates for you automatically from the XML Web service's WSDL document or file. The proxy class accepts a method name and argument value(s) from the client and transforms the method call to a SOAP request message, if the service supports SOAP transport. Otherwise, the class uses HTTP POST or GET as the transport. The proxy class returns the response message to the client.

The proxy class for a Web reference is similar to the SOAP Toolkit's `SoapClient` object, but the properties and methods of the ASP.NET proxy class differ greatly. For example, ASP.NET proxy classes provide methods for asynchronous execution and properties to let you specify client credentials and certificates for secure XML Web services. Chapter 10 explains how to take advantage of asynchronous execution and methods to secure XML Web services.

The Add Web Reference dialog makes it easy to locate and add references to XML Web services. The process is even simpler than adding references to upgraded Visual Basic .NET class DLLs. Microsoft's proprietary Disco methodology generates the equivalent of a repository of ASP.NET services on your local Web server by searching for files with a .vsdisco extension and displaying links to these files in an Available References list. You click the link to the *ServiceName*.vsdisco file whose service you want to add, which displays its WSDL document and its description, if you added descriptive text for the service. Otherwise, only a list of methods appears.

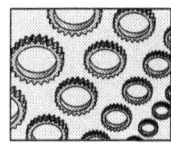

NOTE

The Add Web Reference dialog also lets you search the Microsoft production and test UDDI directories or type the URL to a remote .asmx or .wsdl file in the Address text box. This chapter covers adding local services and remote services from http://www.oakleaf.ws/oce/. You use the UDDI features in the Chapter 11 examples.

Clicking Add Reference adds to Solution Explorer a Web Reference node for the service you specify, creates a WebReferences folder and *ClassName* subfolder, and closes the Add Web Reference dialog. The default *ClassName* is *servername*1 (typically localhost1), but you can change the default value to a more descriptive name. The name you choose must be unique within the WebReferences folder.

The *ClassName* subfolder contains the following files:

▶ **ServiceName.wsdl**   Is the WSDL document generated by the *ServiceName*.asmx file persisted as a conventional WSDL file

▶ **ClassName.disco**   Is a copy of the service's .vsdisco file

▶ **Reference.map**   Contains the URLs required to display the service's WSDL and documentation

▶ **Reference.vb**   Contains code generated by the Visual Studio .NET designer to provide integrated debugging with the SOAP transport

Right-clicking Solution Explorer's *ClassName* node and choosing Upgrade Web Reference regenerates all the preceding files with any changes you've made to the services outside the client solution.

Adding Web References for Local .ASP.NET Services

With the aid of the Disco service, adding a Web reference to a local service took less than a minute in the RC-1 version. In practice, local XML Web services are uncommon. Production services that replace DCOM components are on intranet servers, not clients. The rationale of Web services is their capability to pass messages through firewalls in an Internet environment. Thus, adding local ASP.NET Web references to a client is a development-only exercise.

To add OCE_TestClient references to the four ASP.NET services you created in the preceding sections, do the following:

1. In the OCE_TestClient solution, choose Project | Add Web Reference to open the dialog.

2. The RC-1 version had a Web Services On Local Web Server link to generate a list of .vsdisco files from the local site's default.vsdisco file. (See Figure 4-9.)

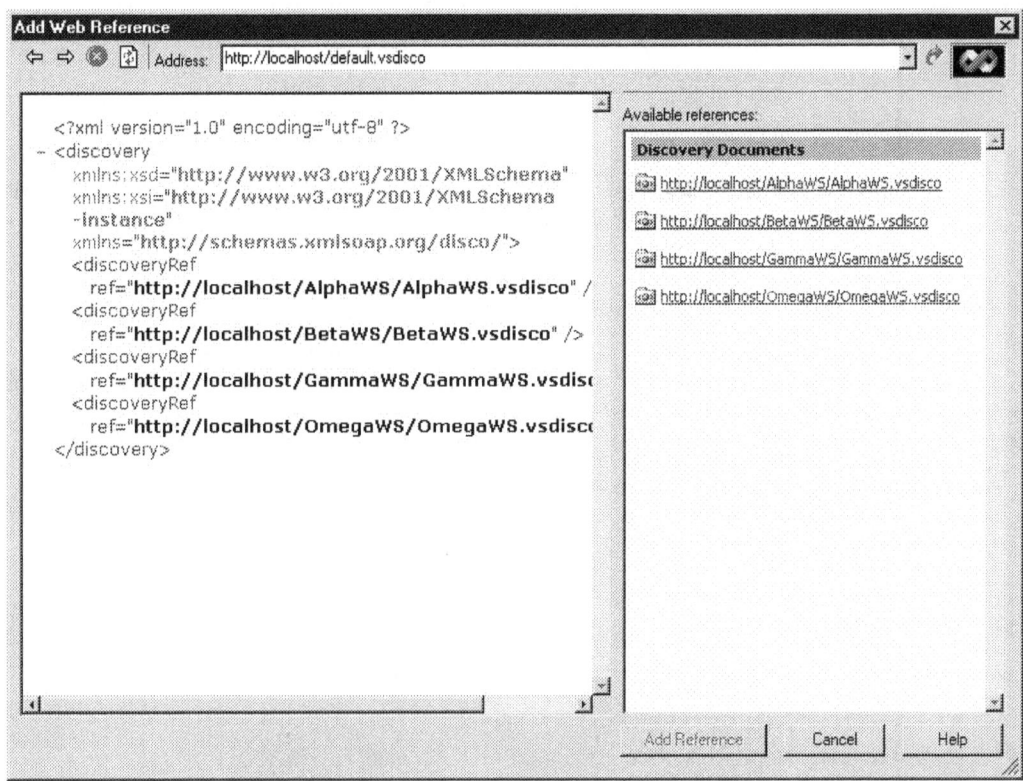

Figure 4-9   *In local Web server mode, pre-release versions of the Add Web Reference dialog box displayed a list of all .vsdisco files on your machine.*

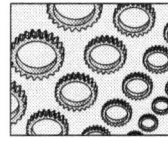

NOTE

Microsoft removed the Web Services On Local Web Server link from the February 13, 2002 release version of Visual Studio .NET. A Microsoft representative at the VSLive! conference in San Francisco stated that the reason for the removal is that the feature "failed to pass the final security tests." It's likely—but not guaranteed—that a secure version of the local Disco search feature will be included in a Visual Studio .NET service pack. In the meantime, you must type the full URL for the ServiceName.asmx file in the text box.

3. Click the AlphaWS.vsdisco link to display the contents of the service's .vsdisco file, and then click the View Contract link to display the .AlphaDist.asmx file's WSDL document.

4. If you added documentation for the service, its methods, or both, go back to the previous page and click View Documentation to display the text. (See Figure 4-10.) Clicking a method name link opens the test form page for the method.

5. Click Add Reference to add the reference to the AlphaWS XML Web service to Solution Explorer and close the dialog box to add the reference as localhost1.

6. In Solution Explorer, rename localhost1 to **AlphaWS**.

7. Repeat steps 1 through 6 for BetaWS, GammaWS, and OmegaWS.

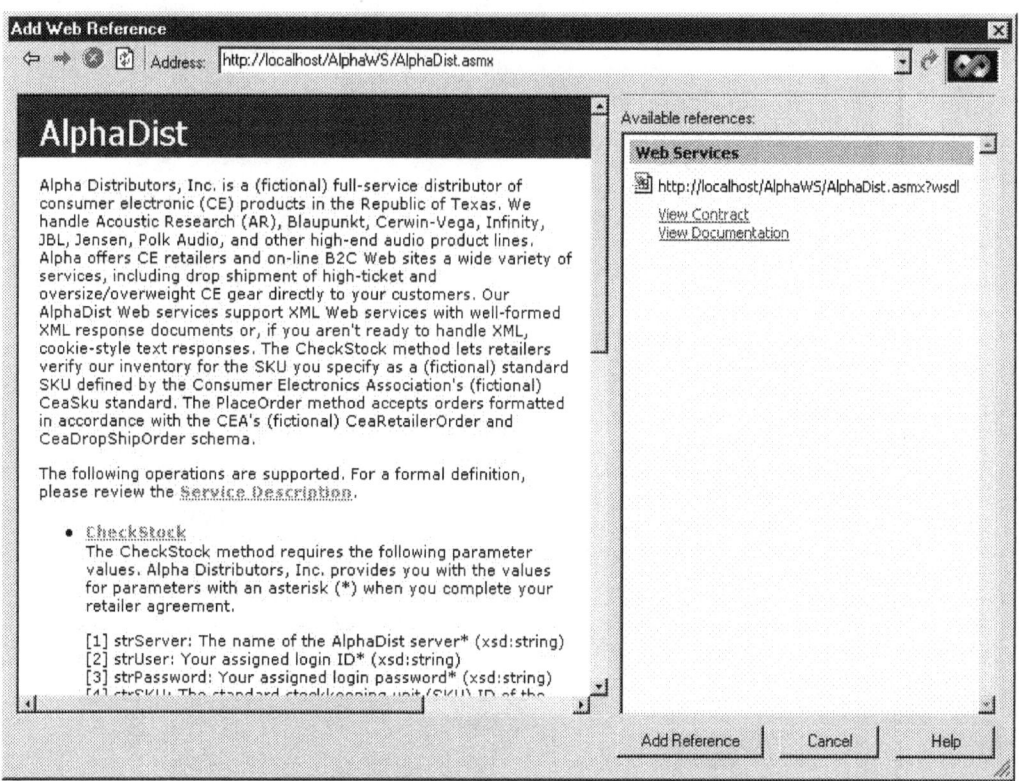

Figure 4-10   *Click the View Documentation link to display the text you added for service and method descriptions.*

Double-clicking the file items under Solution Explorer's Web References node displays their contents. If you add HTML formatting to your service or method descriptions, entities represent characters that are illegal in XML element values, such as < (<), > (&gt) and & (&), as illustrated in Figure 4-11.

Establishing Web References to Remote XML Web Services

Establishing references to remote XML Web services requires that you type the URL to an ASP.NET XML Web service's .asmx file or any other Web service's .wsdl file in the Add Web Reference's Address text box.

For example, typing **http://www.oakleaf.ws/oce/alphaws/alphadist.asmx** as the URL connects to the OakLeaf web site and displays the documentation page for the AlphaDist service. In this case, clicking Add Reference adds a reference with ws.oakleaf.www as the class name, which contorts the URL. You can't have duplicate class names in the Web References folder, so rename the reference to **AlphaWSRem** or the like. To prepare for the examples of the next section, add BetaWSRem, GammaWSRem, and OmegaWSRem references to the OCE_TestClient project.

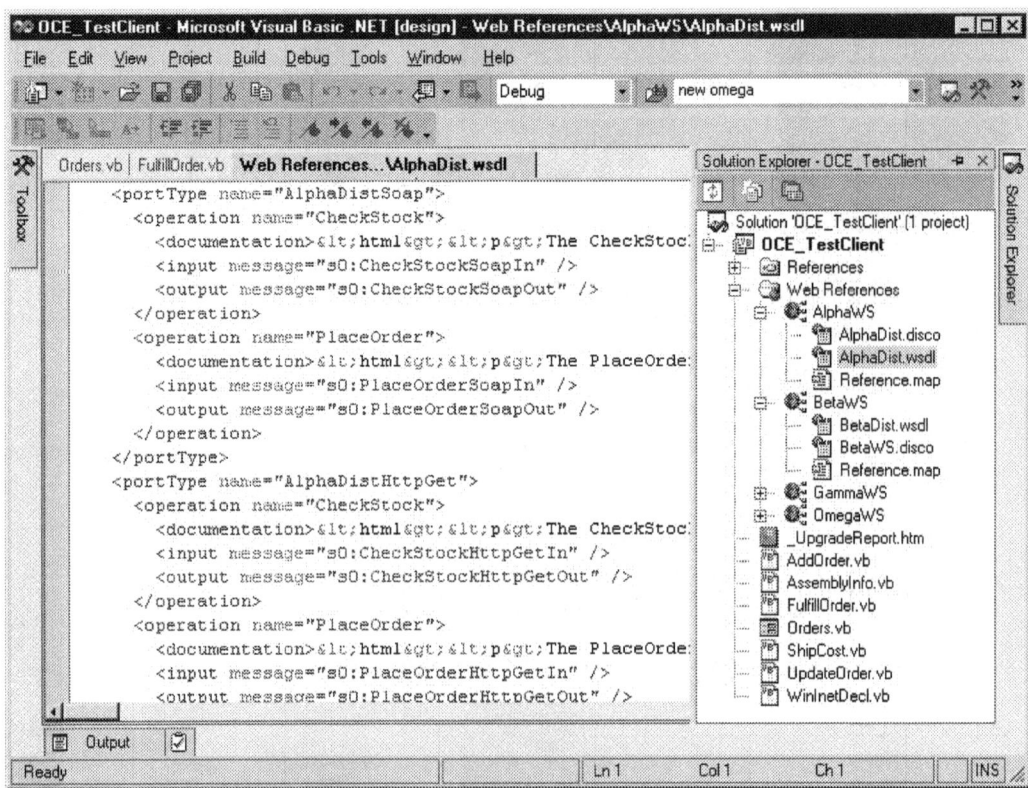

Figure 4-11   *The Web References node contains a subnode for each reference you add to the client project.*

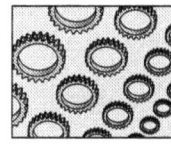

NOTE

The reasoning behind Microsoft's decision to scramble the site URL to create the namespace isn't clear.

To add a Web Reference to any other XML Web service, specify the URL for the WSDL file, such as **http://www.oakleaf.ws/alpha/alphadist.wsdl** for the Chapter 3 COM-based version. In this case, the reference's .disco file is missing because the SOAP Toolkit 2.0 Wizard doesn't generate a .disco file for the service. If you want to compare the performance of ActiveX and ASP.NET XML Web services, add AlphaWSCom and the other two distributor Web references for the remote COM components.

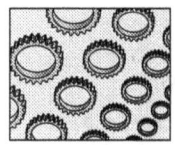

NOTE

The OCE_Client sample project contains the code to run all three types of XML Web services.

Replacing SoapClient with Web Reference Objects

One of the primary advantages of moving to ASP.NET XML Web services is that you treat a Web reference the same as any other .NET object, such as the `OmegaBank` and `AlphaDist` objects of the components that you upgraded early in this chapter. The Visual Basic .NET code to declare and instantiate ASP.NET XML Web service objects is identical to that for ActiveX or .NET components—you change only the object variable and class names. Web references handle all client-side SOAP operations under the covers.

Here are the two lines of generic code to complete an ASP.NET SOAP messaging session:

```
Dim objWebService As New ClassName.ServiceName
strResponse = objWebService.MethodName(typArgument1[, typArgument2[, …]])
```

Upgrading the OCE_TestClient Project to ASP.NET XML Web Services

The OCE_TestClient project and the .NET components you created in the preceding sections demonstrate the ease of moving from Visual Basic .NET components or `SoapClient` code to ASP.NET XML Web services. The following procedure replaces the `SoapClient` code:

1. In the TestClient solution, open the code for Orders.vb and FulfillOrder.vb.

2. Starting with Orders.vb, search with the All Open Document option selected for the three instances of `Dim objOmegaBank` and replace `MSSOAPLib.SoapClient()` with **OmegaWS.OmegaBank()**.

3. Delete or comment the `Call objOmegaBank.mssoapinit(strURL)` line. If your code includes optional `objOmegaBank.ClientProperty ("ServerHTTPRequest") = True` statements, delete or comment them.

4. Search for and comment or delete code that uses the SOAP `faultstring` property.

5. Press F5 to build and run the client, and then click Add Bulk Orders. Select the Use XML Web Services check box. Verify that the Action text box displays periodic "Invoice issued…" messages, which indicate that the two `OmegaBank` methods execute correctly. Click Halt Operation and Close Test Form.

6. In the `clsFulfillOrder.GetDistInventory` function, replace `Dim objSoapClient As New MSSOAPLib.SoapClient()` with the following three declarations:

```
Dim objAlphaWS As New AlphaWS.AlphaDist()
Dim objBetaWS As New BetaWS.BetaDist()
Dim objGammaWS As New GammaWS.GammaDist()
```

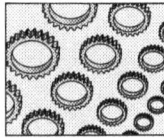

NOTE

Like the `SoapClient` code, you can use the same object with a different URL for each of the three distributors because the code for their XML Web services is identical. The only difference in the WSDL documents for these services is the value of the `<soap:location>` element. Web reference has a `URL` property that lets you specify the URL for the service at runtime. The later "Setting Remote XML Web Service URLs with Code" section discusses the pros and cons of dynamic URLs.

7. Move to the `Select Case` statement, delete or comment the `strServiceURL…` line, and copy the `astrResponse(bytDist, 2)…` line below the `Else` statement to below the `If blnUseWS Then` statement. Change `objAlphaInv` in the copied statement to **objAlphaWS**, and set the last argument to `True.`

CAUTION

If you don't change the `blnXML` argument value from `False` to `True`, successive operations in the `GetDistInventory` function fail, and the function returns `No`.

8. Repeat step 5 for `objBetaWS` and `objGammaWS`. (See Figure 4-12.)

9. Delete or comment all lines in the `If blnUseWS … End If` block below the `End Select` statement. Error handling for ASP.NET XML Web services differs greatly from that for `SoapClient` objects.

10. Repeat step 3 to verify your changes so far. Wait for the creation of at least a few orders having outsourced items to make sure that each XML Web service is working.

11. Repeat steps 4 through 7 for the `Select Case` block of the `SendPurchaseOrder` function, replacing `objDistNameOrder` with **objDistNameWS** in the three statement copies. Don't delete the `If Err.Number = 0 … End If` block in this case. Add a **strResponse = strXML** line above this block.

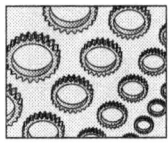

NOTE

The OCE_Client solution has additional references to DistNameWSRem and DistNameWSCom services on the OakLeaf Web site. These services enable performance comparisons of COM and ASP.NET remote XML Web services.

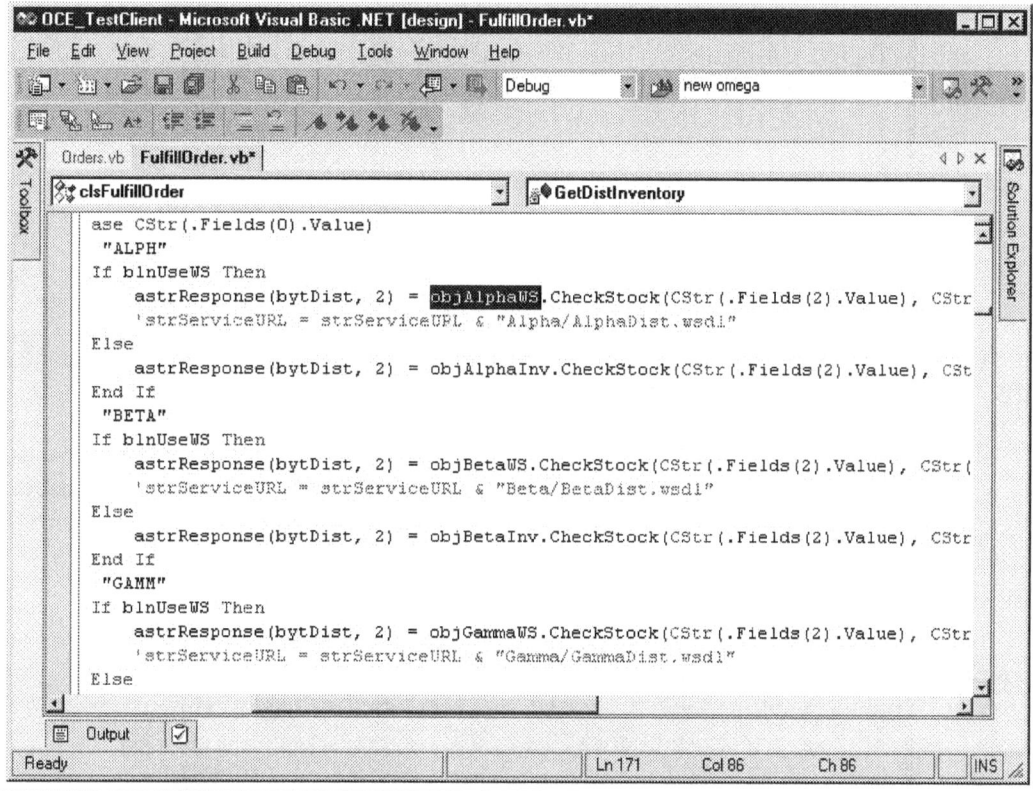

Figure 4-12   *The instructions to process SOAP messages are almost identical to those for calling Visual Basic .NET or ActiveX components.*

Setting Remote XML Web Service URLs with Code

XML Web services represent an evolving technology, and URLs for remote .asmx and .wsdl files are subject to change, often without notice. You can use one of the following three methods to update the URL for a Web reference that has moved:

1. Right-click the *ClassName* node, and choose Properties to open the Properties window for the service's Web reference, as shown here. Change the Web Reference URL to the new location.

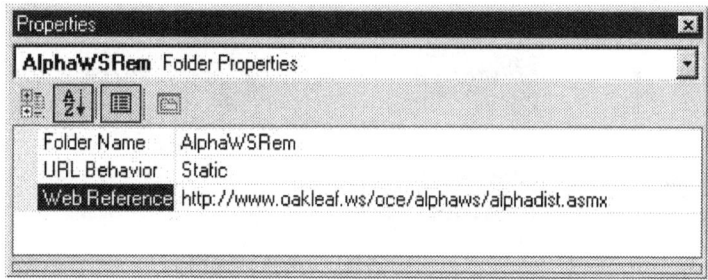

2. Select Dynamic as the URL Behavior property value, and specify the URL in the app.config file. Changing the AlphaWSRem Web reference to a dynamic URL adds the following document to the client's app.config file:

```
<configuration>
  <appSettings>
    <add key="OCE_Client.AlphaWSRem.AlphaDist"
        value="http://www.oakleaf.ws/oce/alphaws/alphadist.asmx"/>
  </appSettings>
</configuration>
```

3. Alter the `value=` URL to change to a new location without modifying your Visual Basic.NET code.

4. Change the value of the *ClassName*.Url property with Visual Basic .NET code.

All three approaches require that the locally stored WSDL files for the services be identical except for the value of the `<soap:address>` element. If the WSDL file has other differences, you receive a runtime error. For example, if you attempt to mix and match ASP.NET .asmx files and COM-based WSDL files that you create with the SOAP Toolkit, the following typical runtime error message replaces the expected SOAP response message:

```
WSDLReader: The operation requested in the Soap message with
soapAction http://omegabank.com/webservices/VerifyOrHold isn't
defined in the WSDL file. This may be because it is in the wrong
namespace or has incorrect case.
```

The OCE_Client solution's Orders.vb project includes code that uses the URL property to change the .asmx file for local and remote consumption of the OmegaBank service. Here's the sample snippet:

```
If blnUseWS Then
    If blnUseOakLeaf Then
        'Use OakLeaf's remote Web services
        strServer = "OAKLEAF-MS7"
        If blnUseCom Then
            'Use the COM-based component's WSDL file
            strVerify = comOmegaBank.VerifyOrHold(strServer, strNetUser, _
                        strNetPwd, 151203, lngOrderID, strCardType, _
                        strCardNumber, strCardName, strZipCode, strExpDate, _
curOrderTotal, False, blnUseWS)
        Else
            strURL = "http://www.oakleaf.ws/oce/omegaws/omegabank.asmx"
        End If
    Else
        strServer = strNetServer
        strURL = "http://localhost/omegaws/omegabank.asmx"
```

```
   End If
   If Not blnUseCom Then
      objOmegaBank.Url = strURL
      strVerify = objOmegaBank.VerifyOrHold(strServer, strNetUser, _
               strNetPwd, 151203, lngOrderID, strCardType, _
               strCardNumber, strCardName, strZipCode, strExpDate,
               curOrderTotal, False, blnUseWS)
   End If
Else …
```

Client code for the AlphaDist, BetaDist, and GammaDist services uses the corresponding Web references' static URL.

Changing the service URL in code is a shortcut that's usually limited to client test harnesses. The benefit is a single block of error-handling code to check for SOAP-related errors in multiple instances of the service, usually at different locations. The downside of changing the service URL with code is the inability to interactively debug the services whose URLs you change.

Debugging Local and Remote ASP.NET XML Web Services

The Visual Studio .NET debugging process for clients having ASP.NET Web references follows the same pattern as that for any other .NET component in your client application. Place a breakpoint on the method call for the service, and press F11 a few times until you finally step into the service's Visual Basic .NET or C# code. Alternatively, hold F11 down until the code document for the service opens. You can add breakpoints in the code document and then remove the method breakpoint in the client code to eliminate the need to step through the call stack.

Remote ASP.NET Service Debugging

You can also debug remote ASP.NET Web services that have debugging enabled, if you have the required credentials and permissions for the server. Following are the setup requirements for debugging an XML Web service running on a remote computer:

▶ Remote Debugging Components must be installed on the server. Visual Studio .NET installs the required components by default.

▶ You must have local Administrator privileges on the remote server, because the ASP.NET process (aspnet_wp.exe) runs under the local SYSTEM account.

▶ Your account must be a member of the local Debugger Users group. By default, the account you used to install Visual Studio .NET on the remote server and the IWAM_*SERVERNAME* account are the only members of this group.

TIP

The online help "Debugging ASP.NET Web Services" topic has more detailed information on how to debug remote XML Web services.

For the examples in this book, the OAKLEAF-MS10 server hosts the test clients and local XML Web services; the remote services run on OAKLEAF-MS7, which also hosts the OakLeaf Web site. Both servers are in the same local Windows 2000 domain (oakleaf.org), so Domain Admins credentials let you step through remote service code. Figure 4-13 illustrates a breakpoint in the remote `OmegaWSRem.VerifyOrHold` method on OAKLEAF-MS7, set from the local OCE_Client project running on OAKLEAF-MS10. You can stop debugging, make changes in the remote service code, and restart the debugging process. Expect a delay for the remote server to interact with the client-side copy of Reference.vb to set up the remote debugging process.

Turning Off Debugging of a Remote XML Web Service

Obviously, you don't want to permit anyone to run production services in debug mode. When you're ready to release your XML Web services for production use, change the Solution

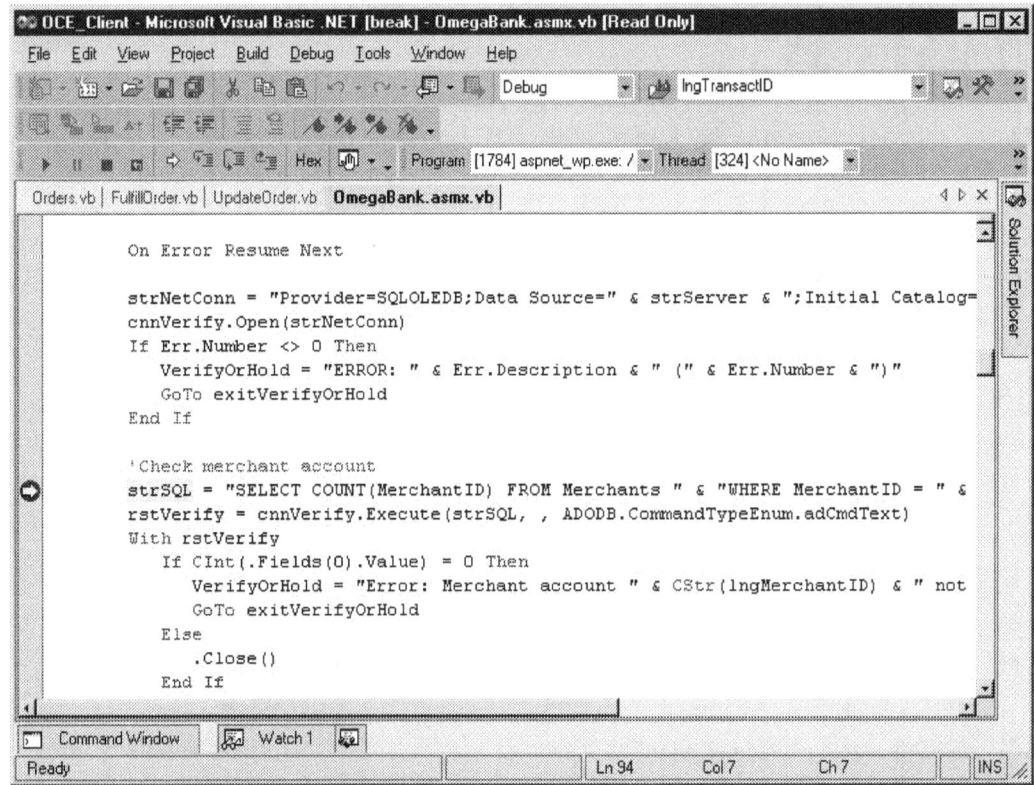

Figure 4-13 *You can set breakpoints and step through the Visual Basic .NET code of a remote XML Web service from the client application.*

Configuration property value from Debug to Release. You can make the change for all ASP.NET projects in your solution by selecting Release in the Solution Configuration list box. Alternatively, select Configuration Manager to open the Configuration Manager dialog box and select Debug or Release for individual projects, as shown here.

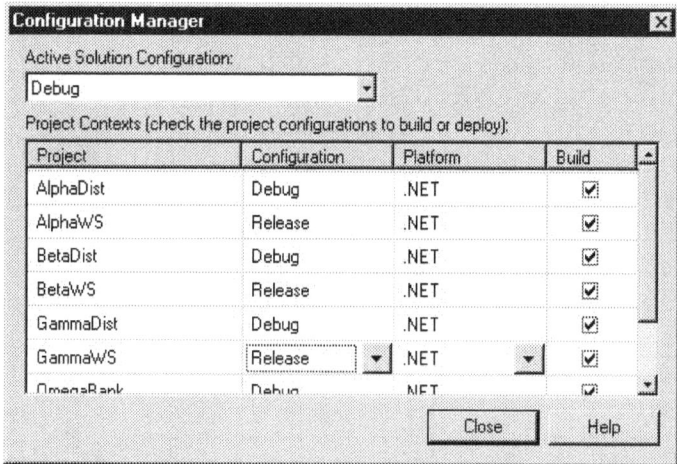

Finally, open the Web.config file for the service and change the value of the `<compilation>` element's `debug` attribute value from `"true"` to `false`, and then rebuild the project.

CAUTION

If you don't make this change, you might find that the remote server's System event log fills with DCOM "General access denied" errors thrown by the Machine Debug Manager (MDM). These messages make it clear that Visual Studio .NET hasn't fully replaced DCOM.

Handling SOAP-Related Errors

The `SoapClient` object has `faultstring` and other `fault...` properties for detecting errors in processing SOAP request messages. Web reference proxy objects don't have corresponding error-handling properties or methods. If the proxy class encounters an error in the request message or the server has a problem generating the designated request message, the class throws a client runtime error with a detailed SOAP error message string as the value of the `Err.Description` property.

The earlier "Setting Remote XML Web Service URLs with Code" section has an example of a detailed error string generated by the `WSDLReader` method. Conventional `On Error GoTo` or inline error handling in the client code handles the disposition of the error.

If prospective users of your XML Web services require custom SOAP fault messages for internally generated errors that are unrelated to runtime error messages, you must add the `System.Web.Services.Protocols` namespace and define custom `SOAPException` objects. As mentioned earlier, Chapter 7 shows you how to specify custom SOAP fault messages.

Consuming ASP.NET XML Web Services with SoapClient Objects

It's easy to adapt Visual Basic 6.0 and ASP projects to substitute ASP.NET XML Web services for COM-based predecessors. The `SoapClient` object handles rpc/encoded and document/literal formats. You can use either or both of the following methods to move clients from COM-based to ASP.NET XML Web services:

▶ Substitute http://*Location/ASPNETServiceName*.asmx?wsdl for the http://*Location/COMServiceName*.wsdl URL as the argument of the obj*Service*.mssoapinit method. In this case, setting the `ServerHTTPRequest` custom `ClientProperty` to `True` is mandatory. You must add the following instruction before calling the `mssoapinit` method:

```
objService.ClientProperty("ServerHTTPRequest") = True
```

CAUTION

If you don't add the preceding line prior to executing the `mssoapinit` *method, you receive this runtime error message: "WSDLReader:Loading of the WSDL file failed HRESULT=0x80070057 - WSDLReader:XML Parser failed at linenumber 0, lineposition 0, reason is: The download of the specified resource has failed. HRESULT=0x1." The* `SoapServer` *object interprets the* `?wsdl` *parameter as a* `GET` *operation request to an ASP listener instead of an ISAPI listener.*

▶ Copy the local *ServiceName*.wsdl file to your XML Web service's virtual directory folder. You create the local *ServiceName*.wsdl file in the *ClientFolder*\Web References*Reference Name* folder when you add a Web Reference to a Visual Basic .NET or ASP.NET project. The earlier "Establishing Web References to Remote XML Web Services" section shows you how to create static WSDL files with client Web references.

TIP

Copying a static WSDL file to the XML Web service's virtual directory folder is the better approach, because potential users of your service expect to connect to a WSDL file. You must have a WSDL to advertise your service in a UDDI registry.

The OCE_OrdersAX project included in the VBWS04.zip sample file has examples of *ServiceName*.wsdl requests to remote services on the OakLeaf web site. Search for "If blnUseASP" with the Current Project option to find the examples. You can redirect the requests to your local Web server by replacing `http://www.oakleaf.ws` with `http://localhost`. Change `.wsdl` to `.asmx?wsdl` to compare performance of direct and indirect WSDL file requests.

Evaluating Performance of Upgraded .NET Clients and XML Web Services

Visual Basic 6.0 applications generate optimized executable files when you accept the default options on the Compile page of the *ProjectName* - Project Properties dialog. By default, Visual Studio .NET compiles your code in debug configuration and doesn't apply optimization methods to improve application performance. Thus, you should rebuild Visual Basic .NET client and XML Web service projects in release configuration and apply optimizations before comparing your application's performance with its COM-based predecessor.

Here's the drill for changing the configuration of client solutions, components, and XML Web services:

1. Open the client solution, OCE_Client.sln for this example, and change the build configuration from Debug to Release.

2. Open the Properties dialog for the client project, select the Configuration Properties, Optimizations page, and select the Enable Optimizations check box.

3. Build the client application.

4. Open the solution that contains your XML Web service(s), Services.sln for this example, and change the build configuration from Debug to Release.

5. Open the Properties dialog for each ASP.NET project, select the Configuration Properties, Optimizations page, and mark the Enable Optimizations check box. For this example, do the same for the four Visual Basic .NET components.

6. Open the Web.config file for each ASP.NET XML Web service and change the value of the `<compilation>` element's `debug` attribute value from `"true"` to `"false."` This change removes the debugging symbols contained in the .pdb file from the compiled code and decreases the size of the compiled service file.

7. Build the XML Web services solution.

8. Rebuild the client application with the optimized services to make sure all components and services are intact.

You're now ready to compare performance of the optimized release version of your .ASP.NET XML Web services and the Visual Basic .NET client application with the COM-based version, OCE_OrdersAX.exe from VBWS04.zip, for this example. The modifications to the code of OCE_OrdersAX.exe, described in the earlier "Moving from Late to Early-Binding" section, establish early-binding for the COM-based services. Tests indicate that changing between early- and late-binding of `SoapClient` objects doesn't measurably affect performance.

 **TIP**

Turn off IIS logging when performing long-running performance tests, if you're short on disk space. The testing regimen to generate the data for the following table created about 100MB of log files.

The following table lists the average execution times in seconds for three test configurations on an 866-MHz Pentium III machine with 512MB RAM, and ATA100 EIDE fixed disk running under Windows 2000 Server. Local results are for 200 or more orders completed; remote data is for 400 or more outsourced orders completed, and are the average for five repetitions of each test. The database tables were initialized after each test. You need at least 100 orders to minimize the influence of component and service compilation time on the .NET results.

Test Configuration	Visual Basic 6.0	Visual Basic .NET/ASP.NET	
Run Simultaneously	Compiled	Debug	Release
Local components	0.63, 0.66	0.58	0.58
Local XML Web Services	1.09, 1.05	0.70	0.71
Remote ASP.NET Services	2.48, 2.46	0.94	0.96
Remote COM Services	2.27, 2.31	0.91	0.90
Run Individually	Compiled	Debug	Release
Local components	0.47	0.47	0.46
Local XML Web Services	0.63	0.57	0.55
Remote ASP.NET Services	1.86	0.75	0.73
Remote COM Services	1.56	0.71	0.70

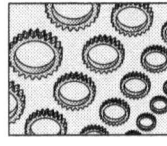

NOTE

The remote results are for services running on the OakLeaf Web server, which was running continuous database update tasks and servicing normal Web site traffic during the test. The client and remote server are connected by the OakLeaf intranet for performance comparisons. The vagaries of Internet packet routing preclude valid comparisons when connecting the client and the XML Web services over the Internet.
There are two results for simultaneous Visual Basic 6.0 tests, because testing repeats for debug and release versions of the .NET implementation.

The difference in performance of the .NET debug and release versions is within experimental error. Thus, it's reasonable to conclude that only very large client applications and XML Web services benefit by removing debug symbols and applying compiler optimization.

The most interesting data in the preceding table is the significant overall performance improvement you achieve by upgrading applications from Visual Basic 6.0 to Visual Basic .NET. The most dramatic performance increase accrues from upgrading a client test harness that accesses remote XML Web services, which emulates a production environment. In these cases, the Visual Basic .NET version runs about 2.5 times faster than its Visual Basic 6.0 predecessor.

Moving from COM-based to ASP.NET components appears to extract a minor performance penalty. The 0.03 second difference, which is very repeatable, might be attributable to the much larger size of the ASP.NET components' WSDL files—due primarily to verbose `<documentation>` elements—or slower processing of ASP.NET's document/literal format than the SOAP Toolkit's RPC/encoded format.

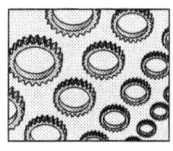
NOTE

A 56-kbps modem connection between the client and the remote XML Web services doesn't degrade performance as badly as you'd expect. The time to complete an order with the Visual Basic .NET client and ASP.NET services averages about 4.5 seconds.

Obviously, your COM-versus-.NET mileage may differ depending on the size and complexity of your client and component code, database server performance, hardware configuration, and network traffic. It's a good bet, however, that client-side performance improvements will more than make up for the minor hit incurred by moving conventional three-tier database applications to XML Web services that run on your intranet.

Moving from ADO 2.5+ to ADO.NET

IN THIS CHAPTER:

Viewing ADO.NET from an ADO Perspective

Working with SqlClient Objects

Test-Driving ADO.NET SqlConnection, SqlCommand, and SqlTransaction Objects

Replacing Recordsets with DataTables

Migrating XML Web Services to ADO.NET

Comparing the Performance of ADO and ADO.NET Components and Services

One of this book's recurring themes is that virtually all production XML Web services interact with databases. The examples in Chapters 3 and 4 typify XML Web services that retrieve data from and update information in database tables. The sample code uses ActiveX Data Objects and the .NET Framework's COM interop(erability) marshalling capabilities to connect to multiple database back ends. The original and upgraded client and XML Web service projects maximize performance by opening read-only, forward-only `ADODB.Recordset` objects (firehose cursors) and executing dynamic T-SQL statements on `ADODB.Connection` objects for `INSERT`, `UPDATE`, and `DELETE` operations. `MSXML2` object or string manipulation code transforms `Recordset` contents to element-centric XML documents.

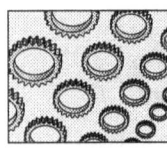

NOTE

The `ADODB.Recordset.Save` method's `adPersistXML` option generates a proprietary Microsoft XML Data-Reduced (XDR) rowset schema and an attribute-centric representation of the `Recordset`'s data. This schema is obsolete, and use of attribute-centric XML to represent rowsets is no longer a generally accepted programming practice. This book doesn't cover SOAP operations with proprietary schemas.

This chapter's primary objective is to show you how to take advantage of ADO.NET features that apply specifically to XML Web services. The emphasis is on migrating Visual Basic .NET code for ASP.NET XML Web services from ADO objects to corresponding ADO.NET classes. Client migration examples precede XML Web service examples, however, because client code is easier to test and debug. The techniques you apply in this chapter represent a major step toward the ultimate objective of replacing all references to COM objects, such as `ADODB` and `MSXML2`, with corresponding .NET Framework class members.

Viewing ADO.NET from an ADO Perspective

ADO.NET substitutes members of the NET Framework's `System.Data` namespace hierarchy for `ADODB.Connection`, `Command`, `Recordset`, `Parameters`, and other ADO objects and collections. ADO.NET abandons cursors in favor of classes that provide client-side cursor equivalents; ADO.NET doesn't let you specify server-side cursors.

This chapter isn't intended to be a dedicated reference and tutorial for ADO.NET objects and their usage. Instead, the chapter concentrates on the practical issues you encounter when moving moderate-sized ADO-based XML Web services to ADO.NET. After you complete the examples, you can determine the extent to which replacing existing ADO code with ADO.NET counterparts improves the performance and scalability of ASP.NET XML Web services and Visual Basic .NET clients.

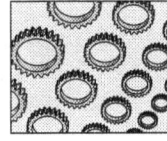

NOTE

ADO.NET Developer's Guide by Mike Otey and Danielle Otey (McGraw-Hill/Osborne, 2002, ISBN 0-07-222357-X) covers all aspects of ADO.NET programming.

Managed Providers

The .NET Framework includes two managed provider namespaces, `System.Data.OleDb` and `System.Data.SqlClient`, and supports `System.Data.Odbc`, which Visual Studio .NET doesn't install. If your service must support ODBC drivers, download and install the bits for `System.Data.Odbc` from http://msdn.microsoft.com/downloads.

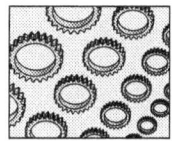

NOTE

Microsoft and most database developers consider ODBC to be legacy technology. OLE DB ultimately will share ODBC's fate as Microsoft and third parties develop fully managed providers for other popular databases. Don't hold your breath waiting for Microsoft to come up with `JetConnection` and related objects; Jet is on life-support and Microsoft is likely to pull the plug when the next version of SQL Server — codenamed Yukon when this book was written — achieves gold-code status.

The managed provider you choose determines the prefix of data connections, commands, readers, adapters, and other classes, except the `DataSet` class and its subclasses, which are contained in the higher `System.Data` namespace.

The `SqlClient` and `OleDb` providers take advantage of connection pooling to improve application performance and scalability. `OleDbConnection` and `SqlConnection` objects don't close automatically when they go out of scope. You must apply the `Close` method to return unused connection objects to the connection pool. You can disable connection pooling by adding an argument to the connection string, but it's a very uncommon practice to disable connection pooling for production XML Web services.

TIP

Don't rely on scoping rules to close database and other objects you open in any programming language. If the object has a `Close` method, apply it as soon as you no longer need the object. The Visual Basic 6.0 and Visual Basic .NET sample code executes the `Close` method on all open data objects as soon as is practical.

The SqlClient Managed Provider

The `SqlClient` managed provider gives high-performance access to Microsoft SQL Server 7.0 and MSDE 1.0 or later. This provider eliminates the overhead of the SQLOLEDB provider and uses SQL Server's native Tabular Data Stream (TDS) protocol to communicate with the database directly.

This book uses SQL Server 2000 for all database examples, so `SqlConnection`, `SqlCommand`, `SqlDataReader`, and `SqlDataAdapter` are the primary ADO.NET objects discussed in this chapter. With a few minor exceptions, the examples also apply to the `OleDb` and `Odbc` managed providers.

The OleDb Managed Provider

You use the `OleDb` provider for all databases except SQL Server, unless you need the Microsoft DataShape provider to process chaptered (hierarchical) rowsets. You specify one of the standard set of MDAC 2.7 OLE DB drivers for Jet, SQL Server, or Oracle databases.

The `OleDb` provider also accommodates third-party OLE DB providers that meet the current OLE DB specification. The `OleDb` provider relies on COM interop for marshalling.

Data Commands and Data Readers

`SqlCommand` and `SqlDataReader` objects operate directly on SQL Server databases and replace most `ADODB.Connection.Execute` operations. An `SqlDataReader` object corresponds to an `ADODB.Recordset` object returned by a firehose cursor but offers better performance, especially when the query returns a large number of records. `SqlDataReader` objects store only one row at a time in memory. An even lighter-weight `SqlCommand.ExecuteScalar` method returns the first column of the first row of a query. `ExecuteScalar` is very useful for returning aggregate values, such as COUNT or SUM, or single values returned from operations, such as checking the available credit of a particular credit or debit card.

TIP

Take advantage of the `ExecuteScalar` method to replace `Recordset` objects that return a single value. Replace your forward-only, read-only `Recordset` objects that return multiple rows, columns, or both with ...`DataReader` objects as the first step in the ADO-to-ADO.NET migration process. The replacement code to create a ...`DataReader` object is quite similar to that for opening a `Recordset` object from a `Command` object.

Another difference from `ADODB.Connection` objects is ADO.NET's use of an `SqlTransaction` object. Instead of applying ADO's conventional `BeginTrans`, `CommitTrans`, and `RollbackTrans` methods on the `Connection` object, you create a named `SqlTransaction` object with the `SqlConnection.BeginTransaction` method, and apply the `Commit` or `Rollback` method to the `SqlTransaction` object. `SqlTransaction` objects support named transactions and savepoints. `OleDbTransaction` and `OdbcTransaction` objects have `Begin`, `Commit`, and `Rollback` methods.

DataAdapter, DataSet, and DataTable Objects

`DataSet` objects represent a very enhanced version of ADO's disconnected `Recordset` objects—an in-memory representation of database tables and their relationships. A `DataSet` is a collection of one or more `DataTable` objects, which hold the data, and can contain optional `DataRelation` and `Constraint` objects. A `DataTable` is the only ADO.NET object that delivers the equivalent of an `ADODB.Recordset` that has a scrollable cursor. A `DataTable` is analogous to a disconnected `Recordset` object you create by specifying batch-optimistic locking.

`DataSets` are a very sophisticated reincarnation of Microsoft's in-memory database (IMDB), which was originally scheduled for inclusion with Windows 2000 Server. You use `DataAdapter` objects to specify the table objects to include and the relationships between the tables. `DataSet` objects also support `DataView` objects, which represent a view over the `DataSet`'s tables.

`DataSet` objects offer the additional advantages of built-in XML serialization and deserialization, and the capability to export XSD schema for the tables and their relations. You can create an `XmlDataDocument` object from the relational data of a `DataSet` object, modify the resulting XML representation of the relational data, and update the database tables with the changes you make to the document. `XmlDataDocument` is a member of the `System.Xml.XmlDocument` namespace, which is one of the subjects of Chapter 7's "System.Xml Member Classes" section. Chapter 10 describes the XSO schemas of `DataSet` objects.

Working with SqlClient Objects

When you create a new Visual Basic .NET Windows Application or ASP.NET Web Service, or upgrade a Visual Basic 6.0 project, Visual Studio .NET automatically adds a project reference to the `System.Data` namespace. To avoid having to type namespace prefixes to class members lower in the hierarchy, add the following `Imports` statements to each project class that contains references to ADODB objects:

```
Imports System.Data.SqlClient   'For SQL Server 7.0+
Imports System.Data.OleDb       'Required only if you use OLE DB providers
Imports System.Data.Odbc        'Requires installing the namespace
Imports System.Data.SqlTypes    'Optional; applies only to SqlClient
```

This book uses SQL Server or MSDE 2000 as the back-end database for all examples, so the sample code uses only `SqlClient` objects.

Replacing ADODB.Connection with SqlConnection and SqlCommand Objects

`ADODB.Connection` objects let you execute SQL statements without creating an `ADODB.Command` object for the connection; ADO.NET doesn't permit this shortcut. First, you create an `SqlConnection` object and open the connection. Then you apply the `CreateCommand` method to create an `SqlCommand` object to execute T-SQL statements.

Following is the generic code for creating new instances of ADO.NET connection and command objects:

```
Dim cnnConnect As SqlConnection = New SqlConnection()
cnnConnect.ConnectionString = strConnect
cnnConnect.Open()
Dim cmmCommand As SqlCommand = cnnConnect.CreateCommand
```

The value of *strConnect* for `SqlConnection` objects is a conventional ADO connection string without the `Provider=SQLOLEDB;` element. The

`SqlConnection.Open()` method doesn't accept ADO-style arguments, so you must specify all connection property values by elements of `strConnect`. Unlike `ADODB.Connection` objects, `SqlConnection` properties are read-only and don't return values until you open the connection. The only property value you can change is `Database`, but you must apply the `ChangeDatabase` method to alter this property value.

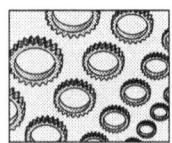

NOTE

Code for the `OleDb` *and* `Odbc` *versions of the objects described in the following sections is identical to the* `SqlClient` *version, except as noted.*

Executing SqlCommands

`SqlCommand` objects are similar to `ADODB.Command` objects. You set the value of the `CommandText` property to the T-SQL statement to execute and the `CommandType` property value to `CommandType.Text`, `CommandType.StoredProcedure`, or `CommandType.TableDirect`. Alternatively, you can specify the T-SQL query as the first argument and an open `SqlConnection` name as the second argument of the `SqlCommand` object.

`SqlCommand` objects support the following `Execute...` methods:

▶ `ExecuteNonQuery` returns an `Integer` value of the number of records affected by SQL `INSERT`, `UPDATE`, and `DELETE` commands.

▶ `ExecuteScalar` returns an `Object` containing the value of the first column of the first row of a query result set. You must convert the `Object` to the datatype of the return variable.

▶ `ExecuteReader` returns an `SqlDataReader` object containing the query result set.

▶ `ExecuteXmlReader` returns an `XmlReader` object that provides quick access to XML data returned by SQL Server 2000, typically by adding the `FOR XML {AUTO|RAW|EXPLICIT} [ELEMENTS]` modifier to a row-returning query. SQL Server 7.0 doesn't support the `FOR XML` modifier.

This chapter's examples use the first three `Execute...` methods. Chapter 7 explains how to take advantage of the `ExecuteXmlReader` method.

Here's the generic code for executing `SqlCommand` objects. The first block executes a T-SQL `INSERT`, `UPDATE`, or `DELETE` statement; the second block returns a scalar value to a variable of a type corresponding to the type conversion function:

```
With cmmCommand
    .CommandText = strSQLUpdate
    .CommandType = CommandType.Text
    intRecordsAffected = .ExecuteNonQuery()
End With
```

```
With cmmCommand
    .CommandText = strSQLQuery
    .CommandType = CommandType.Text
    typScalarVar = CTyp(.ExecuteScalar())
End With
```

Managing Transactions

As mentioned in the earlier "Data Commands and Data Readers" section, ADO.NET transaction management differs considerably from that of ADO. The most significant change is the addition of `OleDBTransaction` and `SqlTransaction` objects for transaction management at the command level. The `SqlClient` provider requires a special `SqlTransaction` object, which supports T-SQL named-transaction syntax. In most other respects, the Visual Basic .NET code required to manipulate `OleDBTransaction` objects is similar to that for `SqlTransaction` objects.

The following generic code demonstrates wrapping multiple `INSERT`, `UPDATE`, or `DELETE` operations on related tables in an SQL Server transaction that's started on an open connection:

```
Dim trnTransaction As SqlTransaction = Nothing
Dim cmmCommand As SqlCommand = cnnConnection.CreateCommand
trnTransaction = _
    cnnConnection.BeginTransaction([IsolationLevel.IsolationType])
With cmmCommand
    .Transaction = trnTransaction   'Attach the SqlTransaction object
    .CommandType = Command.Text
    .CommandText = strSQLInsert1    'Insert a record in the base table
    .ExecuteNonQuery()
    .CommandText = strSQLInsert2    'Insert records in related tables
    .ExecuteNonQuery()

    ...

End With
If Err.Number = 0 Then
    trnTransaction.Commit()
Else
    trnTransaction.Rollback()
End If
```

The `System.Data.IsolationLevel` enumeration defines allowable values of the `BeginTransaction` parameter. The following table lists the enumeration's members, corresponding ADO `adXact...` members, and equivalent T-SQL `SET TRANSACTION LEVEL` modifiers in declining order of transaction integrity, except for `Chaos` and `Unspecified`. `ReadCommitted` is the default `IsolationLevel`.

IsolationLevel	ADO adXact... Member	T-SQL Equivalent
Serializable	adXactSerializable	SERIALIZABLE
RepeatableRead	adXactRepeatableRead	REPEATABLE READ
ReadCommitted	adXactReadCommitted	READ COMMITTED
ReadUncommitted	adXactReadUncommitted	READ UNCOMMITTED
Chaos	adXactChaos	No direct equivalent
Unspecified	adXactUnspecified	None

TIP

If you're not familiar with `IsolationLevel` *terminology, read the .NET Framework SDK's online help topic for the* `System.Data.IsolationLevel` *enumeration or the* `SET TRANSACTION ISOLATION LEVEL` *topic of SQL Server Books Online.*

Working with SqlDataReader Objects

The following generic code creates an `SqlDataReader` object by executing the `SqlCommand.ExecuteDataReader` method:

```
With cmmCommand
    .CommandText = strSQLQuery
    .CommandType = CommandType.Text
    Dim sdrReader As SqlDataReader = .ExecuteReader()
End With
```

Traversing SqlDataReader Rows

Unlike `ADODB.Recordset` objects, `SqlDataReader` objects don't open with the first row selected. You must apply the `Read()` method, which returns `True` if a first or succeeding row exists, to move to the first row. Successive `Read()` method calls have the same effect as invoking ADO's `MoveNext` method. The `sdrReader.Read()` method is equivalent to `Not rstRecordset.EOF`.

The `Item({intFieldIndex|strFieldName})` property returns to an `Object` variable the value of the field whose ordinal position or name you specify. Using the field's ordinal position retrieves the value faster than supplying a name. To obtain an `Object` array of all fields of the current row, substitute the `GetValues(objArray)` method for Item. Set the number of elements of `objArray` equal to the value of the `FieldCount` property.

You iterate the `SqlDataReader` object's query result set with code that's similar to the following:

```
With sdrReader
    Do While .Read()
        objField0Val = .Item(0)         'Single field value
        objFieldName = .Item(strFieldName)
        .GetValues(objArray)  'All field values
```

```
    Loop
    .Close
End With
```

TIP

Don't perform complex data manipulation operations within an `SqlDataReader.Read()` loop. The connection to the database must remain open until the last invocation of `.Item(n)`. Instead, assign the values to a two-dimension `Object` array or `ArrayList`. Close the `SqlDataReader` and `SqlConnection` objects immediately after iteration completes. An alternative to the array approach is opening a `DataSet` object instead of an SqlDataReader. The later " Filling a DataTable with an SQL DataAdapter " section describes how to substitute `DataSets` for `ADODB.Recordset` objects.

Using the Get*Type*Method and Members of the SqlTypes Namespace

You can apply the `.ToString` operator to serialize the `Objects` returned by the `Item` method to `String` variables, as in `strFieldValue = sdrReader.Item(intOrdinal).ToString`. The `ToString` approach doesn't require prior knowledge of the field datatypes of the query result set. A more .NET-compliant, type-safe approach is to invoke the `GetType(intOrdinal)` method, where *Type* is one of the .NET Framework's intrinsic datatypes.

Alternatively, specifying a member of the `SqlTypes` enumeration as the datatype lets you apply the appropriate `GetSqlType(intFieldIndex)` method to avoid mapping native SQL Server datatypes to their .NET equivalents. OleDB and Odbc providers don't support use of `GetSqlType`. In this case, you declare variables `As SqlType`: for example, `Dim curAmount As SqlMoney` to accept the value of a `curAmount = sdrReader.GetSqlMoney(2)` statement. Table 5-1 lists SQL Server datatypes, corresponding `GetType` and `GetSQLType` methods, and .NET native datatypes.

SQL Server Datatype	GetType	GetSQLType	.NET Native Type
bigint	GetInt64	GetSqlInt64	Long
binary	GetBytes	GetSqlBytes	Byte()
bit	GetBoolean	GetSqlBoolean	Boolean
char	GetString	GetSqlString	String
datetime	GetDateTime	GetSqlDateTime	DateTime
decimal	GetDecimal	GetSqlDecimal	Decimal
float	GetDouble	GetSqlDouble	Double
image	GetBytes	GetSqlBytes	Byte()
int	GetInt32	GetSqlInt32	Int32

Table 5-1   *SQL Server datatypes with their **Get**Type and **GetSQL**Type methods, and .NET native datatypes*

SQL Server Datatype	GetType	GetSQLType	.NET Native Type
money	GetDecimal	GetSqlMoney	Decimal
nchar	GetString	GetSqlString	String
ntext	GetString	GetSqlString	String
nvarchar	GetString	GetSqlString	String
real	GetSingle	GetSqlSingle	Single
smalldatetime	GetDateTime	GetSqlDateTime	DateTime
smallint	GetInt16	GetSqlInt16	Short
smallmoney	GetDecimal	GetSqlMoney	Decimal
sql_variant	GetValue	GetSqlValue	Object
test	GetString	GetSqlString	String
timestamp	GetBytes	GetSqlBytes	Byte()
tinyint	GetByte	GetSqlByte	Byte
uniqueidentifier	GetGuid	GetSqlGuid	Guid
varbinary	GetBytes	GetSqlBytes	Byte()
varchar	GetString	GetSqlString	String

Table 5-1   *SQL Server datatypes with their* `GetType` *and* `GetSQLType` *methods, and .NET native datatypes* (continued)

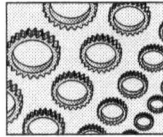

NOTE

You must add an `Imports System.Data.SqlTypes` *instruction to your class to refer to members of the* `SqlTypes` *namespace directly.*

Test-Driving ADO.NET SqlConnection, SqlCommand, and SqlTransaction Objects

Probably the best way of judging whether upgrading existing code to ADO.NET is worth the effort is to begin with an ADO-based client, in this case, the OCE_OrdersADO test harness. The `clsAddOrder.AddNewOrder`, `AddNewOrderConn`, `AddLineItem`, and `AddLineItemConn` methods provide a test bed for passing `SqlConnection` and `SqlTransaction` objects by reference and handling simple T-SQL transactions The migration procedures of the following sections also apply when you write ADO.NET code from scratch.

Downloading and Installing This Chapter's Sample Code

The VBWS05.zip archive, which you can download from this book's entry at http://www.osborne.com/downloads/downloads.shtml, contains a modified version of

Chapter 4's OCE_OrdersNET.sln solution, named OCE_OrdersADO.sln in the
\OCE_OrdersADO folder. OCE_OrdersADO has Web References only to local and
emote ASP.NET XML Web services. Expand VBWS05.zip into a \VBWS05 folder.

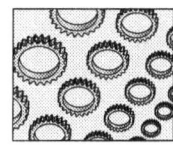

NOTE

*Like in Chapters 3 and 4, this chapter relies on the SQL Server 2000 databases archived in the VBWS_*
OCE.zip file. If you haven't done so already, download VBWS_OCE.zip from http://www.osborne.com/
downloads/downloads.shtml, follow the instructions in Appendix A to attach the database to a local or remote
instance of SQL Server or MSDE 2000, and set up required login accounts and database/table permissions.

VBWS05.zip also includes an \OCE_ClientADO folder with sample code that
incorporates all ADO-to-ADO.NET modifications described in this chapter.
OCE_ClientADO has a Remote ADO 2.7 check box that connects to OakLeaf XML Web
services that do *not* have the ADO-to-ADO.NET upgrades that this chapter demonstrates.
You'll get much more out of this chapter if you modify and test the \OCE_OrdersADO code,
rather than simply inspect and run the \OCE_ClientADO code.

Both sample code versions depend on the existence of local Web References that point to
http://localhost/*virtualdir*/*servicename*.asmx. The references to upgraded remote XML Web
services on the OakLeaf Web site point to the following URLs:

> http://www.oakleaf.ws/AlphaADO/AlphaDist.asmx
>
> http://www.oakleaf.ws/BetaADO/BetaDist.asmx
>
> http://www.oakleaf.ws/GammaADO/GammaDist.asmx
>
> http://www.oakleaf.ws/OmegaADO/OmegaBank.asmx.

OCE_OrdersADO's Web References rely initially on the ASP.NET Web services
described in Chapter 4. The code for Chapter 4's services is located in subfolders of
\VBWS04\OCE_OrdersNET\Services\ and managed by Services.sln in this folder.

If you didn't create the services described in Chapter 4, you must set up the following four
local virtual directories for OCE_OrdersADO.sln:

Virtual Directory	Path to Local Service Project Folder
AlphaWS	\VBWS05\OCE_OrdersADO\Services\AlphaWS
BetaWS	\VBWS05\OCE_OrdersADO\Services\BetaWS
GammaWS	\VBWS05\OCE_OrdersADO\Services\GammaWS
OmegaWS	\VBWS05\OCE_OrdersADO\Services\OmegaWS

To compile and run the upgraded OCE_ClientADO.sln solution, add the following IIS
virtual directories:

Virtual Directory	Path to Local Service Project Folder
AlphaADO	\VBWS05\OCE_ClientADO\Services\AlphaWS
BetaADO	\VBWS05\OCE_ClientADO\Services\BetaWS

Virtual Directory	Path to Local Service Project Folder
GammaADO	\VBWS05\OCE_ClientADO\Services\GammaWS
OmegaADO	\VBWS05\OCE_ClientADO\Services\OmegaWS

Substituting SQLConnection for ADODB.Connection Objects

The first step in migrating existing ADO-based Visual Basic .NET code to ADO.NET is to replace `ADODB.Connection` code with ADO.NET equivalents. Here's the generic process:

1. Add **Imports System.Data.SqlClient** and, optionally, **Imports System.Data.SqlTypes** instructions under your class's `Option Explicit` statement.

2. Replace each instance of `Dim cnnConnection As New ADODB.Connection` or the like, with **Dim cnnConnection As SqlConnection = New SqlConnection()**.

3. Remove the `Provider=SQLOLEB;` element from the connection string (`strConnect`).

4. Replace `cnnConnection.Open(strConnect)` statements with the following two lines:

   ```
   cnnConnection.ConnectionString = strConnect
   cnnConnection.Open()
   ```

5. If you pass the connection by reference to another function or subprocedure, change `As ADODB.Connection` to **As SqlClient.SqlConnection** in the receiving function's or subprocedure's argument list.

Following is the code for `AddOrder.vb`'s `clsAddOrder.AddNewOrder` function after making the changes described in the preceding steps 1 through 4:

```
Public Function AddNewOrder(ByVal strServer As String, _
   ByVal strUser As String, ByVal strPwd As String, _
   ByVal intCustID As Integer, ByVal datOrderDate As Date, _
   ByVal datRequiredDate As Date, ByVal blnPartialShip As Boolean, _
   ByVal bytCardID As Byte, ByVal bytShipToID As Byte, _
   ByVal bytShipTypeID As Byte, ByVal blnSalesTax As Boolean) As Integer

   'Creates and passes a connection to AddNewOrderConn
   Dim cnnOrder As SqlConnection = New SqlConnection()
   On Error Resume Next

   cnnOrder.ConnectionString = "Data Source=" & strServer & _
      ";Initial Catalog=OCE_Cust;UID=" & strUser & ";PWD=" & strPwd
   cnnOrder.Open()
```

```
   If Err.Number <> 0 Then
      'Connection failed
      AddNewOrder = -1
      Exit Function
   End If
   AddNewOrder = AddNewOrderConn(cnnOrder, intCustID, datOrderDate, _
      datRequiredDate, blnPartialShip, bytCardID, bytShipToID, _
      bytShipTypeID, blnSalesTax)
   cnnOrder.Close()
End Function
```

Make the boldface changes in the preceding listing to the `AddNewOrder` function and similar alterations to the `AddLineItems` function. Don't attempt to run the project until you've completed the modifications of the next section.

Replacing the ADODB.Command.Execute Method and Scalar Recordets with an SqlCommand

ADO.NET's added requirement for an `SqlCommand` object to execute SQL statements is offset by the `SqlCommand.ExecuteScalar` method's replacement of `ADODB.Recordset` code to return a single value. The most common uses for single-valued `Recordset`s is returning COUNT and @@IDENTITY values.

Here's the drill for upgrading ADO code for adding a record to a table with an `int` `identity` column and returning the @@IDENTITY value for use when adding line items:

1. Add a **Dim cmm*Command* as SqlCommand = cnn*Connection*.CreateCommand** statement after the cnn*Connection*.Open statement to instantiate an `SqlCommand` object on the open connection.

2. Replace each instance of cnn*Connection*.Execute(str*SQLInsert*, int*Reccnt*, ADODB.CommandTypeEnum.adCmdText) or its equivalent INSERT, UPDATE, or DELETE code with the following lines:

    ```
    With cmmCommand
       .CommandText = strSQL
       .CommandType = CommandType.Text
       intReccnt = .ExecuteNonQuery()
    End With
    ```

3. Replace code for creating ADODB.Recordsets that return a single value, such as rst*Recordset* = cnn*Connection*.Execute(str*SQLIdentity*, , ADODB.CommandTypeEnum.adCmdText) with the following:

    ```
    With cmmCommand
       .CommandText = strSQL
       .CommandType = CommandType.Text
       typScalarValue = CTyp(.ExecuteScalar)
    End With
    ```

4.   Remove unnecessary datatype conversion functions, such as `CLng` for `intReccnt`, which the `Execute...` methods return as an `Integer`.

Following is the code for the `AddNewOrderConn` function after making the preceding revisions and the change to the function's argument list described in step 5 of the preceding section:

```
Public Function AddNewOrderConn(ByRef cnnOrder As
        SqlClient.SqlConnection, _
   ByVal intCustID As Integer, ByVal datOrderDate As Date, _
   ByVal datRequiredDate As Date, ByVal blnPartialShip As Boolean, _
   ByVal bytCardID As Byte, ByVal bytShipToID As Byte, _
   ByVal bytShipTypeID As Byte, ByVal blnSalesTax As Boolean) As Integer

   'Adds a new order; returns OrderID if successful, error code if not.
   Dim cmmOrder As SqlCommand = cnnOrder.CreateCommand
   Dim strSQL As String
   Dim strPartialShip As String
   Dim strSalesTax As String
   Dim intReccnt As Integer
   On Error Resume Next

   If blnPartialShip Then strPartialShip = "1" Else strPartialShip = "0"
   If blnSalesTax Then strSalesTax = "1" Else strSalesTax = "0"
   strSQL = "INSERT Orders(CustID, OrderDate, RequiredShipDate, " & _
      PartialShipOK, CardID, ShipTypeID, SalesTaxApplies, StatusID) " & _
      "VALUES(" & intCustID & ", '" & datOrderDate & "' , "

   If Year(datRequiredDate) = 1899 Then strSQL = strSQL & "NULL" _
      Else strSQL = strSQL & "'" & datRequiredDate & "'"
   strSQL = strSQL & ", " & strPartialShip & ", " & bytCardID & ", " & _
      bytShipTypeID & ", " & strSalesTax & ", 11)"
   With cmmOrder
      .CommandText = strSQL
      .CommandType = CommandType.Text
      lngReccnt = .ExecuteNonQuery()
   End With
   If Err.Number <> 0 Then
      'Execution failed
      AddNewOrderConn = -2
      Exit Function
   End If
   If lngReccnt > 0 Then
      'Get the identity value for the connection
```

```
        strSQL = "SELECT @@identity"
        With cmmOrder
           .CommandText = strSQL
           .CommandType = CommandType.Text
           AddNewOrderConn = CInt(.ExecuteScalar)
        End With
        If Err.Number <> 0 Then
           'Execution failed
           AddNewOrderConn = -3
           Exit Function
        End If
     Else
        'Didn't add order
        AddNewOrderConn = -1
     End If
  End Function
```

As in the preceding section, make the changes shown in boldface to the
AddNewOrderConn and AddLineItemsConn functions. The AddLineItemsConn
function doesn't create a Recordset object, so the ExecuteScalar code isn't
applicable to the function. Open Orders.vb, navigate to the cmdNewOrder_Click event
handler, and change blnTransaction = True to blnTransaction = False.
Build and run your code, and then click the Create Order button to test your work so far.

TIP

If you receive a "Specified cast is not valid" run-time error, you probably forgot to change
blnTransaction to False.

Passing Transaction Objects with Connection Objects

Orders.vb's cmdNewOrder_Click event handler wraps the AddNewOrderConn and
AddItemsConn functions' INSERT operations on the Orders and LineItems tables in a
transaction to prevent adding orders with no line items, or vice versa. Event-handling code
in the frmOrder class manages the transaction, but the SqlCommand objects that perform
the INSERT operations in the clsAddOrder class must have a reference to the
SqlConnection's SqlTransaction object.

The upshot of the need to set the SqlCommand.Transaction property to an
active SqlTransaction object is that you must pass the SqlTransaction object
to each function or subprocedure to which you pass an SqlConnection object. For
this example, the AddNewOrder and AddLineItem functions must deliver a bogus
SqlTransaction object argument to maintain compatibility with calls from
cmdNewOrder_Click.

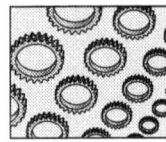

NOTE

If you've wondered why the `cmdNewOrder_Click` and `clsAddOrder` functions have such a convoluted architecture, this and the preceding sections provide the answer. The design permits incremental ADO-to-ADO.NET upgrades: first without a transaction and then wrapped with a transaction. The design, which isn't recommended for production applications, also demonstrates the need for passing `SqlTransaction` with `SqlConnection` objects.

Following is code in the `cmdNewOrder_Click` event handler that illustrates the changes required to start the transaction and create an `SqlTransaction` object:

```
Dim cnnOrder As SqlConnection = New SqlConnection()
Dim trnOrder As SqlTransaction = Nothing
...
If blnTransaction Then
    cnnOrder.ConnectionString = "Data Source=" & strCustServer & _
        ";Initial Catalog=OCE_Cust;UID=" & strCustUser & ";PWD=" &
            strCustPwd
    cnnOrder.Open()
    trnOrder = cnnOrder.BeginTransaction(IsolationLevel.ReadCommitted)
    lngOrderID = AddOrder.AddNewOrderConn(cnnOrder, trnOrder,
        lngCustID, _
        Now, datReqdShipDate, blnPartShipOK, bytCardID, bytShipToID, _
        bytShipTypeID, blnSalesTax)
Else
    lngOrderID = AddOrder.AddNewOrder(strCustServer, strCustUser, _
        strCustPwd, lngCustID, Now, datReqdShipDate, blnPartShipOK, _
        bytCardID, bytShipToID, bytShipTypeID, blnSalesTax)
End If
```

The `cnnOrder` declaration is required because the original class-level `cnnCust` connection is used for other purposes. You also must add the `trnOrder` argument to the later `AddOrder.AddLineItemConn` function call.

Here are the changes to the `clsAddOrder.AddNewOrderConn` function to set the `cmmOrder.Transaction` property:

```
Public Function AddNewOrderConn(ByRef cnnOrder As SqlConnection, _
    ByRef trnOrder As SqlTransaction, ByVal intCustID As Integer, _
    ByVal datOrderDate As Date, ByVal datRequiredDate As Date, _
    ByVal blnPartialShip As Boolean, ByVal bytCardID As Byte, _
    ByVal bytShipToID As Byte, ByVal bytShipTypeID As Byte, _
    ByVal blnSalesTax As Boolean) As Integer
    ...
    With cmmOrder
        .CommandText = strSQL
        .CommandType = CommandType.Text
```

```
If Not trnOrder Is Nothing Then
.Transaction = trnOrder
End If
intReccnt = .ExecuteNonQuery()
    End With
    …
End Function
```

You also must make similar changes to the `clsAddOrder.AddLineItemConn` function.

The `cmdNewOrder_Click` event handler has two `cnnCust.RollbackTrans()` lines; change them to **`trnOrder.Rollback()`**. Change the single instance of `cnnCust.CommitTrans()` to **`trnOrder.Commit()`**, and add **`cnnOrder.Close()`** after the End If line. Add another instance of **`cnnOrder.Close()`** immediately before the End Function line.

TIP

Execute the `Close` method early and often. Invoking `Close` on an unopened or previously closed connection doesn't cause a run-time exception.

To build and run the project, you must conform `clsAddOrder`'s `AddNewOrder` and `AddLineItems` function calls to `AddNewOrderConn` and `AddLineItemsConn` by adding a `Dim {trnOrder|trnItems} As SqlTransaction = Nothing` declaration. Then add the `trnOrder` and `trnItems` arguments to the function calls.

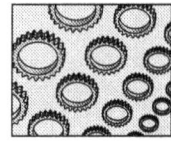

NOTE

The `clsFulfillOrder` class has three operations that require transactions—one in the `CheckOrCommit` function and two in the `ShipItems` function. Upgrading these functions from ADO to ADO.NET is easier than the preceding examples because the transactions are contained within the functions.

Moving from Firehose Cursors to SqlDataReader Objects

The `cmdNewOrder_Click` event handler employs an `ADODB.Recordset` object, `rstCust`, to return the state and ZIP code. These values could be passed to an XML Web service that provides the sales tax percentage imposed by state and local governments. Only the ZIP code is required, but adding the state provides a cross-check for instances where ZIP codes cross state boundaries. Two values preclude use of the `ExecuteScalar` method, so `SqlCommand` and `SqlDataReader` objects are required to replace the `Recordset` object.

The following `cmdNewOrder_Click` code illustrates the modifications you must make to substitute an `SqlDataReader` object for a typical read-only, forward-only `Recordset` created on an `ADODB.Connection` object. The code you replace is commented. The `Do While Not .Read` instruction executes the `Read` method; if the `SqlDataReader` object has no rows, code enters the loop to try another random `lngCustID` value.

```vb
Dim cnnCusts As SqlConnection = New SqlConnection()
Dim rdrCusts As SqlDataReader = Nothing

...

cnnCusts.ConnectionString = "Data Source=" & strCustServer & _
    ";Initial Catalog=OCE_Cust;UID=" & strCustUser & ";PWD=" & strCustPwd
cnnCusts.Open()
Dim cmmCusts As SqlCommand = cnnCusts.CreateCommand
'Set and verify a random customer, get sales tax status and ZIP Code
Randomize()
lngCustID = 1000000 + CInt(25344 * Rnd())
strSQL = "SELECT State, ZIPCode FROM Customers WHERE CustID = " & _
    CStr(lngCustID)
'rstCust = cnnCust.Execute(strSQL, , ADODB.CommandTypeEnum.adCmdText)
With cmmCusts
    .CommandType = CommandType.Text
    .CommandText = strSQL
    rdrCusts = .ExecuteReader
End With
With rdrCusts
    intCtr = 0
    'Do While .EOF
    Do While Not .Read()
        .Close()
        Randomize()
        lngCustID = 1000000 + CInt(25344 * Rnd()) '25,344 customers
        strSQL = "SELECT State, ZIPCode FROM Customers WHERE CustID = " & _
            CStr(lngCustID)
        'rstCust = cnnCust.Execute(strSQL, , _ ADODB.CommandTypeEnum.adCmdText)
        cmmCusts.CommandText = strSQL
        rdrCusts = cmmCusts.ExecuteReader()
        intCtr = intCtr + 1
        If intCtr > 100 Then
            'Bigtime error, bail out
            rdrCusts.Close()
            cnnCusts.Close()
            Exit Sub
        End If
    Loop
    'Check for sales tax
    'If CStr(.Fields(0).Value) = "TX" Then
    If .GetString(0) = "TX" Then
        blnSalesTax = True
        chkSalesTax.CheckState = System.Windows.Forms.CheckState.Checked
    Else
```

```
        blnSalesTax = False
        chkSalesTax.CheckState = System.Windows.Forms.CheckState.Unchecked
    End If
    'strZipCode = CStr(.Fields(1).Value)
    strZipCode = .GetString(1)
    .Close()
End With
...
```

TIP

Use the `GetString` method to serialize `Item` objects returned by character fields, not `Item(intOrdinal).ToString` or `GetSqlString(intOrdinal)`. To use the latter method, you must declare the variable datatype as `SqlString` instead of an ordinary `String`. There's little, if any, performance benefit to use of the `GetSqlType` methods with `SqlDataReader` objects.

The `Recordset` that returns random LineItems data also requires an `SqlDataReader` object. You can replace the other `Recordset` objects in the procedure with values returned by the `ExecuteScalar` method.

Invoking ExecuteReader and ExecuteNonQuery or ExecuteScalar on the Same SqlConnection

Here's an ADO.NET gotcha you're likely to encounter in almost any procedure that combines database lookup and update operations. `ADODB.Recordsets` with firehose cursors disconnect from the database after filling. `SqlDataReader` and `OleDBDataReader` objects maintain the database connection after reading the last row. You must close the connection's `...DataReader` object before you invoke another `Execute...` method. Failure to issue the `Close()` instruction throws a run-time exception, even if you use individual `SqlCommand` objects to open the `SqlDataReader` and invoke the `ExecuteNonQuery` or `ExecuteScalar` method.

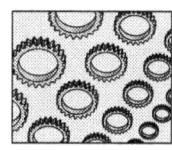

NOTE

A more serious gotcha is the inability to execute nested `SqlDataReader` commands within a `Do While sdrReader.Read ... Loop` structure with a single connection. The next section addresses this issue.

The upgraded `clsFulfillOrder.CheckOrCommit` function provides an example:

```
'Declarations section omitted
strStockConn = "Data Source=" & strServer & _
    ";Initial Catalog=OCE_Prod;UID=" & strUser & ";PWD=" & strPwd
cnnStock.ConnectionString = strStockConn
cnnStock.Open()
If Err.Number <> 0 Then
```

```vb
        'Can't connect
        CheckOrCommit = -1
    End If
    strSQL = "SELECT NetPrice, ShipWeight, Outsourced, BeginningInventory, " & _
        "ReceivedInPeriod, ShippedInPeriod, CommittedNow FROM Products " & _
        "WHERE SKU = '"
    With cnnStock
        Dim cmmStock As SqlCommand = .CreateCommand
        If blnCommit Then
            trnStock = .BeginTransaction
        End If
        For bytItem = 0 To UBound(astrLineItems) - 1
            strSQLItem = strSQL & astrLineItems(bytItem, 0) & "'"
            With cmmStock
                .CommandType = CommandType.Text
                .CommandText = strSQLItem
                If blnCommit Then
                    .Transaction = trnStock
                End If
                sdrStock = .ExecuteReader
            End With
            If Err.Number <> 0 Then
                'Can't execute query
                CheckOrCommit = -1
                GoTo ExitCheckOrCommit
            End If
            With sdrStock
                If .Read Then
                    If .GetBoolean(2) Then
                        'It's outsourced, return the DistID value
                        astrLineItems(bytItem, 2) = GetDistInventory(strServer, _
                            strUser, strPwd, astrLineItems(bytItem, 0), _
                            CByte(astrLineItems(bytItem, 1)), blnUseWS, _
                            blnUseOakLeaf, blnUseCom)
                    Else
                        'Get stock (Beginning + Received - Shipped - Committed)
                        intInStock = .GetInt16(3) + .GetInt16(4) _
                            - .GetInt16(5) - .GetInt16(6)
                        If intInStock >= CByte(astrLineItems(bytItem, 1)) Then
                            astrLineItems(bytItem, 2) = "Yes"
                        Else
                            astrLineItems(bytItem, 2) = "No"
                        End If
                        astrLineItems(bytItem, 3) = .Item(1).ToString
                        If blnCommit Then
                            'Must close the DataReader before ExecuteNonQuery
                            .Close()
                            'Commit the inventory
                            strSQLUpdate = "UPDATE Products SET CommittedNow = " & _
                                "CommittedNow + " & astrLineItems(bytItem, 1) & _
```

```
                              "WHERE SKU = '" & astrLineItems(bytItem, 0) & "'"
                    With cmmStock
                       .CommandText = strSQLUpdate
                       intReccnt = .ExecuteNonQuery()
                    End With
                    If Err.Number <> 0 Or intReccnt <> 1 Then
                       'Unable to commit inventory
                       trnStock.Rollback()
                       CheckOrCommit = -4
                       GoTo ExitCheckOrCommit
                    End If
                 End If
              End If
           Else
              'Can't find item
              CheckOrCommit = -3
              If blnCommit Then
                 trnStock.Rollback()
              End If
              GoTo ExitCheckOrCommit
           End If
           .Close()
        End With
     Next bytItem
     If blnCommit Then
        'Commit the inventory
        trnStock.Commit()
     End If
  End With
  CheckOrCommit = CShort(bytItem)
  'Remainder of code omitted
```

Replacing Recordsets with DataTables

DataSet objects and the DataTables they contain are the cornerstone of .NET data access. As mentioned in the earlier " DataAdapter, DataSet, and DataTable Objects " section, ADO.NET DataTables are similar to disconnected ADODB.Recordset objects but offer much greater versatility. This chapter is devoted to simple data structures returned by queries, so a DataTable suffices.

Filling a DataTable with an SQL DataAdapter

Here are the steps to create and fill a simple DataTable object:

1. Define an SqlConnection object and set its ConnectionString property.

2. Define an SqlDataAdapter object with the SQL statement to return the DataSet's contents and specify the SqlConnection object.

3. Define a new `DataTable` object with a name that reflects its contents.

4. Invoke the `Fill` method of the `SqlDataAdapter` to open the connection, execute the query, fill the `DataTable` with the query result set, and close the connection automatically.

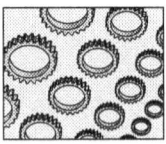

NOTE

If you open the connection prior to invoking the `Fill` method, the connection remains open after filling the `DataTable`.

Following is the generic Visual Basic .NET code that corresponds to the preceding steps:

```
Dim cnnConn As [SqlConnection = ] New SqlConnection(strConnect)
Dim daAdapter As [SqlDataAdapter = ] New SqlDataAdapter(strSQL, cnnConn)
Dim dtTable As [DataTable = ] New DataTable(strName)
daAdapter.Fill(dtTable)
```

NOTE

You can bind a `DataGrid` to a `DataTable` object by setting the `DataGrid`'s `DataSource` property to the `DataTable`. You can also specify a `DataView` over the table and bind the `DataView` to a `DataGrid`. `DataViews` let you sort and filter the table data, and invoke familiar `Find`, `AddNew`, and `Delete` methods. Thus, it's more accurate to say that a `DataView`, not a `DataTable`, is the analog of a disconnected `Recordset`.

Retrieving Values from the DataRowCollection with Code

After filling the `DataTable`, your next step is to traverse its rows and retrieve the values. Unlike `Recordsets`, `DataTables` don't have **MoveNext** or any other **Move…** commands or equivalents, nor do they have a **Fields** collection. Familiar **BOF** and **EOF** properties are also missing. `DataTables` consist of *collections* of `DataRow` and `DataColumn` objects. To access rows, you define an object variable for the `DataRowCollection`, specify the `Rows` property of the `DataTable` as the source of the collection, and then iterate the collection's `Items` with a `For Each …` or `For intCtr = 0 To Collection.Count -1` loop.

Here's the generic Visual Basic .NET code to iterate the rows of the `DataTable` populated in the preceding section and return values to `String` variables:

```
Dim drcRowColl As DataRowCollection = dtTable.Rows
With drcRowColl
   For intRow = 0 to .Count -1
      strCol0 = .Item(intRow)(0).ToString
      …
      strCol4 = .Item(intRow)(4).ToString
```

```
    Next intRow
End With
```

If the table has only a single row, you can shortcut the preceding code by defining a
`DataRow` object as shown here:

```
Dim drRow As DataRow = dtTable.Rows(0)
With drcRow
   strCol0 = .Item(0).ToString
   …
   strCol4 = .Item(4).ToString
End With
```

It's obvious at this point that replacing firehose-cursor `Recordset` objects with
`DataTables` isn't a piece of cake. Instead of a simple `rstData =`
`cnnConn.Execute(strSQL)` instruction, you must instantiate a `DataAdapter` and
`DataRowsCollection` to return individual data values from multiple `DataRow` objects.

If you need information about the table columns, such as the column name for generating
elements of an XML document with code, you open a `DataColumnCollection` object
from the `DataTable`'s `Columns` property, as shown in this example:

```
Dim drcColColl As DataColumnCollection = dtTable.Columns
With drcColColl
   For intCol = 0 to .Count -1
      strName = .Item(intCol).ColumnName
      …
      strType = .Item(intCol).DataType.ToString
   Next intColw
End With
```

The `DataColumnCollection.Item(intCol).ColumnName` property
corresponds to ADO's `Recordset.Fields(intCol).Name`, and
`.Item(intCol).DataType.ToString` is the counterpart to
`.Fields(intCol).Type.`

The built-in XML features of `DataTables` and related objects eliminate much of the
code required to generate XML documents from relational data. The price of `DataSet`
versatility, however, is the additional code for ordinary `Recordset`-style operations.

Substituting a DataTable for the GetDistInventory Method's rstBrand Recordset

The design of the `clsFulfillOrders.GetDistInventory` method requires a list of
distributors for a particular brand to remain open while determining inventory for a particular
SKU. If you replace all `Recordsets` with `SqlDataReaders`, you must provide a
separate connection for `sdrBrand`, which replaces `rstBrand`. Alternatively, you can

create an array or `ArrayList` to hold the DistID values. Another alternative is to replace `rstBrand` with a `DataTable` object, `dtBrand`, as shown in the following example:

```vb
'Declarations section code omitted
strProdConn = "Data Source=" & strProdServer & _
    ";Initial Catalog=OCE_Prod;UID=" & strProdUser & ";PWD=" & strProdPwd
cnnProd.ConnectionString = strProdConn
cnnProd.Open()
If Err.Number = 0 Then
    strSQL = "SELECT BrandID, Cost FROM Products WHERE SKU = '" & _
        strSKU & "'"
    Dim cmmProd As SqlCommand = cnnProd.CreateCommand
    With cmmProd
        .CommandType = CommandType.Text
        .CommandText = strSQL
        sdrProd = .ExecuteReader
    End With
    If sdrProd.Read Then
        strSQL = "SELECT DistID FROM BrandDistributor WHERE BrandID = '" & _
            sdrProd.GetString(0) & "'"
        strBrandID = sdrProd.GetString(0)
        sdrProd.Close()
        Dim daBrand As New SqlDataAdapter(strSQL, cnnProd)
        daBrand.Fill(dtBrand)
        Dim drcBrand As DataRowCollection = dtBrand.Rows
        If drcBrand.Count > 0 Then
            For bytDist = 0 To drcBrand.Count - 1
                'Query each distributor
                strSQL = "SELECT DistID, InventoryWS, ServerName, " & _
                    "[Database], UserName, Password, InventoryWS " & _
                    "FROM Distributors WHERE DistID = '" & _
                    drcBrand(bytDist)(0).ToString & "'"
                With cmmProd
                    .CommandText = strSQL
                    sdrDist = .ExecuteReader
                End With
                With sdrDist
                    '1-based array
                    bytDist = bytDist + 1
                    If .Read Then
                        astrResponse(bytDist, 1) = .GetString(0)
                        Select Case .GetString(0)
                            Case "ALPH"
                                astrResponse(bytDist, 2) = _
                                    objAlpha.CheckStock(.GetString(2), _
                                    .GetString(3), .GetString(4), _
                                    .GetString(5), strSKU, blnUseWS)
                            Case "BETA"
                                astrResponse(bytDist, 2) = _
```

```
                            objBeta.CheckStock(.GetString(2), _
                                .GetString(3), .GetString(4), _
                                .GetString(5), strSKU, blnUseWS)
                        Case "GAMM"
                            astrResponse(bytDist, 2) = _
                                objGamma.CheckStock(.GetString(2), _
                                .GetString(3), .GetString(4), _
                                .GetString(5), strSKU, blnUseWS)
                    End Select
                Else
                    'No distributor for this product
                    astrResponse(bytDist, 1) = "NONE"
                    astrResponse(bytDist, 2) = "Error: No distributor " & _
                        "for SKU " & strSKU
                End If
                If Err.Number <> 0 And _
                        astrResponse(bytDist, 1) <> "NONE" Then
                    astrResponse(bytDist, 1) = "NONE"
                    astrResponse(bytDist, 2) = "ERROR: " & Err.Description
                End If
                .Close()
            End With
        Next bytDist
        'Preferred distributor code omitted
    Else
        astrResponse(bytDist, 1) = "NONE"
        astrResponse(bytDist, 2) = "Error: No distributor for " & _
            "BrandID " & strBrandID
    End If
    Else
        'Shouldn't occur
        astrResponse(bytDist, 1) = "NONE"
        astrResponse(bytDist, 2) = "Error: No record for SKU " & strSKU
    End If
Else
    GetDistInventory = "No"
End If
```

Migrating XML Web Services to ADO.NET

The preceding examples of client-side modifications cover upgrading most single-component XML Web services from ADO to ADO.NET. Following are basic recommendations to maximize performance with ADO.NET:

▶ Always use the `ExecuteScalar` method to return single values.

▶ Use dynamic SQL or stored procedures and the `ExecuteNonQuery` method for `INSERT`, `UPDATE`, and `DELETE` operations.

- ▶ Create `SqlDataReader` objects to return single rows with multiple values and `GetType` methods to deliver the appropriate native .NET datatype. Consider `SqlDataReaders` for multiple-row result sets when your row-processing code is simple.

- ▶ Use `SqlDataAdapters` and `DataTables` only when you need a scrollable cursor or must invoke row-by-row `Execute...` methods on the connection.

- ▶ Reuse your `SqlCommand` objects. Assigning new `CommandText`, `Transaction`, and `Execute...` values is faster than creating a new `SqlCommand` object for each operation.

- ▶ Remove the ADODB reference after you upgrade all ADO code to ADO.NET.

If you have a Windows form test harness that can call .NET components and their corresponding XML Web services, upgrade and test the component before altering the XML Web service code. It's usually easier and faster to debug components than services, and initial ADO-versus-ADO.NET performance comparisons are likely to be more precise. If your ADO.NET component runs faster than the ADO version, it's a safe bet that the upgraded XML Web service will deliver a similar performance improvement. After initial testing, simply copy the upgraded code to the ASP.NET service.

TIP

Remember to add the `Imports System.Data.SqlClient` *directive to each component before modifying the code.*

The OmegaBank .NET Component and Related Web Services

The `OmegaBank` component of OCE-OrdersADO.sln has the highest upgrade priority because each new order invokes the `clsOmegaBank.VerifyOrHold` method at least once. If the customer's credit card passes muster, client code calls `VerifyOrHold` again and, if the items are in stock or partial shipments are allowed, calls `ChargeOrCredit` once when the order ships.

Upgrading the VerifyOrHold Method

The `VerifyOrHold` function illustrates use of the three `...Execute` and several `GetType` methods. A single `SqlCommand` object handles all data-related operations on the connection. Boldface indicates ADO.NET changes to the original Visual Basic .NET code:

```
Public Function VerifyOrHold(ByVal strServer As String, …)
    'Declaration section omitted, except these change
    Dim cnnVerify As New SqlConnection()
    Dim sdrVerify As SqlDataReader
    Dim lngReccnt As Integer 'Was Object

    strNetConn = "Data Source=" & strServer & _
        ";Initial Catalog=OMB_Network;UID=" & strUser & ";PWD=" & strPwd
```

```
cnnVerify.ConnectionString = strNetConn
cnnVerify.Open()
If Err.Number <> 0 Then
   VerifyOrHold = "ERROR: " & Err.Description & " (" & Err.Number & ")"
   GoTo exitVerifyOrHold
End If
'Check merchant account
strSQL = "SELECT COUNT(MerchantID) FROM Merchants " & _
   "WHERE MerchantID = " & CStr(lngMerchantID)
Dim cmmVerify As SqlCommand = cnnVerify.CreateCommand
With cmmVerify
   .CommandType = CommandType.Text
   .CommandText = strSQL
   If CInt(.ExecuteScalar()) = 0 Then
      VerifyOrHold = "Error: Merchant account " & _
         CStr(lngMerchantID) & " not found."
      GoTo exitVerifyOrHold
   End If
   'Check credit-card status
   strSQL = "SELECT Canceled, Issuer, CardName, ZipCode, ExpDate, " & _
      "Available FROM Authorize WHERE CardNumber = '" & _
      strCardNumber & "'"
   .CommandText = strSQL
   sdrVerify = .ExecuteReader
End With
With sdrVerify
   If .Read Then
'Expiration date calculation removed
      datExpDate = CDate(strExpDate)
      curAvailable = .GetDecimal(5)
      'Initial credit-card check
      If .GetBoolean(0) = True Then
         VerifyOrHold = CStr(lngRefNum) & " Declined: " & strIssuer & _
            " " & strCardNumber & " is canceled (19)"
      ElseIf .GetString(1) <> strIssuer Then
         VerifyOrHold = CStr(lngRefNum) & _
            " Declined: Issuer mismatch (18)"
      ElseIf .GetString(2) <> strCardName Then
         VerifyOrHold = CStr(lngRefNum) & _
            " Declined: Cardholder name mismatch (17)"
      ElseIf .GetString(3) <> strZipCode Then
         VerifyOrHold = CStr(lngRefNum) & _
            " Declined: Cardholder ZIP Code mismatch (16)"
      ElseIf .GetDateTime(4) <> datExpDate Then
         VerifyOrHold = CStr(lngRefNum) & _
            " Declined: Expiration date mismatch (15)"
      ElseIf DateDiff(Microsoft.VisualBasic.DateInterval.Day, Today, _
            datExpDate) < 1 Then
         VerifyOrHold = CStr(lngRefNum) & _
```

```
                    " Declined: Card expired " & .GetString(4) & " (13)"
          End If
      Else
          VerifyOrHold = CStr(lngRefNum) & " Error: " & strIssuer & _
             " Card number " & strCardNumber & " not found (0)."
      End If
      .Close()
  End With
If Len(VerifyOrHold) > 0 Then
      GoTo exitVerifyOrHold
  End If
  'Get current available credit
  strSQL = "SELECT SUM(Amount) FROM Transactions WHERE CardNumber = '" & _
      strCardNumber & "' AND AppliedToStatement IS NULL"
  With cmmVerify
      .CommandText = strSQL
      If Not IsDBNull(.ExecuteScalar) Then
          curAvailable = curAvailable + CDec(.ExecuteScalar)
      End If
  End With
  'Check available credit
  If curAvailable < curTransactAmt Then
      VerifyOrHold = CStr(lngRefNum) & _
          " Declined: Insufficient credit available (14)"
      GoTo exitVerifyOrHold
  Else
      VerifyOrHold = CStr(lngRefNum) & " Verify Code: " & _
          CStr(Int(1000 * Rnd())) & "OMB" & CStr(Int(100000 * Rnd())) & _
          " (12)"
  End If
  If blnApplyHold Then
      'Change to debit
      curTransactAmt = -curTransactAmt
      strDateTime = CStr(Now)
      'TypeID 31 is "Hold applied by merchant"
      strSQL = "INSERT Transactions(MerchantID, Reference, CardNumber, " & _
          "TransactionDate, TransactionTypeID, Amount) " & "VALUES(" & _
          CStr(lngMerchantID) & ", " & CStr(lngRefNum) & ", '" & _
          strCardNumber & "', '" & strDateTime & "', 31, " & _
          CStr(curTransactAmt) & ")"
      With cmmVerify
          .CommandText = strSQL
          lngReccnt = .ExecuteNonQuery
      End With
      If lngReccnt = 1 Then
          strSQL = "SELECT @@IDENTITY"
          With cmmVerify
              .CommandText = strSQL
              lngTransactID = CInt(.ExecuteScalar)
```

```
            VerifyOrHold = CStr(lngRefNum) & " Hold on " & _
                Format(-curTransactAmt, "$#,##0.00") & _
                " applied by TRID " & CStr(lngTransactID) & " (12)"
          End With
      Else
          VerifyOrHold = CStr(lngRefNum) & _
              " Error: Unable to apply hold      (99)"
      End If
    End If
exitVerifyOrHold:
    sdrVerify.Close()
    cnnVerify.Close()
End Function
```

Using Get *Type* methods makes the preceding ADO.NET code "cleaner" and easier to read than the original ADO version.

TIP

Upgrade and test each function of a class in sequence. Making numerous changes to several functions and then testing the class makes debugging more difficult.

Upgrading the ChargeOrCredit Method

The `ChargeOrCredit` function uses a `Transaction` object to assure that a charge to a customer's credit card releases the prior hold by reversing its amount or, in the case of a partial shipment, reduces the hold by the amount of the current charge. Adding a record to the Transactions table for each event maintains an audit trail for the customer's account.

```
Public Function ChargeOrCredit(ByVal strServer As String, …)
   'Declaration section omitted, except these changes
   Dim cnnCharge As New SqlConnection()
   Dim sdrCharge As SqlDataReader
   Dim lngReccnt As Integer 'Was Object

   strNetConn = "Data Source=" & strServer & _
     ";Initial Catalog=OMB_Network;UID=" & strUser & ";PWD=" & strPwd
   cnnCharge.ConnectionString = strNetConn
   cnnCharge.Open()
   If Err.Number <> 0 Then
     ChargeOrCredit = "ERROR: " & Err.Description & " (" & Err.Number & ")"
     GoTo exitChargeOrCredit
   End If
   strSQL = "SELECT COUNT(MerchantID) FROM Merchants " & _
     "WHERE MerchantID = " & CStr(lngMerchantID)
   Dim cmmCharge As SqlCommand = cnnCharge.CreateCommand
   With cmmCharge
     .CommandText = strSQL
     If CInt(.ExecuteScalar) = 0 Then
```

```
          ChargeOrCredit = "Error: Merchant account " & _
            CStr(lngMerchantID) & " not found."
          GoTo exitChargeOrCredit
        End If
        strSQL = "SELECT TransactionTypeID, Amount FROM Transactions " & _
"WHERE TransactionID = " & CStr(lngRelTransactID)
        'The following has been restructured
.CommandText = strSQL
        sdrCharge = .ExecuteReader
      End With
      With sdrCharge
        If .Read Then
          'TypeID 31 is "Hold applied by merchant"
          If .GetByte(0) = 31 Then
            strDateTime = CStr(Now)
            If blnReleaseHold Then
              strStatusID = CStr(35) 'Hold Removed by Merchant
              curHoldAmt = -.GetDecimal(1)
            Else
              strStatusID = CStr(34) 'Hold Reduced by Merchant
              curHoldAmt = curTransactAmt
            End If
          Else
            ChargeOrCredit = CStr(lngRefNum) & " Error: Status " & _
              "of reference transaction is not Apply Hold (99)"
            GoTo exitChargeOrCredit
          End If
        Else
          ChargeOrCredit = "Error: Related transaction " & _
            CStr(lngRelTransactID) & " not found."
          GoTo exitChargeOrCredit
        End If
        .Close()
      End With
      With cmmCharge
        trnCharge = cnnCharge.BeginTransaction
        strSQL = "INSERT Transactions(MerchantID, Reference, CardNumber, " & _
          "TransactionDate, TransactionTypeID, Amount, " & _
          "RelatedTransactionID) " & "VALUES(" & CStr(lngMerchantID) & _
          ", " & CStr(lngRefNum) & ", '" & strCardNumber & "', '" & _
          strDateTime & "', 34, " & CStr(curHoldAmt) & ", " & _
          CStr(lngRelTransactID) & ")"
        .Transaction = trnCharge
        .CommandText = strSQL
        lngReccnt = .ExecuteNonQuery
        If lngReccnt <> 1 Then
          'Error
          trnCharge.Rollback()
          ChargeOrCredit = "Error: Unable to commit transaction " & _
```

```
        CStr(lngRelTransactID) & " not found."
      GoTo exitChargeOrCredit
    End If
    'StatusID 32 = Debit by Merchant
    curTransactAmt = -curTransactAmt
    strSQL = "INSERT Transactions(MerchantID, Reference, CardNumber, " & _
      "TransactionDate, TransactionTypeID, Amount, " & _
      "RelatedTransactionID) & _" & "VALUES(" & CStr(lngMerchantID) & _
      ", " & CStr(lngRefNum) & ", '" & strCardNumber & "', '" & _
      strDateTime & "', 32, " & CStr(curTransactAmt) & ", " & _
      CStr(lngRelTransactID) & ")"
    .CommandText = strSQL
    lngReccnt = .ExecuteNonQuery
    If lngReccnt = 1 Then
      trnCharge.Commit()
    Else
      ChargeOrCredit = CStr(lngRefNum) & " Error: Charge " & _
        "transaction didn't commit (99)"
      trnCharge.Rollback()
      GoTo exitChargeOrCredit
    End If
    strSQL = "SELECT @@IDENTITY"
    .Transaction = Nothing
    .CommandText = strSQL
    lngTransactID = CInt(.ExecuteScalar)
    If lngTransactID > 0 Then
      ChargeOrCredit = CStr(lngRefNum) & " Debit " & _
        Format(curTransactAmt, "$#,##0.00") & " applied by TRID " & _
        CStr(lngTransactID) & " (32)"
    Else
      ChargeOrCredit = CStr(lngRefNum) & " Error: Unable " & _
        "to obtain Transaction ID (99)"
    End If
  End With
exitChargeOrCredit:
  sdrCharge.Close()
  cnnCharge.Close()
End Function
```

After you test all component functions, remove the ADODB reference from the component or ASP.NET Web Service project. Rebuild the project to verify that all vestiges of ADO are gone.

Upgrading the Local OmegaBank XML Web Service

The preceding examples apply to modifying code for a .NET component or ASP.NET Web Service. If you use the component-to-service approach for development, add **Imports System.Data.SqlClient** under Imports System.Web.Services, replace the service's original code with the upgraded ADO.NET component code, and remove the project's ADODB reference. In a production environment, copy the original XML Web service project to a new folder, add a new IIS virtual directory that points to the folder, and replace the copied project's code.

TIP

Replace only the code between each existing `Public Function ... End Function` *line to preserve the service's documentation.*

There's a gotcha in the `XCOPY` deployment process when you make copies of Visual Studio .NET solutions for upgrading or other modifications and the solution includes references to .NET components. The component references point to the original files, not the copies you make in the new folder. For example, the OCE_OrdersADO client's local OmegaBankWS Web Reference points to http://localhost/OmegaWS/OmegaBank.asmx, which is located in the \VBWS04\OCE_OrdersNET\Services\OmegaWS folder. If you copy your upgraded component code to ...\OmegaWS\OmegaBank.asmx.vb, you overwrite the original version.

CAUTION

Altering the code of VBWS04 services prevents use of the VBWS04 client test harness for performance comparisons.

If you want to preserve the XML Web service code you created in Chapter 4, do the following:

1. Create four local IIS virtual directories named OmegaNET, AlphaNET, BetaNET, and GammaNET, and point each virtual directory to the corresponding subfolder of \VBWS05\OCE_OrdersADO\Services.

2. Open \VBWS05\OCE_OrdersADO\Services\Services.sln, and remove the AlphaWS, BetaWS, GammaWS, and OmegaWS projects, because the files for these three projects are located in \VBWS04 subfolders and point to the original virtual directories.

3. Open in Notepad each of the *ProjectName*.vbproj.webinfo files for the four services under \VBWS05\OCE_OrdersADO\Services, and change the `<Web URLPath=` attribute value from `http://localhost/`*ServiceWS*`/`*ProjectWS*`.vbproj` to **`http://localhost/`*ServiceNET*`/`*ProjectWS*`.vbproj`**. For example, change `http://localhost/OmegaWS/OmegaWS.vbproj` to **`http://localhost/OmegaNET/OmegaWS.vbproj`**.

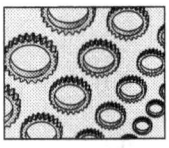

NOTE

If you don't change the `URLPath` *value in the webinfo file, you receive an "Unable to open Web project 'ProjectName'..." error message, and the project won't add to the solution.*

4. Right-click the Solution '*Services*' node, choose Add | Existing Project, and add the four projects under \VBWS05\OCE_OrdersADO\Services.

5. Verify that each project's files are in the correct subfolder by right-clicking the *ServiceName*.asmx file, choosing View Code, and hovering the mouse over the document tab to display its path.

6. Add **Imports System.Data.SqlClient** under Imports System.Web.Services to each of the services.

7. Rebuild Services.sln.

8. Run the client test harness with the Use XML Web Services check box marked to verify that the unmodified Web services operate correctly.

9. Replace the code of \VBWS05\OCE_OrdersNET\Services\OmegaWS\OmegaBank.asmx.vb's two functions with the component function code.

10. Remove the ADODB reference, rebuild the solution, and test the service with the client test harness.

The preceding (laborious) process was used to recreate the \VBWS05\OCE_ClientADO\ Services\Services.sln solution with projects that point to the http://localhost/ *ServiceName*ADO virtual directories.

Distributor .NET Components and XML Web Services

Upgrading the AlphaDist, BetaDist, and GammaDist components and their corresponding XML Web services doesn't offer the potential of a substantial improvement in overall performance. The test client invokes these components or services only for outsourced products, which represent about 17 percent of the SKUs in the OCE_Prod database's Product table. The common CheckStock function provides an example of two useful SqlReader methods that aren't covered in the preceding examples. The modifications of the following sections remove dependence on ADODB from all OCE XML Web services.

Using the GetValues and GetName Methods to Upgrade the CheckStock Function

The ADO.NET upgrade to the CheckStock function takes advantage of the sqlDataReader.GetValues method to return an Object array, which contains the column values as elements. To obtain a corresponding array of column names for elements of XML documents you serialize with code, invoke the GetName(int*Col*) function to return a String value containing the column name.

Following is the upgraded code for the CheckStock method of the three distributor components and corresponding XML Web services. Almost every line in this function requires changing Field(intCtr) references to avarValues(intCtr), astrNames(intCtr), or both, so the modifications aren't shown in boldface.

```
Public Function CheckStock(ByVal strServer As String, ...)
    'The following are modified or added declarations
    Dim cnnInventory As New SqlConnection()
    Dim sdrInventory As SqlDataReader = Nothing
    Dim avarValues(12) As Object
```

```vb
Dim astrNames(12) As String
On Error Resume Next

strConn = "Data Source=" & strServer & ";Initial Catalog=" & _
    strDatabase & ";UID=" & strUser & ";PWD=" & strPassword
cnnInventory.ConnectionString = strConn
cnnInventory.Open()
If Err.Number = 0 Then
    'Get the product data
    strSQL = "SELECT * FROM Products WHERE SKU = '" & strSKU & "'"
    Dim cmmInventory As SqlCommand = cnnInventory.CreateCommand
    With cmmInventory
        .CommandType = CommandType.Text
        .CommandText = strSQL
        sdrInventory = .ExecuteReader
    End With
    With sdrInventory
        If .Read Then
            .GetValues(avarValues)
            For intCol = 0 To 12
                astrNames(intCol) = .GetName(intCol)
            Next intCol
            .Close()
        Else
            CheckStock = "Error: " & strDatabase & _

                " doesn't recognize SKU " & strSKU
            GoTo ExitCheckStock
        End If
    End With
    If blnXML Then
        'Serialize report to XML
        strXML = "<" & strDatabase & "Inventory>" & vbCrLf
        For intCol = 0 To 4
            strXML = strXML & "   <" & astrNames(intCol) & ">" & _
                avarValues(intCol).ToString & "</" & _
                astrNames(intCol) & ">" & vbCrLf
        Next intCol
        For intCol = 5 To 7
            strXML = strXML & "   <" & astrNames(intCol) & ">"
            If IsDBNull(avarValues(intCol)) Then
                'Do nothing
            ElseIf intCol = 7 Then
                'Weight
                strXML = strXML & avarValues(intCol).ToString & " lbs"
            Else
                'Money
                strXML = strXML & _
                    Format(CDec(avarValues(intCol)), "$#,##0.00")
```

```
        End If
        strXML = strXML & "</" & astrNames(intCol) & ">" & vbCrLf
    Next intCol
    For intCol = 9 To 12
        strXML = strXML & "   <" & astrNames(intCol) & ">"
        'AllowanceID
        If CDec(avarValues(9)) > 0 Then
            If intCol = 9 Then
                strXML = strXML & avarValues(9).ToString
            ElseIf intCol = 10 Then
                strXML = strXML & _
                    Format(CDec(avarValues(10)), "$#,##0.00")
            End If
        End If
        If CByte(avarValues(11)) > 0 Then
            If intCol = 11 Then
                strXML = strXML & avarValues(11).ToString
            ElseIf intCol = 12 Then
                strXML = strXML & Format(CSng(avarValues(12)), "#0.0%")
            End If
        End If
        strXML = strXML & "</" & astrNames(intCol) & ">" & vbCrLf
        If intCol = 10 Or intCol = 12 Then
            'Add the allowance type element
            If intCol = 10 Then
                strXML = strXML & "   <AllowanceType>"
            Else
                strXML = strXML & "   <DiscountType>"
            End If
            If (CByte(avarValues(9)) > 0 And intCol = 10) _
                    Or (CByte(avarValues(11)) > 0 And intCol = 12) Then
                strSQL = "SELECT AllowanceDiscount FROM " & _
                    "AllowancesDiscounts WHERE AllowDiscID = " & _
                    avarValues(intCol - 1).ToString
                With cmmInventory
                    .CommandText = strSQL
                    strXML = strXML & CStr(.ExecuteScalar)
                End With
            End If
            If intCol = 10 Then
                strXML = strXML & "</AllowanceType>"
            Else
                strXML = strXML & "</DiscountType>"
            End If
            strXML = strXML & vbCrLf
        End If
    Next intCol
    intCol = 8
    strXML = strXML & "   <" & astrNames(intCol) & "InStock>" & _
```

```
        avarValues(intCol).ToString & "</" & astrNames(intCol) & _
        "InStock>" & vbCrLf
     strXML = strXML & "   <DateTime>" & CStr(Now) & _
        "</DateTime>" & vbCrLf
     strXML = strXML & "</" & strDatabase & "Inventory>" & vbCrLf
     CheckStock = strXML
  Else
     'Return string in cookie format removed for brevity
  End If
Else
  CheckStock = "ERROR: " & Err.Description
End If
ExitCheckStock:
  sdrInventory.Close()
  cnnInventory.Close()
End Function
```

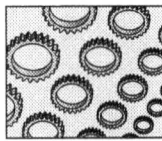

NOTE

The AlphaDist.asmx.vb code in the VBWS05\OCEClient_ADO\Services\AlphaWS folder includes commented original code. The remaining two distributor services don't include the commented code.

Upgrading the PlaceOrder Method

The `PlaceOrder` function requires changing the `ADODB.Connection` to an `SqlConnection` object, and creating an `SqlCommand` object on which you invoke `ExecuteScalar` and `ExecuteNonQuery` methods. The changes are simple, so there's no code example for modifying this function. After you modify and test both functions, don't forget to remove the project's ADODB reference.

Copying Upgraded Code to the Local Distributor XML Web Services

Use the same process to upgrade the AlphaWS, BetaWS, and GammaWS code as you did for OmegaWS in the earlier "Upgrading the Local OmegaBank XML Web Service" section. If you completed all ten steps required to upgrade OmegaBankWS, repeat step 9 for each of the distributor services, and then rebuild and test the solution. As mentioned in the "Upgrading the Local OmegaBank XML Web Service" tip, replace only the code between each existing `Public Function … End Function` lines to preserve the service's documentation. The process is a bit tedious but takes only a few minutes, because the code for each function is identical for all three distributors.

Comparing the Performance of ADO and ADO.NET Components and Services

It takes a substantial time and energy investment to move from ADO to ADO.NET in a production-grade XML Web service. Return on investment (ROI) became the watchword of

IT management in mid-2001 and is likely to remain the primary project selection criterion for the remainder of the decade. If your ADO-based XML Web services meet reliability goals, the only benefit of moving to ADO.NET is better performance. The ROI from improved performance is reduced expenditures for upgraded or additional hardware to handle current or anticipated XML Web service load.

Chapter 4's "Evaluating Performance of Upgraded .NET Clients and XML Web Services" demonstrates that moving from Visual Basic 6.0 COM components with SOAP Toolkit wrappers to ASP.NET Web Services delivers about a 60 percent performance boost. The following table lists the average time in seconds to process about 5000 orders with the original ADO 2.7 (unmodified OCE_OrdersADO) and the upgraded ADO.NET (OCEClientADO) versions.

Configuration	ADO 2.7 Version	ADO.NET Version
Local .NET components	0.461	0.388
Local XML Web services	0.577	0.486
Remote XML Web services (client and service upgrades)	0.704	0.597
Remote XML Web services (service upgrades only)	0.662	0.597

The last table row compares the execution times for the upgraded client calling the original services (Remote ADO 2.7 Services check box marked) and the upgraded services (check box cleared). Partially upgrading the client from ADO to ADO.NET contributes 0.042 seconds of the performance improvement; fully upgrading the services to ADO.NET contributes a 0.135-second gain.

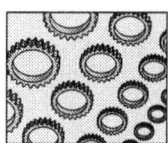

NOTE

The Remote XML Web services transfer data between the client test harness and the IIS server via the 10-Mbps hub of a DSL router. Running the remote tests requires at least an hour each to generate a sufficient number of outsourced orders for meaningful comparisons. Remote comparisons over an Internet connection aren't valid because latency and data rate vary during the tests.

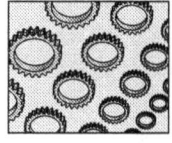

NOTE

*The average amount of a completed order is $1035, and approximately 65 percent of the orders generated complete. Using an average order-processing time of 0.5 seconds, the sample code can handle $1035 * 0.65 * 120 = $80,370 worth of orders per minute. This corresponds to a yearly sales volume of about $40 billion.*

The approximate 15 percent performance boost delivered by moving to ADO.NET includes contributions from the client test harness and component or XML Web service upgrades. Including client-side performance gains with those of the sample services is valid, because typical client-side data access performance improvements also accrue to services of increased complexity. As an example, if OmegaBank's hardware investment to support initial XML Web service usage is $100,000, the return of a 15 percent performance improvement is the lesser of $15,000 or the incremental cost to add 15 percent more capacity, which might range from $5000 to $10,000. Assuming programming, testing, and deployment time for the ADO-to-ADO.NET upgrade totals 20 hours at $150 per hour, the IT investment is $3000. The immediate return ranges from $5000 to $15,000; the cost savings over several years of significant traffic growth is much greater.

Converting XML Web Service Test Clients to ASP.NET

The primary topic of this book is XML Web services, but you also need to know how to design test and production Web pages that consume your XML Web services. Experienced Visual Basic developers are Windows form-oriented, and many find adopting a Web weltanschauung to be disconcerting or worse. It's also uncommon for database component and front-end developers to display graphic arts skills that equal their Visual Basic or VBScript coding wizardry. Thus, Web page design and application coding have diverged into separate—and often conflicting—occupational roles. One way to avoid conflicts is to create utilitarian client pages with the code for consuming your XML Web services and pass them to the graphic artists and usability gurus for the requisite face-lift.

Your technically oriented supervisor is likely to accept results from a Windows test client as proof of performance, reliability, and scalability of your XML Web services. Higher-level managers and executives, on the other hand, probably will demand Web-based evidence. Another benefit of providing a Web-based test harness for XML Web services is the ability to give everyone involved with the project a chance to test the services before you move them into production.

A drawback of traditional Web-based performance tests is that differences between execution time of local components and local or remote XML Web services are masked by random variations in the Web server's page delivery time. ASP.NET's new tracing feature overcomes these problems and enables precise analysis of execution time for individual code blocks behind pages. Tracing alone justifies the time and effort to convert test clients from Windows forms to ASP.NET Web pages.

Fortunately, ASP.NET makes it easy to move existing Windows forms and their underlying Visual Basic .NET code to Web Forms. Even better, the debugging process for ASP.NET projects is almost identical to that for Windows forms and their classes, components, and XML Web services. Experienced ASP VBScript coders will appreciate the demise of performance analysis that requires adding—and then removing—scores of `Response.Write(strElapsedTime)` instructions from scripts.

The primary objective of this chapter is to show you how to migrate moderately complex Visual Basic .NET applications to ASP.NET Web pages with minimum effort and aggravation. The source of the Windows form example is Chapter 5's OCE_ClientADO project. A secondary goal is to demonstrate use of ASP.NET's data-bound server controls and ADO.NET's `DataSet` objects. These server controls emulate in HTML data-bound Windows form and Visual Basic 6.0 controls.

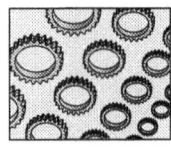

NOTE

This chapter assumes acquaintance with basic ASP.NET Web Form design techniques, but doesn't require ASP coding experience. If Web Forms are totally new to you or you need an ASP.NET tutorial and reference, check out Greg Buczek's ASP.NET Developer's Guide (McGraw-Hill/Osborne, ISBN 0-07-219288-7).

Emulating a Windows Form with a New ASP.NET Web Form

ASP.NET's empty design document is quite similar to that for Windows forms except that it fills the entire page. The Web Form Toolbox contains a collection of native HTML controls and Web forms controls, called *server controls,* which emulate most of those in the Windows form Toolbox. The repertoire of Web forms server controls is adequate for migrating Windows applications that have simple UIs, such as the OakLeaf Consumer Electronics test project. (Adapting applications with multiple complex Windows forms to ASP.NET pages is beyond the scope of this book.)

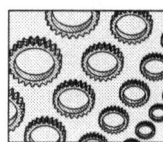

NOTE

Performing the following steps is a tedious, hour-long exercise, so VBWS06.zip contains a prefabricated OCE-Orders.sln solution in the \OCE_OrdersASP folder that does the grunt work for you. Download VBWS06.zip from http://www.osborne.com/downloads/downloads.shtml and expand it into a \VBWS06 folder. The solution depends on code in VBWS05.zip. If you haven't downloaded and installed the contents of VBWS05.zip in a \VBWS05 folder, do so before opening OCE-Orders.sln.

Following is the generic procedure for migrating a simple Windows form to a Web Form; parentheses enclose values used to create the sample OCE-Orders ASP.NET solution:

1. Create a new folder and, optionally, a subfolder for the ASP.NET project (\VBWS06\OCE_OrdersASP).

2. Create a new virtual directory, give the directory an appropriate alias name, and specify the folder or subfolder you created as the source folder (OCE-Orders and \VBWS06\OCE_OrdersASP).

3. Open a new ASP.NET project and specify the folder or subfolder as the source for the project files.

4. Open the *PageName*.aspx Web Form design and *PageName*.aspx.vb code-behind documents (Orders.aspx and Orders.aspx.vb).

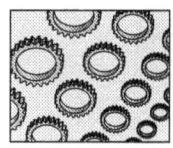

NOTE

The order in which you perform steps 5 through 13 isn't important.

5. Optionally, add a label at the top of the page to identify the form's purpose.

6. Add to the Web Form a set of server controls that corresponds to the controls of the original Windows form. Don't add a Close button; to "close" a Web page, you must close the browser.

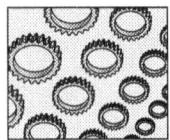

NOTE

The sample Orders.aspx design doesn't include the Windows form's two `DataGrid` controls. You add the server control equivalents in the section "Adding DataGrid Server Controls to Display Line Item and Order Information" near the end of the chapter.

7. Press F4 to open the Properties window and select a control. Assign the `Name` property value of the original controls to the new controls' `ID` property value. Set `Enabled`, `Visible`, and other property values to those of the original control, as shown here for the `cmdNewOrder` button.

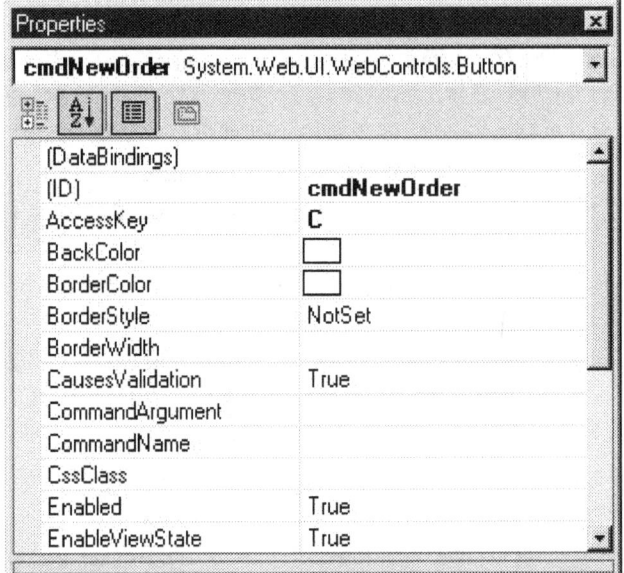

8. Substitute **−1** for the default 0 value of the `TabIndex` property of read-only or other controls you don't want in the tab order. Server controls don't have a `TabStop` property.

9. Right-click the background of the design document to open the DOCUMENT Properties Pages dialog. On the General page, type the title of the page in the Page Title text box.

10. Click the dialog's Color and Margins tab and click the Background text box's builder button (…) to add a background color. `Gainsboro (#dcdcdc)`, as shown here, is a good choice for emulating the default background color of a Windows form.

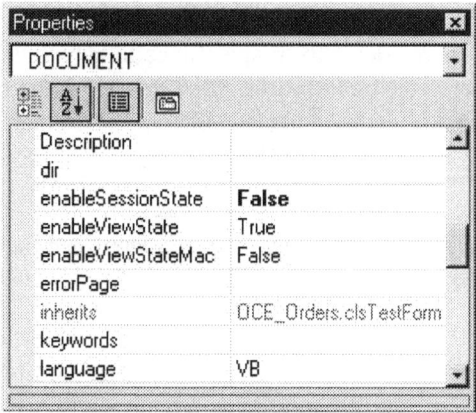

11. With no control selected, press F4 to open the DOCUMENT Properties window, and set the `EnableSessionState` property value to `False` to improve performance (slightly). Verify that `EnableViewState` is `True`, as shown here. This setting causes ASP.NET to save the state of server controls across HTTP requests.

12. Add the COM references required for the project, if any (ADODB and MSXML2 4.0).

13. Add in Solution Explorer class files from the original Windows form project (AddOrder.vb, FulfillOrder.vb, ShipCost.vb, and UpdateOrder.vb from \VBWS05\OCE_ClientADO\Client).

14. Add project references from the Windows form project (ADO.NET versions of AlphaDist.dll, BetaDist.dll, GammaDist.dll, and OmegaBank.dll from \VBWS05\OCE_ClientADO\Services*DistName*\Bin).

TIP

Copy the class files and projects to subfolders of your ASP.NET project if you want your ASP.NET project to be independent of the original Windows form project.

15. Add local Web references (ADO.NET versions of AlphaWS, BetaWS, GammaWS, and OmegaWS).

16. Add remote Web references (http://www.oakleaf.ws/adlphadist.asmx as AlphaWSADO, and so on).

17. Change `Public Class WebForm1` to a more descriptive name (**clsTestForm**).

18. Add the following lines above the `Public Class FormName` declaration:

```
Option Explicit On      'Not present by default (to accommodate VBScript)
Option Strict Off       'Change value to On to check datatype conflicts
Imports System.Data.SqlClient     'For data; you can substitute OleDb
Imports VB = Microsoft.VisualBasic  'Required for residual VB objects
```

19. Build and run the project.

If your class files contain Windows form-specific code, which they should not, you receive error messages during the build process. `DoEvents` is the most common culprit, but `DoEvents` statements don't belong in class files. Remove them.

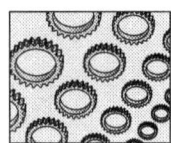

NOTE

At this point, you don't have references to controls in the project, so the build operation doesn't detect errors from missing or misnamed controls.

Figure 6-1 illustrates the Orders.aspx design document at the first stage of the migration.

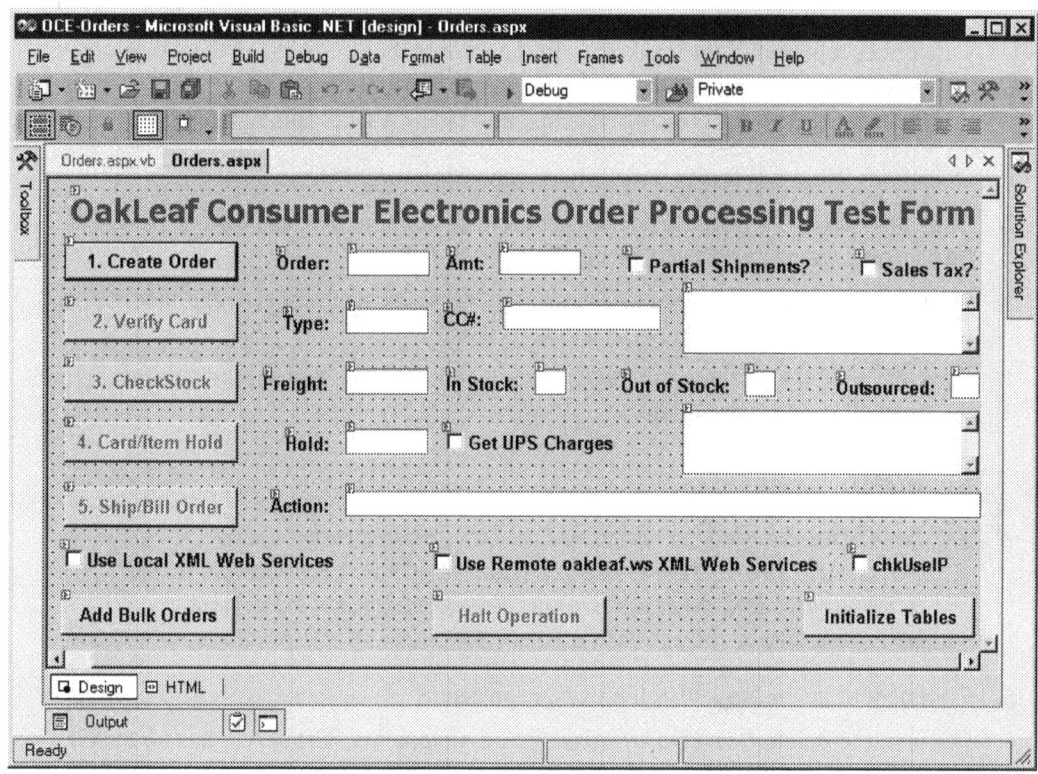

Figure 6-1   *The new Web Form has server controls equivalent to the original Windows form controls, except* `DataGrids`, *at this point.*

Pasting and Fixing Visual Basic .NET Code Behind the Web Form

ASP.NET executes most Visual Basic .NET code, except for instructions that depend on classes defined by the `System.Windows.Forms` namespace, such as message boxes and the Common Dialog controls, which don't have equivalent classes in the `System.Web.UI.WebControls` namespace. A few upgraded Visual Basic 6.0 controls, such as check boxes, have property names and values that differ from the corresponding native .NET versions.

The procedure for migrating Visual Basic .NET code to ASP.NET is similar to that described in Chapter 4 for upgrading Visual Basic .NET components to ASP.NET Web Services.

You copy and paste the Visual Basic .NET code behind the ASP.NET page, build the project, and fix the errors reported in the Task List. In most cases, build errors are easy to fix by changing a property name and value or adding simple workarounds.

Here's the generic drill for copying, pasting, and fixing Visual Basic .NET code:

1. Open your Windows forms project in a second instance of Visual Studio .NET.

2. Copy all form-level variable declarations and paste them below the `Web Form Designer Generated Code` block.

3. Copy the code within the `Form_Load` and `Form_Activated` event handlers, and paste it to the `Page_Load` event handler.

4. Copy the code for all remaining event handlers, functions, and subprocedures, below the `Page_Load` event handler.

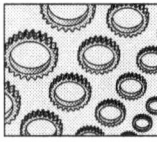

NOTE

The OCE-Client example doesn't include the `FillGrids` subprocedure and the `Form_Activated` and `cmdInitialize_Click` event handlers. The code for initializing the distributor databases requires Windows authentication and isn't necessary in this test scenario.

5. Comment or delete `Me` self-references, if present.

6. Comment or delete *`ControlName`*`.Focus` statements. The server has no means to set focus of a control on a client Web page.

7. Comment or delete `MsgBox` or `MessageBox.Show` statements. If your code relies on a Yes/No or similar response, modify the code to run the most appropriate action.

8. Comment or delete all `System.Windows.Forms.Application.DoEvents` statements.

9. If you upgraded the Windows form from Visual Basic 6.0, replace `chk`*`CheckBox`*`.CheckState = System.Windows.Forms.CheckState .Checked` statements with **`ChkCheckBox.Checked = True`**. Substitute **`False`** for `Unchecked`.

10. Replace `Private Sub chk`*`CheckBox`*`_CheckStateChanged` event handler declarations with **`Private Sub chk`*`CheckBox`*`_CheckedChanged`**. You must also change the `Handles` argument to **`chk`*`CheckBox`*`_CheckedChanged`**.

11. Build the project and fix or work around remaining errors.

12. Run the project to see which features work and which don't.

Figure 6-2 illustrates IE's presentation of the Orders.aspx page after clicking the Create Order and Verify Card buttons. The `OmegaBank` component can't find the card in the Authorize

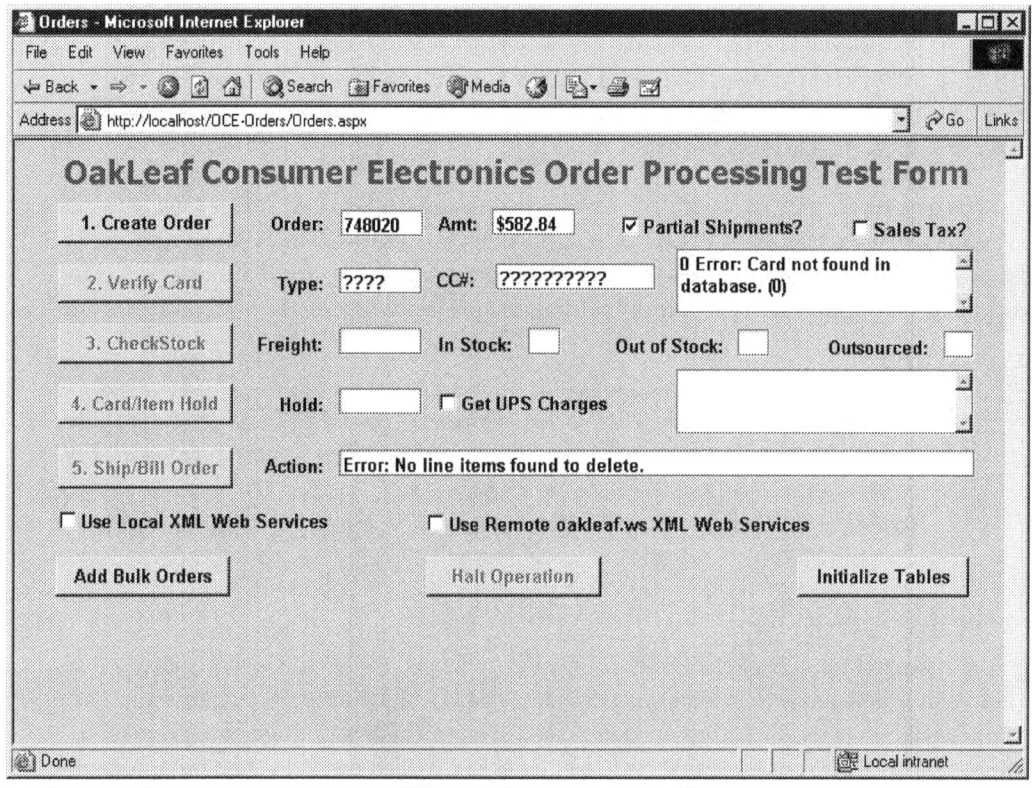

Figure 6-2   *The Verify Card operation doesn't succeed because the OmegaBank component or XML Web service doesn't receive valid credit card credentials.*

database, because the parameters passed to its `VerifyOrHold` method are 0 or empty strings. Welcome to the Web world of semistateless clients—setting `EnableViewState` to `True` protects clients against total statelessness.

Maintaining Variable State Between HTTP Requests

Each click of a `submit` button on the page executes an HTTP request to the server. With `EnableViewState` set to `True`, ASP.NET stores the state of server controls in an instance of the `StateBag` object, and passes these values to a hidden `input` control named `__VIEWSTATE`. Hidden `input` (text box) controls are the classic method for maintaining state between successive HTTP requests. Maintaining the state of server controls extracts a performance toll because the server must send the serialized value of the `StateBag` object with each page.

TIP

Individual server controls have an `EnableViewState` property. You can minimize the performance hit by setting to `False` the `EnableViewState` property of controls whose values are reset by the Web server.

The page-level (previously form-level) variables you declare have values, usually zeroes and empty strings, but don't receive or retain values assigned within event handlers, functions, or subprocedures. In fact, the only purpose page-level declarations serve is to assign variable data types and permit building the project with `Option Explicit On`.

TIP

To see the `StateBag` object's contents, run the project and view the HTML code returned by the server in Notepad. The state values are encrypted. Notice that Microsoft's developers use inconsistent case for HTML tag names: for example `<HTML>`, `<HEAD>`, `<body>`, and `<input>`. XHTML 1.0, the current W3C standard for platform-independent HTML 4.0 code, requires HTML element and attribute names to be lowercase.

Adding the Required TextBox Controls

The workaround for lack of stateful page-level variables is to add hidden `TextBox` server controls to store page-level values you need between HTTP requests. Alternatively, you can use the HTML Toolbox's `Hidden` control. The sample Order.aspx page has several text boxes, such as `txtOrderID` and `txtCardNumber`, which can hold state for `lngOrderID` and `strCardNumber` page-level variables. The `Checked` value of `CheckBox` controls substitutes for `Boolean` variables, such as `blnUseWS` and `blnUseOakLeaf`.

The following table lists the 11 hidden text boxes required for other Orders.aspx page-level variables. Accept the default `Visible` property (`True`) for initial debugging; set `Visible` to `False` when you finish testing.

Variable Name	TextBox ID	Variable Name	TextBox ID
lngCustID	txtCustID	datReqdShipDate	txtReqdShipDate
bytCardID	txtCardID	curItemsTotal	txtItemsTotal
strZipCode	txtZipCode	sngTimer	txtTimer
strCardName	txtCardName	lngCompleted	txtCompleted
datExpDate	txtExpDate	sngTotalTime	txtTotalTime
bytShipToID	txtShipToID		

TIP

Don't attempt to assign variable names as `TextBox ID` values. ASP.NET treats variables like any other object and won't let you duplicate object names within a particular scope—page-level, in this case.

Munging the Test Client Code

Reworking your code to set and retrieve the **Text** property value (**String**) of 15 or so
TextBox and **CheckBox** controls is not fun, and testing the changes is equally dull. Here's
an abbreviated description of the process:

1. Find each instance of the variable in the page.

2. Substitute the following for **Boolean** variable assignments from **CheckBox**es:

   ```
   'If blnVarName Then
   If chkVarName.Checked Then
   ```

3. Substitute the following for other variable type assignments *to* **TextBox**es:

   ```
   'typVarName = typValue
   txtVarName.Text = CStr(typValue)   'CStr isn't required for Strings
   ```

4. Substitute the following for other variable type assignments *from* **TextBox**es:

   ```
   typVarName = CTyp(txtVarName.Text)
   ```

NOTE

*There are numerous examples of the preceding changes in Orders.aspx.vb. Search for "Maintain state"
and "Retrieve state" in the code.*

The code also needs the following modifications to accommodate the change from a
Windows form to a Web Form.

▶ The **Do … Loop** structure in the **cmdBulkOrders_Click** event handler doesn't
work in a Web environment. The Web server executes the loop but doesn't refresh the
page after iterations. Bulk order addition isn't appropriate for end-user testing, so the
workaround—removing the loop—doesn't detract from the application's usefulness.
Changing the **Text** property of the **cmdBulkOrders** button to **Add One Order**
and the **AccessKey** value to **O** conforms the UI to the revised code.

▶ Removing the loop obsoletes the Halt Operations button. However, it's useful to
display average timing results for multiple Add One Order operations. Substituting the
EndBulkOps subprocedure's code for that of **cmdHaltBulkOps_Click** and
changing Halt Operations to **Display Results** solves this problem. Removing the
code that limits data to outsourced items with the Use Remote oakleaf.ws XML Web
Services check box marked makes the data more meaningful to users.

▶ The Use Local XML Web Services check box caption might confuse users, so
remove "Local".

▶ The application doesn't require the **chkUseIP** check box, so it and its associated
code can be deleted.

TIP

When you delete a control from the page design document, ASP.NET might forget to remove its `Protected With Events` *declaration from the class. If your code builds but throws run-time errors after deleting a control, check the declarations section to see if the control declaration is gone. If not, remove it, and delete remaining references to the control in your code.*

▶ The Initialize Tables button isn't used because its event-handling code isn't present. Initializing the tables requires Windows authentication as a system administrator, which (hopefully) you haven't granted to ordinary network users. You can delete the button or substitute a `LinkButton` control that navigates to a help page.

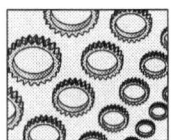

NOTE

In addition to the preceding changes, additional data type conversion functions in the Orders.aspx.vb code permit building the page with `Option Strict On`*.*

Figure 6-3 shows the test client page with the preceding changes, prior to hiding the 11 text boxes that were added in the preceding section. The page design isn't a candidate for a graphic arts award, but the page duplicates almost all operations of the original Windows client test form.

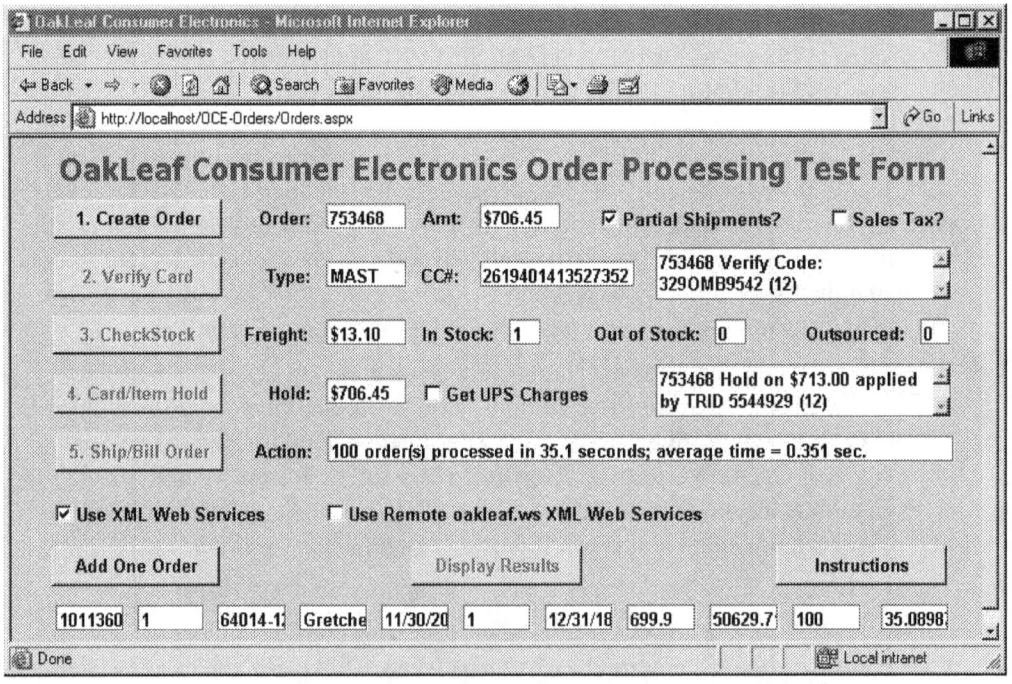

Figure 6-3 *Here's the test harness page before hiding the variable-state text boxes and adding DataGrid controls to display order and line-item data.*

Analyzing Web-Related Behavioral and Performance Changes

It's reasonable to expect behavioral differences between a stateful Windows form application and its stateless ASP.NET counterpart. The unexpected behavior is an apparent improvement in overall performance of the application. Figure 6-3 shows an average time of 0.351 seconds to process 100 orders that consume local XML Web services. The average processing time for the original OCE_Client Windows form application is 0.486 seconds, as measured in Chapter 5's "Comparing the Performance of ADO and ADO.NET Components and Services" section. As you'll discover in the "Testing the Effect of Populating the DataGrids on Client Performance" section at the end of this chapter, the performance improvement is illusory.

Comparing Stepwise and Add One Order Behavior

Clicking the five numbered buttons in sequence defines stepwise order processing. Each button click performs an HTTP POST operation and rerenders the page. You can review preceding pages for each step you complete by clicking the browser's Back button.

Clicking the Add One Order button executes all five cmd*ButtonName*_Click event handlers on the server and then renders the page when the cmdShipOrder_Click event handler completes execution. ASP.NET pages enable the equivalent of Amazon.com's "1-Click*" shopping feature for which Amazon claims U.S. patent protection. Whether the OCE-Orders application infringes U.S. Patent 6,029,141, "Internet-based Customer Referral System" is a subject for attorneys, not developers, to decide.

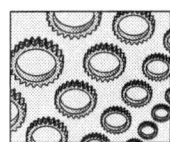

NOTE

To learn more about Amazon.com's controversial patent, go to http://www.delphion.com/ details?pn=US06029141___. The last URL characters are two underscores.

There's a delay of a second or two when you open the page for the first time after rebuilding the project or rebooting the server. The duration of this hiatus for initial page compilation is similar to the initial delay in opening the Windows form version. A much longer initial delay—up to about 10 seconds—to compile and instantiate the local Visual Basic .NET components occurs when you click the Add One Order button. This delay for the ASP.NET page is at least twice as long as for the Windows form version. Fortunately, only the first user of the application incurs this initial performance hit. Subsequent page opening and code execution operations rely on cached components or XML Web services. You can employ combinations of page caching, partial-page caching, and application data caching to improve performance, as described in online help's "ASP.NET Caching Features" topic.

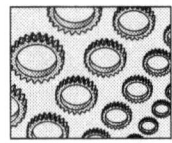

NOTE

When you mark the Use XML Web Services check box, the Use Remote oakleaf.ws XML Web services check box doesn't appear until you click a button that performs a POST operation. You incur a shorter delay when first instantiating ASP.NET XML Web services.

Evaluating ASP.NET's Smart Navigation Feature

Microsoft touts ASP.NET's new Smart Navigation feature as offering the following advantages only to IE 5+ users:

- ▶ Eliminating navigation flashing
- ▶ Persisting scroll bar positioning when moving between pages
- ▶ Persisting control focus when moving between pages
- ▶ Retaining only the last page state in history

You can test the effect of Smart Navigation on the Orders.aspx Web page by pressing F4 to display the DOCUMENT Properties window. Set the `smartNavigation` property to `True`, and click Add One Orders. The screen flashes twice with Smart Navigation enabled and only once with the feature disabled. Clearly, Smart Navigation isn't appropriate for this Web page, so reset the `smartNavigation` property value to `False`.

Targeting Specific Browsers

The DOCUMENT Properties window has a `targetSchema` property with a list box that lets you specify Internet Explorer 5.0, Navigator 4.0, or Internet Explorer 3.02/Navigator 3.0 as the supported browser(s) for the page. The last option is the lowest common browser denominator. If your application must support multiple or antiquated browsers, test each version and modify the design to accommodate differences in HTML interpretation, including unsupported controls.

CAUTION

Changing the `targetSchema` property value relocates and disables or changes the operation of some controls. Don't change this property value from IE 5.0 unless you must create pages for other browsers. This book's sample ASP.NET applications are intended for viewing only in IE 5+.

Tracing Execution at the Page Level

As mentioned near the beginning of this chapter, ASP.NET's tracing features enable detecting code behind the page that acts as a performance bottleneck. To enable page-level tracing, which adds a set of server-generated tables to the bottom of the page, do this:

1. Open the DOCUMENT Properties window, and set the `trace` property value to `True`.

2. Set the `traceMode` property value to `SortByTime` to display the values by their execution sequence instead of alphabetically by name.

3. To prevent the trace data from appearing under the page's controls instead of below them, set the `DOCUMENT` object's `topMargin` property value to a pixel value greater than the bottom of the lowest visible control on the page. For the Orders.aspx page, set the value to about `310px`.

When you open the page and scroll below its controls, you see a trace display similar to that of Figure 6-4. The trace display includes the following tables:

▶ **Request Details**   Provides a summary of the result of the request operation. An HTTP `GET` request opens the page; clicking `submit` buttons executes `POST` operations. If the `enableSessionState` property value is `True`, the table displays the current Session ID value.

▶ **Trace Information**   Lists the execution time for each Web server operation required to render the page. The From First(s) column lists the time in seconds after execution of the `BeginInit` event. The From Last(s) column displays the elapsed time for the operation. The sum of the From Last(s) column values equals the last From First(s) value.

▶ **Control Tree**   Lists each element of the page, the number of HTML bytes required to render each object, and the bytes required to maintain the controls' current `ViewState` property.

▶ **Application State**   Displays application-level variables, such as `HitCounter`, if you've declared them. This table isn't present when tracing the Orders.aspx page.

▶ **Cookies Collection**   Lists the names and values of cookies, such as ASP.NET_SessionID, if your application maintains session state or uses cookies for other purposes. This table isn't present when tracing the Orders.aspx page.

▶ **Headers Collection**   Displays the HTTP headers values for the current session.

▶ **Forms Collection**   Lists the values held by __VIEWSTATE and other text box controls of the form. The `ID` and `Text` property values of the `submit` button are the last members of this collection. This collection appears only for `POST` operations.

▶ **Server Variables**   Lists the values cached by the server for the current session and HTTP operation.

Trace Information is the table you use to evaluate overall application performance and debug bottlenecks. The HTTP `GET` operation timed in Figure 6-4 has an uncommonly long initiation period. After initial compilation, the total server time to open the Orders.aspx page is about 10 milliseconds with a fast server.

For XML Web service test and production clients, it's most important to analyze performance of HTTP `POST` operations that consume services. Clicking Add One Order with the Use XML Web Services and Use Remote oakleaf.ws XML Web Services check boxes marked

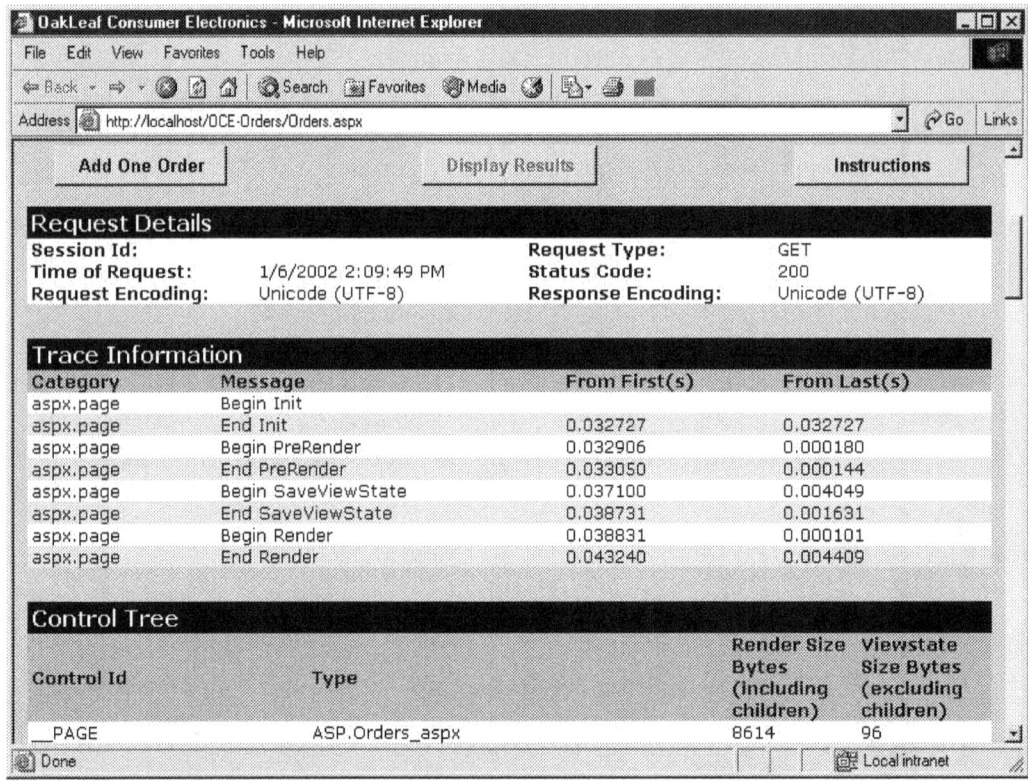

Figure 6-4 *Tracing adds informational and timing tables below your page. This example shows that the server requires about 43 ms to render the opening page.*

produces trace information similar to that shown in Figure 6-5. In this case, the elapsed time of the `PostBackEvent` operation is 525 ms, which represents the elapsed time to execute the code to complete an order with two items outsourced from different distributors. The `PostBack` operation represents 98 percent of the server execution time. Obviously, you need a more granular report to determine the timing of code execution between `Begin Raise PostBackEvent` and `End Raise PostBackEvent`.

NOTE

Trace Information data for the Orders.aspx page lets you verify the timing data displayed in the Action text box. Text box and End Prerender elapsed time values usually track within 1 percent.

Adding Trace.Write Statements to Identify Bottlenecking Culprits

You can improve the granularity of your performance reports by adding `Trace.Write` (`strText`) statements at strategic locations in the code behind your page. With the `trace` property set to `True`, the `strText` values and execution times appear in the Trace

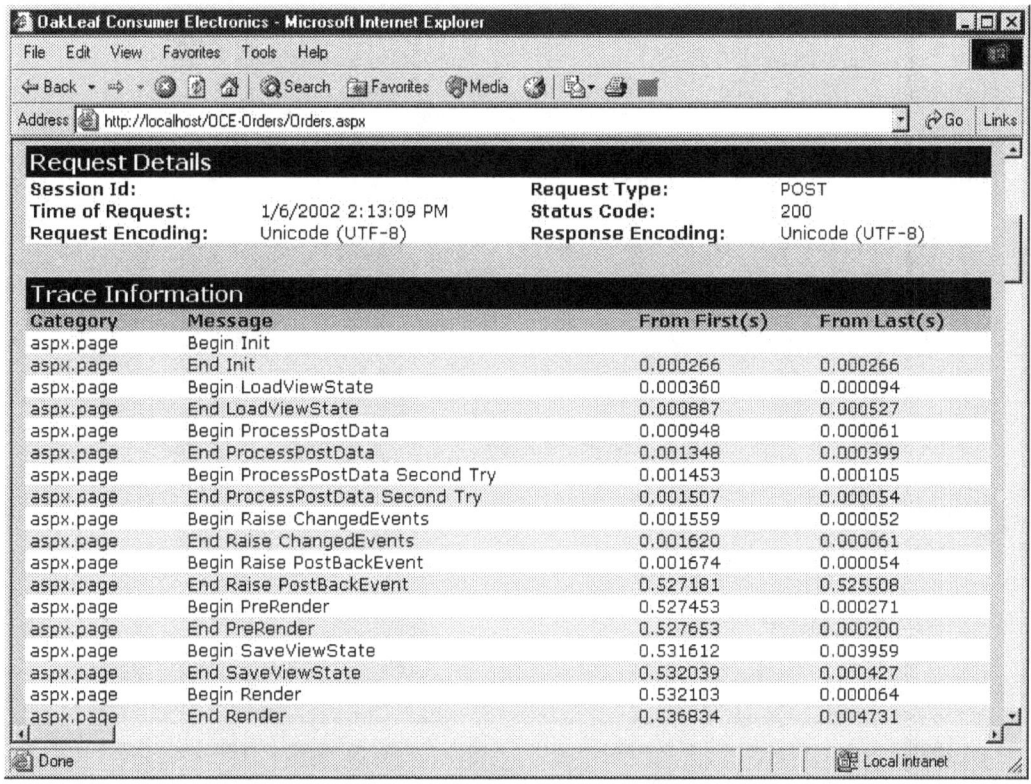

Figure 6-5   *The Trace Information table shown here displays the elapsed time to process an order with four line items, two of which are outsourced from different distributors.*

Information table. If your application has operational variations, you can add code to report the conditions that apply to the execution time values.

As an example, the Orders.aspx page's `cmdAddOrder_Click` event handler includes these two statements at the beginning and end of the code:

```
If Trace.IsEnabled Then
   Trace.Write("Begin New Order")
End If
'Remaining cmdAddOder_Click code goes here
If Trace.IsEnabled Then
   Trace.Write("End New Order " & txtOrderID.Text & " - " & _
      CStr(bytItemID - 1) & " item(s)")
End If
```

The order number lets you relate the timing information to rows in the Orders and LineItems tables. The number of line items provides insight into timing differences that relate to the number of line items per order.

The following code added to the `cmdVerifyCard_Click` event handler reports whether the page uses local Visual Basic .NET components or consumes local or remote XML Web services:

```
If Trace.IsEnabled Then
   strMsg = "Begin Verify Card"
   If chkUseWS.Checked Then
      If chkUseOakLeaf.Checked Then
         strMsg += " - Remote oakleaf.ws services"
      Else
         strMsg += " - Local XML Web services"
      End If
   Else
      strMsg += " - Local components"
   End If
   Trace.Write(strMsg)
End If
'Remaining cmdVerifyCard_Click code goes here
If Trace.IsEnabled Then
   strMsg = "End Verify Card - "
   If bytStatus = 12 Then
      strMsg += "Authorized"
   Else
      strMsg += "Declined"
   End If
   Trace.Write(strMsg)
End If
```

Figure 6-6 illustrates typical timing data for the five major operations involved in completing an OakLeaf order that has two items, one of which is outsourced. The total page delivery time is 484 ms; executing code consumes 469 ms or 97 percent of the delivery time. As you'd expect from the `clsFulfillOrder.ShipOrder` method's complexity, the `cmdShipOrders` function requires 230 ms to execute, which is about 50 percent of the total code execution time.

If you need finer-grained data for operations executed within external classes, add an `Inherits System.Web.UI.Page` directive before the class's first method declaration, and insert `Trace.Write` instructions at strategic locations in the code. Classes usually receive argument values representing stateful `TextBox` values, so the lack of access to server controls from classes isn't a concern.

When you add timing data for class methods, it's a good practice to identify the timed operation as a submember of the calling page's operation. Figure 6-7 illustrates the results for `Trace.Write` statements—prefixed with an asterisk—that execute within methods of the `clsFulfillOrder` class. A quick review of the timing results of Figure 6-7 indicates that no single operation is causing a performance bottleneck. The longest-running operation (103 ms) is generating two XML invoices, which is the most complex element of the `ShipOrder` method.

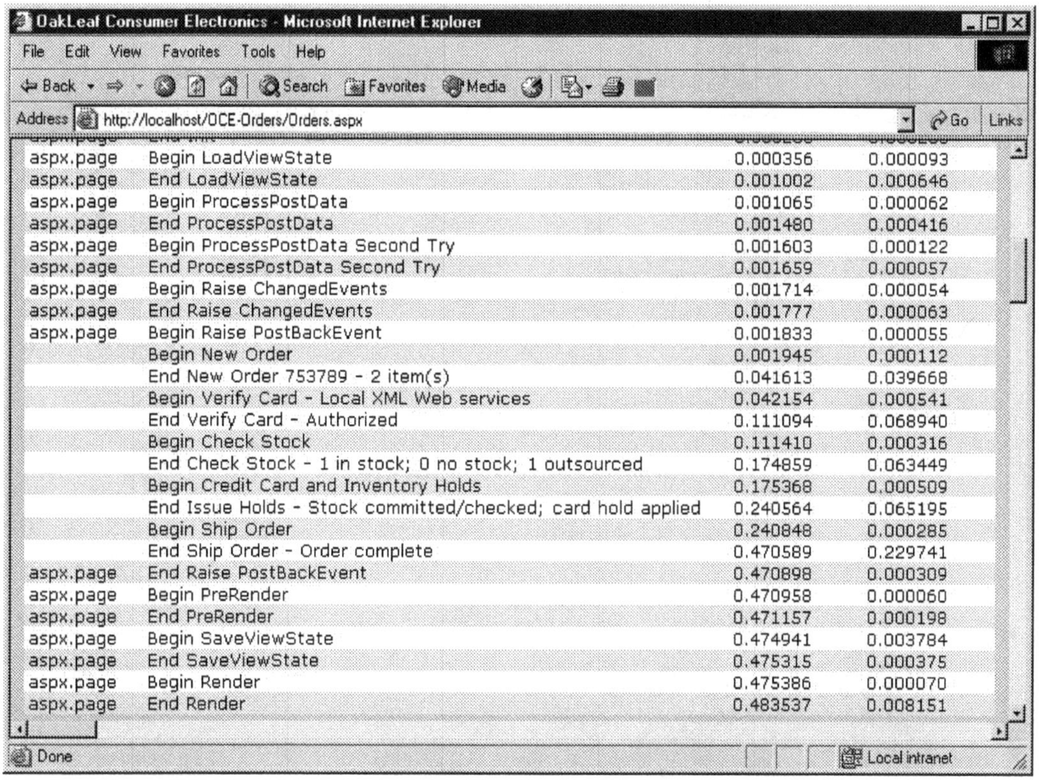

aspx.page	Begin LoadViewState	0.000356	0.000093
aspx.page	End LoadViewState	0.001002	0.000646
aspx.page	Begin ProcessPostData	0.001065	0.000062
aspx.page	End ProcessPostData	0.001480	0.000416
aspx.page	Begin ProcessPostData Second Try	0.001603	0.000122
aspx.page	End ProcessPostData Second Try	0.001659	0.000057
aspx.page	Begin Raise ChangedEvents	0.001714	0.000054
aspx.page	End Raise ChangedEvents	0.001777	0.000063
aspx.page	Begin Raise PostBackEvent	0.001833	0.000055
	Begin New Order	0.001945	0.000112
	End New Order 753789 - 2 item(s)	0.041613	0.039668
	Begin Verify Card - Local XML Web services	0.042154	0.000541
	End Verify Card - Authorized	0.111094	0.068940
	Begin Check Stock	0.111410	0.000316
	End Check Stock - 1 in stock; 0 no stock; 1 outsourced	0.174859	0.063449
	Begin Credit Card and Inventory Holds	0.175368	0.000509
	End Issue Holds - Stock committed/checked; card hold applied	0.240564	0.065195
	Begin Ship Order	0.240848	0.000285
	End Ship Order - Order complete	0.470589	0.229741
aspx.page	End Raise PostBackEvent	0.470898	0.000309
aspx.page	Begin PreRender	0.470958	0.000060
aspx.page	End PreRender	0.471157	0.000198
aspx.page	Begin SaveViewState	0.474941	0.003784
aspx.page	End SaveViewState	0.475315	0.000375
aspx.page	Begin Render	0.475386	0.000070
aspx.page	End Render	0.483537	0.008151

Figure 6-6 *This example trace for the Orders.aspx page has ten added timing values for the five primary order-processing operations.*

You can also add timing information from components, such as OmegaBank.dll or AlphaDist.dll, called by an ASP.NET page. In this case, you must add a .NET reference to System.Web.dll and an `Imports System.Web` directive to the component code and declare an `HTTPContext` object to return the current page context for the `Trace.Write` method. Following is the generic code for adding trace capability to a component:

```
Imports System
Imports …
Imports System.Web     'Required
Public Class ClassName
   Private ctxHTTP as HttpContext
   Public Sub New()
      ctxHTTP = HttpContext.Current
      ctxHTTP.Trace.Write(strTrace)
   End Sub
   …
End Class
```

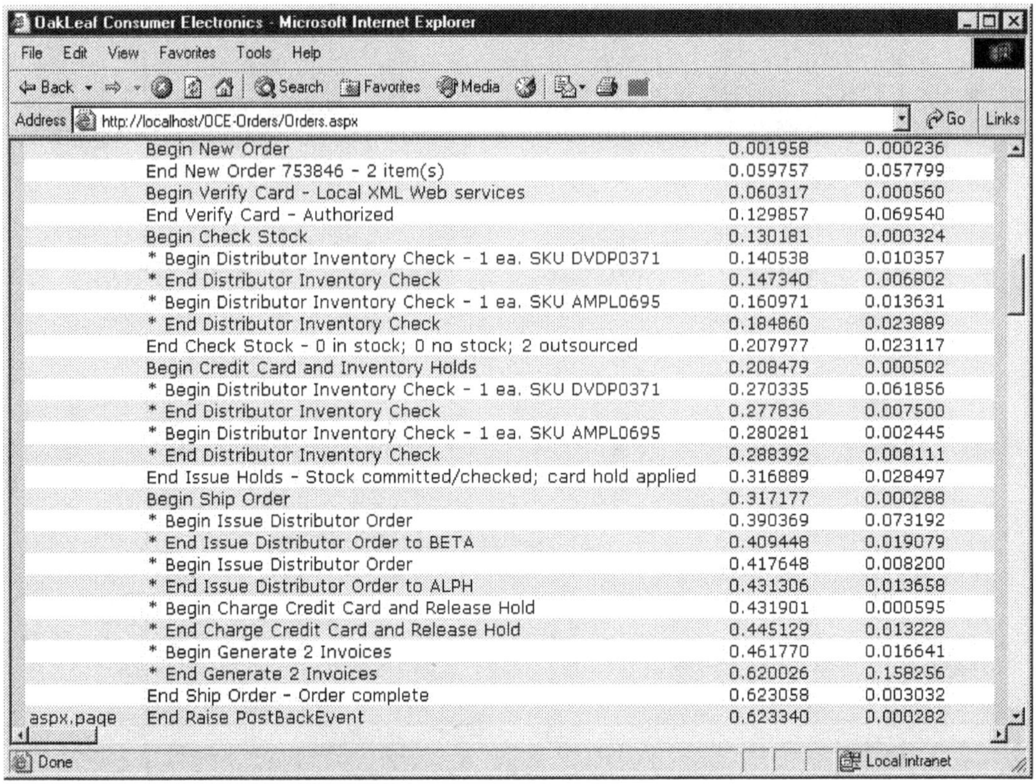

Figure 6-7 Adding `Trace.Write` statements to Visual Basic .NET classes lets you increase the timing granularity of complex operations.

Tracing at the Application Level

Appending tracing information to the bottom of the page probably tells ordinary testers more than they want to know—and more than you want them to know—about the performance of your XML Web services and their test pages. The alternative to page tracing is application tracing, which you enable by modifying entries in your application's web.config file. In addition to hiding page-level tracing from users, application-level tracing lets you specify the maximum number of traces retained in a cache. You can also control whether users can view the trace results.

To enable application-level caching and view multiple tracing pages, do the following:

1. Open the web.config file in your application's folder in Notepad or in a Visual Studio .NET document.

2. Navigate to the line that starts with `<trace enabled="false"`... and change `false` to **true**, as shown here.

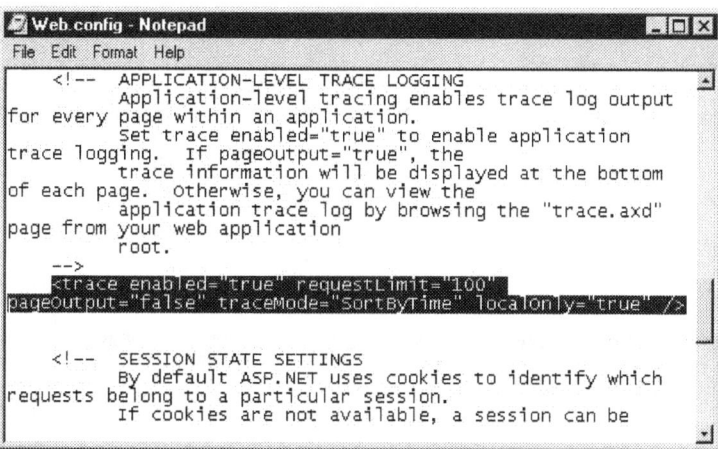

3. If you want to store more than the default ten trace pages in the cache, change the `requestLimit` attribute value from 10 to a larger number.

4. Accept the default values for the remaining `pageOutput`, `traceMode`, and `localOnly` attributes, and save the changes to `web.config`.

TIP

Set the `localOnly` attribute to `True` to allow other testers to view trace information.

5. Open the DOCUMENT Properties window and delete (backspace over) the `trace` property setting.

TIP

Remove—don't change—the `trace` property value. Setting the `trace` property value to `False` in the Properties window overrides the changes you make to the `<trace ... />` element attributes in the web.config file.

6. Run a few sample page executions.

7. Replace the *PageName*.aspx element of the URL with **trace.axd** to open a trace viewer, which has links to the cached trace pages. (See Figure 6-8.)

8. Click the View Details links to open a page that displays the selected trace.

9. Click the Clear Current Trace link to reset the entire list.

If you don't mind writing simple screen-scraping code, you can extract the timing data from multiple traces and save it in a `DataTable` object or an Excel worksheet for statistical

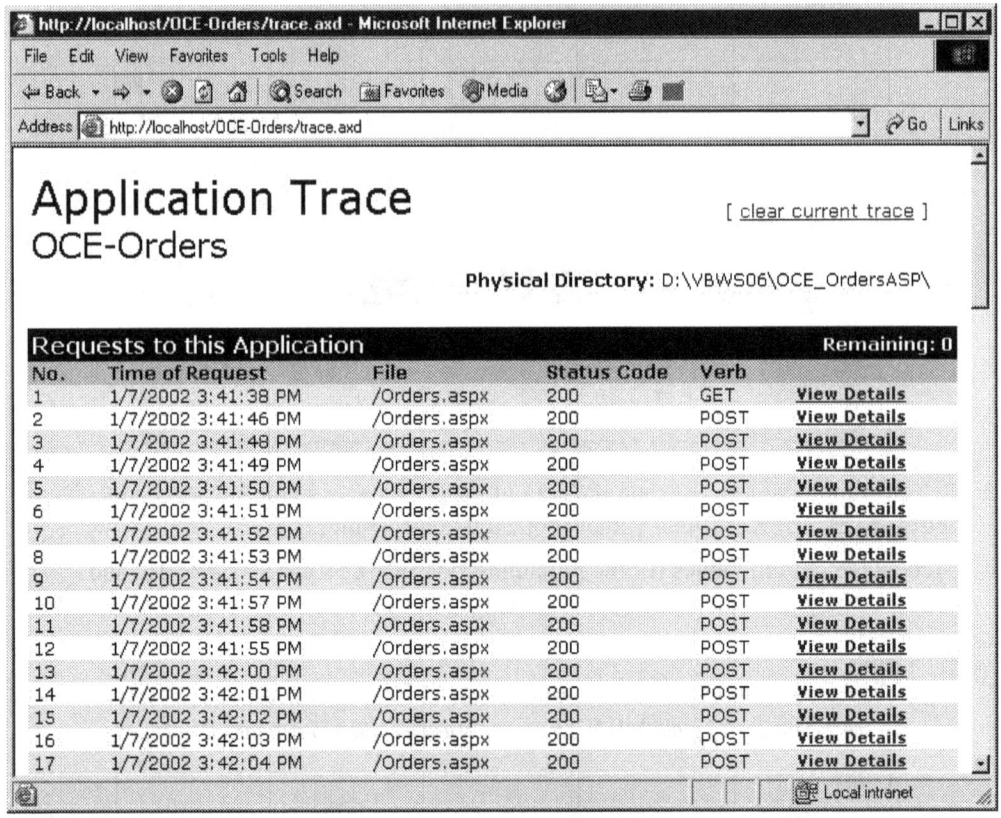

Figure 6-8   *The Application Trace page, which you call with an http://localhost/virtualdir/ trace.axd URL, has links to individually cached trace pages.*

analysis. The URL for individual trace pages is http://localhost/*virtualdir*/trace.axd?id=*n*, where *n* is the 0-based trace sequence number. Alternatively, you can define a custom `System.Diagnostics.TextWriterTraceListener` listener as a child of the `<listeners>` element of the global `<configuration>` file. The custom listener writes the trace data to a log file you specify. See online help's "<trace> Element" topic for more information.

Adding DataGrid Server Controls to Display Line-Item and Order Information

One feature that managers and testers might appreciate is proof that your XML Web services accomplish their objectives. The two ADO-based `DataGrid` controls of the Windows form client let you scroll the field names and corresponding values of the Orders table, and display the LineItems table's fields for each order generated. Adding server control equivalents of the two ADO `DataGrid` controls supplies evidence that records have been added to the two tables and status updates occur as specified. Adding `DataGrid`s to the client page also demonstrates features of the new ASP.NET data-bound server controls, which you bind to `DataTable` objects.

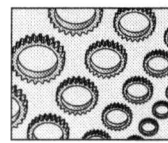

NOTE

Replacing the ADO `DataGrid` controls with server controls normalizes timing data with the original Windows forms test clients. Timing comparisons aren't valid until the Web page performs all functions of the Windows form, as you will see after completing the examples of the following two sections.

Displaying Order Line Items in a DataGrid Server Control

Adding a bound `DataGrid` server control to a page is a piece of cake, and the code to fill the control is no more complex than that to bind an ADO `DataGrid` to a `Recordset` object. Templates make formatting ASP.NET `DataGrid` controls a snap, and column widths of the server-generated HTML tables conform to the data width automatically.

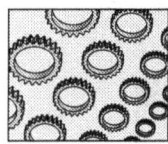

NOTE

The `DataGrids` and the following two code examples aren't included in the OCE-Orders.sln solution in your \VBWS06\OCE_OrdersASP folder. The final version of the project, which has `dgItems`, `dgOrder`, and `dgCustomer DataGrids` and supporting code, is in your \VBWS06\OCE_Client.ASP folder. Before opening OCE-Client.sln, create an OCE-Client virtual directory that points to \VBWS06\OCE_ClientASP. You can open the OCE-Client.sln's Orders.aspx page from links at http://www.oakleaf.ws/ or directly at http://www.oakleaf.ws/oce/.

Following is the generic version of the procedure for adding a bound `DataGrid` server control to a page; the Orders.aspx page serves as an example:

1. Add a `DataGrid` control to the page and assign it a meaningful ID value, **dgItems** for this example.

2. Right-click the control, and choose Auto Format, a template that conforms to the style of your test page. Professional 2, shown here, most closely resembles the OakLeaf page style and colors.

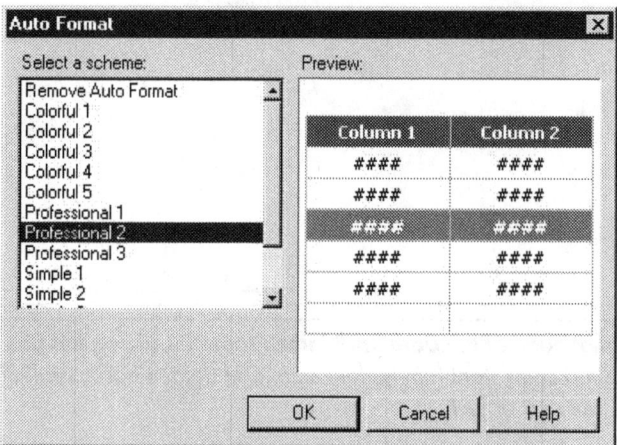

3. Right-click the control again, and choose Property Builder to open the *GridID* Properties dialog, which lets you modify colors, fonts, and other visual properties of the `DataGrid`. To conform the `dgItems` grid's font to OakLeaf style, click the Format button with the DataGrid item selected, and select Verdana and X-Small in the two Font… lists. (See Figure 6-9.)

4. Open the grid's Properties window and set the `EnableViewState` property value to `False`. The server refreshes the data each time you call the subprocedure to fill the grids. Preserving the state of `DataGrid` controls can substantially increase the size of the page's HTML document.

5. Add a subprocedure that creates an `SqlDataAdapter` object to fill a `DataTable` with a query result set.

6. Write the SQL statement to return the required columns. Alias column names for readability, consistent with the width of the data and overall width of the control.

7. Supply the SQL statement and an `SqlConnection` object to the `SqlDataAdapter`.

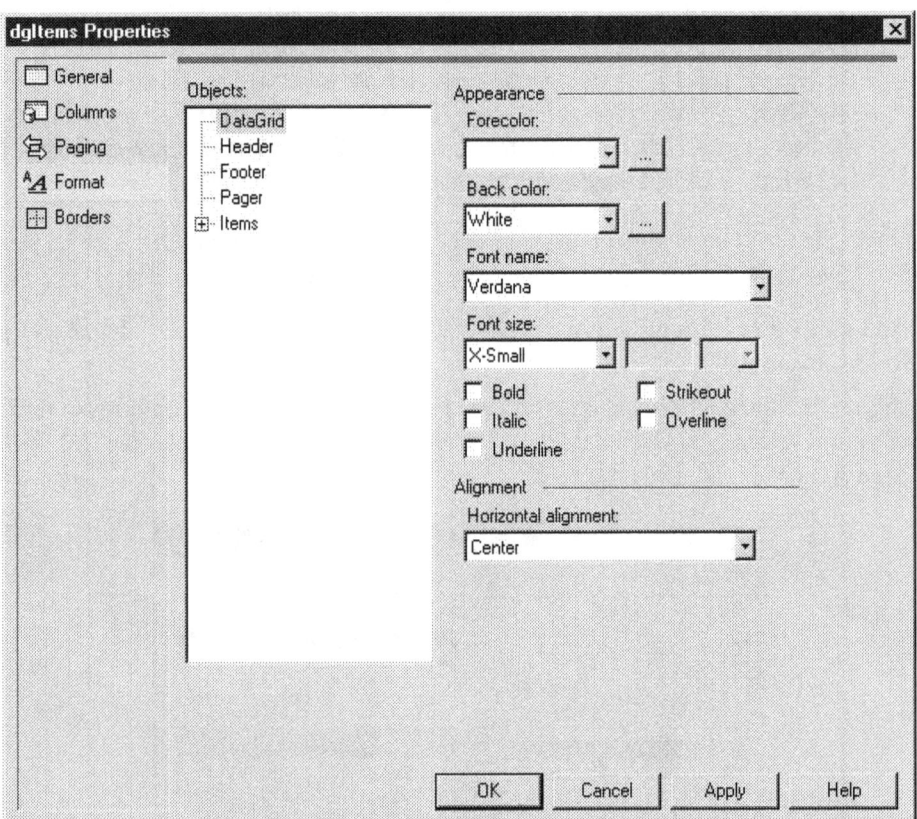

Figure 6-9   *The Format page of the **DataGridName** Properties dialog lets you specify the background color, font family, font size, and default horizontal alignment properties of a `DataGrid` object.*

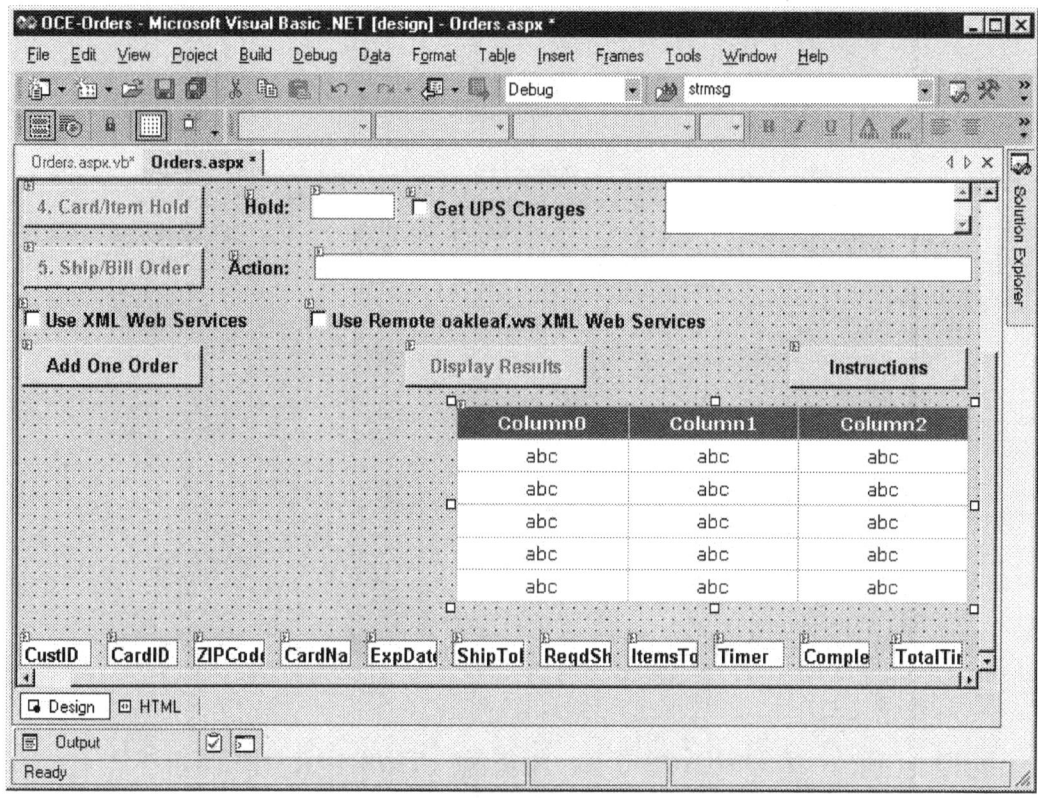

Figure 6-10 *DataGrid controls in the page design document display three columns and five rows when not bound to a data source.*

8. Apply the `SqlDataAdapter.Fill` method to fill the `DataTable`.

9. Specify the `DataTable` as the `DataGrid.DataSource` object, and apply the `DataGrid.DataBind` method to fill the grid.

10. Call the subprocedure to refresh the grid at appropriate locations in the code behind the page. For this example, you replace all previous `Call FillGrids(cnnConnection, rstRecordset)` statements with `Call FillGrids()`.

Figure 6-10 shows the `dgItems` control added to the Orders.aspx page. The header and items rows are centered, and the header background color is set to #266294 to match the OakLeaf label foreground color.

Following is the Visual Basic .NET code to instantiate the required `SqlConnection`, `SqlDataAdapter`, and `DataTable` objects, and bind the `dgLineItems` grid to the `DataTable`:

```
Private Sub FillGrids()
    Dim cnnGrids As New SqlConnection(strCustConn)
    Dim dtItems As New DataTable("LineItems")
```

```
    If Trace.IsEnabled Then
        Trace.Write("* Start Fill Data Grids")
    End If

    'Fill the line items grid
    strSQL = "SELECT ItemID AS [#], Quantity AS Quan, SKU, " + _
        "Outsourced AS [Out?], UnitPrice AS Price, StatusID AS Status, " + _
        "OrderFrom AS Dist FROM LineItems WHERE OrderID = " & txtOrderID.Text
    Dim daItems As New SqlDataAdapter(strSQL, cnnGrids)
    daItems.Fill(dtItems)
    With dgItems
        .DataSource = dtItems
        .DataBind()
    End With

    If Trace.IsEnabled Then
        Trace.Write("* End Fill Data Grids")
    End If
End Sub
```

The `Trace.Write()` methods let you determine the performance hit incurred by the client as a result of the six `FillGrid` calls during the order completion process.

Rolling Your Own DataTable to Display Order Information

Generating a `DataTable` object programmatically and displaying its contents in a `DataGrid` is simpler than the corresponding process for an `ADODB.Recordset` object. Displaying the Orders record makes stepwise order processing meaningful, because StatusID, LastStatusUpdate, LastStatusMessage, and CCTransactionID values change with steps of the order-completion process.

Here's the easy way to add a `dgOrder` grid to the Orders.aspx page:

1. Copy and paste `dgItems` to a new `DataGrid1` server control.

2. Move the new control to the left of the dgItems grid and rename it as **dgOrder**.

3. Change the Horizontal Alignment property values of the Header and Items subobjects to Left.

4. Modify the code for the `FillGrids` subprocedure as shown in the following listing:

```
Private Sub FillGrids()
    Dim cnnGrids As New SqlConnection(strCustConn)
    Dim dtItems As New DataTable("LineItems")
    Dim dtOrder As New DataTable("Order")
    Dim sdrOrder As SqlDataReader
    Dim drOrder As DataRow
    Dim intCtr As Integer
    Dim strReqdDate As String
    If Trace.IsEnabled Then
        Trace.Write("* Start Fill Data Grids")
```

```
        End If
        cnnGrids.Open()
        'Fill the line items grid
        strSQL = "SELECT ItemID AS [#], Quantity AS Quan, SKU, " + _
            "Outsourced AS [Out?], UnitPrice AS Price, StatusID AS Status, " + _
            "OrderFrom AS Dist FROM LineItems WHERE OrderID = " & txtOrderID.Text
        Dim daItems As New SqlDataAdapter(strSQL, cnnGrids)
        daItems.Fill(dtItems)
        With dgItems
            .DataSource = dtItems
            .DataBind()
        End With
        'Create a DataTable from scratch
        With dtOrder
            'Define two columns
            .Columns.Add("Column Name", Type.GetType("System.String"))
            .Columns.Add("Value", Type.GetType("System.String"))
        End With
        'Create an SqlDataReader
        strSQL = "SELECT * FROM Orders WHERE OrderID = " & txtOrderID.Text
        Dim cmmOrder As SqlCommand = cnnGrids.CreateCommand
        With cmmOrder
            .CommandType = CommandType.Text
            .CommandText = strSQL
            sdrOrder = .ExecuteReader
        End With
        With sdrOrder
            .Read()
            For intCtr = 0 To .FieldCount - 1
                'Loop through the fields
                drOrder = dtOrder.NewRow
                drOrder(0) = .GetName(intCtr)
                If intCtr = 3 Then
                    strReqdDate = .Item(intCtr).ToString
                    If InStr(strReqdDate, " ") > 0 Then
                        'Don't include the time
                        drOrder(1) = Left(strReqdDate, InStr(strReqdDate, " ") - 1)
                    End If
                Else
                    drOrder(1) = .Item(intCtr).ToString
                End If
                dtOrder.Rows.Add(drOrder)
            Next intCtr
        End With
        cnnGrids.Close()
        With dgOrder
            .DataSource = dtOrder
            .DataBind()
        End With

        If Trace.IsEnabled Then
            Trace.Write("* End Fill Data Grids")
        End If
    End Sub
```

Figure 6-11 shows the Orders.aspx page with the two added **DataGrid** server controls.

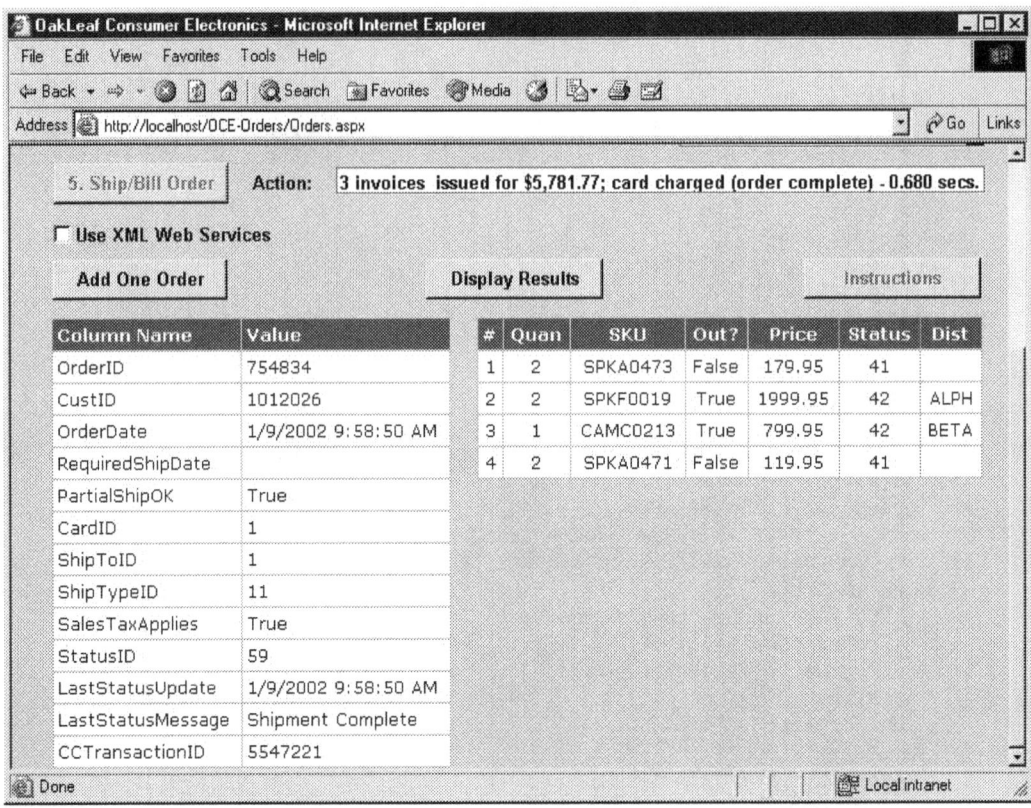

Figure 6-11   *This Orders.aspx page has four items; two items are outsourced to different distributors, which results in the longest completion time for an order.*

Testing the Effect of Populating the DataGrids on Client Performance

At this point, the Orders.aspx page performs the same order-processing operations as the Windows form it replaces. Rerunning the timing tests after adding the two `DataGrid` controls increases the average time to add 100 orders with the Orders.aspx form to 483 ms, which is almost identical to the 486 ms average execution time for the Windows form client. It's reasonable to conclude from this data that the performance of moderately complex ASP.NET Web Forms and their Windows form equivalents is very close to the same, despite the additional code and hidden server controls you need to maintain variable state. Automated performance testing of the two test harness versions in several configurations with several thousand orders proves the conclusion.

Figure 6-12 shows part of the trace results for the Orders.aspx page. The time to generate the initial instance of the two `DataGrid`s is about 16 ms; updates require between 6 and 8 ms each. The total elapsed time in the `FillGrids` subprocedure is about 57 ms, which accounts for about 43 percent of the 132 ms increase in execution time with the two `DataGrid` controls

Figure 6-12   *This trace of the order shown in Figure 6-11 shows the elapsed times for five of the six executions of the* `FillGrids` *subprocedure.*

added. The remainder of the execution time difference is due, in part, to the overhead for trace-caching the `DataGrid` values.

Here's your final take-away from this chapter: when testing the performance of your own or third-party XML Web services under varying conditions, make sure your test clients don't obfuscate the results with differing front-end performance.

Navigating System.Web.Services and System.Xml

IN THIS CHAPTER:

Spelunking the System.Web.Services Namespace

Adding and Processing SOAP Headers

Traversing the System.Xml Namespace

Creating XML Web Services with Microsoft SQLXML 3.0

Most of the preceding chapters covered upgrading existing Visual Basic 6.0 components to XML Web services and Windows form test clients to Visual Basic .NET and ASP.NET. Upgrading existing code to Visual Basic .NET preserves your development investment but doesn't lead to taking full advantage of the XML Web service-related features of the .NET Framework. This and the following two chapters cover creating *de novo* ASP.NET XML Web services and client pages that consume the services. The objective of this chapter is to describe how the members of the `System.Web.Services` and `System.Xml` namespaces fit into the XML Web services picture.

A secondary objective of this chapter is to show you how to use the Microsoft SQXML 3.0 add-on to SQL Server 2000 to generate XML Web services from T-SQL stored procedures, user-defined functions, and template queries. The SQLXML 3.0 example illustrates use of the `XmlTextReader` object to manage attribute-centric XML data streams.

Spelunking the System.Web.Services Namespace

When you create a new ASP.NET Web Service project, the Web Service page designer automatically generates a Service1.asmx file stub and a set of ASP.NET support files. At this point, the service's WSDL document consists of a set of default namespace attributes of the `<definitions>` element, an empty `<types />` element, and a `<service name= "Service1">` element. The `System.Web.Services` namespace contains the classes that the page designer uses to build the default service. The code you add to create and customize `<WebMethod()>` functions also relies on members of the `System.Web.Services` namespace.

The following sections briefly describe the member classes of the `System.Web.Services` class and their properties in approximate order of their participation in the ASP.NET Web Service development process.

System.Web.Services Classes

The top member of the `System.Web.Services` namespace contains classes for setting and retrieving the basic property and attribute values of XML Web services and their methods.

The WebService Class

The `WebService` class gets and, in some cases, sets Web server property values. The most useful of these properties are `Application`, `Session`, and, if your XML Web service requires authentication, `User`. The following table lists the class of the object and common use of each property.

Property	Object Class	Common Uses
Application	HTTPApplicationState	Creating, modifying, and reading application-level variables, such as a total service usage (hit) counter
Context	HTTPContext	Customizing error handling for HTTP requests, tracing, and returning timestamp values for transaction management

Property	Object Class	Common Uses
Server	HTTPServerUtility	Obtaining information and instantiating COM objects on the server
Session	HTTPSessionState	Creating, modifying, and reading session-level variables, such as a session usage counter if you enable session state for a service.
User	IPrincipal	Returning the user's identity, role, and group membership when you specify Windows authentication for the service (shortcut to the HTTPContext.User object)

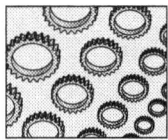

NOTE

The OakLeaf Consumer Electronics example XML Web services at the oakleaf.ws Web site use the Session *property to limit addition of orders to 100 in a single session.*

The WebServiceAttribute Class

Properties of the WebServiceAttribute class represent the attribute values you add as named arguments to the <WebService()> prefix of the class and the name you assign to the class. Property values return System.String objects. ASP.NET sets the values of the Name and Namespace properties when you open a new Web Service project. The following table lists the attributes of the WebServiceAttribute class.

Property	Purpose
Description	Returns the content of the service <documentation> element of the service's WSDL document (empty string)
Name	Returns the name of the Web service class (Service1)
Namespace	Returns the namespace of the Web service (http://tempuri.org/)

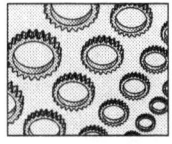

NOTE

System.Web.Services *and subordinate classes that have an* ...Attribute *suffix can't be inherited.*

The WebServiceBindingAttribute Class

The WebServiceBindingAttribute class lets you specify a different remote Web server, name, and namespace for the WSDL document's <binding> element. Property values return String objects. You seldom, if ever, need to alter the default values, so the following table is present only for completeness.

Property	Description
Location	Sets the URL for the binding (http://localhost/WebService1/Service1.asmx?wsdl)
Name	Sets the value of the name attribute of the <binding> element (Service1SOAP)
Namespace	Specifies the value of the namespace attribute of the <binding> element (http://tempuri.org)

The WebMethodAttribute Class

Properties of the `WebMethodAttribute` class represent attribute values that you add as named arguments to the `<WebMethod()>` prefix of the `Public Function` *MethodName* statement. Chapter 4's "Adding XML Web Service Descriptions" section briefly discusses the use of `WebMethodAttribute` properties.

Property	Data Type	Purpose
BufferResponse	Boolean	Specifies whether the server stores the response in memory and sends the message when serialization completes or sends the message as it is serialized (`True`)
CacheDuration	Integer	Sets the number of seconds the server stores requests and responses in memory (`0`, caching disabled)
Description	String	Returns the content of the method's `<documentation>` element of the method's WSDL document (empty string)
EnableSession	Boolean	Specifies whether session state is enabled (False)
MessageName	String	Lets you supply an alias for the function name as the name attribute of the `<service>` element (*MethodName*)
TransactionOption	TransactionOption	Specifies the root transaction context for the service: `Disabled`, `NotSupported`, `Supported`, `Required`, or `RequiresNew` (`Disabled`)

System.Web.Services.Protocols Classes

The `System.Web.Services.Protocols` namespace contains 46 individual classes that support HTTP, MIME, and SOAP transport protocols. This book concentrates on SOAP, which has 16 classes. The following sections group the 16 SOAP class descriptions by their anticipated frequency of use by XML Web service developers—most frequent first.

SoapHeader Classes

The `SoapHeader` class is by far the most useful member of the `System.Web.Services.Protocols` namespace. Defining and processing SOAP headers is the subject of the later "Adding and Processing SOAP Headers" section, but the following table of `SoapHeader...` classes is located here for class presentation consistency.

Class	Purpose and Important Properties
SoapHeaderCollection	Contains the collection of instances of the `SoapHeader` class (enables multiple headers)

Class	Purpose and Important Properties
SoapHeader	Lets you set the values of the `Actor` (empty string), `DidUnderstand` (False), `EncodedMustUnderstand` (0 = "false"), and `MustUnderstand` (False) properties
SoapHeaderAttribute	Lets you set the values of the Direction (In from SoapHeaderDirectionEnumeration), MemberName (empty string), and Required (True) attributes
SoapHeaderException	Throws an exception if the method call sets `MustUnderstand = True` and the method doesn't set `DidUnderstand = True`
SoapUnknownHeader	Contains the data in a SOAP header that wasn't understood by the XML Web service or the SOAP client

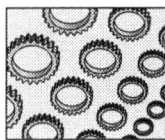

NOTE

View the `SoapHeaderAttribute.Direction` property values (`SoapHeaderDirectionEnumeration.In` and `Out`) from the perspective of the XML Web service. `In` specifies that the service receives the header values from the client. The `InOut` value specifies a bidirectional header.

You must define a class derived from the **SoapHeader** class to add a header. You name the root element of the SOAP header by the name you assign to the derived class, and add header elements as `Public ElementName As DataType` properties. Authentication by user name and password is currently the most common use for SOAP headers. In this case, the client passes the SOAP header values to the server.

SoapDocument and SoapRpc Classes

As you learned in Chapter 4, the default message format for an ASP.NET Web Service is document/literal, which offers operational flexibility but requires an XSD schema for parameters. `SoapDocument...` classes let you change the `Use` value from `Literal` to `Encoded`. `SoapRpc...` classes enable changing the default message format to rpc/encoded. The following table lists only the more important properties of the classes and their default values (in parentheses).

Class	Purpose and Important Properties
SoapDocumentServiceAttribute	Lets you specify values of the `ParameterStyle` (`Wrapped`), `RoutingStyle` (`SoapAction`), and `Use` (`Literal`) attributes
SoapDocumentMethodAttribute	Lets you specify the values of the `Action` (`http://tempuri.org/MethodName`), `Binding` (empty string), `OneWay` (`False`), and `request/response namespace` attributes; and overrides the document-level values for `ParameterStyle` (`Wrapped`) and `Use` (`Literal`) attributes
SoapRpcServiceAttribute	Sets the default message format for the service to rpc/encoded and lets you specify the RoutingStyle attribute (SoapAction)

Class	Purpose and Important Properties
SoapRpcMethodAttribute	Same as the SoapDocumentMethodAttribute class, except for the omission of the Use attribute

TIP

Unless you must use the rpc/encoded format for interoperability with SOAP clients that can't handle document/literal messages, stick with ASP.NET's default `SoapDocument...` attribute values.

SoapExtension Classes

The `SoapExtension...` classes enable capturing and, optionally, modifying a SOAP message at the `BeforeSerialize`, `AfterSerialize`, `BeforeDeserialize`, or `AfterDeserialize` processing stage. `SoapExtensionAttribute` properties don't have default values. The most common current usse of SOAP extensions are message compression, encryption, or both.

Class	Purpose and Important Properties or Methods
SoapExtension	Provides GetInitializer, Initialize, ChainStream, and ProcessMessage methods to intercept and modify messages at the processing stage you specify, in accordance with the priority you establish by the SoapExtensionAttribute class
SoapExtensionAttribute	Lets you set or get the Priority value (Integer) of a SOAP extension

TIP

At http://www.gotdotnet.com/team/rhoward/, Microsoft's Rob Howard has made available several example applications that use the `SoapExtension` methods. The code is C# but it's easy to translate to Visual Basic .NET.

SoapMessage Classes

The `Soap...Message` classes rely on the `SoapExtension` class' `ProcessMessage` method to provide read-write access to most SOAP message elements at one or more of the four message-processing stages. Some elements, such as `Action`, `Exception`, `Stream`, and `Url` are read-only.

Description	Purpose and Important Properties or Methods
SoapMessage	Provides `Action`, `ContentType`, `Exception`, `Headers`, `MethodInfo`, `OneWay`, `Stage`, `Stream`, and `Url` properties to retrieve and set message data for read-write properties
SoapServerMessage	Represents the `SoapMessage` object passed to the `ProcessMessage` method of an XML Web service
SoapClientMessage	Represents the `SOAPMessage` object passed to the `ProcessMessage` method of a `SOAP` client

System.Web.Services.Configuration Classes

ASP.NET uses members of the `System.Web.Services.Configuration` namespace to add service description extensions to the WSDL document for XML Web services that implement `SoapExtension` classes. You use the classes of this namespace and a WSDL extension element to notify clients that they must run a specified SOAP extension to handle the service's response message. The most common use for `System.Web.Services.Configuration` member classes is specifying decryption, expansion, or both methods for SOAP messages that are encrypted and/or compressed.

System.Web.Services.Description Classes

The `System.Web.Services.Description` namespace defines 69 classes and enumerations to represent the elements defined by the WSDL 1.0 specification. ASP.NET uses these classes to generate the WSDL document for an .asmx file. Visual Studio .NET SOAP clients also rely on these classes to create XML Web services proxies from WSDL documents and files.

Invoking the `ServiceDescription.Read(str`*WSDLFile*`)` method parses the specified WSDL document and assigns its elements to members of the `System.Web.Services.Description` namespace. You can substitute a `Stream, String, TextReader`, or `XMLReader` object for a filename. The `Write` method lets you output a modified WSDL document to the same objects. You probably won't need to employ any of these classes when you develop conventional XML Web services, so this section doesn't include a `System.Web.Services.Description` classes list.

System.Web.Services.Discovery Classes

Members of the `System.Web.Services.Discovery` namespace implement the Microsoft Disco service for discovery of XML Web services. The discovery service relies on the contents of local *ServiceName*.disco files on the server you specify. Following is the document contained in the AlphaWS.disco file, which ASP.NET generates for Chapter 5's AlphaWS service:

```xml
<?xml version="1.0" encoding="utf-8"?>
<discovery xmlns:xsd="http://www.w3.org/2001/XMLSchema"
   xmlns:xsi="http://www.w3.org/2001/XMLSchema-instance"
   xmlns="http://schemas.xmlsoap.org/disco/">
   <contractRef ref="http://localhost/AlphaADO/AlphaDist.asmx?wsdl"
      docRef="http://localhost/AlphaADO/AlphaDist.asmx"
      xmlns="http://schemas.xmlsoap.org/disco/scl/" />
</discovery>
```

The `ContractReference` class has `Read` and `ResolveMethod` classes to load a `Stream` object from a *ServiceName*.vsdisco file and verify its validity. Properties of this class are read-only. It's possible—but uncommon—to roll your own .disco `Stream` object with the `Write` method and persist it to a file.

The .vsdisco file that the ASP.NET Web Service project creates for you is adequate for almost all private XML Web services deployed on your intranet. Disco files can handle access by your firm's or client's Web page designers and Windows form developers. Colleagues presumably know the URL for the server(s). If you need to advertise services within your organization, you can establish a private Universal Description, Discovery, and Integration (UDDI) registry. For public access, register the service in one of the public UDDI directories. Chapter 11 describes how to register your services with public UDDI registries.

Adding and Processing SOAP Headers

The basic purpose of SOAP headers is to provide a mechanism for conveying data that's not related directly to the SOAP message payload. As mentioned in the earlier "SoapHeader Classes" section, the most common application for SOAP headers is authentication of service requests by user ID and password strings. Other uses include providing transaction ID values to services that support stateless transactions and exchanging public cryptographic keys.

SOAP headers often replace method arguments, especially for services that use the document/literal format. You gain no significant benefit by replacing rpc/encoded method arguments with header values; it only complicates your service *and* client code. The ADO.NET version of the document/literal OmegaBank service you developed in Chapter 5 is a good candidate to demonstrate replacing arguments that are common to multiple methods with SOAP header values.

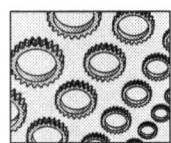

NOTE

You can make the changes described in the following sections to Chapter 5's OmegaBank service and Chapter 6's OCE-Client.sln. Alternatively, download the VBWS07.zip file from <GlobalOMHVbwsSiteReplace>, and expand it into a \VBWS07 folder. Set up a virtual directory for the service named OmegaHdr and point it to the \VBWS07\OmegaHeaders\OmegaWS folder. Add an OCE-Header virtual directory for the client, and point it to the \VBWS07\OmegaHeaders\OCE_Client folder.

Implementing SOAP Headers in XML Web Services

Here's how to add a SOAP header to a new or existing ASP.NET Web Service project, OmegaBank for this example:

1. Add an `Imports System.Web.Services.Protocols` declaration to *ServiceName*.asmx.vb.

2. Add a new class that derives from the `SoapHeader` class. The name of the class defines the SOAP header name. For this example, the first header name is `Authenticate`:

    ```
    Public Class Authenticate
    Inherits SoapHeader
    End Class
    ```

3. Add named properties of the appropriate data type to the class. For this example, header elements replace the `strServerName`, `strUserName`, `strPassword`, and `lngMerchantID` arguments of the `VerifyOrHold` and `ChargeOrCredit` methods:

```
Public Class Authenticate
    Inherits SoapHeader
Public ServerName As String
Public UserName As String
Public Password As String
Public MerchantID As Int32
End Class
```

4. Add a member variable for the derived class prior to the declaration of the first `<WebMethod...>`:

```
Public hdrAuthent As Authenticate
```

5. Add a `SoapHeader('HeaderName')` attribute to the `<WebMethod...` directive of each method that requires the header values. Prefix a comma if your `WebMethod` already has one or more attributes:

```
<WebMethod(Description:='Description text'), _
SoapHeader("hdrAuthent")> _
Public Function VerifyOrHold(Arguments)
```

6. If you want to make the use of the SOAP header optional, add a `Required:=False` attribute value to the `SoapHeader` attribute:

```
SoapHeader("hdrAuthent", Required:=False)> _
```

TIP

Setting the `Required` attribute to `False` lets you test your initially modified service with existing ASP.NET or Windows form clients.

7. Run your modified service and click the Service Description link to verify that the schema elements for the new header values and the header itself appear in the WSDL document.

8. Search for "*HeaderName*" in the WSDL document to find the changes that result from adding the header.

Searching for "Authenticate" in the WSDL document returns the following addition to the `<s:schema>` elements of the `<types>` section, which defines the names and data types of the header values:

```
<s:element name="Authenticate" type="s0:Authenticate" />
s:complexType name="Authenticate">
  <s:sequence>
    <s:element minOccurs="0" maxOccurs="1"
       name="ServerName"  type="s:string" />
```

```
            <s:element minOccurs="0" maxOccurs="1"
               name="UserName" type="s:string" />
            <s:element minOccurs="0" maxOccurs="1"
               name="Password" type="s:string" />
            <s:element minOccurs="1" maxOccurs="1"
               name="MerchantID" type="s:int" />
        </s:sequence>
</s:complexType>
```

Specifying the sample SOAP header adds the following two messages:

```
    <message name="VerifyOrHoldAuthenticate">
        <part name="Authenticate" element="s0:Authenticate" />
    </message>
    ...
    <message name="ChargeOrCreditAuthenticate">
        <part name="Authenticate" element="s0:Authenticate" />
    </message>
```

It also adds a `<soap:header ...>` element to the `<input>` section of each `<binding...>` element:

```
<input>
  <soap:body use="literal" />
  <soap:header d5p1:required="true"
     message="s0:VerifyOrHoldAuthenticate"
     part="Authenticate" use="literal"
     xmlns:d5p1="http://schemas.xmlsoap.org/wsdl/" />
</input>
```

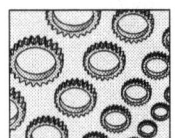

NOTE

The `required="true"` attribute isn't present if you set `Required:=False` in step 6 of the preceding process.

Removing the HTTP GET and POST Protocols from the WSDL Document

When you add required SOAP header elements to the WSDL file, the default method documentation pages substitute a "No test form is available…" message for the input text boxes. Including HTTP GET and POST bindings and ports from the WSDL document reduces its size and prevents you from misleading other developers that these protocols are available for the service.

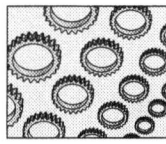

NOTE

The changes described in the following steps have been made to the Web.config file in the VBWS07.zip file.

Here's the drill for removing unsupported protocols from the WSDL file:

1. In Notepad, open the Web.config file for the service.

2. Under the `<system.web>` element, add the following elements:

    ```
    <webServices>
      <protocols>
         <remove name="HttpGet" />
         <remove name="HttpPost" />
      </protocols>
    </webServices>
    ```

CAUTION

The case of the element names must be exactly as shown. If you type `<WebServices>` instead of `<webServices>`, for example, you receive an error message from the debugger when you run the service.

3. Save the changes, run to rebuild the service, and open the WSDL document to verify that all references to `HttpGet` and `HttpPost` are gone.

Testing the Initial SOAP Header Modification with an ASP.NET Client

If you add one or more headers to an ASP.NET XML Web service, the header values become accessible to ASP.NET and Windows forms client applications as members of an early-bound *WebReferenceName.HeaderName* object. The following generic code passes two header values to the service:

```
Dim hdrName As New WebReferenceName.HeaderName()
hdrName.Value1Name = typValue1
hdrName.Value2Name = typValue2
WebReferenceName.HeaderNameValue = hdrName
```

The last line sends the header to the XML Web service, which must receive the header values before the client executes the associated method.

Early-binding a SOAP header enables the Visual Studio .NET editor's Auto List Members feature, which displays all property values you can set or get. In addition to the header values, you can select any of these members from the list: `Actor`, `DidUnderstand`, `EncodedMustUnderstand`, and `MustUnderstand`.

TIP

Add the XML Web service project to your client solution to simplify the modifications to both projects. Temporarily including the service project in your client solution also makes debugging the SOAP header code much easier.

In most cases, you alter existing test or production clients to take advantage of SOAP headers. For this example, you modify the \VBVS06\OCE-ClientASP\OCE-Client.sln solution. Here's the procedure for running an initial test of an XML Web service with optional SOAP headers:

1. If you didn't set the `Required:=False` attribute value in step 6 of the "Implementing SOAP Headers in XML Web Services" section for all service methods, do it now and rebuild the service.

2. Verify that the client test harness works properly in all test modes with your existing XML Web service(s) before making any changes.

3. Add a new Web Reference to the version of the service with the SOAP header(s). For this example, rename the reference **OmegaHdr**.

4. Modify the first instance of the code that calls the original service. In this case, the `cmd_VerifyOrHold` event handler makes the first call to `OmegaWSADO`, so make the following changes to the handler's declarations section:

```
'Dim adoOmegaBank As New OmegaWSADO.OmegaBank()
Dim adoOmegaBank As New OmegaHdr.OmegaBank()
Dim hdrOmegaBank As New OmegaHdr.Authenticate()
```

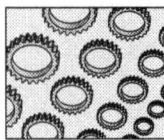

NOTE

Marking the Use XML Web Services check box executes requests to the service specified by the `OmegaHdr` Web Reference, so change the `Checked` value of this check box to `True` to make adoOmegaBank the default service proxy.

5. Prior to executing the `WebSevice` method, set the SOAP header values. Following are the lines you add immediately before the `strVerify = adoOmegaBank.VerifyOrHold(strServer, …)` statement:

```
With hdrOmegaBank
    .ServerName = strNetServer
    .UserName = strNetUser
    .Password = strNetPwd
    .MerchantID = 151203
End With
adoOmegaBank.AuthenticateValue = hdrOmegaBank
```

Here's how the text editor window appears as you add the preceding header values.

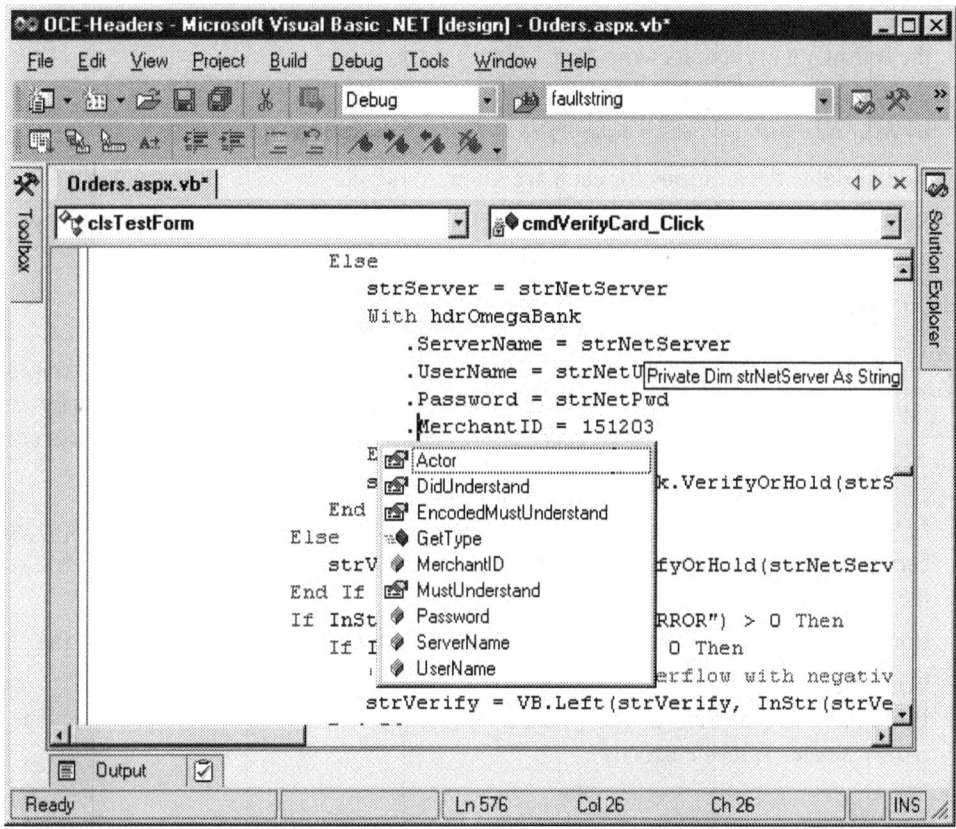

6. Run the project to verify that the client code executes correctly.

At this point, the server doesn't process the header values, so testing only validates client-side SOAP header modifications.

Modifying the XML Web Service to Process Header Values

Altering the method code to substitute SOAP header for method argument values is easy, as demonstrated by the following process for the OmegaBank sample service:

1. Remove the `Required:=False` attribute value from the `WebMethod` directive of the service's method, `VerifyOrHold` for this example.

2. Modify your service's Visual Basic .NET code to use the header values instead of or in addition to the attribute values. For this example, add the following lines immediately after the declarations section of the `VerifyOrHold` function.

```
strServer = hdrAuthent.ServerName
strUserName = hdrAuthent.ServerName
strPassword = hdrAuthent.Password
lngMerchantID = hdrAuthent.MerchantID
```

3. Delete the method arguments that are replaced by header values. In this case, remove the following arguments from `VerifyOrHold`:

```
ByVal strServer As String, ByVal strUser As String,
ByVal strPwd As String, ByVal lngMerchantID As Integer,
```

4. Add variable declarations for each argument removed.

5. Rebuild the service to generate a new WSDL document, and verify that the deleted arguments no longer appear in the schema.

TIP

If your client solution includes the service's project, right-click the service project in Solution Explorer and choose Set As StartUp Project to display the documentation page. Then reset the client project as the startup project. The solution builds without errors because the client's copy of the WSDL file doesn't change when you rebuild the service.

6. In Solution Explorer, right-click the Web Reference, OmegaHdr for this example, and choose Update Web Reference to synchronize the client's copy of the WSDL file with the modified WSDL document.

7. Remove the corresponding arguments from the client instruction that invokes the method.

8. Build and run the client to verify that the modified XML Web service processes the SOAP header values correctly.

TIP

If the Orders.aspx page displays a "Required field/property OmegaBank.AuthenticateValue of SOAP header Authenticate was not set by the client prior to making the call" message in the Verify Card text box, you forgot to add the `adoOmegaBank.AuthenticateValue = hdrOmegaBank` line in step 5 of the preceding section.

You can add additional values, such as `strIssuer`, `strCardNumber`, `strCardName`, and the like to the Authenticate SOAP header, but adding values that are unrelated to the purpose of the header isn't a good SOAP design practice.

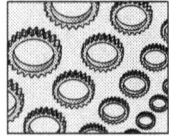

NOTE

Unfortunately, migrating `WebMethod` arguments to SOAP header values doesn't deliver a measurable increase in XML Web service performance.

Traversing the System.Xml Namespace

The `System.Xml` namespace and its member namespaces, especially `System.Xml.Serialization`, contain classes that are very useful for developing complex, production-grade XML Web services for application-integration, B2B, and B2C projects. As mentioned in earlier chapters, this book doesn't include tutorials for XML, XML Schema, XSL/Transform, and other XML derivatives. Thus, the content of the `System.Xml` sections is limited to classes that are germane to developing and consuming XML Web services.

The XML serialization examples of preceding chapters use Visual Basic .NET code to generate element-centric XML documents from `ADODB.Recordset` and `SqlClient.SqlDataReader` objects. OakLeaf Consumer Electronics' sample distributor XML Web services use the COM-based `MSXML2.DomDocument40` and related objects to parse XML order request messages. Members of the `System.Xml` namespaces deliver more elegant object-to-XML serialization techniques and eliminate dependence on MSXML2 COM objects for parsing XML documents.

System.Xml Member Classes

The following table lists the members of the `System.Xml` namespace that most XML Web service developers are likely to use and that the examples of this book employ. If you're familiar with the `MSXML2.DomDocument40` object and `MSXML2.IXMLDOM...` interfaces, you'll find that the properties and methods of the classes are identical or easily translatable to corresponding MSXML2 objects and interfaces.

`System.Xml` Class	Description
`XmlDocument`	Implements the W3C Document Object Model and substitutes for `MSXML2.DomDocument40` and earlier Microsoft XML parsers
`XmlDataDocument`	An extension of the `XmlDocument` class that manipulates as structured XML documents relational data contained in `System.Data.DataSet` objects
`XmlNodeList`	Represents a collection of designated nodes in an XML document
`XmlNode`	Represents a single node in an `XmlNodeList` collection
`XmlTextReader`	An implementation of the `XmlReader` class that provides very fast, forward-only access to a `Stream` object containing an XML document (similar to an `SqlClient.SqlDataReader`)
`XmlNodeReader`	Provides quick access to XML data in a specified `XmlNode` object
`XmlValidatingReader`	An `XmlReader` implementation that enables document validation by XML Schema (XSD), Data Type Definition (DTD), or Microsoft's proprietary (and obsolete) XML-Data Reduced (XDR) documents

Unlike the `MSXML2.DomDocument40` class, `XmlDocument` doesn't load the entire document into memory. Eliminating document caching improves performance and minimizes resource consumption when processing large XML documents. The read-only, forward-only characteristics of `XmlDocument` objects resemble those of the Simple API for XML (SAX) parser, and are optimized for use by production-grade XML Web services.

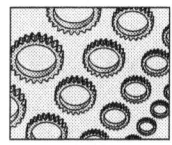

NOTE

The "Creating XML Web Services with Microsoft SQLXML 3.0" section near the end of the chapter shows you how to use an XmlTextReader object to parse attribute-centric XML data streams returned by automatically generated XML Web services from SQL Server 2000 stored procedures. Examples in Chapter 8 also replace MSXML2.DomDocument40 objects with XmlDocument objects.

System.Xml.Serialization Classes

ASP.NET uses the `System.Xml.Serialization.XmlSerializer` class to generate SOAP messages from `WebService`-designated classes at run time. If you aren't satisfied with ASP.NET's serialization of your classes to SOAP messages, you can customize the process with an `XmlSerializer` object to which you apply a set of `Soap...Attribute` objects. You can also deserialize a SOAP message to an object. You're unlikely to need to resort to `XmlSerializer` for common XML Web service implementations, but you should be aware that the .NET Framework offers this option.

The following table lists the objects involved in SOAP message serialization and deserialization.

System.XmlSerialization Classes	Purpose or Description
XmlSerializer	Converts the public properties of any object to an XML document, including a SOAP message, and vice versa, depending on whether you apply the **Serialize** or **Deserialize** method
SoapAttributeAttribute	Serializes a class member as a SOAP attribute
SoapElementAttribute	Serializes a class member as a SOAP element
SoapEnumAttribute	Lets you override the name of a SOAP enumeration member
SoapIgnoreAttribute	Prevents serialization of a public class member
SoapIncludeAttribute	Permits including derived classes in the SOAP message and WSDL document
SoapTypeAttribute	Lets you specify whether to include a particular element type in the SOAP document's schema

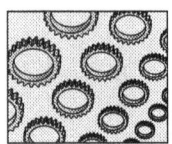

NOTE

The .NET Framework uses most of the remaining classes of the `XmlSerializer` *namespace internally.*

Other System.Xml Classes

The following table lists the other `System.Xml` namespaces whose classes fall beyond the basic scope of this book.

System.XML Namespace	Description
Schema	Represents an XSD schema, and supports W3C XML Schemas for Strrctures and XML Schemas for Datatypes standards. The Schema namespace is similar in structure and use to the more specialized System.Web.Services.Description namespace for WSDL documents.
XPath	Provides the XPath parser and evaluation engine for processing XPath queries.
Xsl	Supports Extensible Stylesheet Transformations (XSLT or XSL/T) in accordance with the W3C XSL Transformations 1.0 recommendation.

The SoapFormatter Class

The `System.Runtime.Serialization.Formatters.Soap.SoapFormatter` class isn't a member of either namespace in this chapter's title, but you should know that the `SoapFormatter` object exists. `SoapFormatter` is a low-level but heavy-duty object that generates an encoded SOAP message from an object, such as an array, to a `Stream` object, and vice versa. .NET remoting uses the `SoapFormatter` for specialized SOAP messaging.

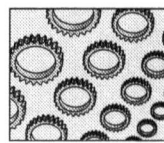

NOTE

The .NET Framework SDK has a Remoting Serialization Sample console application that demonstrates use of the `SoapFormatter`. *You'll find the sample application under the Remoting, Remoting Advanced heading of the page returned by choosing Microsoft .NET Framework SDK | QuickStarts, Tutorials And Samples.*

Creating XML Web Services with Microsoft SQLXML 3.0

Microsoft SQLXML 3.0 is the third in a series of no-charge XML-enabled add-ons for all editions of SQL Server 2000. Microsoft announced SQLXML3 at the October 2001 Professional Developer's Conference (PDC) and released the beta version in late December 2001.

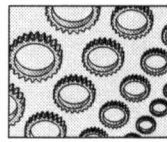

NOTE

For a review of Microsoft's data-related announcements at PDC 2001, go to http://www.oakleaf.ws/a rticles.aspx and click the November 12, 2001, link to read the "Microsoft Unveils .NET Data Futures at PDC 2001" article.

SQLXML 3.0 incorporates the following features introduced by versions 1.0 and 2.0:

► SQLXMLOLEDB data provider to enable ADO clients to process XML data streams returned by `FOR XML {AUTO|RAW} [ELEMENTS]` queries

► HTTP template queries that offer optional XSLT transform capability (For an example of an application that executes template queries, click the Create Powerful Web Reports link at http://www.oakleaf.ws/articles.aspx.)

► Updategrams for specifying `INSERT`, `UPDATE`, and `DELETE` operations by XML documents

► XML views based on XSD (or XDR) annotated schemas

► SQL Managed Classes for executing `SELECT` queries and updating data with Diffgrams

► Bulk loading of XML data into SQL Server 2000 tables

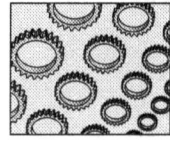

NOTE

SQLXML2's SQLXML Managed Classes are compatible with the Beta 2 version of the .NET Framework. The SQLXML3 upgrade requires a .NET Framework build number of 3423 or greater and won't install under the RC-1 version.

The most important feature added by SQLXML 3.0 is the capability to, in the words of a Microsoft SQL Server product manager, "turn SQL Server [2000] into a gigantic [XML] Web service." SQLXML 3.0's template queries let you turn any SQL Server 2000 stored procedure, user-defined function, or template query into a fully functional XML Web service with minimal effort and in a *very* short time. Most of the work is designing and coding client test harnesses for the services.

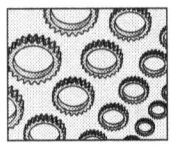

NOTE

If you don't have SQLXML3 installed, download it from the Microsoft Web site at http://msdn.microsoft.com/ sqlxml. You must have an edition of SQL Server 2000 and its client tools installed to complete the SQLXML3 installation.

The SQLXML3 sample application requires downloading and extracting the VBWS07.zip sample files to a \VBWS07 folder on your development computer, as described in the earlier "Adding and Processing SOAP Headers" section. The sample application is located in the \VBWS07\SQLXML3 subfolder.

Adding the Stored Procedures for the XML Web Service

This example requires you to add four T-SQL stored procedures named GetTop10, GetTop25, GetTop50, and GetTop100 to the AlphaDist sample database. The procedures return the SKU, CategoryName, Brand, Model, Description, NetPrice, and Quantity values for products ranked by highest to lowest cost. The only difference between the procedures is the number of rows returned.

Following is the T-SQL statement for the GetTop100 stored procedure, which returns rows from one of the three databases. You don't need to add the FOR XML {AUTO | RAW} modifier, because calling the stored procedure as an XML Web service returns an XML stream in RAW format. If you don't supply category parameter values, the procedures return rows for all six product categories.

```
CREATE PROCEDURE GetTop100
@Cat1 char(4) = 'AMPL',
@Cat2 char(4) = 'DVCC',
@Cat3 char(4) = 'DVDP',
@Cat4 char(4) = 'RCVH',
@Cat5 char(4) = 'SPKF',
@Cat6 char(4) = 'TVRC'
AS
SELECT TOP 100 P.SKU, C.CategoryName AS Category, B.Brand,
      P.Model, P.Description, P.NetPrice, P.Quantity
   FROM Products AS P, Brands AS B, Categories AS C
   WHERE B.BrandID = P.BrandID AND C.CategoryID = P.CategoryID AND
      P.CategoryID IN(@cat1, @cat2, @cat3, @cat4, @cat5, @cat6)
   ORDER BY NetPrice DESC
GO
```

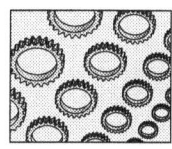

NOTE

The code for the stored procedure and sample client test harness first appeared in the January 29, 2002, issue of Fawcette Technical Publications' .NETInsight newsletter. Click the January 29, 2002, link at http://www.oakleaf.ws/articles.aspx to read the "Generate XML Web Services from Stored Procedures" article, which also describes how to set up and run SQLXML3's sample application.

Your \VBWS07\SQLXML3 folder contains the GetTopProcs.sql script to create the required stored procedures. To add the stored procedures to the AlphaDist database, do the following:

1. Launch SQL Server Query Analyzer, and connect to the server for the OCE sample databases.

2. Select the AlphDist database, choose File | Open, navigate to \VBWS07\SQLXML3, open the GetTopProcs.sql script, and execute it.

3. Launch SQL Enterprise Manager, expand the AlphaDist database node, select the Users node, and double-click AlphaUser to open the Database User Properties - AlphaUser dialog.

4. Click Permissions to open the Permissions page, and mark the EXEC check box for the four added stored procedures.

5. Click OK twice to close the two dialogs and give the AlphaUser login permission to execute the stored procedures.

Setting Up the Virtual Directory

Installing SQLXML3 updates the IIS Virtual Directory Management snap-in by adding XML Web service–related elements to the New Virtual Directory Properties dialog's Virtual Directory page. The Type list gets a new "soap" item, and Web Service Name and Domain Name text boxes provide information required by the Web Services Description Language. Completing the virtual directory setup process creates the *ServiceName*.wsdl file for the service and a *ServiceName*.ssc service configuration file. The .ssc file stores information on the document output type, `raw` for this example, and the names and parameters for each procedure you include in the .wsdl file.

To set up a virtual directory for the four `GetTopN` stored procedures in the AlphaDist database, do the following:

1. Create a folder in which to save the .wsdl and .ssc files, \SQLXML for this example.

2. Choose Programs | SQLXML 3.0 | Configure IIS Support to open the IIS Virtual Directory Management for SQLXML 3.0 snap-in.

3. Right-click the Default Web Site node and choose New | Virtual Directory to open the New Virtual Directory Properties dialog.

4. On the General page, type **SQLXML** in the Virtual Directory Name text box and specify *d:***\SQLXML** as the Local Path.

5. Click the Security tab and type **AlphaUser** in the User Name text box and **Alpha#123** in the Password and Confirm Password text boxes.

6. Click the Data Source tab, accept (local) or specify an SQL Server 2000 instance, clear the Use Default Database for Current Login check box, and select AlphaDist in the Database list.

7. Click the Settings tab and mark the Allow POST check box.

8. Click the Virtual Names tab and, with the <New virtual name> item selected, type **Alpha** in the Name text box. Then open the Type list and choose the soap item. These actions set the defaults in the Web Service Name and Domain Name text boxes: Alpha and the NetBIOS name of the IIS server.

9. Click the Path browse button to open the Browse for Folder dialog, navigate to the *d*:\SQLXML folder, and click OK.

10. Click Save to save the settings, add the Alpha service to the Defined Virtual Names list, and enable the three other command buttons. (See Figure 7-1.)

11. Click Configure to open the Soap [sic] Virtual Name Configuration dialog, and click the builder button to the right of the SP/Template text box to open the SOAP Stored Procedure Mapping dialog. (See Figure 7-2.)

12. Select a stored procedure to add as a service method, click OK to close the dialog, and click Save to add the stored procedure's name to the Methods list.

TIP

You can change the name of the method that executes the stored procedure by altering the value of the Method Name text box.

13. Repeat steps 11 and 12 for the remaining three stored procedures. The configuration dialog appears as shown in Figure 7-3.

14. Click OK twice to close the two dialogs and create the Alpha.wsdl and Alpha.ssc files.

15. Inspect the WSDL file in IE by typing **http://*ServerName*/SQLXML/Alpha?wsdl** as the URL; typing **http://*localhost*/SQLXML/alpha?wsdl** also works. Open the unformatted Alpha.ssc file in Notepad to review its contents.

Running the SQLXML3 Windows Form Project

The SqlXml3.sln solution is a Windows form application that lets you select the stored procedure to execute as an XML Web service method and the categories to include in the attribute-centric XML rowset document returned by the service. A `DataGrid` control displays the attribute values of each row returned. A check box lets you run an identical XML Web service from the OakLeaf Web site. (See Figure 7-4.) Two text boxes display the time to consume the local or remote XML Web service and the total time from clicking the Retrieve Data button until the `DataGrid`'s population completes.

The ASP.NET Web Form version of the application at http://www.oakleaf.ws/sqlxml3/ alphadist.aspx duplicates most of the functions of the Windows form version, but it doesn't

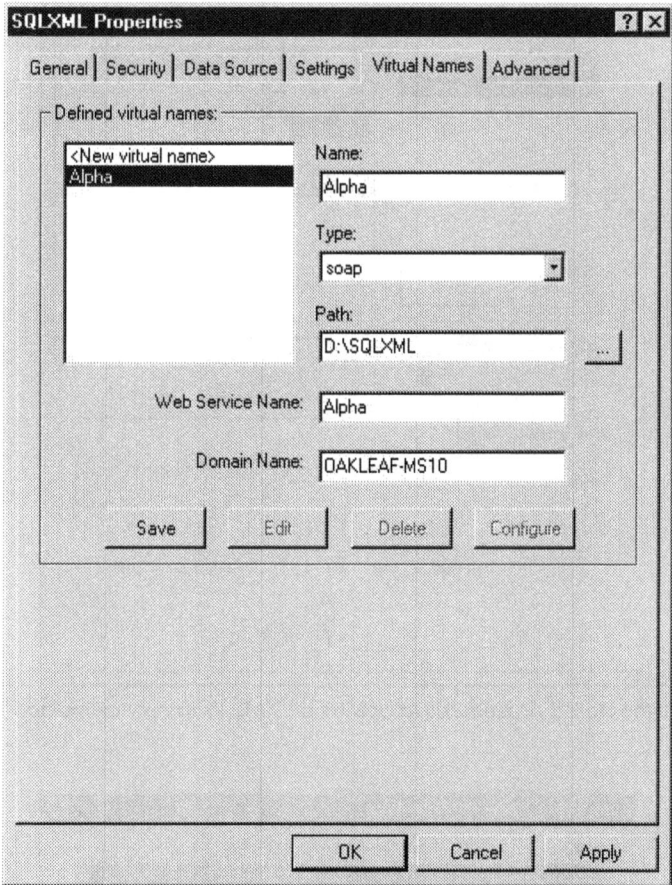

Figure 7-1   *The basic settings for the sample SQLXML3 XML Web service are shown here in edit mode so you can see the values. (The text boxes are disabled after you click Save.)*

report XML Web service execution time. (See Figure 7-5.) Conversion from a Windows form to a Web Form project followed the process described in Chapter 6.

Performance testing of the sample SQLXML3 XML Web services proves that Microsoft's developers paid close attention to performance tuning. On the test machine used to write this book's applications, the average time is 30 ms to return 10 rows from a local or network server. The average time to return 100 rows is 80 ms. As you increase the number of rows returned, populating the grid consumes an increasing percentage of total processing time.

Processing Attribute-Centric XML Data Documents with the XmlTextReader

The default format of rowsets returned by SQLWML3 XML Web services corresponds to adding the `FOR XML RAW` modifier to the stored procedure's `SELECT` statement. Accepting default format, rather than adding the `FOR XML AUTO, ELEMENTS` modifier, doesn't blow up applications that process the rowset as a conventional `ADODB.Recordset` or

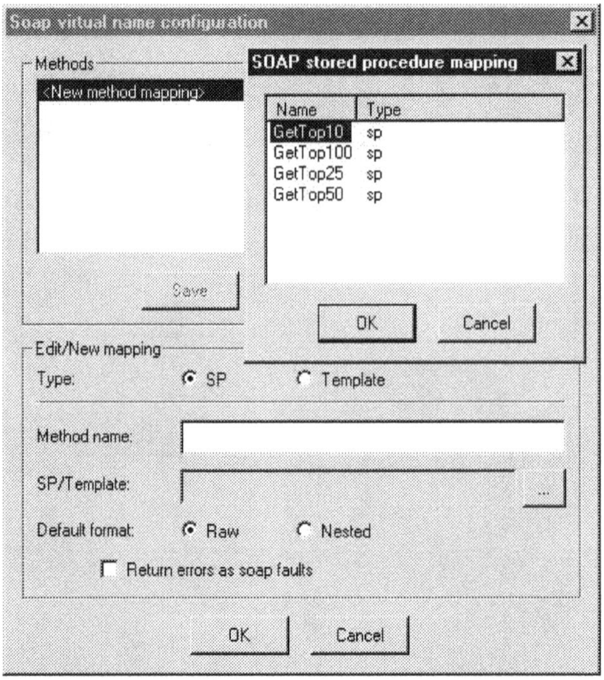

Figure 7-2   *Select the stored procedures to add as an XML Web service method in this dialog.*

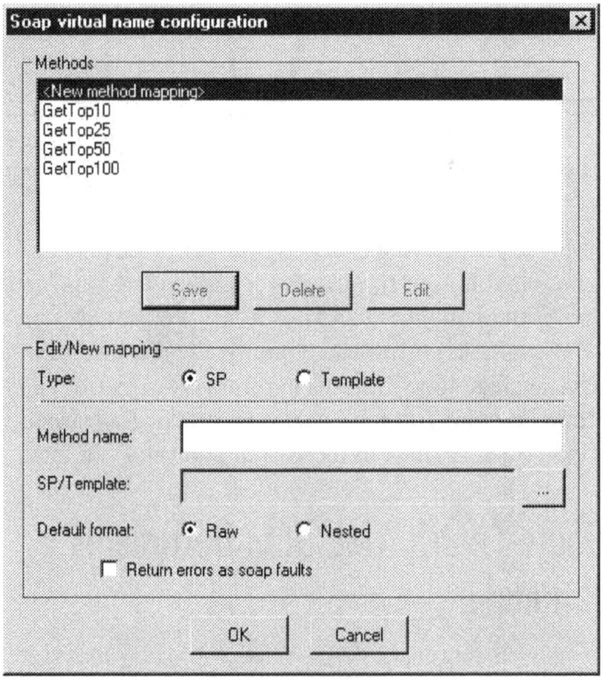

Figure 7-3   *The Soap Virtual Name Configuration dialog appears as shown here after adding the four stored procedures.*

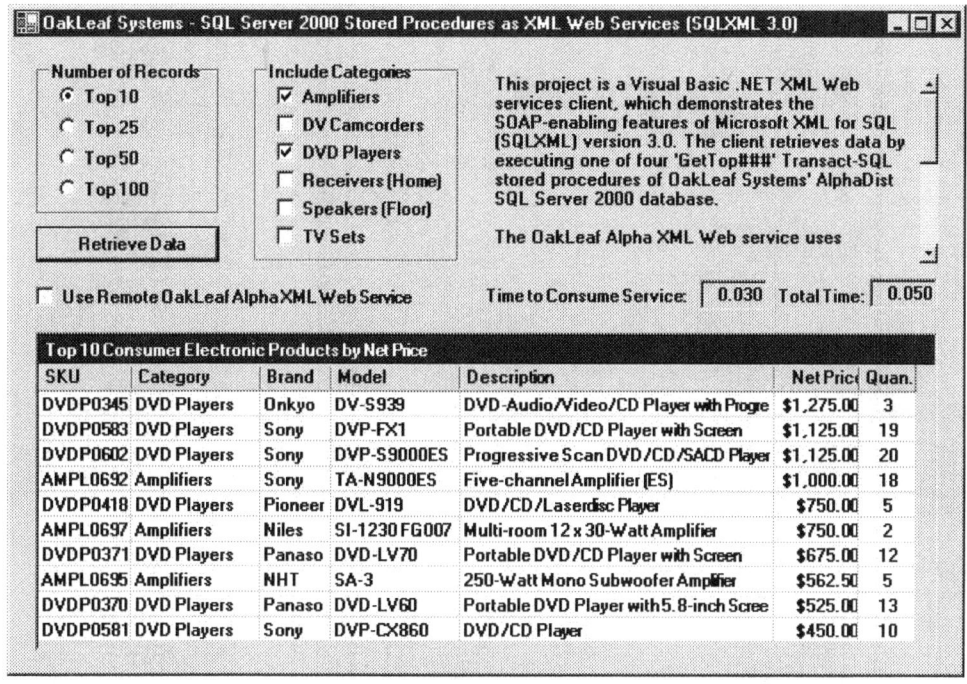

Figure 7-4   *Clicking the Retrieve Data button of the SqlXml3.exe application with default selections returns the data shown here.*

.NET Framework `DataTable` object. Another advantage of attribute-centric over element-centric XML data documents is size; attribute-centric XML rowset documents are often 30 percent to 50 percent smaller than the element-centric version.

Following are the first four rows of the XML document returned by SQLXML3's default settings:

```
<SqlXml>
    <row SKU="DVDP0345" Category="DVD Players" Brand="Onkyo"
        Model="DV-S939" Description="DVD-Audio/Video/CD Player with
        Progressive" NetPrice="1275" Quantity="3" />
    <row SKU="DVDP0583" Category="DVD Players" Brand="Sony"
        Model="DVP-FX1" Description="Portable DVD/CD Player with Screen"
        NetPrice="1125" Quantity="19" />
    <row SKU="DVDP0602" Category="DVD Players" Brand="Sony"
        Model="DVP-S9000ES" Description="Progressive Scan DVD/CD/SACD
        Player (ES)" NetPrice="1125" Quantity="20" />
    <row SKU="AMPL0692" Category="Amplifiers" Brand="Sony"
        Model="TA-N9000ES" Description="Five-channel Amplifier (ES)"
        NetPrice="1000" Quantity="18" />
    ...
</SqlXml>
```

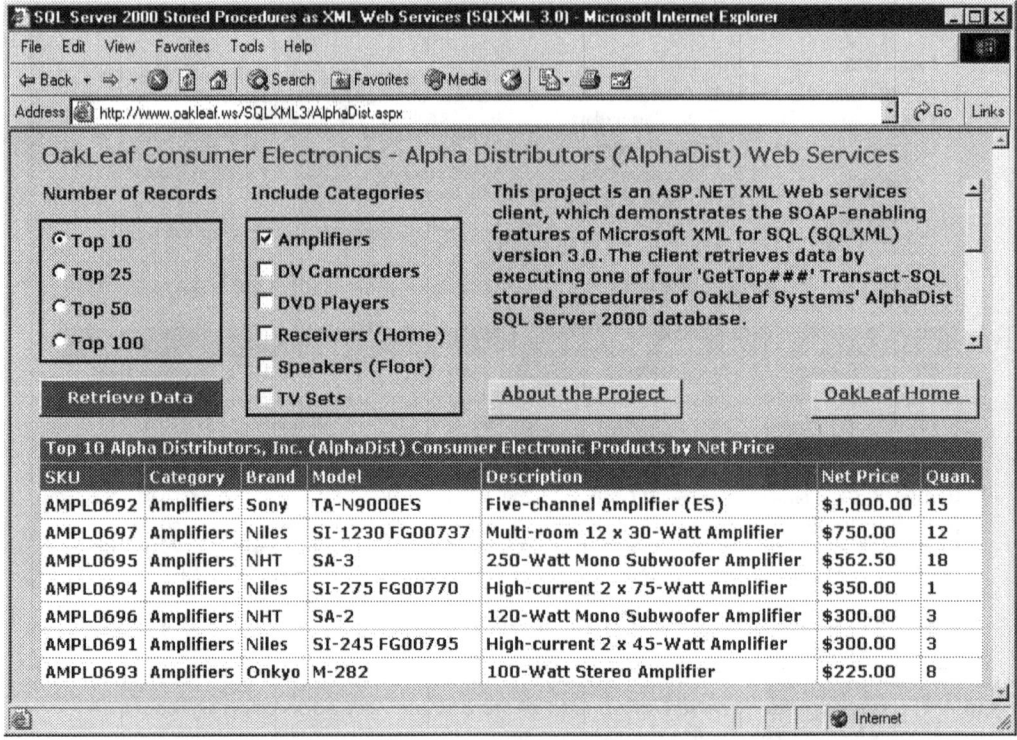

Figure 7-5   *The ASP.NET version of SqlXml3.exe on the OakLeaf Web site returns data from local XML Web services.*

SQLXML3 delivers an `SqlResultStream`, which can contain multiple rowsets returned by a single service method as members of an array (`objResult` in the following code example). You use a `System.Io.StringReader` object to convert the XML representation of individual rowsets to deliver a `Stream` object (`srdData`) to an `XmlTextReader` object, and then apply the `Read` method to return elements. The stored procedures return only a single rowset (`objResult(0)`), and you skip the first element (`<SqlXml>`) when processing the data. The `GetAttribute(n).ToString` method delivers the attribute value to the appropriate column of a `DataRow` object that you append to a `DataTable` for each valid row.

NOTE

The code that sets the `Columns` and `DataSource` properties of the `DataTable` object (`dtProds`) executes in the `Public Sub New()` event handler.

Here's the Visual Basic .NET code for the Retrieve Data button's `cmdExecute_Click` event handler. Most code that isn't germane to understanding rowset document processing has been deleted for brevity.

```
Private Sub cmdExecute_Click(ByVal sender As System.Object, _
        ByVal e As System.EventArgs) Handles cmdExecute.Click
    Dim prxRemote As New AlphaRemote.Alpha()   'OakLeaf Alpha service
    Dim prxLocal As New AlphaLocal.Alpha()     'Local Alpha service
    Dim prxAlpha As Object
    Dim objResult As New Object()
    Dim xmlData As System.Xml.XmlElement
    Dim msgRemote As AlphaRemote.SqlMessage
    Dim msgLocal As AlphaLocal.SqlMessage
    Dim msgError As Object
    Dim srdData As StringReader
    Dim xtrData As XmlTextReader
    Dim drProds As DataRow
    Dim dblTime As Double
    Dim dblConsume As Double
    Dim dblTotal As Double

    Dim strHeader As String
    Dim intRetVal As Integer
    Dim strXmlData As String
    Dim strData As String
    Dim strRow As String
    Dim strError As String
    Dim intCol As Integer
    Dim strCol As String

    txtErrors.Visible = False
    txtHelp.Visible = True
    txtConsume.Text = ""
    txtTotal.Text = ""
    dtProds.Clear()

    'Product category selection code removed for brevity
    If chkRemote.Checked Then
        'Use the OakLeaf Alpha service
        prxAlpha = prxRemote
        msgError = msgRemote
    Else
        prxAlpha = prxLocal
        msgError = msgLocal
    End If
    dblTime = Timer

    'Rows returned
    If optTop10.Checked Then
```

```vb
        objResult = prxAlpha.GetTop10(strCat1, strCat2, strCat3, _
            strCat4, strCat5, strCat6, intRetVal)
        strHeader = "Top 10 "
    ElseIf optTop25.Checked Then
        objResult = prxAlpha.GetTop25(strCat1, strCat2, strCat3, _
            strCat4, strCat5, strCat6, intRetVal)
        strHeader = "Top 25 "
    ElseIf optTop50.Checked Then
        objResult = prxAlpha.GetTop50(strCat1, strCat2, strCat3, _
            strCat4, strCat5, strCat6, intRetVal)
        strHeader = "Top 50 "
    ElseIf optTop100.Checked Then
        objResult = prxAlpha.GetTop100(strCat1, strCat2, strCat3, _
            strCat4, strCat5, strCat6, intRetVal)
        strHeader = "Top 100 "
    End If
    strHeader += "Consumer Electronic Products by Net Price"
    dgProds.CaptionText = strHeader

    'Process the single XmlElement (late binding)
    If UBound(objResult) = 0 Then
        If objResult(0).GetType().ToString() = _
                "System.Xml.XmlElement" Then
            dblConsume = Timer - dblTime
            xmlData = objResult(0)
            'Retrieve all rows as a String
            strXmlData = xmlData.OuterXml
            'Create a Stream from the String
            srdData = New StringReader(strXmlData)
            'Load the XmlTextWriter with the Stream
            xtrData = New XmlTextReader(srdData)
            With xtrData
                'Skip the first row
                .Read()
                'Read the rest of the stream
                Do While xtrData.Read()
                    drProds = dtProds.NewRow
                    If .AttributeCount > 0 Then
                        For intCol = 0 To .AttributeCount - 1
                            'Load the attribute values
                            strCol = .GetAttribute(intCol).ToString
                            If intCol = 5 Then
                                strCol = Format(CDec(strCol), "$#,##0.00")
```

```
                    End If
                    drProds(intCol) = strCol
                Next intCol
                dtProds.Rows.Add(drProds)
            End If
        Loop
    End With
    dblTotal = Timer - dblTime
    txtConsume.Text = Format(dblConsume, "#0.000")
    txtTotal.Text = Format(dblTotal, "#0.000")
    Else
        'Error handling code removed for brevity
    End If
  Else
    'No records returned
    'Error handling code removed for brevity
  End If
End Sub
```

The relationship of the SQLXML3 sections of this chapter to the System.Xml namespace might appear tenuous, but you'll find that the XmlTextReader and other System.Xml classes play an important role in the XML Web services and test client applications of the remaining chapters.

Delivering Reports with XML Web Services

IN THIS CHAPTER:

Creating Business Intelligence Reports

Developing XML Web Services for Data Reporting

Exploring the CTHarness Crosstab Report Project

Migrating Test Harness Code to the XML Web Service

Most XML Web services you created and modified in the preceding chapters originated as sample ActiveX components. The Upgrade Wizard handles migrating Visual Basic 6.0 code to Visual Basic .NET pseudocode quite well, but your projects rely on references to the `Microsoft.VisualBasic.Compatibility` and `Microsoft.VisualBasic.Compatibility.Data` namespaces to support obsolescent objects, properties, methods, and constructs. Your ASP.NET XML Web services don't gain the full benefits offered by Visual Studio .NET and the .NET Framework until you bite the bullet and write new services from scratch in Visual Basic .NET.

TIP

You might find it practical to remove Upgrade Wizard and Visual Basic 6.0 detritus from simple to moderately complex services, but the investment to upgrade large, complex services — especially those that depend on other COM or COM+ objects — isn't likely to deliver adequate performance, reliability, or scalability dividends.

Another side effect of upgrading ActiveX components to ASP.NET Web services is reliance on passing multiple method argument values to the service. Old habits die hard, so experienced Visual Basic component developers might tend to continue using RPC-style method calls to deliver document/literal response messages. Best practices for production XML Web services dictate that request *and* response messages be self-describing. Cryptic RPC-style argument names with conventional datatype prefixes—such as `lngRelTransactID`—seldom qualify as self-describing. The *XML* prefix of XML Web services, as used in this book, requires SOAP as the messaging protocol, HTTP as the transport, and well-formed XML documents for at least the response message.

Generating reports from data contained in relational tables, is especially suited to demonstrating the use of XML documents as request and response messages. The objective of this chapter is to show you how to design document/literal XML Web services for generating summary financial or technical reports. Time-series crosstab reports are one of the most popular summary report formats, so this chapter's example is a crosstab report generated from OakLeaf Consumer Electronics order data. To evaluate the performance of the XML Web service, you need a lot of orders that have dates spanning the time-series periods. Thus, this chapter includes a Windows form application to backdate orders over a range of dates you specify.

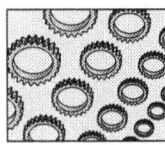

NOTE

The sample code for this chapter is contained in VBWS08.zip, which you can download from http://www. osborne.com/downloads/downloads.shtml. Expand the files for the three example projects — BackdateOrders, CTHarness, and CTReports — into a \VBWS08 folder. Create a new virtual directory named ReportsWS and point its source to the \VBWS08\ReportsWS folder before you open the CTHarness.sln solution.

Creating Business Intelligence Reports

Business intelligence (BI) might seem like an oxymoron to Visual Basic developers, but delivering BI reports to users is destined to become one of the primary applications for XML

Web services. BI is an all-encompassing term for processes that transform raw business data into information that managers and executives use to measure business performance. According to Microsoft's Bill Baker, BI applications account for about 50 percent of SQL Server license revenue.

The primary benefit of XML as the BI message format is the ability to transform data returned from queries against relational and online analytical processing (OLAP) databases to suit a wide range of user and device requirements. Using SOAP over HTTP lets users retrieve BI information via a wired or wireless Internet connection and display it on conventional or pocket PCs, personal organizers, or cell phones.

Emulating Historical Order and Invoice Data

BI reports require historical data, regardless of whether the report is intended to analyze past business activities or project future trends. Chapter 5's OCE-Client bulk order entry application adds orders as quickly as possible. Simulating historical data requires backdating orders over multiple reporting periods, such as months or quarters, to enable generation of sample time-series reports. Time-series is the most widely used BI report format.

To be meaningful, historical data for reports must be representative of real-world transactions and take into account the rate of business growth or decline. It's assumed that OakLeaf Consumer Electronics' Web storefront is successful and business is increasing at an exponential rate—reminiscent of the early days of B2C Web sites. Backdating orders to the beginning of a reporting period requires synchronizing records in related tables with each order date and time. For example, OmegaBank's transaction records for credit holds must have the correct order date and time; records for credit card debits and credit hold releases must correspond to the shipping (invoice) date and time. Similarly, dates and times of purchase orders to distributors must correspond to order `DateTime` values. OCE fulfills orders from 8:00 A.M. to 5:00 P.M. Orders received by 3:00 P.M. ship the same day from local inventory or by drop shipment from a distributor.

BackdateOrders.sln is a Visual Basic .NET Windows form utility, which lets you start backdating OCE orders from any starting date you want, and redate the orders and related records based on a starting value for orders received per day. The defaults are January 1 of the preceding year and two orders per day to start. You can set the rate of increase of the number of orders per day. The default is 0.2—one or more order per day every five days. You need a total of about 14,000 orders to generate one year of data with the default settings. Figure 8-1 shows the BackdateOrder.vb form after clicking the Connect button.

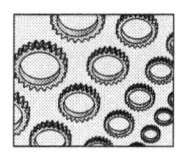

NOTE

The BackdateOrders project isn't a speed demon, despite its use of `SqlCommand` objects to update the records. It takes approximately 45 minutes for a moderate-performance (833-MHz Pentium III) machine to update 14,000 orders and their related records (a total of about 55,000 records). That's considerably faster, however, than adding the 14,000 records, which consumes nearly two hours.

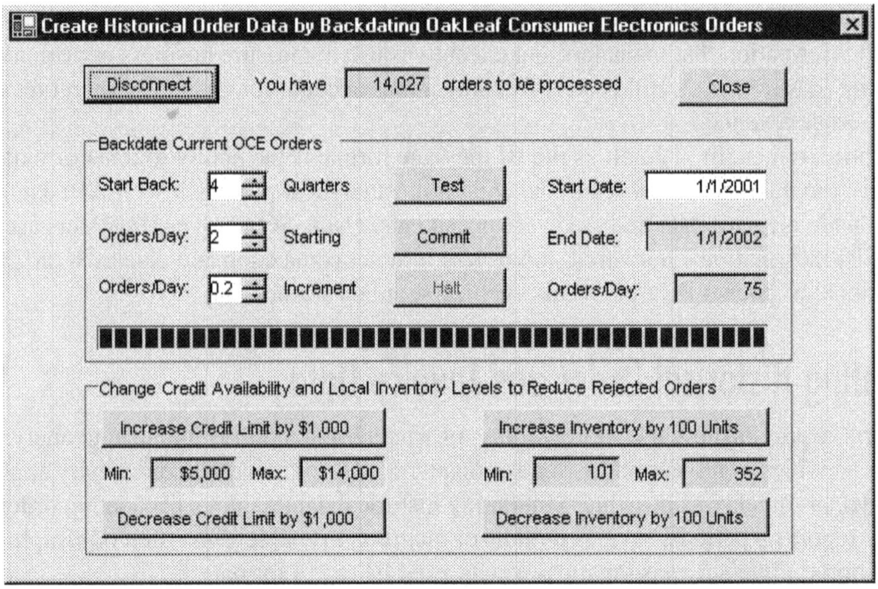

Figure 8-1 *When you click the Connect button, the BackdateOrders form calculates the last order date based on the number of Orders records and the default backdate settings shown here.*

Following are brief descriptions of the functions of the BackdateOrders form controls:

▶ **Connect/Disconnect**   Toggles the state of connections to the OCE_Cust, OCE_Prod, and OMB_Network databases. If your SQL Server instance is on another computer, change (`LOCAL`) to the instance name in the declarations section of the `frmHistory` class.

▶ **Test**   Checks your backdate settings to calculate the End Date and final Orders/Day value. Click Test after changing any settings, including the value of the Start Date text box.

▶ **Commit**   Updates the `datetime` fields of the three databases. The final End Date value is usually a day or two greater than that reported by the Test operation as a result of occasional `datetime` rollovers. A message reports the number of records updated and the elapsed time.

▶ **Halt**   Stops the Commit operation at the end of the update operation for the current order date. You encounter an increasing delay between clicking Halt and stopping the updates as the number of orders per day increases.

▶ **Increase/Decrease Credit Limit By $1,000**   Lets you adjust the ChargeLimit and Available fields of the OMB_Network's Authorize table in $1000 increments. If credit cards are due to expire during order addition, you have the option of adding one year to their expiration date.

▶ **Increase/Decrease Inventory by 100 Units**   Adjusts the `BeginningInventory` value of OCE_Prod database's Products table.

TIP

Use the last two sets of buttons to minimize the number of orders that receive "declined" messages from OmegaBank and out-of-stock reports from the Products table. Reinitialize and regenerate the tables with OCE-Client if you want the new settings to apply to all orders.

The BackdateOrders.vb project's `frmHistory` form contains almost 1000 lines of code and doesn't provide error handling. Following is the code for the `cmdCommit_Click` event handler that processes the updates. The listing demonstrates how to use several new methods and properties of the .NET `DateTime` object, such as `AddDays` and `Hour`, which make working with dates and times much more straightforward in Visual Basic .NET than its predecessors. Manipulating dates and times is a very important component of BI report services.

```
Private Sub cmdCommitDates_Click(ByVal sender As System.Object, _
     ByVal e As System.EventArgs) Handles cmdCommitDates.Click
   'Spread the order/invoice/transaction dates from the beginning date
   Dim cnnOrders As New SqlConnection()
   Dim cmmOrders As New SqlCommand()
   Dim rdrOrders As SqlDataReader
   Dim intOrderID As Int32
   Dim intOPD As Int32
   Dim decOPDIncr As Decimal
   Dim intOPDCurr As Int32
   Dim datOrder As DateTime
   Dim datInvoice As DateTime
   Dim intCtr As Int32
   Dim intDays As Int32
   Dim intRecsAff As Int32
   Dim dblTime As Double
   Dim intMins As Int32
   Dim strMsg As String

   cmdClose.Enabled = False
   cmdHalt.Enabled = True
   Call ControlState(False)
   Me.Cursor = Cursors.WaitCursor
   intOPD = CInt(updOPDStart.Value)
   decOPDIncr = updOPDIncr.Value
   datOrder = CDate(txtStartDate.Text)
   intMins = DatePart(DateInterval.Minute, Now)
   With cnnOrders
      .ConnectionString = strCustConn
      .Open()
   End With
   With cmmCust
      .CommandTimeout = 150 'To accommodate slow machines
      .Connection = cnnCust
      .CommandType = CommandType.Text
      .CommandText = "SELECT OrderID, RequiredShipDate " + _
```

```vbnet
            "FROM Orders ORDER BY OrderID"
        rdrOrders = .ExecuteReader()
    End With
    With cmmOrders
        .Connection = cnnOrders
        .CommandType = CommandType.Text
    End With
    With cmmNet
        .Connection = cnnNet
        .CommandType = CommandType.Text
    End With

    pgbBulk.Value = 0
    intCtr = 0
    intDays = 0
    With rdrOrders
        While .Read
            Randomize()
            intOrderID = rdrOrders.GetInt32(0)
            'Current value of orders/day
            intOPDCurr = CInt(CDec(intDays) * decOPDIncr) + intOPD
            'Spread orders uniformly over 23 hours
            dblTime = 23 / CSng(intOPDCurr)
            datOrder = datOrder.AddHours(dblTime)
            'Update the OrderDate and RequiredShipDate values
            strSQL = "UPDATE Orders SET OrderDate ='" + CStr(datOrder)
            If Not IsDBNull(rdrOrders(1)) Then
                strSQL += "', RequiredShipDate ='" + _
                    CStr(datOrder.AddDays(7))
            End If
            strSQL += "', LastStatusUpdate ='" + _
                CStr(datOrder.AddSeconds(5))
            strSQL += "' WHERE OrderID = " + CStr(intOrderID)
            With cmmOrders
                .CommandText = strSQL
                intRecsAff += .ExecuteNonQuery()
            End With
            'Fix-up the invoice date/time
            If datOrder.Hour < 8 Then
                'Orders received before 8:00 a.m.
                datInvoice = datOrder.AddHours(9 - datOrder.Hour + _
                    (Rnd() * 8))
            ElseIf datOrder.Hour > 15 Then
                'Orders after 3:00 p.m. are processed the next morning
                datInvoice = datOrder.AddHours(-datOrder.Hour + 8 + _
                    (Rnd() * 4))
                datInvoice = datInvoice.AddDays(1)
            Else
                'Orders are processed as received
```

```
      datInvoice = datOrder.AddHours(1 + Rnd())
   End If
   'Update the purchase order date/time
   strSQL = "UPDATE PurchaseOrders SET OrderDate = '" + _
      CStr(datOrder.AddSeconds(1 + (2 * Rnd())))
   strSQL += "' WHERE ReferenceID = " + CStr(intOrderID)
   With cmmProd
      .CommandText = strSQL
      intRecsAff += .ExecuteNonQuery()
   End With
   'Update the invoice OrderDate and ShipDate values
   strSQL = "UPDATE Invoices SET OrderDate ='" + CStr(datOrder)
   strSQL += "', ShipDate = '" + CStr(datInvoice)
   strSQL += "' WHERE OrderID = " + CStr(intOrderID)
   With cmmOrders
      .CommandText = strSQL
      intRecsAff += .ExecuteNonQuery()
   End With
   'Conform the transaction dates and times
   strSQL = "UPDATE Transactions SET TransactionDate ='" + _
      CStr(datOrder.AddSeconds(1 + (2 * Rnd())))
   strSQL += "' WHERE Reference = " + CStr(intOrderID) + _
      " AND TransactionTypeID = 31"
   'Update the hold
   With cmmNet
      .CommandText = strSQL
      intRecsAff += .ExecuteNonQuery()
   End With
   strSQL = "UPDATE Transactions SET TransactionDate ='" + _
      CStr(datInvoice.AddSeconds(1 + (2 * Rnd())))
   strSQL += "' WHERE Reference = " + CStr(intOrderID) + _
      " AND TransactionTypeID > 31"
   'Release the hold and debit the card
   With cmmNet
      .CommandText = strSQL
      intRecsAff += .ExecuteNonQuery()
   End With
   If intCtr >= intOPDCurr Then
      'Next day, so reset the time to 00:00 and add a day
      datOrder = datOrder.AddHours(-datOrder.Hour)
      datOrder = datOrder.AddDays(1)
      intDays += 1
      txtOPD.Text = CStr(intCtr)
      intCtr = 0
      Application.DoEvents()
      If blnHalt Then
         Exit While
      End If
   End If
```

```
            intCtr += 1
            pgbBulk.Value += 1
        End While
        rdrOrders.Close()
        txtEndDate.Text = Format(datOrder, "Short Date")
    End With
    cnnOrders.Close()
    cmdClose.Enabled = True
    cmdHalt.Enabled = False
    Call ControlState(True)
    Me.Cursor = Cursors.Default
    intMins = DatePart(DateInterval.Minute, Now) - intMins
    If intMins <= 0 Then
        intMins = intMins + 60
    End If
    strMsg = Format(intRecsAff, "#,##0") + " records updated in " + _
        CStr(intMins) + " minutes."
    MsgBox(strMsg, MsgBoxStyle.OKOnly, "Backdating Operation Complete")
End Sub
```

TIP

If you take the BackdateOrders project and the SQL Server instance with the OCE database and run them on different computers, change the three instances of (LOCAL) in the declarations section of BackdateOrders.vb to the server's NetBIOS or instance name. Using two computers cuts the update time by 50 percent or more on a fast network with minimal traffic.

Architecting XML BI Report Documents

Crosstab is the common name for time-series and other summary reports derived from SQL aggregate queries. Crosstab reports are a grid of numeric totals that represent, for example, months or quarters in columns, and categories of goods sold, geographical regions, salespersons, or other classification criteria in rows. Grand totals of row and column data—called *crossfoot* totals—are optional but are almost always included in crosstab reports. The capability to automatically generate crosstab queries with Jet-specific TRANSFORM and PIVOT operators has been one of the primary contributors to Microsoft Access' success in the desktop database market. PivotTables deliver the equivalent of crosstab queries, but clients must have Excel installed to view and manipulate them.

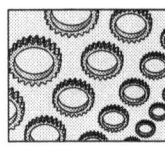

NOTE

The Office Web Components (OWC) are a lightweight version of the Excel PivotTable feature that let you generate PivotCharts automatically. The Office 2000 version of OWC requires clients to have an Office license to view the components; the Office XP version lets unlicensed clients view but not manipulate PivotTables and PivotCharts.

Unfortunately, the SQL Server development team has steadfastly refused to add
TRANSFORM and PIVOT operators to T-SQL. Thus, you must write conventional T-SQL
aggregate queries and transform the result set to the XML equivalent of a Jet crosstab query.
Following is a sample T-SQL statement to return a row for the total value of orders received
in the four quarters of 2001 from each of the 12 states in which OCE does business:

```
SELECT TOP 100 PERCENT State, SUM(Quantity * UnitPrice) AS Amount,
    DATENAME(year, OrderDate) + 'Q' +
    DATENAME(quarter, OrderDate) AS Quarter
FROM Customers
    INNER JOIN Orders ON Customers.CustID = Orders.CustID
    INNER JOIN LineItems ON Orders.OrderID = LineItems.OrderID
WHERE OrderDate BETWEEN '01/01/2001' AND '12/31/2001 12:59:59PM'
GROUP BY State, DATENAME(year, OrderDate) + 'Q' +
    DATENAME(quarter, OrderDate)
ORDER BY State, Quarter
```

TIP

Be sure to add `12:59:59PM` *to the ending* `datetime` *value. If you don't, the result set won't
include values for the last day of the reporting period.*

The query returns 48 rows from the OCE_Cust database's Orders table that has orders
backdated to 1/1/2001; the following table displays the first and last four rows of the result set.

State	Amount	Quarter
CO	166419.1	2001Q1
CO	343470.4	2001Q2
CO	648837.7	2001Q3
CO	889339.95	2001Q4
...		
WY	11448.95	2001Q1
WY	29451.15	2001Q2
WY	93822.4	2001Q3
WY	110851.6	2001Q4

The gotcha with the preceding query is missing rows for states and quarters that have
0 amounts. If you change the starting date to '06/01/2000', you receive the same rowset.
Jet crosstab queries offer the IN predicate to create a fixed set of columns, but IN doesn't
solve the problem with disappearing rows. You must add code to assure that missing result
set columns and rows appear as empty or 0 attribute or element values. Rounding and
formatting values, and generating row and column crossfoot totals also require code.

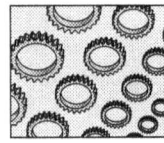

NOTE

You can duplicate Jet crosstab query result sets with T-SQL stored procedures, but the process isn't a simple task. The "Upsize Jet Crosstab Queries" article from the October 2001 issue of Visual Studio Magazine illustrates one approach. (Click the October 2001 link on the http://www.oakleaf.ws/articles.aspx page.) The Relational Access Companion (originally Replacement for Access Crosstabs) shareware application, which you can download from http://rac4sql.home.attbi.com/, is an alternative method.

Attribute-Centric Response Documents

The next step in the summary report design process is to determine the style of the XML response document. Attribute-centric is the simplest XML document format for representing crosstab reports, as illustrated by the following example:

```
<rows xmlns='oakleaf.ws/services/crosstabs/attribute' />
   <row header='State' col1='2001Q1' col2='2001Q2'
      col3='2001Q3' col4='2001Q4' total='Totals' />
   <row header='CO' col1='$10,000' col2='$15,000'
      col3='$20,000' col4='$25,000" total='$70,000' />
   <row header='IA' col1='10,000' col2='15,000'
      col3='20,000' col4='25,000" total='$70,000' />
   ...
   <row header='Totals' col1='$600,000' col2='$900,000'
      col3='$1,200,000' col4='$1,800,000' total='$4,500,000'/>
</rows>
```

The first row provides the column headers, and the remaining rows supply row headers, summary values, and totals. Attribute-centric documents are more compact than their element-centric equivalents and are relatively easy to generate with `XmlTextWriter` objects or Visual Basic .NET code. However, it's a good XML document design practice to deliver data as element values and *metadata* (data about the data) as attribute values. Attribute-centric documents violate this principle.

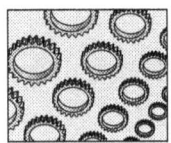

NOTE

The missing dollar signs in columns 2 through 5 of the second and remaining rows for states conforms the data to the common format that accountants use when preparing worksheets. Dollar signs prefix amounts in the first data row and all total values.

Element-Centric Response Documents

Element-centric documents require you to write more `XmlTextWriter` code than the attribute-centric version and have additional tag overhead. The upside of element-centric format is the capability to add attributes that have values for element positioning in presentation documents, such as an Excel worksheet, or displaying the results of drilldown operations. *Drilldown* is the term applied to the process of presenting increasing levels of detail for an individual summary value. For example, the first drilldown level of a quarterly summary report is monthly data; successive levels are weekly, daily, and hourly.

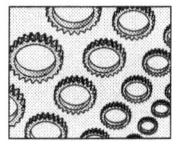

NOTE

The .NETInsight newsletter's "Use XML Attributes to Navigate Data" article describes how the OakLeaf Code of Federal Regulations site uses attribute values for drilldown operations on XML table of contents documents. Go to http://www.oakleaf.ws/articles.aspx and click the article's link. Chapter 9 also covers DHTML navigation methods based on attributes.

The following element-centric document example includes unique `id` attribute values for worksheet cell positioning and `st`, `yr`, and `qt` values for drilldown operations:

```
<crosstab xmlns='oakleaf.ws/services/crosstabs/element' >
   <header>
     <row>
        <col id='R1C1'>State</col>
        <col id='R1C2'>2001Q1</col>
        <col id='R1C3'>2001Q2</col>
        <col id='R1C4'>2001Q3</col>
        <col id='R1C5'>2001Q4</col>
        <col id='R1C6'>Totals</col>
     </row>
   <header>
   <data>
     <row>
        <col id='R2C1'>CO</col>
        <col id='R2C2' st='CO' yr='2001' qt='1'>$10,000</col>
        <col id='R2C3' st='CO' yr='2001' qt='2'>$15,000</col>
        <col id='R2C4' st='CO' yr='2001' qt='3'>$20,000</col>
        <col id='R2C5' st='CO' yr='2001' qt='4'>$25,000</col>
        <col id='R2C6'>$70,000</col>
     </row>
     <row>
        <col id='R3C1'>IA</col>
        <col id='R3C2' st='IA' yr='2001' qt='1'>$10,000</col>
        <col id='R3C3' st='IA' yr='2001' qt='2'>15,000</col>
        <col id='R3C4' st='IA' yr='2001' qt='3'>20,000</col>
        <col id='R3C5' st='IA' yr='2001' qt='4'>25,000</col>
        <col id='R2C6'>$70,000</col>
     </row>
     ...
     <row>
        <col id='R13C1'>Totals</col>
        <col id='R13C2'>$600,000</col>
        <col id='R13C3'>$900,000</col>
        <col id='R13C4'>$1,200,000</col>
        <col id='R13C5'>$1,800,000</col>
        <col id='R13C6'>$4,500,000</col>
```

```
      </row>
   </data>
</crosstab>
```

Another benefit of document-centric XML format is easy transformation to XHTML table code. For example, replacing `crosstab` with `table`, `header` with `th`, and `col` with `td` in the preceding document displays an unformatted table. Chapter 9 also covers transformation of XML documents to XHTML for presentation.

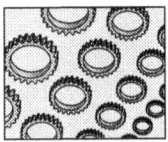

NOTE

For an example of an XML document that was transformed to XHTML with Visual Basic .NET code, go to http://www.oakleaf.ws/cfr/about.aspx and scroll to the "Sample XML TOC Document" and "Sample XHTML Presentation Code" sections.

Developing XML Web Services for Data Reporting

After you decide on a response document structure for crosstab or similar summary financial reports, the following steps complete the XML Web service development process:

1. Specify SOAP header names and values for authentication and authorization.
2. Design the request document to maximize reporting flexibility.
3. Create a test harness to generate the request document.
4. Write and test the code to generate the T-SQL summary queries.
5. Devise the strategy to transform the query result set to the XML response document.
6. Write code to implement the XML transformation strategy.
7. Copy the test-harness code to an ASP.NET Web Service project and add the code required to implement the XML Web service.
8. Add an XML Web service proxy to the test harness and verify that the service works correctly.
9. Design an ASP.NET page to replace the test harness, copy applicable test-harness code to the page, and alter the code for use with Web Forms.

You can start with an ASP.NET client test harness, but Windows forms expedite testing code modifications and let you use Visual Studio .NET's Windows form controls. Another alternative is to write service code in an ASP.NET Web Service project, but doing so adds more overhead to the initial testing process.

Specifying the SOAP Header

The SOAP header for the service handles user authentication with `UserName` and `Password` values. The `ServerName` value maintains consistency with previous OCE projects but probably wouldn't be required in a production application. The SOAP header is the only authentication source, so clients must provide the header values.

The following `Authenticate` header class is a slightly modified version of the class described in Chapter 7's "Implementing SOAP Headers in XML Web Services" section:

```
Public Class Authenticate
    Inherits SoapHeader
    Public ServerName As String
    Public UserName As String
    Public Password As String
End Class
```

Designing the XML Request Document

The request document design requires an element for each value that's required to specify report formats. Your XML Web service should be capable of generating the widest possible report varieties within a given class, such as crosstab-style financial reports. The penance for designing a service without ad hoc reporting flexibility is writing a new XML Web service for each new or modified report your client or manager requests.

TIP

Anticipate users' future requests by including element values to specify features you might add later. Like COM interfaces, the XML request document should be immutable. If you change the request document structure, you must update every client application and Web page that consumes the XML Web service. Design client applications and pages with future enhancements in mind, so they can handle minor changes to the response document structure.

Following is a sample element-centric request document that specifies the default crosstab query for the examples developed in the subsequent sections:

```
<crosstab xmlns='http://oakleaf.ws/services/crosstabs/request' >
    <title>2001 Quarterly Orders by State</title>
    <timeseries>
        <datatable>Orders</datatable>
        <rowsby>State</rowsby>
        <startdate>1/1/2001</startdate>
        <starttime>00:00:00AM</starttime>
        <interval>Quarter</interval>
        <datacolumns>4</datacolumns>
        <count>No</count>
        <avgvalue>No</avgvalue>
        <rowtotals>Yes</rowtotals>
        <coltotals>Yes</coltotals>
        <nulltozero>Yes</nulltozero>
        <format>XML</format>
```

```
    </timeseries>
</crosstab>
```

This chapter's examples don't use the `<datatable>`, `<count>`, `<avgvalue>`, and `<format>` element values.

Analyzing Windows Form Test-Harness Requirements

For this chapter's examples, the test harness serves as the development environment until you deploy the final XML Web service and design client pages or Windows applications. A test harness for a time-series report service should fulfill the following objectives:

▶ Emulate user report format selections, such as source of values, starting date, date intervals, number of reporting periods, and whether to include row totals, column totals, or both.

▶ Generate dynamic SQL aggregate query statements to return summary data based on format selections.

▶ Transform the query result set into an intermediate structure, if necessary, that's easy to transform again to the XML response document structure.

▶ Generate XML response documents and verify that the documents are well-formed and conform to the document specification or schema. (Validation to an XSD schema is optional.)

▶ Transform XML to XHTML if the service generates a Web page directly.

▶ Deliver performance data for query and transformation code execution to provide benchmarks for XML Web service performance comparisons.

▶ Serve as a proxy client for consuming the final XML Web service and evaluating its speed of execution.

Crosstab reports generated from T-SQL aggregate queries require an intermediary structure because of the potential for missing column and row data, which was mentioned in the earlier "Architecting XML BI Report Documents" section. XML purists prefer XML tools, such as the `XmlTextWriter`, for creating documents and hand-coded XSLT for transforming XML to XHTML. Pragmatic Visual Basic programmers usually opt for string manipulation code to accomplish both transformations. The examples of this chapter are intended for the latter group.

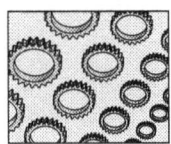

NOTE

The Client form of the CFRClient.exe application, which Appendix B describes, is an example of an ornate test harness. The test harness was used to develop the original Visual Basic 6.0 code for transforming the SGML version of the U.S. Code of Federal Regulations to XML and XHTML documents.

Exploring the CTHarness Crosstab Report Project

CTHarness.sln in your \VBWS08\CTHarness folder is a Windows form project to demonstrate the test-harness design principles of the preceding sections. When you run the project, the upper-right text box displays the default request document. (See Figure 8-2.) Controls on the frmHarness form let you modify the request document. For example, you can select Quarter, Month, Week, or Day in the Interval combo box. Changes to the report interval set default values of the Data Columns NumericUpDown control. Right-clicking the text box uses IE's MSXML parser to verify that the request document is well-formed.

The default value in the Starting Date text box is 1/1/2001, which corresponds to the default starting date used by the BackdateOrders project, except for weekly reports. Weekly reports require Sunday starting dates, such as 12/31/2000 or 1/7/2001. SQL Server considers 12/31/2000 to be week 1 of 2001, so the code special-cases weeks that cross year boundaries.

Reading the Request Document

The TimeSeriesReport function is the only method that the XML Web service will expose. You use a StringReader to create a Stream object from the request document (RequestDoc), and then pass the Stream to an XmlTextReader, which extracts the element values to form-level String variables. The XmlTextReader.ReadElementString method accepts an optional

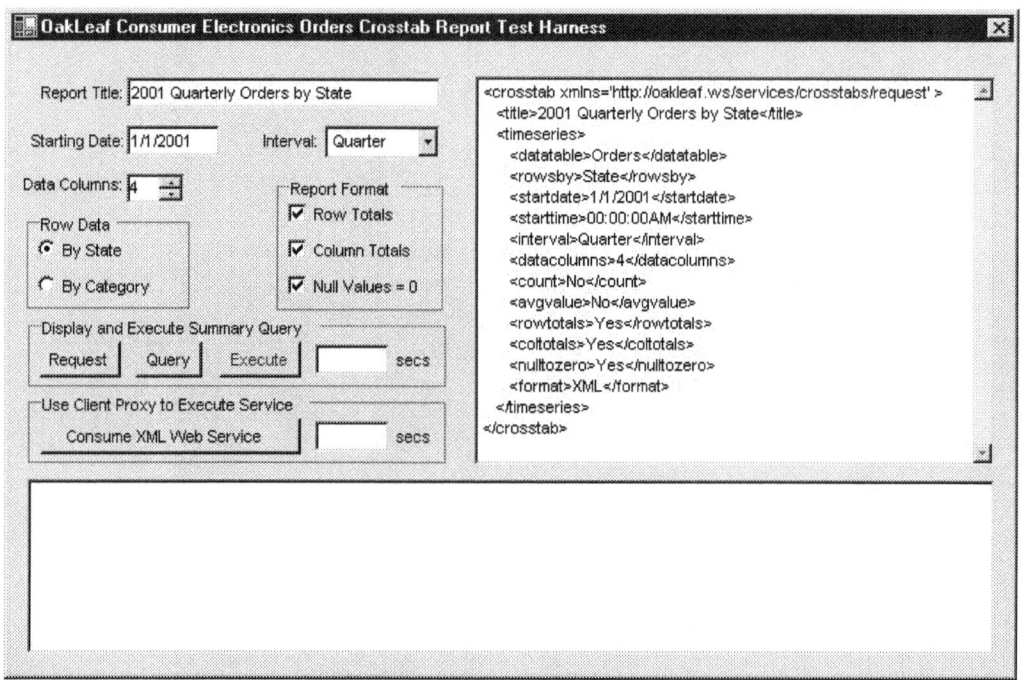

Figure 8-2   *The CTHarness project opens with the default 2001 Quarterly Orders by State request document.*

str*ElementName* argument to verify that the element being read corresponds to the variable that receives its value.

Here's the code for the `TimeSeriesReport` function of the ReportsWS.asmx project:

```
Public Function TimeSeriesReport(ByVal RequestDoc As String) As String
'Read the request document and verify its elements
   Dim srdRequest As StringReader = Nothing
   Dim xtrRequest As XmlTextReader = Nothing
   Dim strTemp As String
   Dim strSQL As String
   Dim strResponse As String
   Try
      srdRequest = New StringReader(RequestDoc)
      xtrRequest = New XmlTextReader(srdRequest)
      With xtrRequest
         'strTemp reads elements not used at this point
         .MoveToContent()   'Root
         .Read()            'Skip <timeseries>
         strTitle = .ReadElementString("title")
         .Read()            'Skip
         .Read()            'Skip
         strTemp = .ReadElementString("datatable")
         If .ReadElementString("rowsby") = "State" Then
            blnRowTotals = True
         Else
            blnRowTotals = False
         End If
         strStartDate = .ReadElementString("startdate")
         strStartTime = .ReadElementString("starttime")
         strInterval = .ReadElementString("interval")
         strDataCols = .ReadElementString("datacolumns")
         strTemp = .ReadElementString("count")
         strTemp = .ReadElementString("avgvalue")
         If .ReadElementString("rowtotals") = "Yes" Then
            blnRowTotals = True
         Else
            blnRowTotals = False
         End If
         If .ReadElementString("coltotals") = "Yes" Then
            blnColTotals = True
         Else
            blnColTotals = False
         End If
         If .ReadElementString("nulltozero") = "Yes" Then
```

```
            blnNullToZero = True
        Else
            blnNullToZero = False
        End If
    End With
  Catch
    'No error processing at this point
  Finally
    srdRequest.Close()
    xtrRequest.Close()
  End Try
  'Generate the T-SQL statement
  strSQL = WriteOrdersQuery()
  'Execute the query and return the report document
  strResponse = GenerateReport(strSQL)
  Return strResponse
End Function
```

Conventional Visual Basic .NET string searches with the `InStr` function are an alternative to the `TimeSeriesReport` approach, but `XmlTextReader` code is simpler to write and much easier for others to read and understand.

Generating the Summary Query

The `WriteOrdersQuery` function uses the form-level variables from the `OrdersTimeSeries` function to construct the summary query to return a result set similar to that described in the earlier "Architecting XML BI Report Documents" section. Following is the code of the `WriteQuery` function:

```
Private Function WriteOrdersQuery() As String
   'Generate the T-SQL query from form-level request document values
   Dim strSelect As String
   Dim strField As String
   Dim strHeader As String
   Dim strPeriod As String
   Dim strYear As String
   Dim datLastDate As DateTime
   Dim strFrom As String
   Dim strWhere As String
   Dim strGroup As String
   Dim strOrder As String
   Dim strSQL As String

   datLastDate = datStartDate
   strFrom = "FROM Customers " + _
      "INNER JOIN Orders ON Customers.CustID = Orders.CustID " + _
      "INNER JOIN LineItems ON Orders.OrderID = LineItems.OrderID "
```

```vb
strSelect = "SELECT TOP 100 PERCENT "
strYear = "DATEPART(year, OrderDate)"
strWhere = "WHERE (OrderDate BETWEEN '" + strStartDate + _
    " " + strStartTime + "' AND '"
strGroup = "GROUP BY "
strOrder = "ORDER BY "
If blnStates Then
   strField = "State"
   strSelect += strField + ", "
Else
   strField = "SUBSTRING(SKU, 1, 4)"
   strSelect += strField + " AS Category, "
End If
strGroup += strField + ", "
strOrder += strField + ", "

Select Case strInterval
   Case "Quarter"
      strHeader = "DATENAME(year, OrderDate) + 'Q' + _
         DATENAME(quarter, OrderDate)"
      strPeriod = "DATEPART(quarter, OrderDate)"
      datLastDate = datLastDate.AddMonths(3 * CInt(strDataCols))
   Case "Month"
      strHeader = "SUBSTRING(DATENAME(month, OrderDate), 1, 3) + _
         ' ' + DATENAME(year, OrderDate)"
      strPeriod = "DATEPART(month, OrderDate)"
      datLastDate = datLastDate.AddMonths(CInt(strDataCols))
   Case "Week"
      strHeader = "DATENAME(year, OrderDate) + 'W' + _
         DATENAME(week, OrderDate)"
      strPeriod = "DATEPART(week, OrderDate)"
      datLastDate = datLastDate.AddDays(7 * CInt(strDataCols))
   Case "Day"
      strHeader = "CAST(DATEPART(mm, OrderDate) AS varchar) + _
         '/' + CAST(DATEPART(dd, OrderDate) AS varchar) + _
         '/' + CAST(DATEPART(yy, OrderDate) AS varchar)"
      strPeriod = "DATEPART(dy, OrderDate)"
      datLastDate = datLastDate.AddDays(CInt(strDataCols))
End Select
datLastDate = datLastDate.AddSeconds(-1)
strGroup += strPeriod + ", " + strYear + ", " + strHeader + " "
strOrder += strPeriod + ", " + strYear + ", " + strHeader + " "
strPeriod += " AS Period, " + strYear + " AS Year "
strSelect += strHeader + " AS Header, COUNT(Orders.OrderID) AS Orders, _
    ROUND(SUM(Quantity * UnitPrice), 0) AS Amount, " + strPeriod
strWhere += Format(datLastDate, "M/d/yyyy hh:mm:ss tt") + _
    "') AND LineItems.Deleted = 0 "
```

```
        strSQL = strSelect + strCrLf + strFrom + strCrLf + strWhere + _
            strCrLf + strGroup + strCrLf + strOrder
        Return strSQL
End Function
```

Clicking the Query button replaces the text box's XML source document with the T-SQL summary query and enables the Execute button. Following is the SQL statement to generate a weekly report for the first 13 weeks of 2001, including Sunday, December 31, 2000:

```
SELECT TOP 100 PERCENT State, DATENAME(year, OrderDate) + 'W' +
    DATENAME(week, OrderDate) AS Header, COUNT(Orders.OrderID) AS Orders,
    ROUND(SUM(Quantity * UnitPrice), 0) AS Amount,
    DATEPART(week, OrderDate) AS Period, DATEPART(year, OrderDate) AS Year
FROM Customers
    INNER JOIN Orders ON Customers.CustID = Orders.CustID
    INNER JOIN LineItems ON Orders.OrderID = LineItems.OrderID
WHERE (OrderDate BETWEEN '12/31/2000 00:00:00 AM' AND
    '3/31/2001 11:59:59 PM') AND LineItems.Deleted = 0
GROUP BY State, DATEPART(week, OrderDate), DATEPART(year, OrderDate),
    DATENAME(year, OrderDate) + 'W' + DATENAME(week, OrderDate)
ORDER BY State, DATEPART(week, OrderDate), DATEPART(year, OrderDate),
    DATENAME(year, OrderDate) + 'W' + DATENAME(week, OrderDate)
```

The following table shows the partial query result set for Wyoming. The table values illustrate the missing-row problem for states and periods that have no orders. When you run a daily report for the first week of 2001, the result set omits rows for several states.

State	Header	Orders	Amount	Period	Year
...	...	...	...	...	...
WY	2001W2	1	100.0000	2	2001
WY	2001W6	3	3270.0000	6	2001
WY	2001W7	4	1830.0000	7	2001
WY	2001W8	6	3550.0000	8	2001
WY	2001W10	2	1500.0000	10	2001
WY	2001W11	1	200.0000	11	2001
WY	2001W12	1	1000.0000	12	2001

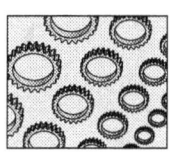

NOTE

The Orders column, which the examples of this chapter don't use, lets you calculate the average order value. You need the Period and Year columns to sort monthly reports correctly; otherwise, the headings appear in alphabetical month name order.

Creating and Populating an Intermediate Crosstab Array

An effective approach for handling missing data cells and entire states is to construct a two-dimensional array of all rows and columns for the specified report and populate the array with formatted values. Following is an overview of the process:

1. Define an array of two ranks. The upper bound of the first rank (rows) is the number elements plus 1. Assign the second rank (columns) the number of data columns plus 1. The extra row and column hold column and row totals, respectively.

2. Fill the first (0) column of each row with the fixed row headers—for this example, States, the 12 state abbreviations, and Totals.

3. Add code to fill the remaining columns of the first (0) row of the array with calculated value column headers for the time series—for this example, 2001W1...2001W13 and Totals. The fixed row headers and calculated column headers, except Totals, must match the query result set's Header values exactly.

4. Fill the value elements of the array with 0.

5. Add SqlConnection, SqlCommand, and SqlDataReader objects to execute the query and return a read-only, forward-only rowset.

6. Iterate the rowset and overwrite the 0 values with Amount values at the position where the row and column headers of the record match those of the array.

7. Loop through the columns and then the rows to populate Totals elements.

8. Apply the appropriate currency format to all values, including Totals.

Following is the code within the GenerateReport function to create and populate the array. Array declarations and code to add the row headers are omitted for brevity:

```
'Generate the time-series column headers
For intCol = 1 To CInt(strDataCols)
   Select Case strInterval
      Case "Quarter"
         datPeriod = datStartDate.AddMonths(3 * (intCol - 1))
         astrCT(0, intCol) = CStr(datPeriod.Year) + "Q" + _
            CStr((datPeriod.Month \ 3) + 1)
      Case "Month"
         datPeriod = datStartDate.AddMonths(intCol - 1)
         astrCT(0, intCol) = Format(datPeriod, "MMM") + _
            " " + CStr(datPeriod.Year)
      Case "Week"
         datPeriod = datStartDate.AddDays(7 * (intCol - 1))
         If datStartDate = #12/31/2000# And intCol = 1 Then
            'Special case for 2001, which starts on Monday
            astrCT(0, intCol) = "2001W1"
         Else
            astrCT(0, intCol) = CStr(datPeriod.Year) + _
               "W" + CStr((datPeriod.DayOfYear \ 7) + 1)
```

```vbnet
                End If
            Case "Day"
                datPeriod = datStartDate.AddDays(intCol - 1)
                astrCT(0, intCol) = Format(datPeriod, "M/d/yyyy")
        End Select
    Next intCol
    astrCT(0, CInt(strDataCols) + 1) = "Totals"

    'Fill array with 0s
    For intRow = 1 To UBound(astrCT, 1)
        For intCol = 1 To UBound(astrCT, 2)
            astrCT(intRow, intCol) = "0"
        Next intCol
    Next intRow

    'Connect and create an SqlDataReader
    With cnnCT
        .ConnectionString = "Data Source=" + ServerName + _
            ";Initial Catalog=OCE_Cust;UID=" + UserName + ";PWD=" + Password
        .Open()
        cmmCT = .CreateCommand
    End With
    With cmmCT
        .CommandType = CommandType.Text
        .CommandText = strSQL
        sdrCT = .ExecuteReader
    End With
    With sdrCT
        While .Read
            'Iterate the rowset and plug values into the proper cell
            For intRow = 1 To UBound(astrCT, 1)
                'Find the row
                If sdrCT.GetString(0) = astrCT(intRow, 0) Then
                    Exit For
                End If
            Next intRow
            For intCol = 1 To UBound(astrCT, 2)
                'Find the column
                If sdrCT.GetString(1) = astrCT(0, intCol) Then
                    Exit For
                End If
            Next intCol
            If intRow < UBound(astrCT, 1) And intCol < UBound(astrCT, 2) Then
                'Found the cell; add the value without decimal fraction
                astrCT(intRow, intCol) = CStr(CInt(sdrCT.GetDecimal(3)))
            Else
                'No-match error is for testing with a breakpoint
                strTemp = sdrCT.GetString(0) + ", " + sdrCT.GetString(1) + _
                    ", " + CStr(sdrCT.GetDecimal(3))
```

```
      End If
   End While
End With
sdrCT.Close()
cnnCT.Close()

'Get row totals
For intRow = 1 To UBound(astrCT, 1) - 1
   intTotal = 0
   For intCol = 1 To UBound(astrCT, 2) - 1
      intTotal += CInt(astrCT(intRow, intCol))
   Next intCol
   astrCT(intRow, UBound(astrCT, 2)) = CStr(intTotal)
Next intRow

'Get column totals (including crossfoot total)
For intCol = 1 To UBound(astrCT, 2)
   intTotal = 0
   For intRow = 1 To UBound(astrCT, 1) - 1
      intTotal += CInt(astrCT(intRow, intCol))
   Next intRow
   astrCT(UBound(astrCT, 1), intCol) = CStr(intTotal)
Next intCol

'Format rows and columns
For intRow = 1 To UBound(astrCT, 1)
   For intCol = 1 To UBound(astrCT, 2)
      If intRow = 1 Or intRow = UBound(astrCT, 1)
            Or intCol = UBound(astrCT, 2) Then
         astrCT(intRow, intCol) =
            Format(CInt(astrCT(intRow, intCol)), "$#,##0")
      Else
         astrCT(intRow, intCol) =
            Format(CInt(astrCT(intRow, intCol)), "#,##0")
      End If
   Next intCol
Next intRow
```

The *Array*.BinarySearch method is faster than iterating each rank to find a match, but the method applies only to single-dimension arrays. Crosstab queries seldom have more than 52 elements per rank, so you don't incur a significant performance hit from the iteration process. You can use the GenerateReport function with other SQL statements that return time-series result sets, such as a sales report generated from invoices.

Producing the XML Response Document

The final step in the test process is to generate the XML response document and test to see how well formed it is. Click the Execute button to display a semiformatted version of the

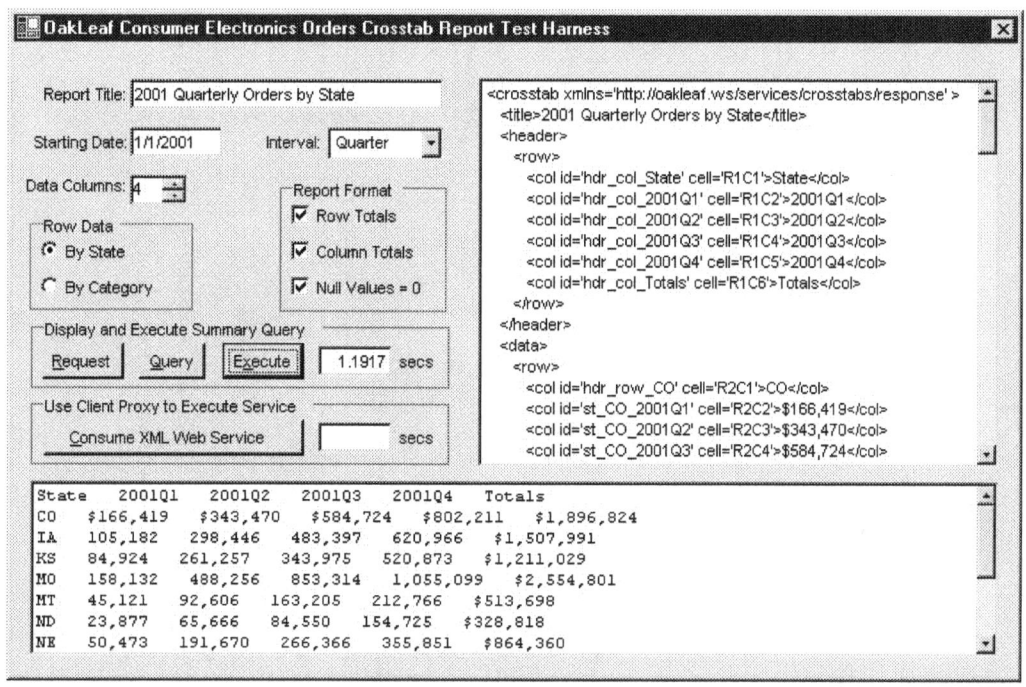

Figure 8-3   *Executing the query displays the array elements in the list box and the response document in the text box.*

array in the bottom list box and the XML response document in the upper-right text box. (See Figure 8-3.) Right-clicking the text box displays the response document in IE 5.0+.

The Visual Basic .NET code to transform the array to an XML response document is almost trivial, as the following excerpt from the `GenerateReport` function demonstrates. Omitting totals and supplying element attribute values are responsible for a substantial part of the code.

```
'Generate the response document
strXML = "<crosstab xmlns='http://oakleaf.ws/services/crosstabs/response' >" +
strCrLf
For intRow = 0 To UBound(astrCT, 1)
   If intRow = UBound(astrCT, 1) And Not blnColTotals Then
      Exit For
   End If
   If intRow = 0 Then
      'Title
      strXML += "   <title>" + strTitle + "</title>" + strCrLf
      'Header
      strXML += "   <header>" + strCrLf + Space(6) + "<row>" + strCrLf
      For intCol = 0 To UBound(astrCT, 2)
         If intCol = UBound(astrCT, 2) And Not blnRowTotals Then
            Exit For
         End If
```

```vb
            strAttrib = "id='hdr_col_" + astrCT(0, intCol) + _
                "' cell='R1C" + CStr(intCol + 1) + "'"
            strXML += Space(9) + "<col " + strAttrib + ">" + _
                astrCT(intRow, intCol) + "</col>" + strCrLf
        Next intCol
        strXML += Space(6) + "</row>" + strCrLf + "    </header>" + strCrLf
        strXML += "    <data>" + strCrLf
    Else
        'Data rows
        strXML += Space(6) + "<row>" + strCrLf
        For intCol = 0 To UBound(astrCT, 2)
            If intCol = UBound(astrCT, 2) And Not blnRowTotals Then
                Exit For
            End If
            If intRow = UBound(astrCT, 1) Or intCol = UBound(astrCT, 2) Then
                strAttrib = "id='total' cell='R" + CStr(intRow + 1) + _
                    "C" + CStr(intCol + 1) + "'"
            Else
                If intCol > 0 Then
                    If blnStates Then
                        strAttrib = "id='st_"
                    Else
                        strAttrib = "id='cat_"
                    End If
                    strAttrib += astrCT(intRow, 0) + "_" + astrCT(0, intCol)
                Else
                    strAttrib = "id='hdr_row_" + astrCT(intRow, 0)
                End If
                strAttrib += "' cell='R" + CStr(intRow + 1) + "C" + _
                    CStr(intCol + 1) + "'"
            End If
            If (astrCT(intRow, intCol) = "0" Or _
                    astrCT(intRow, intCol) = "$0") And Not blnNullToZero Then
                'Empty element for zero values
                strXML += Space(9) + "<col " + strAttrib + "></col>" + strCrLf
            Else
                strXML += Space(9) + "<col " + strAttrib + ">" + _
                    astrCT(intRow, intCol) + "</col>" + strCrLf
            End If
        Next intCol
        strXML += Space(6) + "</row>" + strCrLf
    End If
Next intRow
'Close the tags
strXML += "    </data>" + strCrLf
strXML += "</crosstab>"
```

TIP

Use the `System.Text.StringBuilder` object to improve XML Web service performance with XML documents that have more than 100,000 or so characters. .NET `String` objects are immutable, so you create and destroy a `String` each time you perform a concatenation. The `StringBuilder.Append` method enables incremental construction of long strings.

Generating XML response documents with conventional string manipulation code instead of an `XmlTextWriter` object lets you add custom formatting—called *whitespace*—to make your response documents more readable in text editors. HTTP 1.1 compression creates tokens to represent whitespace elements, so adding spaces and CR/LF pairs doesn't significantly affect transport time. XML parsers ignore whitespace by default; IE 5.0+ provides a stylesheet to format XML documents for presentation.

TIP

The `txtDoc_MouseDown` event handler demonstrates how to replace VBScript's `FileSystemObject` with the .NET Framework's `System.Io.File` and `StreamWriter` objects.

Migrating Test-Harness Code to the XML Web Service

The process of moving test-harness code to an ASP.NET XML Web service is similar to that described in Chapter 6 for upgraded ActiveX components. Here's the drill for creating the service from the Windows form project:

1. Add a folder and a new virtual directory for the service, and disable session state. For the sample code, the folder is \VBWS08\ReportsWS and the virtual directory name is ReportsWS. Assign a different name, such as ReportsCT, if you perform the following steps.

2. Open a new ASP.NET Web Service at http://localhost/ReportsWS, and rename Service1.asmx to **ReportsWS.asmx**.

3. In the ReportsWs.asmx.vb document, delete the sample code, set `Option Explicit On` and `Option Strict On`, and add the following code below the `Imports System.Web.Services` line:

```
Imports System.Web.Services.Protocols
Imports System.Data.SqlClient
Imports System.Xml
Imports System.IO

Public Class Authenticate
    Inherits SoapHeader
    Public ServerName As String
    Public UserName As String
```

```
    Public Password As String
End Class
```

4. Change `http://tempuri.org` to a more appropriate service namespace, **`http://oakleaf.ws/services/crosstabs/`** for this example, and change the class name to **ReportsWS**.

5. Copy `frmHarness`' form-level variable declarations for the documents and T-SQL query after the `Inherits System.Web.Services.WebService` statement.

6. Add `Public hdrAuthent As Authenticate` below the variable declarations.

7. Copy the `TimeSeriesReport, WriteOrdersQuery`, and `GenerateReport` functions below the `Web Services Designer Generated Code` region.

8. Remove harness-specific statements, such as references to text box controls.

9. Add a **`hdrAuthent.`** prefix to the `ServerName, UserName`, and `Password` values in the `.ConnectionString = ...` line of the `GenerateReport` function.

10. Run the project to check your work so far.

You haven't designated a `WebMethod`, so IE displays an empty ReportsWS form and a very abbreviated WSDL document.

Designating the WebMethod and Enabling Tracing

To expose the `TimeSeriesReport` function as a `WebMethod` with a required SOAP header, add optional descriptions for the method and service, and enable performance tracing, do the following:

1. Add the following as a single-line prefix to the `Public Function` statement:

```
<WebMethod(Description:="Optional text"), _
SoapHeader("hdrAuthent")>
```

2. Add an optional **`Description:="Optional text`"** argument to the `WebService` attribute.

3. Open the Web.config file, and change `<trace enabled ="false"` to **"true"**; if you want others to be able to view the trace log, change `localonly=` **"true"** to **"false"**. The default Trace.axd file for ASP.NET XML Web services doesn't return meaningful timing results, but you might find the information in the Control Tree and Server Variables report sections interesting.

4. Optionally, add the following elements under the `<system.web>` element:

```
<webServices>
   <protocols>
      <remove name="HttpGet" />
      <remove name="HttpPost" />
   </protocols>
</webServices>
```

5. Close the Web.config file and save your changes.

6. Add `Trace.WriteLine("Start operation name")` statements at strategic locations in the code, and a `Trace.WriteLine("End operation name")` statement prior to the last `End Function` statement of `GenerateReport`.

7. Run the project, proofread your descriptive text, and verify that the contents of the WSDL document are appropriate for the service.

The WSDL file for services that employ XML request documents is considerably simpler than those for RPC-style requests, especially as the number of arguments increases. The downside of XML request documents is that the WSDL file no longer describes the input parameters and their datatypes. Thus, users of the service need a complete specification for the source document. Regardless of the request style, users need a spec for the response document, so adding request document details isn't a major chore. In either case, it's a good practice to supply client-side developers with an XSD file to enable validation of the required XML document(s). Chapter 10's "Validating XML Request and Response Messages with XSD Schema" section shows you how to add validation code to services and their consumers.

Adding the Web Reference to the Test Harness and Testing Performance

The test harness needs a Web Reference to create a client proxy for the ReportsWS service and code to supply the required SOAP header values. Do the following to enable the test harness to consume the ReportsWS service:

1. Add a Web Reference to the XML Web service. For this example, the reference name is OCEReports.

2. Add to the test harness the code similar to the following listing to supply the required header values and request document, and accept the response document.

3. Compare the execution times for the test harness' original code and consumption of the XML Web service.

Following is the code for the `cmdResponse_Click` event handler of `frmHarness`:

```
Private Sub cmdResponse_Click(ByVal sender As System.Object, _
    ByVal e As System.EventArgs) Handles cmdResponse.Click
  'Retrieve the XML response document from the ReportsWS service
  'Uncomment the following lines to enable the XML Web service proxy
  Dim xwsReport As New OCEReports.ReportsWS()
  Dim hdrReport As New OCEReports.Authenticate()

  dblTimer = Microsoft.VisualBasic.Timer
  With hdrReport
    .ServerName = "(local)"
    .UserName = "CustUser"
    .Password = "Cust#123"
  End With
```

```
    xwsReport.AuthenticateValue = hdrReport
    txtDoc.Text = Replace(xwsReport.TimeSeriesReport(strXML), _
        Chr(10), strCrLf)
    dblTimer = Microsoft.VisualBasic.Timer - dblTimer
    txtWSTime.Text = Format(dblTimer, "0.0000")

    'Comment out the following line when using the Web service
    'txtDoc.Text = TimeSeriesReport(strXML)
End Sub
```

The sample CTHarness project doesn't include a Web Reference for the ReportWS service, and all code in the **cmdResponse_Click** event handler is commented. Add a Web Reference to ReportWS.asmx or the service you created from CTHarness code, and uncomment the client proxy code in the event handler. Comment out the last line, as shown in the preceding listing. Alternatively, you can connect to the remote ReportWS service on the OakLeaf Web site by adding a Web Reference to http://www.oakleaf.ws/reportsws/reportsws.asmx?wsdl.

When the service runs on the same machine as the harness, successive execution times differ by about 50 ms after compiling the ASP.NET service and caching the SQL Server connection and query. Your results will vary depending on server hardware and the network location of the test harness, Web service, and SQL Server instance. The CTHarness project proves that you don't incur a significant performance penalty when you convert typical data-intensive Visual Basic .NET applications from conventional fat-client Windows forms to XML Web services.

Designing the Presentation Layer for XML Web Services

Chapter 1's "Beyond the Web Services Hype" and "Web Services Architectures" sections classify XML Web services by the location of the consuming application— client or server. It's too early in the XML Web services adoption cycle to determine with any precision the ultimate distribution of services targeted on the server-to-server and server-to-client scenarios. It's a safe bet, however, that Windows, Linux, UNIX, and Macintosh clients will consume a *lot* of Web services during the first decade of the twenty-first century.

ASP.NET Web Forms are the most practical method for delivering XML Web services to client computers running under different operating systems. Thus, the primary objective of this chapter is to outline the design methodology and provide examples of ASP.NET Web applications as production-quality consumers of XML Web services. These design principles also apply, at least in part, to Microsoft Office XP XML Web service consumers, such as Excel, Outlook, Access, and even Word 2002.

Creating Production-Grade ASP.NET Pages for XML Web Services

Most Visual Basic .NET Windows form and ASP.NET Web form examples in the previous chapters have been test harnessed for the data-intensive XML Web services you created. The audience for these forms is developers and testers, not ordinary users. Designing and coding production-grade pages that consume XML Web services require much more attention to page layout and usability than simple test harnesses. Like Windows forms, ASP.NET Web applications require extensive testing to assure that the page design and execution of your Visual Basic .NET code correspond to your audience's expectations.

As noted in several preceding chapters, most Visual Basic programmers aren't professional Web page designers. With the release of Visual Studio .NET and the tough economic climate of 2001–2002, many—if not most—Visual Basic .NET programmers will face the challenge of coding *and* designing Web pages. The following sections describe the four-phase design and coding methodologies that were used to create this book's example ASP.NET Web applications.

TIP

If you're an accomplished Web page designer, skip to the "Transforming XML Crosstab Reports to Formatted Tables" section.

Phase 1: Initial Page Layout and Code to Consume the XML Web Service

The first phase of the page design methodology is to get a basic ASP.NET service consumer up and running. Following are the initial steps in the process for creating an ASP.NET XML Web service consumer:

1. Add `Option Explicit On`, `Option Strict On`, and `Imports...` statements for nondefault namespaces to the top of *PageName*.asmx.vb.

2. Add Web References to the XML Web service(s) for the page.

3. Temporarily add the XML Web service project to the solution for debugging.

4. Set the value of the `enableSessionState` property of the page `DOCUMENT` to `False`, unless you *must* maintain the user's session state.

5. Add Web server controls to set required SOAP header values, if you use headers, and supply element values for the request document. Position controls in the left-to-right, top-to-bottom sequence that corresponds to the logical data input sequence.

6. Select all controls and apply a common font. Most Web designers prefer sans-serif control fonts. Most ASP.NET examples in this book use Verdana X-Small for controls and larger sizes for page headings.

TIP

Use a serif font—typically Times New Roman—for large bodies of text. Newspapers use serif fonts for body text to aid readability, especially with smaller font sizes. Don't use more than two font families on a single page or in the collection of pages that make up a single application.

7. Set the `enableViewState` value to `False` for controls whose state you don't need to maintain between HTTP `POST` operations. In most cases, the only stateful controls are those that supply required SOAP header values, such as user name and password.

8. Temporarily set the `AutoPostBack` property value to `True` for controls that alter other control values. Extra server round trips aren't important at this point. You can add client-side script to handle control interactions later in the development process.

9. Add a `submit` button for the page's `form` elements, and write the Visual Basic .NET code to generate the SOAP header and request document element values.

10. Add a temporary multiline `TextBox` server control and code to the page to display the XML response document. If you use output or in/out SOAP headers, add temporary single-line text boxes to display their values for debugging.

11. Verify that the response document conforms to combinations of control settings that are appropriate to the form's purpose.

12. Verify that the layout remains consistent with other common screen resolutions and font sizes, such as 1024×768 and 1280×960 with large fonts. To support persons with visual disability, check layout with different Internet Explorer Text Size settings in multiple resolutions.

13. Remove the temporary XML Web service project from the solution and the temporary `TextBox` control(s) from the page. Comment code that refers to the deleted controls.

Accommodating different font sizes is one of the toughest problems with Web Forms that contain server controls having fixed sizes and positions. You can prevent users from changing browser font sizes by hard-coding font sizes in the default Styles.css style sheet that ASP.NET creates for each Web application. In this case, you replace the relative `font-size: #.#em;` attribute value with `font-size: ##.#pt;` for measurement in points, or `font-size: ##px;` for pixels. The OakLeaf Web site uses this method to freeze the font size of navigation tables and explanatory text.

TIP

You can't control users' replacement of Small Fonts with Large Fonts in the Display Properties dialog. If you need to accommodate laptop users who specify Large Fonts on 1024×768 LCD screens, try designing your page in 800x600 resolution and add about 20 percent extra width to each control and the space between controls.

Phase 2: Displaying the Response Document

The second phase deals with transforming the response document from XML to [X]HTML or the objects required by the server control(s) you select for presentation. If your XML Web service returns a serialized `DataSet` or `DataTable` object, you can bind the XML response document directly to a `DataGrid` control. Otherwise, you need to write an XSL transform or add Visual Basic .NET procedural code to extract and manipulate the element values.

The following steps are oriented to presenting reports but apply in general to most ASP.NET service consumers:

1. Add the Web server controls required to display the response document. For custom reports, the most common data containers are `Table` or `DataGrid` controls.

2. Set preliminary values for basic formatting properties that apply to the document display control as a whole. For tables, starting values for these properties are `Font`, `BorderColor` (`Black`), `BorderStyle` (`Solid`), `BorderWidth` (`1px`), `CellPadding` (`3`), and `CellSpacing` (`0`). Use a standard or custom template to format `DataGrid` controls.

3. Write the *minimum* amount of code required to fill the document display control. Don't be concerned with individual cell formatting, adding `id` attribute values, table headers, and other accouterments at this point.

4. Verify that the document display control behaves as expected with various combinations of control settings. For reports, apply reasonableness tests to the values displayed in the control.

5. Perform a quick check of the display control with different resolutions and text sizes.

Reasonableness tests are especially important when code behind the page performs calculations or modifies in any way the data contained in the response document's elements. Many developers and financial analysts have joined the ranks of the unemployed by supplying management with Windows forms, Web pages, or Excel worksheets that deliver patently erroneous information.

TIP

Beware of XML Web services that deliver bad data. For example, failing to reset row or column total counters when creating services that deliver crosstab reports results in total values that are about double the correct values. To demonstrate this type of computational error, comment one or both of the `intTotal = 0` *instructions of ReportsWS.asmx.vb's* `GenerateReport` *function, rebuild the ReportsWS project, and check the values of the totals cells for column or row 3 or higher.*

Phase 3: Adding Formatting and Navigation Features

Proper formatting of controls and alignment of table cells that display numeric values are the signs of a professional Web page designer. Following are recommendations for formatting the tables of financial and technical reports:

- ▶ Right-align all numeric columns, and add thousands separators to cell values.
- ▶ Right-align numeric column header strings.
- ▶ Add currency symbols for totals rows and columns.
- ▶ Don't add currency symbols to table cells whose values contribute to the totals, except for the first row. Adding currency symbols to all numeric cells in the first row of a worksheet is a standard practice of accountants.
- ▶ Round summary values to the nearest dollar, pound, euro, or other currencies that use decimal fractions. Consider rounding the following to thousands: lira, Colombian pesos, Venezuelan bolivars, South Korean won, and currencies having similar purchasing power.
- ▶ Use minus signs for negative numbers in technical reports; for U.S. financial reports, use parentheses.

Interpage navigation methods should be consistent within an entire site, if possible, and at least within related subsites. For example, the OakLeaf Web site uses table-based navigation methods, some of which are based on client-side ECMAScript code. All but a few pages of the site have a consistent header design; primary navigation rows follow the header table.

Phase 4: Tweaking the Final Page Design and Accommodating Netscape Browsers

Following are a few final recommendations for tidying the page and, if necessary, supporting other browsers:

- ▶ Add a `Label` control to serve as a page title.
- ▶ Use ASP.NET's Format I Align commands to adjust the spacing, size, and location of control.

▶ Add `ToolTip` text to explain the function of each control that requires user entry or value selection. `DropDownList` controls don't have a `ToolTip` property; add the `ToolTip` text to the control's caption label.

▶ If your client application must support Netscape Navigator browsers, verify page presentation in Navigator 4.0+. If you encounter layout problems, try creating a copy of the page with the `DOCUMENT` object's `targetSchema` property value set to `Navigator 4.0`. You might need to make substantial modifications to server controls and their underlying code.

▶ Ask a colleague with graphic design experience to review your application. A second or third opinion on the close-to-final design can prevent embarrassment when you put the project in production.

NOTE

This book's ASP.NET Web applications have not been tested, nor are they intended for use with Netscape browsers.

Transforming XML Crosstab Reports to Formatted Tables

An example of the four-phase development process described in the preceding sections is creating a production ASP.NET front end for the ReportsWS XML Web service you built in Chapter 8. The following sections describe the development of the CTReports ASP.NET Web Application, which is based in part on Chapter 8's CTHarness.sln solution. CTReports.sln contains multiple CTOrders*.aspx pages to demonstrate the development process.

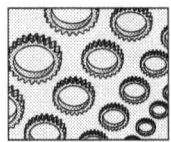

NOTE

Create a \VBWS09 folder, download VBWS09.zip from <GlobalOMHVbwsSiteReplace>, and extract the files into \VBWS09. Create a virtual directory named CTReports that points to the \VBWS09\CTReports folder before you attempt to open CTReports.sln. If you didn't download and extract \VBWS08.zip into a \VBWS08 folder, do it now, and create a virtual directory named ReportsWS that points to the \VBWS08\ReportsWS folder. To generate meaningful data for the crosstab reports, run the BackdateOrders project, as described in Chapter 8's "Emulating Historical Order and Invoice Data" section. Alternatively, mark the Remote check box to consume the ReportsWS service from the OakLeaf Web site. The examples of this chapter are generated from about 14,000 backdated Orders records.

Phase 1: Generating and Sending the Request Document

Most server controls of the initial CTOrders1.aspx page correspond to the Windows form controls of the CTHarness.vb form. One exception is replacement of the `txtStartDate` text box by three `DropDownList` controls to set the starting month, day, and year for the report. Web users are accustomed to selecting credit card expiration dates from lists of months and years. Unlike text boxes, you can limit day selections from `DropDownList` controls to 31, but your code must test values greater than 28 against the month and year selected.

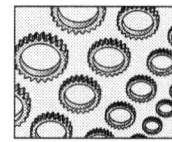

NOTE

A `Calendar` control is an alternative to setting the starting date with `DropDownList`. The server control version of the `Calendar` control requires a round trip to the Web server for each date change, and the control isn't graphically attractive because of HTML rendering limitations.

The `ddlInterval` list interacts with the `ddlDataCols` list to set the default number of data columns for quarterly (4), monthly (12), weekly (13), and daily (7) reports. Changing the report interval requires a server round trip to set the default `ddlDataCols` value. The `ddlInterval_SelectedIndexChanged` event handler contains the code to set the `ddlDataCols` list value.

The settings of the server controls, except the `chkRemote` check box, set the three required SOAP header values and element values of the request document. Following is the code for the `cmdResponse_Click` event handler, which generates the request document, consumes the ReportsWS XML Web service, and displays the response document in a text box.

```
Private Sub cmdResponse_Click(ByVal sender As System.Object, _
      ByVal e As System.EventArgs) Handles cmdResponse.Click
   'Create XML request document
   'Retrieve the XML response document from the ReportsWS service
   Dim xwsReport As New OCEReports.ReportsWS()
   Dim hdrReport As New OCEReports.Authenticate()
   Dim strResponse As String

   'Generate the title
   strTitle = ddlYear.SelectedItem.Value.ToString + " " + _
            ddlInterval.SelectedItem.Value.ToString + _
            " Orders by " + rblRowsBy.SelectedItem.Value.ToString

   'Set the start date
   strStartDate = ddlMonth.SelectedItem.Value.ToString + "/" + _
              ddlDay.SelectedItem.Value.ToString + "/" + _
              ddlYear.SelectedItem.Value.ToString
   'Assign the formatting criteria
   If cblFormat.Items(0).Selected Then
      strRowTotals = "Yes"
   Else
      strRowTotals = "No"
   End If
   If cblFormat.Items(1).Selected Then
      strColTotals = "Yes"
   Else
      strColTotals = "No"
   End If
   If cblFormat.Items(2).Selected Then
      strNullToZero = "Yes"
```

```vb
        Else
            strNullToZero = "No"
        End If
        'Generate the request document
        strXML = "<crosstab xmlns=" + _
                "'http://oakleaf.ws/services/crosstabs/request' >" + strCrLf + _
                "    <title>" + strTitle + "</title>" + strCrLf + _
                "    <timeseries> " + strCrLf + _
                "        <datatable>Orders</datatable>" + strCrLf + _
                "        <rowsby>" + rblRowsBy.SelectedItem.Value.ToString + _
                    "</rowsby>" + strCrLf + _
                "        <startdate>" + strStartDate + "</startdate>" + _
                    strCrLf + _
                "        <starttime>00:00:00AM</starttime>" + strCrLf + _
                "        <interval>" + ddlInterval.SelectedItem.ToString + _
                    "</interval>" + strCrLf + _
                "        <datacolumns>" + ddlDataCols.SelectedItem.ToString + _
                    "</datacolumns>" + strCrLf + _
                "        <count>No</count>" + strCrLf + _
                "        <avgvalue>No</avgvalue>" + strCrLf + _
                "        <rowtotals>" + strRowTotals + "</rowtotals>" + _
                    strCrLf + _
                "        <coltotals>" + strColTotals + "</coltotals>" + _
                    strCrLf + _
                "        <nulltozero>" + strNullToZero + "</nulltozero>" + _
                    strCrLf + _
                "        <format>XML</format>" + strCrLf + _
                "    </timeseries>" + strCrLf + _
                "</crosstab>"
        'RemoteWS code removed for brevity
        With hdrReport
            'Supply the SOAP header values
            .ServerName = "(local)"
            .UserName = txtUserID.Text
            .Password = txtPassword.Text
        End With
        'Send the soap header and request document
        xwsReport.AuthenticateValue = hdrReport
        txtDoc.Text = Replace(xwsReport.TimeSeriesReport(strXML), _
            Chr(10), strCrLf)
    End Sub
```

TIP

In Solution Explorer, right-click the page you want to build and choose Set As Start Page. The default start page for the CTReports.sln solution is CTOrders1.aspx.

Figure 9-1 shows the first-phase CTOrders1.aspx page after clicking the Get Report button with default control values. For a more detailed description of the ReportsWS response document, see Chapter 8's "Producing the XML Response Document" section.

TIP

A `TextBox` control with the `TextMode` value set to `Password` doesn't return the default value you assign in design mode. If you want to provide a temporary default password for testing, assign it to the `Text` property with code in the `Page_Load` event handler.

Phase 2: Populating the Table with an XmlTextReader Object

The `Table` server control is the logical candidate for presenting crosstab and other financial reports, because it's easy to format specific cells for the type of data they contain. Another advantage of the `Table` control is the capability to assign `id` values for DHTML drill-down navigation.

The `Table` control has an object model that's consistent with other list-type server controls, such as the `RadioButtonList` and `CheckBoxList`. Table controls consist of a `TableRows` collection, which contains a `TableCells` collection. To add a row to a

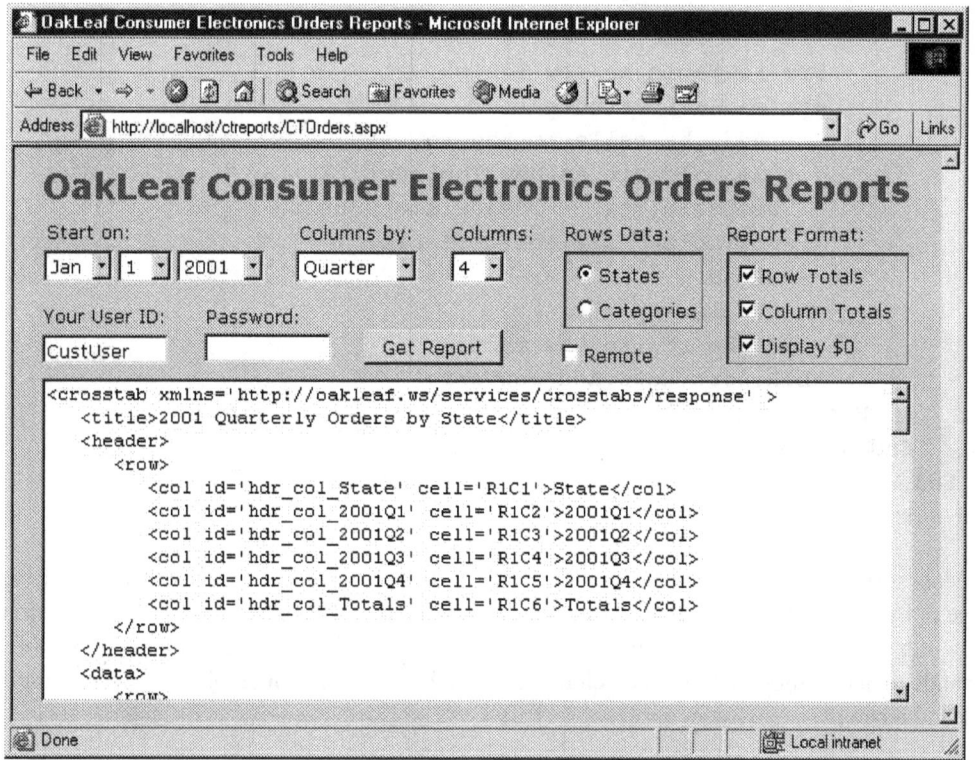

Figure 9-1   *The initial version of the ASP.NET page displays the response document in a text box.*

table, you create a new `TableRow` object, add new `TableCell` objects to the row, and then add the `TableRow` object to the `Table` control.

An `XmlTextReader` object is the best choice for passing response document element values to table cells. Only elements containing header and data values have attributes, so you can use the `XmlTextReader.HasAttribute` property to skip lines in the ReportsWS document that don't contain cell or header values. The following code in CTOrder2.aspx adds the cells' values and rows without adding the title header or specifying cell formatting:

```
Private Sub FillTable(ByVal strResponse As String)
    'Fill the table with the crosstab data
    Dim srdTable As StringReader = Nothing
    Dim xtrTable As XmlTextReader = Nothing
    Dim strTitle As String

    srdTable = New StringReader(strResponse)
    xtrTable = New XmlTextReader(srdTable)
    With xtrTable
        .Read()  '<crosstab>
        .Read()  '<title>
        strTitle = .ReadElementString("title")
        While .Read
            If .HasAttributes Then
                'It's a cell, create a row
                Dim rowTable As New TableRow()
                While .HasAttributes
                    'Add the cells to the row
                    Dim celTable As New TableCell()
                    celTable.Text = .ReadElementString
                    rowTable.Cells.Add(celTable)
                    .Read()
                End While
                'Add the row to the table
                tblReport.Rows.Add(rowTable)
            End If
        End While
    End With
End Sub
```

Most server controls have fixed width and height, which you determine during the design stage or by setting property values with code. `DataGrid` and `Table` controls are exceptions; the width and height you set are minimum values. As you add rows and columns, the table expands to accommodate the added elements. (See Figure 9-2.) The table isn't visible until you add a row.

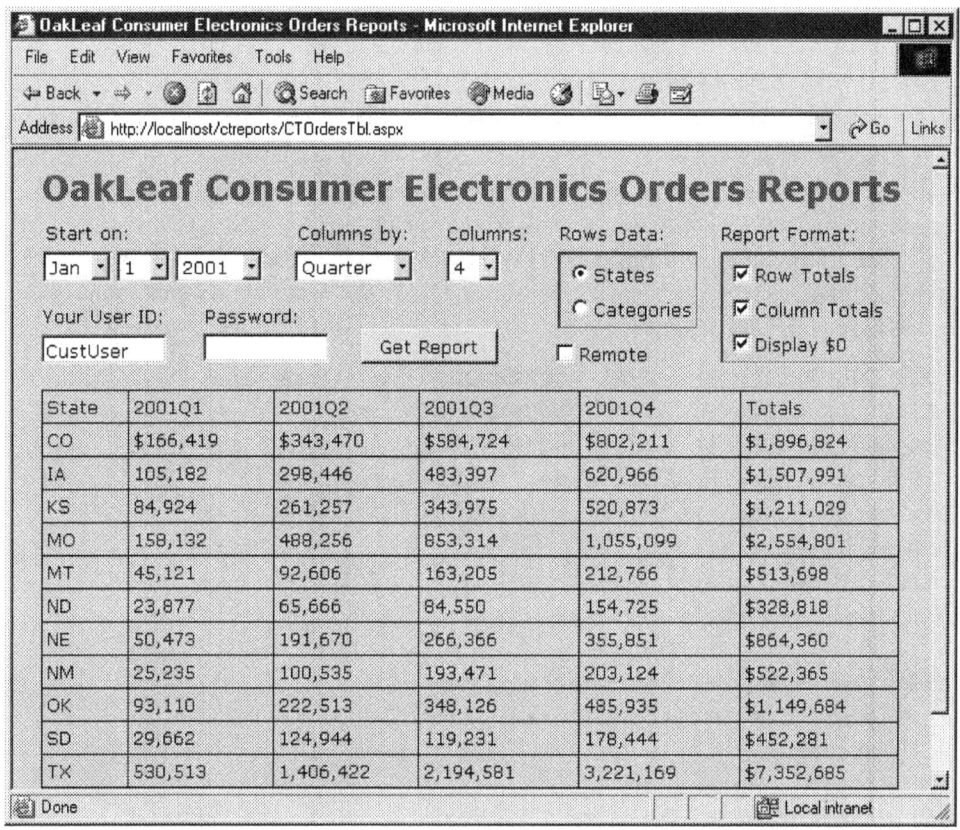

Figure 9-2 *The second development phase adds an unformatted table to display the document values.*

TIP

Set the `EnableViewState` *property value of the table to* `False` *to minimize the size of the* `PropertyBag` *string. The server regenerates the table data for each form submission.*

Phase 3: Formatting the Table and Adding Attribute Values

The next steps are to add the title as a table header row, format the data cells by centering the first column, and right-aligning the remaining currency columns. The table illustrated in Figure 9-2 has very low contrast, so specify `WhiteSmoke` or another lighter color as the table's background color. The standard OakLeaf style for table and column headers is white type against a gray-blue background, which you specify by passing decimal RGB values (0 to 255) as argument values of the `System.Drawing.Color.FromArgb()` method.

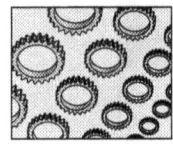

NOTE

Argb is an abbreviation for alpha (transparency), red, blue, and green. When you pass three argument values to the overloaded `FromArgb()` *method, the method interprets the values as red, blue, and green.*

Adding a header that spans multiple columns requires specifying a `TableHeaderRow` object and setting its `ColumnSpan` property value, which corresponds to HTML's `colspan` attribute. The following code from the CTOrders3.aspx page adds a centered title header, alters the column headers row's colors, centers the first (row headers) column, and right-aligns the remaining columns:

```
Private Sub FillTable(ByVal strResponse As String)
    'Fill the table with the crosstab data
    Dim srdTable As StringReader = Nothing
    Dim xtrTable As XmlTextReader = Nothing
    Dim celTable As TableCell = Nothing
    Dim strTitle As String
    Dim blnFirstCol As Boolean
    Dim blnColHeader As Boolean

    srdTable = New StringReader(strResponse)
    xtrTable = New XmlTextReader(srdTable)
    With xtrTable
        .Read()   '<crosstab>
        .Read()   '<title>
        strTitle = "OakLeaf Consumer Electronics " + _
            .ReadElementString("title")
        'Add a title header row
        Dim rowHeader As New TableRow()
        Dim celHeader As New TableHeaderCell()
        With celHeader
            'Center and apply standard OakLeaf colors to the header
            .HorizontalAlign = HorizontalAlign.Center
            'Decimal value for #266294 plus 20% luminance
            .BackColor = Color.FromArgb(50, 110, 160)
            .ForeColor = Color.White
            .ID = "title"
            If strColTotals = "Yes" Then
                'Set the colspan attribute value
                .ColumnSpan = ddlDataCols.SelectedIndex + 3
            Else
                .ColumnSpan = ddlDataCols.SelectedIndex + 2
            End If
            .Text() = strTitle
            'Add the title header row
```

```vb
            rowHeader.Cells.Add(celHeader)
            tblReport.Rows.Add(rowHeader)
        End With
        blnColHeader = True
        While .Read
            If .HasAttributes Then
                'It's a cell, create a row
                blnFirstCol = True
                Dim rowTable As New TableRow()
                rowTable.HorizontalAlign = HorizontalAlign.Right
                While .HasAttributes
                    'Add the cells to the row
                    If blnColHeader Then
                        'Apply standard OakLeaf colors to the header
                        Dim celColHeader As New TableHeaderCell()
                        With celColHeader
                            .BackColor = Color.FromArgb(50, 110, 160)
                            .ForeColor = Color.White
                        End With
                        celTable = celColHeader
                    Else
                        celTable = New TableCell()
                    End If
                    With celTable
                        If blnFirstCol Then
                            .HorizontalAlign = HorizontalAlign.Center
                        End If
                        'id attribute
                        .ID = xtrTable.GetAttribute(0).ToString
                        .Text = xtrTable.ReadElementString
                    End With
                    rowTable.Cells.Add(celTable)
                    .Read()
                    blnFirstCol = False
                End While
                'Add the row to the table
                tblReport.Rows.Add(rowTable)
                blnColHeader = False
            End If
        End While
    End With
End Sub
```

Figure 9-3 shows the new and improved appearance of CTOrders3.aspx's tblReport control.

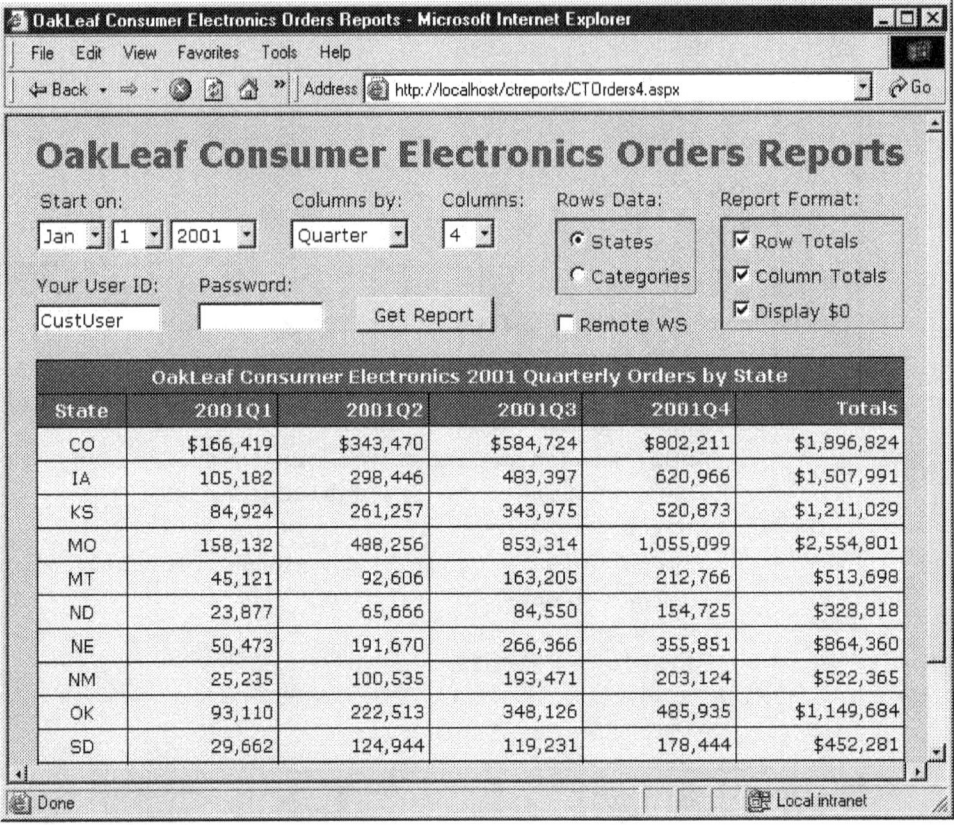

Figure 9-3 *Aligning table cells, changing the background color, and emphasizing the title and column header rows make the table's contents more readable.*

Phase 4: Aligning Valid Starting Dates to Calendar Boundaries

The final steps of the design add usability features, such as ToolTip text for controls, assure that users can't make invalid selections, and, optionally, enable application-level tracing. The CTReports.sln solution's CTOrders4.aspx page incorporates these added features.

The most important additions to the cmdResponse subprocedure's code are correcting invalid starting dates, such as February 31, 2001, and aligning starting dates on calendar boundaries. For example, quarterly data must start on the first day of a calendar quarter, monthly data on the first day of the month, and weekly data on Sunday. Daily reports don't need a starting date restriction. The following abbreviated listing accomplishes these objectives:

```
Private Sub cmdResponse_Click(ByVal sender As System.Object, _
     ByVal e As System.EventArgs) Handles cmdResponse.Click
  'Create XML request document
  'Retrieve the XML response document from the ReportsWS service
  Dim xwsReport As New RemReports.ReportsWS()
  Dim hdrReport As New RemReports.Authenticate()
```

```
Dim strResponse As String
Dim datStartDate As DateTime

If Trace.IsEnabled Then
   'Optional tracing code
   Trace.Write("Start prepare request")
End If


'Generate the title
strTitle = ddlYear.SelectedItem.Value.ToString + " " + _
   ddlInterval.SelectedItem.Value.ToString + _
   " Orders by " + rblRowsBy.SelectedItem.Value.ToString

'Validate day value
With ddlMonth.SelectedItem
   If .ToString = "Feb" And ddlDay.SelectedIndex > 27 Then
      ddlDay.SelectedIndex = 27
   End If
   If InStr("Apr Jun Sep Nov", .ToString) > 0 And _
         ddlDay.SelectedIndex = 30 Then
      '30 days hath September...
      ddlDay.SelectedIndex = 29
   End If
End With


'Start reports on calendar boundaries and set date dropdowns
Select Case ddlInterval.SelectedItem.ToString
   Case "Quarter"
      ddlDay.SelectedIndex = 0
      If InStr("1369", ddlMonth.SelectedItem.Value.ToString) = 0 _
            Then
         Select Case Val(ddlMonth.SelectedItem.Value.ToString)
            Case Is > 9
               ddlMonth.SelectedIndex = 8
            Case Is > 6
               ddlMonth.SelectedIndex = 5
            Case Is > 3
               ddlMonth.SelectedIndex = 2
            Case Else
               ddlMonth.SelectedIndex = 0
         End Select
      End If
   Case "Month"
      'First of month
      ddlDay.SelectedIndex = 0
   Case "Week"
      'Go to the preceding Sunday
      strStartDate = ddlMonth.SelectedItem.Value.ToString + "/" + _
                  ddlDay.SelectedItem.Value.ToString + "/" + _
```

```
                    ddlYear.SelectedItem.Value.ToString
        datStartDate = CDate(strStartDate)
        If datStartDate.DayOfWeek <> DayOfWeek.Sunday And _
            datStartDate <> #1/1/2001# Then
          '1/1/2001 is special-cased by the XML Web service
          datStartDate = datStartDate.AddDays(- _
            CInt(datStartDate.DayOfWeek))
          If datStartDate = #12/31/2000# Then
            ddlMonth.SelectedIndex = 0
            ddlDay.SelectedIndex = 0
            ddlYear.SelectedIndex = 1
          Else
            ddlMonth.SelectedIndex = datStartDate.Month - 1
            ddlDay.SelectedIndex = datStartDate.Day - 1
          End If
        End If
    End Select

    'Set the start date
    strStartDate = ddlMonth.SelectedItem.Value.ToString + "/" + _
                ddlDay.SelectedItem.Value.ToString + "/" + _
                ddlYear.SelectedItem.Value.ToString
    'Assign the formatting criteria (omitted)
    'Generate the request document (omitted)
    If Trace.IsEnabled Then
        Trace.Write("Start send request")
    End If
    With hdrReport
        'Supply the SOAP header values
        .ServerName = "OAKLEAF-MS7"
        .UserName = txtUserID.Text
        .Password = txtPassword.Text
    End With
    xwsReport.AuthenticateValue = hdrReport
    strResponse = xwsReport.TimeSeriesReport(strXML)
    If Trace.IsEnabled Then
        Trace.Write("End receive response")
        Trace.Write("Start fill table")
    End If
    Call FillTable(strResponse)
    If Trace.IsEnabled Then
        Trace.Write("End fill table")
    End If
End Sub
```

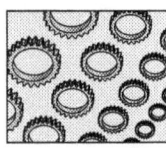

NOTE

The preceding code changes the `DropDownList`'s selected item at the server if the date selected by the user isn't appropriate for the specified interval. Users see the corrected starting date when the page refreshes.

Drilling Down with DHTML Navigation

Chapter 8's "Element-Centric Response Documents" section briefly describes addition of attribute values to element-centric XML and XHTML response documents. Attribute values applied to table rows or cells enable drill-down navigation by clicking an [X]HTML element. VBScript or ECMAScript code that runs on the client executes an HTTP GET or POST request with the element's id value argument to a response document. The response document interprets the id value and sends a request message to the appropriate XML Web service, which returns an XML or XHTML response document.

The OakLeaf CFR project, which the "OakLeaf Systems' Online Code of Federal Regulations" section of Chapter 1 describes in detail, uses DHTML-based navigation to drill down through the title, subtitle, chapter, subchapter, and part hierarchy of the 204-volume U.S. CFR. The ultimate destination is the text of a particular section of the CFR, which ranges in size between about 1000 to more than 500,000 characters. TOC navigation uses id attribute values in ti#st#[ch#sc#[pn#]]format, where # is a letter, number, or, if not a subtitle or subchapter, an underscore. For example, a DHTML-generated http://www.oakleaf.ws/cfr/opentoc.aspx?tocid=ti7stA URL returns the TOC of chapters and subchapters for title 7, subtitle A, "Office of the Secretary of Agriculture," which has parts but no chapters or subchapters.

The CFR project's ASP.NET Web applications consume the following three XML Web services from the OakLeaf Web site:

▶ **CFRTocWS**   Delivers tables of contents for CFR titles and subtitles, chapters and subchapters, and parts, depending on the value of the tocid argument passed to the OpenTOC.aspx page and supplied as the strID argument of the GetTOCByID method. You can specify generic XML or OakLeaf-specific XHTML as the response document format. TOC documents rely on the CFRToc.css stylesheet for XHTML element formatting. The XHTML document uses table row elements for navigation.

▶ **CFRSectWS**   Delivers XML or fully formatted XHTML CFR section text response documents in response to strID values that contain a trailing sn (section number) attribute value. Attribute values provide reverse navigation by a header table to part, chapter, and title parent elements in the TOC hierarchy. Text attribute values supply formatting instructions for the very inconsistent outline hierarchy of CFR sections prepared by independent federal agencies. The CFRSect.css style sheet specifies formats for the table elements and section paragraphs.

▶ **CFRSearchWS**   Performs SQL Server 2000 full-text searches of the demonstration database's CFR section text and, optionally, TOCs. The Search.aspx page lets you type a search string, such as *satellite NEAR broadcast* (the default), specify the maximum number of hits (up to 100), and the lowest starting point in the hierarchy (*sections* is the default). The GetSearchResults method returns an X[HT]ML response document to the Results.aspx page, which contains table rows that link to sections, TOCs, or both.

The WSDL documents for the three CFR...WS services contain extensive HTML-formatted documentation, which includes links to explanatory pages on the OakLeaf Web site. You can view the WSDL documents from links at http://www.oakleaf.ws/cfr/about.aspx or in the Microsoft UDDI Registry (http://uddi.microsoft.com/). Search the Registry with OakLeaf as the business name.

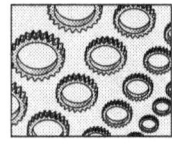

NOTE

The \VBWS09\CFR-Final subfolder includes all Visual Basic .NET code and supporting files for the ASP.NET demonstration version of the CFR client application. Before you open the CFR-Final.sln solution, create an IIS virtual directory named CFR that points to the \VBWS09\CFR-Final folder. The license agreement for this code restricts its use to intranets and prohibits access to the project or any of its components from the public Internet. See the License.txt file for usage restrictions.

The Client-Side Navigation Script

Client-side ECMAScript code in the CFRToc.htc HTML component (behavior) file implements the TOC navigation process from the titles to the section text level. DHTML behaviors let you use a single script for multiple pages and prevent exposing your script code in the HTML source file.

The script highlights the current row with the onMouseOver event handler (onmouseover function) and returns the row to its original state with the onMouseOut handler (onmouseout). The onClick handler (onclick) generates the URL to retrieve the specified TOC or section text. The script affects elements contained only within a tbody section, which lets you add inactive rows that contain optional anchor tags for conventional navigation. The following CFRToc.htc code is based on a sample Microsoft DHTML behavior script written by Dave Massey:

```
<public:event name="onrowselect" ID="rowSelect" />
<public:property name="hlColor" />
<public:property name="slColor" />
<public:property name="txColor" />
<PUBLIC:ATTACH EVENT="ondetach" ONEVENT="cleanup()" />
<script language="jscript">
var currRow = -1;
var selRow = -1;
var strHostURL = "http://localhost/cfr/";
var strTOCPage = "opentoc.aspx?tocid=";

if (element.tagName == 'TBODY')
{
    element.attachEvent('onmouseover', onMouseOver);
    element.attachEvent('onmouseout', onMouseOut);
    element.attachEvent('onclick', onClick);
}
function cleanup()
{
    hilite(-1);
```

```
        element.detachEvent('onmouseover', onMouseOver);
        element.detachEvent('onmouseout', onMouseOut);
        element.detachEvent('onclick', onClick);
}
function onClick()
{
    srcElem = window.event.srcElement;
    //crawl up the tree to find the table row
    while (srcElem.tagName != "TR" && srcElem.tagName != "TBODY")
        srcElem = srcElem.parentElement;
    if(srcElem.tagName != "TR") return;
    if(srcElem.rowIndex == 0 ) return;
    if (selRow != -1) selRow.runtimeStyle.backgroundColor = '';
        srcElem.runtimeStyle.backgroundColor = slColor;
        selRow = srcElem;
    var oEvent = createEventObject();
    oEvent.selected = selRow;
    rowSelect.fire(oEvent);
    //Navigation
    switch(srcElem.id){
        case "search" :
            window.location.href = strHostURL + "search.aspx";
            break;
        case "home" :
            window.location.href = strHostURL + "default.aspx";
            break;
        case "help" :
            window.location.href = strHostURL + "help.aspx";
            break;
        case "about" :
            window.location.href = strHostURL + "about.aspx";
            break;
        case "noText" :
            alert("The text of this section is not available");
            break;
        case "hasSubs" :
            alert("This title only has subtitles. Please click a subtitle.");
            break;
case "reserved" :
            alert("This element is reserved. Please make another selection.");
break;
default :
window.location.href = strHostURL + strTOCPage + srcElem.id;
```

```
      }
   }
function onMouseOver()
{
   srcElem = window.event.srcElement;
   //crawl up to find the row
   while (srcElem.tagName != "TR" && srcElem.tagName != "TBODY")
      srcElem = srcElem.parentElement;
   if(srcElem.tagName != "TR") return;
   if (srcElem.rowIndex > 0)
      hilite(srcElem);
   else
      hilite(-1);
}
function onMouseOut()
{
   // Make sure we catch exit from the table
   hilite(-1, -1);
}
function hilite(newRow)
{
   if (hlColor != null )
   {
      if (currRow != -1 && currRow!=selRow)
      {
         currRow.runtimeStyle.backgroundColor = '';
         currRow.runtimeStyle.color = '';
         currRow.runtimeStyle.textDecoration = '';
         currRow.runtimeStyle.cursor = '';
      }
      if (newRow != -1 && newRow!=selRow)
      {
         newRow.runtimeStyle.backgroundColor = hlColor;
         newRow.runtimeStyle.color = txColor;
         newRow.runtimeStyle.textDecoration = 'underline';
         newRow.runtimeStyle.cursor = 'hand';
      }
   }
   currRow = newRow;
}
</script>
```

The CFR project demonstrates the primary benefit of HTML component files: the preceding code in a single file handles client-side navigation operations for the OpenTOC.aspx, Search.aspx, and Results.aspx pages. Changes you make to the script in CFRToc.htc affect all pages that specify the behavior.

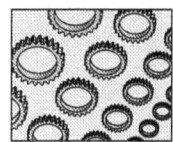

NOTE

DHTML behaviors require IE 5.0+ and don't work with other browsers. Thus, you can substitute VBScript for ECMAScript in HTML component files. If you need Netscape Navigator compatibility, you must add ECMAScript code to your page to perform the navigation operations.

Visual Basic .NET Code Behind the OpenTOC.aspx Page

The CFR project originated as a Visual Basic 6.0 application, which used ASP and VBScript for presentation, and ActiveX middle-tier components to handle XML data access, transformation to XHTML, and a full-text search of the CFRSQL database. The code behind the OpenTOC.aspx page was copied from the VBScript of the earlier OpenTOC.asp version and modified to conform to Visual Basic .NET standards.

Following is the OpenTOC.aspx.vb code, which delivers an XHTML page from the CFRTocWS or CFRSectWS service; the value of the `strId` element passed by the HTML component's `onclick` function determines the service that's consumed:

```
Option Explicit On
Option Strict On

Public Class OpenTOC
    Inherits System.Web.UI.Page

#Region " Web Form Designer Generated Code "
    Public strID As String
    Public strConnect As String
    Public strXHTML As String
    Public strURL As String

    Private Sub Page_Load(ByVal sender As System.Object, _
        ByVal e As System.EventArgs) Handles MyBase.Load
        'Remote OakLeaf CFRTocWS and CFRSectWS XML Web services
        Dim xwsTOC As New CFRTocWS.CFRToc()
        Dim xwsSect As New CFRSectWS.CFRSect()

        Response.Buffer = True
        Response.Expires = 0

        strConnect = CStr(Application("strConnect"))
        strURL = CStr(Application("strCFRURL"))

        strID = Request.QueryString("TocID")
        If strID = "" Then
```

```
               'Default to titles
               strID = "ti0"
         End If


         If InStr(strID, "sn") > 0 Then
             'Retrieve the section text
             Server.ScriptTimeout = 300
             Trace.Write("Start GetSectById service")
             strXHTML = xwsSect.GetSectById(strConnect, "XHTML", strID)
             Trace.Write("End GetSectById service")
             Server.ScriptTimeout = 90
         Else
             'Retrieve the TOC by level
             Trace.Write("Start GetTocById service")
             strXHTML = xwsTOC.GetTocById(strConnect, "", "XHTML", strID)
             Trace.Write("End GetTocById service")
             If Len(strXHTML) < 500 Then
                 'Returned an error string
                 If InStr(strXHTML, "ERROR: Table of contents missing") > 0 Then
'Try subtitles if no chapter specified
                     If InStr(strID, "ch") = 0 Then
                         'Try the first subtitle
                         strID = Replace(strID, "st_", "")
                         strID = strID & "stA"
                         strXHTML = xwsTOC.GetTocById(strConnect, "", _
                             "XHTML", strID)
                     End If
                 End If
             End If
         End If
         'Open the XHTML document
         Trace.Write("Start Write XHTML page")
         Response.Write(strXHTML)
         Trace.Write("End Write XHTML page")
     End Sub
End Class
```

Visual Basic .NET Code for the GetTocById and GetTocByLevel Web Methods

The CFRTocWS XML Web service exposes two methods: GetTocById and GetTocByLevel. GetTocById accepts the value of the strID argument and generates the argument values required by the `GetTocByLevel` function, which generates the T-SQL statement to return the XML TOC document.

To minimize the size of the database, `varchar` fields store TOCs having less than 7900 characters; `text` fields store longer TOCs. Most TOCs are less than 7900 characters and require only one SQL Server round trip. The current version of the CFR project uses MDAC 2.7 components for data access.

Following is the Visual Basic .NET code for the `GetTocById` and `GetTocByLevel` methods:

```vbnet
<WebMethod>Public Function GetTocById(ByVal strConnect As String, _
     ByVal strURL As String, ByVal strTOCType As String, _
     ByVal strId As String) As String
  'Translate the Id string to GetTocByLevel arguments
  'Sending an empty Id string or "ti0" returns the Titles TOC
  Dim strTitleId As String
  Dim strSubtitleId As String
  Dim strChapterId As String
  Dim strSubchapterId As String
  Dim strPartId As String
  Dim strTest As String

  'Error processing not implemented
  If InStr(strId, "ti") > 0 Then
     strTitleId = Mid(strId, InStr(strId, "ti") + 2)
     If InStr(strId, "st") > 0 Then
        strTitleId = Left(strTitleId, InStr(strTitleId, "st") - 1)
        strSubtitleId = Mid(strId, InStr(strId,_"st") + 2)
        If InStr(strId, "ch") > 0 Then
           strSubtitleId = Left(strSubtitleId, InStr(strSubtitleId, "ch")
              - 1)
           strChapterId = Mid(strId, InStr(strId, "ch") + 2)
           If InStr(strId, "sc") > 0 Then
              strChapterId = Left(strChapterId,_InStr(strChapterId, "sc")
                 - 1)
              strSubchapterId = Mid(strId, InStr(strId, "sc") + 2)
              If InStr(strId, "pn") > 0 Then
                 strSubchapterId = Left(strSubchapterId, _
                    InStr(strSubchapterId, "pn") - 1)
                 strPartId = Mid(strId, InStr(strId, "pn") + 2)
              End If
           End If
        End If
     End If
  End If

  'Translate underscores to hyphens
  If strSubtitleId = "_" Then
```

```
            strSubtitleId = "-"
        End If
        If strSubchapterId = "_" Then
            strSubchapterId = "-"
        End If
        GetTocById = GetTocByLevel(strConnect, strTitleId, strSubtitleId, _
            strChapterId, strSubchapterId, strPartId, strTOCType)
End Function

<WebMethod>Public Function GetTocByLevel(ByVal strConnect As String, _
        ByVal strTitleId As String, ByVal strSubtitleId As String, _
        ByVal strChapterId As String, ByVal strSubchapterId As String, _
        ByVal strPartId As String, ByVal strTOCType As String) As String
    'Return the TOC at the specified level
    Dim strDoc As String
    Dim strSQL As String
    On Error GoTo TocByLevelErr

    If Val(strTitleId) > 0 Then
        If Val(strPartId) > 0 Or strPartId = "0" Then
            'Parts level (there are some Part 0s)
            strSQL = "SELECT TOCChar FROM Parts WHERE TitleID = " & _
                Val(strTitleId) & " AND PartID = '" & strPartId & "'"
        Else
            If Val(strChapterId) > 0 Then
                'Chapter level
                If Len(strSubchapterId) = 0 Or Trim(strSubchapterId) = "-" Then
                    strSQL = "SELECT TOCChar FROM Chapters WHERE TitleID = " & _
                        Val(strTitleId) & " AND SubtitleID = '" & strSubtitleId & _
                        "' AND ChapterID = '" & strChapterId & "'"
                Else
                    'Subchapter level
                    strSQL = "SELECT TOCChar FROM Subchapters WHERE TitleID = " & _
                        Val(strTitleId) & " AND SubtitleID = '" & strSubtitleId & _
                        "' AND ChapterID = '" & strChapterId & _
                        "' AND SubchapterID = '" & strSubchapterId & "'"
                End If
            Else
                'Title level
                If Len(strSubtitleId) = 0 Or Trim(strSubtitleId) = "-" Then
                    strSQL = "SELECT TOCChar FROM Titles WHERE TitleID = " & _
                        Val(strTitleId)
                Else
                    'Subtitle level
                    strSQL = "SELECT TOCChar FROM Subtitles WHERE TitleID = " & _
                        Val(strTitleId) & " AND SubtitleID = '" & _
                        strSubtitleId & "'"
                End If
            End If
        End If
```

```
          End If
   Else
      'TitlesTOC has only one record
      strSQL = "SELECT TOCText FROM TitlesTOC"
   End If
   With cnnCFR
      If .State = ADODB.ObjectStateEnum.adStateClosed Then
         'Open the connection
         .CommandTimeout = 300
         .Open(strConnect)
      End If
   End With
   bln2ndPass = False
   Do
      With rstClient
         If .State = ADODB.ObjectStateEnum.adStateOpen Then
            .Close
         End If
      End With
      rstClient = cnnCFR.Execute(strSQL, , ADODB.CommandTypeEnum.adCmdText)
      With rstClient
         If .EOF Then
            Exit Do
         Else
            If IsDBNull(.Fields(0).Value) Then
               If bln2ndPass Then
                  Exit Do
               End If
               If InStr(strSQL, "TOCChar") > 0 Then
                  strSQL = Replace(strSQL, "TOCChar", "TOCText")
                  bln2ndPass = True
               Else
                  Exit Do
               End If
            Else
               If strTOCType <> "XHTML" Then
                  If Len(CStr(.Fields(0).Value)) > 100 Then
                     GetTocByLevel = CStr(.Fields(0).Value)
                  Else
                     GetTocByLevel = "ERROR: Table of contents missing."
                  End If
                  GoTo TocByLevelExit
               Else
                  strDoc = CStr(.Fields(0).Value)
               End If
               Exit Do
            End If
         End If
      End With
```

```
      Loop
      'Release the connection early
      With rstClient
         If .State = ADODB.ObjectStateEnum.adStateOpen Then
            .Close()
         End If
      End With
      With cnnCFR
         If .State = ADODB.ObjectStateEnum.adStateOpen Then
            .Close()
         End If
      End With
      If Len(strDoc) > 100 Then
         GetTocByLevel = TransformXMLToc(strDoc)
      Else
         GetTocByLevel = "ERROR: Table of contents missing."
      End If
      GoTo TocByLevelExit
TocByLevelErr:
      GetTocByLevel = "ERROR: " & Err.Description & " (" & Err.Number & ")"
      GoTo TocByLevelExit
TocByLevelExit:
      'Make sure objects are closed
      With rstClient
         If .State = ADODB.ObjectStateEnum.adStateOpen Then
            .Close()
         End If
      End With
      With cnnCFR
         If .State = ADODB.ObjectStateEnum.adStateOpen Then
            .Close()
         End If
      End With
End Function
```

The private `TransformXMLToc` method, which generates the XHTML version of the response document, uses procedural Visual Basic .NET code—not XSL/T—because of irregularities in the TOC structure. For example, title 7, subtitle A, has parts but no chapters. Similarly, code transforms the XML section documents to XHTML because the outline structure of the original SGML documents is very inconsistent between the contributing federal agencies.

Creating XML Web Services with Crystal Reports

Visual Studio .NET includes an upgraded version of Visual Studio 6.0's Crystal Reports application. Crystal Reports 8.5 for Visual Studio .NET supports XML Web services for reporting. Like previous Visual Studio versions, the bundled product is restricted to five concurrent users and installation on a single Web server. You must purchase additional licenses from Crystal Decisions if your scalability requirements exceed these limits.

Creating a Crystal Reports XML Web service and ASP.NET consumer is a four-step process:

1. Create an SQL Server 2000 data source for the report. In most cases, a view is a better choice than linked related tables. You can also specify a `DataSet` object as the report's data source.

2. Use the embedded Crystal Reports designer to lay out the report and generate the report file.

3. Publish the report as an XML Web service.

4. Create an ASP.NET or Windows form application with the Crystal Reports Viewer, add a Web Reference to the Crystal XML Web service, and bind the Web Reference to the Viewer.

The following sections describe in detail the procedures for each of the preceding four steps. The example is a Crystal Reports clone of the 2001 Quarterly Orders by State version of the crosstab XML Web service you created in Chapter 8.

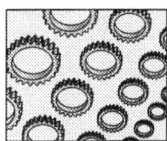

NOTE

The \VBWS09\CrystalWS folder has subfolders for each of the completed projects described in the following sections.

Creating the vw2001OrdersByQuarter View

It's easier to use SQL Server views than dynamic SQL as the data source for `Crystal Decisions` objects. Do the following to start the report project and create a view against the OCE-Cust sample database as a data source:

1. Open a new Visual Basic .NET Windows Application project, CrystalCT for this example. Creating and testing Crystal Reports objects in a Windows form is faster than in an ASP.NET page.

2. In Server Explorer, right-click the Data Connections node, and choose Add Connection to open the Data Link Properties dialog.

3. Accept the default SQL Server OLE DB data provider, complete the Connection page, test the connection, and click OK to close the dialog. For this example, the database is OCE_Cust on a local instance of SQL Server or MSDE 2000.

TIP

Use SQL Server authentication and type the user ID and password for a `db_datareader` *account if you want to enable everyone to access the report by providing a password in the form's logon dialog. Choosing Windows Integrated Authentication speeds the development process.*

4. Right-click the Views node and choose New View to open the daVinci database toolset's view design panes.

5. Design the view in the Diagram and Grid panes or type the T-SQL statement for the view in the SQL pane. For this example, the T-SQL statement is as follows:

```
SELECT TOP 100 PERCENT State, ROUND(SUM(Quantity * UnitPrice), 0)
    AS Amount, DATENAME(year, OrderDate) + 'Q' +
    DATENAME(quarter, OrderDate) AS Quarter
FROM Customers
    INNER JOIN Orders ON Customers.CustID = Orders.CustID
    INNER JOIN LineItems ON Orders.OrderID = LineItems.OrderID
WHERE OrderDate BETWEEN '01/01/2001' AND '12/31/2001 12:59:59PM'
GROUP BY State, DATENAME(year, OrderDate) + 'Q' +
    DATENAME(quarter, OrderDate)
ORDER BY State, Quarter
```

6. Execute the statement, and verify that it returns the values you need for the report.

7. Save the view as **vw2001OrdersByQuarter** for this example, and close Server Explorer.

The only difference between the preceding T-SQL query and that of the Chapter 8 example is the addition of the ROUND function to perform rounding of trailing decimal values on the server. Suppressing decimal values in the report truncates—rather than rounds—the summary values.

Adding a Crosstab Report to the Windows Form

Crystal Reports Experts make it easy to create crosstab reports from views that deliver summary data. Follow these steps to emulate the 2001 Quarterly Orders by State crosstab report with `CrystalDecisions` objects:

1. In Solution Explorer, right-click the CrystalCT project, choose Add New Item, and scroll to and double-click the Crystal Report item to start Crystal Reports. Register the product or click Register Later if the Registration Wizard dialog opens.

2. In the Crystal Report Gallery dialog, double-click Cross-Tab in the Choose An Expert list to open the Cross-Tab Report Expert tabbed dialog.

3. On the Data page, expand the Connections node, and double-click the connection you created in the preceding section. If the Connections node is empty or you want to use a different connection, double-click the OLE DB (ADO) node, select the Microsoft SQL Server Data Provider, and complete the Connection Information dialog to add a new OLE DB connection.

4. Expand the new connection node, select the view, and click Insert Table to add the view to the Tables In Report pane. (See Figure 9-4.)

5. Click the Cross-Tab tab, and drag the field name items from the Available Fields list to the Rows, Columns, or Summarized Fields lists. For this example, drag State to Rows, Quarter to Columns, and Amount to Summarized Fields. (See Figure 9-5.)

6. Click the Style tab, and select a style that suits your taste. This example uses the Sepia style.

7. Click Finish to display the report in layout mode.

8. Select the Row #1 Name text box and reduce its width. Do the same with the row Total text box. The right-most text box determines the width of the column.

9. Increase the width of the Column #1 Name and column Total text boxes.

10. Select the four ...Quarter.Amount numeric value cells, right-click one of the cells, and choose Format to open the Format dialog. Click the Number tab, select the currency

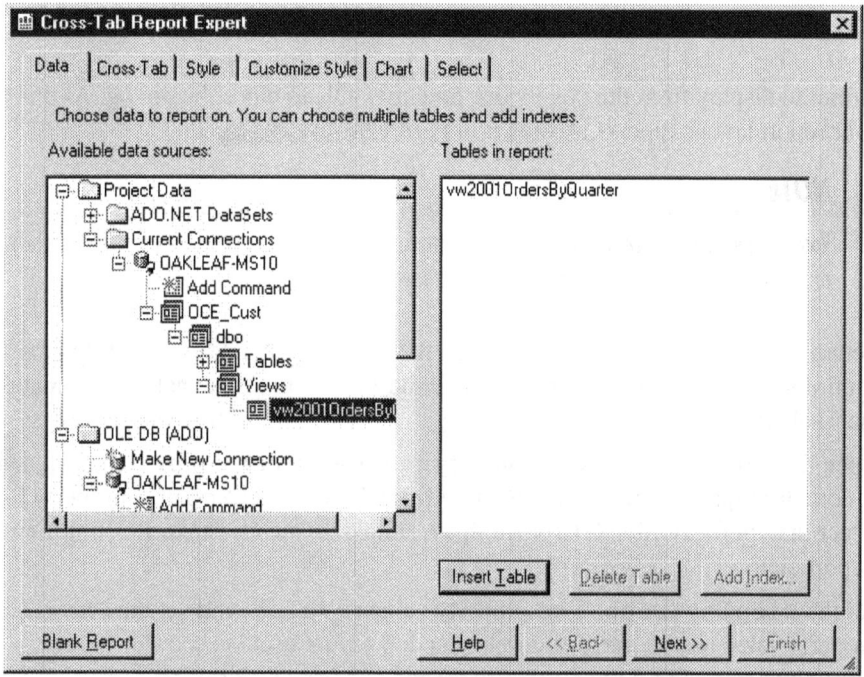

Figure 9-4   *Use an existing Server Explorer connection (shown here) or add a new OLE DB connection and select the table or view to serve as the data source for the report.*

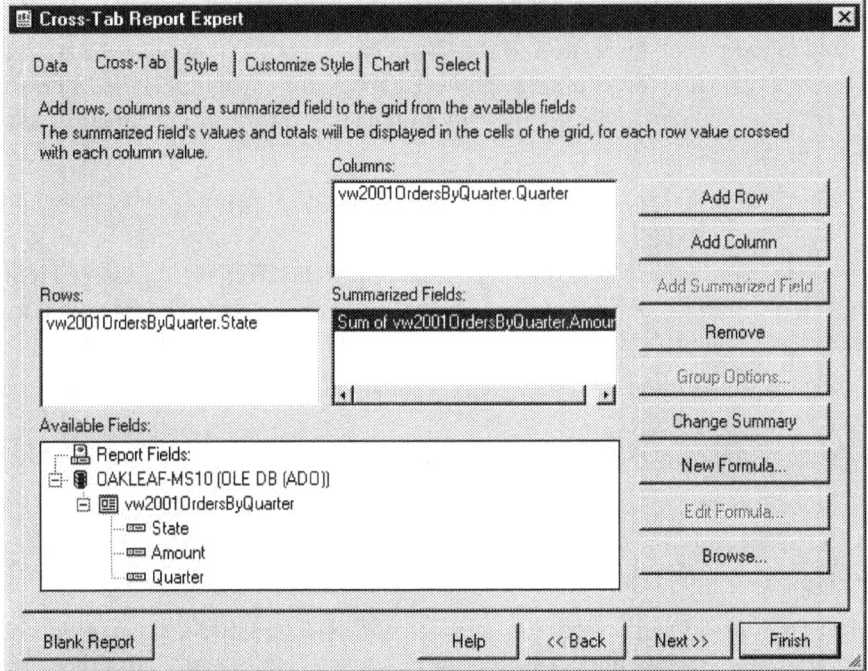

Figure 9-5   *Drag the fields of a summary data view to appropriate list boxes to create a crosstab report.*

format to display from the page's list, and click OK to close the dialog. At this point, your report layout appears as shown in Figure 9-6.

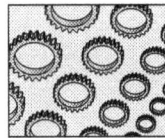

NOTE

You can specify the currency symbol only for totals, and format the remaining cells without the symbol. You can't specify currency symbols for only the first row of data.

11. Return to the form design document, open the Toolbox, and add a Crystal Reports Viewer control to the form. Expand the form and the Viewer to a size that approximates that of the final report.

12. Open the Properties window for the `CrystalReportsViewer1` control, and give it a more descriptive name. Select Browse from the `ReportSource` property list and select the .rpt file, OrdersCT.rpt for this example, in the Open An Existing Crystal Report dialog.

13. Set the `DisplayGroupTree` property value to `False`, and set the `Show...Button` property value to `False` for buttons you don't want users to see.

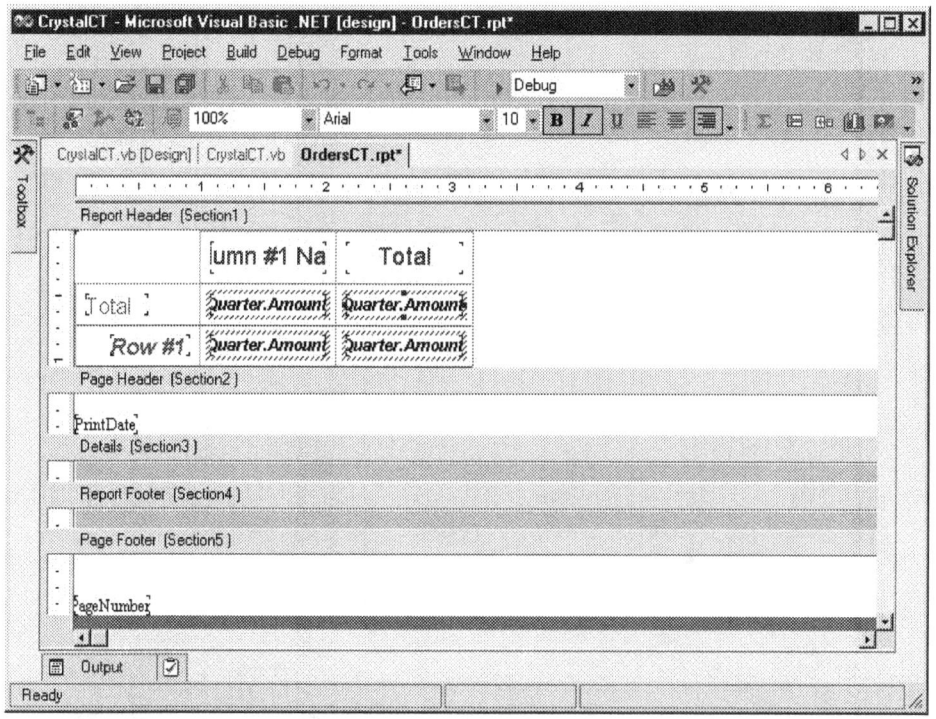

Figure 9-6   *Adjust the width of the text boxes to accommodate the column and field names, and the summary values.*

14. Build and run the project to check your report's data and formatting. Use the Zoom drop-down to change the report's scale. Figure 9-7 shows the report zoomed to 85 percent of full size.

Crystal Reports lets you create charts from crosstab and other types of summary data, and offers built-in drill-down navigation features. If you need reports that are more complex than the simple tabular versions described in the earlier "Transforming XML Crosstab Reports to Formatted Tables" section, Crystal Reports is usually the most cost-effective approach.

Generating the XML Web Service from a Crystal Report

When you add an .rpt file to an ASP.NET Web Service project, Crystal Reports adds a Publish As Web Service command to automatically generate the Visual Basic .NET or C# code for the service. Follow this procedure to create the XML Web service from an existing report:

1. Create a subfolder for the XML Web service and an IIS virtual directory that points to the subfolder. For this example, the virtual directory and subfolder name is CROrdersWS.

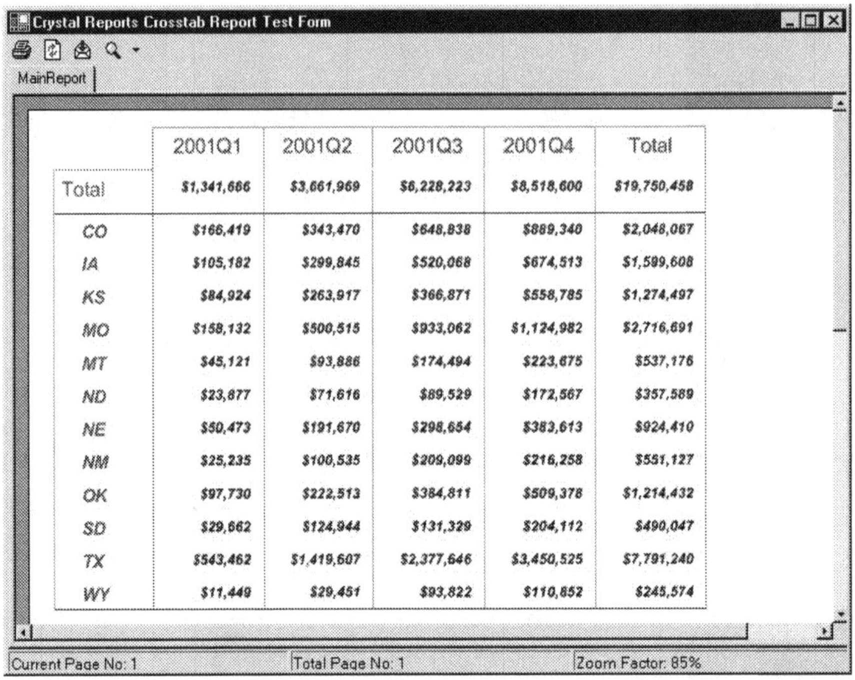

	2001Q1	2001Q2	2001Q3	2001Q4	Total
Total	$1,341,666	$3,661,969	$6,228,223	$8,518,600	$19,750,458
CO	$166,419	$343,470	$648,838	$889,340	$2,048,067
IA	$105,182	$299,845	$520,068	$674,513	$1,599,608
KS	$84,924	$263,917	$366,871	$558,785	$1,274,497
MO	$158,132	$500,515	$933,062	$1,124,982	$2,716,691
MT	$45,121	$93,886	$174,494	$223,675	$537,176
ND	$23,677	$71,616	$89,529	$172,567	$357,589
NE	$50,473	$191,670	$298,654	$383,613	$924,410
NM	$25,235	$100,535	$209,099	$216,258	$551,127
OK	$97,730	$222,513	$384,811	$509,378	$1,214,432
SD	$29,662	$124,944	$131,329	$204,112	$490,047
TX	$543,462	$1,419,607	$2,377,646	$3,450,525	$7,791,240
WY	$11,449	$29,451	$93,822	$110,852	$245,574

Figure 9-7 *Adjust the scale of the report to fit the control size with the Zoom drop-down.*

2. Optionally, copy the .rpt file you created to the new subfolder.
3. Open a new ASP.Net Web Service project with its location at, for this example, http://localhost/CROrdersWS.
4. In Solution Explorer, right-click the project node, choose Add | Add Existing Item to open the Add Existing Item dialog, select All Files (*.*) in the Files Of Type list, and double-click the .rpt file to add it to the project.
5. Right-click the .rpt file and choose Publish As Web Service to add a *ReportName*Service.asmx file to the project. Rename the file to **CROrdersWS.asmx** for this example, and set it as the start page.
6. Optionally, rename Service1.vsdisco to **CROrdersWS.vsdisco**, and delete Service1.asmx from the project.
7. Run the project to display the WSDL documentation page, which offers 11 undocumented methods. `TestReport` is the only method that supports the HTTP `GET` messaging protocol.
8. Click the TestReport link, and then click the Invoke button to verify operation of the report XML Web service. A `<ResponseContext>` message displays the table (view, in this case), server, and database names as XML element values. (See Figure 9-8.)

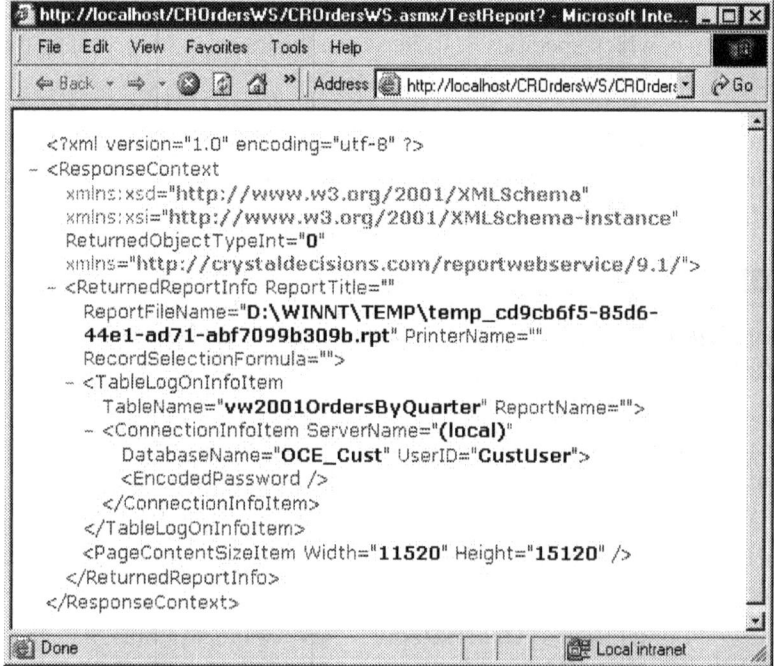

Figure 9-8   *The response document of the* TestReport *method confirms that the Crystal Reports XML Web service is operational.*

Crystal Reports XML Web services generate lengthy document/literal WSDL documents based on autogenerated Visual Basic .NET or C# code behind the .asmx file; the CROrdersWS.wsdl file is 33kB. Online help contains extensive documentation for the four CrystalDecisions namespaces imported by the code.

TIP

Rebuild the ASP.NET Web Service project after making changes to the report design. Otherwise, the WSDL document might not reflect your report modifications.

Designing an ASP.NET Page to Consume the Crystal Reports Service

The Crystal Reports Web Viewer for ASP.NET Web pages does a remarkably good job of generating HTML code to emulate the appearance of reports contained in Windows forms. On the other hand, Crystal Decisions' help files for creating Web and Windows form consumers of Crystal Reports XML Web services leave much to developers' imagination.

Following is the drill for creating an ASP.NET Web Application to consume the sample CROrdersWS service, which specifies SQL Server authentication for access to the OCE-Cust database:

1. Navigate to the \Program Files\Microsoft Visual Studio .NET\Crystal Reports\Views folder and grant the local aspnet_wp account (*ComputerName*\ASPNET) Read & Execute, List Folder Contents, Read, and Write access to the folder.

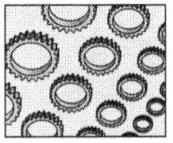

NOTE

Crystal Decisions offers no explanation about why the aspnet_wp account needs Write access to the folder's files.

2. Create a new subfolder for the ASP.NET Web Application and add an IIS virtual directory that points to the folder. For this example, the subfolder is \VBWS09\ CrystalWS\CROrdersCT and the virtual directory name is CROrdersCT.

3. Open a new ASP.NET Web Application, and specify the virtual directory you created as its location.

4. Rename WebForm1.aspx to **OrdersReport.aspx** for this example, and change the DOCUMENT object's `Title` property value to **2001 Quarterly Orders by State**.

5. Add a Web Reference to the Crystal Reports XML Web service, in this case, http://localhost/crordersws/crordersws.asmx. Rename the Web Reference from localhost to **CROrdersWS**.

6. Add a `CrystalReportsViewer` server control to the page. Rename the control to **rptOrdersCT**. Optionally, add a `Label` control with a title for the page.

7. Set the `DisplayGroupTree`, `EnableDrillDown`, `HasDrillUpButton`, `HasGoToPageButton`, `HasPageNavigationButton`, and `HasSearchButton` property values to `False`. Alternatively, set `DisplayToolbar` to `False` and assign an appropriate value, such as 85 (percent) to the `PageZoomFactor` property.

8. Add the following code to OrdersReport.aspx.vb's `Page_Init` subprocedure immediately after the `InitializeComponent()` method call to supply the password for the CustUser login:

```
rptOrdersCT.ReportSource = New CROrdersWS.OrdersCTService()
Dim logOnInfo As TableLogOnInfo
Dim cnnInfo As ConnectionInfo
logOnInfo = rptOrdersCT.LogOnInfo(0)
cnnInfo = logOnInfo.ConnectionInfo
cnnInfo.Password = "Cust#123"
```

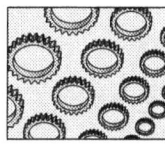

NOTE

The requirement to assign the `ConnectionInfo.Password` property value is buried in online help's "Accessing Secure Databases" topic for Crystal Reports. Search for "TableLogOnInfo" to find the topic. The password is encrypted in the request document. (Refer to Figure 9-8's `<EncodedPassword />` element.)

9. Build and run the project to display the report. Figure 9-9 shows the CROrdersWS report with a fixed 85 percent `ZoomFactor`.

TIP

You can connect the OrdersReport.asmx Web application to the remote OakLeaf XML Web services by changing the CROrdersWS Web Reference to http://www.oakleaf.ws/crorderws/crorderws.asmx.

Like WSDL documents for report services, the HTML documents returned for even simple reports aren't lightweights; the OrdersReport.htm source document is about 106kB. Complex reports can generate 500kB or more of HTML code.

2001 Quarterly Orders by State

	2001Q1	2001Q2	2001Q3	2001Q4	Total
Total	$1,341,666	$3,661,969	$6,228,223	$8,518,600	$19,750,458
CO	$166,419	$343,470	$648,838	$889,340	$2,048,067
IA	$105,182	$299,845	$520,068	$674,513	$1,599,608
KS	$84,924	$263,917	$366,871	$558,785	$1,274,497
MO	$158,132	$500,515	$933,062	$1,124,982	$2,716,691
MT	$45,121	$93,886	$174,494	$223,675	$537,176
ND	$23,877	$71,616	$89,529	$172,567	$357,589
NE	$50,473	$191,670	$298,654	$383,613	$924,410
NM	$25,235	$100,535	$209,099	$216,258	$551,127
OK	$97,730	$222,513	$384,811	$509,378	$1,214,432
SD	$29,662	$124,944	$131,329	$204,112	$490,047
TX	$543,462	$1,419,607	$2,377,646	$3,450,525	$7,791,240
WY	$11,449	$29,451	$93,822	$110,852	$245,574

Figure 9-9 *This crosstab report generated from a Crystal Reports XML Web service has no toolbar.*

Using the Office XP Web Services Toolkit with Excel 2002

The Office XP Web Services Toolkit, which Microsoft released in December 2001 is a COM add-in for VBA-enabled Office applications. The add-in, which installs the Microsoft SOAP Toolkit 2.0 SP2 run-time files on the client, emulates Visual Studio .NET's Add Web Reference dialog. The Web Service References dialog lets you search the Microsoft UDDI Registry by keyword or business name, or type a URL to the WSDL document for a service. If the search is successful or your URL is correct, the add-in displays a list of available services and their methods; a text box displays description text. Selecting a method and clicking Test displays the .axmx page for the service.

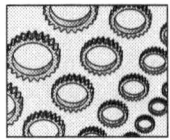

NOTE

You can download the latest version of the Toolkit from http://msdn.microsoft.com/library/ default.asp?url=/nhp/Default.asp?contentid=28000550. You must have Office XP installed on the computer to run the setup program. After installation, running setup again uninstalls the Toolkit.

Figure 9-10 shows the Web Service References dialog for the sample ReportsWS XML Web service. Marking the check box for a service enables the Add button, which you click to autogenerate a class that contains code to create a `SoapClient` proxy object for the specified service and its method(s).

Exploring the Excel 2002 Sample Application

The Toolkit includes documentation for the add-in and sample applications for Excel, Access, and Outlook 2002. None of the sample applications consume services that meet this book's definition of an XML Web service; the SOAP rpc/encoded sample services don't accept or return XML documents. XMethods' sample Java-based Delayed Stock Quotes service at http://services.xmethods.net/soap/urn:xmethods-delayed-quotes.wsdl accepts a stock symbol (`xsd:string`), such as MSFT, and returns the ask price (`xsd:float`), which is delayed by 20 minutes.

NOTE

The XMethods Web site (http://www.xmethods.net) provides access to many sample Web services contributed by XMethods and others. Most of the services use SOAP rpc/encoded format.

The Toolkit installs by default in a \Program Files\Office XP Web Services folder; the Stocks.xls sample application is in the …\1033\Stocks subfolder. Open Stocks.xls and click

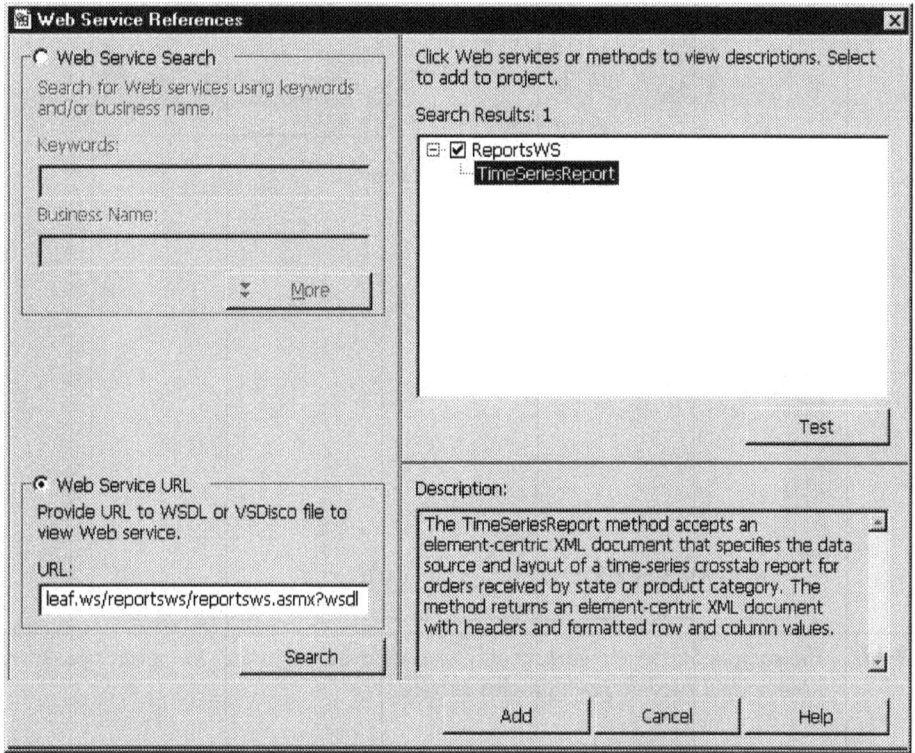

Figure 9-10   *The Office XP Web Services Toolkit's Web Service References dialog displays a list of the services and their methods from a UDDI search or a URL you type in a text box.*

the Get Stock Quotes button to return ask prices for seven computer-related stocks. (See Figure 9-11.)

TIP

Copy the URL from the c_WSDL_URL constant, choose Tools | Web Service Reference to open the dialog, select the Web Service URL option, paste the URL into the text box, and click Search to display the undocumented service and its single getQuote method.

The `cls_netxmethodsservicesst` class module, which has a reference to the Microsoft Soap [sic] Type Library, contains the following subprocedures and function:

▶   `Class_Initialize`   An event handler that creates a `SoapClient` object and invokes the `mssoapinit` method, which specifies the URL to the WSDL file.

▶   `Class_Terminate`   An event handler that sets the `SoapClient` object to `Nothing`.

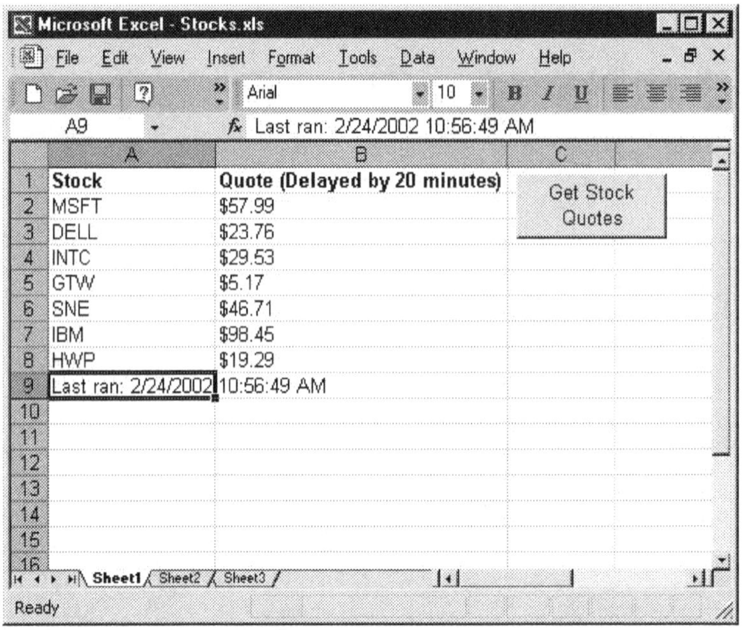

Figure 9-11   *The sample Stocks.xls worksheet returns delayed ask prices for seven stocks from XMethods' Delayed Stock Quotes service.*

▶   *ServiceNameErrorHandler*   An event handler for SOAP and other run-time errors.

▶   wsm_*MethodName*   A function to return the response message, in this case, price of the stock whose symbol you specify by the str_symbol argument value.

Sheet1 of the Stocks.xls workbook contains a GetStockQuotes VBA macro, which iterates column A cells, starting at row 2, and repeatedly executes the wsm_getQuote method until encountering an empty cell.

The sample application is an example of how *not* to design a production-grade XML Web service and consumer application. A more efficient approach is to supply a list of symbols as elements of an XML request document and return the values as elements of an XML response document. In this case, you could encode bid, ask, close, and volume values as attributes, but adding subelements for these values is a better XML Web service programming practice. The downside of complying with the "chunky, not chatty" rule for XML Web services is the client-side VBA required to generate the request and interpret the response documents.

Modifying the ReportsWS Service

Chapter 8's ReportsWS XML Web service uses SOAP headers for authentication, which are cumbersome to implement with the SOAP Toolkit 2.0. You must create an ActiveX component to process each set of SOAP headers your XML Web services require. To make SOAP headers optional and supply default authentication values for the OCE-Cust database, do the following:

1. Open the \VBWS08\ReportsWS\ReportsWS.sln solution, and then open the ReportsWS.asmx.vb document.

2. Make the SOAP header optional by changing the `SoapHeader` attributes of the `TimeSeriesReport` WebMethod from `SoapHeader("hdrAuthent")` to `SoapHeader("hdrAuthent", `**`Required:=False`**`)`.

3. Provide default authentication values if the client doesn't supply SOAP header values by making the following changes shown in bold type to the `GenerateReport` function's connection code:

```
With cnnCT
If hdrAuthent Is Nothing Then
.ConnectionString = "Data Source=(local); " + _
"Initial Catalog=OCE_Cust;UID=CustUser;PWD=Cust#123"
Else
.ConnectionString = "Data Source=" + hdrAuthent.ServerName + _
        ";Initial Catalog=OCE_Cust;UID=" + hdrAuthent.UserName + _
        ";PWD=" + hdrAuthent.Password
End If
.Open()
   cmmCT = .CreateCommand
End With
```

4. Run the project to verify your changes and regenerate the WSDL document.

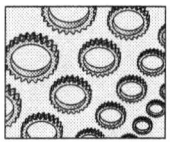

NOTE

Chapter 7's "Implementing SOAP Headers in XML Web Services" section explains how making SOAP headers optional affects the WSDL file.

Displaying XML Web Service Crosstab Reports in an Excel Worksheet

Using the Office XP Web Services Toolkit gives you a chance to test document/literal ASP.NET XML Web services with the SOAP Toolkit 2.0, which is intended primarily for the rpc/encoded format. Creating the Excel client application follows the four-phase development process described at the beginning of the chapter.

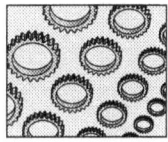

NOTE

The final version of the Crosstab.xls workbook you create in the following sections is located in the \VBWS09\XLCrosstab folder.

Phase 1: Test Consumption of the ReportsWS Service

To create a new Excel workbook, add a reference to the modified ReportsWS XML Web service, and verify that the service behaves as expected, do this:

1. Open a new Excel workbook, save it as **Crosstab.xls**, and press ALT-F11 to open the VBA Editor.

2. Choose Tools | Web Service Reference to open the dialog, select the Web Service URL option, type **http://localhost/reportsws/reportsws.asmx?wsdl** in the URL text box, and click Search to display the service. If you want to use the remote OakLeaf ReportsWS service, change localhost to **www.oakleaf.ws**.

3. Mark and expand the ReportsWS node, select the TimeSeriesReport method, and click Test to display the description document. Click Add to generate the `cls_wsReportsWS` class module.

4. Select Sheet1 and set its (Name) property value to **xlsQtrOrdersSt** and the (sheet) Name property to **2001 Quarterly Orders by State**.

5. Choose Tools | Macros to create a new VBA macro named **QtrOrdersSt** in Module1, and add the following code to Sub `QtrOrdersSt` in the VBA Editor:

```
Sub QtrOrdersSt()
Dim xwsQtrOrders As clsws_ReportsWS
Dim strRequestDoc As String
Dim strResponse As String

Set xwsQtrOrders = New clsws_ReportsWS

strRequestDoc = _
"<crosstab xmlns='http://oakleaf.ws/services/crosstabs/request' >" & _
   "<title>2001 Quarterly Orders by State</title>" & _
   "<timeseries>" & _
      "<datatable>Orders</datatable>" & _
      "<rowsby>State</rowsby>" & _
      "<startdate>1/1/2001</startdate>" & _
      "<starttime>00:00:00AM</starttime>" & _
      "<interval>Quarter</interval>" & _
      "<datacolumns>4</datacolumns>" & _
      "<count>No</count>" & _
      "<avgvalue>No</avgvalue>" & _
      "<rowtotals>Yes</rowtotals>" & _
      "<coltotals>Yes</coltotals>" & _
      "<nulltozero>Yes</nulltozero>" & _
      "<format>XML</format>" & _
   "</timeseries>" & _
"</crosstab>"
strResponse = xwsQtrOrders.wsm_TimeSeriesReport(strRequestDoc)
End Sub
```

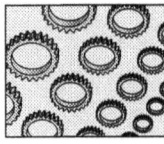

NOTE

You don't need to add the formatting whitespace in the preceding code.

6. Add a breakpoint to the `End Sub` statement and press F5 to compile and run the code. Check the value of `strReponse` in the Immediate window. (See Figure 9-12.)

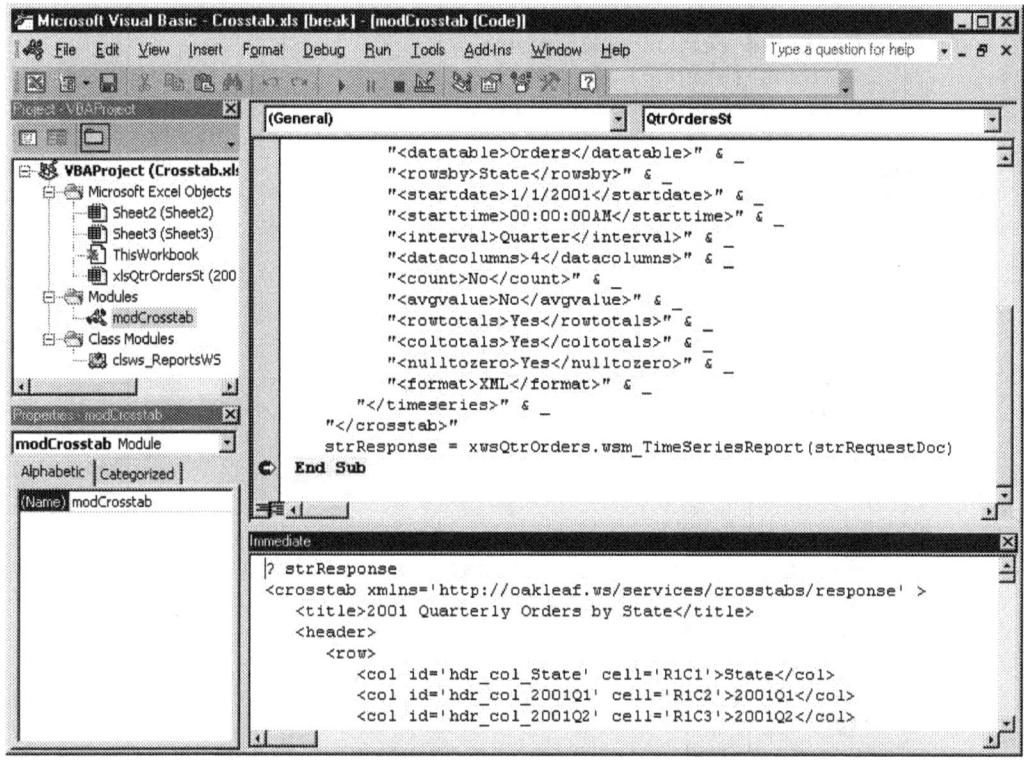

Figure 9-12 *Running the VBA QtrOrdersSt macro returns the expected response document to* `strResponse`.

Phase 2: Extract and Assign the Element Values to Cells

You can use VBA string manipulation code or the MSXML parser to extract element text values from the XML response document. The structure of the ReportsWS XML response document is consistent, so a single subprocedure to populate cell values can serve multiple worksheets. This example uses the `MSXML2` v. 4.0 parser, which loads the entire response document into memory.

1. Add a reference to Microsoft XML v. 4.0 to Module1.

2. Add the following code to extract the element text values and insert it in the appropriate cell of the active worksheet:

```
Private Sub WriteCrosstab(ByVal strDoc As String)
    'Generic code for writing crosstab reports
    Dim domDoc As New MSXML2.DOMDocument40
    Dim domNode As IXMLDOMNode
    Dim domCol As IXMLDOMNodeList
    Dim domRow As IXMLDOMNodeList
    Dim xlsRange As Excel.Range
    Dim intRow As Integer
    Dim intCol As Integer
```

```
With domDoc
   'Load the response document
   .loadXML (strDoc)
   'Specify the header/row node
   Set domNode = .childNodes(0).childNodes(1).childNodes(0)
End With
'Create a node list for the columns
Set domCol = domNode.childNodes
With domCol
   For intCol = 0 To .Length - 1
      'Populate the column headers
      ActiveCell.Value = .Item(intCol).Text
      Set xlsRange = ActiveCell.Offset(0, 1)
      xlsRange.Activate
   Next intCol
End With

'Specify the data node
Set domNode = domDoc.childNodes(0).childNodes(2)
'Create a node list for the rows
Set domRow = domNode.childNodes
For intRow = 0 To domRow.Length - 1
   Set xlsRange = ActiveCell.Offset(1, -intCol)
   xlsRange.Activate
   'Create a node list for the columns of the row
   Set domCol = domRow.Item(intRow).childNodes
   For intCol = 0 To domCol.Length - 1
      'Populate the row header and data cells
      ActiveCell.Value = domCol.Item(intCol).Text
      Set xlsRange = ActiveCell.Offset(0, 1)
      xlsRange.Activate
   Next intCol
Next intRow
Range("A1").Activate
End Sub
```

3. Add a Call WriteCrosstab(strResponse) instruction immediately before the End Sub line of the QtrOrdersSt subprocedure, and remove the breakpoint you set in step 6 of the preceding section.

4. Press F5 to run the macro. Display the worksheet to test your work up to this point. (See Figure 9-13.)

Phase 3: Align and Format the Cells

Excel 2002 automatically detects numeric values, right-aligns the cells, and attempts to apply the correct numeric format. Excel formats cells with currency symbols as currency, but formats other numeric cells as number, which causes the misalignment illustrated in Figure 9-13. Column header cells are right-aligned and, to conform the presentation to the HTML version,

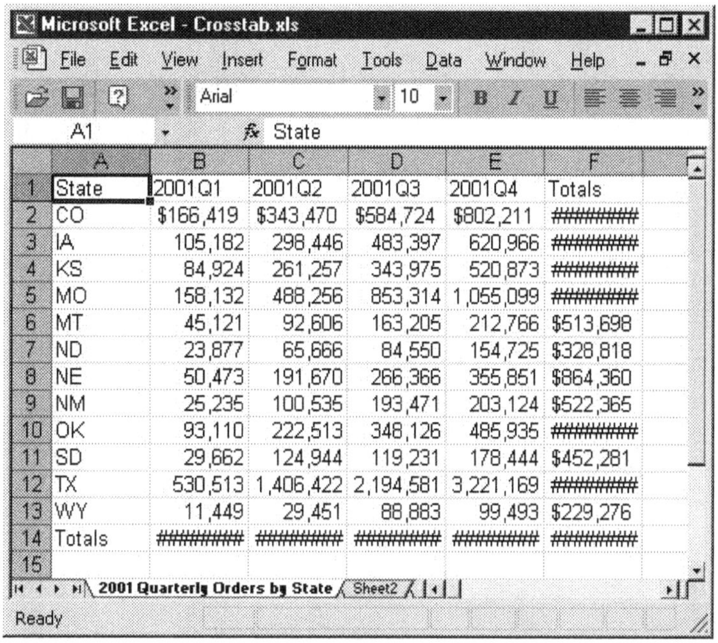

	A	B	C	D	E	F
1	State	2001Q1	2001Q2	2001Q3	2001Q4	Totals
2	CO	$166,419	$343,470	$584,724	$802,211	########
3	IA	105,182	298,446	483,397	620,966	########
4	KS	84,924	261,257	343,975	520,873	########
5	MO	158,132	488,256	853,314	1,055,099	########
6	MT	45,121	92,606	163,205	212,766	$513,698
7	ND	23,877	65,666	84,550	154,725	$328,818
8	NE	50,473	191,670	266,366	355,851	$864,360
9	NM	25,235	100,535	193,471	203,124	$522,365
10	OK	93,110	222,513	348,126	485,935	########
11	SD	29,662	124,944	119,231	178,444	$452,281
12	TX	530,513	1,406,422	2,194,581	3,221,169	########
13	WY	11,449	29,451	88,883	99,493	$229,276
14	Totals	########	########	########	########	########
15						

Figure 9-13 *The crosstab worksheet displays the data delivered by the ReportsWS XML Web service with default Excel formatting.*

the State column needs to be centered. You also need to apply AutoFit to the columns to display currency values of $1 million or more.

To correct the cell alignment, numeric formatting, and column width problems, add the following code to the `WriteCrosstab` subprocedure immediately before the `Range("A1").Activate` instruction:

```
Range(Cells(1, 1), Cells(intRow + 1, intCol + 1)).Columns.AutoFit
Range(Cells(1, 1), Cells(intRow + 1,
   intCol + 1)).HorizontalAlignment = xlRight
Range(Cells(1, 1), Cells(intRow + 1, 1)).HorizontalAlignment = xlCenter
Range(Cells(3, 2), Cells(intRow, intCol)).NumberFormat = _
   "#,##0_);(#,##0)"
```

You can tweak the right-alignment of the column headers by adding a trailing space to the text returned from the `<header>` columns.

After you've fixed the formatting, add a button to execute the QtrOrdersSt macro and, optionally, apply AutoFormat to the worksheet. (See Figure 9-14.) Following is the instruction to AutoFormat the cells:

```
Range(Cells(1, 1), Cells(intRow + 1, intCol)).AutoFormat _
   Format:=xlRangeAutoFormatList2, Number:=True, Font:= True, _
   Alignment:=False, Border:=True, Pattern:=True, Width:=False
```

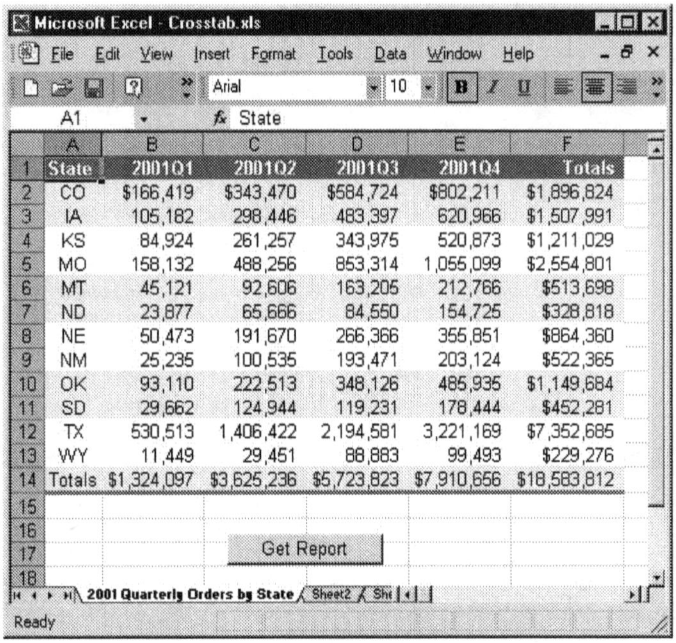

State	2001Q1	2001Q2	2001Q3	2001Q4	Totals
CO	$166,419	$343,470	$584,724	$802,211	$1,896,824
IA	105,182	298,446	483,397	620,966	$1,507,991
KS	84,924	261,257	343,975	520,873	$1,211,029
MO	158,132	488,256	853,314	1,055,099	$2,554,801
MT	45,121	92,606	163,205	212,766	$513,698
ND	23,877	65,666	84,550	154,725	$328,818
NE	50,473	191,670	266,366	355,851	$864,360
NM	25,235	100,535	193,471	203,124	$522,365
OK	93,110	222,513	348,126	485,935	$1,149,684
SD	29,662	124,944	119,231	178,444	$452,281
TX	530,513	1,406,422	2,194,581	3,221,169	$7,352,685
WY	11,449	29,451	88,883	99,493	$229,276
Totals	$1,324,097	$3,625,236	$5,723,823	$7,910,656	$18,583,812

Figure 9-14 *Adding a few lines of VBA code formats the crosstab worksheet. A button lets users refresh the data retrieved from the XML Web service.*

Phase 4: Let Users Specify Crosstab Report Parameters

You can add to the workbook worksheets with modified request documents for different report parameters. The advantage of this approach is that saving the workbook saves the last version of each report.

Alternatively, add an Excel form with controls to emulate those of the ASP.NET Web Application that's described in the earlier "Transforming XML Crosstab Reports to Formatted Tables" section. You'll find that you can cut and paste to the VBA editor a substantial amount of the Visual Basic .NET code from CTOrders4.aspx.vb's `cmdResponse_Click` event handler. The changes for VBA compatibility primarily involve control and property names.

Applying Advanced XML Web Service Techniques

IN THIS CHAPTER:

T his book's preceding chapters and their code examples demonstrate data-intensive rpc/encoded and document/literal XML Web services, but don't delve into issues such as XSD request/response document schemas, message validation, and element datatype checking. The first half of this chapter shows you how to generate and modify XSD schemas for defining XML request and response documents, and how to use the schemas to validate SOAP message payloads. The remainder of the chapter deals with specialized topics, such as changing the SOAP default ASP.NET messaging format, using workarounds for slow or inoperative services, and adding SOAP extensions.

Validating XML Request and Response Messages with XSD Schemas

XML Web services that use the document/literal SOAP messaging format and specify XML documents for request and response messages generate very simple WSDL documents. Simplicity has its price—developers writing applications to consume the service can't gain a clue about the structure of the request and response XML documents from the WSDL file. Thus, you must provide potential users of your XML Web service with descriptions of the documents as XSD schemas, sample documents, or, preferably, both.

Providing developers with XSD schema for request documents enables client-side validation of XML request documents against the schema before making an attempt to consume the service. Similarly, clients can validate XML response documents to verify the structure and datatypes of the element but not, unfortunately, the validity of the data.

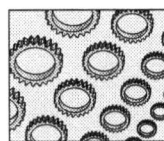

NOTE
Download into a \VBWS10 folder VBWS10.zip from this book's entries at http://www.osborne.com/ downloads/downloads.shtml. Before you open the CTSchema.sln sample solution, create a virtual directory named CTSchema and point its source to the \VBWS10\CTSchema subfolder. Running the project with the original (local) version of the Reports XML Web service generates an error; the later "Programming the XmlValidatingReader Object" section explains the source of the error and how to correct it. Don't open the \VBWS10\ReportsWS\ReportsWS.sln solution until you reach the "Applying Element Datatype Checking to XML Web Services" section near the middle of this chapter.

Generating Schemas with Xsd.exe

The .NET Framework offers a command-line XML Schema Definition Tool (Xsd.exe), which generates XSD schemas from XML files. You can make the resulting schema file (*MessageName*.xsd) available to developers from your Web site. Another option is to incorporate the schema document as a `<pre>` element in the `Description` attribute value of your .asmx page, if it's not too long. A side benefit of generating an XSD schema from typical request and response messages is that Xsd.exe detects violations of XML 1.0 encoding rules. Xsd.exe also enforces Microsoft's rules for creating relational `DataSet` objects from XSD schema.

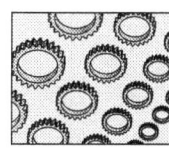

NOTE

Xsd.exe also translates XML Data-Reduced (XDR) schemas to XSD, XSD schemas to `DataSets`, XSD schemas to classes, and classes to XSD schemas.

To create standard XSD schema files from XML documents, using the request and response documents from Chapter 8's ReportsWS XML Web service as examples, do the following:

1. Simplify the command-line entry by adding to your desktop a shortcut to the Visual Studio .NET Command Prompt, if you haven't done so already. Alternatively, copy Xsd.exe from \Program Files\Microsoft Visual Studio .NET\Framework\SDK\Bin to the folder with your XML files, \VBWS11\CTSchema for this example.

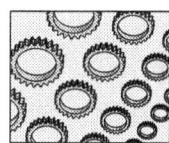

NOTE

VBWS10\CTSchema folder contains the CTRequest.xml and CTResponse.xml files you create in steps 2 through 6.

2. Create breakpoints in your client application at points where you can print the XML request and response strings to the Command window. The client application for this example is Chapter 9's CTOrders4.aspx Web form, and the breakpoints are on the `If chkRemoteWS.Checked Then` and `srdTable = New StringReader(strResponse)` instructions.

3. At the request breakpoint, print the variable to the Command window, open Notepad, copy the XML text without the quotes, and paste it into Notepad.

4. Type the filename with an .xml extension, **CTRequest.xml** for this example, select All Files in the Save As Type list, select UTF-8 in the Encoding list, and save the file in the folder containing Xsd.exe.

5. Repeat step 3 at the response breakpoint, replacing the request text with the response text.

6. Choose Save As, verify the All Files and UTF-8 selections, and save the response document as, for this example, **CTResponse.xml**.

7. Open a command prompt and, for this example, type **xsd CTRequest.xml** to generate the CTRequest.xsd schema file.

8. Open the .xsd file in IE to review its contents, as shown here for CTRequest.xsd.

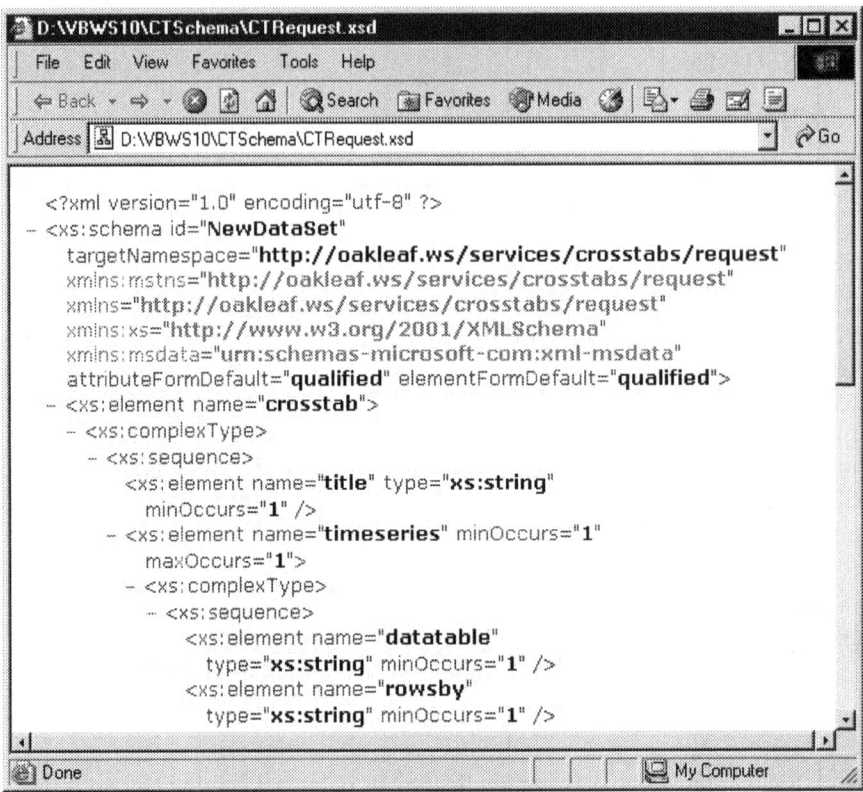

9. Type **xsd CTResponse.xml**. You receive the follow error message:

> "Error: There was an error processing 'CTResponse.xml'. The same table (row) cannot be the child table in two nested relations."

The `XmlTextReader` object of CTReports.aspx.vb's `FillTable` subprocedure doesn't complain about duplication of `<row>` subelements in the `<header>` and `<data>` elements. The problem lies with Xsd.exe's determination to create a schema from which you can generate a `DataSet` object.

Eliminating Nested Relation Errors

Eliminating the nested relation errors in the response document requires renaming the `<row>` and `<col>` elements of the `<header>` section, which is one of the two nested relations; the other is `<data>`. Following in boldface are the changes required to the `<header>` section:

```
<header>
<hdrcols>
    <hdrcol id='hdr_col_State' cell='R1C1'>State</hdrcol>
    <hdrcol id='hdr_col_2001Q1' cell='R1C2'>2001Q1</hdrcol>
    <hdrcol id='hdr_col_2001Q2' cell='R1C3'>2001Q2</hdrcol>
    <hdrcol id='hdr_col_2001Q3' cell='R1C4'>2001Q3</hdrcol>
    <hdrcol id='hdr_col_2001Q4' cell='R1C5'>2001Q4</hdrcol>
    <hdrcol id='hdr_col_Totals' cell='R1C6'>Totals</hdrcol>
</hdrcols>
</header>
```

The replacement element names you choose aren't important; the only requirement is that the names not duplicate those of the `<data>` section. The client application expects a specific sequence of `<header>` and `<data>` values, but the `TimeSeriesReport` method's `XmlTextReader` object doesn't check element names. After you make the changes in Notepad, running xsd CTResponse.xml returns CTResponse.xsd, part of which is shown here.

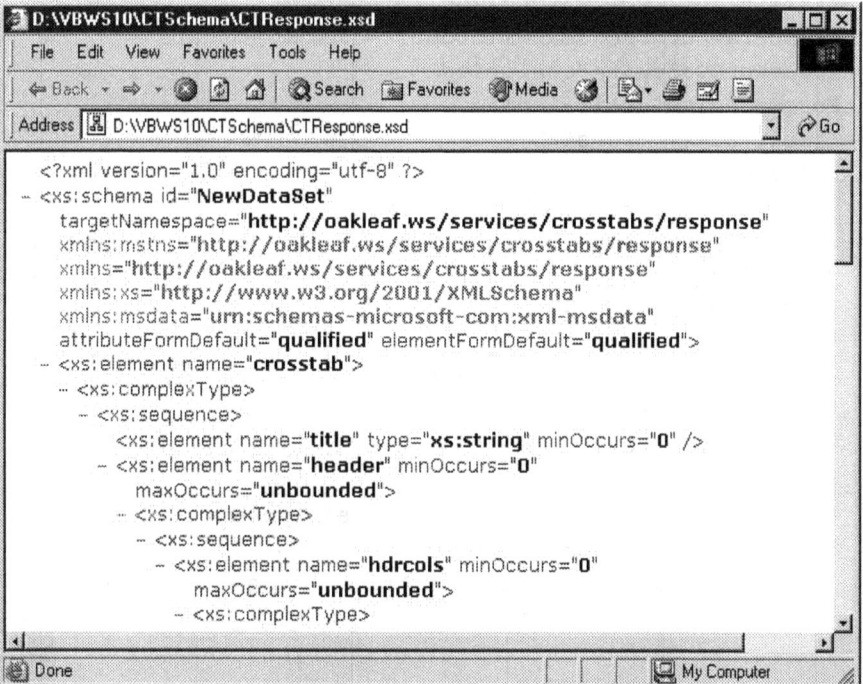

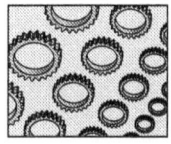

NOTE

The corrected CTResponse.xml file is \VBWS10\CTSchemas\CTResponse1.xml; the schema is CTResponse1.xsd.

Mandating Request Document Elements

The ReportsWS service's `TimeSeriesReport` method requires values for each element of the request document. If an element is missing, the `ReadElementString("element name")` method throws an error because the argument value doesn't match the current element name. Xsd.exe isn't aware of this restriction and designates elements as optional with `minOccurs="0"` attributes.

To require presence of every element in the request document, change the `minOccurs` value to **1** for each of the elements. Change the `TimeSeries` element's `maxOccurs="unbounded"` attribute to `maxOccurs="1"`, because the service accepts only a single report instance. Following is the final version of the CTRequest.xsd schema, which is saved as \VBWS10\CTSchema\CTRequest1.xsd:

```xml
<?xml version="1.0" encoding="utf-8"?>
<xs:schema id="NewDataSet"
    targetNamespace="http://oakleaf.ws/services/crosstabs/request"
    xmlns:mstns="http://oakleaf.ws/services/crosstabs/request"
    xmlns="http://oakleaf.ws/services/crosstabs/request"
    xmlns:xs="http://www.w3.org/2001/XMLSchema"
    xmlns:msdata="urn:schemas-microsoft-com:xml-msdata"
    attributeFormDefault="qualified"
elementFormDefault="qualified">
  <xs:element name="crosstab">
    <xs:complexType>
      <xs:sequence>
        <xs:element name="title" type="xs:string" minOccurs="1" />
        <xs:element name="timeseries" minOccurs="1" maxOccurs="1">
          <xs:complexType>
            <xs:sequence>
              <xs:element name="datatable" type="xs:string"
                minOccurs="1" />
              <xs:element name="rowsby" type="xs:string"
                minOccurs="1" />
              <xs:element name="startdate" type="xs:string"
                minOccurs="1" />
              <xs:element name="starttime" type="xs:string"
                minOccurs="1" />
              <xs:element name="interval" type="xs:string"
                minOccurs="1" />
              <xs:element name="datacolumns" type="xs:string"
                minOccurs="1" />
              <xs:element name="count" type="xs:string"
                minOccurs="1" />
              <xs:element name="avgvalue" type="xs:string"
                minOccurs="1" />
              <xs:element name="rowtotals" type="xs:string"
```

```
                    minOccurs="1" />
              <xs:element name="coltotals" type="xs:string"
                    minOccurs="1" />
              <xs:element name="nulltozero" type="xs:string"
                    minOccurs="1" />
              <xs:element name="format" type="xs:string"
                    minOccurs="1" />
            </xs:sequence>
          </xs:complexType>
        </xs:element>
      </xs:sequence>
    </xs:complexType>
  </xs:element>
  <xs:element name="NewDataSet" msdata:IsDataSet="true">
    <xs:complexType>
      <xs:choice maxOccurs="unbounded">
        <xs:element ref="crosstab" />
      </xs:choice>
    </xs:complexType>
  </xs:element>
</xs:schema>
```

The added `NewDataSet` element at the bottom of the preceding schema is the key to defining relational `DataSet` objects by schemas you create with Xsd.exe and the Visual Studio .NET XML Designer tools. In Visual Studio .NET, `DataSet`s and XSD schemas are interchangeable; a `DataSet` is a deserialized XSD schema. `NewDataSet` is the default name for the `DataSet` object; you can change the name in the XML Designer. The later "Working with Visual Studio .NET's XML Designer" section shows you how to use the XML Designer with XML documents and XSD schemas.

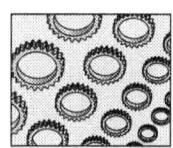

NOTE

Presence of a proprietary element based on the `urn:schemas-microsoft-com:xml-msdata` namespace doesn't affect non-Microsoft-consuming clients, which ignore the `DataSet`-related elements.

Programming the XmlValidatingReader Object

Validating XML request and response documents with XSD schema isn't a simple process. Following is a condensed list of the steps involved:

1. Add an `Imports System.Xml.Schema` instruction to your class. This namespace contains the classes for manipulating XSD and XDR schemas, and Document Type Definitions (DTDs).

2. Declare a class-level variable of the `XmlSchemaCollection` class in the project's initialization event handler—`Page_Load` for an ASP.NET page or `Sub New` for XML Web service and Windows form projects.

3. Cache the schema files for the request and response documents by adding them to the `XmlSchemaCollection` object with the `Add` method. Assign the Universal Resource Name (URN) of the document's namespace as the schema name. You can specify the .xsd file by name or provide a URL to a local or remote .xsd file.

4. In the event handler that generates the request document, create an instance of a `StringReader` object from the request or response document's `String` variable.

5. Populate an `XmlTextReader` object with the `StringReader`, and populate an `XmlValidatingReader` object with the `XmlTextReader`.

6. Add a callback event-handling subprocedure to intercept and report validation errors.

7. Assign the `XmlSchemaCollection` to the `XmlValidatingReader` by invoking its `Schemas.Add(SchemaCollectionName)` method.

8. Attach the validation event handler with the `XmlValidatingReader.AddHandler` method.

9. Execute an `XmlValidatingReader.Read` loop to validate the XML document against the schema specified as the value of the document's `xmlns` attribute.

The following sections use the CTSchema ASP.NET Web form project in your \VBWS10\CTSchema folder to demonstrate client-side XML document validation. The CTSchema.sln solution derives from Chapter 9's CTReports.sln. Most of the validation code in CTSchema.aspx.vb also applies to XML message document validation by ASP.NET XML Web services.

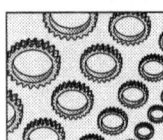

NOTE

The CTSchema ASP.NET client consumes on the local ReportsWS XML Web service's ReportsWS virtual directory, which points to the \VBWS08\ReportsWS folder. If you haven't set up the virtual directory, see the note on the first page of Chapter 8 for downloading instructions.

Caching XSD Schemas in the XmlSchemaCollection

The `XmlSchemaCollection` object provides the `XmlValidatingReader` object with an instance of the schema for the XML document's namespace. Following is the generic code for adding XSD schemas to the collection:

```
Private xscName As XmlSchemaCollection
...
xscName = New XmlSchemaCollection()
xscName.Add(strXMLNamespace1, strFileOrURL1)
xscName.Add(strXMLNamespace2, strFileOrURL2)
...
```

Visual Studio .NET's "XML Schema (XSD) Validation with XmlSchemaCollection" online help topic claims that caching XSD schemas in an `XmlSchemaCollection` improves performance by storing schemas so the application doesn't need to load them into memory for each validation operation. This benefit applies only to Windows forms, because loading ASP.NET pages and instantiating XML Web services reloads the cache. Reloading the cache from a local file is fast—usually 10 to 50 ms—but Internet latency adds a performance hit if you rely on a remote schema file.

Following is the code in CTSchema.aspx.vb's `Page_Load` event handler to load the CTRequest1.xsd and CTRequest2.xsd schemas from a local Web server:

```
xscCrosstabs = New XmlSchemaCollection()
With xscCrosstabs
   'Add the schema files to the cache
   .Add("http://oakleaf.ws/services/crosstabs/request", _
      "http://localhost/CTSchema/CTRequest1.xsd")
   .Add("http://oakleaf.ws/services/crosstabs/response", _
      "http://localhost/CTSchema/CTResponse1.xsd")
End With
```

Adding the XmlValidatingReader

The `XmlValidatingReader` requires an `XmlTextReader`, which in turn requires a `StringReader` to deserialize the XML document, `strXML` for this example. Here's the code in the `cmdResponse_Click` event handler to create `XmlTextReader`:

```
Dim srdRequest As New StringReader(strXML)
Dim xtrRequest As New XmlTextReader(srdRequest)
Dim xvrRequest As New XmlValidatingReader(xtrRequest)
```

Writing the Validation Error Callback Event Handler

The `XmlValidatingReader` object raises an event for each validation error it detects. You must add a callback event-handling subprocedure to serve as an event sink and process the errors. A single event handler can serve multiple validation operations.

For this example, the `ValidationError` handler displays validation error messages in a Label server control and sets the `blnValid` flag to `False`, which terminates the service request operation. Here's the CTSchema code:

```
Private Sub ValidationError(ByVal sender As Object, _
      ByVal args As ValidationEventArgs)
   'Common callback function for intercepting request
   'and response validation errors
   lblError.Text += args.Message.ToString
   lblError.Visible = True
   tblReport.Visible = False
   blnValid = False
End Sub
```

For an XML Web service, returning a custom SOAP fault message with a `SoapFault` object is the best alternative, because an XML error response message won't pass the client's response document validation test. In this case, the consuming client must include code to handle the SOAP fault message.

Performing the Validation

The final validation steps involve attaching the `XmlSchemaCollection` to the `XmlValidatingReader`, specifying the callback event handler, and processing the XML document. Following is the remaining code to validate the request message against the CTRequest1.xsd schema:

```
With xvrRequest
   .Schemas.Add(xscCrosstabs)
   AddHandler .ValidationEventHandler, AddressOf ValidationError
   While .Read
      'Process the document
   End While
   .Close()
End With
```

The `FillTable` method contains the same validation code as that of the `cmdResponse_Click` event handler; the only differences are names of objects.

Testing the Validation Process

Testing the validation process requires more than just running the client application and observing that no errors occur. You must induce an error to verify that the `XmlValidatingReader` and your callback event handler report all errors.

Chapter 8's ReportsWS XML Web service returns response messages that don't conform to the revised XML document structure, which is described in the earlier "Eliminating Nested Relation Errors" section. Thus, attempting to consume your local version of ReportsWS should fire `ValidationError` events. Commenting one of the `<elementName>` lines in the `cmdResponse_Click` event handler's `strXML =` instruction should display a validation error message for the request document.

The `XMLValidatingReader` object fires an event for each error it encounters. When you click CTSchema.aspx's Get Report button with the Remote WS check box cleared, the page displays the eight error messages shown in Figure 10-1, all of which result from element name mismatches for the `<header>` section. The error messages include the namespace URI, which identifies the request or response message as the culprit. The numbers in parenthesis are the line number and character position of the source XML document that failed the validation process.

The OakLeaf Web site's version of ReportsWS returns a response document that conforms to the CTResponse1.xsd schema. Marking the Remote WS check box and clicking Get Report displays the report you specify. The `Description` attribute value of the remote WSDL document at http://www.oakleaf.ws/ReportsWS/ReportsWS.asmx has HTML links

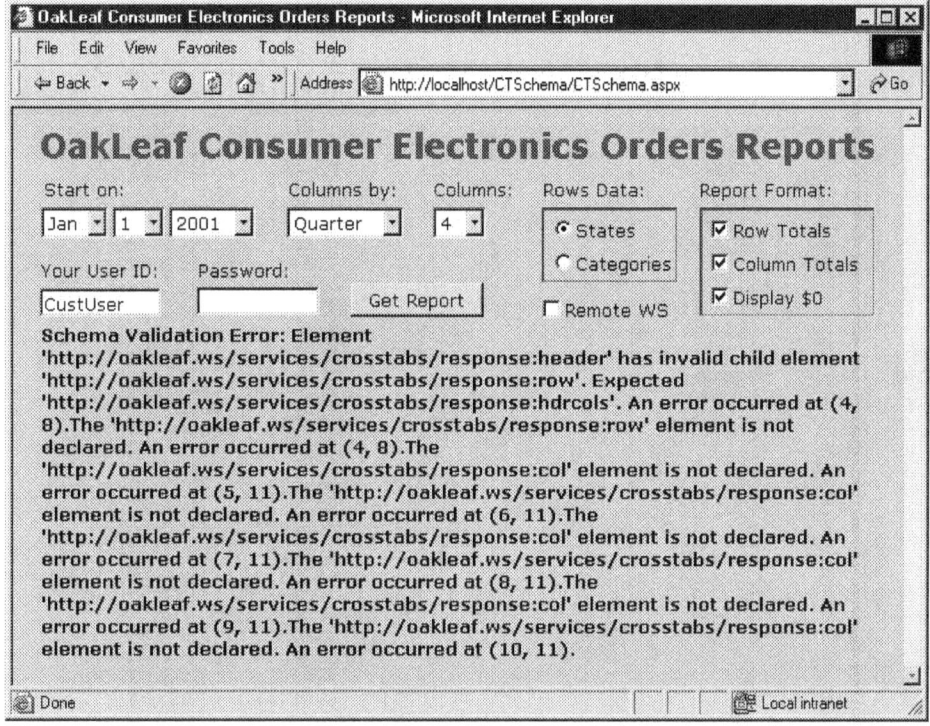

Figure 10-1   *Chapter 8's version of the ReportsWS XML Web service returns response messages that don't conform to the CTResponse1.xsd schema, so you receive the error message shown here.*

to the CTRequest and CTResponse schemas, which are copies of CTRequest1.xsd and CTResponse1.xsd. If you want to test the latency of schema requests over the Internet, substitute **http://www.oakleaf.ws/** for http://localhost/ as the location argument for the XmlSchemaCollection.Add method call.

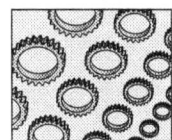

NOTE

The modifications made to the OakLeaf Web site's production version of ReportsWS violate the immutable <WebMethod> rule, which parallels the immutable interface rule for COM components. In this case, Chapter 8's Windows form consumer and Chapter 9's Web Form consumer don't test response message element names, so the changes don't affect these applications. It's a better design practice, however, to add a new <WebMethod> when you change the schema for the XML document the method consumes or produces.

Measuring Validation's Effect on Consumer Performance

CTSchema.aspx.vb includes Trace.Write method calls to measure the elapsed time for caching schemas and performing the two validation operations. Tracing is enabled for the CTSchema project but not for the CTReports.sln solution. You can generate a Trace.axd file from the remote ReportsWS service, but not from your local version. Figure 10-2 shows a trace report for the second client request to return the default crosstab report in a single session.

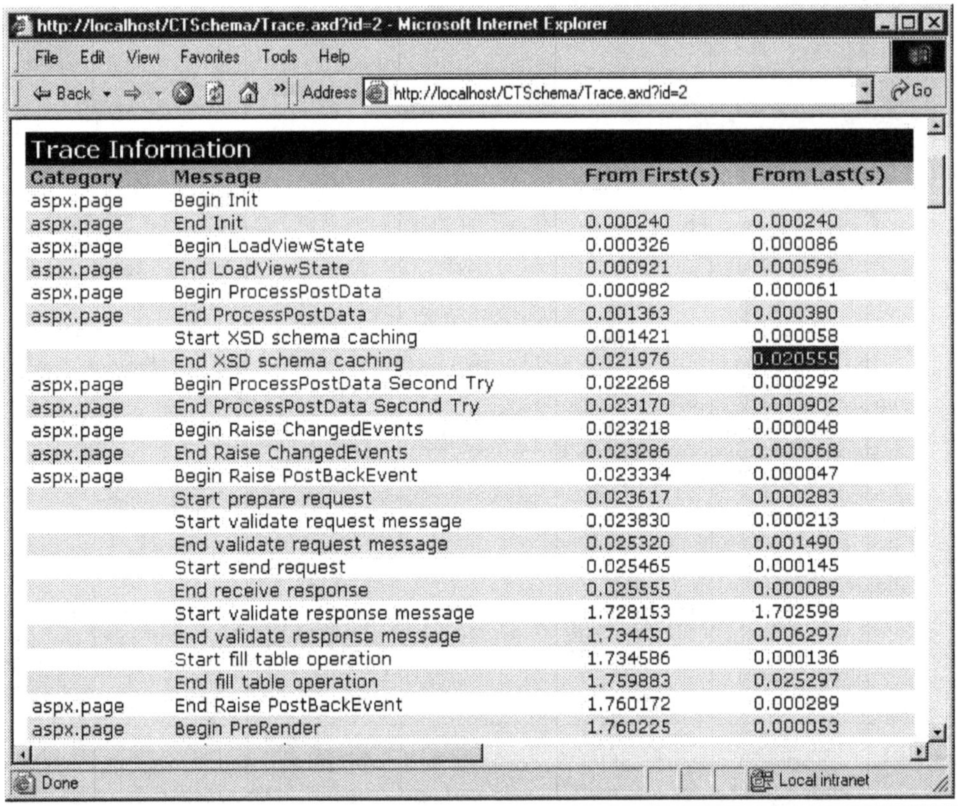

Figure 10-2   *The Trace.axd page shows that caching the XSD schema files requires about 20 ms.*

Validation's overall performance impact is about 25 to 30 ms for a client page running on an 833-MHz server with an UltraDMA/66 IDE drive. You can expect a similar performance hit from adding XSD schema validation code to your XML Web services.

Modifying the Local ReportsWS Service to Permit Tracing

If you modify the code for your local version of the ReportsWS XML Web service to generate a response document that conforms to the CTResponse1.xsd schema, you receive an untrapped Trace error when you click the Get Report button. Trace won't work if duplicate `id` attribute values exist in the page. ReportsWS generates a response document having `id='total'` attribute values for all row and column totals, which the client's `FillTable` subprocedure assigns to table cells.

To fix the Trace problem, comment out ReportsWS.asmx.vb's following two instructions:

```
If intRow = UBound(astrCT, 1) Or intCol = UBound(astrCT, 2) Then
    strAttrib = "id='total' cell='R" + CStr(intRow + 1) + _
        "C" + CStr(intCol + 1) + "'"
```

Replace the lines with this:

```
If intRow = UBound(astrCT, 1) Then
    strAttrib = "id='total_col" + CStr(intCol + 1) + _
       "' cell='R" + CStr(intRow + 1) + "C" + CStr(intCol + 1) + "'"
ElseIf intCol = UBound(astrCT, 2) Then
    strAttrib = "id='total_row" + CStr(intRow + 1) + _
       "' cell='R" + CStr(intRow + 1) + "C" + CStr(intCol + 1) + "'"
```

The preceding changes substitute `total_row#` and `total_col#` for the ambiguous `total` attribute values. CTResponse2.xml is a sample response document returned by the ReportsWS service's modified `TimeSeriesReport` method.

NOTE

Changing attribute values doesn't affect the XML data document's schema. If you modify the attribute name or add or delete attributes, you must recreate the XSD schema.

Working with Visual Studio .NET's XML Designer

Several earlier chapters of this book mention that teaching the fundamentals of XML, as well as XSD, XSL/T, and other XML derivatives, is beyond its scope. On the other hand, many seasoned Visual Basic developers will undoubtedly cut their XML eyeteeth on XML Web services. Thus, Visual Studio .NET's XML Designer warrants at least basic coverage in this chapter on advanced XML Web service techniques.

The XML Designer offers the following three views of XML data and schema documents:

▶ **Schema view**   Displays a relationship diagram of an .xsd schema file and its corresponding typed `DataSet` object. The read-only `DataSet` diagram reflects modifications you make to the XSD schema.

▶ **Data view**   Displays the contents of an XML document in a `DataGrid` control with an inferred XSD schema, which you can save as a *DataDocName*.xsd file. You can edit element values, and add or delete elements.

▶ **XML view**   Displays an XML data or schema document with color coding and error detection. Statement completion is available for .xsd files and .xml data document files that have an associated XSD schema.

The following sections show you how to use the three XML Designer views with the sample XML CTResponse# data documents and schema. The VBWS10\CTSchema folder holds the sample .xml and .xsd files, which are included in the project.

TIP

To associate .xml and .xsd files with your project, in Solution Explorer, right-click the file node and choose Include In Project.

Schema View

Opening an existing XSD file in the Visual Studio .NET IDE automatically displays its schema and `DataSet` diagrams in Schema view. Schema view consists of a set of element boxes connected by lines representing parent-child relationships between elements. An *E* identifies elements, *A* specifies attributes, and *G* represents groups or sequences. Figure 10-3 shows part of the schema page for CTResponse1.xsd. You can change the $xsd:datatype$ of elements and attributes from a drop-down list in the second column of the element box. Clicking the XML button at the bottom of the window displays color-coded text of the schema in the XML editor page.

NOTE

When you save the SchemaName.xsd file, Visual Studio .NET adds a SchemaName.xsx file, which stores the layout of the Schema view.

Figure 10-3 *The Visual Studio .NET IDE's Schema view displays diagrams of XSD documents and corresponding typed **DataSet** objects.*

Right-clicking the page and choosing Preview Data Set opens the Dataset Properties dialog shown here. This dialog represents each element of the schema as a `DataTable` member of the default NewDataSet `DataSet` object.

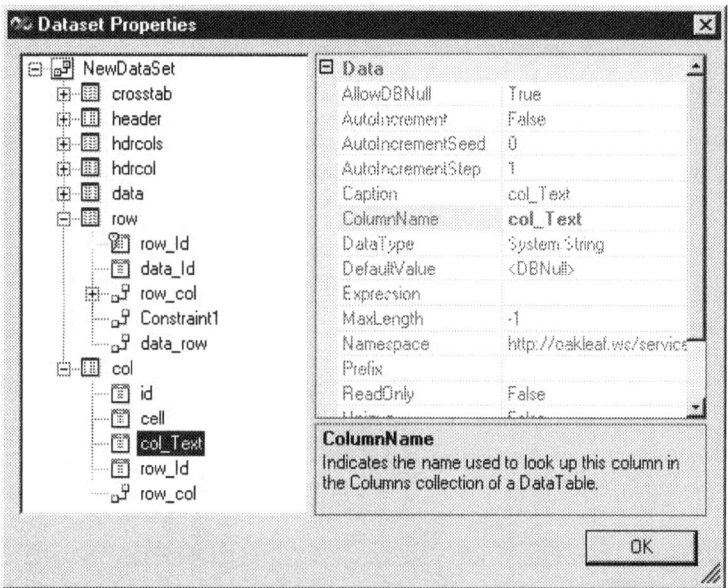

CAUTION

Right-clicking the Schema page for CTResponse1.xsd and choosing Generate Dataset creates a 2000-line Visual Basic .NET `NewDataSet` class (CTResponse1.vb) that contains a multitude of errors, won't build, and prevents your project from running. The Generate Dataset command works correctly with CTRequest1.xsd. If you accidentally create one of these classes, delete the SchemaName.vb file in Solution Explorer.

Data View

Data view lets you display request and response XML data documents in a `DataGrid` control or as text in the XML page. You can generate an XSD schema for the XML document in Data view by clicking the Create Schema button; alternatively, right-click the page and select Create Schema. Creating an XSD schema from a request or response document in Data view is quicker than using Xsd.exe. Like Xsd.exe, you can't create a schema that doesn't pass `DataSet` muster. For example, you receive the error message shown here if you attempt to generate a schema from CTResponse.xml.

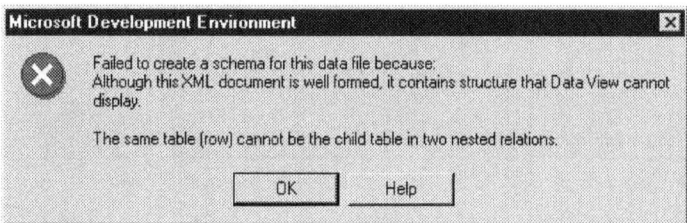

CAUTION

If you include multiple XSD schemas named DataDocName#.xsd — where # is 1 or greater — for a DataDocName.xml data document, Data view loads the numbered schema. For example, when you open CTResponse.xml and CTResponse1.xsd is included in the project, the XML view of CTResponse.xml displays the error message "The active schema does not support the element 'col'" for `<col>` elements of the `<header>` section.

Figure 10-4 shows the first few rows of data in the `<data><rows><cols>` section of the CTResponse1.xml data document. You can edit, add, and delete elements if the operation doesn't violate constraints imposed by the schema, such as `minOccurs="1"` or `maxOccurs="1"`.

XML View

XML view presents color-coded text of the XML data or XSD schema document. Figure 10-5 shows the original CTResponse.xml document in XML view. The squiggly underline and error message report the problem with duplicate `id` values addressed in the earlier "Modifying the

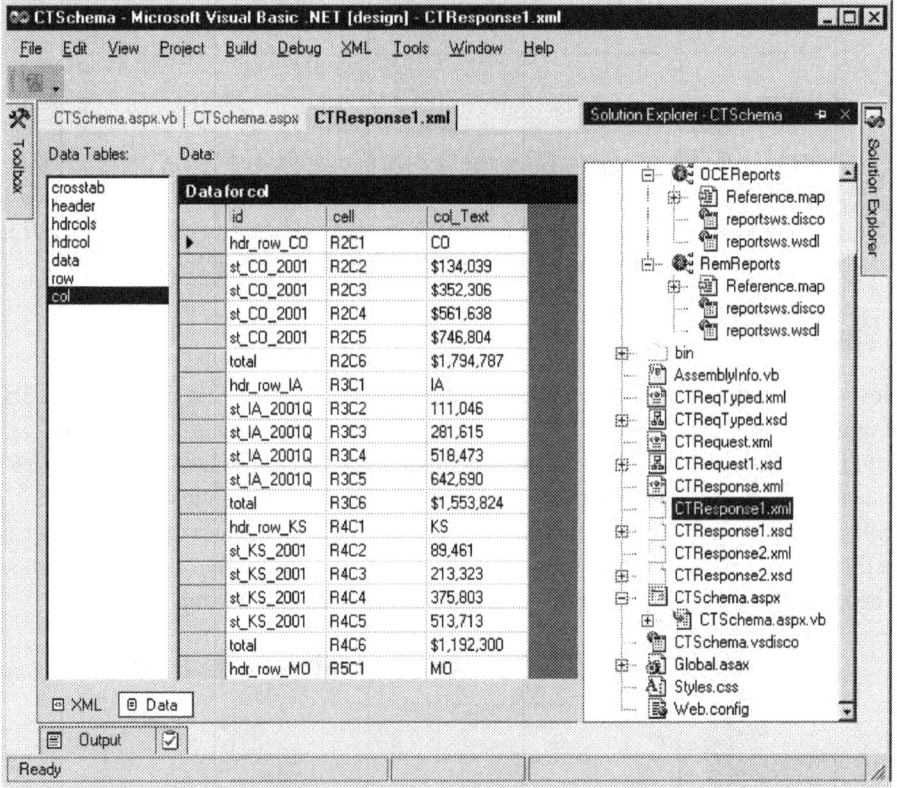

Figure 10-4 *Data view of an XML data document treats the document as a collection of editable DataTable objects.*

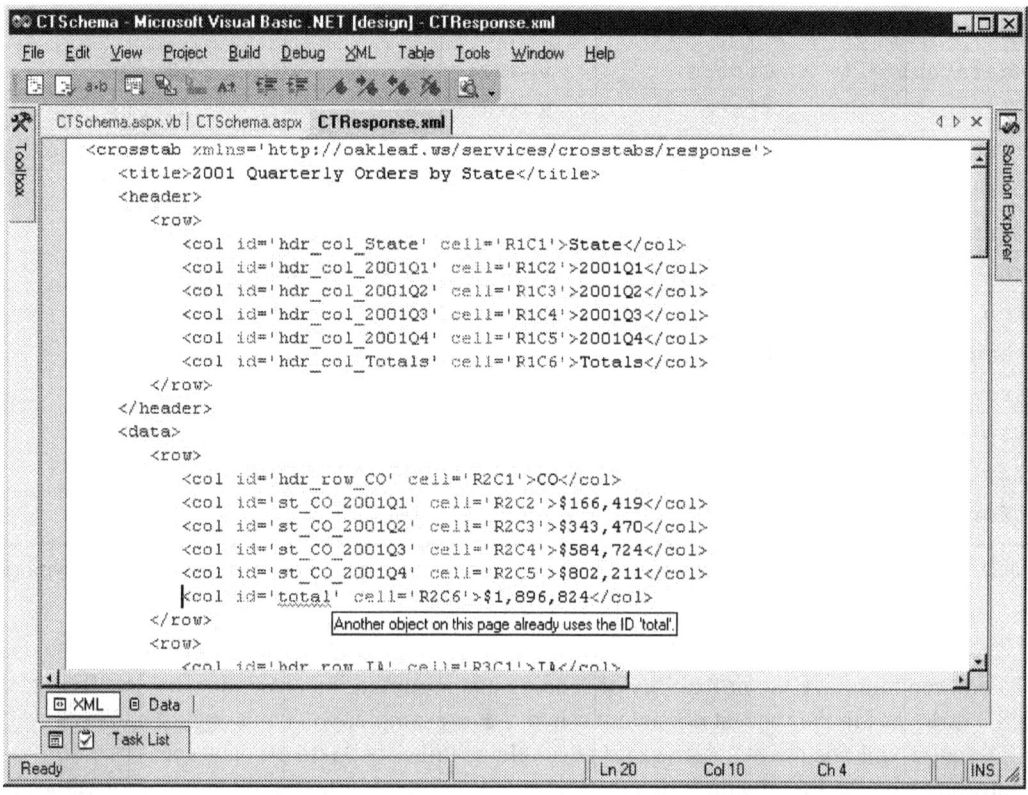

```
<crosstab xmlns='http://oakleaf.ws/services/crosstabs/response'>
    <title>2001 Quarterly Orders by State</title>
    <header>
        <row>
            <col id='hdr_col_State' cell='R1C1'>State</col>
            <col id='hdr_col_2001Q1' cell='R1C2'>2001Q1</col>
            <col id='hdr_col_2001Q2' cell='R1C3'>2001Q2</col>
            <col id='hdr_col_2001Q3' cell='R1C4'>2001Q3</col>
            <col id='hdr_col_2001Q4' cell='R1C5'>2001Q4</col>
            <col id='hdr_col_Totals' cell='R1C6'>Totals</col>
        </row>
    </header>
    <data>
        <row>
            <col id='hdr_row_CO' cell='R2C1'>CO</col>
            <col id='st_CO_2001Q1' cell='R2C2'>$166,419</col>
            <col id='st_CO_2001Q2' cell='R2C3'>$343,470</col>
            <col id='st_CO_2001Q3' cell='R2C4'>$584,724</col>
            <col id='st_CO_2001Q4' cell='R2C5'>$802,211</col>
            <col id='total' cell='R2C6'>$1,896,824</col>
        </row>
        <row>
            <col id='hdr_row_IA' cell='R3C1'>IA</col>
```

Another object on this page already uses the ID 'total'.

Figure 10-5 *XML view displays XML documents as color-coded text and identifies problematic elements similarly to the code editor's handling of Visual Basic .NET syntax errors.*

Local ReportsWS Service to Permit Tracing" section. Right-clicking the page and choosing Synchronize Document Outline opens a Document Outline pane.

Specifying XSD Datatypes in XML Request Documents

The CTRequest.xsd schema for CTRequest.xml documents handles basic document validation, but it can't determine whether the values of the `xsd:string` elements of the datatype are formatted in accordance with the XML Web services requirements. The ReportsWS service's `TimeSeriesReport` method also doesn't test the validity of the element datatypes. A malformed string value in the request document can throw exceptions or—even worse—return an incorrect response document.

TIP

Open W3C's XML Schema Part 2: Datatypes recommendation page at http://www.w3.org/TR/xmlschema-2/ in preparation for making the datatype changes in the following sections.

Element Name	String Value	XSD Datatype	Canonical Value
`<datatable>`	Orders	xsd:string	Orders
`<rowsby>`	State	xsd:string	State
`<startdate>`	1/1/2001	xsd:date	2001-01-01
`<starttime>`	00:00:00AM	xsd:time	00:00:00
`<interval>`	Quarter	xsd:string	Quarter
`<datacolumns>`	4	xsd:nonNegativeIteger	4
`<count>`	No	xsd:boolean	false
`<avgvalue>`	No	xsd:boolean	false
`<rowtotals>`	Yes	xsd:boolean	true
`<coltotals>`	Yes	xsd:boolean	true
`<nulltozero>`	Yes	xsd:boolean	true
`<format>`	XML	xsd:string	XML

Table 10-1   *Suggested Xsd Datatypes and Canonical Representations of Values for Strong-Typing of* `TimeSeriesReport` *Request Documents*

You can minimize the probability of sending and accepting incorrect data by specifying XSD datatypes in the request document schema. For example, you can assign the CTRequest.xml document's `<startdate>` element the `xsd:date` datatype. Unfortunately, the literal values that the `TimeSeriesReport` method expects for values other than `xsd:string` don't correspond to the canonical representation of XSD datatypes. Table 10-1 above lists the XSD datatypes and canonical values required for strong-typing request document data.

Strongly typing element values of request XML documents provides the data-typing benefits of rpc/encoded SOAP message format in messages that use the document/literal format and XML request documents. The techniques described in the following sections also apply to SOAP response documents.

Creating the Strongly Typed Schema

The XML Designer's XML and Data views make it easy to generate an XML schema for a strongly typed request document. Following are the required steps with the CTRequest.xml data document serving as an example:

1. In Solution Explorer, copy and paste CTRequest.xml and rename the copy as **CTReqTyped.xml**.

2. Double-click CTReqTyped.xml to open it in XML view.

3. Right-click the XML page, and choose Create Schema to generate CTReqTyped.xsd.

4. In Solution Explorer, double-click CTReqTyped.xsd to display it in Schema view.

5. Select and expand the `timeseries` box to display all elements.

6. Open the `startdate` element's datatype list and select `date`.

7. Open the `starttime` list and select `time`.

8. Open the `datacolumns` list and select `nonNegativeInteger`.

9. Open the `count` list and select `boolean`.

10. Repeat step 9 for `avgvalue`, `rowtotals`, `coltotals`, and `nulltozero`.

11. Press CTRL-S to save your changes. (See Figure 10-6.)

Like Xsd.exe, the default attribute values for the `timeseries` section are `minOccurs="0"` and `maxOccurs="unbounded"`. To conform the schema to the original CTRequest.xsd version, do this:

1. Open the schema in XML view.

2. In the `timeseries` element line, change 0 to **1** and `unbounded` to **1**.

3. Add **`minOccurs="1"`** to each of the `<xs:sequence>` elements.

4. Press CTRL-S to save your changes. (See Figure 10-7.)

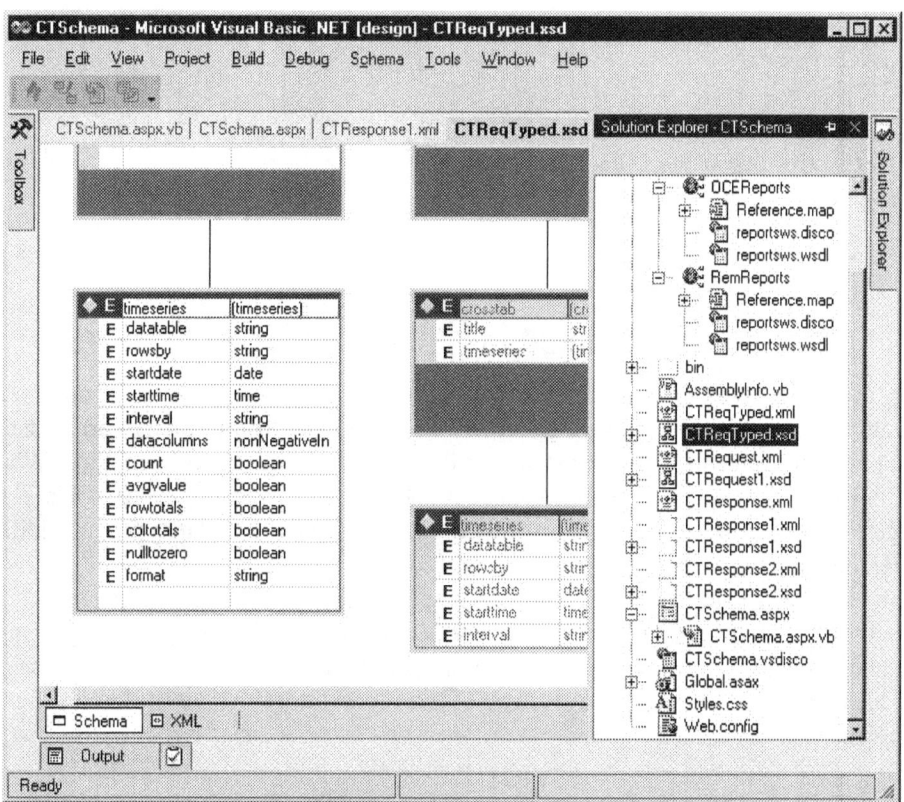

Figure 10-6 *This is the Schema view of CTReqTyped.xsd schema after making the XSD datatype changes listed in Table 10-1.*

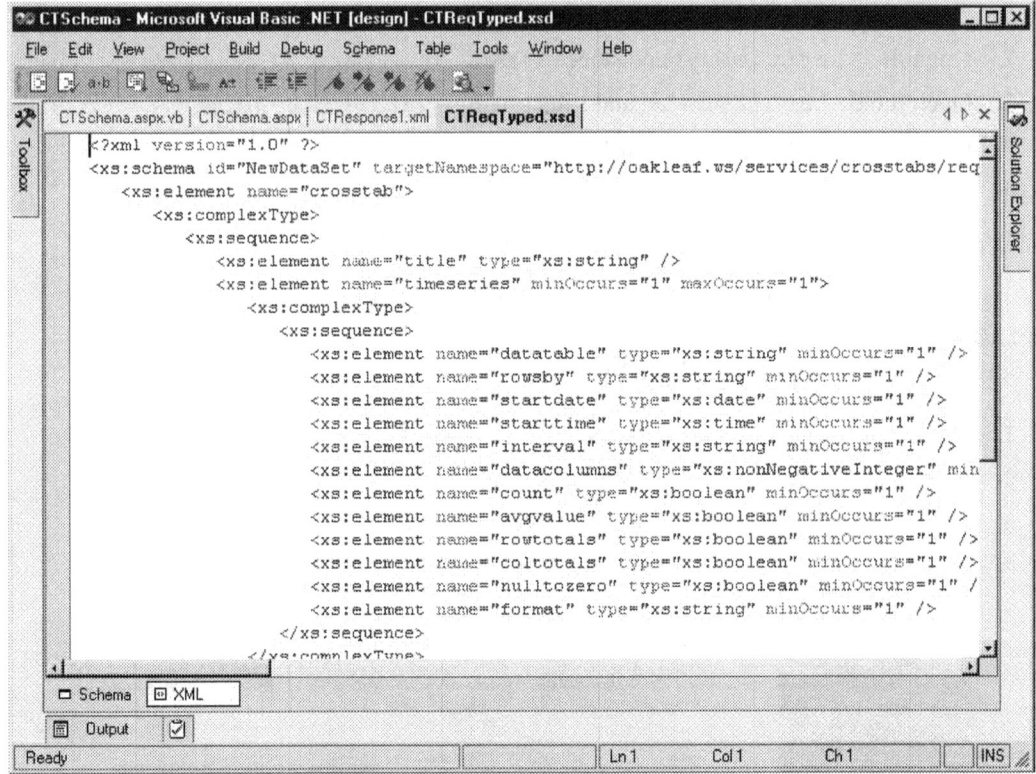

Figure 10-7   *XML view of the CTReqType.xsd file after making the changes described in this section*

Altering the Client Application to Handle the Typed Schema

Making the initial change to CTSchema.aspx.vb to cache CTReqType.xsd instead of CTRequest1.xsd is simple: change `CTRequest1.xsd` to **`CTReqTyped.xsd`** as the second argument value of the first instance of the **`xscCrosstabs.Add`** method. When you click Get Report, you receive the expected error message shown in Figure 10-8. The error message proves that the **`XmlValidatingReader`** validates XSL datatypes, in addition to the XML data document's structure.

To ease the testing process, the **`frmCTReport`** class has a **`Boolean`** flag (**`blnTyped`**) that's set to **`False`** by default. Setting **`blnTyped`** to **`True`** makes the preceding change to the cached schemas, turns off error-checking of the locally cached WSDL files for the Web References, and substitutes code to create an XML request document with canonically correct values.

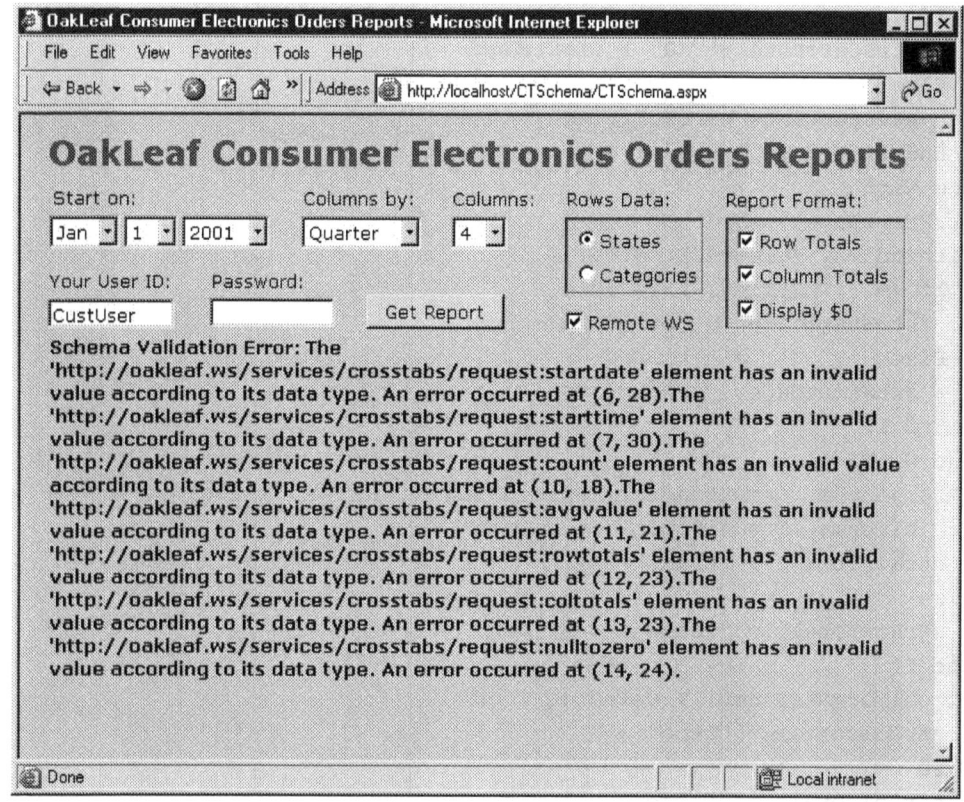

Figure 10-8   *Element values generated by the unmodified CTSchema client cause the*
xsd:datatype errors shown here.

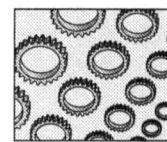

NOTE

A nonfatal 'types' run-time error in the Sub New subprocedure of the Web Reference sometimes occurs
when you change the membership of the XmlSchemaCollection object. If this error
repeats, uncomment On Error Resume Next, and the statement at the beginning of the
cmdResponse_Click event handler ignores the error. In this case, you must temporarily
remove the structured error-handling code near the end of the subprocedure.

Following is the code that the **cmdResponse_Click** event handler needs to generate
an XML document that complies with the strongly typed schema (important changes appear
in boldface):

```
If blnTyped Then
  'Change M/D/YYYY to CCYY-MM-DD
  strStartDate = ddlYear.SelectedItem.Value.ToString + "-"
  With ddlMonth.SelectedItem.Value
```

```
      If Val(.ToString) < 10 Then
        strStartDate += "0" + .ToString
      Else
        strStartDate += .ToString
      End If
    End With
    strStartDate += "-"
    With ddlDay.SelectedItem.Value
      If Val(.ToString) < 10 Then
        strStartDate += "0" + .ToString
      Else
        strStartDate += .ToString
      End If
    End With
    'Assign the formatting criteria using "true" or "false"
    If cblFormat.Items(0).Selected Then
      strRowTotals = "true"
    Else
      strRowTotals = "false"
    End If
    If cblFormat.Items(1).Selected Then
      strColTotals = "true"
    Else
      strColTotals = "false"
    End If
    If cblFormat.Items(2).Selected Then
      strNullToZero = "true"
    Else
      strNullToZero = "false"
    End If
    'Generate the request document with XSD canonical datatypes
    'for default values
    strXML = "<crosstab xmlns='http://oakleaf.ws/services/crosstabs/" + _
      "request' >" + strCrLf + _
      "  <title>" + strTitle + "</title>" + strCrLf + _
      "  <timeseries> " + strCrLf + _
      "    <datatable>Orders</datatable>" + strCrLf + _
      "    <rowsby>" + rblRowsBy.SelectedItem.Value.ToString + _
          "</rowsby>" + strCrLf + _
      "    <startdate>" + strStartDate + "</startdate>" + strCrLf + _
      "    <starttime>00:00:00</starttime>" + strCrLf + _
      "    <interval>" + ddlInterval.SelectedItem.ToString + _
          "</interval>" + strCrLf + _
      "    <datacolumns>" + ddlDataCols.SelectedItem.ToString + _
          "</datacolumns>" + strCrLf + _
```

```
"        <count>false</count>" + strCrLf + _
"        <avgvalue>false</avgvalue>" + strCrLf + _
"        <rowtotals>" + strRowTotals + "</rowtotals>" + strCrLf + _
"        <coltotals>" + strColTotals + "</coltotals>" + strCrLf + _
"        <nulltozero>" + strNullToZero + "</nulltozero>" + strCrLf + _
"        <format>XML</format>" + strCrLf + _
"    </timeseries>" + strCrLf + _
"</crosstab>"
Else
  'Original request document generation code omitted for brevity
End If
```

You must also change the If strRowTotals = "Yes" line in the FillTable
subprocedure to If **strRowTotals = "Yes" Or strRowTotals = "true"** Then to
provide the correct colspan value to the table header.

Surprisingly, the changes to the client code don't prevent the OakLeaf Web site's
production version of the ReportsWS service's TimeSeriesReport from returning a
report; only requested column and row totals are missing.

Fixing the ReportsWS XML Web Service

Fortunately, SQL Server and MSDE 2000 accept the ISO 8601 CCYY-MM-DD xsd:date
datatype and recognize the 24-hour clock format of the xsd:time datatype. Thus, the only
workaround that's required to make the TimeSeriesReport method fully operable is
acceptance of xsd:boolean true and false values as synonyms for Yes and No.

Following is a snippet from the TimeSeriesReport method that shows the change
required to equate true with Yes, using the <rowtotals> xsd:boolean element as
an example:

```
'If .ReadElementString("rowtotals") = "Yes" Then
   'strTemp = .ReadElementString("rowtotals")
If strTemp = "Yes" Or strTemp = "true" Then
   blnRowTotals = True
Else
   blnRowTotals = False
End If
```

Applying Element Datatype Checking to XML Web Services

After you've written and tested the client's strongly typed XML request document and its
XSD schema, validating the request document in the corresponding XML Web service is
basically a copy-and-paste operation. Moving to strong typing in a production environment

usually requires adding a new `<WebMethod>` to avoid breaking the immutable
`<WebMethod>` rule.

TIP

Break monolithic methods into manageable function or subprocedure chunks before you add a new method. The ReportsWS service, for example, separates SOAP message processing, database query generation, and response document construction into a `Public Function` *and two* `Private Subs`.

Cloning Client Schema Validation in a New Method

Following are the generic steps for adding schema-based datatype checking code from a consuming client to an existing XML Web service, using the ReportsWS service as the example:

1. Copy the validation schema (CTReqTyped.xsd) to the service's folder.

2. In the XML Web service project, copy and paste the original `<WebMethod>` function (`TimeSeriesReport`) to a new method and assign the copy a new name (`TimeSeriesValidated`).

3. Alter the `Description` attribute value, if present, to reflect changes to the request document's element values and, if applicable, its structure.

4. Run the service to create a new WSDL document (ReportsWS.asmx).

5. In the consuming client project's Solution Explorer, right-click the Web Method node for the service (OCEReports), and choose Update Web Reference to cache the updated WSDL file.

6. Modify the client code to point to the new method, set `blnTyped` to `False`, and run the client to test the cloned service.

7. Add an `Imports System.Xml.Schema` instruction and `Private xscName As XmlSchemaCollection` declaration to the class.

8. Copy the schema-caching code from the client's `Page_Load` event handler to below `Sub New`'s `InitializeComponent()` call. Modify the URL to point to the validation schema you copied in step 1. The following example points to the OakLeaf remote service's schema:

```
.Add("http://oakleaf.ws/services/crosstabs/request",
    "http://www.oakleaf.ws/ReportsWS/CTReqTyped.xsd")
```

9. Copy the client's callback event handler to the new method, and remove code that isn't applicable to XML Web services, as in this example:

```
Private Sub ValidationError(ByVal sender As Object,
    ByVal args As ValidationEventArgs)
    'Common callback function for intercepting
    'request and response validation errors
    blnValid = False
End Sub
```

10. Copy the validation code from the client to the new service method, and alter the code to suit the XML Web service, as shown here:

```
srdRequest = New StringReader(RequestDoc)
xtrRequest = New XmlTextReader(srdRequest)
Dim xvrRequest As New XmlValidatingReader(xtrRequest)
blnValid = True
With xvrRequest
    .Schemas.Add(xscCrosstabs)
    AddHandler .ValidationEventHandler, AddressOf ValidationError
    While .Read
        'Process the document
    End While
    .Close()
End With
```

11. Run the new service to check for build errors, and then test it with the CTSchema client project.

Replacing Chapter 8's CTReportsWS Service with the Production Version

The \VBSW10\ReportsWS folder contains a production version of the ReportsWS XML Web service from the OakLeaf Web site, which has been modified to run on localhost. You can view the WSDL document for the production version at http://www.oakleaf.ws/ReportsWS/ReportsWS.asmx.

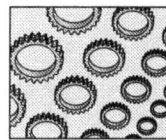

NOTE

Installation instructions for the production version of the ReportsWS service are located here because premature installation of this version prevents illustration of the validation error messages in these earlier sections: "Testing the Validation Process" (refer to Figure 10-1) and "Altering the Client Application to Handle the Typed Schema" (refer to Figure 10-8).

To substitute the production version of the ReportsWS service for Chapter 8's version, which doesn't include the `TimeSeriesValidated` method, do the following:

1. If you added the ReportsWS virtual directory in Chapter 8, change the source for ReportsWS from \VBWS08\ReportsWS to **\VBWS10\ReportsWS**. If you didn't add the virtual directory, create it.

2. Open ReportsWS.sln and change the folder location from D:\VBWS10\ReportsWS to the logical drive for this book's samples.

3. Run ReportsWS.sln to confirm it builds correctly, and regenerate the WSDL document.

4. In the CTSchema client project, right-click the OCEReports Web Reference node and choose Update Web Reference.

5. Open the ReportsWS.wsdl file to confirm that entries for the `TimeSeriesValidated` method are present.

6. Uncomment the following four commented instructions in the `cmdResponse_Click` event handler:

```
'If blnTyped Then
'    Call FillTable(xwsReport.TimeSeriesValidated(strXML))
'Else
     Call FillTable(xwsReport.TimeSeriesReport(strXML))
 'End If
```

7. Test the client with `blnTyped = True` and `blnTyped = False`. Be sure to clear the Remote WS check box to use the local XML Web service.

8. To prevent the client from defaulting to the remote OakLeaf service when `blnTyped = True`, comment the `chkRemoteWS.Checked = True` statement in the `Page_Load` event handler.

9. Optionally, add the ReportsWS.vbproj project to the solution to enable debugging of the local XML Web service.

NOTE

It isn't necessary to change the URL for the CTReqTyped.xsd schema, because the client's version is identical to the service's version.

Verifying the XML Web Service Validation Process

Another rule for schema-based document validation is, to paraphrase Yogi Berra: "It ain't over until it's tested." The only method of verifying that the service's schema validation and type checking tests are functional is to induce an error in the request document. Processing a nonconforming document with the CTSchema client requires temporarily disabling the callback event handler for the request document. The ReportsWS service returns an empty string if the response document fails validation.

To simulate a ReportsWS service validation error, do this:

1. Add a temporary validation callback event handler named `BypassValidation` or the like.

2. Change the `xvrRequest`'s `Add Handler` instruction's `Address Of` name to the name of the temporary validation handler.

3. Add an **AM** suffix to the value of the `<starttime>` element.

4. Run the client with `blnTyped` = `True`. You receive a "root element is missing" server error message because the SOAP response message is empty.

5. Reverse the changes you made in the preceding steps.

NOTE

CTSchema.aspx.vb contains commented code to speed the preceding steps.

A production XML Web service might provide a more elegant method for reporting validation errors, but it's easy to trap "root element is missing" errors with conventional or structured Visual Basic .NET exception handling in the client code.

Substituting rpc/encoded for document/literal SOAP Message Format

All Web service toolkits are *not* created equal. Potential consumers of your XML Web services might be using toolkits that create client proxies only for rpc/encoded SOAP messages. As mentioned in Chapter 12's "The SOAP Builders Group" section, most current SOAP interoperability testing is devoted to the SOAP 1.1 specification's Section 5 encoding rules with simple and complex datatypes. If you must support SOAP toolkits that can't handle document/literal-format SOAP messages, you need to emulate the Microsoft SOAP Toolkit 2.0+ rpc/encoded format.

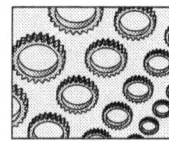

NOTE

Microsoft's decision to make document/literal format the default for Visual Studio .NET XML Web services wasn't based on a toss of a coin. Ultimately, almost all EAI, B2B, and B2C Web services that currently use Section 5 encoding will—or at least should—gravitate to document/literal format, XSD-validated XML request and response documents, and strongly typed element values. This chapter makes it clear that that Visual Studio .NET will accelerate migration to document/literal format.

Fortunately, Visual Studio .NET makes moving from the default document/literal to rpc/encoded format very easy, as the following sections demonstrate.

Creating a Clone of the document/encoded Web Service

The first phase of migration to rpc/encoded form is to clone your original [XML] Web services. The service doesn't need to meet this book's definition of an XML Web service. This section's example uses the AlphaDist XML Web service from the \VBWS05\OCE_Client\Services\AlphaWS folder as the example. AlphaDist qualifies for the XML prefix because the `CheckStock` method optionally returns an XML document, and the `PlaceOrder` method requires an XML request document and optionally returns an XML invoice document as the response.

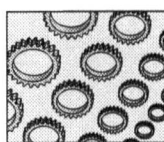

NOTE

AlphaDist, BetaDist, and GammaDist services might be called hybrid XML Web services because their SOAP request messages contain a combination of typed argument values and XML documents.

Following are the steps to create an independent copy of an existing Web service:

1. Create a new folder and a new virtual directory for the rpc/encoded version of your existing [XML] Web service. For this example, create a virtual directory named **AlphaRPC** and point its source to \VBWS05\OCE_ClientADO\Services\AlphaWS, which contains code from the AlphaWS XML Web service you created in Chapter 5.

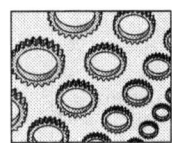

NOTE

The VBWS10\AlphaRPC folder contains the code with the changes described in the following steps.

2. Create a new Web service at the virtual directory's URL, **http://localhost/AlphaRPC** for this example.

3. Copy the *ServiceName*.asmx, *ServiceName*.asmx.resx, and *ServiceName*.asmx.vb files from the original project folder to the new folder. For this example, the files are AlphaDist.asmx, .asmx.resx, and .asmx.vb.

4. In Solution Explorer, delete Service1.asmx, and choose Add | Add Existing Item to open the Add Existing Item dialog.

5. Navigate to the new folder, select Web Files in the Files Of Type list, and add the *ServiceName*.asmx file to the project.

6. Rename the *ServiceName*.aspx file to match your new service name (**AlphaRPC**.aspx), and set it as the start page.

7. Add missing references, if any, change the `Public Class` name to the new service name (**AlphaRPC**), and build the project. For this example, you must add a reference to Microsoft XML, v4.0.

TIP

It's a good service design practice to specify a different namespace for the rpc/encoded version. For this example, an `rpc/` namespace suffix is sufficient. Another alternative is to adopt the URN format for service namespaces, such as `urn:alphadist-com:webservices:rpc`.

8. Click the Service Description link of the WSDL document and verify that its format is document/literal.

Adding the SoapRpcMethod Attribute

To specify Section 5 encoding of methods, you must add an `Imports System.Web.Services.Protocols` statement to the service's class, and then prefix the `<WebMethod>` attribute with the `SoapRpcMethod` attribute. The generic syntax for specifying rpc/encoded style for a Web service method is:

```
<SoapRpcMethod(Action:="ServiceURI"[, _
            RequestNamespace:="RequestURI",
            RequestElementName:="MethodNameRequest",
            ResponseNamespace:="ResponseURI",
            ResponseElementName:="MethodNameResponse"]),
WebMethod([Description:="DescriptionText"])> _
Public Function MethodName() As DataType

    ...

End Function
```

Attribute name/value pairs enclosed in square braces are optional, if you're willing to accept the default values for the `<message>` elements' `name` attribute and the `ServiceURI` as the value of the `targetNamespace` for all messages. The default `name` values are `MethodNameSoapIn` and `MethodNameSoapOut`.

The only modification required to the example AlphaDist XML Web service is to insert the following line attribute value between the `CheckStock` function's opening angle bracket (<) and `WebMethod...>`:

```
SoapRpcMethod(Action:="http://alphadist.com/webservices/rpc/stock/"),
```

See Figure 10-9, and add this line in the same position of the `PlaceOrder` function:

```
SoapRpcMethod(Action:="http://alphadist.com/webservices/rpc/order/"),
```

TIP

Online help's "Customizing SOAP Messages" topic explains more than anyone would want or need to know about the process for migrating from document/literal to rpc/encoded format. What's missing from the topic is a brief explanation of the simple migration approach described in this section. Further customization might make your rpc/encoded service incompatible with at least a few third-party SOAP toolkit client proxy generation approaches.

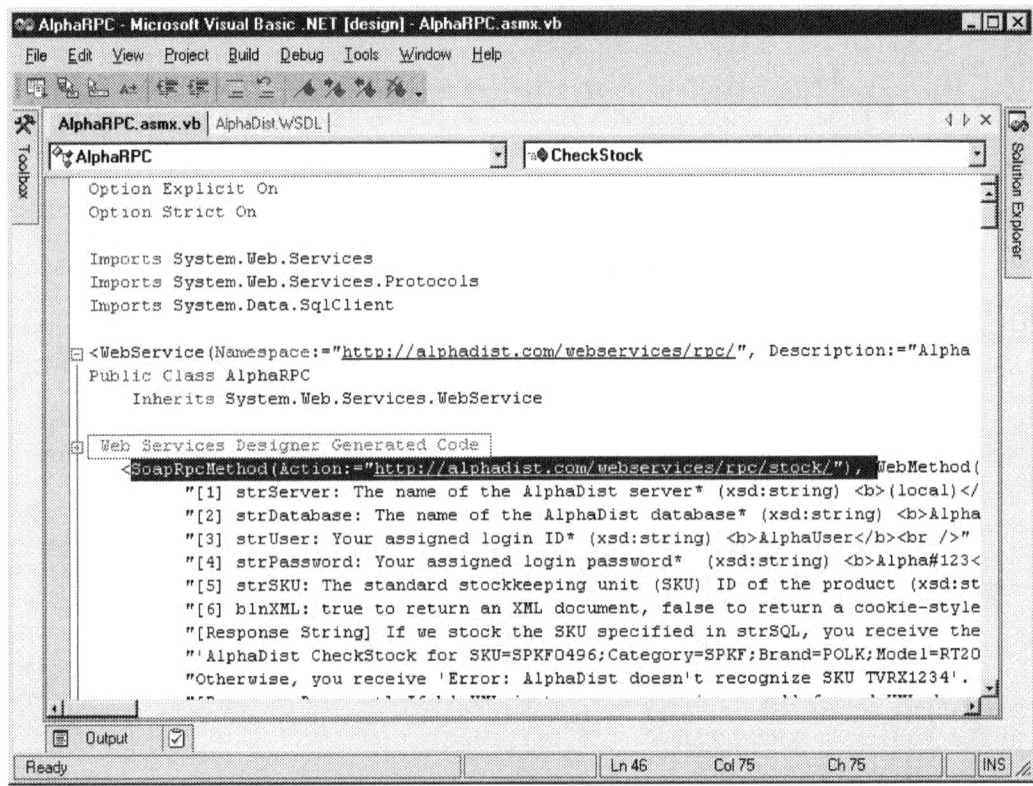

Figure 10-9   *Adding the* `SoapRpcMethod` *attribute with a single* `Action:="MethodNameURI"` *property changes the method from document/literal to rpc/encoded format.*

Run the project and click the Service Description link to display the WSDL document and verify that it conforms to the rpc/encoded format. (See Figure 10-10.)

Type the values shown in Figure 10-11 to return the XML response document.

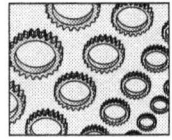

NOTE

The original AlphaDist and rpc/encoded AlphaRPC versions of the service are registered with the UDDI 1.0 nodes. Search with "Alpha Distributors" as the business name.

Testing the Cloned Web Service with a Client Consumer

You have several choices of clients with which to test the new rpc/encoded version of your service. Chapter 5's OCE_Client Windows form client is a good candidate for the testing process because it offers a bulk order addition feature. To substitute the sample AlphaRPC service for the original AlphaDist service in the OCE_Client solution, do the following:

1. Open OCE_Client.sln, right-click Solution Explorer's Web References node, and choose Add Web Reference to open the dialog.

2. Type **http://localhost/alpharpc/alpharpc.asmx** in the Address text box, and click Add Reference to create a proxy.

3. Temporarily rename AlphaWSADO to **AlphaWSOrig**, and localhost to **http://localhost/alpharpc/alpharpc.asmx**.

4. Run the client project. You receive two "Type 'AlphaWSADO.AlphaDist' is not defined" errors in the Task List.

5. Double-click each Task List error item and temporarily replace `AlphaWSADO.AlphaDist()` with `AlphaWSADO.`**`AlphaRPC()`**.

6. Run the project, mark the Use XML Web Services check box, and click Add Bulk Orders to start adding orders to the OCE_Cust database. Add at least 500 orders to assure that you test the rpc/encoded version thoroughly. AlphaDist receives outsourced orders for about 5 percent of the total orders you add.

7. Reverse the changes you made in steps 3, 4, and 5 to return the OCE_Client project to its original condition.

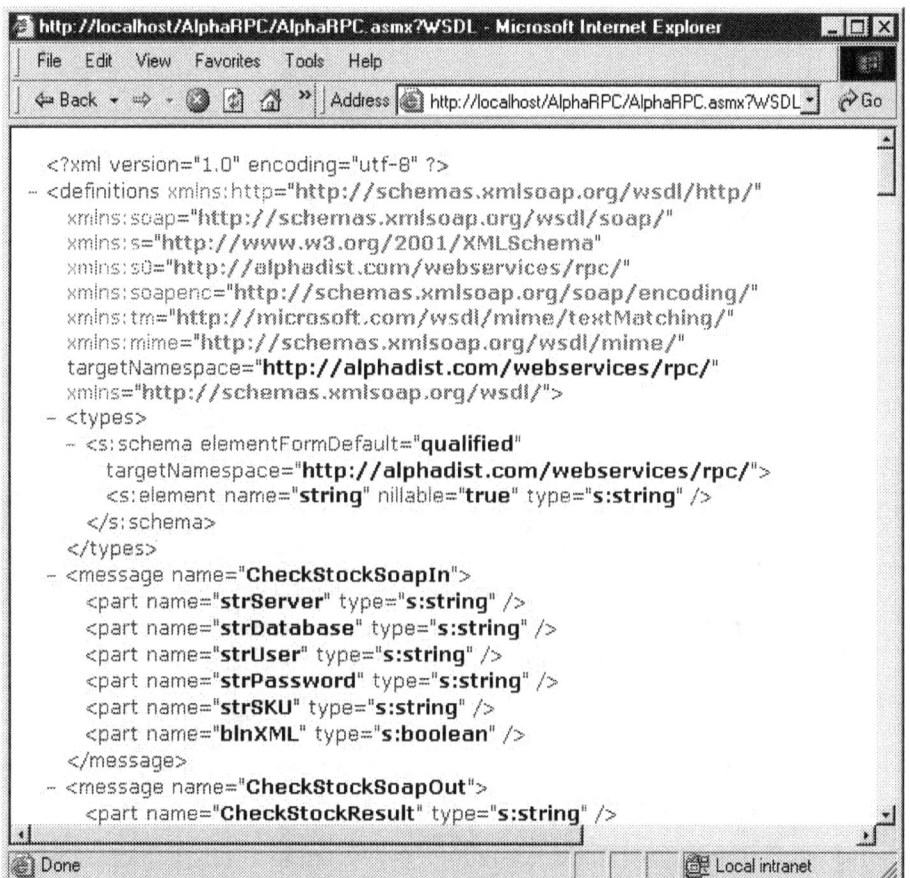

Figure 10-10   *The* `CheckStockSoapIn` *and* `CheckStockSoapOut` *messages prove that the WSDL document uses rpc/encoded SOAP message format.*

```
┌─────────────────────────────────────────────────────────────────┐
│ 🔷 AlphaRPC Web Service - Microsoft Internet Explorer    _ □ ✕   │
├─────────────────────────────────────────────────────────────────┤
│  File   Edit   View   Favorites   Tools   Help                 🖲 │
├─────────────────────────────────────────────────────────────────┤
│ ← Back ▾ → ▾ ◎ ⑳ 🏠 ❯❯ │Address 🔷 alhost/AlphaRPC/AlphaRPC.asmx?op=CheckStock ▾│ 🔗Go │
├─────────────────────────────────────────────────────────────────┤
│                                                                 ▲ │
│  Test                                                            │
│    To test the operation using the HTTP GET protocol, click the 'Invoke' button. │
│                                                                   │
│     Parameter    Value                                            │
│     strServer:   │(local)                                    │    │
│                                                                   │
│     strDatabase: │AlphaDist                                  │    │
│                                                                   │
│     strUser:     │AlphaUser                                  │    │
│                                                                   │
│     strPassword: │Alpha#123                                  │    │
│                                                                   │
│     strSKU:      │SPKF0496                                   │    │
│                                                                   │
│     blnXML:      │true                                       │    │
│                                                                   │
│                                                 │ Invoke │        │
│                                                                   │
│  SOAP                                                             │
│    The following is a sample SOAP request and response. The placeholders shown need to be │
│    replaced with actual values.                                  │
│                                                                   │
│    POST /AlphaRPC/AlphaRPC.asmx HTTP/1.1                          │
│    Host: localhost                                               │
│    Content-Type: text/xml; charset=utf-8                         │
│    Content-Length: length                                       ▼ │
│  ◄                                                             ►   │
├─────────────────────────────────────────────────────────────────┤
│ 🔷 Done                                         🖳 Local intranet  │
└─────────────────────────────────────────────────────────────────┘
```

Figure 10-11   *Type the values shown here in the Test form to return the XML document for a* `CheckStock` *request.*

You don't need to remove the localhost Web Reference from the project, but rename it to AlphaWSRPC or the like so you know what it is when you return to the OCE_Client project.

TIP

Register your rpc/encoded Web service with one or both of the independent registries described in Chapter 12's "Finding Web Services for .NET Interoperability Testing" section. Encourage users of other SOAP toolkits to give your service a try by providing sample values in the documentation for the service. You might have better luck gaining interoperability testers if you copy the ServiceName.wsdl file from a test client's . . .\Web References folder to the service's folder, and specify ServiceName.wsdl rather than ServiceName.asmx as the access point.

Serializing Complex Datatypes

Much of the work of the SOAP Builders coalition is devoted to testing interoperability of rpc/encoded Web services that process complex datatypes, such as arrays, structures, and arrays of structures in SOAP request and response documents. This is a noble effort, but

XML request and response documents are quite capable of emulating such complex datatypes and offer the important benefit of human readability in your code.

Examples in this book's earlier chapters use procedural string-building code to generate XML request and response documents. XML and object purists eschew the string-building approach in favor of serializing class instances. The .NET Framework's `XmlSerializer` class makes generating XML documents from classes almost as easy as building strings. `XmlSerializer` objects generate well-formed, indented XML documents from classes but require about twice as many lines of code for source object declarations, class instantiation, and serializing the top member of the class hierarchy. A side benefit of serializing objects is cleaner, more understandable and maintainable document generation code.

Defining Classes from Existing Documents

The ReportsWS XML Web service's request document is a simple example of an XML document that you can represent by nested classes. Following are the two class declarations for the untyped version of the request document:

```
Public Class clsCT_Untyped
    Public title As String
    Public timeseries As clsTS_Untyped
End Class

Public Class clsTS_Untyped
    Public datatable As String
    Public rowsby As String
    Public startdate As String
    Public starttime As String
    Public interval As String
    Public datacolumns As String
    Public count As String
    Public avgvalue As String
    Public rowtotals As String
    Public coltotals As String
    Public nulltozero As String
    Public format As String
End Class
```

The `clsCT_Untyped` class defines the `<crosstab>` root element of the request document and supplies the `<title>` element value. The `clsTS_Untyped` class specifies the `<timeseries>` section and its elements. The preceding object declarations are located at the bottom of CTSchema.aspx.vb.

The XML request document for OakLeaf Consumer Electronics orders that are outsourced to distributors has a more complex object representation. Chapter 3's "XML Purchase Order Documents" describes the structure of the XML request document. Each of the document's five sections requires a subclass, and the `<LineItems>` sections contain an array of `<Item>`

subelements. The `<CustomerInvoice>` section contains a nested variation of the first four sections. Following are three of the seven class declarations for the purchase order document:

```
Public Class PurchaseOrder
    Public Header As poHeader
    Public BillingAddr As poBillAddr
    Public ShippingAddr As poShipAddr
    Public LineItems As poItem()
    Public CustomerInvoice As poCustInv
End Class


Public Class poHeader
    Public PurchID As Integer
    Public OrderDate As Date
    Public ShipToCustomer As Boolean
    Public RequiredShipDate As Date
    Public ShipPhone As String
    Public ShipID As Integer
    Public PartialShipOK As Boolean
End Class


Public Class poItem
    Public ItemID As Integer
    Public Quantity As Integer
    Public SKU As String
    Public Cost As Decimal
    Public Discount As Decimal
    Public DiscountID As Integer
    Public Allowance As Decimal
    Public AllowanceID As Integer
End Class
```

Serializing the Class Instance

Instantiating an `XmlSerializer` object requires adding an Imports `System.Xml.Serialization` statement and supplying the class type definition as an argument value. You apply the XmlSerializer.Serialize method with `StreamWriter` and `ClassInstance` arguments to save the document to a file or populate a `String` variable. Here's the generic code for serializing a class instance:

```
Dim xsName As New XmlSerializer(GetType(ClassName))
Dim swName As New _
    StreamWriter("\Path\FileName.xml", False)
xsName.Serialize(swName, ClassInstanceName)
swName.Close()
```

The following code in CTSchema.axpx.vb's `cmdResponse_Click` event handler creates instances of the `clsTS_Untyped` and `clsCT_Untyped` classes, assigns element values, and invokes the `XmlSerializer.Serialize` method to save the stream to an XML file:

```
'XmlSerializer untyped demonstration
Dim objTS_Untyped As New clsTS_Untyped()
With objTS_Untyped
    .datatable = "Orders"
    .rowsby = rblRowsBy.SelectedItem.Value.ToString
    .startdate = strStartDate
    .starttime = "00:00:00AM"
    .interval = ddlInterval.SelectedItem.ToString
    .datacolumns = ddlDataCols.SelectedItem.ToString
    .count = "No"
    .avgvalue = "No"
    .rowtotals = strRowTotals
    .coltotals = strColTotals
    .nulltozero = strNullToZero
    .format = "XML"
End With
Dim objCT_Untyped As New clsCT_Untyped()
With objCT_Untyped
    .title = strTitle
    .timeseries = objTS_Untyped
End With
Dim xsReqUntyped As New XmlSerializer(GetType(clsCT_Untyped))
Dim swReqUntyped As New
    StreamWriter("\VBWS10\CTSchema\CT_Untyped.xml", _
    False)
xsReqUntyped.Serialize(swReqUntyped, objCT_Untyped)
swReqUntyped.Close()
Dim srReqUntyped As New
    StreamReader("\VBWS10\CTSchema\CT_Untyped.xml")
'Uncomment to replace strXML with serialized version
'strXML = srReqUntyped.ReadToEnd
srReqUntyped.Close()
```

The preceding code generates the following XML request document:

```
<?xml version="1.0" encoding="utf-8"?>
<clsCT_Untyped xmlns:xsd="http://www.w3.org/2001/XMLSchema"
xmlns:xsi="http://www.w3.org/2001/XMLSchema-instance">
  <title>2001 Quarterly Orders by State</title>
  <timeseries>
    <datatable>Orders</datatable>
```

```
      <rowsby>State</rowsby>
      <startdate>1/1/2001</startdate>
      <starttime>00:00:00AM</starttime>
      <interval>Quarter</interval>
      <datacolumns>4</datacolumns>
      <count>No</count>
      <avgvalue>No</avgvalue>
      <rowtotals>Yes</rowtotals>
      <coltotals>Yes</coltotals>
      <nulltozero>Yes</nulltozero>
      <format>XML</format>
   </timeseries>
</clsCT_Untyped>
```

Adding the XmlRootAttribute to the Class Declaration

The preceding default XML request document is close to what you need, but it
doesn't have the correct root element name (`crosstab`) and namespace attribute
(`xmlns="http://oakleaf.ws/services/crosstabs/request"`) required
for validation by the CTRequest1.xsd schema.

To specify a nondefault root element name and document namespace, add the following
`XmlRootAttribute` prefix to the class declaration:

```
<XmlRootAttribute("RootElementName",
  Namespace:="NamespaceURI", IsNullable:=False)>
```

The `IsNullable` attribute value determines if the element is required; the root element,
of course, is required.

Here's the final version of the `clsCT_Untyped` class declaration:

```
<XmlRootAttribute("crosstab", _
   Namespace:="http://oakleaf.ws/services/crosstabs/request", _
   IsNullable:=False)> _
Public Class clsCT_Untyped
   Public title As String
   Public timeseries As clsTS_Untyped
End Class
```

It returns the following clone of the original untyped XML request document:

```
<?xml version="1.0" encoding="utf-8"?>
<crosstab xmlns:xsd="http://www.w3.org/2001/XMLSchema"
     xmlns:xsi="http://www.w3.org/2001/XMLSchema-instance"
     xmlns="http://oakleaf.ws/services/crosstabs/request">
  <title>2001 Quarterly Orders by State</title>
  <timeseries>
```

```
        <datatable>Orders</datatable>
        <rowsby>State</rowsby>
        <startdate>1/1/2001</startdate>
        <starttime>00:00:00AM</starttime>
        <interval>Quarter</interval>
        <datacolumns>4</datacolumns>
        <count>No</count>
        <avgvalue>No</avgvalue>
        <rowtotals>Yes</rowtotals>
        <coltotals>Yes</coltotals>
        <nulltozero>Yes</nulltozero>
        <format>XML</format>
    </timeseries>
</crosstab>
```

Search for `'strXML = srReqUntyped.ReadToEnd` and uncomment the instruction to replace the procedural version of `strXML`. Executing the `StreamReader` lets you confirm that CTRequest1.xsd successfully validates the serialized version of the XML request document.

Typing Request and Response Classes

CTSchema.aspx.vb's `cmdResponse_Click` event handler sets the values for instances of a second class, `clsCT_Typed`, which substitutes `Integer` and `Boolean` datatypes for `String` where appropriate. Following is the declaration for the `clsTS_Typed` class:

```
Public Class clsTS_Typed
    Public datatable As String
    Public rowsby As String
    Public startdate As String
    Public starttime As String
    Public interval As String
    Public datacolumns As Integer
    Public count As Boolean
    Public avgvalue As Boolean
    Public rowtotals As Boolean
    Public coltotals As Boolean
    Public nulltozero As Boolean
    Public format As String
End Class
```

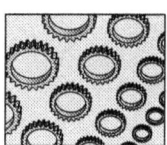

NOTE

To substitute the serialized output of an instance of `clsCT_Typed` *for the procedurally generated request document, set* `blnTyped = True` *and uncomment the* `'strXML = srReqTyped.ReadToEnd` *instruction.*

Unfortunately, you can't strongly type the `startdate` and `starttime` members because `Date` or `DateTime`. `XMLSerializer.Serialize` converts `Date` and `DateTime` members into the `xsd:dateTime` datatype, which represents midnight, January 1, 2001, in ISO 8601 format as `2001-01-01T00:00:00.0000000-08:00` for computers running in the Pacific time zone. The `-08:00` element represents the difference between local and Universal Coordinated Time (UCT, formerly GMT). If you specify the `Date` datatype and set the value of `startdate` with `CDate(strStartDate)`, you receive this validation error message: "The 'http://oakleaf.ws/services/crosstabs/request:startdate' element has an invalid value according to its data type. An error occurred at (7, 51)."

The .NET Framework has no readily discoverable datatype or structure to return only the time in the HH:MM:SS[*FractionalSeconds*] format, which the `xsd:time` datatype requires. For example, Visual Basic .NET's `TimeValue` function returns a `DateTime` structure with the date set to January 1, 1. Unless you specify `xsd:dateTime` in your validation schema, use `Strings` for date and time.

Creating Class Declaration Files with Xsd.exe

You can use Xsd.exe to create a schema from an XML file of a typical request or response document. You then generate a Visual Basic .NET class definition file by issuing this instruction at the command prompt—**xsd.exe** *docname*.**xsd /c[lass] /l[anguage]:VB**—which generates a *docname*.vb file.

If you have a complex document structure, such as the OCE `PurchaseOrder` request document, using Xsd.exe to create the class declaration code is a real time-saver. Editing the *docname*.vb file is much faster and less error-prone than writing class declarations from scratch. The autogenerated class names handle duplicated element names within class hierarchies; you can alter the class names to suit your own naming convention.

Following is the code in OCE_Order.vb for the first three classes of the `PurchaseOrder` document (OCE_Order.xml) generated by executing **xsd.exe OCE_Order.xsd /c /l:VB**:

```
' <autogenerated>
'      This code was generated by a tool.
'      Runtime Version: 1.0.3705.0
'      Changes to this file may cause incorrect behavior and will be lost if
'      the code is regenerated.
' </autogenerated>
Option Strict Off
Option Explicit On
Imports System.Xml.Serialization
'This source code was auto-generated by xsd, Version=1.0.3705.0.

<System.Xml.Serialization.XmlRootAttribute("PurchaseOrder", [Namespace]:="",
IsNullable:=false)>  _
Public Class PurchaseOrder
    <System.Xml.Serialization.XmlElementAttribute("CustomerInvoice")>  _
    Public Items() As PurchaseOrderCustomerInvoice
End Class
```

```
Public Class PurchaseOrderCustomerInvoice
    <System.Xml.Serialization.XmlElementAttribute("Header")>  _
    Public Header() As PurchaseOrderCustomerInvoiceHeader
    <System.Xml.Serialization.XmlElementAttribute("BillingAddr")>  _
    Public BillingAddr() As PurchaseOrderCustomerInvoiceBillingAddr
    <System.Xml.Serialization.XmlElementAttribute("ShippingAddr")>  _
    Public ShippingAddr() As PurchaseOrderCustomerInvoiceShippingAddr
    <System.Xml.Serialization.XmlArrayItemAttribute("Item", _
        GetType(PurchaseOrderCustomerInvoiceLineItemsItem), _
        IsNullable:=false)>  _
    Public LineItems()() As PurchaseOrderCustomerInvoiceLineItemsItem
End Class

Public Class PurchaseOrderCustomerInvoiceHeader
    Public PurchID As String
    Public OrderDate As String
    Public ShipToCustomer As String
    Public RequiredShipDate As String
    Public ShipPhone As String
    Public ShipByID As String
    Public PartialShipOK As String
    Public InvoiceID As String
    Public OrderID As String
    Public CustID As String
    Public ShipDate As String
    Public ShipTypeID As String
    Public TrackingID As String
    Public ShippingCharge As String
    Public SalesTax As String
    Public PartialShipment As String
    Public CardDigits As String
    Public ShipToID As String
    Public StatusID As String
End Class
...
```

The preceding listing omits extra blank lines and `<remarks />` elements from Xsd.exe's autogenerated code. The code adds `System.Xml.Serialization.XmlElementAttribute` values for ordinary elements and `System.Xml.Serialization.XmlArrayItemAttribute` values for elements, such as `Item`, that can occur multiple times within an element.

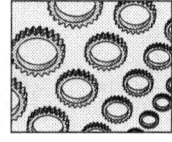

NOTE

The \VBWS10\CTSchema folder contains a sample OCE_Order.xml file from which Xsd.exe created OCE_Order.xsd and OCE_Order.vb.

Strongly Typing Services with DataSets

Passing serialized typed `DataSet` objects as SOAP request and response documents is an alternative to the techniques described in the preceding sections. Typed `DataSet`s have the advantage of not requiring a separate XSD schema file, and client applications can manipulate document values in `DataGrid` controls. Chapter 6's "Rolling Your Own DataTable to Display Order Information" section describes how to create a typed `DataSet`.

The downside of using `DataSet` objects as SOAP message payload is that the `DataSet` object is an element of Microsoft's proprietary .NET Framework technology. `DataSet`s serialize to a Microsoft-specific DiffGram format that contains the original and current values of the `DataSet`'s rows. This technique originated in the XML representation of `ADODB.Recordset` objects with annotated XDR schemas; SQL Server 2000's updategrams use a similar approach. The objective of adopting XML Web services for EAI, B2B, and B2C projects is platform *and* development environment independence. Assuring that commercial XML Web services are vendor-agnostic is more than a good design practice—it's imperative. Reserve your use of `DataSet` objects to conventional Visual Studio .NET Web and Windows form applications and Visual Basic .NET components.

Dealing with Inoperative or Slow Web Services

A major issue with all types of Web services, especially third-party services, is "What happens when the service goes down?" In some cases, such as failure of a server-to-server credit card validation service, your ASP.NET Web storefront is out of business until the validation service comes back online. If the consuming client is a Windows form, the UI freezes until the service responds or the service proxy times out.

Large-scale commercial [XML] Web services providers will use high-end server clusters to assure scalability and reliability of services. In March 2002, Akamai announced a plan to enable enterprises to deploy the company's edge server technology to minimize .NET XML Web services latency. Application service providers (ASPs) are lining up to host high-reliability Web services for organizations that are reluctant to install the hardware and telecommunication infrastructure required to support a new and—when this book was written—commercially unproven technology. Regardless of the deployment method, your own or others' services are subject to Internet vagaries, such as server outages, DNS failures, and varying degrees of network latency.

Deciding Between Synchronous or Asynchronous Processing

This book's ASP.NET and Windows form client examples use synchronous processing for calling XML Web services. Synchronous processing blocks the client's calling thread until the service responds or the service's proxy times out. Synchronous processing is satisfactory for clients that call a single XML Web service which, when operational, takes only a few seconds to respond.

Synchronous processing also applies to clients that call multiple services, which must respond in particular sequence. For example, the OCE client applications require credit card validation before stock checking, credit hold, and order processing. Successive XML Web service invocations are determined by the outcome of the previous service response. Checking stock for an order from a customer with an expired credit card is a waste of resources; processing an order for that customer causes a direct hit on the bottom line.

Asynchronous Web service processing sends the SOAP request message to the client and continues processing successive lines of code until the service responds, the request times out, or `End Sub` or `End Function` is encountered. Asynchronous processing offers these prospective advantages:

▶ The Windows form UI or a server-based consumer component isn't frozen during service request/response processing.

▶ ASP.NET clients' worker threads aren't stalled while waiting for the service to respond. Threads that aren't involved in the Web service interaction are freed for use by other clients.

▶ Clients can make simultaneous calls to multiple services, such as those provided by OCE's three distributors, and choose whether to wait for the first responding service only or for all services to respond.

In reality, Windows form UIs probably *should* freeze while waiting for a service to respond, and ASP.NET pages shouldn't reload until the service responds or times out. This is especially true for sequential processes, such as the OCE order processing examples. The only benefit of asynchronous calls to multiple services is eliminating the timeout delay incurred by one or more services that don't respond.

Adding the code to implement asynchronous service requests isn't unduly time-consuming, as the later "Consuming XML Web Services Asynchronously" section demonstrates. The code for handling interactions between asynchronous services, however, is usually quite complex and difficult to debug.

Adopting a Downed Service Strategy

Design your service-consuming applications or components to deal with the loosely coupled nature of Web services and service failures. Following are the basic elements of a strategy for recovering from service failures, regardless of the source of the problem:

▶ **Timeout notification**   Add an exception handler for synchronous service requests that don't respond within a reasonable multiple of the normal response time. The next section illustrates Visual Basic .NET code to handle timeout exceptions. If you use asynchronous processing, add a `Timer` control to the form to set a limit on the waiting time.

▶ **Backup services**   Add Web References that point to the URL or IP address of backup services, if the provider doesn't offer redirection for a primary service that's out of commission. Add a nested exception handler to try the backup service.

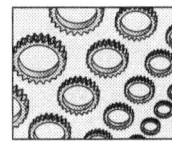

NOTE

The CFRClient program, which Appendix B describes, contains an example of code to change to http://www.ecfrback/..., if the Government Printing Office's primary e-CFR Beta site at http://www.ecfr/... is down.

▶ **Alternative services**   Add Web References and exception-handling code to try alternative services, such as other distributors of a particular product, if the service on which you ordinarily depend times out. For example, OCE's three Texas distributors stock many items in common. If the AlphaDist XML Web service doesn't respond, it's not difficult to add a nested exception handler to the OCE_Client code that checks stock for the required item at BetaDist and GammaDist.

▶ **Service outage logging**   If a service fails to respond after a few requests, persist a record of the failure and, if a backup or alternative service is available, switch to its client proxy. Use the Visual Studio .NET `EventLog` component to add and read custom events or logs for service failures. Add code to periodically retry the primary service.

Processing Synchronous Timeouts

.NET Framework Web service proxy classes are derived from the `WebClientProtocol` base class, which has a `Timeout` property. The default `Timeout` value, `100000` (ms), causes the client to wait 100 seconds for the service to respond. Setting the `Timeout` value to `Timeout.Infinite`, which isn't a good design practice, causes the client to wait forever for a response.

Exceeding the `Timeout` value throws a `System.Net.WebException` error with this message: "The operation has timed out." The following code at the end of CTSchema.aspx.vb's `cmdResponse_Click` event handler traps the timeout exception and displays a message to the user:

```
Try
    'Handle Timeout exception
    If chkRemoteWS.Checked Then
        If blnTyped Then
            'Use the validating version
            Call FillTable(xwsRemote.TimeSeriesValidated(strXML))
        Else
            Call FillTable(xwsRemote.TimeSeriesReport(strXML))
        End If
    Else
        Call FillTable(xwsReport.TimeSeriesReport(strXML))
    End If
Catch errTimout As System.Net.WebException
    'Exception handling code goes here
    lblError.Text = "Web service didn't respond within "
    If chkRemoteWS.Checked Then
```

```
        lblError.Text += CStr(intRemoteTimeout / 1000)
    Else
        lblError.Text += CStr(intLocalTimeout / 1000)
    End If
    lblError.Text += " seconds. Try again or increase the service's " + _
        "Timeout property value."
    lblError.Visible = True
    tblReport.Visible = False
    blnValid = False
End Try
```

To test the exception handler, substitute 1000 or less for the value of the `intLocalTimeout` or `intRemoteTimeout` values in the declarations section of the `frmCTReport` class, and click Get Report. The client application's execution thread is blocked for the `Timeout` period.

TIP

Be sure to set the `Timeout` value to a period that is sufficient to include the delay that occurs when you invoke the service for the first time after a server reboot. Initializing a complex XML Web service can take 15 seconds or more.

Inducing a Delay to Emulate Slow or Nonresponding Services

Before you can test your synchronous or asynchronous code for handling slow or nonresponding services, you need to modify test versions of your XML Web services to add a variable delay interval. An unused or ignored element in the request document, such as ReportsWS's `starttime`, lets you add an optional delay to a production XML Web service without changing the request document structure.

To emulate a delayed service response for testing consuming applications, add code similar to the following snippet to your XML Web service:

```
'Induce a delay equal to the seconds value of starttime to emulate
'a slowly responding service: 00:00:15AM adds a 15 second delay.
If Mid(strStartTime, 7, 2) <> "00" Then
    Dim thdDelay2 As Thread
    thdDelay2 = System.Threading.Thread.CurrentThread
    thdDelay2.Sleep(1000 * CInt(Mid(strStartTime, 7, 2)))
End If
```

The production ReportsWS XML Web service at the OakLeaf Web site includes the preceding code example in the `TimeSeriesReport` method; the `TimeSeriesValidated` method has a slightly modified version. You can induce up to a 59-second response delay by replacing the `starttime` element's seconds value with numbers from 01 to 59.

Consuming XML Web Services Asynchronously

You don't need to modify your XML Web services in any way to change from synchronous to asynchronous processing. It's up to the consumer to determine whether synchronous or asynchronous calls occur and the methods used to make the asynchronous calls.

Visual Studio .NET and the .NET Framework support two methods for consuming XML Web services asynchronously. The simplest approach uses callback processing with an `AsyncDelegate` object to invoke the service on a new thread and an `AsyncCallback` object to specify the event handler that traps the service's response. Asynchronous clients use the following three `AsyncDelegate` methods:

▶ **Invoke** Performs conventional synchronous processing.

▶ **BeginInvoke** Initiates the service request on a new thread, which prevents blocking the calling method's thread.

▶ **EndInvoke** Returns the response document from the service. Calling `EndInvoke` prematurely blocks the calling method's thread until the service responds.

Visual Studio .NET's sample AsyncWebService.sln solution demonstrates the code required to consume a simple random-number service asynchronously. You can copy and install the required files from online help's "XML Web Services: Windows Forms Client-Asynchronous XML Web Service Sample" topic. Following is the code behind the AsyncTestClient project's Form1.vb that executes the **DoSomeWork** method of WebService1:

```
'Declare the delegate function
Public Delegate Function myAsyncDelegate(ByVal intReturn As Integer) _
   As Integer


'Event handler for asynchronous calls
Private Sub cmdWebServAsync_Click(ByVal sender As System.Object, _
   ByVal e As System.EventArgs) Handles cmdWebServAsync.Click

   'Create instance of web service proxy
   'Call the method "DoSomeWork" asynchronously.
   'The first parameter is the value for the actual method call _
   'parameter and the second parameter is the address of the
   'function to be called when the method completes execution.
   'Create instance of web service proxy
   Dim WebServ As New localhost.Service1()
   Dim AsyncCallback As New AsyncCallback(AddressOf Me.MyCallBack)
   Dim AsyncDelegate As New myAsyncDelegate(AddressOf WebServ.DoSomeWork)
   Dim AsyncResult As IAsyncResult
   'Call the web service asynchronously and display the results.
   AsyncResult = AsyncDelegate.BeginInvoke(Int32.Parse(txtDelay.Text), _
```

```
      AsyncCallback, Nothing)
   MessageBox.Show("Async call started", "Asynchronous Call")

End Sub


Private Shared Sub MyCallBack(ByVal ar As System.IAsyncResult)
   Dim AsyncDelegate As myAsyncDelegate
   Dim AsyncResult As AsyncResult
   Dim ReturnValue As Integer

   AsyncResult = CType(ar, AsyncResult)
   AsyncDelegate = AsyncResult.AsyncDelegate()

   'End async call
   ReturnValue = AsyncDelegate.EndInvoke(AsyncResult)

   MessageBox.Show("Asynchronous response has returned with " & _

      "the value: " & ReturnValue.ToString)

End Sub
```

Service1's `DoSomeWork` method imposes a variable delay implemented by code similar to that in the earlier "Inducing a Delay to Emulate Slow or Nonresponding Services" section and returns a random number to the client.

You can adapt the preceding code to change existing synchronous consumers to asynchronous processing. Before you make the decision to apply asynchronous processing to multiple, complex services, use a Web service load simulation tool to determine if moving to the asynchronous model delivers sufficient server scalability to justify the programming and testing effort.

NOTE

The Microsoft Web Application Stress (WAS) tool lets you simulate multiple Web browser clients that access a test or production ASP.NET XML Web service. WAS is the foundation for the stress-testing tool included with Microsoft Application Center Server. You can download a no-charge copy of WAS from http://webtool.rte.microsoft.com. Red Gate Software offers the Advanced .NET Testing System (ANTS), which is specifically intended for testing load capacity and scalability of ASP.NET XML Web services. You can download a trial version of the ANTS <concept> version from http://www.red-gate.com.

Adding SOAP Extensions

SOAP extensions provide a method for intercepting and, optionally, modifying SOAP headers and payload at the four processing stages that are described briefly in Chapter 7's

"SoapExtension Classes" section. You can extend Web services, consuming clients, or both; if the extension modifies the SOAP message, you must implement extensions at the sender and recipient endpoints. For example, if you decide to encrypt SOAP headers and request documents for security, the consumer extension must encrypt the request message and the service must decrypt it. Similarly, the client must be able to decrypt encrypted response messages.

TIP

Don't confuse the .NET Framework's SOAP extensions with the SOAP 1.1 specification's "HTTP Extension Framework" and the "extensions" described in Section 4.2. The SOAP extensions described in this chapter are elements of your Web service and consumer code, and aren't covered by the SOAP specification.

ASP.NET SOAP extensions that modify the SOAP envelope or its payload usually aren't interoperable with client proxies generated by other SOAP toolkits. Unlike SOAP headers, which the service can define as optional with a `SoapHeader("HeaderName", Required:=False)` attribute, extensions that modify messages can't be made optional at either endpoint.

Reviewing Visual Studio .NET's TraceExtension Example

You can add SOAP extensions that don't modify SOAP messages to perform useful functions, such as logging SOAP request and response messages for troubleshooting, intrusion detection, and the like. Online help's "Altering the SOAP Message Using SOAP Extensions" topic includes the Visual Basic .NET code for a SOAP message logging extension named `TraceExtension`. The logging extension serves a purpose similar to the SOAP Toolkit 2.0's Trace Utility, but it doesn't require adding a TCP listening port number to the WSDL file or running a separate program.

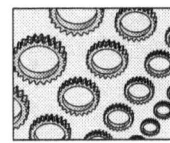

NOTE

The "Altering the SOAP Message Using SOAP Extensions" online help topic contains a full description of the purpose of `TraceExtension`'s classes. TraceExtensionVB.txt in the \VBWS10\ReportsWS folder is a copy of the Visual Basic .NET sample code that's extracted from the help topic.

Making the TraceExtension Example Operable

Unfortunately, you can't simply paste the contents of TraceExtensionVB.txt into your Visual Basic .NET XML Web service or consumer project, add the required SOAP extension attribute to a `WebMethod` call, and log service request and response messages. The sample code is missing the `Sub New` constructor that's required to define the argument for specifying the logging path and filename.

Following is the Visual Basic .NET TraceExtension sample code with the `Sub New` constructor added and changes made to reflect this book's naming conventions. Comments in parentheses refer to subtopics of the "Altering the SOAP Message Using SOAP Extensions" topic:

```vb
'Define an attribute to specify the log file name and location,
'and the extension's priority
'(Help Topic: "Configure the SOAP extension to Run With
'XML Web Service Methods)
<AttributeUsage(AttributeTargets.Method)> Public Class LogMessagesAttribute
    Inherits SoapExtensionAttribute

    'Supply default values
    Private m_intPriority As Integer = 0
    Private m_strLogFile As String = "\VBWS10\ReportsWS\Report.log"

    'Override the default values
    Public Sub New(ByVal strLogFile As String, ByVal intPriority As Integer)
       m_strLogFile = strLogFile
       m_intPriority = intPriority
    End Sub

    Public ReadOnly Property strLogFile() As String
       Get
           strLogFile = m_strLogFile
       End Get
    End Property

    Public Overrides Property Priority() As Integer
       Get
           Priority = m_intPriority
       End Get
       Set(ByVal Value As Integer)
          m_intPriority = Value
       End Set
    End Property

    Public Overrides ReadOnly Property ExtensionType() As Type
       Get
           Return GetType(LogMessages)
       End Get
    End Property
End Class

'Applying the LogMessages("\Path\Name.log", Priority) attribute
'to a WebMethod instantiates the following class derived from SoapExtension
'(Help Topic: "Derive a Class From SoapExtension")
Public Class LogMessages
    Inherits SoapExtension

    Private strLogFile As String
    Private stmSoap As Stream
    Private stmTemp As Stream
    Private lngTicks As Long
```

```vb
Public Overloads Overrides Function GetInitializer(ByVal _
    serviceType As Type) As Object
  'Get the service type
  '(Help Topic: "Initialize SOAP extension specific data")
  Return Nothing
End Function

Public Overloads Overrides Function GetInitializer(ByVal _
   methodInfo As LogicalMethodInfo, _
   ByVal attribute As SoapExtensionAttribute) As Object
   'Get the initializer for the strLogFile attribute
   Dim atrLog As LogMessagesAttribute = _
      CType(attribute, LogMessagesAttribute)
   Return atrLog.strLogFile
End Function

Public Overrides Sub Initialize(ByVal initializer As Object)
   'Get the strLogFile value from the initializer
   strLogFile = initializer.ToString
End Sub

Public Overrides Function ChainStream(ByVal stream As Stream) As Stream
   'Replace the default soap message streams with the stmSoap and stmTemp
   '(Help Topic: "Save a Reference to the Stream Representing
   'Future SOAP messages")
   stmSoap = stream
   stmTemp = New MemoryStream()
   Return stmTemp
End Function

Public Overrides Sub ProcessMessage(ByVal message As SoapMessage)
   'Log the serialized messages at the appropriate stages
   '(Help Topic: "Process the SOAP messages")
   Select Case message.Stage
      Case SoapMessageStage.BeforeDeserialize
         'Get time and write the request message
         'Ticks are 100 ns increments
         lngTicks = DateTime.Now.Ticks
         Call WriteRequest()
      Case SoapMessageStage.AfterDeserialize
         'Do nothing
      Case SoapMessageStage.BeforeSerialize
         'Do nothing
      Case SoapMessageStage.AfterSerialize
         'Get elapsed time and write the response message
         lngTicks = DateTime.Now.Ticks - lngTicks
         Call WriteResponse(lngTicks)
   End Select
End Sub
```

```vb
Sub WriteRequest()
    'Append the request message to the log and
    'return the stream to the service
    CopyStream(stmSoap, stmTemp)
    Dim fsRequest As New FileStream(strLogFile, _
        FileMode.Append, FileAccess.Write)
    Dim swRequest As New StreamWriter(fsRequest)
    swRequest.WriteLine("<!-- SOAP Request at " + _
        DateTime.Now.ToString + " -->")
    swRequest.Flush()
    stmTemp.Position = 0
    CopyStream(stmTemp, fsRequest)
    fsRequest.Close()
    stmTemp.Position = 0
End Sub


Sub WriteResponse(ByVal lngTicks As Long)
    'Append the response message to the log and
    'return the stream to the service
    Dim fsResponse As New FileStream(strLogFile, _
        FileMode.Append, FileAccess.Write)
    Dim swResponse As New StreamWriter(fsResponse)
    With swResponse
        .WriteLine("<!-- SOAP Response at " + _
            DateTime.Now.ToString + " -->")
        .Flush()
        stmTemp.Position = 0
        CopyStream(stmTemp, fsResponse)
        'Divide by 10^7 to convert from 100 ns increments to seconds
        .WriteLine("<!-- Response time = " + _
            CStr(CDbl(lngTicks / 10000000)) + " seconds -->")
        .WriteLine("") 'Empty line
        .Flush()
    End With
    stmTemp.Position = 0
    CopyStream(stmTemp, stmSoap)
    fsResponse.Close()
End Sub

Public Sub CopyStream(ByVal stmSource As Stream, ByVal stmDest As Stream)
    'Copy the stream from the source to the destination
    Dim srSource As New StreamReader(stmSource)
    Dim swDest As New StreamWriter(stmDest)
    swDest.WriteLine(srSource.ReadToEnd())
    swDest.Flush()
End Sub
End Class
```

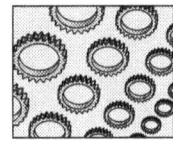

NOTE

The Sub New constructor has an `intPriority` argument for establishing the relative priority of multiple SOAP extensions. This example has one extension, so the code ignores the `intPriority` value. A 0 value runs an extension before other extensions with larger values. You can also assign SOAP extensions to groups and assign group priority values.

The `LogMessages` SOAP extension includes an added feature—a high-resolution timer that measures the interval in `DateTime.Ticks` from the beginning of request document deserialization to the end of response document serialization. For example, you can determine quite accurately the difference in performance between the validated and nonvalidated `WebMethods`. ASP.NET client-side tracing doesn't provide accurate data when making comparisons that differ by 100 ms or less, because network connectivity affects the trace data. Tracing performance of a service connected via the Internet is at least an order of magnitude less reliable.

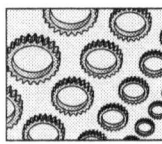

NOTE

`Ticks` represent 200 nanosecond intervals, which the `DateTime` structure uses to determine the date and time. The advantage of using `Ticks` for timing measurements is that `Ticks`—which start at a 0 value at 12:00:00 A.M. on January 1 of the year 1—don't roll over.

Enabling Message Logging and Reading the Log Files

Add the following generic attribute to the `<WebMethod ...>` prefix of `Public Function MethodName()` to enable logging to the *FileName*.log file:

```
LoggingClassName(strFileName[, intPriority])
```

These two instructions implement logging for the two `WebMethods` of the ReportsWS service:

```
<WebMethod(Description:="HTML Text"), _
SoapHeader("hdrAuthent", Required:=False), _
LogMessages("\VBWS10\ReportsWS\TimeSeriesReport.log", 0)> _…

<WebMethod(Description:="HTML Text"), _
SoapHeader("hdrAuthent", Required:=False), _
LogMessages("\VBWS10\ReportsWS\TimeSeriesValidated.log", 0)> _…
```

Following is an example of a log for a single request and response message to and from the ReportsWS XML Web service. The `WriteOutput` subprocedure doesn't add indentation and replaces XML-illegal characters in messages with entities, such as `&lt;` for < and `&gt;` for > in the TimeSeriesReport.log and TimeSeriesValidated.log text files. This sample has formatting added and entities replaced for readability:

```xml
<!-- SOAP Request at 3/28/2002 1:48:52 PM -->
<?xml version="1.0" encoding="utf-8"?>
<soap:Envelope
    xmlns:soap="http://schemas.xmlsoap.org/soap/envelope/"
    xmlns:xsi="http://www.w3.org/2001/XMLSchema-instance"
    xmlns:xsd="http://www.w3.org/2001/XMLSchema">
  <soap:Header><Authenticate
      xmlns="http://oakleaf.ws/services/crosstabs/">
    <ServerName>(local)</ServerName>
    <UserName>CustUser</UserName>
    <Password>Cust#123</Password></Authenticate>
  </soap:Header>
  <soap:Body>
    <TimeSeriesReport
        xmlns="http://oakleaf.ws/services/crosstabs/">
      <RequestDoc>
        <crosstab
            xmlns='http://oakleaf.ws/services/crosstabs/request' >
          <title>2001 Quarterly Orders by State</title>
          <timeseries>
            <datatable>Orders</datatable>
            <rowsby>State</rowsby>
            <startdate>2001-01-01</startdate>
            <starttime>00:00:00</starttime>
            <interval>Quarter</interval>
            <datacolumns>4</datacolumns>
            <count>false</count>
            <avgvalue>false</avgvalue>
            <rowtotals>true</rowtotals>
            <coltotals>true</coltotals>
            <nulltozero>true</nulltozero>
            <format>XML</format>
          </timeseries>
        </crosstab>
      </RequestDoc>
    </TimeSeriesReport>
  </soap:Body>
</soap:Envelope>

<!-- SOAP Response at 3/28/2002 1:48:54 PM -->
<?xml version="1.0" encoding="utf-8"?>
<soap:Envelope xmlns:soap="http://schemas.xmlsoap.org/soap/envelope/"
    xmlns:xsi="http://www.w3.org/2001/XMLSchema-instance"
    xmlns:xsd="http://www.w3.org/2001/XMLSchema">
  <soap:Body><TimeSeriesReportResponse
```

```
            xmlns="http://oakleaf.ws/services/crosstabs/">
        <TimeSeriesReportResult>
            <crosstab xmlns='http://oakleaf.ws/services/crosstabs/response' >
                <title>2001 Quarterly Orders by State</title>
                <header>
                  <hdrcols>
                    <hdrcol id='hdr_col_State' cell='R1C1'>State</hdrcol>
                    <hdrcol id='hdr_col_2001Q1' cell='R1C2'>2001Q1</hdrcol>
                    <hdrcol id='hdr_col_2001Q2' cell='R1C3'>2001Q2</hdrcol>
                    <hdrcol id='hdr_col_2001Q3' cell='R1C4'>2001Q3</hdrcol>
                    <hdrcol id='hdr_col_2001Q4' cell='R1C5'>2001Q4</hdrcol>
                    <hdrcol id='hdr_col_Totals' cell='R1C6'>Totals</hdrcol>
                  </hdrcols>
                </header>
                <data>
                  <row>
                    <col id='hdr_row_CO' cell='R2C1'>CO</col>
                    <col id='st_CO_2001Q1' cell='R2C2'>$166,419</col>
                    <col id='st_CO_2001Q2' cell='R2C3'>$343,470</col>
                    <col id='st_CO_2001Q3' cell='R2C4'>$584,724</col>
                    <col id='st_CO_2001Q4' cell='R2C5'>$802,211</col>
                    <col id='total_row2' cell='R2C6'>$1,896,824</col>
                  </row>
                  <row>
                    <col id='total_col1' cell='R14C1'>Totals</col>
                    <col id='total_col2' cell='R14C2'>$1,324,097</col>
                    <col id='total_col3' cell='R14C3'>$3,625,236</col>
                    <col id='total_col4' cell='R14C4'>$5,723,823</col>
                    <col id='total_col5' cell='R14C5'>$7,910,656</col>
                    <col id='total_col6' cell='R14C6'>$18,583,812</col>
                  </row>
                </data>
            </crosstab>
        </TimeSeriesReportResult>
      </TimeSeriesReportResponse>
    </soap:Body>
  </soap:Envelope>
  <!-- Response time = 1.2317835 seconds -->
```

Writing the code to implement SOAP extensions isn't for the faint of heart, and debugging code that modifies messages is an even more daunting challenge. Until Microsoft adds a "SOAP Extension Wizard" to Visual Studio .NET, consider SOAP extensions a last resort. In most cases, a combination of SOAP headers and procedural code in your XML Web service can handle message modification chores.

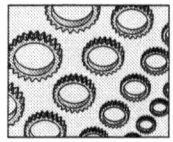

NOTE

Some secure XML Web services that employ encryption—other than today's HTTPS—might require SOAP extensions to manage encryption at service and consumer endpoints. Go to http://www.gotdotnet.com/ team/rhoward/default.aspx and click the Custom ASP.NET SOAP Extension For Encrypting Messages link for an early example written by Microsoft's Rob Howard, who also wrote the `TraceMessage` *extension.*

Caching XML Web Services

Chapter 7's "The WebMethodAttribute Class" section mentions that ASP.NET lets you cache the results of `WebMethods` on the XML Web service's server. Caching provides a substantial performance boost but only for successive, identical request documents or parameter values from the same machine running the consuming application. In this respect, XML Web service caching is very similar to SQL Server's approach to caching query result sets.

The CTOrders and CTSchema ASP.NET consumers might benefit from caching the default quarterly report for 2001, because that's the version most users will try first and might request repeatedly. On the other hand, there's no benefit from caching the four XML Web services that support the OakLeaf Consumer Electronics Order Processing Test Form at http://www.oakleaf.ws/OCE/Orders.aspx. Orders.aspx request documents have random parameter values, so cache hits by consumers have close to a zero probability.

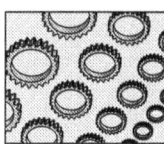

NOTE

Crystal Reports' caching mechanism isn't the same as XML Web service caching. Search online help's index for "caching Crystal Reports" for links to topics on Crystal Reports' caching methods.

To add caching to your ASP.NET XML Web services, add the following attribute to the initial `WebMethod` attribute whose results you want to cache:

```
CacheDuration:=intSeconds
```

For example, the following instruction caches the `TimeSeriesReport` or `TimeSeriesValidated` result for 60 seconds:

```
<WebMethod(Description:="HTML Text", CacheDuration:=60), _
    SoapHeader("hdrAuthent", Required:=False) > _…
```

The first time you click the CTSchema consumer's Get Report button, the service takes a few seconds to respond. Successive clicks return reports almost instantaneously.

The downside of caching XML Web services on the server is consumption of memory resources that might be better devoted to other tasks. If you decide to implement caching of commercial XML Web services, be sure to keep an eye on Task Manager's Physical Memory Available counter on the Performance page when conducting multiple-consumer scalability tests.

Advertising Public Web Services with UDDI

IN THIS CHAPTER:

Touring the Microsoft UDDI 1.0 Registry Site

Registering Services at an Operator Site

Adding a Web Reference from a UDDI Registry

Surveying the UDDI Specifications

Working with the UDDI .Net SDKs

Universal Description, Discovery, and Integration (UDDI) 1.0 and 2.0 are specifications for a set of XML Web services that provide access to searchable public or private databases of Web service descriptions. The most common description of UDDI implementations are "yellow pages" for Web services, but UDDI also implements "white pages" for businesses and "green pages" for service descriptions. UDDI's intent is to provide a means to locate organizations that offer a particular product or service and to describe the Web services that are involved in purchasing the products or services. UDDI is the first large-scale XML Web service intended for public use.

Unlike the print version of the Yellow Pages, there's no charge for advertising your business in the first two public UDDI 1.0 registries run by Microsoft and IBM. All public UDDI registries replicate their content daily, so the only basic difference between the registries is the design of search and administration Web pages. Registering a business doesn't require the organization to provide Web services or the organization and its registered services to exist. It's also possible for unscrupulous individuals to add bogus entries for well-known firms. When this book was written, almost all the 8500 entries in the public UDDI 1.0 registries were spam.

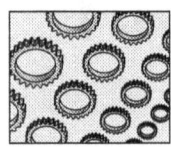

NOTE

*Hewlett-Packard, IBM, Microsoft, NTT Communications, and SAP were conducting beta tests of UDDI 2.0 registries in early 2002. Version 2.0 also permits unmoderated business registrations. For an example of spam in the UDDI 1.0 databases, go to http://uddi.microsoft.com, type **%** in the Search text box, click the arrow to display the first six entries, and read a few more pages.*

Web services pundits assign UDDI stature equal to—and occasionally greater than—the SOAP and WSDL specifications. The hype behind UDDI is that organizations will find Web service-enabled "business partners" by searching the UDDI database for a product or service, and then automating purchases in accordance with a WSDL file and its accompanying documentation, if any. In today's B2B world, most business partners already know one another and will undoubtedly negotiate interoperability of their respective XML Web services directly. A more likely early-adopter scenario is deployment of private UDDI registries by large organizations having many independent XML Web service development teams. Windows .NET Server Beta 3 and later includes an option to create an enterprisewide UDDI 2.0 registry.

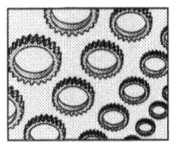

NOTE

Running a private UDDI 2.0 registry under Windows .NET Server Beta 3 or later requires SQL Server or MSDE 2000. You must also download Windows .NET Server UDDI Services Beta 3 or later from the Microsoft Web site.

Touring the Microsoft UDDI 1.0 Registry Site

The best way to understand how UDDI works is to examine a registered business entity that has published a set of fully documented XML Web services. Registrations for the OakLeaf Code of Federal Regulations (CFR) demonstration XML Web services in the Microsoft production (UDDI 1.0) registry serve as examples in the following sections. The Microsoft beta implementation of the UDDI 2.0 registry at http://uddi.rte.microsoft.com/ had a UI that was under construction when this book was written; much of the content of the site was outdated, and there were very few—if any—valid entries for Web services of any type.

TIP

You can publish only one business with a default Level 1 publisher account, which has additional restrictions on the number of other UDDI records you can add. Thus, it's a good practice to view a few complete registrations before you register your organization and the XML web services you offer. Click the Policies and Publishing Restrictions links for more information on Level 1 publishing limits. You can request a Level 2 publisher account by e-mail; the link is at the bottom of the Policies page.

The Business Entity Page

Business entities, also called the "white pages," are the default top-level search element. Figure 11-1 illustrates the relationships between a user account and the elements (called *structures*) of a complete UDDI 1.0 or 2.0 registration. All elements shown in Figure 11-1 apply to UDDI 1.0, except the `publisherAssertion` structure added by the UDDI 2.0 specification. Brackets enclose the XML prefix because the UDDI specification applies to any Web service, and isn't limited to XML Web services that have WSDL files or documents, or use the document/literal style for request and response documents.

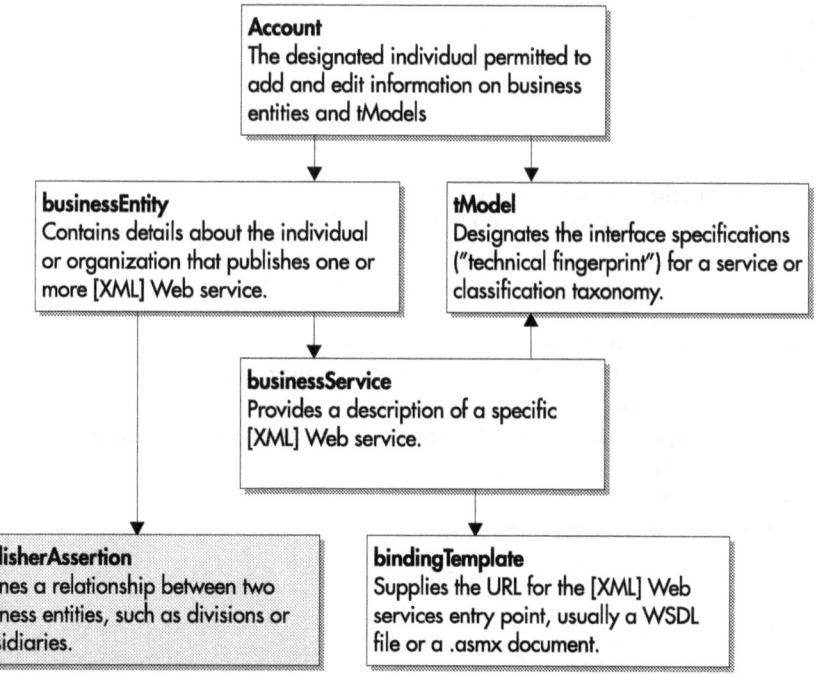

Figure 11-1 *This diagram illustrates the relationships between the UDDI publisher account and the structures (elements) of UDDI 1.0 and UDDI 2.0 registries. (The structure added by UDDI 2.0 is shaded.)*

To start the tour of entries for the OakLeaf `businessEntity` XML document, go to http://uddi.microsoft.com, type **oakleaf** in the Search text box, and press ENTER to display a list of business entities. Click the OakLeaf Systems link to open the Business Entity page. (See Figure 11-2.)

Business Detail and Contacts

The Business Detail section contains the business entity name, a GUID for the entity, and a description of the business. There's no provision in UDDI 1.0 for business entity divisions or subsidiaries. Version 2.0 adds the capability to describe business units, departments, divisions, and subsidiaries, and it supports business and service descriptions in multiple languages.

Following are the elements of OakLeaf Systems' `businessEntity` document that populate the Business Detail section:

```
<?xml version="1.0" encoding="utf-8"?>
<businessEntity xmlns:xsi="http://www.w3.org/2001/XMLSchema-instance"
    xmlns:xsd="http://www.w3.org/2001/XMLSchema"
    businessKey="A1701D8A-AB45-42D7-A0E8-D10C968E2A12"
    operator="Microsoft Corporation" authorizedName="Roger Jennings"
    xmlns="urn:uddi-org:api">
  ...
  <name>OakLeaf Systems</name>
  <description xml:lang="en">Design and Development of Data-Intensive
    XML Web Services and Consuming Applications ("Visual Basic .NET
    XML Web Services Developer's Guide", McGraw-Hill/Osborne,
    ISBN 0-07-222369-3, Spring 2002)</description>
  ...
</businessEntity>
```

The Contacts section contains individual `<contact>` elements for each member of the list; these elements don't have a GUID. Here's the `<contacts>` fragment of the `businessEntity` document:

```
<contacts>
  <contact useType="Info on demo XML Web Services">
    <description xml:lang="en">Principal</description>
    <personName>Roger Jennings</personName>
    <email useType="Plain Text">Roger_Jennings@compuserve.com</email>
    <address sortCode="" useType="">
      <addressLine>Oakland, CA</addressLine>
      <addressLine>USA</addressLine>
    </address>
  </contact>
</contacts>
```

Services

The Services section contains a list of all Web services published by the business entity. The list contains a name, description, and GUID for each `<businessService>` element, as

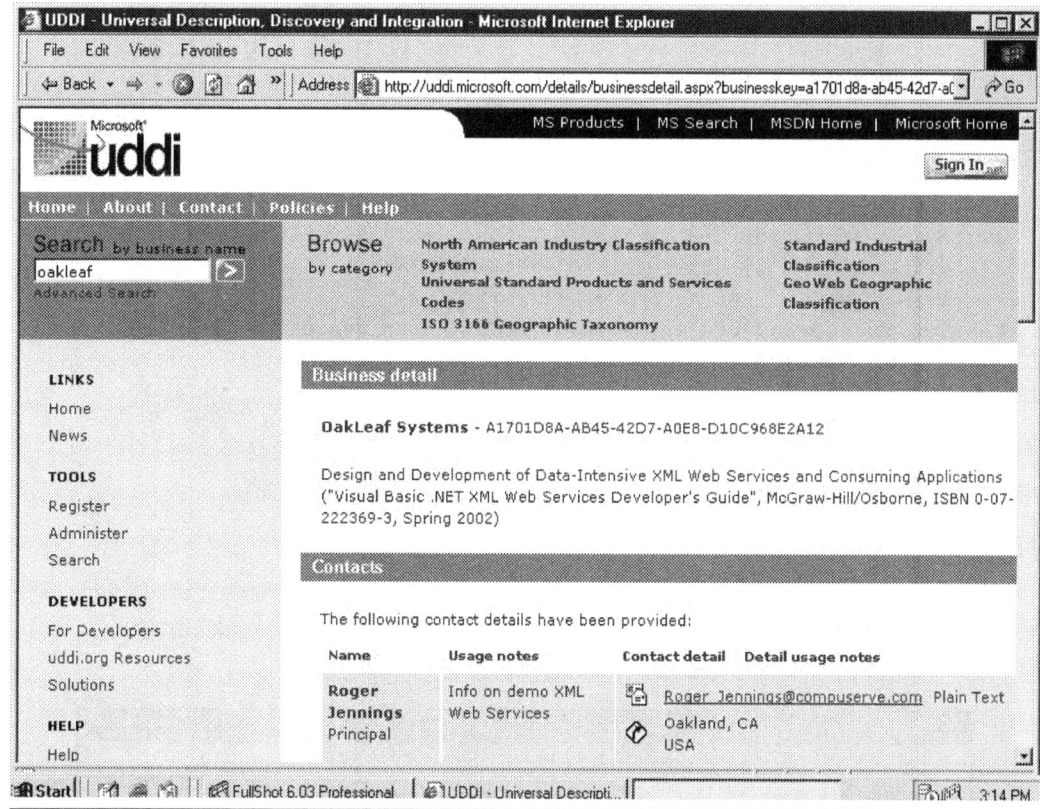

Figure 11-2   *The Microsoft UDDI 1.0 Business Entity page for OakLeaf Systems has six sections, only two of which are shown here.*

shown here. Operators limit Level 1 publishers to two business services per business entity. Clicking a service name link opens a Business Service page.

Name	Description	Service Key
OakLeaf CFR Services	Online Access to the OakLeaf U.S. Code of Federal Regulations delivered as XML or XHTML documents (not an official version of the U.S. CFR)	bf8240a4-a967-4845-b432-466f8944b899
OakLeaf CFR Search Service	Peforms a full-text search of the OakLeaf CFR demonstration database	fc67cac2-4d0c-4e0b-9762-31ebbbb6cb51

Subelements that are described in the later section "The Business Service Page" have been removed from the following `<businessServices>` document fragment for brevity:

```
<businessServices>
 <businessService serviceKey="bf8240a4-a967-4845-b432-466f8944b899"
```

```
        businessKey="a1701d8a-ab45-42d7-a0e8-d10c968e2a12">
    <name>OakLeaf CFR Services</name>
    <description xml:lang="en">Online Access to the OakLeaf U.S. Code of
        Federal Regulations delivered as XML or XHTML documents
        (not an official version of the U.S. CFR)</description>
    ...
  </businessService>
  <businessService serviceKey="fc67cac2-4d0c-4e0b-9762-31ebbbb6cb51"
        businessKey="a1701d8a-ab45-42d7-a0e8-d10c968e2a12">
    <name>OakLeaf CFR Search Service</name>
    <description xml:lang="en">Peforms a full-text search of the
        OakLeaf CFR demonstration database</description>
    ...
  </businessService>
  ...
</businessServices>
```

Business Identifiers

The Business Identifiers section, also part of the "white pages," is intended for adding records that represent identifying codes for the business, such as the Dun & Bradstreet nine-digit D-U-N-S® number for OakLeaf Systems, shown here.

Business Identifiers		
Identifiers are pieces of data that are unique to an individual business e.g. a D-U-N-S® Number. These enable users of the registry to confirm the identity of a listed business.		
Identifier type	**Name**	**Value**
D-U-N-S® Number	OakLeaf Systems	072625135

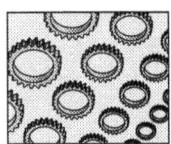

NOTE

You can learn more about D-U-N-S numbers and apply for your own unique numeric identifier at http://www.dunandbradstreet.com/. There's no charge for obtaining a D-U-N-S number.

D&B claims more than 64 million registrations. UDDI 1.0 also recognizes Thomas Register supplier ID codes, which are less commonly used than D-U-N-S numbers. Microsoft's UDDI registry also supports RealNames keywords, which the Office XP Web Services Toolkit expects as values in its Keywords text box. The Advanced Search option lets you locate business entities by identifier name and `keyValue`.

Following is the `<identifierBag>` element for a single D-U-N-S identifier:

```
<identifierBag>
  <keyedReference
```

```
    tModelKey="uuid:8609c81e-ee1f-4d5a-b202-3eb13ad01823" _
    keyName="OakLeaf Systems" keyValue="072625135" />
</identifierBag>
```

The `tModelKey` attribute value identifies D-U-N-S as a taxonomy—one of the three business identifiers supported by UDDI 1.0. UDDI version 2.0 permits trade organizations and businesses to submit additional business identifiers and other taxonomies to the registry operator for public or restricted use. The later " The Instance Detail and tModel Pages" section describes `tModel` documents.

Business Classifications

The Business Classifications section contains a list of industry and geographic location codes based on national and international standards. Business classifications support UDDI's "yellow pages" feature; you can perform an advanced search on any of the following business classification entries. The following table lists UDDI 1.0's standard classification taxonomies.

Code	Taxonomy Name and Source for More Information	Applies To
NAICS	North American Industry Classification Standard (http://www.naics.com/info.htm)	Canada, Mexico, U.S.
UNSPSC	Universal Standard Products and Services Codes (http://eccma.org/unspsc/)	Worldwide
ISO 3166	International Standards Organization Geographic Taxonomy (http://www.iso.ch/iso/en/prods-services/iso3166ma/)	Worldwide
SIC	Standard Industrial Classification (http://www.naics.com/info.htm)	U.S.
GeoWeb	SRI/DARPA Digital Earth Geographic Classification (http://www.dgeo.org/)	Worldwide
UDDI Types	UDDI-specific classifications for `tModels`, such as specification for a Web service—`wsdlSpec` or `soapSpec`	`tModels`

The UDDI 1.0 specification calls NAICS, UNSPSC, and ISO 3166 *core taxonomies*. Six-digit NAICS and hierarchical UNSPSC codes, which the United Nations promulgates, are the preferred industrial classification taxonomies; four-digit SIC codes are obsolete. UNSPSC codes provide more granularity than NAICS, especially for computer-related products and services, as shown here. ISO 3166 country-region codes, such as US-CA, aren't as granular as GeoWeb codes, which let you specify country, state and province, or region and city.

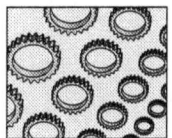 **NOTE**

UDDI Types classifications apply only to `tModels`, and you should not add them as business entity classifications.

Business classifications

Classifications are pieces of data that classify the field of operation of a business or a service e.g. a geographic location or an industry sector. These enable users of the registry to confirm the relevance of a particular entry.

Classification	Name	Value
NAICS	On-Line Information Services	514191
NAICS	Database and Directory Publishers	51114
NAICS	Custom Computer Programming Services	541511
UNSPSC	On line database information retrieval	81.11.19.02.00
UNSPSC	Programming for Visual Basic	81.11.16.01.00
UNSPSC	Internet or intranet server application development services	81.11.15.10.00
UNSPSC	Internet or intranet client application development services	81.11.15.09.00
UNSPSC	ERP or database applications programming services	81.11.15.07.00
ISO 3166 Geographic Taxonomy	California	US-CA

Here are the `<categoryBag>` elements for the OakLeaf Systems business entity:

```
<businessEntity>
  ...
  <categoryBag>
    <keyedReference tModelKey="uuid:c0b9fe13-179f-413d-8a5b-5004db8e5bb2"
      keyName="On-Line Information Services" keyValue="514191" />
    <keyedReference tModelKey="uuid:c0b9fe13-179f-413d-8a5b-5004db8e5bb2"
      keyName="Database and Directory Publishers" keyValue="51114" />
    <keyedReference tModelKey="uuid:c0b9fe13-179f-413d-8a5b-5004db8e5bb2"
      keyName="Custom Computer Programming Services" keyValue="541511" />
    <keyedReference tModelKey="uuid:cd153257-086a-4237-b336-6bdcbdcc6634"
     keyName="On line database information retrieval"
     keyValue="81.11.19.02.00" />
    <keyedReference tModelKey="uuid:cd153257-086a-4237-b336-6bdcbdcc6634"
     keyName="Programming for Visual Basic" keyValue="81.11.16.01.00" />
    <keyedReference tModelKey="uuid:cd153257-086a-4237-b336-6bdcbdcc6634"
      keyName="Internet or intranet server application development services"
      keyValue="81.11.15.10.00" />
    <keyedReference tModelKey="uuid:cd153257-086a-4237-b336-6bdcbdcc6634"
      keyName="Internet or intranet client application development services"
      keyValue="81.11.15.09.00" />
    <keyedReference tModelKey="uuid:cd153257-086a-4237-b336-6bdcbdcc6634"
      keyName="ERP or database applications programming services"
      keyValue="81.11.15.07.00" />
    <keyedReference tModelKey="uuid:4e49a8d6-d5a2-4fc2-93a0-0411d8d19e88"
```

```
        keyName="California" keyValue="US-CA" />
    </categoryBag>
</businessEntity>
```

Like business identification taxonomies, each recognized business classification and geographic location taxonomy has its own `tModel`. The sequence of `<keyedReference>` elements in the `businessEntity` document determines their position in the Business Classifications list.

Discovery URLs

Discovery URLs, the last section of the Business Entity page, provide a link to a source of additional information about the business—usually the default or an About page of the organization's Web site. You can search for a business entity by the value of one or more of its `<discoveryURL>` element(s). Clicking the businessEntity link opens in your browser the complete `businessEntity` document specified by the entity's GUID.

Discovery URLs

Discovery URLs provide a location where details about a particular entity can be found.

Discovery URL	Usage notes
http://www.oakleaf.ws/	OakLeaf XML Web Services Site
http://uddi.microsoft.com/discovery?businessKey=A1701D8A-AB45-42D7-A0E8-D10C968E2A12	businessEntity

The `<discoveryURLs>` element is the last on the Business Entity page, but it's the first subelement of the `businessEntity` document:

```
<businessEntity xmlns:xsi="http://www.w3.org/2001/XMLSchema-instance"
    … />
  <discoveryURLs>
    <discoveryURL useType="OakLeaf XML Web Services Site">
      http://www.oakleaf.ws/</discoveryURL>
    <discoveryURL useType="businessEntity">
      http://uddi.microsoft.com/discovery?
        businessKey=A1701D8A-AB45-42D7-A0E8-D10C968E2A12
    </discoveryURL>
  </discoveryURLs>
```

The `businessEntity` document's `<discoveryURL>` element value opens the XML document in your browser. The Discovery URL is similar to the URL to open OakLeaf Systems' Business Entity page directly: http://uddi.microsoft.com/details/businessdetail.aspx?businesskey=a1701d8a-ab45-42d7-a0e8-d10c968e2a12.

The Business Service Page

Business services are the foundation of UDDI's "green pages" search service. Clicking the OakLeaf CFR Services link opens the Business Service page with Service Detail, Bindings, and Service Classifications sections. The Service Detail section repeats the name, service key, and description from the Services section of the Business Entity page. The Service Classification section enables adding specific NAICS, UNSPSC, or other recognized business and geographical codes for the service. The Bindings section shown here is the key element of the Business Service page.

Bindings

This details the specific access points for this service instance and allows display of additional instance specific details.

Access point	URL type	Description	Binding Key	Instance details
http://www.oakleaf.ws/cfrtocws/cfrtocws.asmx	http	WSDL Document for CFR-TOC service (with description)	A81732D7-450A-40AB-9ECF-89A6F50B20D6	Details
http://www.oakleaf.ws/cfrsectws/cfrsectws.asmx	http	WSDL Document for CFR-Section Service (with description)	7C273DEF-9DBD-4068-9506-DF5DDB09F7F1	Details

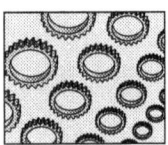

NOTE

Level 1 publishers are limited to two bindings per service. Thus, the three CFR XML Web services are divided into two business services: OakLeaf CFR Services, which has two bindings, and OakLeaf CFR Search Service, which has one. OakLeaf Systems obtained Level 2 status after publishing these services.

Bindings specify an Access Point, URL Type, Binding Key, and an Instance Details link to a Specification Signature (`tModel`), which is the subject of the next section. The value of the `<accessPoint>` element is usually the URL for the WSDL document or file for the service, but the UDDI 1.0 and 2.0 specifications don't require the service description document to use WSDL. UDDI best practices for XML Web services dictate a URL that points to a .wsdl or .asmx file. The value of the `URLType` attribute can be `http`, `https`, `ftp`, `mailto`, `fax`, `phone`, or `other`. The `<bindingKey>` attribute value is a pointer to collection of one or more `tModel`(s) for the service.

Following is the `businessEntity` document fragment for OakLeaf CFR Services; the next section describes the omitted `tModel` elements:

```
<businessServices>
  <businessService serviceKey="bf8240a4-a967-4845-b432-466f8944b899"
      businessKey="a1701d8a-ab45-42d7-a0e8-d10c968e2a12">
    <name>OakLeaf CFR Services</name>
    <description xml:lang="en">Online Access to the OakLeaf U.S. Code
      of Federal Regulations delivered as XML or XHTML documents
      (not an official version of the U.S. CFR)</description>
    <bindingTemplates>
      <bindingTemplate serviceKey="bf8240a4-a967-4845-b432-466f8944b899"
          bindingKey="a81732d7-450a-40ab-9ecf-89a6f50b20d6">
        <description xml:lang="en">WSDL Document for CFR-TOC service
          (with description)</description>
        <accessPoint
          URLType="http">http://www.oakleaf.ws/cfrtocws/cfrtocws.asmx
        </accessPoint>
        <tModelInstanceDetails>
          ...
        </tModelInstanceDetails>
      </bindingTemplate>
      <bindingTemplate serviceKey="bf8240a4-a967-4845-b432-466f8944b899"
          bindingKey="7c273def-9dbd-4068-9506-df5ddb09f7f1">
        <description xml:lang="en">WSDL Document for CFR-Section Service
          (with description)</description>
        <accessPoint
          URLType="http">http://www.oakleaf.ws/cfrsectws/cfrsectws.asmx
        </accessPoint>
        <tModelInstanceDetails>
          ...
        </tModelInstanceDetails>
      </bindingTemplate>
    </bindingTemplates>
    <categoryBag>
      <keyedReference tModelKey="uuid:c0b9fe13-179f-413d-8a5b-5004db8e5bb2"
        keyName="On-Line Information Services" keyValue="514191" />
      <keyedReference tModelKey="uuid:cd153257-086a-4237-b336-6bdcbdcc6634"
        keyName="On line database information retrieval"
        keyValue="81.11.19.02.00" />
      <keyedReference tModelKey="uuid:cd153257-086a-4237-b336-6bdcbdcc6634"
        keyName="Remote database information retrieval"
          keyValue="81.11.19.03.00" />
    </categoryBag>
  </businessService>
  ...
</businessServices>
```

Adding description text, HTML code, or both to the <WebService> and <WebMethod> attributes of your ASP.NET XML Web service is another best practice for services you publish in public or private UDDI registries. Figure 11-3 shows the documentation for the CFRToc

XML Web service. The advantages of specifying the .asmx file for services are that there's no restriction on the length of the description text, and you can use HTML to format the document and add links to pages that contain supporting information for the services. The UDDI specification limits description text to 255 characters.

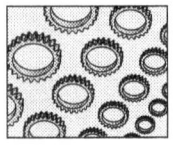

NOTE

The test forms for the CFRToc service's `GetTocByID` *method and CFRSect's* `GetSectByID` *method let you test the service with HTTP* `GET` *operations. Copy the supplied connection string to the strConnect text box and the sample navigation attribute value to the strID text box. Click Invoke to return the XML version of the TOC or section.*

The Instance Detail and tModel Pages

The Instance Details page displays information about one or more **tModels** within a binding template. **tModels** exist independently of business entities, because services provided by

```
CFRToc Web Service - Microsoft Internet Explorer                         _ □ ×
 File   Edit   View   Favorites   Tools   Help
 ← Back  ·  → ·  ◎  ☑  ⌂  »  Address  http://www.oakleaf.ws/cfrtocws/cfrtocws.asmx    ▼  ⬈ Go

 CFRToc

 CFRTocWS is one of three document/literal ASP.NET XML Web services for OakLeaf Systems Code of Federal
 Regulations (CFR) demonstration/development database. The 1-GB SQL Server 2000 database (CFRSQL) contains
 the entire text of the 204 volumes of the CFR as individual structured XML documents, which range in size from
 about 1,000 to more than 500,000 characters. A Visual Basic .NET client handles the transformation from the U.S.
 Government Printing Office's unstructured SGML to well-formed XML documents.

 CFRTocWS provides basic navigation services to XML Web service client applications. The service returns table of
 contents (TOC) documents for individual CFR titles, subtitles, chapters, subchapters, and parts. You can specify XML
 or XHTML as the format for the response document. The XHTML transformation is what you see when navigating the
 OakLeaf CFR Web site.

 Click here for further details about the XML and XHTML response document formats.

 The OakLeaf Systems CFR XML Web services are for demonstration/development use only and do not
 return official content of the U.S. CFR. Click here to go to the official U.S. GPO/NARA eCFR Beta Test
 Site.

 The following operations are supported. For a formal definition, please review the Service Description.

   • GetTocByLevel

     The GetTOCByLevel Web method accepts the following xsd:string arguments:

       ○ strConnect is an OLEDB connection string for the SQL Server 2000 CFRSQL database. The standard
         connection string is Provider=SQLOLEDB;Data Source=OAKLEAF-MS7;Initial
         Catalog=CFRSQL;UID=CFRUser;PWD=charon?123. CFRUser has dbdatareader permissions for the
         database.

       ○ strTitleId is a valid CFR title number (1 through 50, except titles 2 and 6, which are reserved.) If you leave
         this and the remaining TOC arguments empty, the response document is a XML TOC document of all titles
         and subtitles. If you enter a title number, you receive a TOC of chapters and subchapters for the title.

 Done                                                              Internet
```

Figure 11-3   *The OakLeaf CFRToc XML Web service's WSDL document incorporates HTML-formatted description content.*

multiple companies can depend on another organization's `tModel`s. For example, Rosettanet has more than 80 registered `tModel`s for B2B electronic components services. Members of Rosettanet, such as electronic product manufacturers and distributors, integrate these `tModel`s with their own services.

The Instance Details page has Specification Signature, Instance Details, and Overview Document sections, which correspond to element values obtained from the `tModel`. (See Figure 11-4.) If the WSDL document includes a full description of the service, the `<overviewDoc>` element value is usually the URL to the .wsdl or .asmx file for the service. Otherwise, the value is a URL for the service's documentation.

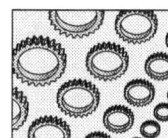

NOTE

The recommended naming convention for `tModel`s is the IETF Uniform Resource Name (URN) Syntax (RFC2141). The IETF defines URNs as "persistent, location-independent, resource identifiers." A review of the `tModel` URNs for Microsoft and other operational services indicates that the UDDI convention is to omit the `urn:` prefix required by RFC2141. OakLeaf URNs are derived from the XML Web service's namespace; for example, the `http://oakleaf.ws/cfr/toc` namespace becomes `oakleaf-ws:cfr:toc:version`. For more information on URN syntax, go to http://www.ietf.org/rfc/rfc2141.txt.

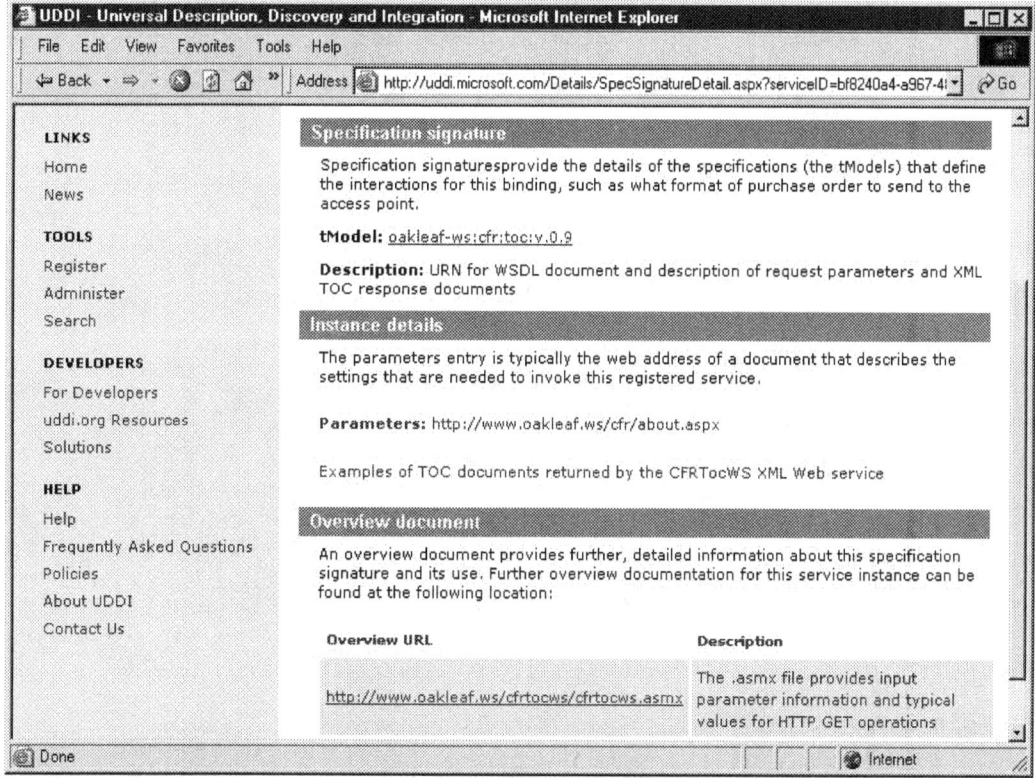

Figure 11-4   *Microsoft's UDDI Instance Details page displays values from the XML Web service's `tModel` registration data.*

Following is the `<bindingTemplate>` document fragment for OakLeaf's CFRToc service with the subelements whose values populate the Instance Details page:

```
<bindingTemplates>
  <bindingTemplate serviceKey="bf8240a4-a967-4845-b432-466f8944b899"
        bindingKey="a81732d7-450a-40ab-9ecf-89a6f50b20d6">
    <description xml:lang="en">
      WSDL Document for CFR-TOC service (with description)
    </description>
    <accessPoint URLType="http">
      http://www.oakleaf.ws/cfrtocws/cfrtocws.asmx
    </accessPoint>
    <tModelInstanceDetails>
      <tModelInstanceInfo
          tModelKey="uuid:b21ab15b-555b-473d-a560-2e30fd4f7e42">
        <description xml:lang="en">
          URN for WSDL document and description of request parameters
          and XML TOC response documents
        </description>
        <instanceDetails>
          <description xml:lang="en">
            Examples of TOC documents returned by the CFRTocWS
            XML Web service
          </description>
          <overviewDoc>
            <description xml:lang="en">
              The .asmx file provides input parameter information and
              typical values for HTTP GET operations
            </description>
            <overviewURL>
              http://www.oakleaf.ws/cfrtocws/cfrtocws.asmx
            </overviewURL>
          </overviewDoc>
            <instanceParms>
              http://www.oakleaf.ws/cfr/about.aspx
            </instanceParms>
        </instanceDetails>
      </tModelInstanceInfo>
    </tModelInstanceDetails>
  </bindingTemplate>
  ...
<bindingTemplates>
```

Deleting a business entity registration removes the organization's `businessEntity` document from the database, but doesn't remove `tModels` that the business itself registered or those to which its services refer. This prevents inadvertent deletion of a `tModel` on which other services depend. Only the publisher of a `tModel` can hide or remove its registration. Hiding a `tModel` prevents it from appearing in a search list, but doesn't affect access to the `tModel` from the Specification Signature section.

The Specification Signature section has a link to the tModel page, which has `tModel` Detail, Overviews, Service Classifications, and Business Identifiers sections. (See Figure 11-5.) Service classifications for `tModel`s are often more specific than those for business entities. Microsoft's UDDI 1.0 Advanced Search feature lets you search for `tModel`s by full or partial name, but not by other attributes. For example, to find all `tModel`s with CFR in their URNs, in Advanced Search, type **%cfr** in the Search For text box and select tModel By Name in the list. Clicking the tModel name in the Search Results list opens a list of business entities that support or consume the service; clicking (details) opens the tModel page.

NOTE

Level 1 publishers are limited to a maximum of ten `tModel`*s.*

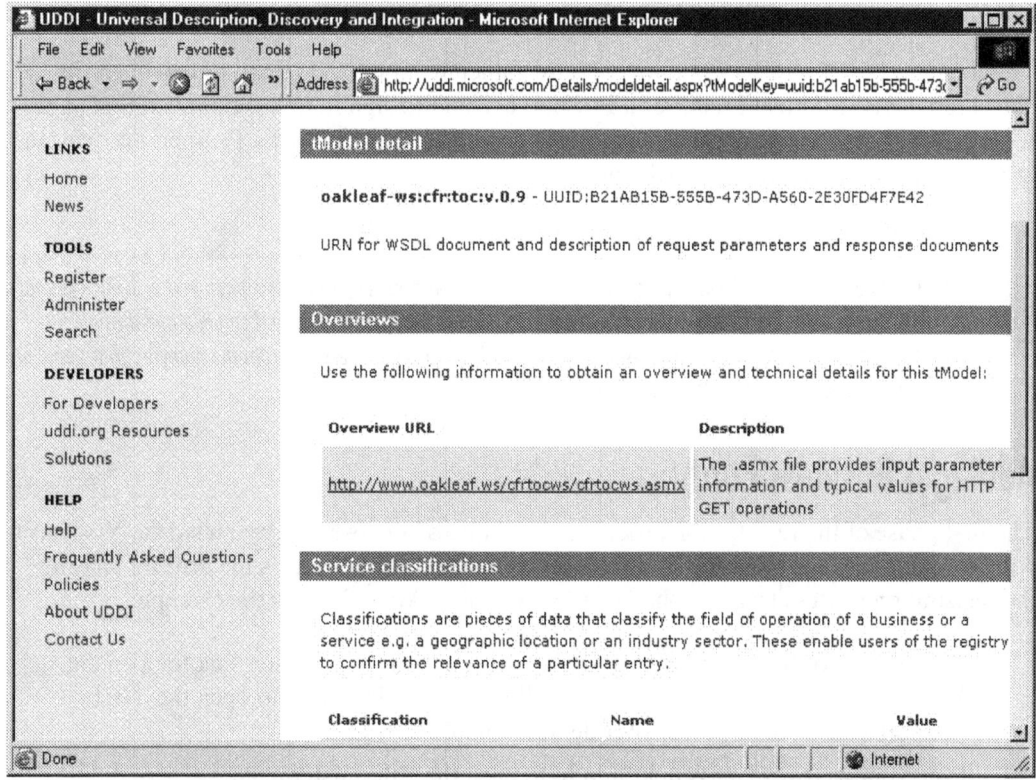

Figure 11-5   *The tModel page displays more information about the* `tModel` *for the service than the Instance Details page. (The Business Identifiers section doesn't appear in this figure.)*

Registering Services at an Operator Site

Unless you need to add a very large number of XML Web services to a public UDDI registry, the most practical approach is to take advantage of the operator's administration pages. Writing production-quality Visual Basic .NET code to publish your services in a UDDI 1.0 registry is a time-consuming process, and you'll need to update your applications when UDDI 2.0 goes live.

The following sections describe how to add a business entity, tModels, service descriptions, and other XML Web service metadata to the Microsoft UDDI 1.0 registry. The process is similar to that for the IBM registry, which has a substantially different UI. Neither of the administration pages have totally intuitive UIs, and Microsoft's site has a few gotchas, which were uncovered when adding the OakLeaf Systems registration. These anomalies account for what might appear as overly detailed step-by-step instructions in the following sections.

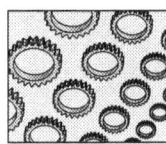

NOTE

If you want to experiment with a business registration or duplicate a registration that exists on a production site, use the Microsoft Test UDDI 1.0 Registry at http://test.uddi.microsoft.com/. It's not good form and might be illegal to counterfeit registrations of Web services that have been registered by their copyright owners or for which you don't have the express, written permission of the copyright owner.

All public UDDI registry operators require authentication to add, edit, or delete entries. Not surprisingly, Microsoft requires a Passport account to sign in to its administration pages. It's a good bet that every serious Visual Basic developer has acquired a Passport account; the following sections assume you have one.

TIP

It's a best practice to document your ASP.NET XML Web services fully with description text or HTML code for the service and its methods before you publish the service in a public registry. Complete and attractively formatted documentation in the .asmx page helps distinguish your services from the many nonfunctional or trivial registrations that litter the UDDI 1.0 registry.

Adding a Business Entity

The first phase of the registration process is to add businessEntity metadata. You can't add any other data until you provide at least the business name. Here's the drill for starting the registration process using Alpha Distributors, Inc., (AlphaDist) as the example:

1. On any page of the Microsoft UDDI 1.0 site, click the Administer link to open the Administration Registration page, and click the Sign In button to open the .NET Passport Sign In dialog with your default e-mail address.

2. Type your password and click Sign In to open the Administer page.

TIP

For security reasons, don't mark the Remember My Password check box when signing in. If you use a cookie to sign in automatically, you might encounter fatal errors when attempting to add or edit elements of your registration.

3. Click the Add A New Business link to open the Business Detail page. Type the business name (required) and an optional brief description of the business in the two text boxes.

4. Click Save to open the Edit Business page, which has Business Detail, Contacts, Services, Identifiers, Business Classifications, and Discovery URLs sections. Only the Business Detail section has content at this point.

5. Scroll to the bottom of the page and click the Add Discovery URL link to open the Discovery URL Detail page. Type the default URL for your Web site or a page that describes your entire range of XML Web services, and add a brief (20 characters or fewer) description of the page as the `useType` attribute value.

TIP

If you don't add `discoveryURL` metadata, the business entity won't be published in the next step, and you must start over. Contrary to the note on the page, Microsoft won't assign a `businessEntity` GUID without a Discovery URL entry.

6. Click Publish to assign a GUID to your business entity and save the data by committing the transaction. Publishing the business entity at this point assures that additional metadata or corrections you enter aren't lost. This step is especially important when you register multiple business entries as a Level 2 publisher.

7. Click Administer to return to the Administer page, and click the Edit link for your business entity. Each business and description you enter, if you're a Level 2 publisher, appears in the Business Name list.

8. Click the Add A Contact link to open the Contact Details page and complete the entries for the person responsible for handling inquires about your XML Web services. Figure 11-6 shows fictitious entries for Alpha Distributors, Inc. (AlphaDist).

9. Click Continue to return to the Business Entity Edit page. To save your addition at this point, click Publish.

TIP

Don't add entries to the Business Services section at this point. A business service requires adding its `tModel` prior to completing a business service registration.

10. If you have a D-U-N-S number or Thomas Supplier ID, scroll to the Identifiers section, click Add An Identifier, and complete the information required by the Add Identifier page.

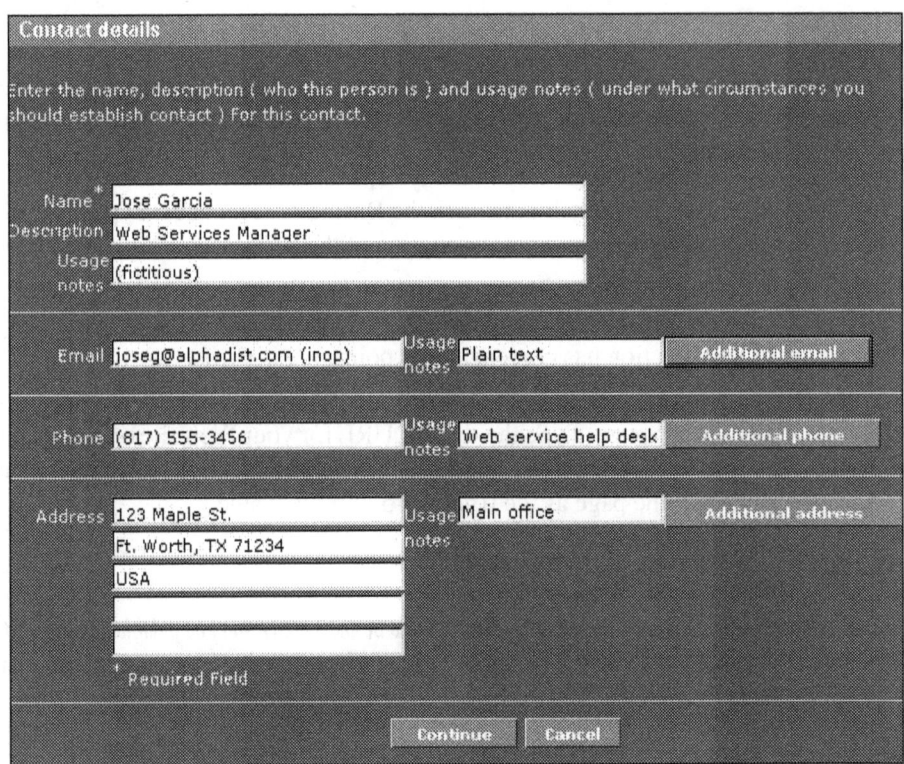

Figure 11-6   *Add contact information for persons who support your services on the Contact Details page. Optionally, add sales or marketing contacts for your products or services.*

TIP

If your organization doesn't have a D-U-N-S number, obtain one from the Dun & Bradstreet Web site at http://www.dunandbradstreet.com. The process usually takes a week or two. One of the ways public registry operators might reduce the amount of spam in the database is by requiring a valid D-U-N-S number that corresponds to the `businessEntity` *information you submit.*

Specifying Business and Geographical Classifications

As noted in the earlier "Business Classifications" section, you can add classifications for the five supported taxonomies and RealNames keywords, if you have one. You should include NAICS, UNSPSC, and ISO 3166 classifications; SIC is optional, and RealNames keywords are expensive.

Following is the process for navigating the hierarchies to the closest business classification codes for consumer electronics distributors:

1. In the Business Classifications section, click the Add A Classification link, and click the NAICS link of the Add Classification page.

2. For this example, click the More Records: 2 link to display the Wholesale Trade class. Click the link, and then click the Wholesale Trade, Durable Goods link.

3. Click the Electrical Goods Wholesalers link and click the Electrical Appliance, Television, And Radio Set Wholesalers link, which is the closest description for consumer electronics distributors.

4. Click the Add This Classification link to add the NAICS 42162 code to the Classification list and return to the Business Entity page.

TIP

Make sure you click Add This Classification for each entry. The preceding step is easy to forget after navigating through multiple classification hierarchies.

5. Repeat step 1, but click the UNSPSC link. The closest UNSPSC category is Domestic Appliances and Supplies and Consumer Electronic Products, Consumer Electronics, Audio and Visual Equipment. Click Add This Classification to add UNSPSC code 52.16.15.00.00 to the Classification link and return to the Business Entity page.

TIP

The Audio and Visual Equipment classification has many subclasses for products that AlphaDist distributes. The degree of granularity you specify for a classification is a matter of business judgment and the number of entries you must add to cover specific product types. UNSPSC codes don't distinguish manufacturing, distributing, or retailing organizations.

6. Repeat step 1, but click the ISO 3166 link and then World. If your XML Web services have worldwide scope, click Add This Classification. AlphaDist's territory is limited to Texas, so navigate to page 12 of the World classification, click United States, click Page 3, Texas, and Add This Classification.

7. Optionally, publish your additions at this point to preserve them.

Registering tModels of Your Services

As mentioned in the earlier section "The Instance Detail and tModel Pages," `tModel` metadata exists independently of business services. All `tModels` you add with your Passport administrative account appear in the Add A New tModel list. Before you add entries to the Business Services section, register a `tModel` for each XML Web service you intend to publish.

TIP

Copy the entries you make for the `tModel` registration to Notepad to preserve them for duplicate `tModel` entries you must add in the next section.

Here are the steps for `tModel` registration, which use the AlphaDist service you created in Chapter 5 as an example:

1. On the Administer page, click the Add A New tModel link to open the `tModel` editing page.

2. In the tModel Detail section, type a URN-style service name for the new tModel, preferably derived from the namespace you assigned to the service. The AlphaDist namespace is `http://alphadist.com/webservices/`, which translates to `alphadist-com:webservices` in the URN format for `tModels`. A colon-separated version number is optional.

3. Add a brief description of your XML Web service and its methods.

4. In the Overview Document section, type the URL to the WSDL document or files for the service, **http://www.oakleaf.ws/AlphaADO/AlphaDist.asmx** for this example.

TIP

*If you haven't added documentation to your XML web service, add **?wsdl** to the URL for the .asmx file to display the WSDL contents instead of the Documentation page.*

5. Add a description of the of the overview document. (See Figure 11-7.)

6. Click Continue to return to the `tModel` editing page.

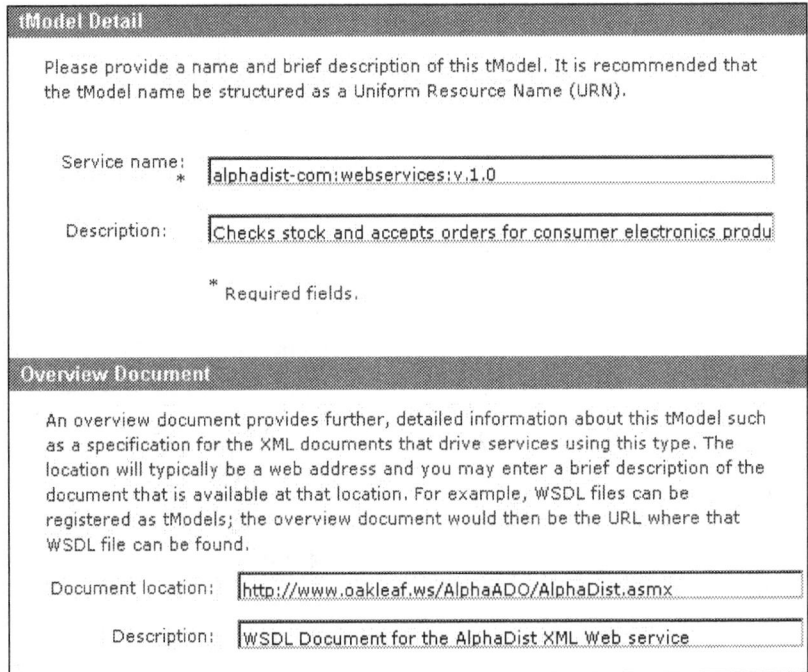

Figure 11-7   *Define the `tModel` for your service in this detail page.*

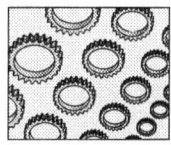

NOTE

If you've added `tModels` for other services, the business classifications and business identifiers will default to those of the last `tModel` you added. If the values don't apply to the new `tModel`, remove the entries.

7. Add NAICS, UNSPSC, and ISO 3166 classifications for the service, as described in the preceding section, and add your D-U-N-S business identifier.

8. Add a `wsdlSpec` classification by navigating in the UDDI Types Taxonomy classifications to the Specification For A Web Service node and then to the Specification For A Web Service Described In WSDL item. Click Add This Classification. (See Figure 11-8.)

CAUTION

If you don't add the `wsdlSpec` classification, your `tModel` registration won't appear in a search of the Microsoft UDDI registry by Visual Studio .NET's Add Web Reference dialog.

9. Click Publish to add the `tModel` to the database, and click Continue to return to the Administer page.

TIP

If you have several `tModels` to publish, add them all at this point. You'll save time when adding business services to your Business Entity page.

Service classifications

Classifications are pieces of data that classify the field of operation of a business or a service e.g. a geographic location or an industry sector. These enable users of the registry to confirm the relevance of a particular entry.

Classification	Name	Value	Action
NAICS	Electrical Appliance, Television, and Radio Set Wholesalers	42162	Remove
UNSPSC	Audio and visual equipment	52.16.15.00.00	Remove
ISO 3166 Geographic Taxonomy	Texas	US-TX	Remove
UDDI Types Taxonomy	Specification for a web service described in WSDL	wsdlSpec	Remove

---

Figure 11-8   *Add the UDDI Types Taxonomy's wsdlSpec classification to every XML Web service you register in any UDDI registry.*

Adding Business Services

The final step in the registration process is to add business services that have pointers to the tModels you've added. To add a service, do this:

1. On the Administer page, click the link to your business entity, and click Add A Service in the Services section to open the Service Detail page.

2. Add a name and detailed description for the service of up to 255 characters, and click Continue to open the Service editing page.

3. In the Bindings section, click the Define New Binding link to open the Binding editing page.

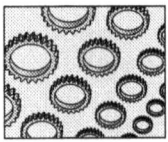

NOTE

Unfortunately, the Microsoft UDDI 1.0 administration pages don't supply default tModel *attributes if you omit entries in steps 5 through 10.*

4. Type or paste the URL of the .asmx file for your XML Web service in the Access Point text box, **http://www.oakleaf.ws/AlphaADO/AlphaDist.asmx** for this example. Accept the default HTTP protocol in the URL Type list, and add a description of the service. (See Figure 11-9.) Click Continue.

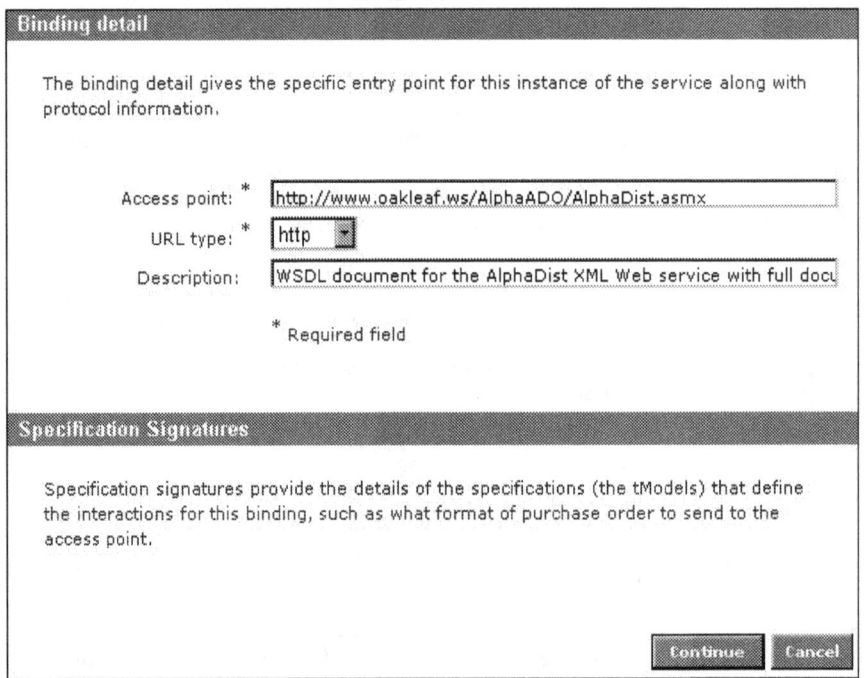

Binding detail

The binding detail gives the specific entry point for this instance of the service along with protocol information.

Access point: * http://www.oakleaf.ws/AlphaADO/AlphaDist.asmx

URL type: * http

Description: WSDL document for the AlphaDist XML Web service with full docu

* Required field

Specification Signatures

Specification signatures provide the details of the specifications (the tModels) that define the interactions for this binding, such as what format of purchase order to send to the access point.

Continue   Cancel

Figure 11-9 *The first page for adding a business service defines the location of its WSDL document or files and lets you add a description of the service.*

5. In the Specification Signatures page, click the Add Specification Signature link to open the Find page. Type the URN for the service's `tModel` in the text box, and click Continue to open the Select page.

TIP

Type the first few characters of the URN to find the `tModel`. UDDI searches append a percent sign (%) wildcard to your entry.

6. Select the `tModel` in the list box and click Continue to open the Instance Details editing page.

7. Complete the Edit Specification Signature section by adding the description of the `tModel`. This is the value you entered in step 3 of the preceding section.

8. Complete the Instance Details section by adding the URL to the .asmx page and the description of the page (not the service).

9. Complete the Overview Document section by adding the URL and description for the `tModel` in steps 4 and 5 of the preceding section. (See Figure 11-10.)

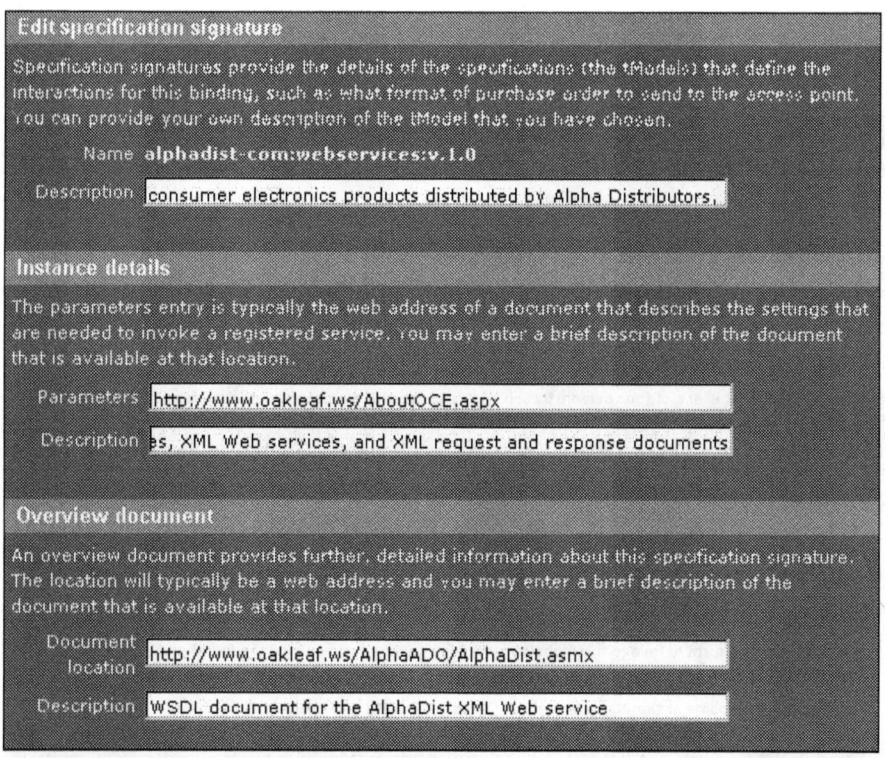

Figure 11-10   *The Instance Details editing page binds the `tModel` to the business service when you publish your additions.*

10. Click Continue three times to return to the Business Entity page, and click Publish to add the business service for the `tModel`.

You can bind a business service to multiple `tModel`s. As an example, the OakLeaf CFR Services business service has bindings to the `oakleaf-ws:cfr:toc` and `oakleaf-ws:cfr:section tModel`s. Level 1 publishers are limited to two bindings per business service.

After you publish new or modified entries in the registry, click the Search link in the left frame and search for your business name. Proofread all text you entered, and follow all the links to confirm that the URLs you typed lead to the expected page. Figure 11-11 shows the AlphaDist.asmx page opened by clicking the Access Point link. Beta Electronics Corp. and Gamma Distributors, Inc., business entities are also present in the Microsoft UDDI 1.0 Registry. The test page for the `CheckStock` method of the three services is operational.

Adding a Web Reference from a UDDI Registry

Adding a `tModel` with a `wsdlSpec` classification makes your registered XML Web services visible to the search feature of the Add Web Reference dialog. To search for your

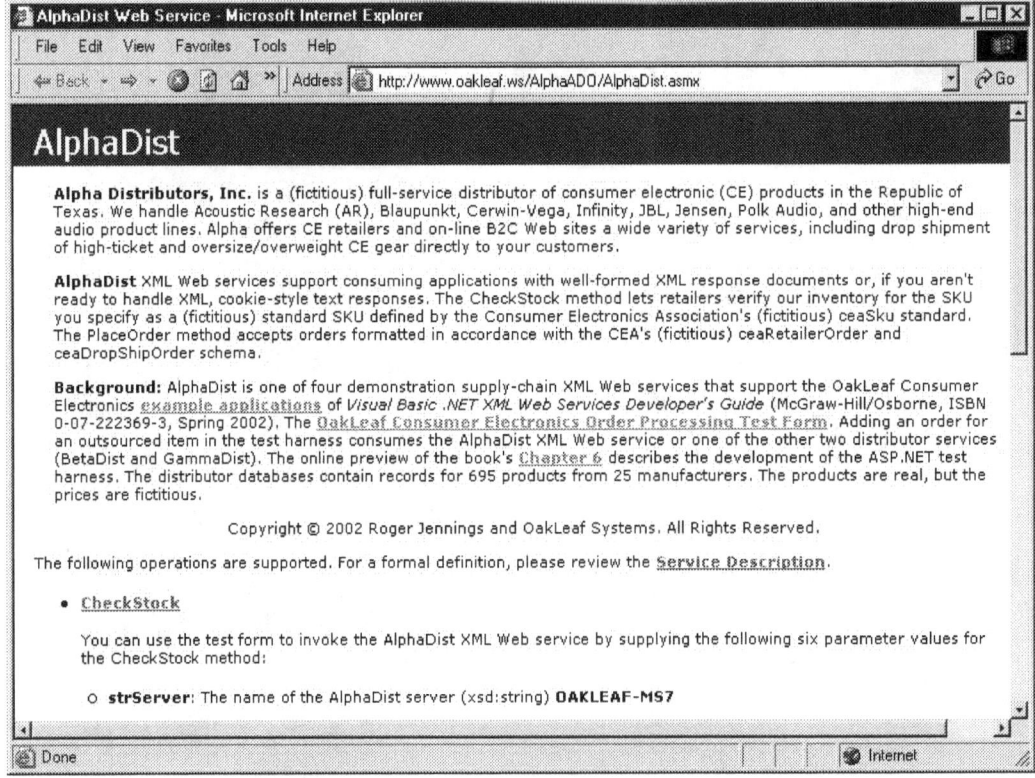

Figure 11-11   *The WSDL document for the AlphaDist XML Web service has a complete HTML-encoded description of the service and its two methods.*

tModels and verify their accessibility to developers using Visual Studio .NET, do the
following:

1. In a Visual Studio .NET project, right-click Solution Explorer's References node, and
   choose Add Web Reference.
2. Click the UDDI Directory link to open the Search page, type your business name in the
   text box, and click Search to open a tree view containing a node for each of the XML
   Web services you've registered. This example uses the two OakLeaf CFR services.
3. Expand the nodes to display tModel item(s) for the services. (See Figure 11-12.)
4. Click one of the tModel items to replace the tree view with the WSDL document. If
   the WSDL file passes Microsoft muster, the Add Reference button is enabled. (See
   Figure 11-13.)

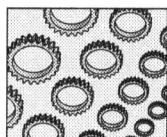

NOTE

*Many WSDL files in the UDDI 1.0 production registry aren't accessible or don't conform to Visual Studio
.NET's standards for validating WSDL documents. Chapter 12 describes techniques for working with
third-party Web services that the Add Web Reference dialog refuses.*

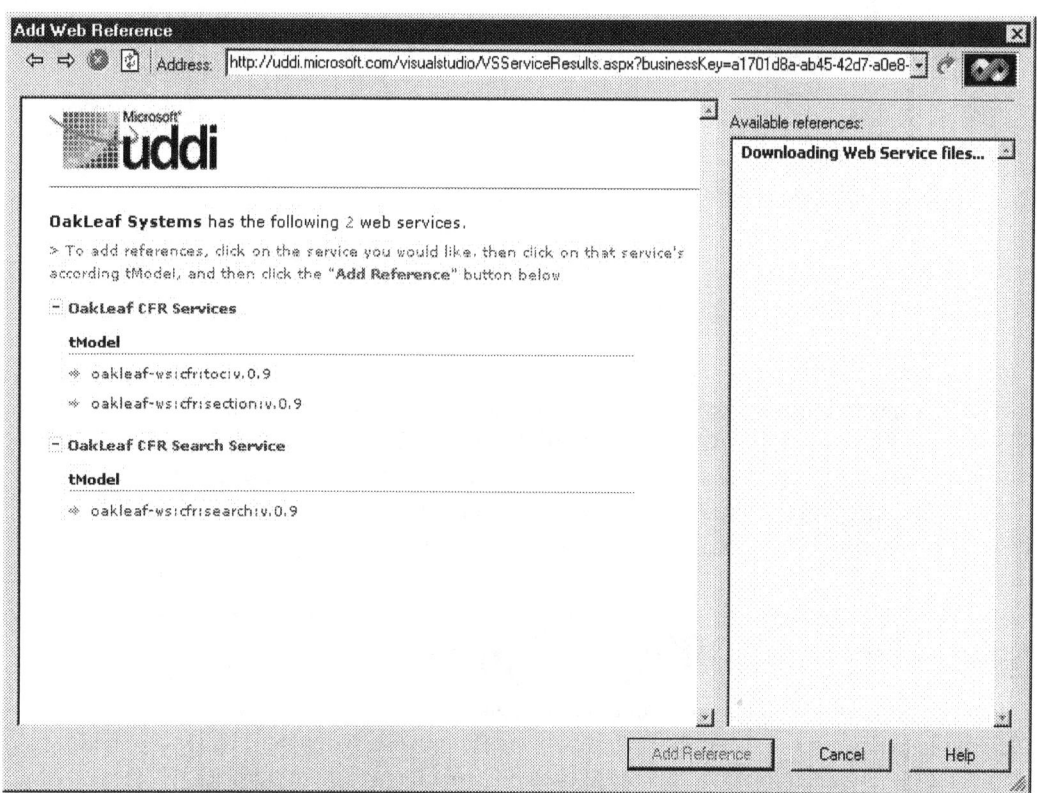

Figure 11-12   *The Add Web Reference dialog's tree view pane displays tModels for your
published XML Web services.*

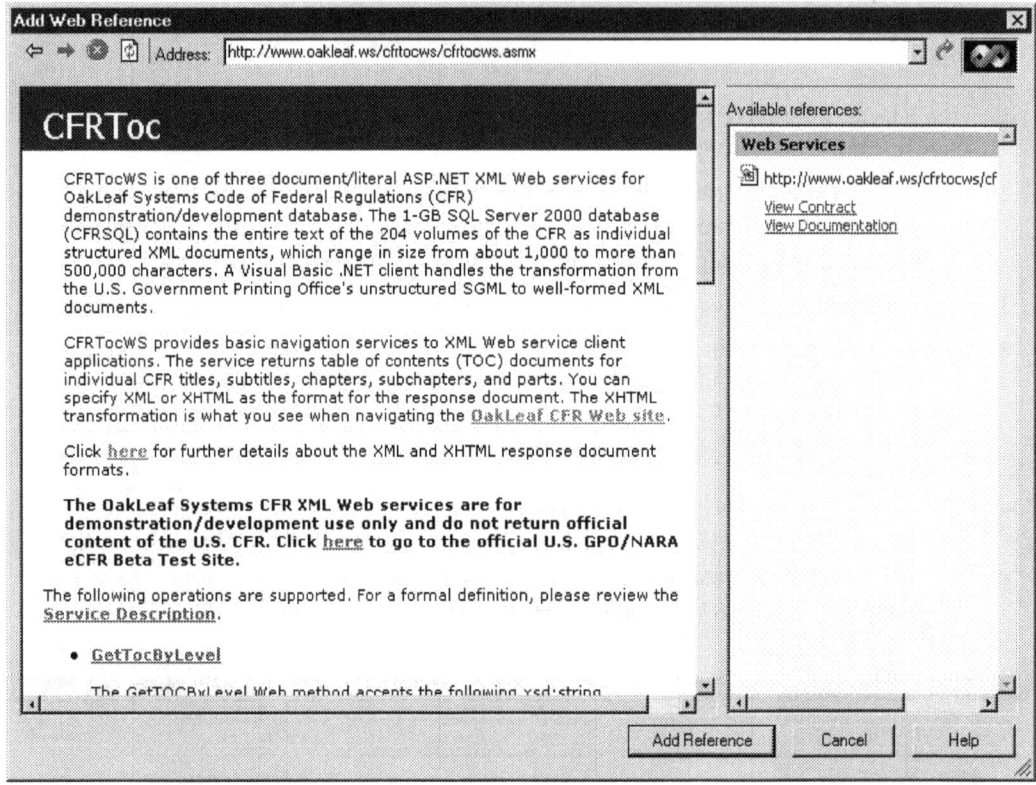

Figure 11-13   *A WSDL file or document that validates to Microsoft's WSDL schema standards enables the Add Reference button to create a SOAP client proxy.*

5. Click the back button to return to the tree view, and verify that each service you registered returns the correct WSDL document.

When this book was written, only 164 of the 1994 `tModels` in the UDDI 1.0 production registry had a `wsdlSpec` classification. Most of these 164 `tModels` returned HTTP 404 errors or had other problems that prevented display of the WSDL file or document. Many accessible WSDL documents failed Visual Studio .NET's validation rules. For example, you can't create a SOAP client proxy for the http://www.alanbushtrust.org.uk/soap/compositions.wsdl file for the UK-based Alan Bush Compositions Web Service.

Surveying the UDDI Specifications

Uddi.org (http://www.uddi.org) is an industry consortium responsible for developing and maintaining the UDDI 1.0 and 2.0 specifications. Microsoft, Ariba, and IBM were uddi.org's founders; the organization now has more than 300 members. The organization's purported goal is to turn the UDDI specification over to an Internet standards organization. When this book was written, uddi.org had not disclosed the organization or timetable for the transfer.

You don't need to understand—or even scan—the UDDI specifications if your only objective is to search for existing services or use one of the operator sites to add registrations for tModels and business entities. You'll have a better idea of what's going on behind the scenes during the registration process, however, after a brief review of the three UDDI specifications that are common to versions 1.0 and 2.0. Go to http://www.uddi.org/specification.html for a complete list of UDDI version 1.0 and 2.0 specifications in .doc and .pdf formats, and XML schemas in .xsd format.

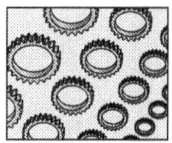

NOTE

Public and private UDDI registries replace Microsoft's proprietary Disco search feature, which disappeared with the release version of Visual Studio .NET. If you're interested in implementing a private UDDI registry for your organization, start with a review of the UDDI 2.0 Operators Specification.

UDDI 1.0 and 2.0 Common Specifications

If you're interested in UDDI-enabling Web or Windows form clients, you need a basic understanding of the three specification documents that are common to UDDI versions 1.0 and 2.0. The documents that the following three sections describe are complementary. They are intended as a guide for writing applications that access a public or private UDDI registry programmatically.

Programmer's API Specification

The programmer's API specification contains an overview of UDDI design principles, which correspond to this book's definition of an XML Web service. UDDI uses the SOAP document/literal messaging format. The API is divided into two groups of methods: Inquiry API and Publish API. The Inquiry API uses HTTP as the transport and doesn't require authentication. The Publish API requires a site-specific user authentication process and requires HTTPS for security.

The Inquiry API supports the following three HTTP query patterns, which don't require user authentication:

► **Browse** Supports searches for business entities, services, bindings, and tModels.

► **Drill-down** Returns the detail structure for a specified business, service, binding, or tModel.

► **Invocation** Updates the caller's locally cached bindingDetail information for a service, in the event that the location of the service changes.

Following is the generic syntax for the SOAP request document's payload for UDDI 1.0's find_business method:

```
<find_business  generic="1.0" [ maxRows="nn" ] xmlns
   ="urn:uddi-org:api" >   [<findQualifiers/>]
   <name/> | <identifierBag/> | <categoryBag/> |
```

```
          <tModelBag/>  |  <discoveryURLs>
</find_business>
```

Elements other than `<findQualifiers>` are mutually exclusive; that is, you can specify only one search criterion.

The UDDI 2.0 version of the `find_business` method lets you search for multiple names and use any combination of search elements. The response message includes businesses that match any search term. Here's the UDDI 2.0 syntax for the request document:

```
<find_business [maxRows="nn"] generic="2.0" xmlns
   ="urn:uddi-org:api_v2" >
   [<findQualifiers/>]
   [<name/> [<name/>]…]
   [<discoveryURLs/>]
   [<identifierBag/>]
   [<categoryBag/>]
   [<tModelBag/>]
</find_business>
```

The `Microsoft.Uddi.Api` namespace has a `FindBusiness` object to generate the preceding XML structure and its attribute values, and send the request document to the URL for the UDDI directory. The later section "Working with the UDDI .Net SDKs" illustrates use of the `Uddi` 1.0 managed classes and a simple Visual Basic .NET application to search public UDDI registries.

The four basic methods of the Publish API let you add a new business entity, service, binding, or `tModel`, edit existing detail information retrieved by the `get_elementDetail` method, or delete existing elements.

The following table lists the four sets of related methods of the Inquiry API and Publish API of UDDI versions 1.0 and 2.0.

Inquiry API Query Patterns		Publish API	
Browse	**Drill-Down**	**Add or Edit**	**Remove or Hide**
find_binding	get_bindingDetail	save_binding	delete_binding
find_business	get_businessDetail	save_business	delete_business
find_service	get_serviceDetail	save_service	delete_service
find_tModel	get_tModelDetail	save_tModel	delete_tModel

UDDI 2.0 adds the capability to search for related businesses and supports `publisherAssertions` to confirm relationships between businesses. For example, Oakleaf Systems might assert a relationship with Alpha Distributors, Inc., and the other fictitious business entities that support the OakLeaf Consumer Electronics sample applications. For the relationships to be visible to the `find_relatedBusinesses` method, UDDI 2.0 requires reciprocal `publisherAssertions`. Related businesses can share `businessService` references, which the specification calls *service projections*. The following table lists additional

methods for browse query patterns, `publisherAssertions`, and account authentication. An asterisk (*) follow methods added by the UDDI 2.0 specification.

Browse	Publisher Assertions	Authentication
find_relatedBusinesses*	add_publisherAssertions*	get_authToken
get_businessDetailExt	delete_publisherAssertions*	discard_authToken
get_registeredInfo	get_assertionStatusReport*	

The `get_businessDetailExt` method applies only to private UDDI registries that add additional elements to the `businessDetail` structure; `get_registeredInfo` returns a short form of the `get_businessDetail` structure. The `get_assertionStatusReport` method returns elements that reveal the status of all assertions for business entities under the control of a single account. The `get_authToken` method is a logon request that returns an authentication token for subsequent publishing operations; `discard_authToken` is a message to the site operator that the token is no longer valid for publishing.

Data Structure Reference

The Data Structure Reference provides response document `<element>` subschemas for substructures of each of the four UDDI 1.0 structures and UDDI 2.0's `publisherAssertion` structure. The subschemas conform to the 2001 final version of the XSD Schema specification. Following is the subschema for the `businessEntity` structure, which is the same for versions 1.0 and 2.0:

```
<element name = "businessEntity">
   <complexType>
      <sequence>
         <element ref = "discoveryURLs" minOccurs = "0"/>
         <element ref = "name" maxOccurs = "unbounded"/>
         <element ref = "description" minOccurs = "0"
                                         maxOccurs = "unbounded"/>
         <element ref = "contacts" minOccurs = "0"/>
         <element ref = "businessServices" minOccurs = "0"/>
         <element ref = "identifierBag" minOccurs = "0"/>
         <element ref = "categoryBag" minOccurs = "0"/>
      </sequence>
      <attribute ref = "businessKey" use = "required"/>
      <attribute ref = "operator"/>
      <attribute ref = "authorizedName">
   </complexType>
</element>
```

XML Schema

The XML Schema for UDDI 2.0 defines 25 request and 15 response documents for which the Data Structure Reference provides detailed descriptions. Figure 11-14 shows 26 of the almost 800 lines of the uddi_v2.xsd file.

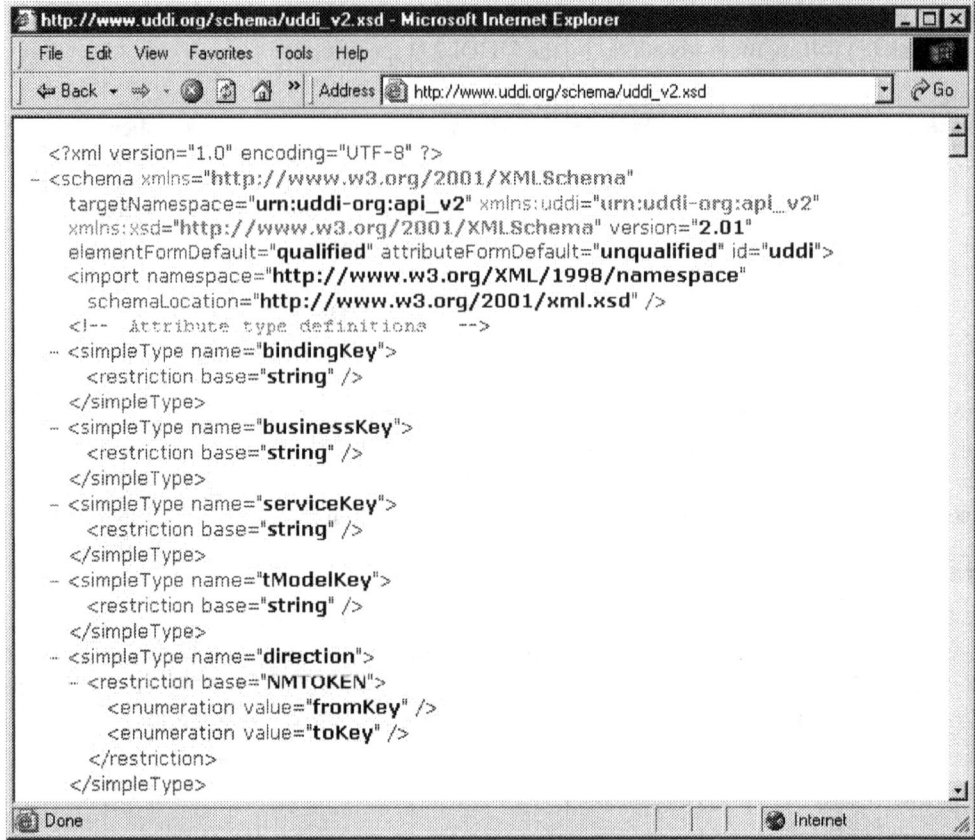

Figure 11-14 *Internet Explorer displays this UDDI 2.0 schema when you click the link to the uddi_v2.xsd file.*

Specifications Added to UDDI 2.0

UDDI 2.0 adds the following set of four documents that apply only to operators of public and large private registries:

▶ **Replication Specification** Defines the interfaces required to implement interoperator (public) or intersite (private) replication of UDDI 2.0 registration data.

▶ **XML Replication Schema** An XSD file that contains the schema required to support the Replication Specification.

▶ **Operator's Specification** Defines the security and data management requirements of public UDDI nodes, and policies for transferring custody of user accounts.

▶ **XML Custody Schema** An XSD file that contains the schema for transferring user accounts between public or private operators.

These specifications and schemas are of interest primarily to operators of public sites or private operators who must replicate registration data between database management systems supplied by different vendors. SQL Server 2000 replication is adequate for organizations that have standardized on Microsoft products.

Working with the UDDI .Net SDKs

Microsoft offers UDDI .Net SDKs for versions 1.0 and 2.0 of the UDDI specification as an add-in for the release version of Visual Studio .NET. All SDK versions install a managed code class library to streamline development of UDDI-enabled applications. If you intend to write UDDI-enabled Visual Basic .NET applications, download and install the version that's appropriate for your operating system.

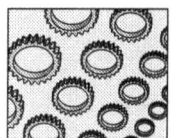

NOTE

According to Microsoft, the UDDI Developer Edition, which was part of the UDDI SDK version 1.5.2, is no longer available for download because it isn't operable with newer versions of the SDK for UDDI 1.0. Version 1.5.2 works only with Visual Studio .NET Beta 2. Tests with version 1.76 of the SDK confirm this statement. If you want to experiment with a private UDDI registry, you must install Windows .NET Server Beta 3 or later, Visual Studio .NET, and UDDI.NET SDK 2.0 Beta 1.

UDDI .NET SDK 1.76 Beta

When this book was written, UDDI.NET SDK 1.76 Beta was the latest version of the SDK that's compatible with UDDI 1.0, the release version of Visual Studio .NET, and the .NET Framework. You can download the latest version of the SDK for UDDI 1.0 public or test registries at http://msdn.microsoft.com/uddi/. The SDK installs a UDDI .NET SDK Help file, a sample UDDIExplorer C# project, and adds `Microsoft.Uddi` namespaces to the .NET Framework. Documentation for many items remains "[t]o be delivered" from online help, despite the long gestation period of this SDK. For example, there's no reference information for members of the `Microsoft.Uddi` namespaces.

The elegance of Microsoft's UDDI 1.0 object model more than compensates for the lack of documentation. The `Microsoft.Uddi` namespace provides methods that correspond to each UDDI 1.0 API member. Microsoft's method-naming convention eliminates the underscore that follows the verb—`find_businessDetail` translates to `FindBusinessDetail`. Members of the `Microsoft.Uddi.Api`, `.Authentication`, `.Binding`, `.Business`, `.Service`, and `.ServiceDetail` namespaces provide serialization and deserialization services for the UDDI 1.0 data structures.

Microsoft's UDDIExplorer C# Example

UDDIExplorer won't win any UI design awards and doesn't include the publish, delete, and registry cleanup features of UDDI .NET SDK version 1.52. UDDIExplorer invokes only the UDDI 1.0 Inquiry API's browse and drill-down query patterns to populate a `TreeView` control with the results of *find_structure* and *get_structure* invocations. UDDIExplorer's combo box lets you select the Microsoft test and production registries, the IBM production registry, or a local UDDI 1.0 registry. The application's developer apparently forgot to remove the local entry when Microsoft decided to eliminate the UDDI Developer Edition from version 1.76 of the SDK.

The UDDIExplorerVB Visual Basic .NET Example

UDDIExplorerVB.sln is a quick-and-dirty port of Microsoft's C# example application to Visual Basic .NET. The modifications consist of conforming form and control names to this book's standards, removing error-handling code, and reorganizing subprocedure sequences. Figure 11-15 shows UDDIExplorerVB displaying the OakLeaf business services from the IBM production registry at http://www-3.ibm.com/services/uddi/inquiryapi.

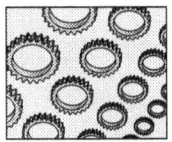

> ### NOTE
> You can download the UDDIExplorerVB project as VBWS11.zip from this book's entry at http://www.osborne.com/downloads/downloads.shtml. Expand the files into a \VBWS11 folder.

Clicking Submit sets the authentication method and URL for the registry that you specify in the combo box and executes `frmUddi`'s `find_business` or `find_tModel` subprocedure, depending on the option you select. Following is the code for `find_business`, which

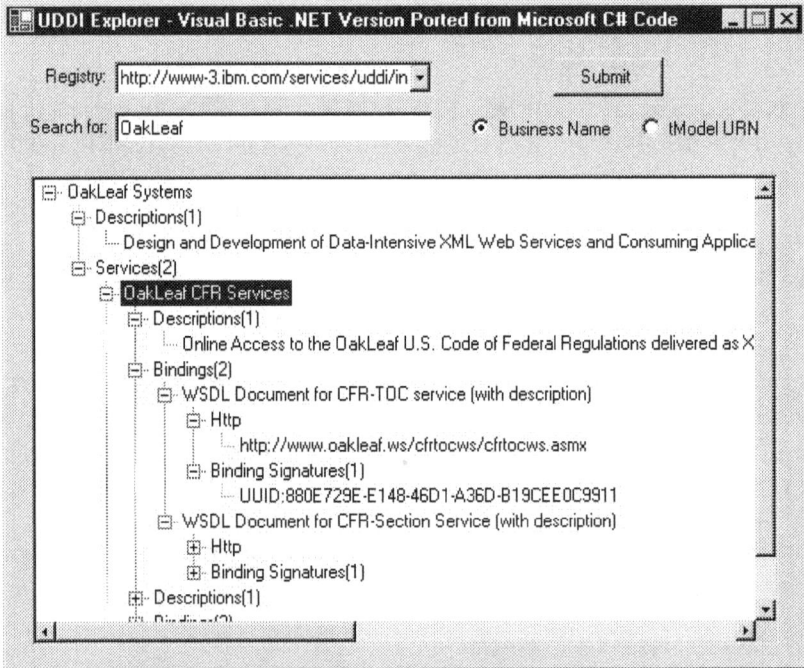

Figure 11-15   *The Visual Basic .NET version of Microsoft's UDDIExplorer C# application displays the OakLeaf registrations in a* `TreeView` *control.*

sends a search term to the registry and adds to the `TreeView` control `BusinessInfo` and `ServiceInfo` data for matching business entities:

```
Private Sub find_business()
   ' Construct a find_business message
   Dim bl As BusinessList
   Dim d As Description
   Dim bi As BusinessInfo
   Dim si As ServiceInfo

   trvUddi.BeginUpdate()
   Dim fb As New FindBusiness()
   fb.Name = txtSearch.Text
   bl = fb.Send()
   trvUddi.Nodes.Clear()

   If bl.BusinessInfos.Count = 0 Then
      trvUddi.Nodes.Add(New TreeNode("No Businesses were found"))
   Else
      ' Add information about businesses found to tree
      For Each bi In bl.BusinessInfos
         trvUddi.Nodes.Add(New TreeNode(bi.Name))
         If bi.Descriptions.Count > 0 Then
            trvUddi.Nodes(bl.BusinessInfos.IndexOf(bi)).Nodes. _
               Add(New TreeNode("Descriptions(" +
               CStr(bi.Descriptions.Count) + ")"))
            For Each d In bi.Descriptions
               ' Adding descriptions
               trvUddi.Nodes(bl.BusinessInfos.IndexOf(bi)). _
                  Nodes(0).Nodes.Add(d.Text)
            Next d
         End If
         If bi.ServiceInfos.Count > 0 Then
            ' Adding info about services exposed by the business
            trvUddi.Nodes(bl.BusinessInfos.IndexOf(bi)).Nodes. _
               Add(New TreeNode("Services" + "(" + _
               CStr(bi.ServiceInfos.Count) + ")"))
            For Each si In bi.ServiceInfos
               trvUddi.Nodes(bl.BusinessInfos.IndexOf(bi)). _
                  Nodes(1).Nodes.Add(si.Name)
               trvUddi.Nodes(bl.BusinessInfos.IndexOf(bi)). _
                  Nodes(1).Nodes(bi.ServiceInfos.IndexOf(si)).Tag = _
                  si.ServiceKey
            Next si
         End If
```

```
      Next bi
   End If
   trvUddi.EndUpdate()
End Sub
```

When you click to expand a `ServiceInfo` node, the `get_serviceDetail` subprocedure sends the corresponding message to the registry and adds `BusinessService`, `BindingTemplate`, and `tModel` nodes, and `Description` data to the `TreeView` control. Following is the code for `get_serviceDetail`:

```
Private Sub get_serviceDetail()
   ' Construct a get_serviceDetail message and retrieve service
   Dim sd As ServiceDetail
   Dim service As BusinessService
   Dim d As Description
   Dim bt As BindingTemplate
   Dim desc As Description
   Dim tmii As TModelInstanceInfo
   Dim tn1 As TreeNode

   Dim gsd As New GetServiceDetail()
   gsd.ServiceKeys.Add(trvUddi.SelectedNode.Tag.ToString())
   sd = gsd.Send()

   For Each service In sd.BusinessServices
      ' Show service descriptions
      Dim tn As New TreeNode("Descriptions(" + _
         CStr(service.Descriptions.Count) + ")")

      For Each d In service.Descriptions
         tn.Nodes.Add(d.Text)
         trvUddi.SelectedNode.Nodes.Add(tn)
         ' Show binding template information
         tn1 = New TreeNode()
         tn1.Text = "Bindings(" + CStr(service.BindingTemplates.Count) + ")"
         For Each bt In service.BindingTemplates
            Dim tn2 As New TreeNode()
            For Each desc In bt.Descriptions
               tn2.Text = desc.Text
               If Not bt.AccessPoint Is Nothing Then
                  tn2.Nodes.Add(bt.AccessPoint.URLType.ToString())
                  tn2.Nodes(0).Nodes.Add(bt.AccessPoint.Text)
               End If

               If bt.TModelInstanceDetail.TModelInstanceInfos.Count > 0 Then
                  tn2.Nodes.Add("Binding Signatures(" + _
                     CStr(bt.TModelInstanceDetail. _
                     TModelInstanceInfos.Count) + ")")
                  For Each tmii In bt.TModelInstanceDetail. _
```

```
                        TModelInstanceInfos
                    tn2.Nodes(1).Nodes.Add(tmii.TModelKey)
                Next tmii
                tn1.Nodes.Add(tn2)
            End If
        Next desc
      Next bt
    Next d
    trvUddi.SelectedNode.Nodes.Add(tn1)
  Next service
End Sub
```

Most of the code in the two preceding listings is devoted to populating the `TreeView` control. Only a few lines of code are necessary to connect to the registry, and retrieve and iterate the collections.

UDDI .NET SDK 2.0 Beta 1

According to a February 8, 2000, posting by Microsoft in the microsoft.public.uddi.programming newsgroup, UDDI .NET SDK 2.0 Beta 1 "…is intended as a technology preview for developers interested in early access to an implementation of that specification." Version 2.0 of the SDK works only with UDDI 2.0 test registries.

Microsoft promises that a future beta version will accommodate UDDI 1.0 and 2.0 registries. In the meantime, the Beta 1 version of the 2.0 SDK is missing more documentation than UDDI .NET SDK 1.76. If you're planning to implement a private UDDI 2.0 registry with Microsoft .NET Server, consider postponing your project until Microsoft releases a fully documented, production-quality version of this SDK and public UDDI 2.0 registries go live with the release—not a beta—version.

Interoperating with Third-Party Web Services

IN THIS CHAPTER:

Chapter 1's "Beyond the Web Services Hype" section concludes that enterprise application integration (EAI) projects will be the first major market for XML Web services. The theory is that XML, XSD, SOAP, WSDL, and HTTP[S] will pave the way to standards-based data interchange between information islands in a sea of disparate operating systems. It's common for multinational corporations to have divisions and subsidiaries that run five or more different relational database management systems under UNIX, Windows, and, increasingly, Linux operating systems. A uniform, standards-based system for secure information exchange over the Internet promises a substantial reduction of EAI development cost, longer lifetime for completed EAI projects, and decreased telecommunication expenses.

The reality is that achieving EAI nirvana with XML Web services requires a substantial amount of upfront investment in developer training and establishing internal standards for SOAP message schemas. Integration of third-party XML Web services and schemas for SOAP XML message payloads generates additional complication and expense.

Visual Studio .NET's Web Reference feature makes creating SOAP client proxies for ASP.NET XML Web services easy. IBM's WebSphere Studio Application Developer software includes Java XML tools and support for creating XML Web services. Cooperation between Microsoft and IBM in the development of the SOAP and WSDL specifications should result in few, if any, interoperability problems with XML Web services created with these two development tools. There are many other client- and server-side SOAP implementations in varying stages of development. The probability is about zero that Visual Studio .NET service consumers will interoperate with *all* SOAP implementations. By the time SOAP 1.2 and WSDL 1.2 become candidate recommendations, it's a good bet that most commercial rpc/encoded Web services will interoperate at the version 1.1 level. The outlook is not as clear for document/literal SOAP implementations.

TIP

For an interesting comparison between the Microsoft and IBM approaches to XML Web service development tools, read the "How IBM WebSphere Studio Application Developer Compares with Microsoft Visual Studio .NET" white paper at http://www7b.boulder.ibm.com/wsdd/techjournal/0202_kraft/kraft.html.

Standardizing Web Service Interoperability

Web services are based on standards, but that doesn't mean that a Web service created with a Java- or Perl-based SOAP implementation will interoperate correctly—or at all—with a Visual Studio .NET client proxy.

For example, the Alan Bush Compositions Web Service at http://www.alanbushtrust.org.uk/soap/compositions.wsdl doesn't pass the Add Web Reference dialog's tests. The Add Reference button is disabled and the Available References page states, "No Web References were found on this page." This behavior was probably caused by the developer's use of an early version of the Microsoft SOAP Toolkit to create the WSDL file, which contains an `xmlns:stk=` "http://schemas.microsoft.com/soap-toolkit/wsdl-extension" namespace declaration. (See Figure 12-1.)

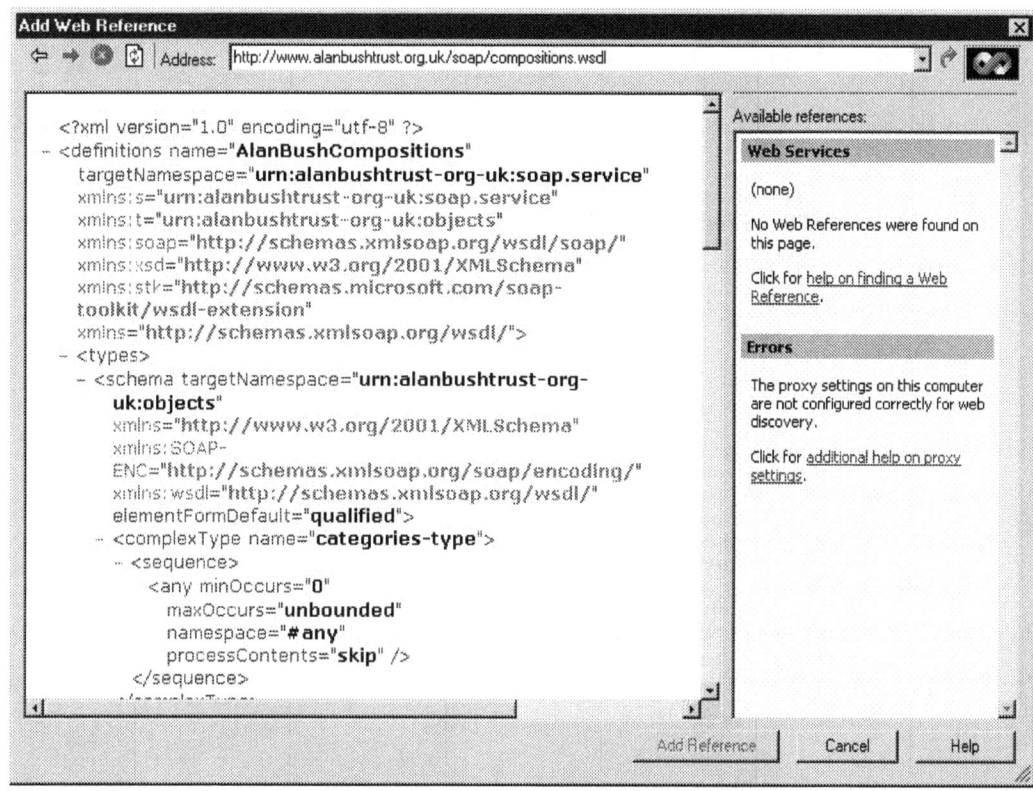

Figure 12-1   *The Add Web Reference page won't accept this WSDL file, which was apparently created by an early version of the SOAP Toolkit.*

The Add Web Reference dialog has no problem with the http://www.oakleaf.ws/cfr-soap/ cfrsearchws.wsdl file, which was created with the SOAP Toolkit 2.0. The ASP.NET/SOAP Toolkit version of the OakLeaf CFR XML Web services at http://www.oakleaf.ws/cfr-aspx/ default.aspx successfully creates a Web Reference from the WSDL and WSML files. (See Figure 12-2.)

TIP

Use the `ValidateWSDL` method of Microsoft's WsdlVerify XML Web service at http://www.gotdotnet.com/ services/wsdl/wsdlverify.asmx to verify a WSDL file or document against the WSDL 1.1 specification.

In some cases, the WSDL file passes Add Web Reference dialog muster, but the autogenerated client proxy returns SOAP errors when you execute it. The PHP-based newsgroup reader Web service at http://www.codecraze.com/soap/nntp.wsdl has an assortment of issues that prevent the Visual Studio .NET client proxy from generating an operable SOAP request message.

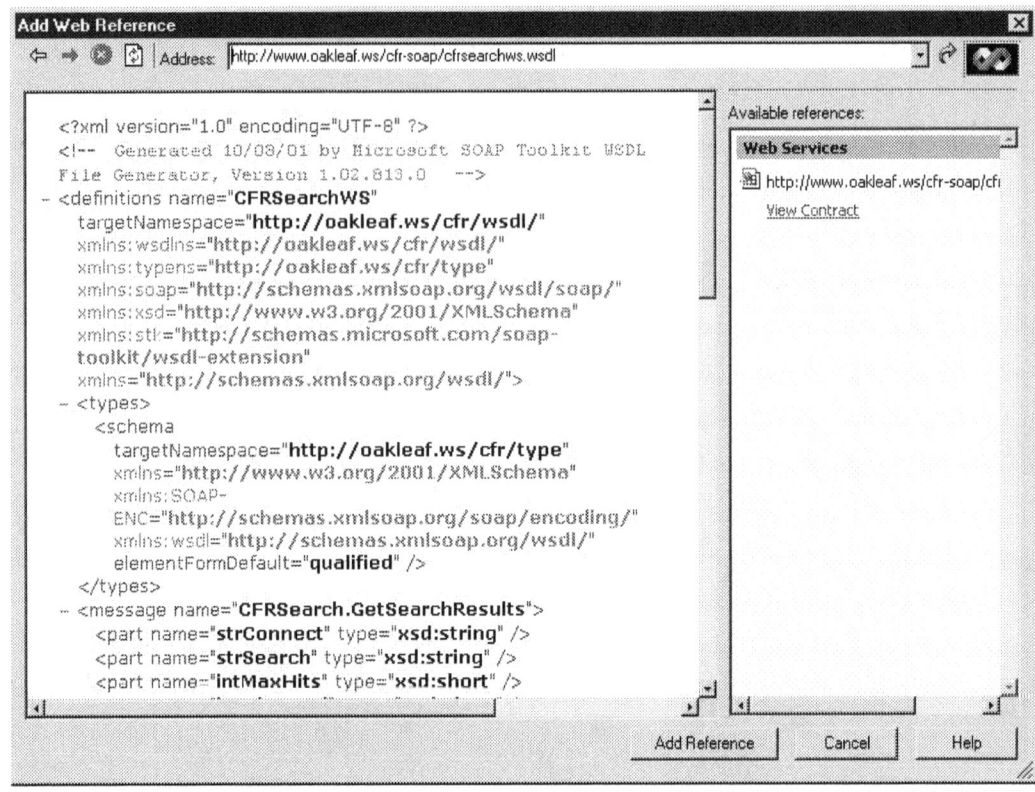

Figure 12-2   A WSDL file created with the SOAP Toolkit 2.0 generates an operable .NET Web Reference.

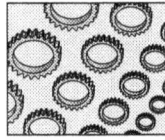

NOTE

Dan Wahlin's "Integrate .NET into Other Platforms" XML Magazine article explains the gyrations required to manually create a .NET client proxy for nntp.wsdl. You can read the article at http://www.fawcette.com/xmlmag/2002_03/magazine/columns/integration/dwahlin/.

The Web Services Interoperability Organization

Microsoft and IBM, together with Accenture, BEA Systems, Fujitsu, Hewlett-Packard, Intel, Oracle, and SAP announced formation of the Web Services Interoperability Organization (WS-I) on February 5, 2002. The organization's Web site (http://www.ws-i.org) describes WS-I as "… an open, industry organization chartered to promote Web services interoperability across platforms, operating systems, and programming languages." As of mid-February 2002, WS-I had a total of 40 corporate members.

WS-I's mission is "to provide implementation guidance to support customers deploying Web services, promote consistent and reliable interoperability among Web services, and articulate a common industry vision for Web services." The first step in the process is establishing a set of profiles to define the standards that apply to interoperable Web services. WS-I's "Web Service Profiles - An Introduction" white paper describes profiles as "… a named group of Web services specifications at specific version levels, along with conventions about how they work together."

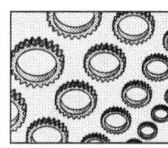

NOTE

WS-I doesn't apply the XML prefix to Web services in its documentation and presentations. Similarly, this chapter omits the XML prefix when referring to Web services in general and particularly to rpc/encoded-style services that don't return XML response documents.

The first of the WS-I core profiles collection is *WS-I Basic Web services*, which requires adherence to XML Schema 1.0, SOAP 1.1, WSDL 1.1, and UDDI 1.0 standards. Working groups will be assigned to establish conventions and best practices for the Basic profile. WS-I also promises to deliver scenarios, which represent practical examples of applications of the profiles, and tools for analyzing WSDL files and SOAP messages for conformance to a specified profile. When this book was written, WS-I was in the formative stage and offered only introductory documentation.

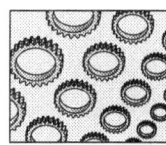

NOTE

Sun Microsystems is conspicuous by its absence from the founders list. In March 2002, Sun claimed to have been a late invitee to WS-I and was considering joining the organization. Eric Knorr's article at http://techupdate.zdnet.com/techupdate/stories/main/0,14179,2853078,00.html has additional background on the controversy.

The SOAP Builders Group

SOAP Builders is a Yahoo! group devoted to testing rpc/encoded Web service interoperability between the many SOAP implementations currently available for UNIX, Linux, and Windows. Tony Hong, one of the founders of the XMethods site (http://www.xmethods.net), started the group in January 2001. To join SOAP Builders as a guest, go to http://groups.yahoo.com/group/soapbuilders/.

When this book was written, the XMethods site listed almost 50 SOAP server and client implementations, many of which have limited or no support for document/literal-style services. Thus, the group's Interoperability Lab test suite concentrates on Section 5 encoding and support for simple and complex datatypes. The specifications and WSDL documents for the Interoperability Lab's Round 2 are at http://www.whitemesa.com/interop.htm. If you're working with rpc/encoded services, such as those created by the Microsoft SOAP Toolkit 2.0, consider joining the SOAP Builders group.

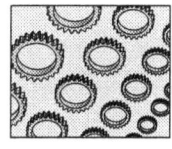

NOTE

The PerfextXML Web site (http://www.perfectxml.com/soap.asp) offers several links to sites dealing with SOAP and WSDL interoperability issues.

Finding Web Services for .NET Interoperability Testing

Web services are in their infancy and, when this book was written, relatively few production Web services were available for public consumption. Production UDDI registries have entries for only a small subset of publicly accessible Web services. Many Web sites have links to a few special-interest services. The following two sites have databases with entries for 100 or more demonstration Web services.

The XMethods Site

The XMethods site at http://www.xmethods.com/ has a list of publicly accessible Web services classified by rpc/encoded and document/literal formats. (See Figure 12-3.) XMethods, Inc., was founded by Tony and James Hong in late 2000, and has become one of the most popular independent (non-UDDI) Web service registries.

Clicking a service name opens a page that displays detailed information on the service, and provides links to a WSDL analyzer and, for rpc/encoded-style services, an RPC profile page. Some services have links to sample client applications. The site offers an eclectic mix

Publisher	Style	Service Name	Description
eltegra.com	RPC	Monthly Car Payment	Calculates your monthly car payment
toti	RPC	Verbix -- verb conjugations	Verb conjugations in tens of languages
tbjohnray	RPC	Modulus Checker	Checks a string of digits using the 10-modulus alg—
tbjohnray	RPC	Captain Haddocks Curser	Generates random curses from Captain Haddock in languages
jamsterdam	DOC	Orbitarium	retrieves positions of the Sun, Moon, and Planets f and time
esynaps	DOC	Miss Proxy "the programmer"	Cartoon strip service
cchenoweth	DOC	Delayed Stock Quotes	Pulls 15 minute delayed Stock Quotes
cchenoweth	DOC	Postal Address Correction	Will correct U.S. Postal Addresses
hsaurin	DOC	Unisys Weather Web Service	Retrieves the weather forecast from the Unisys W center
simonfell	RPC	Weblogs Watcher	a notifications interface for weblogs.com
esynaps	DOC	eSynapsSearch	Search for Web Services Articles/Sample Code/Co
xml-webservices.net	DOC	Financial Calc	Serves some interesting financial calculations
richsolutions.com	DOC	RichPayments.NET	ePayment Web Service that suports credit cards, c and check services
sonnemaf	DOC	Html2Xml	Converts HTML to XML
jcono	DOC	Local Time	Local time for a zip code
systinet.com	RPC	FreeDbService	SOAP interface for freedb web site
juicesoftware.com	RPC	Juice Temperature Service	Returns the current temperature for the specified z
juicesoftware.com	RPC	Juice Snapshot Service	Returns a market snapshot for the specified ticker

Figure 12-3   *The XMethods Web site provides links to detailed information for more than 100 publicly accessible Web services.*

of services for Visual Studio .NET interoperability testing, and has links to many services created with Java and Perl SOAP implementations.

You don't need to register to browse the XMethods site, which offers user-contributed tutorials on 13 popular SOAP implementations, including Java-based Apache SOAP, CapeConnect, GLUE, XMLBus, and WASP. Adding your XML Web service to the XMethods database requires free registration.

The SalCentral Web Services Brokerage

SalCentral at http://www.whatwebservice.com/ claims to be "The Napster of Web Services." SalCentral's database contains a list of public Web services that you can browse by category, organization name, or WSDL file version (1.0 or 1.1). In early 2002, the site had entries for about 300 services, most of which had accessible WSDL documents. Figure 12-4 shows entries for services in the Database category.

SalCentral offers free registration of your Web services and provides a free watch service, which sends you an e-mail alert if your Web service is out of commission. The site also offers Web service developers a paid subscription and authentication service for

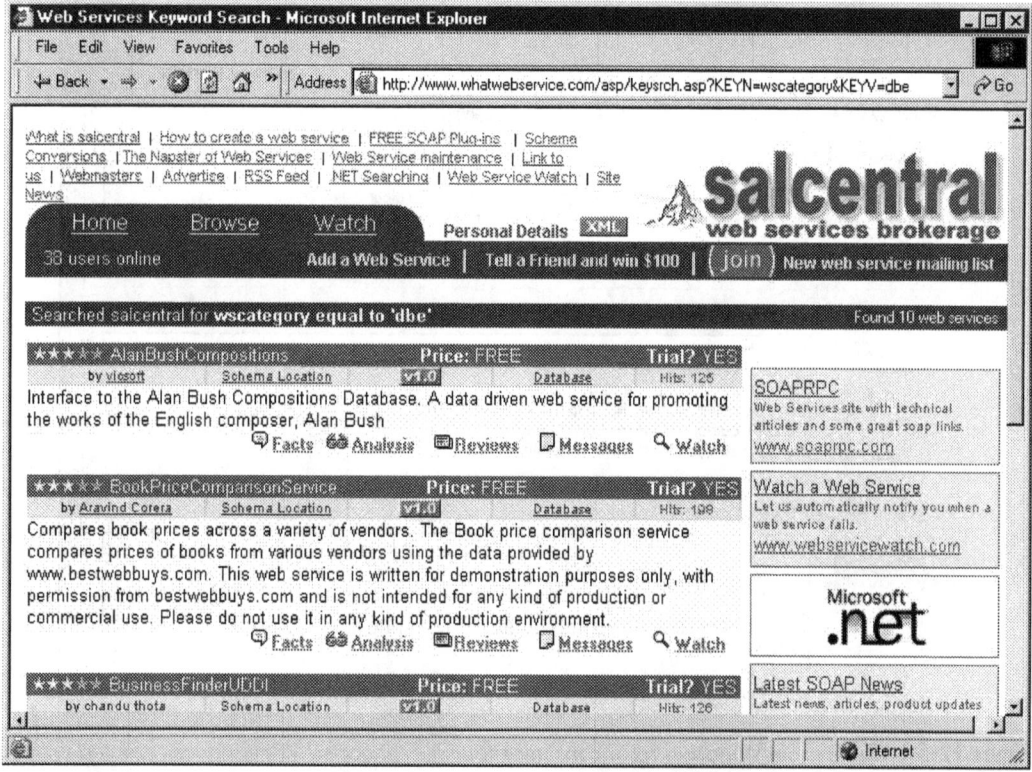

Figure 12-4   *The SalCentral site classifies registered Web services by use categories, such as Database (shown here).*

per-use Web service charges. Free registration is required to search and advertise Web services on the SalCentral site.

Testing Interoperability with a Windows Form Consumer

The easiest way to perform WSDL-based interoperability tests with Web services created by SOAP implementations other than the .NET Framework is to create a Visual Basic .NET Windows consumer client. If the WSDL file enables the Add Web Reference dialog's Add Reference button, the chances are better than 80 percent or so that you can create an operable rpc/encoded Web Reference for the service.

Figure 12-5 shows a Windows form for testing four rpc/encoded Web services that were registered on the XMethods site when this book was written. The developers created the services with Delphi, CapeClear, and Apache SOAP toolkits; the CapeClear and Apache registrations include brief documentation. Default values return the response messages shown in Figure 12-5.

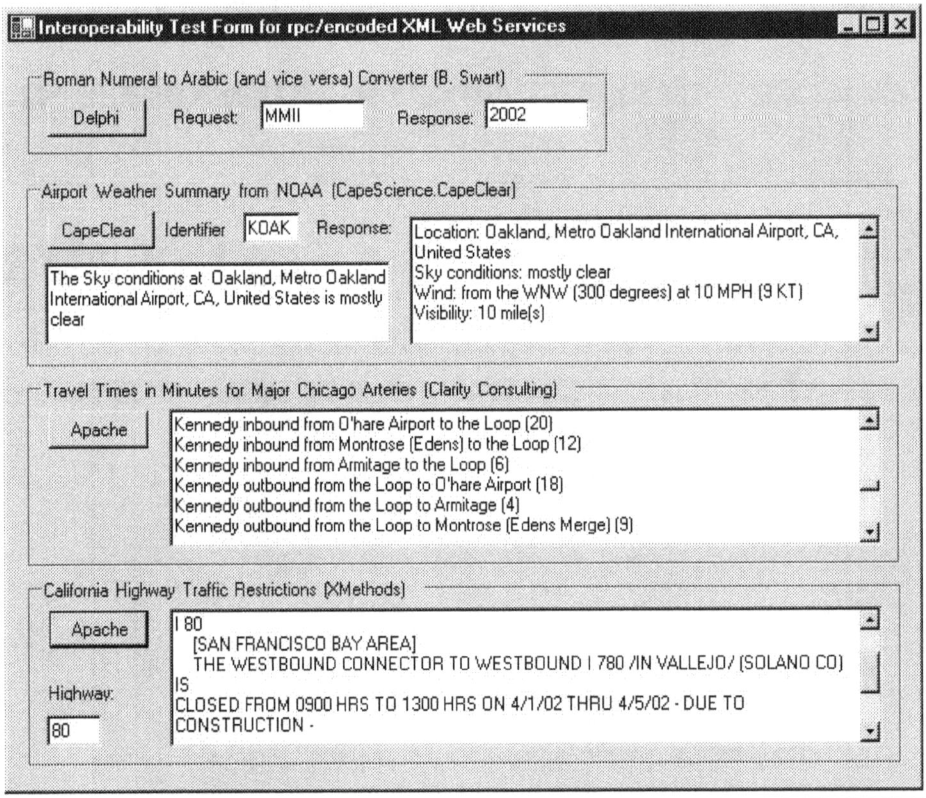

Figure 12-5 *This simple Windows form consumes four rpc/encoded Web services created with three SOAP toolkits.*

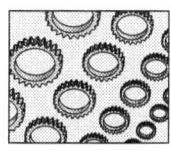

NOTE

The InteropTest.sln solution is in the VBWS12.zip archive, which you can download from this book's entry at http://www.osborne.com/downloads/downloads.shtml. Create a \VBWS12 folder and expand the file into it to create the \VBWS12\InteropTest folder which contains the source code.

Following is the code behind the InteropTest Web service consumer form:

```
Option Explicit On
Option Strict On
Public Class frmInterop
    Inherits System.Windows.Forms.Form
    'Designer code omitted
    Private strCrLf As String = Chr(13) + Chr(10)

    Private Sub cmbDelphi_Click(ByVal sender As System.Object, _
        ByVal e As System.EventArgs) Handles cmbDelphi.Click
        'Roman Numeral Conversion (Delphi SOAP)
        Dim wsDelphi As New DelphiRomanArabic.IRomanservice()
        Dim curCurrent As Cursor = Cursor.Current
        Me.Cursor.Current = Cursors.WaitCursor
        With txtDelphiReq
            If Val(.Text) > 0 Then
                'It's an integer
                txtDelphiResp.Text = wsDelphi.IntToRoman(CInt(.Text))
            Else
'It's a Roman numeral
.Text = UCase(.Text)
txtDelphiResp.Text = CStr(wsDelphi.RomanToInt(.Text))
End If
End With
        Me.Cursor.Current = curCurrent
    End Sub

    Private Sub cmbCapeClear_Click(ByVal sender As System.Object, _
        ByVal e As System.EventArgs) Handles cmbCapeClear.Click
        'Airport weather reporting service (CapeClear SOAP)
        Dim objSummary As New CapeClearWeather.WeatherSummary()
        Dim wsWeather As New CapeClearWeather.AirportWeather()
        Dim curCurrent As Cursor = Cursor.Current
        Me.Cursor.Current = Cursors.WaitCursor
        With txtCapeResp
            objSummary = wsWeather.getSummary(txtCapeReq.Text)
            'Extract the individual values for the summary
            .Text = "Location: " + objSummary.location + strCrLf
            .Text += "Sky condition: " + objSummary.sky + strCrLf
            .Text += "Wind: " + objSummary.wind + strCrLf
```

```
            .Text += "Visibility: " + objSummary.visibility + strCrLf
            .Text += "Barometric pressure: " + objSummary.pressure + strCrLf
            .Text += "Humidity: " + objSummary.humidity
            txtSky.Text = wsWeather.getSkyConditions(txtCapeReq.Text)
        End With
        Me.Cursor.Current = curCurrent
    End Sub


    Private Sub cmbApache_Click(ByVal sender As System.Object, _
            ByVal e As System.EventArgs) Handles cmbApache.Click
        'Chicago traffic conditions (Apache SOAP)
        Dim wsApache As New ChicagoTraffic.ChicagoTravelTimesService()
        Dim curCurrent As Cursor = Cursor.Current
        Me.Cursor.Current = Cursors.WaitCursor
        txtApacheResp.Text = Replace(wsApache.GetTravelTimes, _
            Chr(10), strCrLf)
        Me.Cursor.Current = curCurrent
    End Sub


    Private Sub cmbApache2_Click(ByVal sender As System.Object, _
            ByVal e As System.EventArgs) Handles cmbApache2.Click
        'California traffic restrictions (Apache SOAP)
        Dim wsTraffic As New CaliforniaTraffic.CATrafficService()
        Dim curCurrent As Cursor = Cursor.Current
        Me.Cursor.Current = Cursors.WaitCursor
        txtApacheCA.Text = Replace(wsTraffic.getTraffic(txtHighway.Text), _
            Chr(10), strCrLf)
        Me.Cursor.Current = curCurrent
    End Sub
End Class
```

Following are brief descriptions of the four rpc/encoded Web services:

▶ **Roman Numeral to Arabic Converter (Delphi SOAP)** Accepts an uppercase or lowercase Roman numeral or an integer and returns an integer or Roman numeral.

▶ **Airport Weather Summary (CapeClear SOAP)** Accepts an International Civil Air Organization (ICAO) four-letter station code and returns a weather summary and the sky condition for the location. Location codes are the three-letter airport identifier with a K prefix. The National Weather Service provides lists of station codes by state at http://www.nws.noaa.gov/oso/siteloc.shtml. It takes a few seconds for this service to respond.

▶ **Chicago Travel Times (Apache SOAP)** Returns a list of travel times between locations of major Chicago highways. This service demonstrates the use of the `Imports` directive in WSDL documents; the `ChicagoTraffic` Web Reference has two WSDL files.

▶ **California Traffic Restrictions (Apache SOAP)** Accepts a numeric State, U.S., or Interstate highway number and returns from the California Department of Transportation (CalTrans) a list of impediments on the route.

The CapeClear and Apache SOAP examples are screen-scrapers that repurpose as Web services public information available from Web sites. The example screen-scraping services are trivial, but XML Web services are well suited to commercial content syndication.

CAUTION

Don't create publicly-accessible XML Web services from copyrighted content unless you have permission of the copyright holder. Almost all content on the Web is copyrighted, except that provided by federal and some state sites.

Taking Advantage of Standard Schemas

Developing XSD schemas is probably the most labor-intensive component of an EAI project that involves XML response or request documents, or both. You or your colleagues must develop a set of XSD schemas that represent the XML-formatted data to be exchanged at each step in the EAI workflow. Each schema must represent current business practices accurately and permit extension for future procedural changes. Schema extensions must be backwardly compatible to prevent breaking deployed application components.

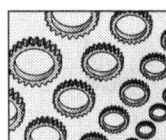

NOTE

Chapter 10's "Validating XML Request and Response Messages with XSD Schemas" section describes how to use XSD schemas to validate request and response documents for Visual Studio .NET XML Web services.

XML is firmly established as the *lingua franca* of document interchange. Trade groups, professional associations, and government agencies have formed working groups to establish standard schemas for a wide variety of XML documents. These schemas target the range from standardized documents, such as quarterly and annual financial reports, to specialized documents that are applicable to a particular industry or profession. Before you embark on developing a proprietary schema for EAI or B2B XML Web services, attempt to locate a standard XML schema that applies to the business process you're integrating. The following sections describe a typical standardized schema and sources for locating special-purpose XSD schemas for EAI and B2B projects.

Extensible Business Report Language

The Extensible Business Report Language (XBRL) is a standard XSD schema that's intended primarily for representing data in financial reports—balance sheets, profit and loss statements, and statements of cash flow—as XML documents. XBRL is the result of an American Institute of Certified Public Accountants (AICPA) project to develop a prototype set of XML financial documents (XFRML). XBRL is managed by an international project committee made up of the AICPA and its international counterparts, software publishers, and financial institutions; Microsoft, IBM, and Oracle are members. XBRL's Web site (http://www.xbrl.org) offers extensive documentation for the current XBRL 2.0 version.

The most obvious benefit of supplying financial data as an XML document that's validated against a standard XSD schema is analytical accuracy. Traditionally, members of the financial information supply chain—investment brokers, analysts, regulators, and lenders—rely on printed and Web-based reports as sources of financial data. Manual data entry and screen-scraping applications are a source of potential errors in subsequent analyses. XBRL provides a single source of financial data for a particular firm and reporting period. Recipients can use XSL/T or procedural code to transform the XML data into formats ranging from fully formatted [X]HTML Web pages to Excel worksheets.

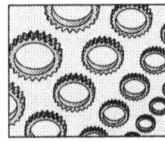

NOTE

Authentication of XBRL documents will be an important element as the standard schema gains acceptance in the financial community. The XML-Signature Syntax and Processing specification (http://www.w3.org/TR/xmldsig-core/), which W3C issued as a candidate recommendation on February 12, 2002, might be used to verify the source of the XBRL document and ensure that the original data hasn't undergone unauthorized changes.

Figure 12-6 shows the XML Financial Statement Viewer at http://www.xbrl.org/us/gaap/ci/2000-07-31/Sample/Viewer.htm. The Viewer displays HTML transformations of a balance sheet, income statement, stockholders' equity statement, and statement of cash flow. You can

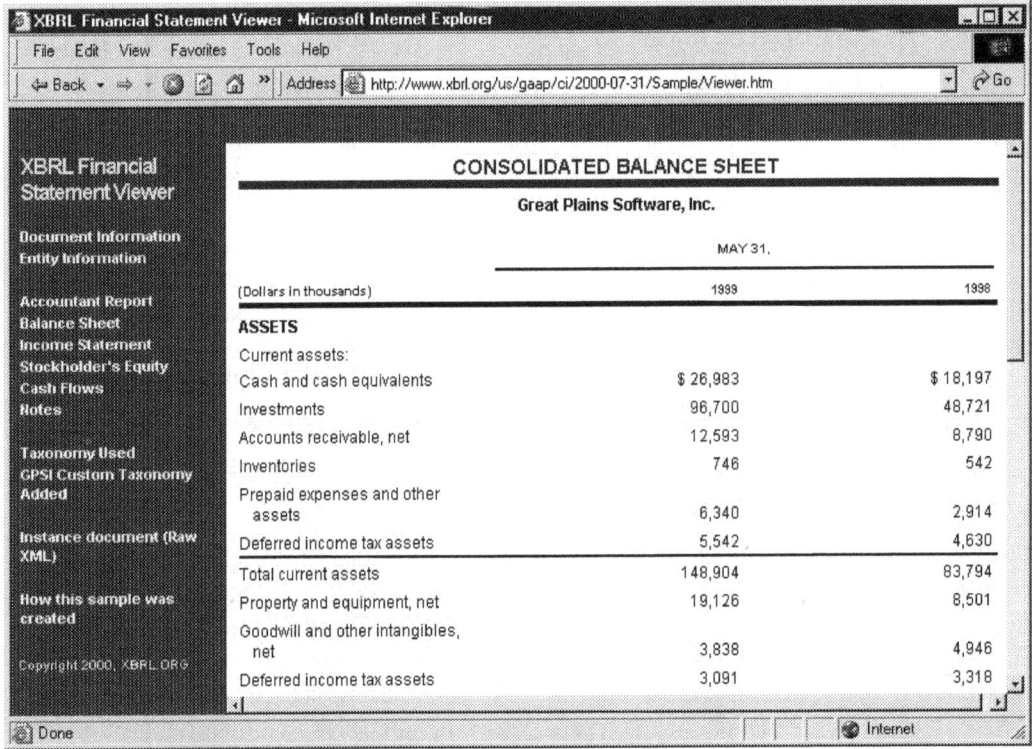

Figure 12-6   *The XBRL.org site's XML Financial Statement Viewer shows Great Plains Software, Inc.'s XBRL balance sheet documents for May 31, 1999, and May 31, 1998, transformed to HTML.*

also read the XBRL taxonomy for U.S. Generally Accepted Accounting Practices (GAAP) and the XML source document for the reports.

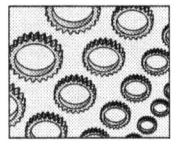

NOTE

The XML Financial Statement Viewer is an example of an ASP application that transforms XBRL-encoded data into HTML pages. The application uses Visual Basic and the XML DOM to generate the HTML with procedural code. This approach is similar to the OakLeaf CFR project's transformation of XML tables of contents and section text to XHTML, which is described in Chapter 9's "Visual Basic .NET Code Behind the OpenTOC.aspx Page" section.

Microsoft is among the first publicly traded corporations to provide financial reports as XBRL documents. The Microsoft Investor Relations XBRL Information page at http://www.microsoft.com/msft/xbrlinfo.htm has links to XBRL press releases and FAQs. The "XBRL Formatted Downloads" section at the bottom of the page has links to XBRL 2.0 documents for the current fiscal year's quarterly reports and the last annual report. Figure 12-7 shows a part of the report—the elements that relate to determining Microsoft's gross profit for the second quarter of fiscal year 2002.

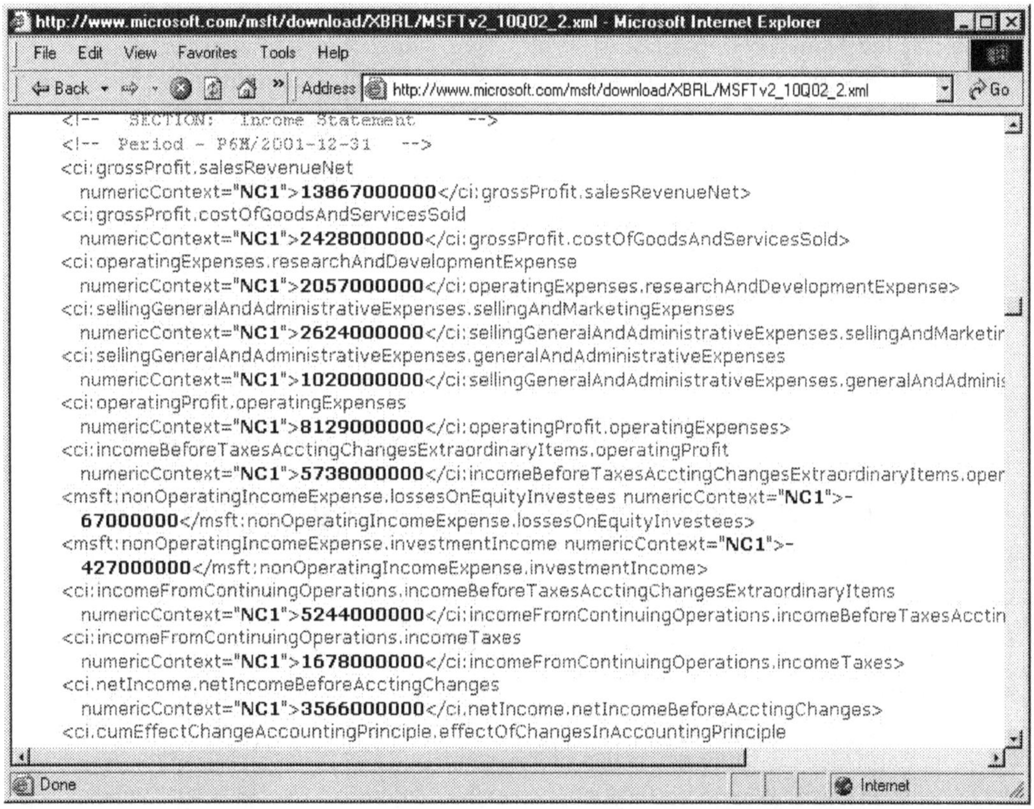

```
http://www.microsoft.com/msft/download/XBRL/MSFTv2_10Q02_2.xml - Microsoft Internet Explorer
File   Edit   View   Favorites   Tools   Help
Back  ⇨  ⊗  ⬜  ⌂  »  Address  http://www.microsoft.com/msft/download/XBRL/MSFTv2_10Q02_2.xml  ⮕ Go

<!--   SECTION:   Income Statement   -->
<!-- Period - P6M/2001-12-31   -->
<ci:grossProfit.salesRevenueNet
  numericContext="NC1">13867000000</ci:grossProfit.salesRevenueNet>
<ci:grossProfit.costOfGoodsAndServicesSold
  numericContext="NC1">2428000000</ci:grossProfit.costOfGoodsAndServicesSold>
<ci:operatingExpenses.researchAndDevelopmentExpense
  numericContext="NC1">2057000000</ci:operatingExpenses.researchAndDevelopmentExpense>
<ci:sellingGeneralAndAdministrativeExpenses.sellingAndMarketingExpenses
  numericContext="NC1">2624000000</ci:sellingGeneralAndAdministrativeExpenses.sellingAndMarketir
<ci:sellingGeneralAndAdministrativeExpenses.generalAndAdministrativeExpenses
  numericContext="NC1">1020000000</ci:sellingGeneralAndAdministrativeExpenses.generalAndAdminis
<ci:operatingProfit.operatingExpenses
  numericContext="NC1">8129000000</ci:operatingProfit.operatingExpenses>
<ci:incomeBeforeTaxesAcctingChangesExtraordinaryItems.operatingProfit
  numericContext="NC1">5738000000</ci:incomeBeforeTaxesAcctingChangesExtraordinaryItems.oper
<msft:nonOperatingIncomeExpense.lossesOnEquityInvestees numericContext="NC1">-
  67000000</msft:nonOperatingIncomeExpense.lossesOnEquityInvestees>
<msft:nonOperatingIncomeExpense.investmentIncome numericContext="NC1">-
  427000000</msft:nonOperatingIncomeExpense.investmentIncome>
<ci:incomeFromContinuingOperations.incomeBeforeTaxesAcctingChangesExtraordinaryItems
  numericContext="NC1">5244000000</ci:incomeFromContinuingOperations.incomeBeforeTaxesAcctin
<ci:incomeFromContinuingOperations.incomeTaxes
  numericContext="NC1">1678000000</ci:incomeFromContinuingOperations.incomeTaxes>
<ci:netIncome.netIncomeBeforeAcctingChanges
  numericContext="NC1">3566000000</ci:netIncome.netIncomeBeforeAcctingChanges>
<ci:cumEffectChangeAccountingPrinciple.effectOfChangesInAccountingPrinciple

Done                                                      Internet
```

Figure 12-7   *These elements of the XBRL 2.0 document for Microsoft's 2002Q2 quarterly report have unformatted numerical values for computing gross profit.*

XML Web services are an ideal method for returning XML documents in raw form or formatted as XHTML by the appropriate XSL/T document. For example, the request document might include elements to define the type and date of the report, and the desired format, such as raw XBRL 2.0, comma-separated values, or XHTML for PCs, handheld devices, or cell phones. Microsoft promises demonstration tools and Web pages to show off XBRL's potential for financial reporting.

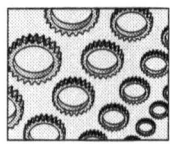

NOTE

XBRL is probably the most significant of the standard schemas that were published when this book was written. All publishers of accounting software for mid-size and larger businesses will undoubtedly add XBRL-compliant publishing features to their products.

Electronic Business XML (ebXML)

Electronic Business XML (ebXML) is more than a set of vocabularies, schemas, and related documents. The ebXML effort is directed to providing an alternative to the current Electronic Document Interchange (EDI) system, which relies primarily on private, proprietary, and expensive value-added networks (VANs) to interconnect large manufacturers, distributors, and retailers. The United Nations Directories for Electronic Data Interchange for Administration, Commerce, and Transport (UN/EDIFACT, http://www.unece.org/trade/untdid/) coordinates worldwide EDI standards. The United Nations Centre for Trade Facilitation and Electronic Business (UN/CEFACT, http://www.unece.org/cefact/) has similar responsibility for ebXML standards.

UN/CEFACT and the Organization for the Advancement of Structured Information Standards (OASIS, http://www.oasis-open.org) jointly sponsor ebXML, which is an organization devoted to establishing a "single global electronic market" that's based on ebXML standards. These standards include a registry service, messaging and collaboration protocols, and interoperability of implementations. OASIS and UN/CEFACT plan to deliver in May 2001 the following ebXML specifications:

▶ Business Process Methodology

▶ Technical Architecture

▶ Core Components

▶ Transport/Routing and Packaging

▶ Registry and Repository

▶ Trading Partners

▶ Security

Much of ebXML's work parallels that of Microsoft and IBM for generic Web services and the GXA extensions that are described in Chapter 1's "Microsoft Global XML Web Service Architecture Extensions" section. The ebXML registry service offers features similar to UDDI's;

messaging uses SOAP with extensions, and implementation interoperability ploughs the same ground as WS-I.

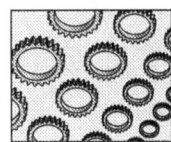

NOTE

Version 2.0c of the ebXML Message Service Specification consists of core Packaging Specification, ebXML SOAP Envelope Extensions, Error Handling, Security, and SyncReply elements. The spec also offers additional features, such as reliable messaging, message status service, message order, and multihop message routing. You can read the ebXML position paper and view accompanying slides at http://www.w3.org/2001/03/wsws-program. This page for the April 2002 W3C Web Services Workshop has links to several other presentations and position papers that involve interoperability issues.

Sun Microsystems is an outspoken proponent of ebXML, which competes with Microsoft's BizTalk Server and the BizTalk Framework. A third-party BizTalk adapter produced by iWay (http://www.iwaysoftware.com) provides ebXML registry services; the iWay Transformation Engine supports ebXML and EDI messages.

XML.org's Schema Registry

XML.org is a portal site hosted by OASIS at http://www.xml.org. The stated purpose of XML.org is "… to minimize overlap and duplication in XML languages and XML standard initiatives by providing public access to XML information and XML [s]chemas."

The XML.org site provides a registry search service at http://www.xml.org/xml/registry.jsp that lets you specify the document type, such as XSD, XDR, or DTD. Try a search on a keyword that's specific to your industry or service. The search page also has direct links to about 100 ebXML specifications classified by industry.

TIP

XML.org and OASIS host Robin Cover's Cover Pages (http://xml.coverpages.org/sgmlnew.html), which publishes news on SGML and XML topics. The Cover Pages provide the most up-to-date and detailed information on activities that relate to XML Web services.

BizTalk.org's Schema Registry

BizTalk.org is a Microsoft-sponsored Web site (http://www.biztalk.org) intended to "… provide resources for learning about and using Extensible Markup Language (XML) for [e]nterprise [a]pplication [i]ntegration (EAI) and business-to-business (B2B) document exchange." The content of the site consists primarily of propaganda for BizTalk Server and the BizTalk Framework. The site also offers a registry of close to 500 user-contributed schemas, almost all of which are in Microsoft's proprietary XDR format.

As the BizTalk community gradually moves from XDR to the XSD format, you can expect the percentage of contributed XSD schemas to increase. BizTalk Server 2002's BizTalk Framework 2.0 supports SOAP 1.1, and XML Schema 1.0 Parts 1 and 2. BizTalk Server 2000+ includes an XDR to XSD conversion script.

Exploring a Commercial ASP.NET Web Service

RichSolutions, Inc., was one of the first organizations to publish a commercial ASP.NET Web Service. The company introduced the RichPayments.NET Web service on February 13, 2001, the official release date of Visual Studio .NET. RichPayments.NET handles credit card, debit card, check verification, and federal Electronic Benefits Transfer (EBT) transactions. Obviously, you won't have problems interoperating with the RichPayments.NET Web services.

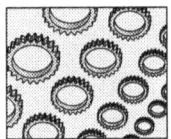

NOTE

For more information on EBT and the Benefit Security Card, which is currently available in only eight southern states, go to http://www.fms.treas.gov/ebt/.

You can view RichPayment's fully documented WSDL document at http://www.richsolutions. com/richpayments/richpay.asmx. The five methods return a `Response` structure that contains an `xsd:int Result` code and up to 20 additional `xsd:string` values.

RichSolutions offers the following demonstration programs, which you can download after free registration:

▶   A Visual Basic .NET test consumer application with forms to demonstrate the four RichPayments Web service methods.

▶   Visual Basic .NET Windows form and ASP.NET sample consumers of a secure credit card number validation service (http://www.richsolutions.com/richpayments/ richcardValidator.asmx).

▶   RichPayments.NET SDK version 2.1, which includes three ActiveX DLLs and a Visual Basic 6.0 application. The SDK components emulate the Visual Basic .NET test application.

Figure 12-8 shows the CreditTxForm for credit card processing after completing a $10.00 transaction. The Transaction Type list lets you select a Sale, Return, Void, Auth(orize), or Force transaction. The message box displays the response from the initial card validation (Good) and the Sale transaction (Response: Approved; Approval Code: DEMO-1; and AVS Match: Issuer Did Not Perform AVS).

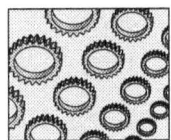

NOTE

The `VerifyOrHold` and `ChargeOrCredit` methods of the OakLeaf OCE project's OmegaBankWS Web services perform operations similar to RichPayments' `ProcessCreditCard` method, but the OmegaBankWS service doesn't comply with industry-standard processes or terminology.

The RSWin_VB.sln solution defaults to demonstration mode, which uses Demo as the user name and password. To run the service in training mode, which more closely simulates actual transactions, request a user account and password from RichSolutions, Inc.

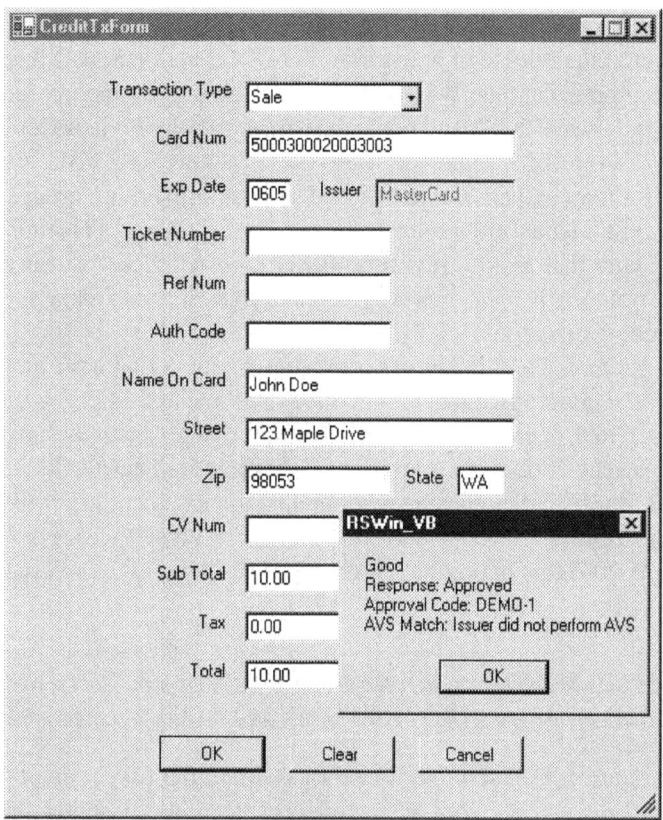

Figure 12-8   *The RichSolutions Visual Basic .NET test harness for the RichPayments Web service displays the result of a sample $10.00 credit card transaction.*

Projecting the Future of XML Web Services

If you gauge the future of a technology by totaling the column inches of related trade press articles or the number of books with "Web Services" in their titles, XML Web services is a *killer* application. On the other hand, if you measure a technology's deadliness by the number of its current commercial deployments, you'd probably conclude that XML Web services has missed its target.

It's premature to judge the ultimate success of XML Web services a few months after release of the first development tools that fully support creating and consuming services at the WS-I Basic profile. When this book was written, most Visual Basic developers were in the training-wheels stage with Visual Basic .NET, ASP.NET, and ADO.NET. The Microsoft SOAP 2.0 Toolkit gives Visual Basic 6.0 developers an entry point for creating Web services, but difficulties with creating and consuming document/literal-style services and handling SOAP headers relegate the Toolkit to legacy status.

It's unlikely that large organizations will place XML Web services for EAI into full production status until the release of at least the SOAP 1.2 and WSDL 1.2 specifications as W3C candidate recommendations. W3C's Web Services Activity incorporated the XML Protocol Activity in January 2002, and now consists of a Web Services Coordination Group with representatives from IBM, Microsoft, Sun Microsystems, and W3C, and Web Services Architecture, XML Protocol, and Web Services Description working groups. The working groups held their first teleconferences in February 2002 and began issuing initial draft recommendations later that month. It will probably require at least a year to resolve the divergent interests of the W3C's Web Services Activity membership and issue final SOAP 1.2 and WSDL 1.2 recommendations.

An encouraging sign is the number of software publishers that have announced their intention to add Web services features to—or have implemented SOAP 1.1 and WSDL 1.1 in—packaged B2B, CRM, document management, and office productivity software. Microsoft's Office XP Web Services Toolkit is a step in the right direction, despite its reliance on the SOAP Toolkit 2.0. Hardly a day goes by without an announcement in *InfoWorld* magazine that *Company X*'s *Product Y* does or will soon support Web services. For example, from March 1 to March 8, 2002, the magazine's Web site ran 13 articles with Web services content.

TIP

InfoWorld's editorial staff appears to have a decided Web services bent. Click the Web Services entry under the Subject Indexes heading at http://www.infoworld.com/ to check the current article list.

Even if the market for Web services doesn't live up to the rosy projections of market researchers that the "Beyond the Web Services Hype" section of Chapter 1 describes, there's no question that the XML Web services technologies described in this book portend a major shift in the architecture of distributed, data-intensive applications. If you've worked your way through all—or even most of—this book's sample applications, you'll be well prepared for the forthcoming migration from proprietary component architectures to interoperable XML Web services based on W3C-standard SOAP, WSDL, XSD, and other related specifications.

Installing the Sample Databases

IN THIS CHAPTER:

Downloading and Installing the OakLeaf Consumer Electronics Databases

Installing the CFRSQL Database

This book requires installation of a set of six SQL Server 2000 sample databases to support the OakLeaf Consumer Electronics (OCE) sample applications. Installation of the OakLeaf Code of Federal Regulations (CFRSQL) database is optional. All databases run under any SQL Server 2000 version, including the Microsoft Data Engine (MSDE) 2000. MSDE doesn't include the full-text search feature, so you can't implement the search page of the OakLeaf Online CFR project if you use MSDE.

TIP

Apply SQL Server 2000 Service Pack 2 or later if you haven't installed it previously. You can download the latest SP from http://www.microsoft.com/sql/.

Attaching and managing the databases requires SQL Enterprise Manager (EntMan), which isn't included with MSDE or Visual Studio .NET. You can download the SQL Server 2000 Evaluation Edition, which includes EntMan, from http://www.microsoft.com/ sql/evaluation/ trial/2000/. The license for this edition expires in 120 days, so install only the Client Tools, not SQL Server.

Downloading and Installing the OakLeaf Consumer Electronics Databases

Here's the procedure for installing the six databases required to support the B2C and B2B XML Web services for the OakLeaf Consumer Electronics (OCE) examples of this book:

1. Download the VBWS_OCE.zip file from the book's entry at http://www.osborne.com/ downloads/downloads.shtml. The size of the archive file is about 11MB. The expanded files consume about 42MB and can expand to at least 100MB.

2. Expand the six databases (.mdf) and their log (.ldf) files into your \Program Files\ Microsoft SQL Server\MSSQL[$*InstanceName*]\Data folder.

TIP

If you're short of space on the default drive, you can install the files to any folder of any local physical drive.

3. Launch EntMan with Windows authentication and expand your local server node. Your server logon account must have system administrator (sa) privileges for the server.

TIP

If this is a new EntMan installation, right-click the SQL Server Group node, and choose New SQL Server Registration to open the Registered SQL Server Properties dialog. Select (local) from the Server list, and click OK to add a (LOCAL)(WindowsNT) node.

4. Right-click the Databases node, and choose All Tasks | Attach Database to open the Attach Database - (LOCAL) dialog.

5. Click the browse button to the left of the Verify button to open the Browse For Existing File - (LOCAL) dialog, and navigate to the drive and folder that contains the data and log files. Select AlphaDist.mdf and click OK to return to the Attach Database dialog.

6. Select your administrative login ID from the Specify Database Owner list, as shown here, and click OK to attach the database and acknowledge the "success" message.

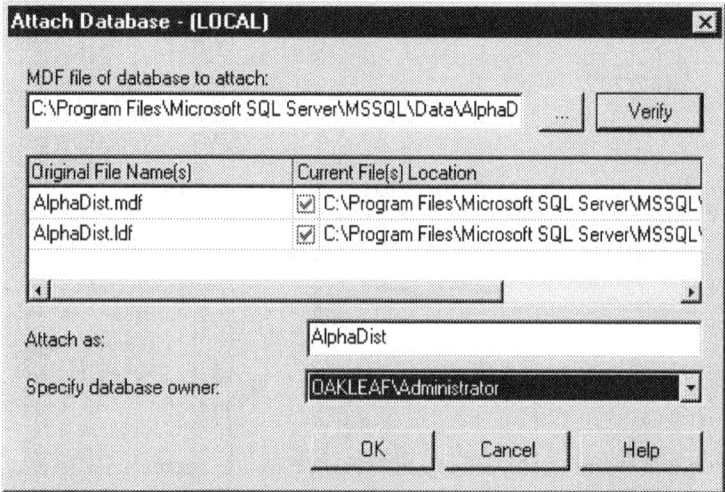

CAUTION

Make sure to specify your administrative account—typically DOMAIN/Administrator—in the preceding step. The database owner (dbo) defaults to the first login ID in alphabetical order. If you accidentally use DatabaseUser as the dbo, you might not be able to add the DatabaseUser login. In this case, you must detach the database and start over.

7. Repeat steps 4 through 6 for the BetaDist.mdf, GammaDist.mdf, OMB_Network.mdf, OCE_Cust.mdf, and OCE_Prod.mdf databases.

Adding SQL Server Logins and Database Users

Now that you've attached the databases, you must add the individual login IDs and passwords for six databases. The XML Web services use the login ID and password for authentication. The services in the early chapters of the book use SQL Server authentication; later chapters send the login ID and password in the SOAP header section. The following table lists the login entries you make for the six databases:

Login ID	Password	Default Database	Optional Secure Permissions
AlphaUser	Alpha#123	AlphaDist	SELECT on all Products columns, UPDATE only on Quantity column
BetaUser	Beta#123	BetaDist	SELECT on all Products columns, UPDATE only on Quantity column
GammaUser	Gamma#123	GammaDist	SELECT on all Products columns, UPDATE only on Quantity column
CustUser	Cust#123	OCE_Cust	SELECT on all tables; INSERT and UPDATE on Invoices, LineItems, Orders, and OrdersInvoices
NetUser	Net#123	OMB_Network	SELECT on all tables; INSERT only on Transactions table
ProdUser	Prod#123	OCE_Prod	SELECT on all tables except Products, INSERT and UPDATE on PurchaseOrders and POLineItems, SELECT on all columns, and UPDATE only on CommittedNow and ShippedInPeriod columns of Products

   To add the login IDs and passwords to the server and add the user ID to each database, follow these steps:

1. Expand the Security node of the server, right-click the Logins item, and choose New Login to open the SQL Server Login Properties - New Login dialog.

2. Type **AlphaUser** in the Name text box, select the SQL Server authentication option, type **Alpha#123** as the password, and select AlphaDist as the default database, as illustrated here.

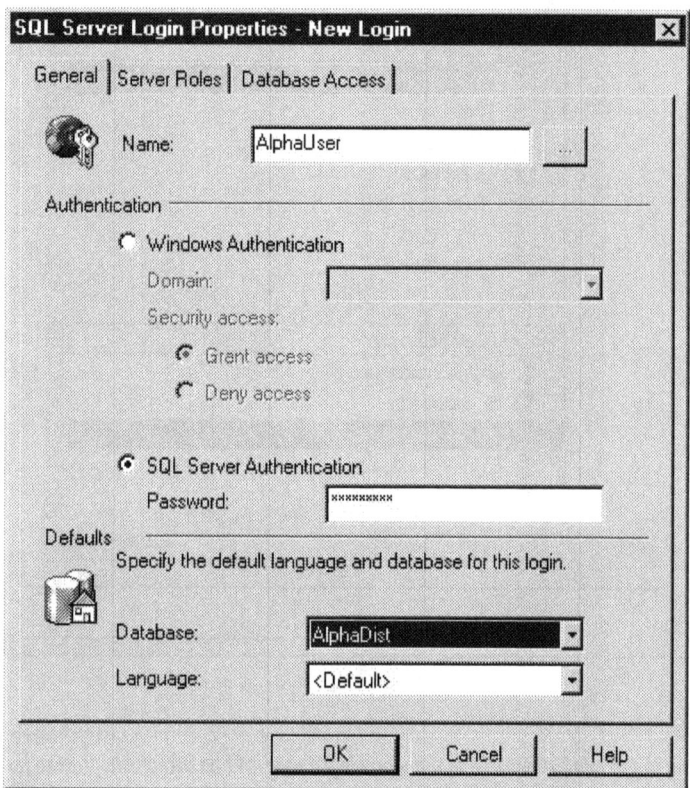

3. Click the Database Access tab, mark the Permit check box for the AlphaDist database to add AlphaUser to the User column, and mark the Db_datareader and Db_datawriter check boxes in the Permit In Database Role list, as shown in the next illustration.

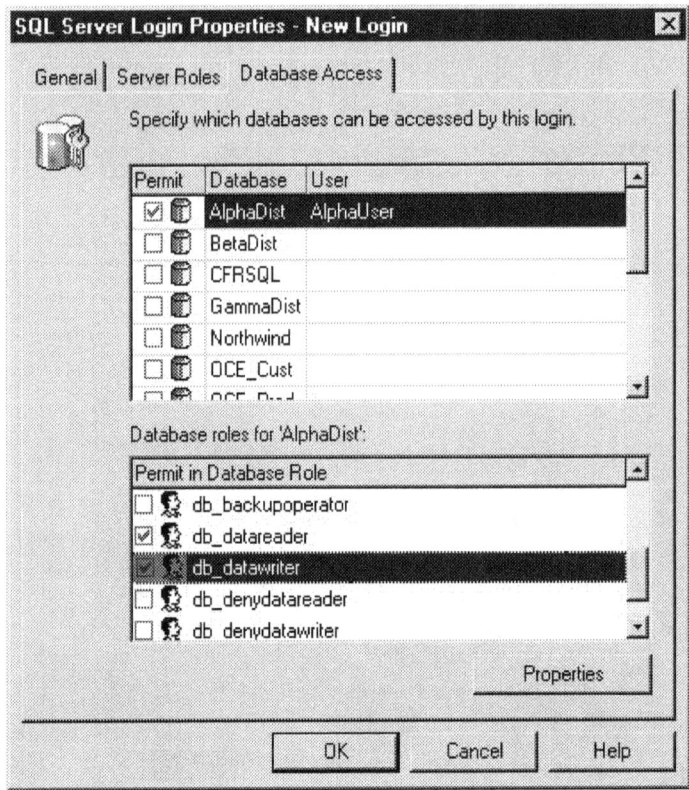

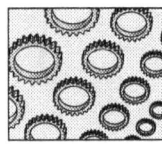

NOTE

Assigning the db_datawriter role to a nonprivileged user isn't an acceptable practice for a secure database. For production databases, specify SELECT, INSERT, UPDATE, and, especially, DELETE permissions for each table and, for UPDATEs (and possibly SELECTs), individual columns. (See the Optional Secure Permissions column of the preceding table.) The tables of the remote databases you access by the XML Web services of the http://www.oakleaf.ws/oce/ site have individual user permissions for each table and, where applicable, columns.

4. Click OK to add the new login ID, confirm the password, and click OK to add the new AlphaUser login and add AlphaUser to the Users group of the AlphaDist database.

5. Repeat steps 1 through 5 for BetaUser, GammaUser, NetUser, CustUser, ProdUser, and NetUser. (Refer to the preceding table.)

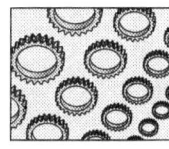

NOTE

This tedious database installation process is required to emulate a production-grade configuration and to enable secure logins to local and remote XML Web services with different security configurations. (When grumbling about the installation process, which requires about 15 minutes, consider the tedium involved in creating these databases.)

Verifying Correct Installation of the Databases

The `frmOrders` form of Chapter 3's OCE_Orders and OCE_OrdersAX Visual Basic 6.0 projects and Chapter 4's NET_Orders and NET_OrdersAX upgraded Visual Basic .NET projects include code to test for presence of the databases and verify required `SELECT`, `INSERT`, and `UPDATE` permissions for each login.

To verify proper installation and configuration of the databases, do this:

1. Download VBWS03.zip (for Visual Basic 6.0) or VBWS04.zip (for Visual Basic .Net) from the McGraw-Hill/Osborne FTP site at http://www.osborne.com/downoads/ downloads.shtml. If you've already downloaded either or both of these files, skip to step 3.

2. Extract the contents of the VBWS0?.zip file to a \VBWS03 or \VBWS04 folder (or any folder of your choice), preferably on the machine with the instance of SQL Server to which you attached the databases.

3. Run OCE_Order.exe or NET_Orders.exe from the installation folder, if the file is on the machine running SQL Server. Otherwise, open `frmOrders` and replace all instances of (`LOCAL`) with the NetBIOS name of the server, and run the project from the IDE.

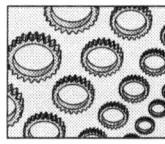

NOTE

The `cmdInitialize` subprocedure contains the database test code.

4. Click Initialize and acknowledge the message for testing the SQL Server logins and their permissions, and reset the databases to their original condition. If you completed the installation process correctly, you receive this message.

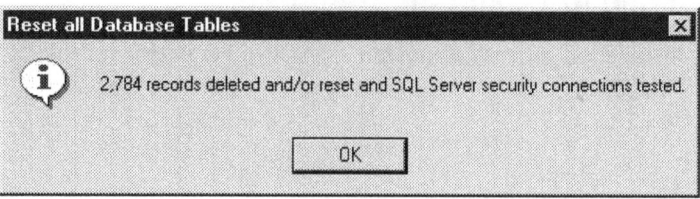

5. If you receive an error message, such as that shown here, expand the Users node of the offending database, and verify that the *Database*User SQL Server login has db_ datareader and db_datawriter permissions. Correct the user permissions and try again.

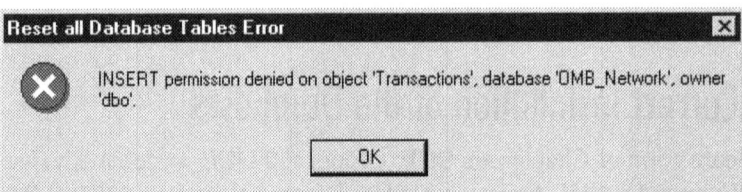

Reset all Database Tables Error

INSERT permission denied on object 'Transactions', database 'OMB_Network', owner 'dbo'.

OK

TIP

Don't try to change database user roles in the SQL Server Login Properties - UserName dialog. You can't change database roles in this dialog after you create the new login.

Installing the CFRSQL Database

Installation of the CFRSQL database for the OakLeaf CFR project is optional, because you have read-only access to all the tables as XML Web services from the ASP.NET CFR client application that's included in VBWS09.zip's CFR-Final subfolder. You might find it interesting, however, to examine and run the Visual Basic 6.0 and Visual Basic .NET code that generates the XML table of contents and section text documents. Another incentive for downloading the CFRSQL database is lack of a high-speed Internet connection. The fully populated CFRSQL database is close to 1GB. The abbreviated downloadable version expands to fewer than 50MB.

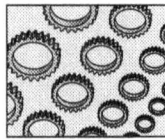

NOTE

The downloadable version of CFRSQL has tables of contents (TOCs) and sections only for Title 47-Telecommunication. You can add as many additional records as your patience permits. Downloading the entire CFR from the Government Printing Office's Electronic CFR (e-CFR) Beta site takes about a week with a DSL connection.

Downloading and Attaching the Database

Fortunately, the installation process is much less involved than that for the OCE projects' databases. Here's the drill:

1. Download VBWS_CFR.zip (9MB) from this book's entry at http://www.osborne.com/ downloads/downloads.shtml, and expand it into the \Program Files\Microsoft SQL Server\ MSSQL[*#InstanceName*]\Data\ folder, or wherever you have space for it.

2. Open EntMan, and attach the CFRSQL.mdf file to the database with your Windows system administrative account as the database owner.

3. Add a **CFRUser** login and **charon?123** as the password. Add the db_datareader role so you can use this book's applications that rely on SQL Server security to read the data.

Setting Up a Full-Text Search

If you run CFRSQL under any SQL Server version other than MSDE, you can enable a full-text search of the tables of contents and section text. Disk space requirements for the catalogs vary with database size. The Mssearch.exe service must be running to enable full-text search services. The fully populated CFRSQL database has 125MB of catalogs. Do the following to add full-text indexing on the tables of contents and section text of the CFRSQL's tables:

1. In EntMan, select the CFRSQL database, and choose Tools | SQL Query Analyzer to open a Query window with the CFRSQL database selected.

2. Enable a full-text search on the database by typing **sp_fulltext_database 'enable'** in the upper query pane and pressing F5 to execute the query. Close Query Analyzer, and don't save the changes.

3. Expand the CFRSQL node.

4. Right-click the Full-Text Catalogs item, and choose New Full-Text Catalog to open the New Full-Text Catalog - Properties dialog.

5. Type **CFRToc** in the Name text box, accept the default location for the catalogs, and click OK to add the catalog for the XML TOCs.

6. Repeat steps 4 and 5, but change the Name entry to **CFRSect** to add the catalog for the XML section text.

7. Click the Tables node to display a list of CFRSQL's tables in the right pane.

8. Right-click the Chapters table entry and choose Full-Text Index Table | Define Full-Text Indexing On A Table to start the Full-Text Indexing Wizard. Click Next.

9. Accept the default IX_Chapters unique index on the table, and click Next.

10. In the Select Table Columns dialog, mark the TOCChar and TOCText check boxes, as shown here. Click Next.

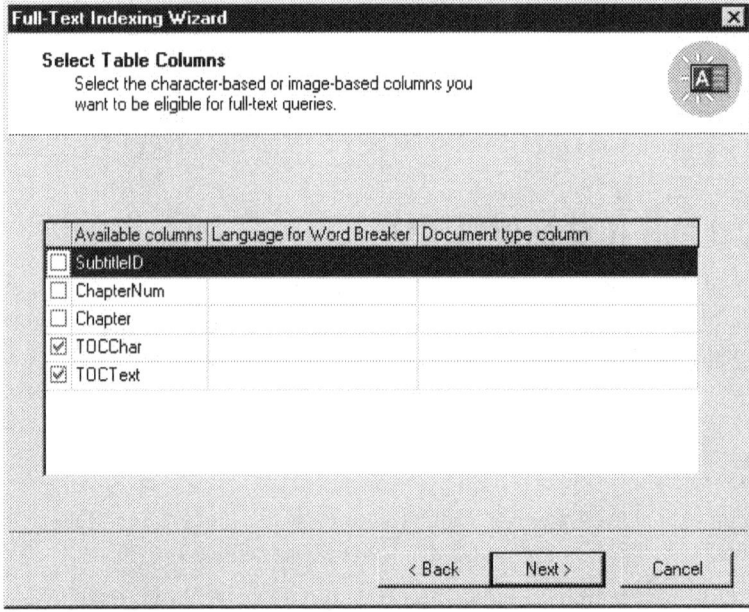

11. Accept the default CFRToc catalog, click Next twice, and then click Finish to add the indexes on the table's columns to the catalog. Acknowledge the "success" message.

12. Repeat steps 8 through 11 for the Parts, Subchapters, Subtitles, TitlesTOC, and Titles tables. The TitlesTOC table doesn't have a TOCChar field.

13. Right-click the Sections table, start the Wizard, and click Next twice.

14. In the Select Table Columns dialog, mark the SectText and SectChar check boxes, and click Next.

15. In the Select A Catalog dialog, select CFRSect in the Select Full-Text Catalog list.

CAUTION

If you don't select CFRSect in this step, full-text indexing won't work correctly.

16. Click Next twice, and then click Finish to generate the full-text catalog for the XML section text. Acknowledge the "success" message.

17. Click CFRSQL's Full Text Catalogs node to display the two catalogs you created in the right pane.

18. Right-click the CFRToc catalog, choose Start Full Population, and click OK to confirm background population has started. Populating this catalog requires about 5 minutes on a fast machine.

19. Repeat step 18 for the CFRSect catalog, which requires about 10 minutes.

After you add new CFR parts and sections to the database, you must rerun steps 18 and 19 to add the new items to the catalogs. Schedule an SQL Agent task to repopulate the catalogs automatically by double-clicking the catalog item to open its Properties dialog and clicking the Schedules tab. Click New Catalog Schedule to open a dialog that lets you specify the frequency and time for repopulation.

Appendix B shows you how to use the CFRClient application to add parts and sections from the U.S. Government Printing Office's e-CFR database.

Expanding the CFRSQL Database with CFRClient

IN THIS CHAPTER:

Installing the CFRClient Project and Solution

Running the CFRClient

Using the Client Emulator Form

The OakLeaf Online Code of Federal Regulations database (CFRSQL), which you install by using the procedure described in Appendix A, contains parts, sections, and section text for only a single title of the U.S. CFR—Title 47 - Telecommunication. The CFRClient.vbp project enables adding parts, sections, and section text for additional titles, starting with Title 1 - General Provisions. The client also generates XML tables of contents (TOCs) at the title, subtitle, chapter, subchapter, and part levels. If you have the patience to add data and TOCs for all titles, the database expands to about 850MB, plus about 150MB for full-text search catalogs. MSDE 2000 doesn't include SQL Server's full-text search feature.

TIP

To learn more about the structure and size of the electronic and print CFR versions, go to http://www.oakleaf.ws/cfr/ and scroll to the "About the U.S. Code of Federal Regulations" section.

The CFRClient.vbp project is the management and testing tool for the OakLeaf Web site's implementation of the original COM-based version of the Online CFR at http://www.oakleaf.ws/cfr-com/. VBWSAB.zip contains the Visual Basic 6.0 code for CFRClient.vbp and upgraded Visual Basic .NET code for CFRClient.sln. To aid the upgrade process, the Visual Basic 6.0 code uses datatype conversion functions for all `ADODB.Recordset` field variables and doesn't have `Variant` variables. Removing `Set objName = Nothing` statements, deleting an extra `Else` added by the Upgrade Wizard, and making minor modifications for changes in behavior of list boxes took care of run-time exceptions. The upgrade process requires fewer than 30 minutes, including these fixes.

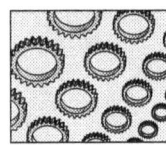

NOTE

Microsoft recommends not upgrading complex Visual Basic 6.0 applications to Visual Basic .NET, unless you need to add specific .NET features. Upgrading the CFRClient.vbp to Visual Basic .NET indicates that the Wizard handles the upgrade of a 5700-line project quite well. The _UpgradeReport.htm page lists the issues detected during the upgrade. The six design errors reported for CFRClient.frm are bogus; all `lstName.ItemData` values are set at run time, not design time, and the upgrade from the `ItemData` property to the `SetItemData` method succeeds.

Both versions include the .asp, .htm, .css, .htc, and other files required to emulate the CFR-COM version of the OakLeaf CFR project. The terms of the copyright license (License.txt) limit your use of the code to personal educational purposes. The license specifically prohibits you from making the copyrighted .asp, .htm, and other Web-related files accessible from the public Internet. You can, however, create your own version of the Online CFR by authoring Web pages that connect to the three OakLeaf XML Web services at http://www.oakleaf.ws/cfr/.

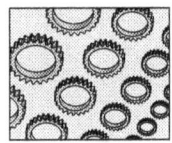

NOTE

Both CFRClient versions require installation of the Microsoft SOAP Toolkit 2.0+ before you open the project or solution.

Installing the CFRClient Project and Solution

Following is the procedure for downloading, installing, and testing the two CFRClient versions:

1. If you haven't downloaded and installed the CFRSQL database, follow the instructions in Appendix A's "Installing the CFRSQL Database" section. You can't run either version of the CFRClient project without the SQL Server 2000 database.

2. Download the VBWSAB.zip file (870MB) from this book's entry at http://www.osborne.com/downloads/downloads.shtml.

3. Expand the archive into a folder named CFRClient or the like, which creates a CFRClient.NET subfolder for the Visual Basic .NET version's code.

4. Read the License.txt file.

5. Open the CCFRSearch.vbp project, recompile CCFRSearch.dll to register the ActiveX DLL, close the project, and save your changes.

6. Repeat step 5 for CCFRSect.vbp and CCFRToc.vbp. Both versions use these three ActiveX DLLs.

7. Open CFRClient.vbp, and verify that the three CFR - ... references point to the DLLs in the project folder. If the location is incorrect, clear the references' check boxes, close and save the project, and reopen it.

8. If the SQL Server 2000 instance running the CFRSQL database isn't on this computer, open the code for **frmCFRClient**, and change the (LOCAL) entry in the following line of the **cmdConnect_Click** event handler to the NetBIOS name of the server.

   ```
   gstrConnect = "Provider=SQLOLEDB;Integrated Security=SSPI;Data
   Source=(LOCAL);Initial Catalog=CFRSQL"
   ```

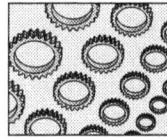

NOTE

Change the preceding line in the ...\CFRClient.NET folder's code for frmClient.vb, if your SQL Server instance is on another machine.

9. Compile and run CFRClient.vbp.

10. Click the Connect button to verify that you can connect to the local instance of the CFRSQL database. Run-time error messages at this point indicate that the CFRSQL database isn't configured correctly.

11. Open ...\CFRClient.NET\CFRClient.sln and press F5 to build and execute the solution.

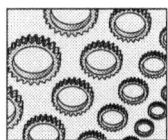

NOTE

The CFRClient program is a development and testing tool, so it doesn't include run-time error-handling code. Running CFRClient from the IDE is the recommended approach until you verify proper execution of the code on your computer.

Running the CFRClient

To test-drive either of the two CFRClient versions, do this:

1. Click the Connect button to make the connection to your local, abbreviated copy of CFRSQL, and populate the titles and chapters lists at the top of the window.

2. In the titles list, scroll to 47 - Telecommunication and double-click the item to display the title's chapters and subchapters in the chapters list.

3. Double-click a chapter or subchapter item, such as C - Broadcast Radio Services, to display the chapter's parts in the lower-left list box. A marked check box indicates that the part has section records in the database.

4. Double-click a part item, such as 76 - Cable Television Service, to list the part's sections in the lower-right list box. Sections with marked check boxes have section text in the section records.

NOTE

Double-clicking a title, section, or part item displays the XML table of contents for the object in the main text box.

5. Double-click a marked section, such as 76.56 - Signal Carriage Obligations, to display the XML section text in the main text box. (See Figure B-1.)

6. Double-click the main text box to displays its contents in IE 5.0+. (See Figure B-2.)

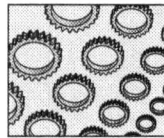

NOTE

Marking the Updates check box before clicking Connect invokes the CFRUpdates .GetPartsAffected method, which opens the Government Printing Office (GPO) List of CFR Parts Affected Today page at http://www.access.gpo.gov/nara/lsa/lsatoday.html. Code scrapes the page to extract the title and part number changed, and adds records to the PartsAffected table. Clicking the Get Updates button retrieves all sections for each updated part on Monday through Friday. On the average, the GPO updates about ten parts per workday, which can require downloading several hundred sections when only a few sections might have changed.

Adding Part Records to the Database

The CFR is a dynamic document—the federal agencies responsible for the CFR titles add and delete parts frequently. The authoritative sources for current parts and their sections are the GPO's CFR browsing pages, such as http://www.access .gpo.gov/nara/cfr/cfrhtml_00/Title_ 7/ 7tab_00.html. Adding parts and sections and periodically verifying the database contents requires a full pass through the 50 titles, 28 subtitles, 375 chapters, and 799 subchapters of the CFR.

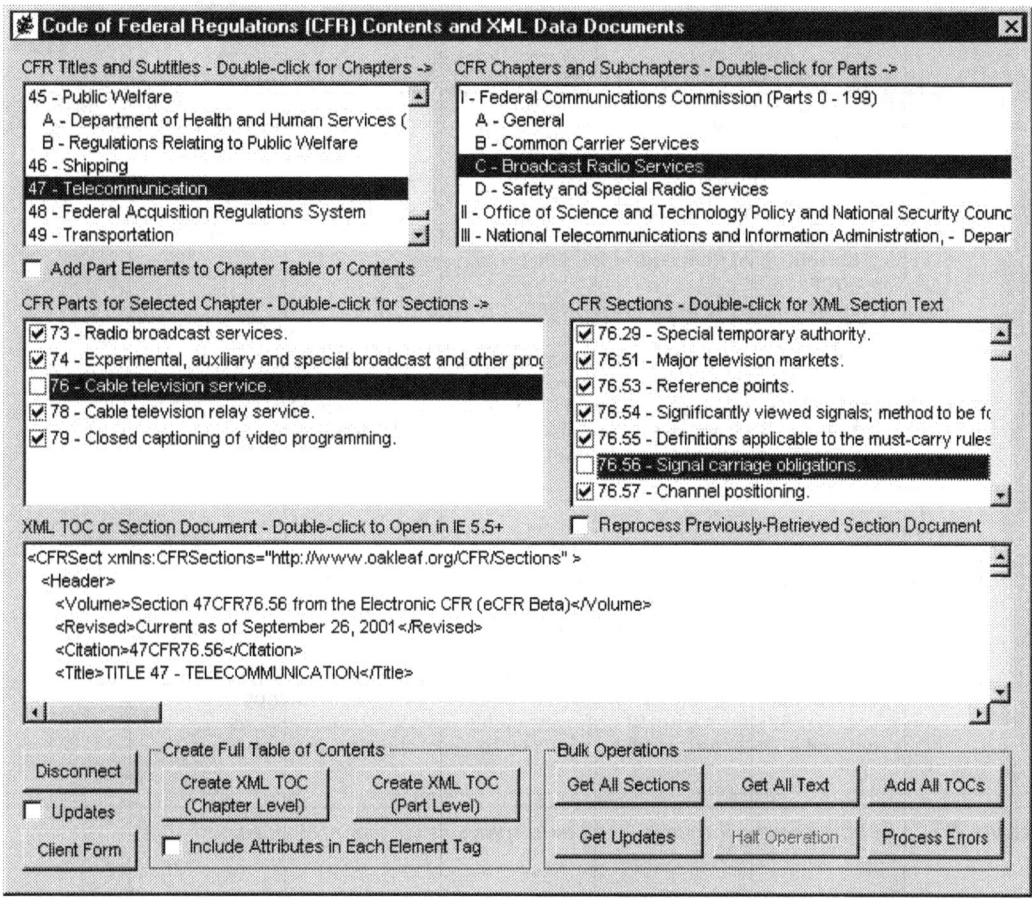

Figure B-1   *The four list boxes display the titles and subtitles, chapters and subchapters, parts, and sections of the CFR.*

Click the Get All Sections button to execute code in the `frmCFRClient` `.cmdGetSections_Click` event handler that scrapes the Browse page for each title, navigates to the Browse Parts page (http://www.access .gpo.gov/nara/ cfr/ cfrhtml_ 00/Title_7/ 7cfrv1_00.html), and then to the Part page (http://www.access .gpo.gov/nara/ cfr/ cfrhtml_ 00/Title_7/7cfr1_00.html). Scraping the Part page adds one record to the Parts table and multiple records to the Sections table. The CFR has about 8000 parts; adding or verifying all the part and section records requires about 24 hours with a DSL connection to the Internet.

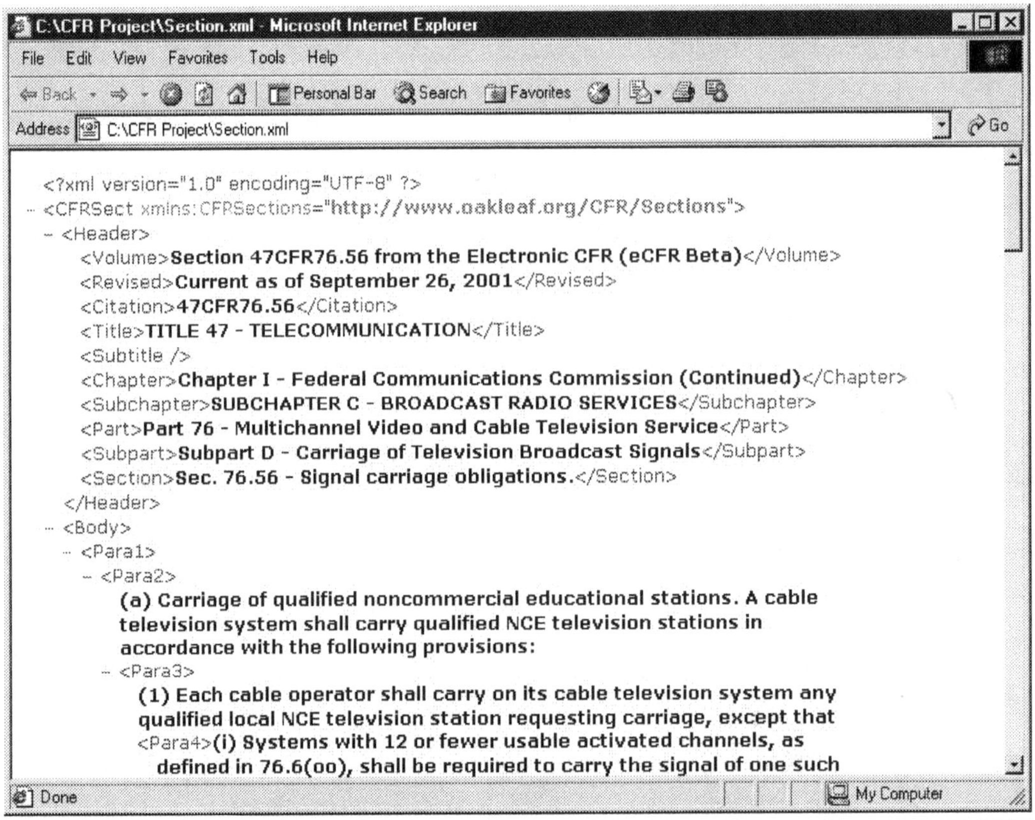

```
C:\CFR Project\Section.xml - Microsoft Internet Explorer                    _ □ ×

 File   Edit   View   Favorites   Tools   Help

 ← Back  →   ·   ⊗  ⌂  ⌂  │  ⊞ Personal Bar   ⊛ Search  ⌂ Favorites  ⊛  │  ⧉·  ⊜  ⬚

 Address  ⌂ C:\CFR Project\Section.xml                               ▼   ⬗ Go

    <?xml version="1.0" encoding="UTF-8" ?>
  - <CFRSect xmlns:CFRSections="http://www.oakleaf.org/CFR/Sections">
   - <Header>
       <Volume>Section 47CFR76.56 from the Electronic CFR (eCFR Beta)</Volume>
       <Revised>Current as of September 26, 2001</Revised>
       <Citation>47CFR76.56</Citation>
       <Title>TITLE 47 - TELECOMMUNICATION</Title>
       <Subtitle />
       <Chapter>Chapter I - Federal Communications Commission (Continued)</Chapter>
       <Subchapter>SUBCHAPTER C - BROADCAST RADIO SERVICES</Subchapter>
       <Part>Part 76 - Multichannel Video and Cable Television Service</Part>
       <Subpart>Subpart D - Carriage of Television Broadcast Signals</Subpart>
       <Section>Sec. 76.56 - Signal carriage obligations.</Section>
     </Header>
   - <Body>
    - <Para1>
     - <Para2>
         (a) Carriage of qualified noncommercial educational stations. A cable
         television system shall carry qualified NCE television stations in
         accordance with the following provisions:
       - <Para3>
           (1) Each cable operator shall carry on its cable television system any
           qualified local NCE television station requesting carriage, except that
           <Para4>(i) Systems with 12 or fewer usable activated channels, as
             defined in 76.6(oo), shall be required to carry the signal of one such

 ⬚ Done                                                            ⬚ My Computer
```

Figure B-2   *Double-clicking the main text box displays its current XML document in IE.*

Adding Section Text to the Database

After adding the section records, you add the section's text as an XML document to the Sections table. The GPO's e-CFR database contains SGML and HTML versions of each section. The `CFRGetSection.ECFRFormatXML` method transforms the SGML text to a well-formed XML document that preserves the hierarchical (outline) structure of the original document by nesting child subparagraphs within parent paragraphs. The SGML text uses 325 special GPO and standard ISO 8879 character references, such as `&para;` (the pilcrow or paragraph sign), which the code translates to ISO 8879 numeric entities— `&#182;` in this case. Failure to convert character references to numeric entities generates malformed XML. Another hurdle is handling unclosed SGML tags and nonstandard outline structures, such as jumps from level 2 to level 4 in the paragraph hierarchy.

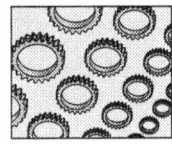

NOTE

The `ECFRFormatXML` method isn't perfect. Approximately 0.1 percent of the sections have XML parsing errors in this version of the CFRClient program. The process errors feature isn't implemented at this point in the program's development.

Click the Get All Text button to iterate the Sections table for records without section text or that contain text that has parsing errors. The `CFRGetSection.UpdateSectionText` method retrieves the SGML text from the e-CFR database, passes it to the `CFRGetSection` `.ECFRFormatXML` method, and stores documents having frewer than 8000 characters in the SectChar `varchar` field. The SectText `text` field stores longer documents.

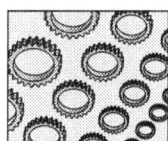

NOTE

If the code can't connect to the GPO's production database, it reverts to the backup database. Downloading text from the backup database can be a very slow process.

Figure B-3 shows the client form in the process of downloading and transforming SGML documents. The main text box displays the XML document or an error

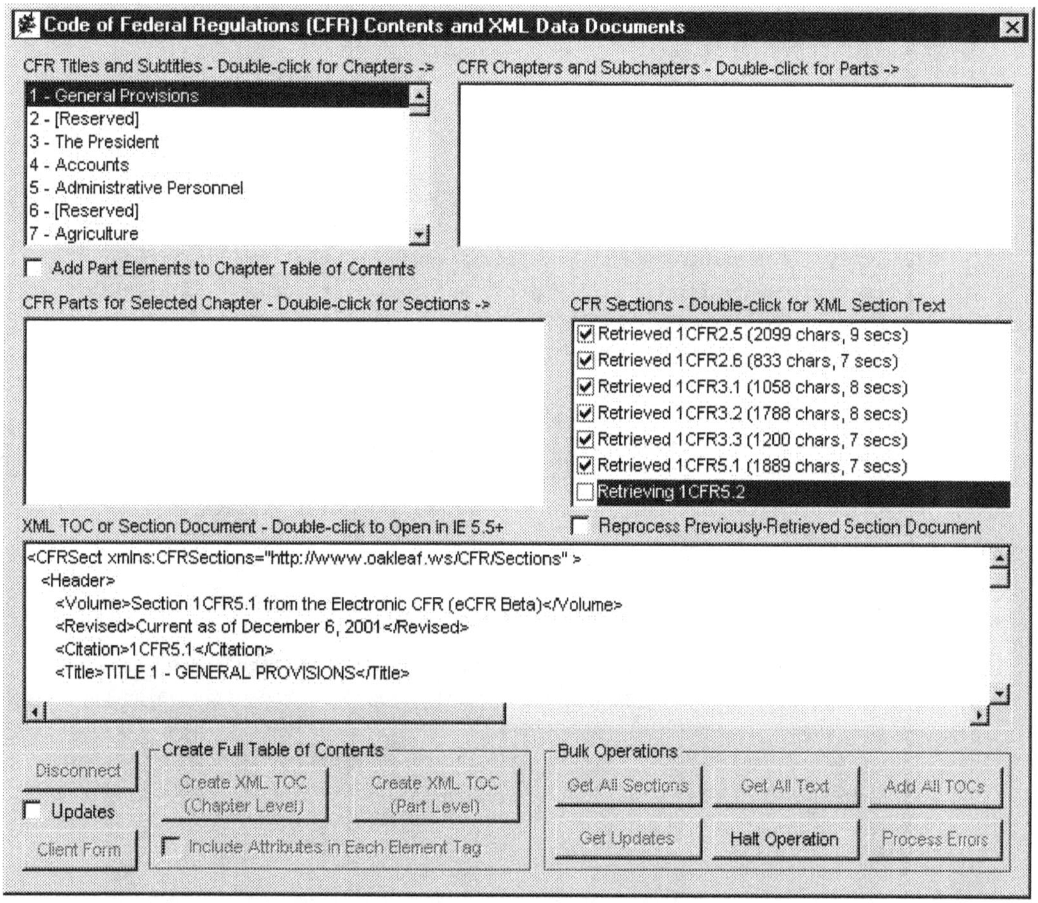

Code of Federal Regulations (CFR) Contents and XML Data Documents

CFR Titles and Subtitles - Double-click for Chapters ->

```
1 - General Provisions
2 - [Reserved]
3 - The President
4 - Accounts
5 - Administrative Personnel
6 - [Reserved]
7 - Agriculture
```

CFR Chapters and Subchapters - Double-click for Parts ->

☐ Add Part Elements to Chapter Table of Contents

CFR Parts for Selected Chapter - Double-click for Sections ->

CFR Sections - Double-click for XML Section Text

☑ Retrieved 1CFR2.5 (2099 chars, 9 secs)
☑ Retrieved 1CFR2.6 (833 chars, 7 secs)
☑ Retrieved 1CFR3.1 (1058 chars, 8 secs)
☑ Retrieved 1CFR3.2 (1788 chars, 8 secs)
☑ Retrieved 1CFR3.3 (1200 chars, 7 secs)
☑ Retrieved 1CFR5.1 (1889 chars, 7 secs)
☐ Retrieving 1CFR5.2

XML TOC or Section Document - Double-click to Open in IE 5.5+   ☐ Reprocess Previously-Retrieved Section Document

```
<CFRSect xmlns:CFRSections="http://www.oakleaf.ws/CFR/Sections" >
  <Header>
    <Volume>Section 1CFR5.1 from the Electronic CFR (eCFR Beta)</Volume>
    <Revised>Current as of December 6, 2001</Revised>
    <Citation>1CFR5.1</Citation>
    <Title>TITLE 1 - GENERAL PROVISIONS</Title>
```

Disconnect	Create Full Table of Contents		Bulk Operations		
☐ Updates	Create XML TOC (Chapter Level)	Create XML TOC (Part Level)	Get All Sections	Get All Text	Add All TOCs
Client Form	☐ Include Attributes in Each Element Tag		Get Updates	Halt Operation	Process Errors

Figure B-3   *The Sections list displays the progress of section text retieval.*

message if a parsing problem occurs. Following is an example of a typical section document:

```xml
<?xml version="1.0" encoding = "UTF-8" ?>
<CFRSect xmlns:CFRSections="http://www.oakleaf.ws/CFR/Sections" >
    <Header>
        <Volume>Title 1 from Electronic CFR (eCFR Beta)</Volume>
        <Revised>Current as of December 15, 2001</Revised>
        <Citation>1CFR2.5</Citation>
        <Title>1 - GENERAL PROVISIONS</Title>
        <Subtitle></Subtitle>
        <Chapter>Chapter I - Administrative Committee of the Federal
            Register</Chapter>
        <Subchapter>SUBCHAPTER A - GENERAL</Subchapter>
        <Part>Part 2 - General Information</Part>
        <Subpart></Subpart>
        <Section>Sec. 2.5 - Publication of statutes, regulations, and related
            documents.</Section>
    </Header>
    <Body>
        <Para1>
            <Para2>
                (a) The Director of the Federal Register is responsible for the central
                filing of the original acts enacted by Congress and the original documents
                containing Executive orders and proclamations of the President, other
                Presidential documents, regulations, and notices of proposed rulemaking and
                other notices, submitted to the Director by officials of the executive branch
                of the Federal Government.
            </Para2>
            <Para2>
                (b) Based on the acts and documents filed under paragraph (a) of this
                section, the Office of the Federal Register publishes the "slip laws," the
                "United States Statutes at Large," the daily Federal Register and the 'Code
                of Federal Regulations.'

            </Para2>
            <Para2>
                (c) Based on source materials that are officially related to the acts and
                documents filed under paragraph (a) of this section, the Office also publishes
                "The United States Government Manual," the "Public Papers of the Presidents of
                the United States," the "Weekly Compilation of Presidential Documents," the
                "Federal Register Index," and the "LSA (List of CFR Sections Affected)".
            </Para2>
        </Para1>
    </Body>
    <FedReg>
        [37 FR 23603, Nov. 4, 1972, as amended at 54 FR 9676, Mar. 7, 1989]
    </FedReg>
</CFRSect>
```

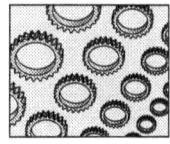

NOTE

The average length of an XML section document is about 2000 characters, but some documents have more than 300,000 characters. Storing all documents in a `text` *field, which stores data in one-page (8000 char) blocks, would increase the size of the database from about 850MB to more than 3GB.*

Over a 24-hour period, the average time to download and transform a section from the e-CFR production database is about 20 seconds. The CFR contains about 173,000 sections and appendixes, so it takes close to 1000 hours to populate the entire database.

TIP

When the GPO changes to the backup database, which the program detects, the download time can increase to 2 minutes or more. The GPO often switches to the backup database during eastern-time working hours, so downloading section text at night is the better tactic.

Generating Tables of Contents

After you download as much section text as your patience permits, click the Add All TOCs button to generate the TOCs for each CFR element (except sections), starting at Title 1. Each element tag that identifies a specific document element has a unique `id` attribute, such as `id='ti1st_ch1scApn2'`, for Web page navigation and document retrieval. The CCFRSect .dll's `GetSectByID` and `GetSection` methods translate the `id` value into an SQL `WHERE` clause to return the document. Additional attributes provide a human-readable translation of the `id` code.

Following is a typical XML TOC document:

```
<?xml version="1.0" encoding = "UTF-8" ?>
<CFRToc xmlns:CFRContents="http://www.oakleaf.ws/CFR/Contents" >
 <Titles>
  <Title id='ti1st_' TitleID='1' >
   1 - GENERAL PROVISIONS
   <Chapters>
    <Chapter id='ti1st_ch1sc_' TitleID='1' SubtitleID='-' ChapterID='1' >
     I - Administrative Committee of the Federal Register (Parts 1 - 49)
      <Subchapters>
       <Subchapter id='ti1st_ch1scA ' TitleID='1' SubtitleID='-' ChapterID='1' SubchapterID='A' >
        A - GENERAL
        <Parts>
         <Part id='ti1st_ch1scApn2' TitleID='1' SubtitleID='-' ChapterID='1'
             SubchapterID='A' PartID='2' >
          2 - General Information
          <Sections>
           <Section id='ti1st_ch1scApn2sn1' TitleID='1' PartID='2'
             SectionID='1' Citation='1CFR2.1' HasText='Yes' >
            2.1 - Scope and purpose.
```

```
        </Section>
        <Section id='ti1st_ch1scApn2sn2' TitleID='1' PartID='2'
          SectionID='2' Citation='1CFR2.2' HasText='Yes' >
        2.2 - Administrative Committee of the Federal Register.
        </Section>
        <Section id='ti1st_ch1scApn2sn3' TitleID='1' PartID='2'
          SectionID='3' Citation='1CFR2.3' HasText='Yes' >
        2.3 - Office of the Federal Register; location; office hours.
        </Section>
        <Section id='ti1st_ch1scApn2sn4' TitleID='1' PartID='2'
          SectionID='4' Citation='1CFR2.4' HasText='Yes' >
        2.4 - General authority of Director.
        </Section>
        <Section id='ti1st_ch1scApn2sn5' TitleID='1' PartID='2'
          SectionID='5' Citation='1CFR2.5' HasText='Yes' >
        2.5 - Publication of statutes, regulations, and related documents.
        </Section>
        <Section id='ti1st_ch1scApn2sn6' TitleID='1' PartID='2'
          SectionID='6' Citation='1CFR2.6' HasText='Yes' >
        2.6 - Unrestricted use.
        </Section>
       </Sections>
      </Part>
     </Parts>
    </Subchapter>
   </Subchapters>
  </Chapter>
 </Chapters>
 </Title>
 </Titles>
</CFRToc>
```

Using the Client Emulator Form

Click the Client Form button to open a modal window (`frmClientEmulator`) for testing document retrieval from the CFRSQL database and the transformation from XML to XHTML for presentation. If you've enabled full-text indexing, the text box displays catalog statistics and displays the controls for testing the search feature, as shown for the OakLeaf production database in Figure B-4. Otherwise, the search controls are hidden.

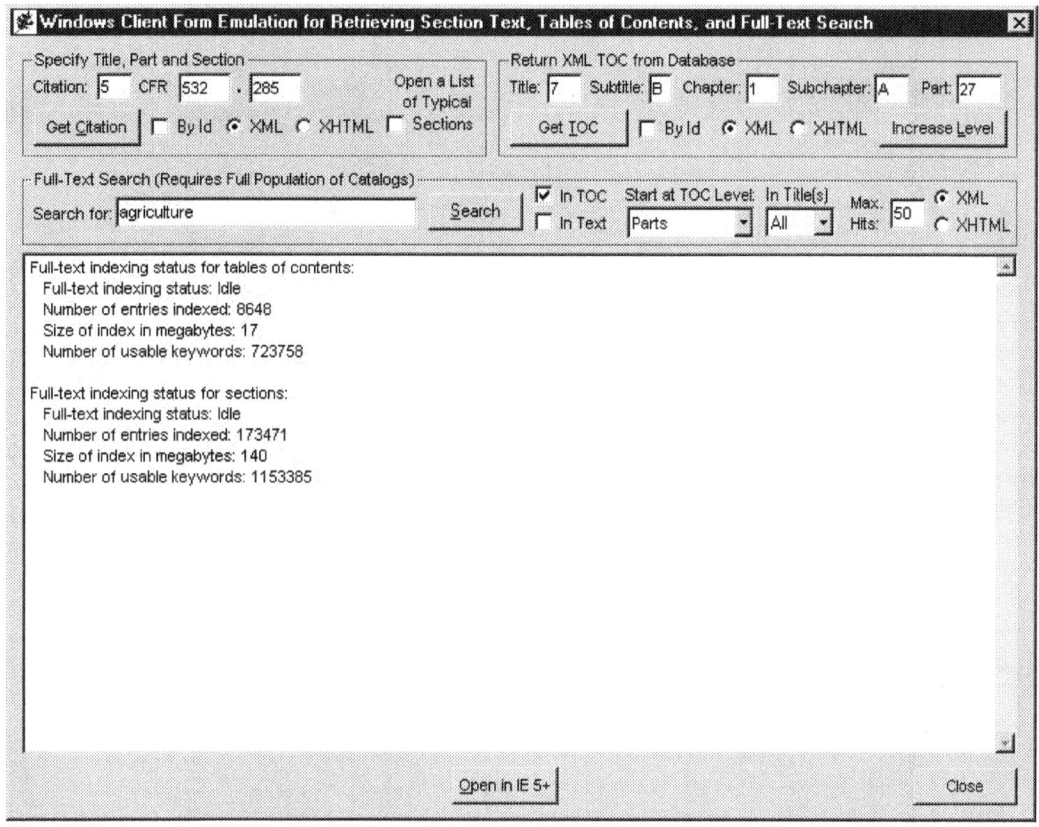

Figure B-4   *These catalog statistics are for the fully populated CFRSQL database that supports the OakLeaf CFR XML Web services.*

Displaying Section Documents

Mark the Open A List Of Typical Sections check box and select a section from the list to display in the text box. If the section text isn't present in your local copy of the CFRSQL database, code in the `frmClientEmulator.cmdGetDoc_Click` event handler creates a `SoapClient` object, connects to http://www.oakleaf.ws/cfr/cfrsectws.asmx?wsdl, and invokes the `GetSection` method to return the XML document. (See Figure B-5.) Marking the By Id check box invokes the `GetSectionByID` method, which has fewer arguments. Click the Open In IE 5+ button to display the formatted XML document with IE's XML presentation style sheet.

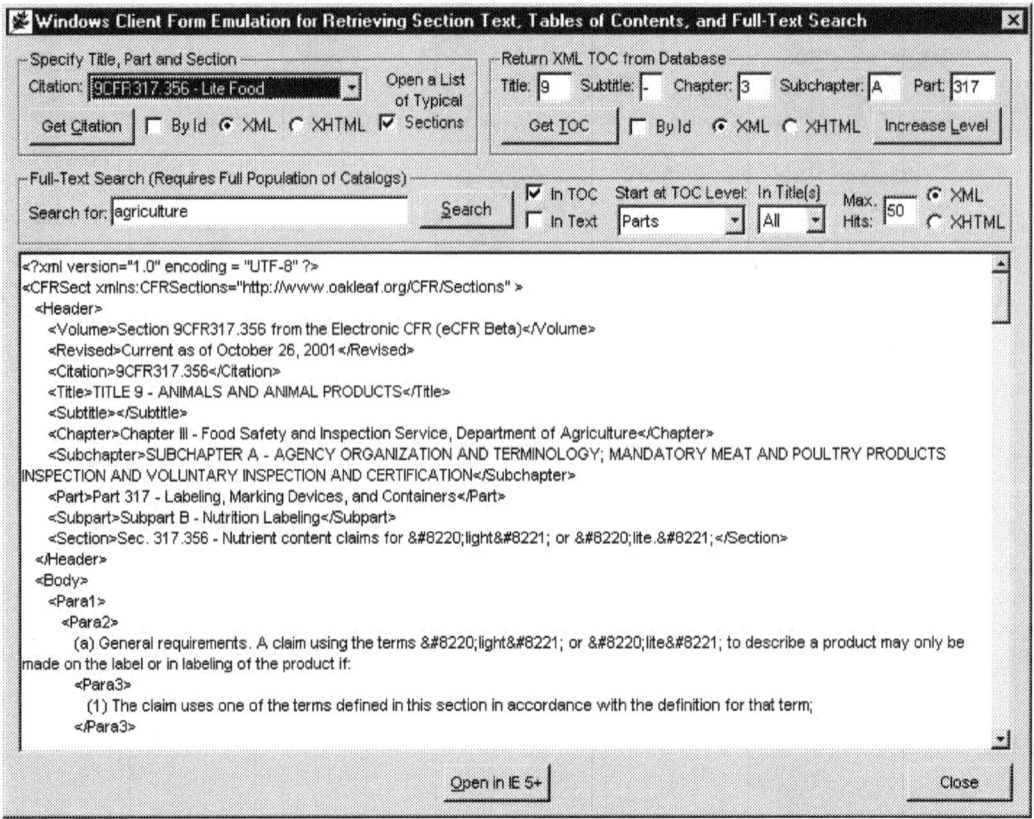

Figure B-5   *The text box displays the XML document for the section you select in the list box. Notice the entities that replace the open and closing quotation marks around* light *and* lite.

Selecting the XHTML option returns a well-formed—but not verified—XHTML document to create the Web page. (See Figure B-6.) Double-click the text box to display a clone of the OakLeaf Web site's section page.

Displaying Tables of Contents

The text of the Title, Subtitle, Chapter, Subchapter, and Part text boxes synchronize with the section you select. Click the Get TOC button to invoke the CCFRToc.dll's `GetTocByLevel` or `GetTocById` method to display or the XML TOC document.

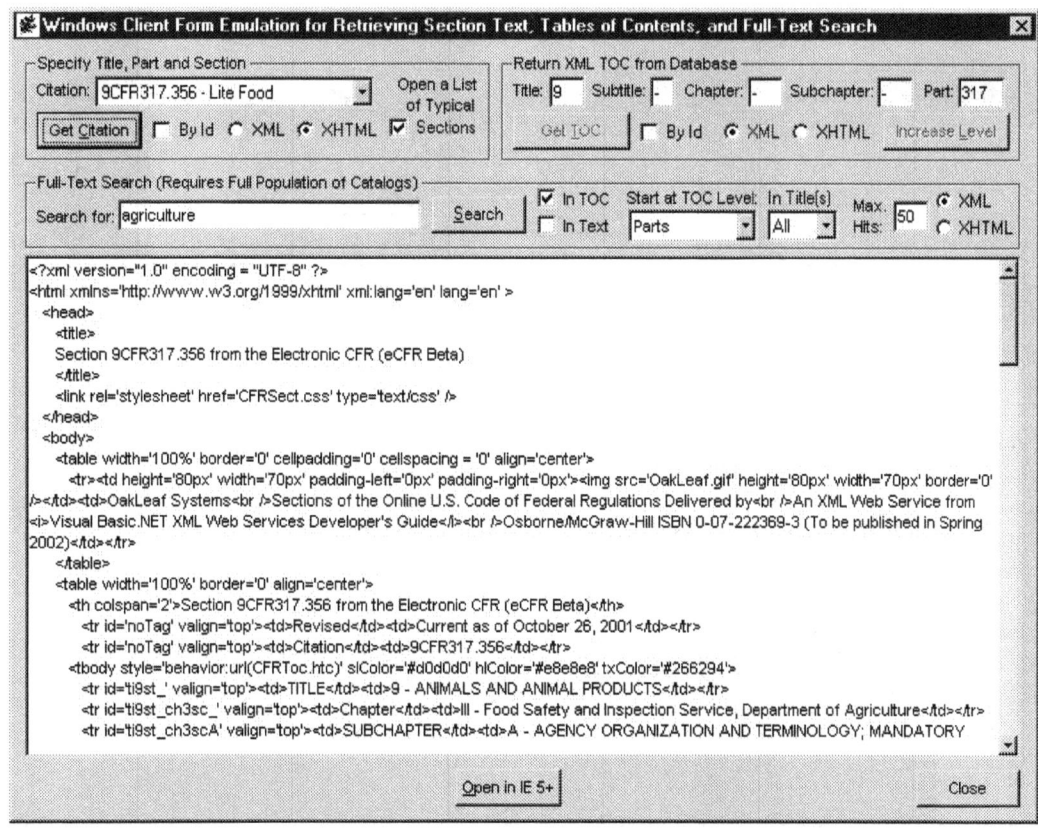

Figure B-6   *The XHTML transformation of the XML document delivers the document's Web page presentation.*

(See Figure B-7.) Click the Increase Level button to move up through the TOC hierarchy. Selecting the XHTML option returns the presentation version of the document. A `SoapClient` object returns missing TOCs from the OakLeaf Web site.

Performing a Full-Text Search

If you've installed a full-text search and have populated the catalogs for Title 47 - Telecommunication, mark the In TOC and In Text check boxes, type **satellite NEAR broadcast** in the Search For text box, and click Search. The CCFRSearch.dll's

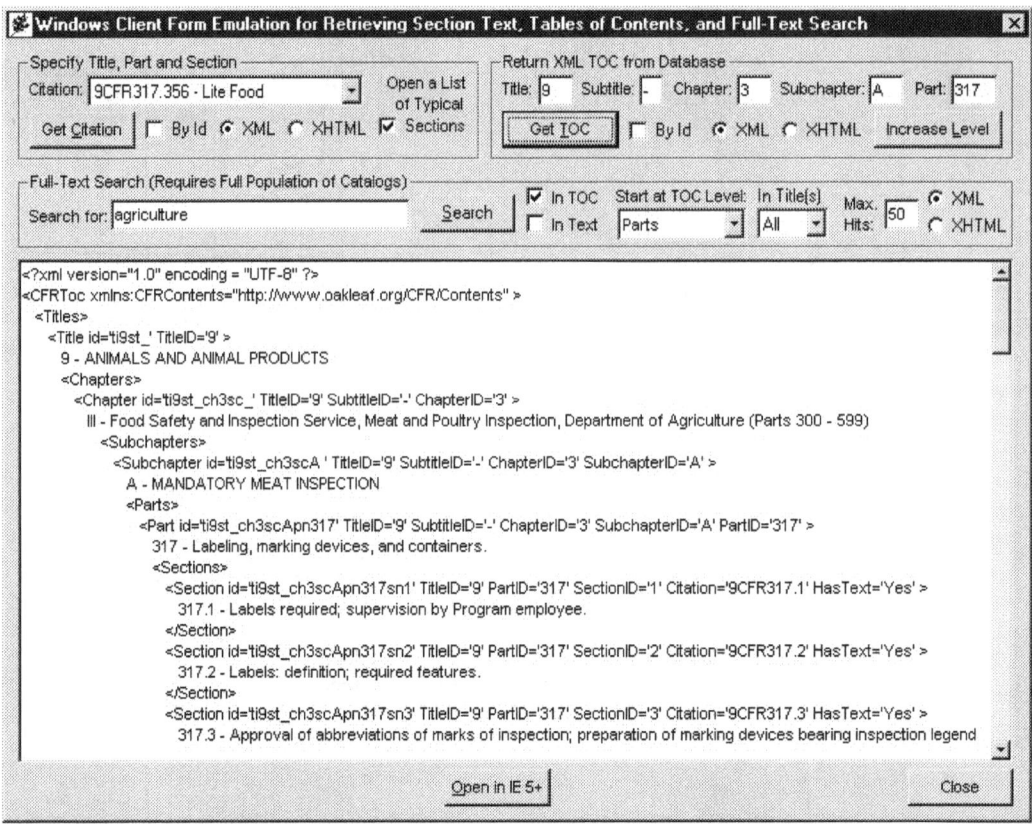

Figure B-7 *The table of contents shown here is at the lowest (parts) level of the TOC hierarchy.*

`GetSearchResults` method search returns the search XML document to the main text box. (See Figure B-8.)

The `GetSearchResults` method generates a `UNION` query to create a `Recordset` containing the composite primary key values and element names for matching TOCs and sections. Except for the Titles TOC, the query must check the `varchar` and `text` document fields for a match; the Titles TOC has only a `varchar` document field.

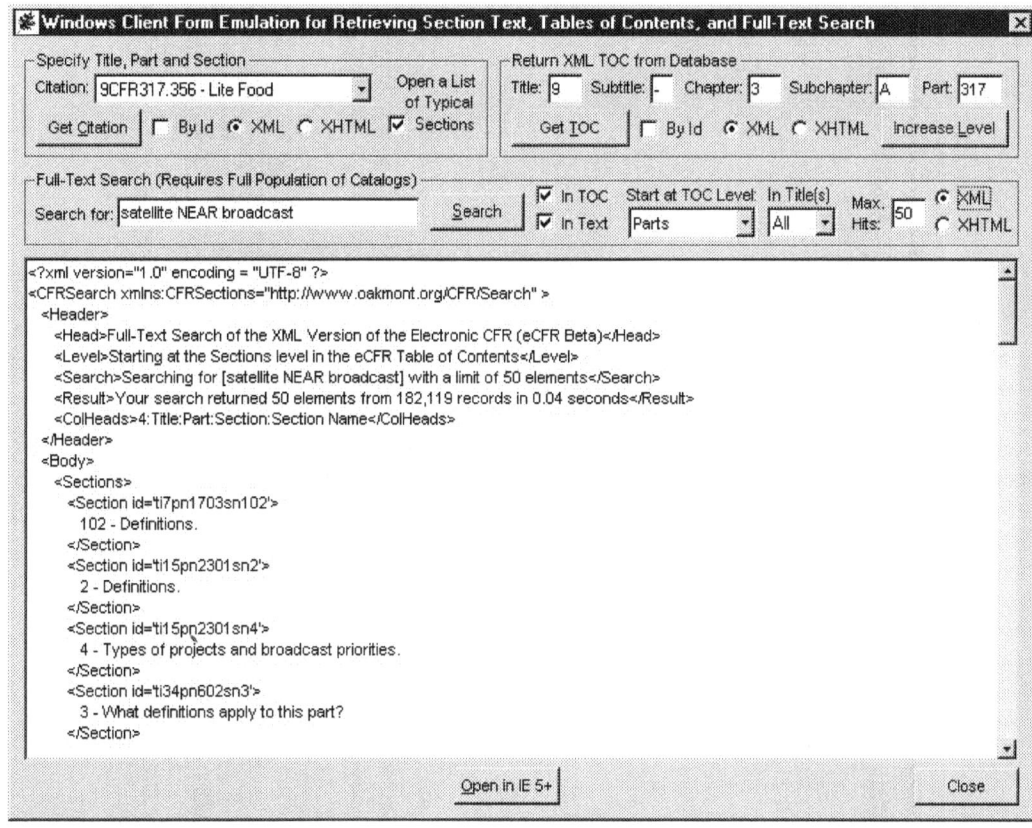

Figure B-8   *The full-text search document contains id attribute values for retrieving the selected section document.*

Following is the SQL statement for the first five of the nine UNION queries required to guarantee that the query will return at least 50 matches, if found:

```
SELECT TOP 50 TitleID, SubtitleID, ChapterID, SubchapterID, PartID, Part
   FROM Parts
   WHERE CONTAINS(TOCText, 'satellite NEAR broadcast') AND TitleID = 47
UNION SELECT TOP 50 TitleID, SubtitleID, ChapterID, SubchapterID,
      PartID, Part
   FROM Parts
```

```
   WHERE CONTAINS(TOCChar, 'satellite NEAR broadcast') AND TitleID = 47
UNION SELECT TOP 50 TitleID, SubtitleID, ChapterID, SubchapterID,
     Subchapter , "-"
   FROM SubChapters
   WHERE CONTAINS(TOCText, 'satellite NEAR broadcast') AND TitleID = 47
UNION SELECT TOP 50 TitleID, SubtitleID, ChapterID, SubchapterID,
     Subchapter, "-"
   FROM SubChapters
   WHERE CONTAINS(TOCChar, 'satellite NEAR broadcast') AND TitleID = 47
UNION SELECT TOP 50 TitleID, SubtitleID, ChapterID, SubchapterID, "-", "-"
   FROM Chapters
   WHERE CONTAINS(TOCText, 'satellite NEAR broadcast') AND TitleID = 47
UNION SELECT TOP 50 ...
```

The CONTAINS function in the WHERE clauses is specific to the SQL Server full-text search. Additional GetSearchResults method code prioritizes the rows returned by the query in section, part, subchapter, chapter, subtitle, and title sequence.

Index

T

INTERNATIONAL CONTACT INFORMATION

AUSTRALIA
McGraw-Hill Book Company Australia Pty. Ltd.
TEL +61-2-9417-9899
FAX +61-2-9417-5687
http://www.mcgraw-hill.com.au
books-it_sydney@mcgraw-hill.com

CANADA
McGraw-Hill Ryerson Ltd.
TEL +905-430-5000
FAX +905-430-5020
http://www.mcgrawhill.ca

GREECE, MIDDLE EAST, NORTHERN AFRICA
McGraw-Hill Hellas
TEL +30-1-656-0990-3-4
FAX +30-1-654-5525

MEXICO (Also serving Latin America)
McGraw-Hill Interamericana Editores S.A. de C.V.
TEL +525-117-1583
FAX +525-117-1589
http://www.mcgraw-hill.com.mx
fernando_castellanos@mcgraw-hill.com

SINGAPORE (Serving Asia)
McGraw-Hill Book Company
TEL +65-863-1580
FAX +65-862-3354
http://www.mcgraw-hill.com.sg
mghasia@mcgraw-hill.com

SOUTH AFRICA
McGraw-Hill South Africa
TEL +27-11-622-7512
FAX +27-11-622-9045
robyn_swanepoel@mcgraw-hill.com

UNITED KINGDOM & EUROPE (Excluding Southern Europe)
McGraw-Hill Education Europe
TEL +44-1-628-502500
FAX +44-1-628-770224
http://www.mcgraw-hill.co.uk
computing_neurope@mcgraw-hill.com

ALL OTHER INQUIRIES Contact:
Osborne/McGraw-Hill
TEL +1-510-549-6600
FAX +1-510-883-7600
http://www.osborne.com
omg_international@mcgraw-hill.com

www.ingramcontent.com/pod-product-compliance
Lightning Source LLC
Chambersburg PA
CBHW080132060326
40689CB00018B/3763